Modern Competing Ideologies

MODERN COMPETING IDEOLOGIES

L. Earl Shaw, Editor
University of Minnesota

Introduction by Steven Thomas Seitz

D. C. HEATH AND COMPANY
Lexington, Massachusetts Toronto London

Published simultaneously in Canada.

Printed in the United States of America.

International Standard Book Number: 0–669–81869–0

Library of Congress Catalog Card Number: 73–44

To my students at the University of Minnesota
in the hope that they have learned as much
from me as I have learned from them

Preface

Mark Twain reputedly once wired the Associated Press that that agency's report of his death was an exaggeration. Likewise, rumors about the death or "end of ideology" have been exaggerated. From college campuses to labor halls, from lily white suburbs to black ghettos, from the industrial nations of the West to the developing nations of Indochina, we hear ideology speak. Whether due to a case of mistaken identity in the death reports or a rather swift resurrection, there is little doubt today that ideology is alive and doing well.

It is the editor's belief in the inevitable and significant role of ideology that has prompted the preparation of this book. Ideology is not used here in a pejorative sense; indeed, all men are ideological to a degree. Ideologies for given individuals may vary in their rationalness, comprehensiveness, coherence, systematization, or emotional attachment. But for all men—to some extent—ideologies, which are a blending of the empirical and the normative, help them to understand, evaluate and direct or prescribe political activity.

The specific event that prompted a survey of the literature in the field was an assignment to teach an undergraduate course on contemporary ideologies. I became convinced that though there were several quite adequate secondary interpretations of the various ideologies or collections of readings on one ideology, there was not available in one volume a good collection of the original sources of the major ideologies today competing for men's minds and wills. I believe it is imperative to read the original texts and, as much as possible, to transport ourselves into the relevant historical and cultural context to fully understand the appeal, impact, and validity of an ideology.

A few comments about the book's organization and contents are in order. An introduction by Steven Seitz of Florida State University analyzes the nature and function of ideologies in the modern nation–state. The introductory notes to each chapter provide brief discussions of (a) the way in which each ideology views man, society, and the state, (b) the varieties of experience, both personal and historical, from which the ideological model in a given chapter has been abstracted, as well as the social vantage point from which it is offered and defended, and (c) a brief introduction to each selection in the various chapters.

The selections for each chapter offer a variety of diverse viewpoints within the scope of the particular ideology under consideration. Some rather lengthy selections are included in their entirety to allow the reader to see the depth, detail, and wholeness of the argument offered. Another central concern in the selection of the essays was to make them relevant to the American context. In all chapters I have selected at least one American writer. For further reading on a given ideology the reader is directed to the original sources of the readings as well as the selected bibliography at the end of each chapter.

The focus of this reader is on *political* ideologies; thus various economic systems have been integrated on the basis of both their political relevance and the implicit assumptions they make regarding the role of state and government. For example, rather than devote a separate chapter to socialism, we include this system under both communism and democratic socialism.

The reader might wonder about the disproportionately large number of selections on democracy as opposed to those on fascism, racism, and communism. In a sense each of Chapters IV through VII deals with a different ideology, though each carries *democracy* in the title. In fact, several different ideologies exist which correspond in practice to democratic institutions. In many political struggles today all who participate claim to carry the democratic banner. Democracy has become an honorific term; nobody in recent times, except possibly the fascists, have preferred explicitly to be antidemocratic. UNESCO, in a study a few years ago asking scholars from around the world to state and define their political preferences, found that while there is remarkable, indeed almost unanimous, agreement on the desirability of democracy, there is remarkable diversity in understanding what democracy entails.

No categorization of modern ideologies will satisfy everyone. The categories presented here are not exhaustive or even mutually exclusive. But they do offer a means whereby to delineate the various emphases seen in recent and present ideological struggles.

I would also like to take this opportunity to express my appreciation and gratitude to Steve Seitz and Betty Shaw. Steve's contribution went well beyond the introductory essay to include extensive involvement in each stage and aspect of the project. Without his enormous contribution, the completion of this project would have been significantly delayed or possibly even aborted. My wife aided me in the editing of the articles and from time to time offered her own criticism of the project. In addition, she performed much of the secretarial work, such as typing and securing permissions, which is associated with a project like this one.

Finally, a special word of appreciation is in order to those authors and publishers who so graciously permitted their materials to be reprinted.

L. Earl Shaw

Contents

Modern Competing Ideologies

Introduction

Political Ideologies and the Essence of Politics

STEVEN THOMAS SEITZ

Historical Origins

An analysis of *ideology* properly begins with two important developments in the sixteenth and seventeenth centuries, almost two hundred years before the term ideology was coined. Both developments were directed against the power and ascendancy of the Catholic church. The first was the development of a new theory of knowledge. Perhaps the earliest exponent of this new theory of knowledge was Francis Bacon, an English philosopher of the late sixteenth and early seventeenth centuries. In *Novum Organum* Bacon argues that the mind, or Reason, suffers from various distortions, making it difficult to discover "Truth." Bacon felt that if these distortions or "idols" were swept away, then Reason would be free to see the world as it "really" is.

The new theory of knowledge was brought to fruition in the late seventeenth century by another English philosopher, John Locke. In his famous *Essay Concerning Human Understanding,* Locke argues that the whole of our knowledge is derived solely from sensory experience. He sees the human mind, at birth, as a *tabula rasa* or blank tablet upon which experiences are recorded and gradually transformed into general ideas. Indeed, it was through Locke that the attack on Catholic doctrine became explicit: First, he maintains, there are no innate ideas. Further, the way to discover "truth" is through the senses, not through blind faith in the authority and doctrine of the Catholic church.

The second important development, predating the first use of the term ideology, was the growth of the absolutist state in the sixteenth and seventeenth centuries. Early medieval philosophy and theology of the Western tradition rested personal authority—whether of the monarch or the Pope—

upon the laws of nature, a fundamental law binding upon all men.[1] By so doing medieval thought struck a synthesis between secular and religious powers. In the later middle ages, however, this medieval synthesis succumbed to rapid social changes; the slow development of custom proved quite inadequate to the changing times. Based on a law that could not be changed by law-making bodies, the medieval institutions gradually gave way to the unfettered law-making institutions of the sovereign nation-state. This subtle shift from the authority of law to the authority of persons was, in turn, reflected in both the Jesuit and the Calvinist theology of the day. Lindsay summarizes the consequences of this historic change: [2]

> Once this fundamental assumption of the supremacy of the law over personal authority was abandoned, the medieval balance between Church and State—both authorities under law—broke down. When that happened, the logical conclusion of the belief that the State was dependent upon morality, when combined with the acceptance of a common moral authority, was Papal absolutism. This was one of those logical conclusions whose practical results are so disastrous that they lead to the repudiation of the premises on which they are based. Papal absolutism led and was bound to lead to the absolutism of the monarch, and the repudiation of the authority of the Pope led to the throwing away of the baby of morality along with the bath water of Papal absolutism.

The absolutism of the monarch admitted neither limitation nor guidance by an "international" morality, at least not one prescribed by the Pope. This led to a rather serious problem: were there no limits to the caprice of the monarch? Exponents of the new theory of knowledge were to answer, in fact, that there were limits, discoverable through human reason, on the discretionary powers of the monarch. Locke had already proposed such a political doctrine in his *Two Treatises on Civil Government.* A core assumption linked that doctrine with the new theory of knowledge: man can, by means of his unencumbered reason, discover "natural" or inalienable rights.

The focus of attention now shifts to France at the end of the eighteenth century. Like England, France played a major role in repudiating the role of any "international" authority such as that prevalent in the sixteenth century. France, like England, had become master of its own house at a very early stage.[3] Unlike England, however, France found it exceedingly difficult to reduce the power of the Catholic church within its borders. It is perhaps to be expected, therefore, that the French variant of the new theory of knowledge and its associated political doctrine, with the implicit attack on the Catholic church and Catholic doctrine, did not develop in France until approximately a century after similar developments in England.

In France, the new theory of knowledge was argued by the French philos-

[1] A. D. Lindsay, *The Modern Democratic State* (New York: Oxford University Press, 1962; 1943), p. 67.
[2] *Ibid.*, p. 67.
[3] *Ibid.*, pp. 65–66.

opher Destutt de Tracy, at the end of the eighteenth century. And it was de Tracy who coined the term ideology. De Tracy believed that ideas could be purified if they were reduced to sense perceptions. Like the British empiricists, de Tracy and his colleagues argued that truth depended solely upon sensory experience rather than upon the faith and authority demanded by the Catholic church. These philosophers, often referred to as the Ideologues, attempted to develop a political theory based on the new theory of knowledge. As a guide for political activity, the new political theory sought, among other things, to define the limits of autocracy. Needless to say, the Ideologues faced strong opposition from supporters of both the Church and the royal family. With Napoleon the Ideologues had originally gained favor; in time, he too turned upon them with a vengeance.

Toward the end of the eighteenth century the ideologues established the National Institute, dedicated to the application of ideology in legislation and government. Among the Institute members was the young Napoleon Bonaparte, hailed by many as a savior from the wars and intrigues besetting French society. (During the Revolutionary years through the Reign of Terror, the Ideologues had supported the moderate republican Girondist interests and those of other bourgeois forces in power.) Although the Ideologues had supported Napoleon's coup d'état in France, Napoleon, once in power, found the doctrine of the Ideologues—rooted as it was in the religious conflicts of the preceding centuries—quite at odds with his autocratic policies. Reacting to the strenuous objections of his erstwhile supporters, Napoleon derided their philosophy as "visionary moonshine" and "idealistic trash." Then, through bribes, purges, and insults, underscored by a compact made by Napoleon with the Catholic church, Napoleon stripped the Ideologues of all but the formal vestiges of power. Although de Tracy had failed in France, he hoped that, through the efforts of Thomas Jefferson, the United States of America would pursue the principles of ideology which he and his colleagues had developed.[4]

Until the reign of Napoleon, therefore, the term ideology stood for a science devoted to the removal of any prejudice or bias which might stand in the way of objective social analysis and proper social reform. Ideology was, properly speaking, a guide for attending to the arrangements of society. Through the attacks and mockery which Napoleon directed at the Ideologues, the term soon came to have pejorative connotations. As a case for dramatic irony, these pejorative connotations allowed later writers, the most outstanding of whom was Karl Marx, to use the term ideology in a sense almost precisely opposite from the claims of the doctrine it had originally described. Thus ideology came to mean those prejudices and biases which obstruct

[4] For a more detailed discussion of the Ideologues, see Jay W. Stein, "Beginnings of 'Ideology,'" *South Atlantic Quarterly,* Vol. *55* (1956); also, see Joseph Roucek, "A History of the Concept of Ideology," *Journal of the History of Ideas, 5* (1944). The French forerunners of the Ideologues were the philosophés.

the processes of objective reason. For Marx, these ideological prejudices and biases were reflections of class interests.

Marx argued that the production of ideas and conceptions—of consciousness itself—was directly interwoven with the material activities and material relationships among men.[5] Thought is held to be a direct result of man's material behavior (his mode of production). Marx and Engels write:[6]

> The phantoms formed in the human brain, too, are necessary sublimations of man's material life-process which is empirically verifiable and connected with material premises. Morality, religion, metaphysics, and all the rest of ideology and their corresponding forms of consciousness no longer seem to be independent. They have no history or development. Rather, men who develop their material production and their material relationships alter their thinking and the products of their thinking along with their real existence. Consciousness does not determine life, but life determines consciousness.

A close reading of the *German Ideology,* written by Karl Marx and Friedrich Engels, reveals two distinct, albeit related, uses of the concept ideology. In the first use, ideology is thought which has been detached from the class relations which gave it birth; in this sense, *ideological thought* is thought arising from the material activities and material relations of a class of men, which has been attributed an existence independent of the class in which it is rooted.[7] In the second use, ideology is thought which is distorted precisely because it is intricately bound with the material activities and material relations of a given class. Each class has its own consciousness, a way of imagining itself and other classes; merely reflecting the interests of a given class, this is ideological thought, for it does not portray men as they really are.[8] Ideology, as Marx and Engels state the point, amounts to either a distorted interpretation of the history of man or a complete abstraction from the history of man.[9]

Both insights were crucial: that thought is distorted because it is bound up with the material activities and material relations of class provided Marx with a political weapon of unexpected potential; that thought is a distorted abstraction of human experience provided several writers, Mannheim among them, with a clue to the nature of thought itself. Both Marx and Mannheim assume that some thought, although abstracted from experience, is free of distortion. Such thought is "scientific." To that assumption we shall turn in the following section. It remains at this point to discuss the relation between Marx's insights and the subsequent deployment of those insights.

[5] Karl Marx and Friedrich Engels, *The German Ideology,* in Lloyd D. Easton and Kurt H. Guddat (ed.; trans.) *Writings of the Young Marx on Philosophy and Society* (Garden City, New York: Anchor Books, 1967), p. 414.
[6] *Ibid.*, p. 415.
[7] *Ibid.*, p. 439.
[8] *Ibid.*, pp. 414–415.
[9] *Ibid.*, p. 408.

Marx was extremely effective in using his insight that thought is distorted through an individual's position in the class structure of society. Marx argued that the ideas of those opposing Marxism were dependent upon a given socio-historical setting. This allowed him to assert, in turn, that various social doctrines of his day were biased and distorted representations of and guides to the arrangements of society. Although Marx claimed that his doctrine was scientific, and hence free of bias and distortion, the opponents of Marxism rejoined Marx by pointing out that if the thought of various groups is rooted in the group's socio-historical position, then the same must also hold true for Marxist thought. By assailing other positions as ideological, Marx's social and political theory soon faced a similar challenge. (The issue here can be carried one step further. What is the status of Marx's insight that thought is distorted by the socio-historical position of the thinker? Is that insight scientific or ideological?)

As a clue to the nature of thought, Marx's insight that thought is a distorted abstraction from human experience—distorted in the sense that it does not capture all of human experience—was further developed by Karl Mannheim. Mannheim transformed Marx's theory of ideology into the sociology of knowledge: a method of research in social and intellectual history.[10] Like Marx, Mannheim emphasized the dependence of thought on the social situation, although Mannheim tended to include in social situation not only the mode and relations of production but also the more vague notions of group life and group existence. Like Marx, Mannheim saw the genesis of thought to be rooted in action. And with Marx, Mannheim agreed that ruling groups can in their thinking become so interest-bound to their social situation that they are no longer able to see certain "facts" that are basically incompatible with their dominant mode of thought. Mannheim argues that such deception is not confined to unwitting disguises of the facts; these deceptions may also be conscious lies on the part of the ruling group. Such deceptions about the "facts," whether they be unwitting or conscious and deliberate, Mannheim classifies as examples of the "particular conception of ideology."[11] When speaking of the "particular conception of ideology," it is generally assumed that the parties to a dispute over "facts" share common criteria of validity. That is to say, it is still possible to refute lies and correct error by reference to a standard set of criteria used in ascertaining the validity of claims by each party to the dispute.

In contrast to examples of the "particular conception of ideology," there are no common criteria of validity when we speak of disputes rooted in differing "total conceptions of ideology."[12] Here each historical epoch is said to have its own intellectual world; and within each historical epoch, differing

[10] Karl Mannheim, *Ideology and Utopia* (New York: Harcourt, Brace and World, Inc., 1936), pp. 77–78.
[11] *Ibid.*, pp. 55–57.
[12] *Ibid.*, p. 57.

social strata have different categories through which to see the world. When we speak of "total conceptions of ideology," Mannheim points out, we are speaking of fundamentally divergent thought-systems, each based on different modes of experience and interpretation. As a method of research in social and intellectual history, the total conception of ideology seeks to comprehend thought in the concrete setting of a historically and socially given situation. The essence of such an approach to knowledge is simply this: a large part of thought and knowledge can be correctly understood only if the existing modes of thought are not separated from the context of group life and group action.

Perhaps a final word is in order suggesting why it is important to have some idea of the history of a particular concept such as ideology. From Humpty Dumpty we have all learned that a word may mean anything we want it to mean. But this is hardly conducive to communication or understanding. The historical usage of a term becomes quite important when stipulating the definition of a concept, assuming that communication and understanding are important guidelines in "making a word mean anything we want it to mean." A stipulative definition of ideology would, with an eye to the historical usage of the concept, include: (a) since the time of Napoleon, the notion that ideology refers to thought rooted in a socio-historical context, (b) the notion that ideology is an abstraction from human experience, and (c) the notion that ideology is a guide to social and political action. These three notions form the core of the concept ideology as it is used here.

Ideology as Knowledge

The presence of so many competing ideologies in the modern world raises a question relative to historical usage (a) which, as Mannheim suggests, is fundamental to human thought: how is it possible that human beings, all with similar thought processes and all concerned with the same world, can produce such divergent conceptions of that world?[13] (There is little reason to believe that significant qualitative differences exist among human minds, whether those differences be racial, social, or individual.[14]) Mannheim's answer to this question is that all knowledge is relational; knowledge can only be understood through an examination of the relation between the thinker and his social and historical context. Mannheim's concern is not the isolated individual thinker; rather, Mannheim focuses upon men in certain

[13] *Ibid.*, p. 9.
[14] This debate still continues, however. For a couple of more recent articles tending to disconfirm the existence of qualitative differences among human minds, see: Claude Lévi-Strauss, "The Science of the Concrete," in Claude Lévi-Strauss, *The Savage Mind* (Chicago: The University of Chicago Press, 1966), pp. 1–33; and John Osgood Field and Ronald E. Anderson, "Ideology in the Public's Conceptualization of the 1964 Election," *Public Opinion Quarterly* (Fall 1969).

groups who, through endless responses to the situations of their common existence, develop a particular form of knowledge.[15]

If all—or most—knowledge is relational, then a second problem arises: how do we know what is true or false, objective or biased, in this knowledge? [16] The problem raised here has, over the years, come to be widely known as Mannheim's paradox. Broadly stated the problem becomes: where does science begin and ideology end? [17] Mannheim cautions that relationism—the idea that systems of meaning are possible only within a historical context—must not be confused with philosophical relativism. Relationism signifies that criteria of rightness and wrongness are valid only within the context of a given socio-historical situation. Philosophical relativism denies the validity of all such standards.[18] Mannheim's solution to this paradox is two-fold. On the one hand, he hopes that advances in sociological research into the nature of ideology will reveal the various interrelations between and among social positions, motives, and various points of view.[19] On the other hand, he places great faith in the ability of the intellectual, who, according to Mannheim, does not have a fixed class position, thus enabling the intellectual to gain a more total conception of the historical process.[20]

Whether Mannheim's proposed solutions to his paradox are adequate—and it is doubtful that they are—is not of immediate concern here. It is clear, however, that only knowledge which encompasses a complete conception of the vastly complex arrangements of society and the historical process can even approximate what Mannheim calls "scientific knowledge." None of the current ideologies can make such a sweeping claim, even though the Marxists do make such a claim. Political ideologies, as we know them, rest upon value judgments, which are intricately tied with social position, motive, and point of view.[21] There is some reason to believe that this is characteristic of all forms of knowledge, including the "scientific," as we shall briefly note below.[22] As Mannheim so wisely observes: although epistemology is the basis of all empirical sciences, it derives its principles only from the data supplied through the empirical sciences.[23] The larger point still remains, of course, that since ideologies are bound with a group's social position, motives, and point of view, and since no ideology can make a claim to being "scientific" in Mannheim's sense, it is therefore clear that ideologies are only partial views of the total social and historical process. As Mannheim

[15] Karl Mannheim, *Ideology and Utopia,* p. 3.
[16] *Ibid.,* p. 79.
[17] *Ibid.,* Chapter 3: "The Prospects for a Scientific Politics."
[18] *Ibid.,* p. 283.
[19] *Ibid.,* p. 189.
[20] *Ibid.,* pp. 153–164.
[21] *Ibid.,* pp. 88–89.
[22] See Thomas Kuhn, *The Structure of Scientific Revolutions,* Vol. *II,* No. 2: *International Encyclopedia of Unified Science* (2d ed., enlarged; Chicago: University of Chicago Press, 1970).
[23] Mannheim, *Ideology and Utopia,* p. 292.

states, "All points of view in politics are but partial points of view because historical totality is always too comprehensive to be grasped by any one of the individual points of view which emerge out of it." [24]

Ideology and Politics

Relative to the first historical usage (a)—that ideology is thought rooted in a socio-historical context—an ideology is a form of knowledge, however biased and incomplete that knowledge might be. Next, relative to the second historical usage (b)—that ideology is an abstraction from human experience—let us define the concept ideology with further precision; (1) ideologies are abstract pictures of man, society, and the state, as imagined by a given group of people in a concrete socio-historical position, (2) ideologies are abstract pictures of how man, society, and state ought to be, based on the perspective of a given group in its concrete socio-historical setting, (3) ideologies are vehicles used to explain human, social, and political "reality," however inadequate or inaccurate the explanation. Ideologies, in sum, represent the various ways different groups think about man, the relations among men, and the institutions of the modern nation–state. In this sense each ideology presents a somewhat different picture of man, society, and state. Mannheim argues: [25]

> The divergence of political theories is accounted for mainly by the fact that the different positions and social vantage points as they emerge in the stream of social life enable one from its particular point in the stream to recognize the stream itself. Thus, at different times, different elementary social interests emerge and accordingly different objects of attention in the total structure are illuminated and viewed as if these were the only ones that existed.

Ideologies, as noted in definition (2), involve some notion of how man, society, and the state ought to be. Because they involve such a notion, ideologies provide standards or guidelines by means of which we judge man, society, and state as they are imagined to be, in terms of what the particular group holds that man, society, and state ought to be. Because of this potential tension between existing conditions and the "ideal," we arrive at a fourth definition, i.e., that ideologies are programs, however incomplete, aimed at changing the current condition of man, society, and the state, into the ideal state of affairs envisioned by the programs' adherents. With this last clarification we capture the essence of the third historical usage (c): that ideology is a guide to social and political action. Ideologies in short tell us, whether implicitly or explicitly, what is, why it is, what ought to be, and (in case of any gaps between the real and the ideal) how to move from what is to what ought to be.

[24] *Ibid.*, p. 151.
[25] *Ibid.*, p. 151.

Our concept of ideology in the social sciences is not without parallel to a similar concept in the natural sciences: what Thomas Kuhn has called "paradigms." Kuhn defines "paradigm" as the entire set of beliefs, values, and techniques shared by the members of any given scientific community.[26] Just as ideologies reflect the "consciousness" of certain groups in concrete socio-historical circumstances, so also paradigms reflect a large area of scientific experience at a given point in time.[27] Just as ideologies tell us something about man, society, and the state, so paradigms tell scientists something about the entities that nature does and does not contain.[28] And paradigms provide the scientist with standards and criteria of legitimacy, much like ideologies. Finally, paradigms provide directions for research, again in an almost amazing parallel to the directions for political action provided by ideologies.

Perhaps it is appropriate to clarify the sense in which ideologies are rooted in a socio-historical context [historical usage (a)] and at the same time abstracted from that experience [historical usage (b)]. Ideological thought develops through the endless responses of a group of people to common situations. The distinguished English conservative Michael Oakeshott agrees on this point, arguing that the system of abstract ideas called "ideologies" are abstractions from some kind of concrete activity.[29] Some political ideologies, according to Oakeshott, are abstractions from the political traditions of a society, while others originate out of such activity as war, religion, or the conduct of industry.[30] There is a simple point to be made here: ideologies are not the purely rational products of intellectual premeditation.[31] As guides to further political activity, therefore, ideologies in effect presume some previous activity of one form or another.

This brings us to the third core notion of the concept ideology: that ideologies are guides to social and political action. In what sense can it be said that ideologies are guides to action? Politics, once again to draw from Oakeshott, is the activity of attending to the general arrangements of a set of people whom chance or choice have brought together.[32] Politics—the attending to the arrangements of society—is an activity which, like any other activity, must be learned and hence requires some form of knowledge.[33] In earlier societies, this knowledge differed little from the examples provided by tradition. With the rise of industrialism, the concomitant decay of feudalism, and the growth of the modern nation–state, however, tradition proved

[26] Thomas Kuhn, *The Structure of Scientific Revolutions*, p. 175.
[27] *Ibid.*, p. 125.
[28] *Ibid.*, p. 109.
[29] Michael Oakeshott, "Political Education," in Michael Oakeshott, *Rationalism in Politics* (New York: Basic Books Publishing Company, Inc., 1962), p. 121.
[30] *Ibid.*, p. 121.
[31] See also Oakeshott, "Political Education," pp. 118–119.
[32] *Ibid.*, p. 112.
[33] *Ibid.*, p. 113.

an insufficient guide for political activity. In the discussion of the historical origins of the concept ideology we saw that the inability of custom to adapt in the face of rapid social change led to the breakdown of the medieval synthesis between church and state, thereby marking the growth of the absolutist state of the sixteenth and seventeenth centuries. This same inflexibility made tradition a poor source of knowledge, particularly within the context of the rapid change so characteristic of modern industrial states. There is a rather obvious connection between the rise of ideology as a guide to political and social action and the need for such a guide.

There are further limitations on tradition as a guide to political action in the modern nation–state. Tradition often assumes a congruency of character and life style foreign to the societies governed by the institutions of the modern nation–state. As a corollary of this point, the growth of industrialism marked a rapid division of labor in society. The immediate consequence of this change meant that the arrangements of society had become vastly more complicated than ever before. This meant, in turn, that there were simply more niches in society from which to view the various arrangements of society.

The rapid change and complexity characterizing the modern nation–state tend to underscore the basic inadequacy of tradition as a guide to political action: tradition is most relevant to those societies in which the dominant institutions of government serve merely to interpret the law. In the modern nation–state, the dominant political institutions serve to make law. Tradition tends to be, more often than not, at odds with the latter task of making laws when compared with the former task of merely interpreting the law.

With the growth of the modern nation–state, then, political ideologies provided the knowledge necessary for attending to the arrangements of society. As the Chicago anthropologist Clifford Geertz once wrote: "the function of ideology is to make an autonomous politics possible by providing the authoritative concepts that render it meaningful, the suasive images by means of which it can be sensibly grasped." [34] And as Geertz so rightly observes, ideologies first emerged and became important guides to political action precisely at the point where the political system freed itself from tradition, conventional morality, and religion.[35] That type of political system includes, as we saw above, the modern nation–state.

Perhaps it is necessary, at this point, to consider briefly the essential characteristics of the modern nation–state. The state is, most generally, an association: a group of people united together for the pursuit of common goals or purposes. But more specifically, membership in the state is compulsory. Further, the purposes of the state are more comprehensive than

[34] Clifford Geertz, "Ideology as a Cultural System," in David Apter (ed.), *Ideology and Discontent* (New York: The Free Press, 1964), p. 63.
[35] *Ibid.*, pp. 63–64.

other associations: the state attempts to make rules and law for society as a whole. Characterized by a fairly well-defined territorial area, the state claims to exercise sovereignty through government as the agency of the modern nation–state.

So what can be said of ideologies as guides to political action in the modern nation–state? Recall that ideologies are rooted in various socio-historical contexts. As such, ideologies are not "scientific": they do not represent the totality and complexity of the arrangements of society. Ideologies are biased and partial: they tend to reflect the interests of a given group of people jointly struggling with common problems in a given socio-historical context. Yet the state purports to make rules and laws for society as a whole; as an association, the state purports to pursue purposes more comprehensive than those of other associations.

The tension here is quite apparent. On the one hand, ideologies as guides to political action are incomplete and tend to favor the interests of one group in society. On the other hand, ideologies guide political action in the modern nation–state, which not only claims more comprehensive purposes than other associations but, further, proceeds to make rules and laws for society as a whole. The immediate consequence is that the state, whether unwittingly or consciously, tends to govern in the interests of the few while supposedly governing in the interests of all members of society. This is a tendency endemic to the politics of the modern nation–state.

Historically speaking, however, this tendency has not gone unchecked by the various institutions of the modern nation–state. The crucial development, in this respect, has been the rise of democratic institutions wihin the modern nation–state. Several characteristics are commonly associated with these democratic institutions. First, final power is in some manner placed in the hands of the people; as a corollary, government is in some way responsible to the people. Second, there is some effective selection of the rulers by the public; broadly speaking, popular sovereignty has some effect on the general direction of public policy. The mechanisms securing such effective selection of rulers and the general direction of public policy include universal suffrage, periodic elections, secret elections, and some equitable form of representation (including proportional representation and the one man, one vote principle). Third, democratic institutions have come to be associated with alternative party government characterized by a willingness to abide by electoral decision. Fourth, the government possesses limited powers, usually defined by a constitution, whether written or unwritten. Fifth, democratic institutions are marked by freedom of discussion and criticism to determine who is to represent the people. Finally, a fundamental rule of law exists, which involves more than a constitution and an independent judiciary; the rulers themselves must obey the law, and citizens are guaranteed the opportunity to seek redress against actions of the government.

Democratic institutions are not a sure guarantee against the tendency, in the modern nation–state, to govern in the interests of the few, perhaps at the expense of the many. They do, however, provide a minimal corrective against this tendency. There is a rather clear connection between the growth in importance of ideologies as guides to political action and the rise of democratic institutions in the modern nation–state. In this sense it is best to consider democracy primarily as a set of institutions, to which have been added ideologies that incorporate the various functions fulfilled by the democratic institutions.

The Future of Ideology

Not too many years ago several intellectuals, among them Daniel Bell, argued that ideologies were exhausted. The modern era, they felt, marked the end of ideologies.[36] It is quite apparent in their work that these writers did not use the word "ideology" in precisely the same manner as it has been used here. Yet it is perhaps instructive to examine briefly why these men thought ideology was on the decline. The core of the decline thesis seems to be that "ideological conflict," "utopian thinking," and the rigid polarization of modern society are slowly becoming less significant in modern politics. This change is often attributed to the growth of bureaucracy and affluence in Western society, coupled with the concomitant tendency to minimize class conflict.[37]

If we were to reconstruct the decline thesis in terms of the historical meaning of the term "ideology," it would involve two essential premises. First, the content of "ideological thinking" is becoming increasingly similar. That is to say, ideologies appear to be reflecting, better and better, the vast complexity of the total arrangements of society. The second premise would be that ideologies are becoming less necessary as guides to political action: the problem of politics is fast becoming a mere technical problem. That is, politics is being reduced to a problem of technology.

There is little reason to believe that either of these premises can be taken seriously today. The events of the 1960s and 1970s clearly indicate that "ideological politics" still exist. The immensely productive capitalist system may have alleviated much of the original tension between worker and producer, but that conflict is not the last. Today, for example, we are faced with a relatively new problem: where do we impose the limits on capitalist production? This is the central issue of ecology and environmentalism. And the politics of consumer protection readily indicate that capitalist enter-

[36] See, for example, Daniel Bell, *The End of Ideology* (New York: The Free Press, 1960).
[37] See Seymour Martin Lipset, "The Changing Class Structure and Contemporary European Politics," *Daedalus* (Vol. 93, 1964); and S. M. Lipset, *Political Man* (New York: Doubleday and Company, 1960).

prise is still not responsive to all the various interests of the consumer.

And there are uglier issues marring the American political battlefield. The issue of race and racial equality shows little sign of diminishing for some years to come. Further, we still contend with the critical issues of war and peace. These problems hardly demonstrate an increasing similarity in "ideological thinking." And these problems are, first and foremost, problems requiring value judgments, which technology simply cannot provide. What, then, can be said about the end-of-ideology thesis?

On the positive side, the end-of-ideology thesis draws attention to the role of bureaucracy in supporting the function of democratic institutions: serving as a minimal corrective on the biases inherent in ideologies as guides to political action. With its characteristic division of intellectual labor, and hence the potential to assimilate more information than any single human mind, bureaucracy helps secure equal treatment before the law and in the policy process. Of course, bureaucracy, like democracy, cannot guarantee such equal treatment. But far more must be said on the negative side. The decline-of-ideology thesis is itself an ideology, rooted in American pragmatism and the philosophy of positivism; like all ideologies, it serves the interests of a particular group, in this case, the intellectuals, bringing them closer to the heavenly city of their so earthly philosophy.

It has now been several centuries since the countries of the world, to say nothing of individual men, have shared a common conception of man, society, and state.[38] Ideological conflicts are not, of course, limited to those between nations; in several countries of Europe, in addition to the United States of America, ideological conflict persists within the societies of the various nations.[39] The simple point is that ideology will continue to influence both foreign and domestic affairs for some time to come.

Unless a new source of political knowledge is discovered—and such a discovery seems quite unlikely—ideologies will continue to serve as guides to political action, perhaps as long as the institutions of the modern nation–state continue to exist. And as long as ideologies serve as guides to political action, there will be a need for democratic institutions to check the tendency of ideologies to guide political action in favor of the few rather than in favor of all citizens, unless, in turn, a new means of checking this tendency can be deployed. To borrow a phrase from the late Reinhold Niebuhr: democracy is a method for finding proximate solutions to insoluble problems.[40]

[38] For a brief discussion, see Michael Oakeshott (ed.), *The Social and Political Doctrines of Contemporary Europe* (New York: The Macmillan Co., 1947), pp. xi–xxiii.
[39] For an interesting approach to ideological conflict in society see Samuel Barnes, "Ideology and the Organization of Conflict," *The Journal of Politics* (Vol. *28,* 1966), pp. 513–530.
[40] This is greatly out of the context within which Niebuhr expressed it. See Reinhold Niebuhr, *The Children of Light and the Children of Darkness* (New York: Charles Scribner's Sons, 1960; 1944), p. 118.

Bibliography

Apter, David (ed.). *Ideology and Discontent.* New York: Free Press, 1964.

Bell, Daniel. *The End of Ideology.* Rev. ed. New York: Free Press, 1962.

Brecht, Arnold. *Political Theory: The Foundations of Twentieth Century Political Thought.* Princeton, N.J.: Princeton University Press, 1959.

Christenson, Reo, *et al. Ideologies and Modern Politics.* New York: Dodd, Mead and Co., 1971.

Cohen, Carl (ed.). *Communism, Fascism and Democracy: The Theoretical Foundations.* 2d ed. New York: Random House, 1972.

Connolly, William E. *Political Science and Ideology.* New York: Atherton, 1967.

Cox, Richard H. (ed.). *Ideology, Politics and Political Theory.* Belmont, Calif.: Wadsworth Publishing Co., 1969. Includes good bibliography, pp. 369–373.

Dolbeare, Kenneth M., and Dolbeare, Patricia, with Hadley, Jane. *American Ideologies: The Competing Political Beliefs of the 1970's.* 2d ed. Chicago: Markham Publishing Co., 1973.

Dolbeare, Kenneth M., Dolbeare, Patricia, and Hadley, Jane. (eds.). *Readings in American Ideologies.* Chicago: Markham, 1973.

Ebenstein, William. *Today's Isms.* 6th ed. Englewood Cliffs, N.J.: Prentice-Hall, 1970.

Germino, Dante. *Beyond Ideology.* New York: Harper and Row, 1967.

Groth, Alexander J. *Major Ideologies.* New York: John Wiley and Sons, 1971.

Hallowell, John H. *Main Currents in Modern Political Thought.* New York: Holt, Rinehart and Winston, 1960.

Ingersoll, David T. *Communism, Fascism and Democracy.* Columbus, Ohio: Charles E. Merrill Publishing Co., 1971.

Kohn, Hans. *Political Ideologies of the Twentieth Century.* 3rd ed. New York: Harper and Row, 1966.

Lane, Robert E. *Political Ideology: Why the Common Man Believes What He Does.* New York: Free Press, 1962.

LaPalombara, Joseph. "Decline of Ideology: A Dissent and an Interpretation," *American Political Science Review LX* (March 1966): 5–16.

Lichtheim, George. *The Concept of Ideology and Other Essays.* New York: Random House, 1967.

Mannheim, Karl. *Ideology and Utopia: An Introduction to the Sociology of Knowledge.* Translated by Louis Wirth and Edward Shils. New York: Harcourt, Brace, 1936.

Marx, Max. *Modern Ideologies.* New York: St. Martin's Press, 1973.

McClosky, Herbert. "Consensus and Ideology in American Politics," *American Political Science Review LVIII* (June 1964): 361–382.

Merelman, Richard M. "The Development of Political Ideology: A Framework for the Analysis of Political Socialization," *American Political Science Review LXIII* (September 1969): 750–767.

Preston, N. S. *Politics, Economics and Power: Ideology and Practice Under Capitalism, Socialism and Fascism.* New York: Macmillan, 1967.

Rejai, Mostafa (ed.). *Decline of Ideology?* New York: Atherton, 1971.

Rokeach, Milton. *The Open and Closed Mind.* New York: Basic Books, 1960.

Sargent, L. T. *Contemporary Political Ideologies.* Rev. ed. Homewood, Ill.: The Dorsey Press, 1972.

Sartori, Giovanni. "Politics, Ideology and Belief Systems," *American Political Science Review LXIII* (June 1969): 398–441.

Shils, Edward. "The Concept and Functions of Ideology," *International Encyclopedia of Social Sciences.* Edited by David Sills. New York: Macmillan and Free Press, 1968, Vol. *VII*, pp. 66–76.

Shklar, Judith. *After Utopia: The Decline of Political Faith.* Princeton, N.J.: Princeton University Press, 1957.

Sigmund, Paul (ed.). *The Ideologies of Developing Nations.* 2d rev. ed. New York: Praeger, 1972.

Ward, Barbara. *Nationalism and Ideology.* New York: W. W. Norton & Co., 1966.

Watkins, Frederick M. *The Age of Ideology: Political Thought, 1750 to the Present.* Englewood Cliffs, N.J.: Prentice-Hall, 1965.

Waxman, Chaim (ed.). *The End of Ideology Debate.* New York: Funk and Wagnalls, 1968.

I Fascism and Racism

No political ideologies offer a more clearly defined religious conception of man, society, and the state than fascism and racism. The comparative study of religions reveals that a fundamental aspect of all religions is the spiritual expression of the corporate identity of a particular group. To state this another way, the basis of all spiritual expression is the ability to recognize ourselves in others and the ability to discern how our group differs from others. Although this notion of a "spiritual expression of a corporate identity" can be found in other political ideologies—Marx's conception of "class" is a good example—the notion forms the very essence of fascist and racist thought.

In fascist and racist doctrine the corporate identity is usually the state (as in fascism), or the race (as in the various forms of racism), or a curious combination of the two (as in naziism). Such a corporate identity emphasizes the spiritual integration and organic unity of the group or community in question. In somewhat less mystical terms, this means that the group is thought to have a unity of purpose because it has a unity of existence. The group, analogous with a human being, has its own distinct "personality" and "will." Conceived as a spiritual phenomenon, the group is exalted in moral value until it assumes a reality and significance above any of its constituent members. By emphasizing the transcendental or spiritual nature of the particular group in question, the fascists and racists exaggerate the importance of the corporate identity, often at the expense of the individual members.

As political ideologies, fascism and racism represent attempts to impose, often where it does not exist, a conciliation of interests and a unity of purpose. It is in this respect that fascism and racism are products of political activity peculiar to the modern nation–state. As guides for political action, both fascism and racism presume the centralization of power and authority so characteristic of the modern nation–state, particularly in times of war. And both emphasize the unity of purpose implicit in the notion of sovereignty as it has evolved with the growth of the institutions of the modern nation–state.

The principal means through which the corporate identity is forged, in both doctrine and practice, is the exercise of force and coercion, made possible through the concentration of power in the institutions of the modern nation–state. Of course an appeal is made to a common spiritual identity—much like the appeal of any nationalistic doctrine—through shared but often meaningless symbols. The crucial point is, however, that the harmony of interests and the unity of purpose presupposed by the fascist and racist doctrines are more "spiritual" than real. That is to say, there is little basis in fact for the supposed common identity of interests across the vast sections of a society.

In the absence of a common purpose and unity of interests, fascist and racist political activity becomes a conscious effort to realize the interests of a particular group, whether those be the interests of a political elite or the supposed interests of a certain race or nation. Fascists and racists deliberately attend to those arrangements of society which are most supportive or most conducive to their alleged group interests, usually at the cost and deprivation of vast sections of society as a whole.

The readings to follow clearly demonstrate the various aspects of fascism and racism discussed above. The first selection is by Benito Mussolini, leader of the Italian Fascist Party before and during the Second World War. Mussolini argues that the spiritual identity of man is the nation and country. The state, according to Mussolini, is the true expression of the individual. In fascist doctrine all interests are conciliated in the unity of the state. Emphasizing the importance of political elites in directing the activities of the state, Mussolini finds that the "people" are realized only through the consciousness and will of the few—or perhaps of one only. Depicting the fascist state as a will expressing power and empire, Mussolini sees the state as the creator of "right." The individual, in consequence, owes to the state absolute duty and obedience.

Like Mussolini, Dennis, the most articulate American proponent of fascism, emphasizes the importance of educative institutions—such as schools, the press, and radio—as agents of social control. By means of these institutions, Dennis argues, we can harmonize the development of an individual's mind and character with the purposes embodied in the national plan. Manipulating the thought and feeling of the masses, the dominant elites can fit groups of people into schemes of social organization conducive to the goals of the elites. (These elite goals constitute the presumed unity of purpose in society.) At the same time, according to Dennis, this manipulation of thought and feeling assures the elites that the people will like the arrangements of society constructed through the "national plan."

Quite consistent with the fascist doctrine of Mussolini and Dennis, Adolf Hitler emphasizes the primary importance of subordinating the interests of ego (the individual) to those of the community. Unlike the fascists, however, who see man as a spiritual expression of nation and country, Hitler argues that the basis of community is a self-sacrificing will to give one's labor and possibly even one's life for the community. This self-sacrificing will, according to Hitler, is a racial characteristic most strongly developed in the Aryan. As a culture-creating race in Hitler's schema, the Aryans transform egoism into selfless caring for the Aryan community. Hitler further identifies the Aryan race or folk with the German nation. By so doing he seeks to show that those races, such as the Jews, which he accuses of defiling the Aryan race, also cause a similar decline in the German nation. Thus, unlike fascist ideology, Hitler's ideology combines a curious mixture of biological models of evolutionary activity with models abstracted from the activities of the modern nation–state.

Paralleling Hitler's discussion of the Aryan race, Hiram Evans, who in 1926 was Imperial Wizard and Emperor of the Knights of the Ku Klux Klan, maintains that the Nordic race in America is the source of modern civilization. Like Hitler, Evans identifies an alien component in Nordic society which, although sharing the Nordic heritage and prosperity, betrays the Nordic interests. These aliens, Evans imagines, because of instincts, character, and thought fixed by centuries of racial selection and development, work only for the interests of their own peoples. Arguing that diverse races can never live together in harmony, while asserting some fundamental ties between nation and race, Evans issues an urgent plea for patriotism: America for Americans—just as Hitler seeks a German state for the German nation and the Aryan race.

1 The Doctrine of Fascism

BENITO MUSSOLINI

Fundamental Ideas

Like every sound political conception, Fascism is both practice and thought; action in which a doctrine is immanent, and a doctrine which, arising out of a given system of historical forces, remains embedded in them and works there from within. Hence it has a form correlative to the contingencies of place and time, but it has also a content of thought which raises it to a formula of truth in the higher level of the history of thought. In the world one does not act spiritually as a human will dominating other wills without a conception of the transient and particular reality under which it is necessary to act, and of the permanent and universal reality in which the first has its being and its life. In order to know men it is necessary to know man; and in order to know man it is necessary to know reality and its laws. There is no concept of the State which is not fundamentally a concept of life: philosophy or intuition, a system of ideas which develops logically or is gathered up into a vision or into a faith, but which is always, at least virtually, an organic conception of the world.

Thus Fascism could not be understood in many of its practical manifestations as a party organization, as a system of education, as a discipline, if it were not always looked at in the light of its whole way of conceiving life, a spiritualized way. The world seen through Fascism is not this material world which appears on the surface, in which man is an individual separated from all others and standing by himself, and in which he is governed by a natural law which makes him instinctively live a life of selfish and momentary pleasure. The man of Fascism is an individual who is nation and fatherland, which is a moral law, binding together individuals and the generations into a tradition and a mission, suppressing the instinct for a life enclosed within the brief round of pleasure in order to restore within duty a higher life free from the limits of time and space: a life in which the individual, through the denial of himself, through the sacrifice of his own private interests, through death itself, realizes that completely spiritual existence in which his value as a man lies.

Therefore it is a spiritualized conception, itself the result of the general reaction of modern times against the flabby materialistic positivism of the

SOURCE: Benito Mussolini, "The Doctrine of Fascism," from *The Social and Political Doctrines of Contemporary Europe*, ed. Michael Oakeshott. Reprinted by permission of Oxford University Press © 1949.

nineteenth century. Anti-positivistic, but positive: not sceptical, nor agnostic, nor pessimistic, nor passively optimistic, as are, in general, the doctrines (all negative) that put the centre of life outside man, who with his free will can and must create his own world. Fascism desires an active man, one engaged in activity with all his energies: it desires a man virilely conscious of the difficulties that exist in action and ready to face them. It conceives of life as a struggle, considering that it behoves man to conquer for himself that life truly worthy of him, creating first of all in himself the instrument (physical, moral, intellectual) in order to construct it. Thus for the single individual, thus for the nation, thus for humanity. Hence the high value of culture in all its forms (art, religion, science), and the enormous importance of education. Hence also the essential value of work, with which man conquers nature and creates the human world (economic, political, moral, intellectual).

This positive conception of life is clearly an ethical conception. It covers the whole of reality, not merely the human activity which controls it. No action can be divorced from moral judgement; there is nothing in the world which can be deprived of the value which belongs to everything in its relation to moral ends. Life, therefore, as conceived by the Fascist, is serious, austere, religious: the whole of it is poised in a world supported by the moral and responsible forces of the spirit. The Fascist disdains the "comfortable" life.

Fascism is a religious conception in which man is seen in his immanent relationship with a superior law and with an objective Will that transcends the particular individual and raises him to conscious membership of a spiritual society. Whoever has seen in the religious politics of the Fascist regime nothing but mere opportunism has not understood that Fascism besides being a system of government is also, and above all, a system of thought.

Fascism is an historical conception, in which man is what he is only in so far as he works with the spiritual process in which he finds himself, in the family or social group, in the nation and in the history in which all nations collaborate. From this follows the great value of tradition, in memories, in language, in customs, in the standards of social life. Outside history man is nothing. Consequently Fascism is opposed to all the individualistic abstractions of a materialistic nature like those of the eighteenth century; and it is opposed to all Jacobin utopias and innovations. It does not consider that "happiness" is possible upon earth, as it appeared to be in the desire of the economic literature of the eighteenth century, and hence it rejects all teleological theories according to which mankind would reach a definitive stabilized condition at a certain period in history. This implies putting oneself outside history and life, which is a continual change and coming to be. Politically, Fascism wishes to be a realistic doctrine; practically, it aspires to solve only the problems which arise historically of themselves and that of themselves find or suggest their own solution. To act among men, as to act in the natural world, it is necessary to enter into the process of reality and to master the already operating forces.

Against individualism, the Fascist conception is for the State; and it is for the individual in so far as he coincides with the State, which is the conscience and universal will of man in his historical existence. It is opposed to classical Liberalism, which arose from the necessity of reacting against absolutism, and which brought its historical purpose to an end when the State was transformed into the conscience and will of the people. Liberalism denied the State in the interests of the particular individual; Fascism reaffirms the State as the true reality of the individual. And if liberty is to be the attribute of the real man, and not of that abstract puppet envisaged by individualistic Liberalism, Fascism is for liberty. And for the only liberty which can be a real thing, the liberty of the State and of the individual within the State. Therefore, for the Fascist, everything is in the State, and nothing human or spiritual exists, much less has value, outside the State. In this sense Fascism is totalitarian, and the Fascist State, the synthesis and unity of all values, interprets, develops and gives strength to the whole life of the people.

Outside the State there can be neither individuals nor groups (political parties, associations, syndicates, classes). Therefore Fascism is opposed to Socialism, which confines the movement of history within the class struggle and ignores the unity of classes established in one economic and moral reality in the State; and analogously it is opposed to class syndicalism. Fascism recognizes the real exigencies for which the socialist and syndicalist movement arose, but while recognizing them wishes to bring them under the control of the State and give them a purpose within the corporative system of interests reconciled within the unity of the State.

Individuals form classes according to the similarity of their interests, they form syndicates according to differentiated economic activities within these interests; but they form first, and above all, the State, which is not to be thought of numerically as the sum-total of individuals forming the majority of a nation. And consequently Fascism is opposed to Democracy, which equates the nation to the majority, lowering it to the level of that majority; nevertheless it is the purest form of democracy if the nation is conceived, as it should be, qualitatively and not quantitatively, as the most powerful idea (most powerful because most moral, most coherent, most true) which acts within the nation as the conscience and the will of a few, even of One, which ideal tends to become active within the conscience and the will of all—that is to say, of all those who rightly constitute a nation by reason of nature, history or race, and have set out upon the same line of development and spiritual formation as one conscience and one sole will. Not a race,[1] nor a geographically determined region, but as a community historically perpetu-

[1] "Race; it is an emotion, not a reality; ninety-five per cent of it is emotion."—Mussolini.

ating itself, a multitude unified by a single idea, which is the will to existence and to power: consciousness of itself, personality.

This higher personality is truly the nation in so far as it is the State. It is not the nation that generates the State, as according to the old naturalistic concept which served as the basis of the political theories of the national States of the nineteenth century. Rather the nation is created by the State, which gives to the people, conscious of its own moral unity, a will and therefore an effective existence. The right of a nation to independence derives not from a literary and ideal consciousness of its own being, still less from a more or less unconscious and inert acceptance of a *de facto* situation, but from an active consciousness, from a political will in action and ready to demonstrate its own rights: that is to say, from a state already coming into being. The State, in fact, as the universal ethical will, is the creator of right.

The nation as the State is an ethical reality which exists and lives in so far as it develops. To arrest its development is to kill it. Therefore, the State is not only the authority which governs and gives the form of laws and the value of spiritual life to the wills of the individuals, but it is also a power that makes its will felt abroad, making it known and respected, in other words, demonstrating the fact of its universality in all the necessary directions of its development. It is consequently organization and expansion, at least virtually. Thus it can be likened to the human will which knows no limits to its development and realizes itself in testing its own limitlessness.

The Fascist State, the highest and most powerful form of personality, is a force, but a spiritual force, which takes over all the forms of the moral and intellectual life of man. It cannot therefore confine itself simply to the functions of order and supervision as Liberalism desired. It is not simply a mechanism which limits the sphere of the supposed liberties of the individual. It is the form, the inner standard and the discipline of the whole person; it saturates the will as well as the intelligence. Its principle, the central inspiration of the human personality living in the civil community, pierces into the depths and makes its home in the heart of the man of action as well as of the thinker, of the artist as well as of the scientist: it is the soul of the soul.

Fascism, in short, is not only the giver of laws and the founder of institutions, but the educator and promoter of spiritual life. It wants to remake, not the forms of human life, but its content, man, character, faith. And to this end it requires discipline and authority that can enter into the spirits of men and there govern unopposed. Its sign, therefore, is the Lictors' rods, the symbol of unity, of strength and justice.

Political and Social Doctrine

When in the now distant March of 1919 I summoned to Milan, through the columns of the *Popolo d'Italia,* my surviving supporters who had followed me since the constitution of the Fasces of Revolutionary Action, founded in January 1915, there was no specific doctrinal plan in my mind. I had known and lived through only one doctrine, that of the Socialism of 1903–4 up to the winter of 1914, almost ten years. My experience in this had been that of a follower and of a leader, but not that of a theoretician. My doctrine, even in that period, had been a doctrine of action. . . .

. . . Fascism was not given out to the wet nurse of a doctrine elaborated beforehand round a table: it was born of the need for action; it was not a party, but in its first two years it was a movement against all parties. The name which I gave to the organization defined its characteristics. Nevertheless, whoever rereads, in the now crumpled pages of the time, the account of the constituent assembly of the *Fasci italiani di Combattimento* will not find a doctrine, but a series of suggestions, of anticipations, of admonitions, which when freed from the inevitable vein of contingency, were destined later, after a few years, to develop into a series of doctrinal attitudes which made of Fascism a self-sufficient political doctrine able to face all others, both past and present. "If the bourgeoisie," I said at that time, "thinks to find us a lightning-conductor, it is mistaken. We must go forward in opposition to Labour. . . . We want to accustom the working classes to being under a leader, to convince them also that it is not easy to direct an industry or a commercial undertaking successfully. . . . We shall fight against technical and spiritual retrogression. . . . The successors of the present regime still being undecided, we must not be unwilling to fight for it. We must hasten; when the present regime is superseded, we must be the ones to take its place. The right of succession belongs to us because we pushed the country into the War and we lead it to victory. The present method of political representation cannot be sufficient for us, we wish for a direct representation of individual interests. . . ."

The years preceding the March on Rome were years during which the necessity of action did not tolerate enquiries or complete elaborations of doctrine. Battles were being fought in the cities and villages. There were discussions, but—and this is more sacred and important—there were deaths. People knew how to die. The doctrine—beautiful, well-formed, divided into chapters and paragraphs and surrounded by a commentary—might be missing; but there was present something more decisive to supplant it—Faith. Nevertheless, he who recalls the past with the aid of books, articles, votes in Parliament, the major and the minor speeches, he who knows how to investigate and weigh evidence, will find that the foundations of the doctrine were laid while the battle was raging. It was precisely in these years that Fascist thought armed itself, refined itself, moving towards one organization of its own. The problems of the individual and the State; the problems of authority and liberty; political and social problems and those more specifically national; the struggle against liberal, democratic, socialist, Masonic, demagogic doctrines was carried on at the same time as the "punitive expeditions". But since the "system" was lacking, adversaries ingenuously denied that Fascism had any power to make a doctrine of its own, while the doctrine rose up, even though tumultuously, at first under the aspect of a violent and dogmatic negation, as happens to all ideas that break new ground, then under the positive aspect of a constructive policy which, during the years 1926, 1927, 1928, was realized in the laws and institutions of the regime.

Fascism is to-day clearly defined not only as a regime but as a doctrine. And I mean by this that Fascism to-day, self-critical as well as critical of other movements, has an unequivocal point of view of its own, a criterion, and hence an aim, in face of all the material and intellectual problems which oppress the people of the world.

Above all, Fascism, in so far as it considers and observes the future and the development of humanity quite apart from the political considerations of the moment, believes neither in the possibility nor in the utility of perpetual peace. It thus repudiates the doctrine of Pacifism—born of a renunciation of the struggle and an act of cowardice in the face of sacrifice. War alone brings up to their highest tension all human energies and puts the stamp of nobility upon the peoples who have the courage to meet it. All other trials are substitutes, which never really put a man in front of himself in the alternative of life and death. A doctrine, therefore, which begins with a prejudice in favour of peace is foreign to Fascism; as are foreign to the Fascism, even though acceptable by reason of the utility which they might have in given political situations, all internationalistic and socialistic systems which, as history proves, can be blown to the winds when emotional, idealistic and practical movements storm the hearts of peoples. Fascism carries over this anti-pacifist spirit even into the lives of individuals. The proud motto of the Squadrista, "Me ne frego", written on the bandages of a wound is an act of philosophy which is not only stoical, it is the epitome of a doctrine that is not only political: it is education for combat, the acceptance of the risks which it brings; it is a new way of life for Italy. Thus the Fascist accepts and loves life, he knows nothing of suicide and despises it; he looks on life as duty, ascent, conquest: life which must be noble and full: lived for oneself, but above all for those others near and far away, present and future.

The "demographic" policy of the regime follows from these premises. Even the Fascist does in fact love his neighbour, but this "neighbour" is not for him a vague and ill-defined concept; love for one's neighbour does not exclude necessary educational severities, and still less differentiations and distances. Fascism rejects universal concord, and, since it lives in the community of civilized peoples, it keeps them vigilantly and suspiciously before its eyes, it follows their states of mind and the changes in their interests and it does not let itself be deceived by temporary and fallacious appearances.

Such a conception of life makes Fascism the precise negation of that doctrine which formed the basis of the so-called Scientific or Marxian Socialism: the doctrine of historical materialism, according to which the history of human civilizations can be explained only as the struggle of interest between the different social groups and as arising out of change in the means and instruments of production. That economic improvements—discoveries of raw materials, new methods of work, scientific inventions—should have an importance of their own, no one denies, but that they should suffice to explain human history to the exclusion of all other factors is absurd: Fascism believes, now and always, in holiness and in heroism, that is in acts in which no economic motive—remote or immediate—plays a part. With this negation of historical materialism, according to which men would be only by-products of history, who appear and disappear on the surface of the waves while in the depths the real directive forces are at work, there is also denied the immutable and irreparable "class struggle" which is the natural product of this economic conception of history, and above all it is denied that the class struggle can be the primary agent of social changes. Socialism, being thus wounded in these two primary tenets of its doctrine, nothing of it is left save the sentimental aspiration—old as humanity—towards a social order in which the sufferings and the pains of the humblest folk could be alleviated. But here Fascism rejects the concept of an economic "happiness" which would be realized socialistically and almost automatically at a given moment of economic evolution by assuring to all a maximum prosperity. Fascism denies the possibility of the materialistic conception of "happiness" and leaves it to the economists of the first half of the eighteenth century; it denies, that is, the equation of prosperity with happiness, which would transform men into animals with one sole preoccupation: that of being well-fed and fat, degraded in consequence to a merely physical existence.

After Socialism, Fascism attacks the whole complex of democratic ideologies and rejects them both in their theoretical premises and in their applications or practical manifestations. Fascism denies that the majority, through the mere fact of being a majority, can rule human societies; it denies that this majority can govern by means of a periodical consultation; it affirms the irremediable, fruitful and beneficent inequality of men, who cannot be levelled by such a mechanical and extrinsic fact as universal suffrage. By democratic regimes we mean those in which from time to time the people is given the illusion of being sovereign, while true effective sovereignty lies in other, perhaps irresponsible and secret, forces. Democracy is a regime without a king, but with very many kings, perhaps more exclusive, tyrannical and violent than one king even though a tyrant. This explains why Fascism, although before 1922 for reasons of expediency it made a gesture of republicanism, renounced it before the March on Rome, convinced that the question of the political forms of a State is not pre-eminent to-day, and that studying past and present monarchies, past and present Republics it becomes clear that monarchy and republic are not to be judged *sub specie aeternitatis,* but represent forms in which the political evolution, the history, the tradition, the psychology of a given country are manifested. Now Fascism overcomes the antithesis between monarchy and republic which retarded the movements of democracy, burdening the former with every defect and defending the latter as the regime of perfection. Now it has been seen that there are inherently reactionary and absolutistic republics, and monarchies that welcome the most daring political and social innovations.

"Reason, Science", said Renan (who was inspired before Fascism existed) in one of his philosophical Meditations, "are products of humanity, but to expect reason directly from the people and through the people is a chimera. It is not necessary for the existence of reason that everybody should know it. In any case, if such an initiation should be made, it would not be made by means of base democracy, which apparently must lead to the extinction of every difficult culture, and every higher discipline. The principle that society exists only for the prosperity and the liberty of individuals who compose it does not seem to conform with the plans of nature, plans in which the species alone is taken into consideration and the individual seems to be sacrificed. It is strongly to be feared lest the last word of democracy thus understood (I hasten to say that it can also be understood in other ways) would be a social state in which a degenerate mass would have no other care than to enjoy the ignoble pleasures of vulgar men."

Thus far Renan. Fascism rejects in democracy the absurd conventional lie of political equalitarianism clothed in the dress of collective irresponsibility and the myth of happiness and indefinite progress. But if democracy can be understood in other ways, that is, if democracy means not to relegate the people to the periphery of the State, then Fascism could be defined as an "organized, centralized, authoritarian democracy".

In face of Liberal doctrines, Fascism takes up an attitude of absolute opposition both in the field of politics and in that of economics. . . . From 1870–1915 there occurs the period in which the very priests of the new creed had to confess the twilight of their religion: defeated as it was by decadence in literature, by activism in practice. Activism: that is to say, Nationalism, Futurism, Fascism. The "Liberal" century, after having accumulated an infinity of Gordian knots, tried to untie them by the hecatomb of the World War. Never before has any religion imposed such a cruel sacrifice. Were the gods of Liberalism thirsty for blood? Now Liberalism is about to close the doors of its deserted temples because the peoples feel that its agnosticism in economics, its indifferentism in politics and in morals, would lead, as they have led, the States to certain ruin. In this way one can understand why all the political experiences of the contemporary world are anti-Liberal, and it is supremely ridiculous to wish on that account to class them outside of history; as if history were a hunting ground reserved to Liberalism and its professors, as if Liberalism were the definitive and no longer surpassable message of civilization.

But the Fascist repudiations of Socialism, Democracy, Liberalism must not make one think that Fascism wishes to make the world return to what it was before 1789, the year which has been indicated as the year of the beginning of the liberal-democratic age. One does not go backwards. The Fascist doctrine has not chosen De Maistre as its prophet. Monarchical absolutism is a thing of the past and so also is every theocracy. So also feudal privileges and division into impenetrable and isolated castes have had their day. The theory of Fascist authority has nothing to do with the police State. A party that governs a nation in a totalitarian way is a new fact in history. References and comparisons are not possible. Fascism takes over from the ruins of Liberal Socialistic democratic doctrines those elements which still have a living value. It preserves those that can be called the established facts of history, it rejects all the rest, that is to say the idea of a doctrine which holds good for all times and all peoples. If it is admitted that the nineteenth century has been the century of Socialism, Liberalism and Democracy, it does not follow that the twentieth must also be the century of Liberalism, Socialism and Democracy. Political doctrines pass; peoples remain. It is to be expected that this century may be that of authority, a century of the "Right", a Fascist century. If the nineteenth was the century of the individual (Liberalism means individualism) it may be expected that this one may be the century of "collectivism" and therefore the century of the State. That a new doctrine should use the still vital elements of other doctrines is perfectly logical. No doctrine is born quite new, shining, never before seen. Now doctrine can boast of an absolute "originality". It is bound, even if only historically, to other doctrines that have been, and to develop into other doctrines that will be. Thus the scientific socialism of Marx is bound to the Utopian Socialism of the Fouriers, the Owens and the Saint-Simons; thus the Liberalism of the nineteenth century is connected with the whole "Enlightenment" of the eighteenth century. Thus the doctrines of democracy are bound to the *Encyclopédie.* Every doctrine tends to direct the activity of men towards a determined objective; but the activity of man reacts upon the doctrine, transforms it, adapts it to new necessities or transcends it. The doctrine itself, therefore, must be, not words, but an act of life. Hence, the pragmatic veins in Fascism, its will to power, its will to be, its attitude in the face of the fact of "violence" and of its own courage.

The keystone of Fascist doctrine is the conception of the State, of its essence, of its tasks, of its ends. For Fascism the State is an absolute before which individuals and groups are relative. Individuals and groups are "thinkable" in so far as they are within the State. The Liberal State does not direct the interplay and the material and spiritual development of the groups, but limits itself to registering the results; the Fascist State has a consciousness of its own, a will of its own, on this account it is called an "ethical" State. In 1929, at the first quinquennial assembly of the regime, I said: "For Fascism, the State is not the night-watchman who is concerned only with the personal security of the citizens; nor is it an organization for purely material ends, such as that of guaranteeing a certain degree of prosperity and a relatively peaceful social order, to achieve which a council of administration would be sufficient, nor is it a creation of mere politics with no contact with the material and complex reality of the lives of individuals and the life of peoples. The State, as conceived by Fascism and as it acts, is a spiritual and moral fact because it makes concrete the political, juridical, economic organization of the nation and such an organization is, in its origin and in its development, a manifestation of the spirit. The State is the guarantor of internal and external security, but it is also the guardian and the transmitter of the spirit of the people as it has been elaborated through the centuries in language, custom, faith. The State is not only present, it is also past, and above all future. It is the State which, transcending the brief limit of individual lives, represents the immanent conscience of the nation. The forms in which States express themselves change, but the necessity of the State remains. It is the State which educates citizens for civic virtue, makes them conscious of their mission, calls them to unity; harmonizes their interests in justice; hands on the achievements of thought in the sciences, the arts, in law, in human solidarity; it carries men from the elementary life of the tribe to the highest human expression of power which is Empire; it entrusts to the ages the names of those who died for its integrity or in obedience to its laws; it puts forward as an example and recommends to the generations that are to come the leaders who increased its territory and the men of genius who gave it glory. When the sense of the State declines and the disintegrating and centrifugal tendencies of individuals and groups prevail, national societies move to their decline."

From 1929 up to the present day these doctrinal positions have been strengthened by the whole economico-political evolution of the world. It is the State alone that grows in size, in power. It is the State alone that can solve the dramatic contradictions of capitalism. What is called the crisis cannot be overcome except by the State, within the State. . . . But when one says liberalism, one says the individual; when one says Fascism, one says the State. But the Fascist State is unique; it is an original creation. It is not reactionary, but revolutionary in that it anticipates the solutions of certain universal problems. These problems are no longer seen in the same light: in the sphere of politics they are removed from party rivalries, from the supreme power of parliament, from the irresponsibility of assemblies; in the sphere of economics they are removed from the sphere of the syndicates' activities—activities that were ever widening their scope and increasing their power both on the workers' side and on the employers'—removed from their struggles and their designs; in the moral sphere they are divorced from ideas of the need for order, discipline and obedience, and lifted into the plane of the moral commandments of the fatherland. Fascism desires the State to be strong, organic and at the same time founded on a wide popular basis. The Fascist State has also claimed for itself the field of economics and, through the corporative, social and educational institutions which it has created, the meaning of the State reaches out to and includes the farthest off-shoots; and within the State, framed in their respective organizations, there revolve all the political, economic and spiritual forces of the nation. A State founded on millions of individuals who recognize it, feel it, are ready to serve it, is not the tyrannical State of the medieval lord. It has nothing in common with the absolutist States that existed either before or after 1789. In the Fascist State the individual is not suppressed, but rather multiplied, just as in a regiment a soldier is not weakened but multiplied by the number of his comrades. The Fascist State organizes the nation, but it leaves sufficient scope to individuals; it has limited useless or harmful liberties and has preserved those that are essential. It cannot be the individual who decides in this matter, but only the State.

The Fascist State does not remain indifferent to the fact of religion in general and to that particular positive religion which is Italian Catholicism. The State has no theology, but it has an ethic. In the Fascist State religion is looked upon as one of the deepest manifestations of the spirit; it is, therefore, not only respected, but defended and protected. The Fascist State does not create a "God" of its own, as Robespierre once, at the height of the Convention's foolishness, wished to do; nor does it vainly seek, like Bolshevism, to expel religion from the minds of men; Fascism respects the God of the ascetics, of the saints, of the heroes, and also God as seen and prayed to by the simple and primitive heart of the people.

The Fascist State is a will to power and to government. In it the tradition of Rome is an idea that has force. In the doctrine of Fascism Empire is not only a territorial, military or mercantile expression, but spiritual or moral. One can think of an empire, that is to say a nation that directly or indirectly leads other nations, without needing to conquer a single square kilometre of territory. For Fascism the tendency to Empire, that is to say, to the expansion of nations, is a manifestation of vitality; its opposite, staying at home, is a sign of decadence: peoples who rise or re-rise are imperialist, peoples who die are renunciatory. Fascism is the doctrine that is most fitted to represent the aims, the states of mind, of a people, like the Italian people, rising again after many centuries of abandonment or slavery to foreigners. But Empire calls for discipline, co-ordination of forces, duty and sacrifice; this explains many aspects of the practical working of the regime and the direction of many of the forces of the State and the necessary severity shown to those who would wish to oppose this spontaneous and destined impulse of the Italy of the twentieth century, to oppose it in the name of the superseded ideologies of the nineteenth, repudiated wherever great experiments of political and social transformation have been courageously attempted: especially where, as now, peoples thirst for authority, for leadership, for order. If every age has its own doctrine, it is apparent from a thousand signs that the doctrine of the present age is Fascism. That it is a doctrine of life is shown by the fact that it has resuscitated a faith. That this faith has conquered minds is proved by the fact that Fascism has had its dead and its martyrs.

Fascism henceforward has in the world the universality of all those doctrines which, by fulfilling themselves, have significance in the history of the human spirit.

1932

2 Control: Making Good Citizens

LAWRENCE DENNIS

Continuing the discussion of social control, we shall be concerned with the processes of education, indoctrination, and inculcation of right attitudes. We may, then, divide all human institutions into those in which education is purposive, or done with certain purposes pursued by those in charge of the institution, and those institutions in which education is nonpurposive and purely, or chiefly, incidental. The school is one institution which most people will readily admit has this purpose and educates with definite purposes. . . .

Before entering upon a brief discussion of education by the school as one of the important agencies of social control or government, let us run over one or two considerations which link up certain other institutions with the school as educators with social purposes. The church, the press, the theater, the moving picture, and the radio undoubtedly do more educating than the school, if for no other reason than that they educate people throughout their entire lifetimes. These institutions also educate with definite social purposes. Sometimes these purposes harmonize with the larger purposes of the social plan, and sometimes they certainly do not. In the fascist view of things, all institutional formation of character, mind, social attitudes, and opinions with a social purpose, must harmonize with, and not be antagonistic to, the larger purposes of the national plan. This means that fascism holds that no institution forming people's minds, characters, and attitudes should have among its purposes or effects the unfitting of people for good citizenship as the State defines good citizenship.

It is obviously impossible to list all the offenses which purposive edu-

SOURCE: from pp. 211–228 in *The Coming American Fascism* by Lawrence Dennis. Copyright, 1936 by Harper & Row, Publishers. Reprinted by permission of Harper & Row, Publishers.

cation, whether by the church, school, or radio, can commit against the national interest. It is only possible, in a brief space, to outline certain guiding principles in reference to purposive education by powerful social institutions. The first consideration in order of logical approach, perhaps, is the one most ignored, or openly denied, by liberalism. It is the consideration that institutions like the church, the radio, or the press, to mention only three examples, do form people's minds and social attitudes with definite social purposes which are determined by the persons in charge of the institution, or, more particularly, by the persons in charge of the particular unit of the institution in question. No one can work on a farm or in a bakery without getting a good deal of education from the experience, but the social attitudes acquired while undergoing these experiences may vary greatly. Few persons, however, can read the Hearst papers daily, or tune in daily on certain radio programs, or attend weekly certain churches, without having their social attitudes and opinions markedly determined by these experiences. In the cases of a majority of those constantly exposed to one of these institutional educators with a purpose, it may be said that most of their opinions and attitudes will be derived almost entirely from two or three of these.

From the consideration just stated follows a second one, that given units of some of these important institutional educators or opinion- and attitude-formers are largely—at times, wholly—controlled by powerful persons or economic interests for private ends which are not always consistent with public ends. These rich persons who can own a newspaper, buy time over national hook-ups, and command the resources of expensive publicity experts, or these powerful interests which, because of their economic power as advertisers and contributors to persons and institutions, can dictate largely the policies of churches, newspapers, moving pictures, and radio, or of cultural leaders, can and do, through the sheer might of money, use these educational institutions or leaders to make people think and feel as it suits their interests. The facts are matters of such common knowledge, and have been exposed so many times and in so many connections, that it seems superfluous to support the foregoing generalizations with detailed examples. The consideration, then, that people by the million are being made to think, feel, and vote as powerful economic interests desire, through the use of the character-, mind-, and attitude-forming techniques of important institutions, constitutes one of the best refutations of liberal premises and one of the strongest arguments for fascism.

Liberalism talks freedom of the press, the pulpit, the radio and, in fact, all the institutions which educate people and form social attitudes. But liberalism cannot make such freedom a reality in a world of present-day complexities of economic organization and of present-day inequalities of economic power. Fascism does not talk in preposterous terms of a freedom which is non-existent and impossible to maintain, but rather in terms of a social discipline which it is possible for the State to impose in the name of a given ideal of national interest. So far as freedom is concerned (if that term in the abstract and by itself can ever have much meaning) it may be said that the people as a whole have most freedom where they have most opportunities to do what they like, and where they most like to do the things they have opportunities to do. Liberal freedom in practice today means, among other things, freedom for powerful economic interests to manipulate public opinion, and the social attitudes of the masses, to suit selfish private or corporate ends. It cannot be shown that a large measure of freedom for such manipulation gives the people as a whole more freedom than a drastic State discipline of it in the public interest would afford.

Stated somewhat differently, the question really is: Who shall manipulate the opinions, feelings, and attitudes of the masses?—for manipulated they must and will be in a civilization as complex and highly organized as ours. Is it preferable to have mass opinions, feelings, and social attitudes manipulated by powerful private interests for personal or minority group ends, or to have mass opinions guided by a national State in the pursuit of some idealized plan of social well-being and order? In this connection, the case against the manipulation of mass opinions and social attitudes by private or corporate interests pursuing personal or minority group ends, is that these manipulators have no concern with, or responsibility for, public order. They ask freedom to use economic power to manipulate mass opinions and emotions, but decline all responsibility for the social consequences. The State, or those in charge of government, can never act with such irresponsibility, for, after all, it is those in charge of government—not those in charge of countinghouses—who, in a crisis, must deal with the hungry and unemployed mob and must ensure that the trains run and the banks reopen.

Liberal theory may be said to regard the great social institutions through which the characters, minds, and attitudes of the people are formed somewhat as one might have regarded the village well in a 17th century English hamlet. The well was free for every one, who could take from it as much water as he wanted. It was run by no one, and had no social purpose. It was a social institution which was just used by every one as he saw fit, and which was never, as a practical matter, subject to serious misuse or abuse by any one. For one thing, water in England was abundant. For another, people in 17th century England used comparatively little water, and had no reason to misuse the well. Any selfish person who might have thought of establishing a monopoly over the well would have been dealt with adequately by the town constables—if not by a few strong-armed villagers.

Up to about the middle of the 19th century the press and the platform, like the village well, were, more or less, institutions available for the free and equal use of those competent to use them. When rich men patronized the arts and letters, their demands and impositions were of socially slight significance. Once the monopoly of the State religion was broken sufficiently to allow substantial tolerance of other forms of worship (from about the beginning of the 18th century in England) different social ideas then current competed in a fairly free market and on terms of a considerable degree of equality.

The radical British liberals, utopians, socialists, and idealists of the late 18th and early 19th centuries had practically as much access to the public mind as the extreme conservatives. For the small elite of literate persons to whom such ideas were accessible, there was considerable freedom both in presenting and accepting ideas. Capitalists had not yet begun to use mass propaganda. In England, they controlled Parliament through the rotten boroughs, in which a handful of personal employees or friends of the lord of the manor would elect him or his designate. With the reform of the rotten boroughs in England toward the middle of the 19th century, with the enlargement of the franchise, and with the growth of population of the United States from the time of Andrew Jackson on, the powerful economic interests began to find it necessary to buy political control more and more through the instrumentalities of those institutions now under discussion, namely, those which educate with definite social purposes.

Up to the middle of the 19th century the masses had not acquired enough economic importance or buying power to make it worth while for capitalists to buy up control of the colleges, newspapers, and intellectual leaders as instruments of mass control, business promotion, and property protection. Up to the beginning of the era of nearly universal literacy and suffrage, the consumers of intellectual products were a critical, discriminating, and strongly opinionated elite. They were persons of high personal cultivaton and well-grounded tastes. On the intellectual elite of the 17th and 18th centuries the arts of modern advertising and propaganda would have been largely wasted. The 18th century Americans who read the heavy political literature of that period, such as was produced by the Adamses, Jefferson, Monroe, Hamilton, and Franklin, would have furnished no market for the arts of the contributors to the popular publications of our day.

Those Americans of the elite were doubtless wrong in their opinions as often, or as much, as the Americans of today, but they were able to expound and defend their opinions. Whereas the masses who get their opinions from subsidized institutions at the present time can only repeat them parrot-like in the terms in which advertising and propagandizing technique have planted such ideas in their minds. Most of the liberal assumptions about freedom of speech and the press presuppose that the written and spoken word is addressed mainly to an elite which maintains high standards of critical judgment.

Modern democracy and mass purchasing power, really, are most to be blamed for the creation of a selfish interest in the control and use of the institutions which can be made to educate with any desired purposes. The modern lobby is the creature of liberal democracy. It pays to advertise. It pays to educate the public to your purposes. Because it pays to educate the public to suit anti-social purposes, the liberal assumptions are fallacious and in this respect the fascist principles are inevitable. The more money you can make, the more you can control public education. Fascism does not seek to end the control of might, but it does aim at ending the control of irresponsible might such as is so often exercised under liberal capitalism.

Under a desirable form of fascism for Americans, national interest should not require the same drastic measures of suppression and assimilation of institutions as have been taken in Germany in connection with the church, the press, the theater, the moving picture, and the radio. Adequate observance of the essential principle for public order simply means in this connection that all institutions which educate with a social purpose must be careful to avoid educating people to be bad citizens and must coöperate with the State in its attempts to fit people for good citizenship. There are a great many differences of opinion, taste, and personal behavior consistent with satisfactory observance of the principle just stated. Different people can have different ways to suit their different types of personality and different personal aptitudes. Different people can also be educated to be good citizens in different ways, or through playing different rôles.

It is not a difficult matter to pick out a hundred lessons in bad citizenship which are being given currently by our educative press, movies, radio, or schools. What is needed in this respect is less talk about an abstract freedom, which is essentially anarchy if really applied, and more effort to develop a rational technique of control through purposive education, with a view to making such education serve the ends of social welfare and order. Such effort must not be restricted to the field of child training but must be exercised in the entire field of purposive education of adults. Every social institution which is used to educate people with definite social purposes must be made to coöperate with the national plan. There must be no anti-social formation of character, mind, or group attitudes by any institution if it can be prevented. The rest of this chapter is devoted to a discussion of the problem of educational control, with reference especially to the school, which is a recognized educator with a social purpose. Most of what is said here in connection with the school . . . will be found to apply equally to all institutions which are used to educate with definite social purposes.[1]

> To say that the school should be used to influence positively attitudes favoring one or another type of social living seems to me merely the making of the trite observation that the school ought to do what it has always done and what it cannot help doing. The school cannot help imparting knowledge of social facts or ideas. That, of course, is its special business. But it is also one of the daily

[1] Dennis took the concluding quotation from an article he contributed to a symposium entitled "Indoctrination, the Task Before the American School," in *The Social Frontier, a Journal of Educational Criticism and Reconstruction,* January 1935.—Ed.

performances of every human institution. It is not the peculiar feature of the school that it educates. Its most distinctive peculiarity is that it educates with consciously conceived and willed purposes. Those purposes are mainly to serve the supposed interests of the prevailing social order, or, really, certain interests conceived and willed by the dominant classes. It is one of the peculiar delusions that the school is the chief educator of the community. All human institutions are educators. The school, however, unlike the market place, for instance, educates with avowed purposes.

An academically popular superstition about the school is the notion that social facts or ideas are objects which the school can dispense like cigarettes wrapped in cellophane. Facts and ideas are not objects. They are personal experiences. Social facts or ideas are not things existing outside and independently of the knowing, understanding, or judging person. To whatever extent the school teaches social facts, the school causes persons to undergo certain peculiarly personal experiences which involve the processes of the reason and the emotions, or processes which take place in the torso as well as the skull. Ideas about patriotism, religion, sex, and art are apprehended mainly in the sub-cranial areas. One of the conditions precedent to the occurrence of the learning, knowing, thinking, or judging experiences is the continuous maintenance of a set of attitudes towards the prevailing type of social living and towards any other social scheme actually operative somewhere in the world or merely imagined, should such other scheme or schemes condition the given experience of the person.

To suppose a person knowing a social fact independently of an attitude towards the social scheme in which he lives, and towards other social schemes which may affect his thinking and feeling, is as senseless as it would be to talk of weighing an object which was assumed to be floating through space an infinite and, hence, unknown distance from any planet. What gives sense to a personal experience (call it intellectual or emotional as you will) with a social fact or idea, is the relation or attitude of the person to his own and other social planets. We must reckon with the attraction or pull and also the repulsion of the social system operating on the individual in order to teach him a social fact.

In the processes of education or knowledge and thought we can do things only with persons equipped with attitudes towards the social scheme. Every educational experience affects such attitudes and is affected by them, just as the movement of every object on this planet affects the earth's gravity and is affected by it. A person not equipped with and using, every moment of his conscious life, and particularly in respect to every intellectual experience, a set of attitudes towards the social scheme, is a hopeless idiot. He is not the mythical student with the objective mind.

The school is expressly charged with the function of contributing to the formation of attitudes as a part of the processes of causing persons to undergo the experiences of learning, thinking, and judging. As the school specialist is normally the hired man and an instrument of government of those who exercise a directive influence over government in the broadest sense of the term, the school normally aims to create right attitudes towards the prevailing social order.

Right, of course, is always a relative. A right attitude is an attitude which suits the purposes of the conceptual scheme of some person or the purpose of causing some given course of events to happen. There are, naturally, as many right attitudes or as many rights as there are conceptual schemes or courses of events, the realization of which would constitute a purpose to be served. Where such purposes conflict, whatever serves the realization of one's own preferred scheme is one's own standard of right. Civilization or social order is a matter of having a large group of people accept the same scheme or right. As a practical matter, any realizable scheme of interests or purposes of an individual, however selfish or reprehensible the person or the purposes may be considered, has to be a scheme which integrates the person in a social pattern.

Therefore, all rational or realizable personal schemes are social or collectivistic. They cannot have the qualities of a specious individualism which are found in the contrary-to-fact hypotheses of certain confused minds. The isolated-man-on-a-desert-isle situation is never a reality. Most of the talk about individualism versus collectivism going the rounds today is a sheer confusion of terms, ideas, and issues. A working capitalism, for instance, is *ex-hypothesi* and according to Adam Smith, a collectivism of freedom of contract. If it breaks down, it breaks down because its collectivistic characteristics fail, or, specifically, because the motives and mechanisms of the free market in their operation no longer secure the collectivistic result of an efficient and social coöperation of the factors of production.

Why these motives and mechanisms so fail, or why capitalism fails in its collectivism, is another story. For the explanation you can try Marx, J. A. Hobson, Spengler, or Freud. The first purpose of any social scheme is to work. Whatever makes it work is right for it. If it works well as a system, it must involve the coöperation of a lot of people, for whom it must work well enough to secure their coöperation. People may coöperate with the social scheme by fleecing or being fleeced, by sending their first born to Groton or throwing him into the Ganges.

The right attitudes which the school is supposed to inculcate are those which suit the purposes of the system, or make it work. If the social order is destroying itself, or, to be more accurate, if it is being destroyed by agencies and forces which are integral parts of its organic life, it will naturally follow that the well run school will serve those purposes.

It may be objected that suicide cannot be a rational purpose of anyone or anything. But why not? In the life cycle of a human being, processes innate in his being begin destroying him as soon as he reaches maturity and achieve their work forty to a hundred years later. These processes are constantly killing Platos and Edisons, and breeding Jukes and Dillingers. It just is not one of the purposes of the course of events we may call life to make one person or one civilization live forever. The school will be as instrumental in the processes of culture degeneration as in the processes of culture generation. The idea that the right sort of education will preserve a civilization from decay is as absurd as the notion that the right sort of medicine or science will keep people from ever dying.

In a dying civilization the school will naturally be the tool of the decadent elite until the vigorous barbarians of the new order, also of the elite (the outs over any length of time are always barbarians), capture the state and the government.

If a realist feels moved to change his civilization he may seek spiritual leadership or political power, or both. In the one case, he may go into the wilderness and eat locusts and wild honey; in the other case, he may pick the crown of France out of the gutter with the point of his sword. In neither case will the drama of his passion for power over men be played in the rôle of an instrument of the order he abhors or despises.

In government or politics, ultimately you either buy or shoot your way, or both. The cross, the crescent, the hammer and sickle, and the swastika, alike, have shot their way to power. The social revolutionist usually cannot buy his way; often he or his disciple can shoot his way. The school man can do neither. He follows those who can and do buy or shoot their way.

There have been civilizations in which men at times cumulated successfully the functions of school teaching, political command, and spiritual leadership. Medieval Christendom, with its all-embracing spiritual synthesis, furnishes an example. Modern capitalism, by carrying to absurd extremes the principles of division of labor or specialization, separation instead of coördination of powers, and atomic fractionalization instead of purposive synthesis of social factors, has rendered this cumulation of the governing functions of the priest, the teacher, the soldier, and the administrator quite impossible. Hence, political government tends to be the work of specialists whose type pattern is the Tammany politician; economic government tends to be the work of specialists whose type pattern is a man of the Mitchell or Insull sort; while teaching tends to be the work of specialists whose type pattern is a frustrated old maid.

It is, of course, possible for the superman to pass from the school to the White House, just as a Persian in the present century passed from stable boy to king. The points, however, is that the school, under modern capitalism, cannot be integrated with the highest mechanisms or personalities of government and social control. Exceptionally, a prophet or spiritual leader at war with the existing order, instead of serving as its docile instrument of mass conditioning for three square meals a day, will cumulate the functions of minor prophecy and petty pedagogy. If he continues to do so, it is because his influence is too negligible to warrant his dismissal. Ultimately, the *amour propre,* even of a very minor prophet, will require some substantial tribute to his effectiveness, such as a sensational dismissal can afford. Major prophets must either be crucified or crowned (king of kings and lord of lords) or both, for only such supreme tributes can satisfy the ego of a man big enough to impose his ideal on his fellow men.

The social ideal of the prevailing system should be made explicit by the school. A contrary ideal should not be given a chance of success with any significant number of students. The educational theory that a scale of views and situations should be presented to the student in the hope that attitudes requisite for orderly social living under the given scheme will develop by the processes of individual selection is wholly fallacious. Either the theory is a misrepresentation of what is actually undertaken and accomplished in the educational enterprise, or else the theory is a statement of what has never been practised and what, if tried out, would result immediately in social anarchy. It is hard enough to preserve sanity in the machine age. The difficulties ought not to be aggravated by gratuitous misrepresentations of the educational process.

Keeping sane requires that we recognize as the chief end of social agencies, including the school, the maintenance and enrichment of the social order, not the production of individuals as isolated entities, or disembodied personalities endowed with the faculty of living in or out of the social scheme as they may choose. The chief function of purposive education has to do with catching human beings in their formative years and integrating them into the social scheme as far as that can be done in youth. The end of this integration is a social order, not the formation of a lot of personal entities supposedly free either to fit themselves into society or not, mainly as the preference of each may incline him. As Hobbes taught, life is the war of all against all. One of the ends of any civilization is to mitigate the evils of this anarchy by resolving considerable groups of people into workable schemes of social organization which permit of social coöperation and the consequent enjoyment of some degree of order and peace in the world during lengthy periods of time.

Now, few persons in the first twenty or thirty years of their lives, even if given access to the world's fund of social knowledge and Socrates for a tutor, could evolve a workable conceptual scheme of society of their own into which to fit themselves. And, if a number of people worked out such schemes, the schemes would all differ, whereas only one scheme of society could be operative for a large group. The problem of civilization is to make one social scheme operative for a given people, and this means, among other requisites, that it must be made explicit. The problem of the school is to help fit people into that scheme. Any opposite philosophy of civilization and education is absurd, impractical, and vicious. It is absurd, because no social order that has order can allow its schools to train people in ways deliberately calculated to make large numbers of them enemies of the social order. It is absurd because the premise of an individual in awful isolation from his group, is untenable for any useful hypothesis of social organization. Such an individual cannot exist.

The theory of educating individuals rather than citizens is impractical for the same reasons. And it is vicious because it involves an educational technique of false rationalizations and deceit which contributes to mental and emotional unbalance, and because it creates a large number of enemies of the social order who do not become creative revolutionists but frustrated escapists, futilely flitting between a real world where they are unfulfilled and a fantasy world of wishful thinking where nothing is ever fulfilled except insanity.

The escapists produced by an educational technique combining the worst of Bentham and Marx with the best of neither become split personalities. Part of the time they are trying to adjust themselves to a bread and butter job, and the other part of the time they are trying to adjust social reality to personal fantasy by impotent manifestations of hate and bitterness. Because we admire Socrates and Jesus is no reason why we should suppose that the purpose of the school, necessarily conducted by a host of salaried mediocrities, is to create social rebels. The social rebels will happen just as surely as civilizations rise and fall, or as men are born and die. They will happen in spite of the school, not because of it.

The school must be one of the instruments of government of the group culture. The group culture should be the expression of the will of the dominant element of the elite, whose values are validated by the power to enforce them. This method of validating values is the only one by which an argument can ever be ended and coöperative activity made possible. You can have social order only to the extent that you can settle arguments or end conflicts, even if only temporarily. The boundaries of the dominant elite and the rebellious elite mark the only significant class cleavage. The masses divide naturally among the warring groups of the elite. As the elite are the leaders, the directives lie with them. Directions of social trends are determined by them. Education does not make or unmake the elite. It equips them and increases their social distance from the masses. It raises their potentialities as instruments of creation, destruction, and combat, processes which make up the mysterious drama of life.

Purposive education and the technique of mass guidance are purely instrumental in the many enterprises of the leaders. These instrumentalities neither select nor validate ultimate values. Nor do they materially determine ultimate results of conflicts. No single instrumentality won the War. A preponderance of force factors determined it. Both sides used the same factors—machine guns, schools, tanks, press, etc. There can be no conflict except between classes or groups which have approximately the same instruments or force factors. (God and Justice are with all the belligerents.) This is a fact that Marxists disregard. There is no important conflict today between the hungry and well-fed in America, because command and possession of the force factors is with the well-fed. Foxes and rabbits don't fight. Today fighting has to be done by soldiers. Decisive conflict is between those who can command soldiers—not mere voters or trade union members.

A kind, humane civilization should realize the following two conditions. First, it must suit my purposes as a person, or it must give me a suitable function as an individual. Every individual must be the center of his ethical or social scheme. For an individual there can be no validity to a social scheme in which he has no place. Whether the scheme suits him and whether he suits the scheme depends mainly on who he is and what social conditioning has made him. Let not this placing of the individual at the center of his own ethical system be called individualism. It is the purest collectivism. Any collectivism must successfully integrate a considerable number of individuals, for each of whom the collectivism centers around himself and his rôle. This merely means that the social scheme fits the individual and the individual fits the scheme. The point is that if the scheme works, those in charge of the social scheme will purposively direct most of the fitting, and some of their most useful fitters will be the schoolman and the priest. God, right, truth, and beauty are personal experiences.

To be successfully adjusted, an individual does not have to have two cars or even a full stomach. He merely needs to have a place, or, to belong. The social system may fit me and I may fit it, I being a barefooted, penitent pilgrim, a missionary to the lepers, or a plumed knight in shining armor. People don't mind suffering. On the contrary, some of them love to suffer all of the time, and all of them love to suffer some of the time. What people cannot endure is not belonging. The tragedy of capitalism—unemployment—does not inhere in the phenomena of want and privation, but in the spiritual disintegration of large numbers of people from the group culture. Hitler can feed millions of his people acorns, and, yet, if he integrates them in a spiritual union with their community, they will be happier than they were while receiving generous doles from a régime which gave them no such spiritual integration with the herd. In so far as the school is a force for spiritual integration it is mightier than the dole.

A second set of requisites of a humane civilization is that the dominant elite should know what they want, that they should give the people what they think best for the people, and that they should make the people both like and fit the scheme. The elite always determine what the masses get. Nowhere is this more apparent than in present-day Communist Russia, which enjoys an oversimplified dictatorship of the proletariat (and of everybody else in Russia) by certain of the elite. The elite leaders are a permanent power-holding or power-seeking class. When one set of the elite kicks out another, it is merely the old story of "The King is dead! Long live the King!" The average man goes on doing as he is told. It makes little difference to him whether his surplus goes to building private yachts for capitalists or an air fleet for the Soviet Commissars. Whatever the elite impose on the people, they should use good educational technique to make the people like. Whatever the elite demand of the people, they should use good educational technique to enable the people to do. This is the work of purposive education. Conditioning a people to like what they have and to do their part is a simple exercise in educational technique. The real difficulty arises not out of the inadequacy of educational technique but out of the failure of the elite to have unity in emotional responses or intellectual clarity as to ultimate values and objectives. In these matters the instrumental or purposive education of the school is of minor importance. The struggle for existence must educate and unify men's hearts and clarify their minds in ways to produce a dominant or efficient group of the elite.

In so far as the school does a good job for its masters, who are never the schoolmasters, the school population will be in the rear-guard of social revolution. The education of the struggle for existence, however, sometimes gets at the student population, as it has done in most European countries which have not so effectively insulated their youth against the currents of social ideas, as the country club atmosphere of our colleges, or the kindergarten atmosphere of our lower schools, have done for our youth. In America today, the important social education is going on in shanty town, the bread line, the code conferences, mortgage foreclosure sales, and the relief committees. The social teaching of the schools, particularly in economics, ethics, and law, is largely out of date, contrary to experience, irrelevant, and trivial. So are most of the teachers. The American schools have no teachers of the social importance of educators like the late Huey Long and Father Coughlin. The pupils of the latter will fight and die for what they are being taught; the school pupil may vicariously fight on the playing fields for dear old Siwash, but he won't fight for what Siwash professors are teaching. The founders of Siwash had a fighting faith; but the endowed pensioners of Siwash deem it bad form to have a conviction.

There is an irony and a moral in the social insignificance of the American school in the present crisis. No school has ever been more popularized, praised, petted, or pampered with money. It has been the kept darling of the plutocracy and the idolized plaything of the masses. In the main, neither group has numbered many devotees of any scheme of civilized values. Serious interest in the school has centered around getting a technical preparation, or useful connections for money-making, or else around getting a job in the schools. For the masses, the school is a necessary process to enable them to read signs and advertisements. For the more favored the school has been a playground.

The moral is obvious. The school realizes its highest possibilities only as the instrument of a dominant elite who not only have cultural values but who also are prepared to express them in the manifold enterprises of social control, which include fighting and governing as well as teaching.

The American school will come into its own when it becomes alive with the spirit of men of strong convictions and iron wills to achieve. The school will be an instrument of a high culture when it recognizes fulfillment, achievement, and deeds to be the test of truth, right, and beauty, not normative verbalisms, the precise meaning and correct application of which men can and will go on disagreeing about to the end of time. In short, the school can only attain its highest dignity or fulfill its noblest destiny as an integrated part of the creative machinery of a civilization.

1936

3 Nation and Race

ADOLF HITLER

There are some truths which are so obvious that for this very reason they are not seen or at least not recognized by ordinary people. They sometimes pass by such truisms as though blind and are most astonished when someone suddenly discovers what everyone really ought to know. Columbus's eggs lie around by the hundreds of thousands, but Columbuses are met with less frequently.

Thus men without exception wander about in the garden of Nature; they imagine that they know practically everything and yet with few exceptions pass blindly by one of the most patent principles of Nature's rule: the inner segregation of the species of all living beings on this earth.

Even the most superficial observation shows that Nature's restricted form of propagation and increase is an almost rigid basic law of all the innumerable forms of expression of her vital urge. Every animal mates only with a member of the same species. The titmouse seeks the titmouse, the finch the finch, the stork the stork, the field mouse the field mouse, the dormouse the dormouse, the wolf the she-wolf, etc.

Only unusual circumstances can change this, primarily the compulsion of captivity or any other cause that makes it impossible to mate within the same species. But then Nature begins to resist this with all possible means, and her most visible protest consists either in refusing further capacity for propagation to bastards or in limiting the fertility of later offspring; in most cases, however, she takes away the power of resistance to disease or hostile attacks.

This is only too natural.

Any crossing of two beings not at exactly the same level produces a medium between the level of the two parents. This means: the offspring will probably stand higher than the racially lower parent, but not as high as the higher one. Consequently, it will later succumb in the struggle against the higher level. Such mating is contrary to the will of Nature for a higher breeding of all life. The precondition for this does not lie in associating superior and inferior, but in the total victory of the former. The stronger must dominate and not blend with the weaker, thus sacrificing his own greatness. Only the born weakling can view this as cruel, but he after all

SOURCE: from Adolf Hitler, *Mein Kampf,* translated and edited by Ralph Manheim, pp. 284–291, 293–307, 312, 315–316, 325, 327–329. Editor's notes have been deleted. Reprinted by permission of Houghton Mifflin Company, copyright © 1943, renewed 1971 by Houghton Mifflin Company, and courtesy of Hutchinson Ltd., London.

is only a weak and limited man; for if this law did not prevail, any conceivable higher development of organic living beings would be unthinkable.

The consequence of this racial purity, universally valid in Nature, is not only the sharp outward delimitation of the various races, but their uniform character in themselves. The fox is always a fox, the goose a goose, the tiger a tiger, etc., and the difference can lie at most in the varying measure of force, strength, intelligence, dexterity, endurance, etc., of the individual specimens. But you will never find a fox who in his inner attitude might, for example, show humanitarian tendencies toward geese, as similarly there is no cat with a friendly inclination toward mice.

Therefore, here, too, the struggle among themselves arises less from inner aversion than from hunger and love. In both cases, Nature looks on calmly, with satisfaction, in fact. In the struggle for daily bread all those who are weak and sickly or less determined succumb, while the struggle of the males for the female grants the right or opportunity to propagate only to the healthiest. And struggle is always a means for improving a species' health and power of resistance and, therefore, a cause of its higher development.

If the process were different, all further and higher development would cease and the opposite would occur. For, since the inferior always predominates numerically over the best, if both had the same possibility of preserving life and propagating, the inferior would multiply so much more rapidly that in the end the best would inevitably be driven into the background, unless a correction of this state of affairs were undertaken. Nature does just this by subjecting the weaker part to such severe living conditions that by them alone the number is limited, and by not permitting the remainder to increase promiscuously, but making a new and ruthless choice according to strength and health.

No more than Nature desires the mating of weaker with stronger individuals, even less does she desire the blending of a higher with a lower race, since, if she did, her whole work of higher breeding, over perhaps hundreds of thousands of years, might be ruined with one blow.

Historical experience offers countless proofs of this. It shows with terrifying clarity that in every mingling of Aryan blood with that of lower peoples the result was the end of the cultured people. North America, whose population consists in by far the largest part of Germanic elements who mixed but little with the lower colored peoples, shows a different humanity and culture from Central and South America, where the predominantly Latin immigrants often mixed with the aborigines on a large scale. By this one example, we can clearly and distinctly recognize the effect of racial mixture. The Germanic inhabitant of the American continent, who has remained racially pure and unmixed, rose to be master of the continent; he will remain the master as long as he does not fall a victim to defilement of the blood.

The result of all racial crossing is therefore in brief always the following:

a) Lowering of the level of the higher race;
b) Physical and intellectual regression and hence the beginning of a slowly but surely progressing sickness.

To bring about such a development is, then, nothing else but to sin against the will of the eternal creator.

And as a sin this act is rewarded.

When man attempts to rebel against the iron logic of Nature, he comes into struggle with the principles to which he himself owes his existence as a man. And this attack must lead to his own doom.

Here, of course, we encounter the objection of the modern pacifist, as truly Jewish in its effrontery as it is stupid! 'Man's rôle is to overcome Nature!'

Millions thoughtlessly parrot this Jewish nonsense and end up by really imagining that they themselves represent a kind of conqueror of Nature; though in this they dispose of no other weapon than an idea, and at that such a miserable one, that if it were true no world at all would be conceivable.

But quite aside from the fact that man has never yet conquered Nature in anything, but at most has caught hold of and tried to lift one or another corner of her immense gigantic veil of eternal riddles and secrets, that in reality he invents nothing but only discovers everything, that he does not dominate Nature, but has only risen on the basis of his knowledge of various laws and secrets of Nature to be lord over those other living creatures who lack this knowledge—quite aside from all this, an idea cannot overcome the preconditions for the development and being of humanity, since the idea itself depends only on man. Without human beings there is no human idea in this world, therefore, the idea as such is always conditioned by the presence of human beings and hence of all the laws which created the precondition for their existence.

And not only that! Certain ideas are even tied up with certain men. This applies most of all to those ideas whose content originates, not in an exact scientific truth, but in the world of emotion, or, as it is so beautifully and clearly expressed today, reflects an 'inner experience.' All these ideas, which have nothing to do with cold logic as such, but represent only pure expressions of feeling, ethical conceptions, etc., are chained to the existence of men, to whose intellectual imagination and creative power they owe their existence. Precisely in this case the preservation of these definite races and men is the precondition for the existence of these ideas. . . .

. . . this planet once moved through the ether for millions of years without human beings and it can do so again some day if men forget that they owe their higher existence, not to the ideas of a few crazy ideologists, but to the knowledge and ruthless application of Nature's stern and rigid laws.

Everything we admire on this earth today—science and art, technology and inventions—is only the creative product of a few peoples and originally perhaps of *one* race. On them depends the existence of this whole culture. If they perish, the beauty of this earth will sink into the grave with them.

However much the soil, for example, can influence men, the result of the influence will always be different depending on the races in question. . . .

All great cultures of the past perished only because the originally creative race died out from blood poisoning.

The ultimate cause of such a decline was their forgetting that all culture depends on men and not conversely; hence that to preserve a certain culture the man who creates it must be preserved. This preservation is bound up with the rigid law of necessity and the right to victory of the best and stronger in this world.

Those who want to live, let them fight, and those who do not want to fight in this world of eternal struggle do not deserve to live.

Even if this were hard—that is how it is! Assuredly, however, by far the harder fate is that which strikes the man who thinks he can overcome Nature, but in the last analysis only mocks her. Distress, misfortune, and diseases are her answer.

The man who misjudges and disregards the racial laws actually forfeits the happiness that seems destined to be his. He thwarts the triumphal march of the best race and hence also the precondition for all human progress, and remains, in consequence, burdened with all the sensibility of man, in the animal realm of helpless misery.

• • •

It is idle to argue which race or races were the original representative of human culture and hence the real founders of all that we sum up under the word 'humanity.' It is simpler to raise this question with regard to the present, and here an easy, clear answer results. All the human culture, all the results of art, science, and technology that we see before us today, are almost exclusively the creative product of the Aryan. This very fact admits of the not unfounded inference that he alone was the founder of all higher humanity, therefore representing the prototype of all that we understand by the word 'man.' He is the Prometheus of mankind from whose bright forehead the divine spark of genius has sprung at all times, forever kindling anew that fire of knowledge which illumined the night of silent mysteries and thus caused man to climb the path to mastery over the other beings of this earth. Exclude him—and perhaps after a few thousand years darkness will again descend on the earth, human culture will pass, and the world turn to a desert.

If we were to divide mankind into three groups, the founders of culture, the bearers of culture, the destroyers of culture, only the Aryan could be considered as the representative of the first group. From him originate the foundations and walls of all human creation, and only the outward form and color are determined by the changing traits of character of the various peoples. He provides the mightiest building stones and plans for all human progress and only the execution corresponds to the nature of the varying men and races. In a few decades, for example, the entire east of Asia will possess a culture whose ultimate foundation will be Hellenic spirit and Germanic technology, just as much as in Europe. Only the *outward* form—in part at least—will bear the features of Asiatic character....

If beginning today all further Aryan influence on Japan should stop, assuming that Europe and America should perish, Japan's present rise in science and technology might continue for a short time; but even in a few years the well would dry up, the Japanese special character would gain, but the present culture would freeze and sink back into the slumber from which it was awakened seven decades ago by the wave of Aryan culture. Therefore, just as the present Japanese development owes its life to Aryan origin, long ago in the gray past foreign influence and foreign spirit awakened the Japanese culture of that time. The best proof of this is furnished by the fact of its subsequent sclerosis and total petrifaction. This can occur in a people only when the original creative racial nucleus has been lost, or if the external influence which furnished the impetus and the material for the first development in the cultural field was later lacking. But if it is established that a people receives the most essential basic materials of its culture from foreign races, that it assimilates and adapts them, and that then, if further external influence is lacking, it rigidifies again and again, such a race may be designated as *'culture-bearing,'* but never as *'culture-creating.'* An examination of the various peoples from this standpoint points to the fact that practically none of them were originally *culture-founding*, but almost always *culture-bearing*.

• • •

As in daily life the so-called genius requires a special cause, indeed, often a positive impetus, to make him shine, likewise the genius-race in the life of peoples. In the monotony of everyday life even significant men often seem insignificant, hardly rising above the average of their environment; as soon, however, as they are approached by a situation in which others lose hope or go astray, the genius rises manifestly from the inconspicuous average child, not seldom to the amazement of all those who had hitherto seen him in the pettiness of bourgeois life—and that is why the prophet seldom has any honor in his own country. Nowhere have we better occasion to observe this than in war. From apparently harmless children, in difficult hours when others lose hope, suddenly heroes shoot up with death-defying determination and an icy cool presence of mind. If this hour of trial had not come, hardly anyone would ever have guessed that a young hero was hidden in this beardless boy. It nearly always takes some stimulus to bring the genius on the scene. The hammer-stroke of Fate which throws one man to the ground suddenly strikes steel in another, and when the shell of everyday life is broken, the previously hidden kernel lies open before the eyes of the astonished world. The world then resists and does not want to believe that the type which is apparently identical with it is suddenly a very different being; a process which is repeated with every eminent son of man.

Though an inventor, for example, establishes his fame only on the day of his invention, it is a mistake to think that genius as such entered into the man only at this hour—the spark of genius exists in the brain of the truly creative man from the hour of his birth. True genius is always inborn and never cultivated, let alone learned.

As already emphasized, this applies not only to the individual man but also to the race. Creatively active peoples always have a fundamental creative gift, even if it should not be recognizable to the eyes of superficial observers. Here, too, outward recognition is possible only in consequence of accomplished deeds, since the rest of the world is not capable of recognizing genius in itself, but sees only its visible manifestations in the form of inventions, discoveries, buildings, pictures, etc.; here again it often takes a long time before the world can fight its way through to this knowledge. Just as in the life of the outstanding individual, genius or extraordinary ability strives for practical realization only when spurred on by special occasions, likewise in the life of nations the creative forces and capacities which are present can often be exploited only when definite preconditions invite.

We see this most distinctly in connection with the race which has been and is the bearer of human cultural development—the Aryans. As soon as Fate leads them toward special conditions, their latent abilities begin to develop in a more and more rapid sequence and to mold themselves into tangible forms. The cultures which they found in such cases are nearly always decisively determined by the existing soil, the given climate, and—the subjected people. This last item, to be sure, is almost the most decisive. The more primitive the technical foundations for a cultural activity, the more necessary is the presence of human helpers who, organizationally assembled and employed, must replace the force of the machine. Without this possibility of using lower human beings, the Aryan would never have been able to take his first steps toward his future culture; just as without the help of various suitable beasts which he knew how to tame, he would not have arrived at a technology which is now gradually permitting him to do without these beasts. The saying, 'The Moor has worked off his debt, the Moor can go,' unfortunately has only too deep a meaning. For thousands of years the horse had to serve man and help him lay the foundations of a development which now, in consequence of the motor car, is making the horse superfluous.

In a few years his activity will have ceased, but without his previous collaboration man might have had a hard time getting where he is today.

Thus, for the formation of higher cultures the existence of lower human types was one of the most essential preconditions, since they alone were able to compensate for the lack of technical aids without which a higher development is not conceivable. It is certain that the first culture of humanity was based less on the tamed animal than on the use of lower human beings.

• • •

. . . it is no accident that the first cultures arose in places where the Aryan, in his encounters with lower peoples, subjugated them and bent them to his will. They then became the first technical instrument in the service of a developing culture.

• • •

The question of the inner causes of the Aryan's importance can be answered to the effect that they are to be sought less in a natural instinct of self-preservation than in the special type of its expression. The will to live, subjectively viewed, is everywhere equal and different only in the form of its actual expression. In the most primitive living creatures the instinct of self-preservation does not go beyond concern for their own ego. Egoism, as we designate this urge, goes so far that it even embraces time; the moment itself claims everything, granting nothing to the coming hours. In this condition the animal lives only for himself, seeks food only for his present hunger, and fights only for his own life. As long as the instinct of self-preservation expresses itself in this way, every basis is lacking for the formation of a group, even the most primitive form of family. Even a community between male and female beyond pure mating, demands an extension of the instinct of self-preservation, since concern and struggle for the ego are now directed toward the second party; the male sometimes seeks food for the female, too, but for the most part both seek nourishment for the young. Nearly always one comes to the defense of the other, and thus the first, though infinitely simple, forms of a sense of sacrifice result. As soon as this sense extends beyond the narrow limits of the family, the basis for the formation of larger organisms and finally formal states is created.

In the lowest peoples of the earth this quality is present only to a very slight extent, so that often they do not go beyond the formation of the family. The greater the readiness to subordinate purely personal interests, the higher rises the ability to establish comprehensive communities.

This self-sacrificing will to give one's personal labor and if necessary one's own life for others is most strongly developed in the Aryan. The Aryan is not greatest in his mental qualities as such, but in the extent of his willingness to put all his abilities in the service of the community. In him the instinct of self-preservation has reached the noblest form, since he willingly subordinates his own ego to the life of the community and, if the hour demands, even sacrifices it.

• • •

This state of mind, which subordinates the interests of the ego to the conservation of the community, is really the first premise for every truly human culture. From it alone can arise all the great works of mankind, which bring the founder little reward, but the richest blessings to posterity. Yes, from it alone can we understand how so many are able to bear up faithfully under a scanty life which imposes on them nothing but poverty and frugality, but gives the community the foundations of its existence. Every worker, every peasant, every inventor, official, etc., who works without ever being able to achieve any happiness or prosperity for himself, is a representative of this lofty idea, even if the deeper meaning of his activity remains hidden in him.

What applies to work as the foundation of human sustenance and all human progress is true to an even greater degree for the defense of man and his culture. In giving one's own life for the existence of the community lies the crown of all sense of sacrifice. It is this alone that prevents what human hands have built from being overthrown by human hands or destroyed by Nature.

Our own German language possesses a word which magnificently designates this kind of activity: *Pflichterfüllung* (fulfillment of duty); it means not to be self-sufficient but to serve the community.

The basic attitude from which such activity arises, we call—to distinguish it from egoism and selfishness—idealism. By this we understand only the individual's capacity to make sacrifices for the community, for his fellow men.

How necessary it is to keep realizing that idealism does not represent a superfluous expression of emotion, but that in truth it has been, is, and will be, the premise for what we designate as human culture, yes, that it alone created the concept of 'man'! It is to this inner attitude that the Aryan owes his position in this world, and to it the world owes man; for it alone formed from pure spirit the creative force which, by a unique pairing of the brutal fist and the intellectual genius, created the monuments of human culture.

Without his idealistic attitude all, even the most dazzling faculties of the intellect, would remain mere intellect as such—outward appearance without inner value, and never creative force.

But, since true idealism is nothing but the subordination of the interests and life of the individual to the community, and this in turn is the precondition for the creation of organizational forms of all kinds, it corresponds in its innermost depths to the ultimate will of Nature. It alone leads men to voluntary recognition of the privilege of force and strength, and thus makes them into a dust particle of that order which shapes and forms the whole universe.

• • •

The mightiest counterpart to the Aryan is represented by the Jew. In hardly any people in the world is the instinct of self-preservation developed more strongly than in the so-called 'chosen.' Of this, the mere fact of the survival of this race may be considered the best proof. Where is the people which in the last two thousand years has been exposed to so slight changes of inner disposition, character, etc., as the Jewish people? What people, finally, has gone through greater upheavals than this one—and nevertheless issued from the mightiest catastrophes of mankind unchanged? What an infinitely tough will to live and preserve the species speaks from these facts!

The mental qualities of the Jew have been schooled in the course of many centuries. Today he passes as 'smart,' and this in a certain sense he has been at all times. But his intelligence is not the result of his own development, but of visual instruction through foreigners. For the human mind cannot climb to the top without steps; for every step upward he needs the foundation of the past, and this in the comprehensive sense in which it can be revealed only in general culture. All thinking is based only in small part on man's own knowledge, and mostly on the experience of the time that has preceded. The general cultural level provides the individual man, without his noticing it as a rule, with such a profusion of preliminary knowledge that, thus armed, he can more easily take further steps of his own. . . .

Since the Jew—for reasons which will at once become apparent—was never in possession of a culture of his own, the foundations of his intellectual work were always provided by others. His intellect at all times developed through the cultural world surrounding him.

The reverse process never took place.

For if the Jewish people's instinct of self-preservation is not smaller but larger than that of other peoples, if his intellectual faculties can easily arouse the impression that they are equal to the intellectual gifts of other races, he lacks completely the most essential requirement for a cultured people, the idealistic attitude.

In the Jewish people the will to self-sacrifice does not go beyond the individual's naked instinct of self-preservation. Their apparently great sense of solidarity is based on the very primitive herd instinct that is seen in many other living creatures in this world. It is a noteworthy fact that the herd instinct leads to mutual support only as long as a common danger makes this seem useful or inevitable. The same pack of wolves which has just fallen on its prey together disintegrates when hunger abates into its individual beasts. The same is true of horses which try to defend themselves against an assailant in a body, but scatter again as soon as the danger is past.

It is similar with the Jew. His sense of sacrifice is only apparent. It exists only as long as the existence of the individual makes it absolutely necessary. However, as soon as the common enemy is conquered, the danger threatening all averted and the booty hidden, the apparent harmony of the Jews among themselves ceases, again making way for their old causal tendencies. The Jew is only united when a common danger forces him to be or a common booty entices him; if these two grounds are lacking, the qualities of the crassest egoism come into their own, and in the twinkling of an eye the united people turns into a horde of rats, fighting bloodily among themselves.

If the Jews were alone in this world, they would stifle in filth and offal; they would try to get ahead of one another in hate-filled struggle and exterminate one another, in so far as the absolute absence of all sense of self-sacrifice, expressing itself in their cowardice, did not turn battle into comedy here too.

So it is absolutely wrong to infer any ideal sense of sacrifice in the Jews from the fact that they stand together in struggle, or, better expressed, in the plundering of their fellow men.

Here again the Jew is led by nothing but the naked egoism of the individual.

That is why the Jewish state—which should be the living organism for preserving and increasing a race—is completely unlimited as to territory. For a state formation to have a definite spatial setting always presupposes an idealistic attitude on the part of the state-race, and especially a correct interpretation of the concept of work. In the exact measure in which this attitude is lacking, any attempt at forming, even of preserving, a spatially delimited state fails. And thus the basis on which alone culture can arise is lacking.

Hence the Jewish people, despite all apparent intellectual qualities, is without any true culture, and especially without any culture of its own. For what sham culture the Jew today possesses is the property of other peoples, and for the most part it is ruined in his hands.

In judging the Jewish people's attitude on the question of human culture, the most essential characteristic we must always bear in mind is that there has never been a Jewish art and accordingly there is none today either; that above all the two queens of all the arts, architecture and music, owe nothing original to the Jews. What they do accomplish in the field of art is either patchwork or intellectual theft. Thus, the Jew lacks those qualities which distinguish the races that are creative and hence culturally blessed.

To what an extent the Jew takes over foreign culture, imitating or rather ruining it, can be seen from the fact that he is mostly found in the art which seems to require least original invention, the art of acting. But even here, in reality, he is only a 'juggler,' or rather an ape; for even here he lacks the last touch that is required for real greatness; even here he is not the creative genius, but a superficial imitator, and all the twists and tricks that he uses are powerless to conceal the inner lifelessness of his creative gift. Here the Jewish press most lovingly helps him along by raising such a roar of hosannahs about even the most mediocre bungler, just so long as he is a Jew, that the rest of the world actually ends up by thinking that they have an artist before them, while in truth it is only a pitiful comedian.

No, the Jew possesses no culture-creating force of any sort, since the idealism, without which there is no true higher development of man, is not present in him and never was present. Hence his intellect will never have a constructive effect, but will be destructive, and in very rare cases perhaps will at most be stimulating, but then as the prototype of the 'force which always wants evil and nevertheless creates good.' Not through him does any progress of mankind occur, but in spite of him.

Since the Jew never possessed a state with definite territorial limits and therefore never called a culture his own, the conception arose that this was a people which should be reckoned among the ranks of the *nomads.* This is a fallacy as great as it is dangerous. The nomad does possess a definitely limited living space, only he does not cultivate it like a sedentary peasant, but lives from the yield of his herds with which he wanders about in his territory. The outward reason for this is to be found in the small fertility of a soil which simply does not permit of settlement. The deeper cause, however, lies in the disparity between the technical culture of an age or people and the natural poverty of a living space. There are territories in which even the Aryan is enabled only by his technology, developed in the course of more than a thousand years, to live in regular settlements, to master broad stretches of soil and obtain from it the requirements of life. If he did not possess this technology, either he would have to avoid these territories or likewise have to struggle along as a nomad in perpetual wandering, provided that his thousand-year-old education and habit of settled residence did not make this seem simply unbearable to him. We must bear in mind that in the time when the American continent was being opened up, numerous Aryans fought for their livelihood as trappers, hunters, etc., and often in larger troops with wife and children, always on the move, so that their existence was completely like that of the nomads. But as soon as their increasing number and better implements permitted them to clear the wild soil and make a stand against the natives, more and more settlements sprang up in the land.

Probably the Aryan was also first a nomad, settling in the course of time, but for that very reason he was never a Jew! No, the Jew is no nomad; for the nomad had also a definite attitude toward the concept of work which could serve as a basis for his later development in so far as the necessary intellectual premises were present. In him the basic idealistic view is present, even if in infinite dilution, hence in his whole being he may seem strange to the Aryan peoples, but not unattractive. In the Jew, however, this attitude is not at all present; for that reason he was never a nomad, but only and always a *parasite* in the body of other peoples. That he sometimes left his previous living space has nothing to do with his own purpose, but results from the fact that from time to time he was thrown out by the host nations he had misused. His spreading is a typical phenomenon for all parasites; he always seeks a new feeding ground for his race.

This, however, has nothing to do with nomadism, for the reason that a Jew never thinks of leaving a territory that he has occupied, but remains where he is, and he sits so fast that even by force it is very hard to drive him out. His extension to ever-new countries occurs only in the moment in which certain conditions for his existence are there present, without which —unlike the nomad—he would not change his residence. He is and remains the typical parasite, a sponger who like a noxious bacillus keeps spreading as soon as a favorable medium invites him. And the effect of his existence is also like that of sponges: wherever he appears, the host people dies out after a shorter or longer period.

Thus, the Jew of all times has lived in the states of other peoples, and there formed his own state, which, to be sure, habitually sailed under the disguise of 'religious community' as long as outward circumstances made a complete revelation of his nature seem inadvisable. But as soon as he felt strong enough to do without the protective cloak, he always dropped the veil and suddenly became what so many of the others previously did not want to believe and see: the Jew.

The Jew's life as a parasite in the body of other nations and states explains a characteristic which once caused Schopenhauer, as has already been mentioned, to call him the 'great master in lying.' Existence impels the Jew to lie, and to lie perpetually, just as it compels the inhabitants of the northern countries to wear warm clothing.

His life within other peoples can only endure for any length of time if he succeeds in arousing the opinion that he is not a people but a 'religious community,' though of a special sort.

And this is the first great lie.

In order to carry on his existence as a parasite on other peoples, he is forced to deny his inner nature. The more intelligent the individual Jew is, the more he will succeed in this deception. Indeed, things can go so far that large parts of the host people will end by seriously believing that the Jew is really a Frenchman or an Englishman, a German or an Italian, though of a special religious faith. Especially state authorities, which always seem animated by the historical fraction of wisdom, most easily fall a victim to this infinite deception. Independent thinking sometimes seems to these circles a true sin against holy advancement, so that we may not be surprised if even today a Bavarian state ministry, for example, still has not the faintest idea that the Jews are members of a *people* and not of a *'religion'* though a glance at the Jew's own newspapers should indicate this even to the most modest mind. The *Jewish Echo* is not yet an official organ, of course, and consequently is unauthoritative as far as the intelligence of one of these government potentates is concerned.

The Jew has always been a people with definite racial characteristics and never a religion; only in order to get ahead he early sought for a means which could distract unpleasant attention from his person. And what would have been more expedient and at the same time more innocent than the 'embezzled' concept of a religious community? For here, too, everything is borrowed or rather stolen. Due to his own original special nature, the Jew cannot possess a religious institution, if for no other reason because he lacks idealism in any form, and hence belief in a hereafter is absolutely foreign to him. And a religion in the Aryan sense cannot be imagined which lacks the conviction of survival after death in some form. Indeed, the Talmud is not a book to prepare a man for the hereafter, but only for a practical and profitable life in this world.

The Jewish religious doctrine consists primarily in prescriptions for keeping the blood of Jewry pure and for regulating the relation of Jews among themselves, but even more with the rest of the world; in other words, with non-Jews. But even here it is by no means ethical problems that are involved, but extremely modest economic ones. Concerning the moral value of Jewish religious instruction, there are today and have been at all times rather exhaustive studies (not by Jews; the drivel of the Jews themselves on the subject is, of course, adapted to its purpose) which make this kind of religion seem positively monstrous according to Aryan conceptions. The best characterization is provided by the product of this religious education, the Jew himself. His life is only of this world, and his spirit is inwardly as alien to true Christianity as his nature two thousand years previous was to the great founder of the new doctrine. Of course, the latter made no secret of his attitude toward the Jewish people, and when necessary he even took to the whip to drive from the temple of the Lord this adversary of all humanity, who then as always saw in religion nothing but an instrument for his business existence. In return, Christ was nailed to the cross, while our present-day party Christians debase themselves to begging for Jewish votes at elections and later try to arrange political swindles with atheistic Jewish parties—and this against their own nation.

On this first and greatest lie, that the Jews are not a race but a religion, more and more lies are based in necessary consequence. Among them is the lie with regard to the language of the Jew. For him it is not a means for expressing his thoughts, but a means for concealing them. When he speaks French, he thinks Jewish, and while he turns out German verses, in his life he only expresses the nature of his nationality. As long as the Jew has not become the master of the other peoples, he must speak their languages whether he likes it or not, but as soon as they became his slaves, they would all have to learn a universal language (Esperanto, for instance!), so that by this additional means the Jews could more easily dominate them!

• • •

. . . In the course of more than a thousand years he has learned the language of the host people to such an extent that he now thinks he can venture in [the] future to emphasize his Judaism less and place his 'Germanism' more in the foreground; for ridiculous, nay; insane, as it may seem at first, he nevertheless has the effrontery to turn 'Germanic,' in this case a 'German.' With this begins one of the most infamous deceptions that anyone could conceive of. Since of Germanism he possesses really nothing but the art of stammering its language—and in the most frightful way—but apart from this has never mixed with the Germans, his whole Germanism rests on the language alone. Race, however, does not lie in the language, but exclusively in the blood, which no one knows better than the Jew, who attaches very little importance to the preservation of his language, but all importance to keeping his blood pure. A man can change his language without any trouble—that is, he can use another language; but in his new language he will express the old ideas; his inner nature is not changed. This is best shown by the Jew who can speak a thousand languages and nevertheless remains a Jew. His traits of character have remained the same, whether two thousand years ago as a grain dealer in Ostia, speaking Roman, or whether as a flour profiteer of today, jabbering German with a Jewish accent. It is always the same Jew. That this obvious fact is not understood by a ministerial secretary or higher police official is also self-evident, for there is scarcely any creature with less instinct and intelligence running around in the world today than these servants of our present model state authority.

• • •

. . . [The Jew] always represents himself personally as having an infinite thirst for knowledge, praises all progress, mostly, to be sure, the progress that leads to the ruin of others; for he judges all knowledge and all development only according to its possibilities for advancing his nation, and where this is lacking, he is the inexorable mortal enemy of all light, a hater of all true culture. He uses all the knowledge he acquires in the schools of other peoples, exclusively for the benefit of his race.

And this nationality he guards as never before. While he seems to overflow with 'enlightenment,' 'progress,' 'freedom,' 'humanity,' etc., he himself practices the severest segregation of his race. To be sure, he sometimes palms off his women on influential Christians, but as a matter of principle he always keeps his male line pure. He poisons the blood of others, but preserves his own. The Jew almost never marries a Christian woman; it is the Christian who marries a Jewess. The bastards, however, take after the Jewish side. Especially a part of the high nobility degenerates completely.

The Jew is perfectly aware of this, and therefore systematically carries on this mode of 'disarming' the intellectual leader class of his racial adversaries. In order to mask his activity and lull his victims, however, he talks more and more of the equality of all men without regard to race and color. The fools begin to believe him.

• • •

With satanic joy in his face, the black-haired Jewish youth lurks in wait for the unsuspecting girl whom he defiles with his blood, thus stealing her from her people. With every means he tries to destroy the racial foundations of the people he has set out to subjugate. Just as he himself systematically ruins women and girls, he does not shrink back from pulling down the blood barriers for others, even on a large scale. It was and it is Jews who bring the Negroes into the Rhineland, always with the same secret thought and clear aim of ruining the hated white race by the necessarily resulting bastardization, throwing it down from its cultural and political height, and himself rising to be its master.

For a racially pure people which is conscious of its blood can never be enslaved by the Jew. In this world he will forever be master over bastards and bastards alone.

And so he tries systematically to lower the racial level by a continuous poisoning of individuals.

• • •

If we pass all the causes of the German collapse in review, the ultimate and most decisive remains the failure to recognize the racial problem and especially the Jewish menace.

The defeats on the battlefield in August, 1918, would have been child's play to bear. They stood in no proportion to the victories of our people. It was not they that caused our downfall; no, it was brought about by that power which prepared these defeats by systematically over many decades robbing our people of the political and moral instincts and forces which alone make nations capable and hence worthy of existence.

In heedlessly ignoring the question of the preservation of the racial foundations of our nation, the old Reich disregarded the sole right which gives life in this world. Peoples which bastardize themselves, or let themselves be bastardized, sin against the will of eternal Providence, and when their ruin is encompassed by a stronger enemy it is not an injustice done to them, but only the restoration of justice. If a people no longer wants to respect the Nature-given qualities of its being which root in its blood, it has no further right to complain over the loss of its earthly existence.

Everything on this earth is capable of improvement. Every defeat can become the father of a subsequent victory, every lost war the cause of a later resurgence, every hardship the fertilization of human energy, and from every oppression the forces for a new spiritual rebirth can come—as long as the blood is preserved pure.

The lost purity of the blood alone destroys inner happiness forever, plunges man into the abyss for all time, and the consequences can never more be eliminated from body and spirit.

Only by examining and comparing all other problems of life in the light of this one question shall we see how absurdly petty they are by this standard. They are all limited in time—but the question of preserving or not preserving the purity of the blood will endure as long as there are men.

All really significant symptoms of decay of the pre-War period can in the last analysis be reduced to racial causes.

Whether we consider questions of general justice or cankers of economic life, symptoms of cultural decline or processes of political degeneration, questions of faulty schooling or the bad influence exerted on grown-ups by the press, etc., everywhere and always it is fundamentally the disregard of the racial needs of our own people or failure to see a foreign racial menace.

And that is why all attempts at reform, all works for social relief and political exertions, all economic expansion and every apparent increase of intellectual knowledge were futile as far as their results were concerned. The nation, and the organism which enables and preserves its life on this earth, the state, did not grow inwardly healthier, but obviously languished more and more. All the illusory prosperity of the old Reich could not hide its inner weakness, and every attempt really to strengthen the Reich failed again and again, due to disregarding the most important question.

It would be a mistake to believe that the adherents of the various political tendencies which were tinkering around on the German national body—yes, even a certain section of the leaders—were bad or malevolent men in themselves. Their activity was condemned to sterility only because the best of them saw at most the forms of our general disease and tried to combat them, but blindly ignored the virus. Anyone who systematically follows the old Reich's line of political development is bound to arrive, upon calm examination, at the realization that even at the time of the unification, hence the rise of the German nation, the inner decay was already in full swing, and that despite all apparent political successes and despite increasing economic wealth, the general situation was deteriorating from year to year. If nothing else, the elections for the Reichstag announced, with their outward swelling of the Marxist vote, the steadily approaching inward and hence also outward collapse. All the successes of the so-called bourgeois parties were worthless, not only because even with so-called bourgeois electoral victories they were unable to halt the numerical growth of the Marxist flood, but because they themselves above all now bore the ferments of decay in their own bodies. Without suspecting it, the bourgeois world itself was inwardly infected with the deadly poison of Marxist ideas and its resistance often sprang more from the competitor's envy of ambitious leaders than from a fundamental rejection of adversaries determined to fight to the utmost. In these long years there was only one who kept up an imperturbable, unflagging fight, and this was the *Jew.* His Star of David rose higher and higher in proportion as our people's will for self-preservation vanished.

Therefore, in August, 1914, it was not a people resolved to attack which rushed to the battlefield; no, it was only the last flicker of the national instinct of self-preservation in face of the progressing pacifist-Marxist paralysis of our national body. Since even in these days of destiny, our people did not recognize the inner enemy, all outward resistance was in vain and Providence did not bestow her reward on the victorious sword, but followed the law of eternal retribution.

On the basis of this inner realization, there took form in our new movement the leading principles as well as the tendency, which in our conviction were alone capable, not only of halting the decline of the German people, but of creating the granite foundation upon which some day a state will rest which represents, not an alien mechanism of economic concerns and interests, but a national organism:

A Germanic State of the
German Nation

1924

4 The Klan's Fight for Americanism

HIRAM WESLEY EVANS

The Ku Klux Klan on last Thanksgiving Day passed its tenth anniversary. In one decade it has made a place and won a record for achievement which are almost, if not quite, unique in the history of great popular movements. It has not merely grown from a handful to a membership of millions, from poverty to riches, from obscurity to great influence, from fumbling impotence to the leadership in the greatest cause now before the American people. All these are important, but not vital.

What is vital is that in these years the Klan has shown a power to reform and cleanse itself from within, to formulate and vitalize fundamental instincts into concrete thought and purposeful action, to meet changing conditions with

SOURCE: from Hiram Wesley Evans, "The Klan's Fight for Americanism," *North American Review,* Vol. 223 (1926), pp. 33–63. Reprinted by permission of The University of Northern Iowa.

adaptability but without weakness, to speak for and to lead the common people of America and, finally, to operate through the application of practical patriotism to public life with increasing success, and along the only constructive lines to be found in the present welter of our national thought.

By these things the Klan has proved not only its ability to live, but its right to life and influence. It has already lasted longer than any similar movement; its tenth birthday finds it stronger than ever before, with its worst weaknesses conquered or being eliminated, and so well prepared for the future that it may fairly be said to stand merely on the threshold of its life and service.

The greatest achievement so far has been to formulate, focus, and gain recognition for an idea—the idea of preserving and developing America first and chiefly for the benefit of the children of the pioneers who made America, and only and definitely along the lines of the purpose and spirit of those pioneers. The Klan cannot claim to have created this idea: it has long been a vague stirring in the souls of the plain people. But the Klan can fairly claim to have given it purpose, method, direction and a vehicle. When the Klan first appeared the nation was in the confusion of sudden awakening from the lovely dream of the melting pot, disorganized and helpless before the invasion of aliens and alien ideas. After ten years of the Klan it is in arms for defense. This is our great achievement.

The second is more selfish; we have won the leadership in the movement for Americanism. Except for a few lonesome voices, almost drowned by the clamor of the alien and the alien-minded "Liberal," the Klan alone faces the invader. This is not to say that the Klan has gathered into its membership all who are ready to fight for America. The Klan is the champion, but it is not merely an organization. It is an idea, a faith, a purpose, an organized crusade. No recruit to the cause has ever been really lost. Though men and women drop from the ranks they remain with us in purpose, and can be depended on fully in any crisis. Also, there are many millions who have never joined, but who think and feel and—when called on—fight with us. This is our real strength, and no one who ignores it can hope to understand America today.

Other achievements of these ten years have been the education of the millions of our own membership in citizenship, the suppression of much lawlessness and increase of good government wherever we have become strong, the restriction of immigration, and the defeat of the Catholic attempt to seize the Democratic party. All these we have helped, and all are important.

The outstanding proof of both our influence and our service, however, has been in creating, outside our ranks as well as in them, not merely the growing national concentration on the problems of Americanism, but also a growing sentiment against radicalism, cosmopolitanism, and alienism of all kinds. We have produced instead a sane and progressive conservatism along national lines. We have enlisted our racial instincts for the work of preserving and developing our American traditions and customs. This was most strikingly shown in the elections last fall, when the conservative reaction amazed all politicians—especially the LaFollette rout in the Northwest. This reaction added enormously to the plurality of the President, the size of which was the great surprise of the election.

I wish it might fairly be claimed that the Klan from the beginning had this vision of its mission. Instead the beginnings were groping and futile, as well as feeble; they involved errors which long prevented any important achievement. The chief idea of the founders seems to have been merely to start a new fraternal society, based on rather vague sentiments of brotherhood among white Americans, and of loyalty to the nation and to Protestantism. There was also a sentimental reverence for the Klan of the 'Sixties which led to revival of the old name and some of the ritual. There was finally the basic idea of white supremacy, but this was also at the time a mere sentiment, except as it applied to some Negro unrest.

But along with these ideas there shortly appeared others far from laudable. The Klan had remained weak, gaining barely 10,000 members in the first few years. Then the possibility of profit, both in cash and in power, was seen, and soon resulted in a "selling plan" based partly on Southern affection for the old Klan, partly on social conditions in the South, but chiefly on the possibility of inflaming prejudices. They began to "sell hate at $10 a package".

To us who know the Klan today, its influence, purpose and future, the fact that it can have grown from such beginnings is nothing less than a miracle, possible only through one of those mysterious interventions in human affairs which are called Providence. The fact is, as we see now, that beneath the stupid or dangerous oratory of those early leaders lay certain fundamental truths, quite unseen by them, and then hardly bigger than the vital germ in a grain of corn, but which matured automatically.

The hate and invisible government ideas, however, were what gave the Klan its first great growth, enlisted some 100,000 members, provided wealth for a few leaders, and brought down upon the organization the condemnation of most of the country, leaving it a reputation from which it has not yet recovered. But even before outside indignation had appeared there began an inside reaction, caused by abuses and excesses and by the first stirrings of the purposes which now dominate. Thus began the reform of the Klan by itself, which gained steadily until it won full control in 1922. It laid the basis for the astounding growth of the last three years, and for the present immense influence.

This reform did more than merely rectify the old abuses; it developed into full life the hidden but vital germs, and released one of the most irresistible forces in human affairs, the fundamental instinct of race pride and loyalty—what Lothrop Stoddard calls "the imperious urge of superior heredity". Closely associated with it are two other instincts vital to success among the northern races: patriotism, stimulated to unusual activity by the hyphenism revealed in the World War; and spiritual independence, a revival of the individualism which sprang up just as the Nordic races began to assert themselves in their great blossoming of the last four centuries, and which found its chief expression in Protestantism. These ideas gave direction and guidance to the reforms demanded by the rank and file three years ago. They have been further developed, made more definite and more purposeful, and they are the soul of the Klan today.

The direct reforms brought about were several. First was the stopping of any exercise of "invisible government". This was reinforced by a change in the oath, by which all Klansmen are sworn to uphold legally constituted officers in enforcing the law at all times. One result of this is to be seen in the decrease of lawlessness in Klan territory. We can justly claim credit for the remarkable improvement as regards lynching in the last two years.

The elimination of private profit for officers of the Klan came next and with it went a democratizing of the order. The Klan, being chiefly an organized crusade, cannot operate efficiently on a purely democratic basis, but the autocracy of the early years has been replaced by a system approximating that of the American Government in its early years; final power in the hands of the rank and file, but full power of leadership in the officers they choose.

Another most important reform was a complete change in the method of "propagation"—of recruiting and spreading our gospel. In the early days this had been done very secretively, a high percentage of money had gone to the kleagles—the "sales agents"—there had been a high-pressure appeal to sentimentality, hatred and the invisible government idea, and a tendency to emphasize numbers rather than quality of recruits. Today, instead, the evangelistic emphasis is put on Americanism, Protestant Christianity, and action through government machinery; an increasing number of field agents are on salary, lists of possible members are carefully weeded out before any are approached, and those found worthwhile are won by personal work, backed by open discussion. This has, to be sure, cut down the number of new members accepted, but has greatly increased quality and loyalty, and it has brought amazing gains in strength, particularly in the Mid-West and North.

Most important of all has been the formulation of the true Klan purposes into definite principles. This has been a gradual process. We in the lead found ourselves with a following inspired in many ways beyond our understanding, with beliefs and purposes which they themselves only vaguely understood and could not express, but for the fulfilment of which they depended on us. We found ourselves, too, at the head of an army with unguessable influence to produce results for which responsibility would rest on us—the leaders—but which we had not foreseen and for which we were not prepared. As the solemn responsibility to give right leadership to these millions, and to make right use of this influence, was brought home to us, we were compelled to analyze, put into definite words, and give purpose to these half conscious impulses.

The Klan, therefore, has now come to speak for the great mass of Americans of the old pioneer stock. We believe that it does fairly and faithfully represent them, and our proof lies in their support. To understand the Klan, then, it is necessary to understand the character and present mind of the mass of old-stock Americans. The mass, it must be remembered, as distinguished from the intellectually mongrelized "Liberals".

These are, in the first place, a blend of various peoples of the so-called Nordic race, the race which, with all its faults, has given the world almost the whole of modern civilization. The Klan does not try to represent any people but these.

There is no need to recount the virtues of the American pioneers; but it is too often forgotten that in the pioneer period a selective process of intense rigor went on. From the first only hardy, adventurous and strong men and women dared the pioneer dangers; from among these all but the best died swiftly, so that the new Nordic blend which became the American race was bred up to a point probably the highest in history. This remarkable race character, along with the new-won continent and the new-created nation, made the inheritance of the old-stock Americans the richest ever given to a generation of men.

In spite of it, however, these Nordic Americans for the last generation have found themselves increasingly uncomfortable, and finally deeply distressed. There appeared first confusion in thought and opinion, a groping and hesitancy about national affairs and private life alike, in sharp contrast to the clear, straightforward purposes of our earlier years. There was futility in religion, too, which was in many ways even more distressing. Presently we began to find that we were dealing with strange ideas; policies that always sounded well, but somehow always made us still more uncomfortable.

Finally came the moral breakdown that has been going on for two decades. One by one all our traditional moral standards went by the boards, or were so disregarded that they ceased to be binding. The sacredness of our Sabbath, of our homes, of chastity, and finally even of our right to teach our own children in our own schools fundamental facts and truths were torn away from us. Those who maintained the old standards did so only in the face of constant ridicule.

Along with this went economic distress. The assurance for the future of our children dwindled. We found our great cities and the control of much of our industry and commerce taken over by strangers, who stacked the cards of success and prosperity against us. Shortly they came to dominate our government. The *bloc* system by which this was done is now familiar to all. Every kind of inhabitant except the Americans gathered in groups which operated as units in politics, under orders of corrupt, self-seeking and un-American leaders, who both by purchase and threat enforced their demands on politicians. Thus it came about that the interests of Americans were always the last to be considered by either national or city governments, and that the native Americans were constantly discriminated against, in business, in legislation and in administrative government.

So the Nordic American today is a stranger in large parts of the land his fathers gave him. Moreover, he is a most unwelcome stranger, one much spit upon, and one to whom even the right to have his own opinions and to work for his own interests is now denied with jeers and revilings. "We must Americanize the Americans," a distinguished immigrant said recently. Can anything more clearly show the state to which the real American has fallen in this country which was once his own?

Our falling birthrate, the result of all this, is proof of our distress. We no longer feel that we can be fair to children we bring into the world, unless we can make sure from the start that they shall have capital or education or both, so that they need never compete with those who now fill the lower rungs of the ladder of success. We dare no longer risk letting our youth "make its own way" in the conditions under which we live. So even our unborn children are being crowded out of their birthright!

All this has been true for years, but it was the World War that gave us our first hint of the real cause of our troubles, and began to crystallize our ideas. The war revealed that millions whom we had allowed to share our heritage and prosperity, and whom we had assumed had become part of us, were in fact not wholly so. They had other loyalties: each was willing—anxious!—to sacrifice the interests of the country that had given him shelter to the interests of the one he was supposed to have cast off; each in fact did use the freedom and political power we had given him against ourselves whenever he could see any profit for his older loyalty.

This, of course, was chiefly in international affairs, and the excitement caused by the discovery of disloyalty subsided rapidly after the war ended. But it was not forgotten by the Nordic Americans. They had been awakened and alarmed; they began to suspect that the hyphenism which had been shown was only a part of what existed; their quiet was not that of renewed sleep, but of strong men waiting very watchfully. And presently they began to form decisions about all those aliens who were Americans for profit only.

They decided that even the crossing of salt water did not dim a single spot on a leopard; that an alien usually remains an alien no matter what is done to him, what veneer of education he gets, what oaths he takes, nor what public attitudes he adopts. They decided that the melting pot was a ghastly failure, and remembered that the very name was coined by a member of one of the races—the Jews—which most determinedly refuses to melt. They decided that in every way, as well as in politics, the alien in the vast majority of cases is unalterably fixed in his instincts, character, thought and interests by centuries of racial selection and development, that he thinks first for his own people, works only with and for them, cares entirely for their interests, considers himself always one of them, and never an American.

They decided that in character, instincts, thoughts, and purposes—in his whole soul—an alien remains fixedly alien to America and all it means.

They saw, too, that the alien was tearing down the American standard of living, especially in the lower walks. It became clear that while the American can out-work the alien, the alien can so far under-live the American as to force him out of all competitive labor. So they came to realize that the Nordic can easily survive and rule and increase if he holds for himself the advantages won by strength and daring of his ancestors in times of stress and peril, but that if he surrenders those advantages to the peoples who could not share the stress, he will soon be driven below the level at which he can exist by their low standards, low living and fast breeding. And they saw that the low standard aliens of Eastern and Southern Europe were doing just that thing to us.

They learned, though more slowly, that alien ideas are just as dangerous to us as the aliens themselves, no matter how plausible such ideas may sound. With most of the plain people this conclusion is based simply on the fact that the alien ideas do not work well for them. Others went deeper and came to understand that the differences in racial background, in breeding, instinct, character and emotional point of view are more important than logic. So ideas which may be perfectly healthy for an alien may also be poisonous for Americans.

Finally they learned the great secret of the propagandists; that success in corrupting public opinion depends on putting out the subversive ideas without revealing their source. They came to suspect that "prejudice" against foreign ideas is really a protective device of nature against mental food that may be indigestible. They saw, finally, that the alien leaders in America act on this theory, and that there is a steady flood of alien ideas being spread over the country, always carefully disguised as American.

As they learned all this the Nordic Americans have been gradually arousing themselves to defend their homes and their own kind of civilization. They have not known just how to go about it; the idealist philanthropy and good-natured generosity which led to the philosophy of the melting pot have died hard. Resistance to the peaceful invasion of the immigrant is no such simple matter as snatching up weapons and defending frontiers, nor has it much spectacular emotionalism to draw men to the colors.

The old-stock Americans are learning, however. They have begun to arm themselves for this new type of warfare. Most important, they have broken away from the fetters of the false ideals and philanthropy which put aliens ahead of their own children and their own race.

To do this they have had to reject completely—and perhaps for the moment the rejection is a bit too complete—the whole body of "Liberal" ideas which they had followed with such simple, unquestioning faith. The first and immediate cause of the break with Liberalism was that it had provided no defense against the alien invasion, but instead had excused it—even defended it against Americanism. Liberalism is today charged in the mind of most Americans with nothing less than national, racial and spiritual treason.

But this is only the last of many causes of distrust. The plain people now see that Liberalism has come completely under the dominance of weaklings and parasites whose alien "idealism" reaches its logical peak in the Bolshevist platform of "produce as little as you can, beg or steal from those who do produce, and kill the producer for thinking he is better than you." Not that all Liberalism goes so far, but it all seems to be on that road. The average Liberal idea is apparently that those who can produce should carry the unfit, and let the unfit rule them.

This aberration would have been impossible, of course, if American Liberalism had kept its feet on the ground. Instead it became wholly academic, lost all touch with the plain people, disowned its instincts and common sense, and lived in a world of pure, high, groundless logic.

Worse yet, this became a world without moral standards. Our forefathers had standards—the Liberals today say they were narrow!—and they had consciences and knew that Liberalism must be kept within fixed bounds. They knew that tolerance of things that touch the foundations of the home, of decency, of patriotism or of race loyalty is not lovely but deadly. Modern American Liberalism has no such bounds. If it has a conscience it hides it shamefacedly; if it has any standards it conceals them well. If it has any convictions—but why be absurd? Its boast is that it has none except conviction in its own decadent religion of Liberalism toward everything; toward the right of every man to make a fool or degenerate of himself and to try to corrupt others; in the right of any one to pull the foundations from under the house or poison the wells; in the right of children to play with matches in a powdermill!

The old-stock Americans believe in Liberalism, but not in this thing. It has undermined their Constitution and their national customs and institutions, it has corrupted the morals of their children, it has vitiated their thought, it has degenerated and perverted their education, it has tried to destroy their God. They want no more of it. They are trying to get back to decency and common sense.

The old-stock "plain people" are no longer alone in their belief as to the nature of the dangers, their causes, and the folly of Liberal thought. Recently men of great education and mind, students of wide reputation, have come to see all this as the plain Americans saw it years before. This was stated by Madison Grant:

> The Nordic race . . . if it takes warning in time, may face the future with assurance. Fight it must, but let the fight be not a civil war against its own blood kindred but against the dangerous foreign races, whether they advance sword in hand

> or in the more insidious guise of beggars at our gates, pleading for admittance to share our prosperity. If we continue to allow them to enter they will in time drive us out of our own land by the mere force of breeding.
>
> The great hope of the future here in America lies in the realization of the working classes that competition of the Nordic with the alien is fatal, whether the latter be the lowly immigrant from Southern or Eastern Europe, or the more obviously dangerous Oriental, against whose standards of living the white man cannot compete. In this country we must look to such of our people—our farmers and artisans—as are still of American blood, to recognize and meet this danger.
>
> Our present condition is the result of following the leadership of idealists and philanthropic doctrinaires.

The chief of Mr. Grant's demands, that the un-American alien be barred out, has already been partly accomplished. It is established as our national policy by overwhelming vote of Congress, after years of delay won by the aliens already here through the political power we gave them. The Klan is proud that it was able to aid this work, which was vital.

But the plain people realize also that merely stopping the alien flood does not restore Americanism, nor even secure us against final utter defeat. America must also defend herself against the enemy within, or we shall be corrupted and conquered by those to whom we have already given shelter.

The first danger is that we shall be overwhelmed, as Mr. Grant forecasts, by the aliens' "mere force of breeding". With the present birthrate, the Nordic stock will have become a hopeless minority within fifty years, and will within two hundred have been choked to death, like grain among weeds. Unless some means is found of making the Nordic feel safe in having children, we are already doomed.

An equal danger is from disunity, so strikingly shown during the war and from a mongrelization of thought and purpose. It is not merely foreign policy that is involved; it is all our thought at home, our morals, education, social conduct—everything. We are already confused and disunited in every way; the alien groups themselves, and the skilful alien propaganda, are both tearing steadily at all that makes for unity in nationhood, or for the soul of Americanism. If the word "integrity" can still be used in its original meaning of singleness of purpose or thought, then we as a nation have lost all integrity. Yet our old American motto includes the words ". . . divided we fall!"

One more point about the present attitude of the old-stock American: he has revived and increased his long-standing distrust of the Roman Catholic Church. It is for this that the native Americans, and the Klan as their leader, are most often denounced as intolerant and prejudiced. This is not because we oppose the Catholic more than we do the alien, but because our enemies recognize that patriotism and race loyalty cannot safely be denounced, while our own tradition of religious freedom gives them an opening here, if they can sufficiently confuse the issue.

The fact is, of course, that our quarrel with the Catholics is not religious but political. The Nordic race is, as is well known, almost entirely Protestant, and there remains in its mental heritage an anti-Catholic attitude based on lack of sympathy with the Catholic psychology, on the historic opposition of the Roman Church to the Nordics' struggle for freedom and achievement, and on the memories of persecutions. But this strictly religious prejudice is not now active in America, and so far as I can learn, never has been. I do not know of a single manifestation in recent times of hostility to any Catholic because of his religion, nor to the Catholic Church because of its beliefs. Certainly the American has always granted to the Catholic not only full religious liberty, without interference or abuse either public or private, but also every civil, social and political equality. Neither the present day Protestant nor the Klan wishes to change this in any degree.

The only possible exception to this statement is worth mentioning only because some people give it far too much importance. This has been in the publication of vicious and ignorant anti-Catholic papers, with small circulation and minute influence. These publications, by the way, the Klan has denounced and helped suppress. If the Catholic Church would do as much by *Tolerance* and some of the equally vicious and ignorant sheets published under its aegis, it could come into court against the American people with cleaner hands.

The real indictment against the Roman Church is that it is, fundamentally and irredeemably, in its leadership, in politics, in thought, and largely in membership, actually and actively alien, un-American and usually anti-American. The old-stock Americans, with the exception of the few such of Catholic faith—who are in a class by themselves, standing tragically torn between their faith and their racial and national patriotism—see in the Roman Church today the chief leader of alienism, and the most dangerous alien power with a foothold inside our boundaries. It is this and nothing else that has revived hostility to Catholicism. By no stretch of the imagination can it fairly be called religious prejudice, though, now that the hostility has become active, it does derive some strength from the religious schism.

We Americans see many evidences of Catholic alienism. We believe that its official position and its dogma, its theocratic autocracy and its claim to full authority in temporal as well as spiritual matters, all make it impossible for it as a church, or for its members if they obey it, to coöperate in a free democracy in which Church and State have been separated. It is true that in this country the Roman Church speaks very softly on these points, so that many Catholics do not know them. It is also true that the Roman priests preach Americanism, subject to their own conception of Americanism, of course. But the Roman Church itself makes a point of the divine and unalterable character of its dogma, it has never seen fit to abandon officially any of these un-American attitudes, and it still teaches them in other countries. Until it does renounce them, we cannot believe anything except that they all remain in force, ready to be called into action whenever feasible, and temporarily hushed up only for expediency.

The hierarchical government of the Roman Church is equally at odds with Americanism. The Pope and the whole hierarchy have been for centuries almost wholly Italian. It is nonsense to suppose that a man, by entering a church, loses his race or national loyalties. The Roman Church today, therefore, is just what its name says—Roman; and it is impossible for its hierarchy or the policies they dictate to be in real sympathy with Americanism. Worse, the Italians have proven to be one of the least assimilable of people. The autocratic nature of the Catholic Church organization, and its suppression of free conscience or free decision, need not be discussed; they are unquestioned. Thus it is fundamental to the Roman Church to demand a supreme loyalty, overshadowing national or race loyalty, to a power that is inevitably alien, and which at the best must inevitably inculcate ideals un-American if not actively anti-American.

We find, too, that even in America, the majority of the leaders and of the priests of the Roman Church are either foreign born, or of foreign parentage and training. They, like other aliens, are unable to teach Americanism if they wish, because both race and education prevent their understanding what it is. The service they give it, even if sincere, can at best produce only confusion of thought. Who would ask an American, for instance, to try to teach Italians their own language, history, and patriotism, even without the complication of religion?

Another difficulty is that the Catholic Church here constantly represents, speaks for and cares for the interests of a large body of alien peoples. Most immigration of recent years, so unassimilable and fundamentally un-American, has been Catholic. The Catholics of American stock have been submerged and almost lost; the aliens and their interests dictate all policies of the Roman Church which are not dictated from Rome itself.

Also, the Roman Church seems to take pains to prevent the assimilation of these people. Its parochial schools, its foreign born priests, the obstacles it places in the way of marriage with Protestants unless the children are bound in advance to Romanism, its persistent use of the foreign languages in church and school, its habit of grouping aliens together and thus creating insoluble alien masses—all these things strongly impede Americanization. Of course they also strengthen and solidify the Catholic Church, and make its work easier, and so are very natural, but the fact remains that they are hostile to Americanism.

Finally, there is the undeniable fact that the Roman Church takes an active part in American politics. It has not been content to accept in good faith the separation of Church and State, and constantly tries through political means to win advantages for itself and its people—in other words, to be a political power in America, as well as a spiritual power. Denials of

Catholic activity in politics are too absurd to need discussion. The "Catholic vote" is as well recognized a factor as the "dry vote". All politicians take it for granted.

The facts are that almost everywhere, and especially in the great industrial centers where the Catholics are strongest, they vote almost as a unit, under control of leaders of their own faith, always in support of the interests of the Catholic Church and of Catholic candidates without regard to other interests, and always also in support of alienism whenever there is an issue raised. They vote, in short, not as American citizens, but as aliens and Catholics! They form the biggest, strongest, most cohesive of all the alien *blocs.* On many occasions they form alliances with other alien *blocs* against American interests, as with the Jews in New York today, and with others in the case of the recent opposition to immigration restriction. Incidentally they have been responsible for some of the worst abuses in American politics, and today are the chief support of such machines as that of Brennan in Chicago, Curley in Boston and Tammany in New York.

All this might occur without direct sanction from the Roman Church, though that would not make it less a "Catholic" menace. But the evidence is that the Church acts directly and often controls these activities. The appearance of Roman clergy in "inside" political councils, the occasional necessity of "seeing" a prelate to accomplish political results, and above all the fact that during the fight in the Democratic National Convention of 1924 the hotel lobbies and the corridors of Madison Square Garden were suddenly black with priests, all seem to prove that the Catholic Church acts in politics *as a church,* and that it must bear responsibility for these evils.

This is the indictment of the old-stock Americans against the Roman Church. If at any time it should clear its skirts, should prove its willingness to become American in America, and to be politically an equal among equals with other religious bodies, then Americans would make no indictment of it whatever. But until it does these things it must be opposed as must all other agencies which stand against America's destiny.

Just a word about the American Catholics, of whom there are a few hundred thousand only. From the time of the Reformation on there have always been Catholics (like Lord Howard, who commanded the English fleet against the Armada, despite the Pope's bulls) who have put race and national patriotism ahead of loyalty, not to their faith, but to the self-created Roman hierarchy. There are such in America today, and always have been. With these the American people have no quarrel whatever. They, even the Klan, have supported some of them at the polls, and will continue to do so.

But these people are not "good Catholics" in the eyes of the hierarchy. They are really in a tragic situation. They are pulled on one side by their faith and on the other by the deepest racial and patriotic instincts. If there should be a crisis they would be torn between them. They are put into this position not by their religion but by the autocratic hierarchy which uses their faith as a weapon to enforce its own power; which demands not only faith and piety, but subservience, as the price of salvation. What they may do in a crisis no man can forecast, but whatever it may be, they will deserve nothing but the deepest sympathy.

This is the general state of mind of the Nordic Americans of the pioneer stock today. Many of them do not understand the reasons for their beliefs so fully as I have stated them, but the state of mind is there beyond doubt, and the reasons are true at all vital points. It is inevitable that these people are now in revolt. This is the movement to which the Klan, more through Providence than its own wisdom, has begun to give leadership.

The Ku Klux Klan, in short, is an organization which gives expression, direction and purpose to the most vital instincts, hopes and resentments of the old-stock Americans, provides them with leadership, and is enlisting and preparing them for militant, constructive action toward fulfilling their racial and national destiny. Madison Grant summed up in a single sentence the grievances, purpose and type of membership of the Klan: "Our farmers and artisans . . . of American blood, to recognize and meet this danger." The Klan literally is once more the embattled American farmer and artisan, coördinated into a disciplined and growing army, and launched upon a definite crusade for Americanism!

This Providential history of the Klan, and the Providential place it has come to hold, give it certain definite characteristics. The disadvantages that go with them, as well as the advantages, may as well be admitted at once.

We are a movement of the plain people, very weak in the matter of culture, intellectual support, and trained leadership. We are demanding, and we expect to win, a return of power into the hands of the everyday, not highly cultured, not overly intellectualized, but entirely unspoiled and not de-Americanized, average citizen of the old stock. Our members and leaders are all of this class—the opposition of the intellectuals and liberals who held the leadership, betrayed Americanism, and from whom we expect to wrest control, is almost automatic.

This is undoubtedly a weakness. It lays us open to the charge of being "hicks" and "rubes" and "drivers of second-hand Fords". We admit it. Far worse, it makes it hard for us to state our case and advocate our crusade in the most effective way, for most of us lack skill in language. Worst of all, the need of trained leaders constantly hampers our progress and leads to serious blunders and internal troubles. If the Klan ever should fail it would be from this cause. All this we on the inside know far better than our critics, and regret more. Our leadership is improving, but for many years the Klan will be seeking better leaders, and the leaders praying for greater wisdom.

Serious as this is, and strange though our attitude may seem to the intellectuals, it does not worry us greatly. Every popular movement has suffered from just this handicap, yet the popular movements have been the mainsprings of progress, and have usually had to win against the "best people" of their time. Moreover, we can depend on getting this intellectual backing shortly. It is notable that when the plain people begin to win with one of their movements, such as the Klan, the very intellectuals who have scoffed and fought most bitterly presently begin to dig up sound—at least well-sounding!—logic in support of the success. The movement, so far as can be judged, is neither hurt nor helped by this process.

Another weakness is that we have not been able, as yet, to bring home to the whole membership the need of continuous work on organization programmes both local and national. They are too prone to work only at times of crisis and excitement, and then to feel they can let down. Partly, of course, this is inherent in the evangelistic quality of our crusade. It is "strong medicine", highly emotional, and presently brings on a period of reaction and lethargy. All crusaders and evangelists know this: the whole country saw it after the war. The Klan will not be fully entrenched till it has passed this reaction period, and steadied down for the long pull. That time is only beginning for most of the Klan, which really is hardly three years old.

But we have no fear of the outcome. Since we indulge ourselves in convictions, we are not frightened by our weaknesses. We hold the conviction that right will win if backed with vigor and consecration. We are increasing our consecration and learning to make better use of our vigor. We are sure of the fundamental rightness of our cause, as it concerns both ourselves and the progress of the world. We believe that there can be no question of the right of the children of the men who made America to own and control America. We believe that when we allowed others to share our heritage, it was by our own generosity and by no right of theirs. We believe that therefore we have every right to protect ourselves when we find that they are betraying our trust and endangering us. We believe, in short, that we have the right to make America *American* and for Americans.

We believe also that only through this kind of a nation, and through development along these lines, can we best serve America, the whole world today, and the greater world yet unborn. We believe the hand of God was in the creation of the American stock and nation. We believe, too, in the right and duty of every man to fight for himself, his own children, his own nation and race. We believe in the parable of the talents, and mean to keep and use those entrusted to us—the race, spirit and nationhood of America!

Finally we believe in the vitality and driving power of our race: a faith based on the record of the Nordics throughout all history, and especially in America. J. P. Morgan had a motto which said, in effect, "Never bet against the future of America." We believe it is equally unsafe to bet against the future of any stock of the Nordic race, especially so finely blended and highly bred a stock as that of the sons of the pioneers. Handicaps, weaknesses, enemies and all, we will win!

Our critics have accused us of being merely a "protest movement", of being frightened; they say we fear alien competition, are in a panic because we cannot hold our own against the foreigners. That is partly true. We are a protest movement—protesting against being robbed. We are afraid of competition with peoples who would destroy our standard of living. We are suffering in many ways, we have been betrayed by our trusted leaders, we are half beaten already. But we are not frightened nor in a panic. We have merely awakened to the fact that we must fight for our own. We are going to fight—and win!

The Klan does not believe that the fact that it is emotional and instinctive, rather than coldly intellectual, is a weakness. All action comes from emotion, rather than from ratiocination. Our emotions and the instincts on which they are based have been bred into us for thousands of years; far longer than reason has had a place in the human brain. They are the many-times distilled product of experience; they still operate much more surely and promptly than reason can. For centuries those who obeyed them have lived and carried on the race; those in whom they were weak, or who failed to obey, have died. They are the foundations of our American civilization, even more than our great historic documents; they can be trusted where the fine-haired reasoning of the denatured intellectuals cannot.

Thus the Klan goes back to the American racial instincts, and to the common sense which is their first product, as the basis of its beliefs and methods. The fundamentals of our thought are convictions, not mere opinions. We are pleased that modern research is finding scientific backing for these convictions. We do not need them ourselves; we know that we are right in the same sense that a good Christian knows that he has been saved and that Christ lives—a thing which the intellectual can never understand. These convictions are no more to be argued about than is our love for our children; we are merely willing to state them for the enlightenment and conversion of others.

There are three of these great racial instincts, vital elements in both the historic and the present attempts to build an America which shall fulfill the aspirations and justify the heroism of the men who made the nation. These are the instincts of loyalty to the white race, to the traditions of America, and to the spirit of Protestantism, which has been an essential part of Americanism ever since the days of Roanoke and Plymouth Rock. They are condensed into the Klan slogan: "Native, white, Protestant supremacy."

First in the Klansman's mind is patriotism—America for Americans. He believes religiously that a betrayal of Americanism or the American race is treason to the most sacred of trusts, a trust from his fathers and a trust from God. He believes, too, that Americanism can only be achieved if the pioneer stock is kept pure. There is more than race pride in this. Mongrelization has been proven bad. It is only between closely related stocks of the same race that interbreeding has improved men; the kind of interbreeding that went on in the early days of America between English, Dutch, German, Huguenot, Irish and Scotch.

Racial integrity is a very definite thing to the Klansman. It means even more than good citizenship, for a man may be in all ways a good citizen and yet a poor American, unless he has racial understanding of Americanism, and instinctive loyalty to it. It is in no way a reflection on any man to say that he is un-American; it is merely a statement that he is not one of us. It is often not even wise to try to make an American of the best of aliens. What he is may be spoiled without his becoming American. The races and stocks of men are as distinct as breeds of animals, and every boy knows that if one tries to train a bulldog to herd sheep, he has in the end neither a good bulldog nor a good collie.

Americanism, to the Klansman, is a thing of the spirit, a purpose and a point of view, that can only come through instinctive racial understanding. It has, to be sure, certain defined principles, but he does not believe that many aliens understand those principles, even when they use our words in talking about them. Democracy is one, fairdealing, impartial justice, equal opportunity, religious liberty, independence, self-reliance, courage, endurance, acceptance of individual responsibility as well as individual rewards for effort, willingness to sacrifice for the good of his family, his nation and his race before anything else but God, dependence on enlightened conscience for guidance, the right to unhampered development—these are fundamental. But within the bounds they fix there must be the utmost freedom, tolerance, liberalism. In short, the Klansman believes in the greatest possible diversity and individualism within the limits of the American spirit. But he believes also that few aliens can understand that spirit, that fewer try to, and that there must be resistance, intolerance even, toward anything that threatens it, or the fundamental national unity based upon it.

The second word in the Klansman's trilogy is "white." The white race must be supreme, not only in America but in the world. This is equally undebatable, except on the ground that the races might live together, each with full regard for the rights and interests of others, and that those rights and interests would never conflict. Such an idea, of course, is absurd; the colored races today, such as Japan, are clamoring not for equality but for their supremacy. The whole history of the world, on its broader lines, has been one of race conflicts, wars, subjugation or extinction. This is not pretty, and certainly disagrees with the maudlin theories of cosmopolitanism, but it is truth. The world has been so made that each race must fight for its life, must conquer, accept slavery or die. The Klansman believes that the whites will not become slaves, and he does not intend to die before his time.

Moreover, the future of progress and civilization depends on the continued supremacy of the white race. The forward movement of the world for centuries has come entirely from it. Other races each had its chance and either failed or stuck fast, while white civilization shows no sign of having reached its limit. Until the whites falter, or some colored civilization has a miracle of awakening, there is not a single colored stock that can claim even equality with the white; much less supremacy.

The third of the Klan principles is that Protestantism must be supreme; that Rome shall not rule America. The Klansman believes this not merely because he is a Protestant, nor even because the Colonies that are now our nation were settled for the purpose of wresting America from the control of Rome and establishing a land of free conscience. He believes it also because Protestantism is an essential part of Americanism; without it America could never have been created and without it she cannot go forward. Roman rule would kill it.

Protestantism contains more than religion. It is the expression in religion of the same spirit of independence, self-reliance and freedom which are the highest achievements of the Nordic race. It sprang into being automatically at the time of the great "upsurgence" of strength in the Nordic peoples that opened the spurt of civilization in the fifteenth century. It has been a distinctly Nordic religion, and it has been through this religion that the Nordics have found strength to take leadership of all whites and the supremacy of the earth. Its destruction is the deepest purpose of all other peoples, as that would mean the end of Nordic rule.

It is the only religion that permits the unhampered individual development and the unhampered conscience and action which were necessary in the settling of America. Our pioneers were all Protestants, except for an occasional Irishman—Protestants by nature if not by religion—for though French and Spanish dared and explored and showed great heroism, they made little of the land their own. America was Protestant from birth.

She must remain Protestant, if the Nordic stock is to finish its destiny. We of the old-stock Americans could not work—and the work is mostly ours to do, if the record of the past proves anything—if we become priest-ridden, if we had to submit our consciences and limit our activities and suppress our thoughts at the command of any man, much less of a man sitting upon Seven Hills thousands of miles away. This we will not permit. Rome shall not rule us. Protestantism must be supreme.

Let it be clear what is meant by "supremacy". It is nothing more than power of control, under just laws. It is not imperialism, far less is it autocracy or even aristocracy of a race or stock of men. What it does mean is that we insist on our inherited right to insure our own safety, individually and as a race, to secure the future of our children, to maintain and develop our racial heritage in our own, white, Protestant, American way, without interference.

Just how we of the Klan will accomplish this we do not yet know. Our first task has been to organize and this is not yet quite accomplished. But already we are beginning our second stage, which is to meet, stop and remove the invader and leave ourselves free once more. In the strict sense we have no programme. We are not ready for one and have not put our minds to it. No such popular movement ever springs full-panoplied from the head of any man or group. For some time we must be opportunists, meeting the enemy wherever he attacks and attacking where we can. This course, so far, has accomplished much more than could have been done by a hard and fast programme. We expect to continue it.

There are, however, certain general principles and purposes which are always kept in view. Enough has been said about pioneer Americanism. Another constant aim is better citizenship. The Klan holds that no man can be either a good Klansman or a good American without being a good citizen. A large part of our work is to preach this, and no man can be a Klansman long without feeling it.

Another constant objective is good government, locally and nationally. The Klansman is pledged to support law and order, and it is also a part of his duty to see that both law and officers are as good as possible. We believe that every man and woman should keep well-informed on all public matters, and take an active and direct part in all public affairs. There is nothing spectacular about this; it is merely good citizenship on the job. The Klan, however, never attempts to dictate the votes of its members, but does furnish information about men and measures.

In the National Government our interest is along the same lines, with special emphasis on anti-alien and pro-American legislation. Also, far more than in local affairs, we take pains to support men who understand and are loyal to the best American traditions. Apart from that the Klan takes no interest in any government matters except those having a direct bearing on decency and honesty.

We take great pains in all these matters never to be made use of—at least not twice!—by any man, party or faction. We have no political interests except Americanism, and do not belong in or with any party or faction. We do support a certain American type of man, and will support any group which draws the right kind of an issue. If there is no such issue, and no choice between candidates from the American point of view, we keep out. It is true that some men have been able to make use of the Klan once, but it has always reacted against them.

It is inevitable that most of the active work of the Klan, outside our own ranks, should be in public affairs. By no other means can most of our demands be accomplished. And it is against this patriotic activity that the most violent criticisms have been made. We are accused of injecting old prejudices, hatred, race and religion into politics, of creating an un-American class division, of trying to profit by race and religious enmities, of violating the principle of equality, and of ruining the Democratic party.

Most of these charges are not worth answering. So long as politicians cater to alien racial and religious groups, it is the merest self-defense to have also a Protestant and an American "vote" and to make it respected.

The hatred and prejudice are, as has been evident to every candid person, displayed by our enemies and not by us.

As to the charge that the Klan brought race and religion into politics, that simply is not true. That was done by the very people who are now accusing us, because we are cutting into the profits they had been making in politics out of *their* races and *their* religions. Race and religion have for years been used by the aliens as political platforms. The Klan is in no way responsible for this condition. We merely recognized it when others dared not, and we fight it in the open. Our belief is that any man who runs for office or asks political favors, or advocates policies or carries on any other political activity, either as a member of any racial or religious group, or in the interests of or under orders from such a group or of any non-American interest whatever, should be opposed for that very reason. The Klan's ambition is to get race and religion out of politics, and that cannot be done so long as there is any profit in exploiting them. It therefore fights every attempt to use them.

This vicious kind of politics has mostly been more or less secret. We of the Klan wish we could claim credit for bringing the scandal into the open, but we cannot even do that. The open issue was raised for the first time on a national scale at the Democratic National Convention of 1924. This was the doing of the Catholic politicians, who seized upon Catholicism as a cement for holding the anti-McAdoo forces together. The bitter cleavage that followed was inevitable, and it was they—the Catholic leaders—who so nearly wrecked the party and were quite ready to wreck it completely if that would have helped their local Catholic machines.

One of the Klan's chief interests is in education. We believe that it is the duty of government to insure to every child opportunity to develop its natural abilities to their utmost. We wish to go to the very limit in the improvement of the public schools; so far that there will be no excuse except snobbery for the private schools.

Further, the Klan wishes to restore the Bible to the school, not only because it is part of the world's great heritage in literature and philosophy and has profoundly influenced all white civilization, but because it is the basis on which all Christian religions are built, and to which they must look for their authority. The Klan believes in the right of each child to pass for itself on the ultimate authority behind the creed he is asked to adopt; it believes in preserving to all children their right to religious volition, to full freedom of choice. This is impossible if they are barred from the Bible. We oppose any means by which any priesthood keeps its hold on power by suppressing, hiding or garbling the fundamental Christian revelation.

This is one of the reasons for the Klan's objection to parochial schools of any church. They very readily become mere agencies of propaganda. Another reason is that in many the teaching is in the hands of aliens, who cannot possibly understand Americanism or train Americans to citizenship. In many, even, the textbooks have been so perverted that Americanism is falsified, distorted and betrayed. The Klan would like to see all such schools closed. If they cannot be abolished, the Klan aims to bring them under control of the State, so as to eliminate these evils, insure religious volition, and enforce the teaching of true Americanism.

This, then, is the mental attitude, the purpose and the plan of the Klan today, and it is against this position of ours, and against nothing else, that charges of bigotry, narrowness, intolerance and prejudice can fairly be brought. Charges made on other grounds need not be discussed, but we of the Klan are prepared to admit that some of these charges are at least partly justified.

This does not mean merely that there are "bigots and fanatics" among us. There certainly are; we are weeding them out, but we have some left, and others will join in spite of our utmost care. The fault is serious but not fatal. Every such movement has them, as Roosevelt found when he dubbed the similar nuisances in his own movement "the lunatic fringe".

Nor does this mean, either, an admission of the charges of those who deny to Americans the right—which every alien claims and uses—to speak his mind freely and criticize things about him. Jews or Catholics are lavish with their caustic criticism of anything American. Nothing is immune; our great men, our historic struggles and sacrifices, our customs and personal traits, our "Puritan consciences"—all have been scarified without mercy. Yet the least criticism of these same vitriolic critics or of their people brings howls of "anti-Semitic" or "anti-Catholic". We of the Klan pay no attention to those who argue with epithets only. They thereby admit their weakness. And we are still waiting for some one to try to answer us with facts and reasons.

Aside from these things, however, we of the Klan admit that we are intolerant and narrow in a certain sense. We do not think our intolerance is so serious as that of our enemies. It is not an intolerance that tries to prevent free speech or free assembly. The Klan has never broken up a meeting, nor tried to drive a speaker to cover, nor started a riot, nor attacked a procession or parade, nor murdered men for belonging to the Knights of Columbus or the B'nai B'rith.

And we deny that either bigotry or prejudice enters into our intolerance or our narrowness. We are intolerant of everything that strikes at the foundations of our race, our country or our freedom of worship. We are narrowly opposed to the use of anything alien—race, loyalty to any foreign power or to any religion whatever—as a means to win political power. We are prejudiced against any attempt to use the privileges and opportunities which aliens hold only through our generosity as levers to force us to change our civilization, to wrest from us control of our own country, to exploit us for the benefit of any foreign power—religious or secular—and especially to use America as a tool or cat's-paw for the advantage of any side in the hatreds and quarrels of the Old World. This is our intolerance; based on the sound instincts which have saved us many times from the follies of the intellectuals. We admit it. More and worse, we are proud of it.

But this is all of our intolerance. We do not wish harm to any man, even to those we fight. We have no desire to abuse, enslave, exploit or deny any legal, political or social right to any man of any religion, race or color. We grant them full freedom—except freedom to destroy our own freedom and ourselves. In many ways we honor and respect them. Every race has many fine and admirable traits, each has made notable achievements. There is much for us to learn from each of them. But we do insist that we may learn what we choose, and what will best fit the peculiar genius of our own race, rather than have them choose our lessons for us, and then ram them down our throats.

The attitude of the Klan toward outsiders is derived logically from these beliefs. From all Americans except the racial and spiritual expatriates we expect eventual support. Of the expatriates nothing can be hoped. They are men without a country and proud of it.

The Negro, the Klan considers a special duty and problem of the white American. He is among us through no wish of his; we owe it to him and to ourselves to give him full protection and opportunity. But his limitations are evident; we will not permit him to gain sufficient power to control our civilization. Neither will we delude him with promises of social equality which we know can never be realized. The Klan looks forward to the day when the Negro problem will have been solved on some much saner basis than miscegenation, and when every State will enforce laws making any sex relations between a white and a colored person a crime.

For the alien in general we have sympathy, opportunity, justice, but no permanent welcome unless he becomes truly American. It is our duty to see that he has every chance for this, and we shall be glad to accept him if he does. We hold no rancor against him; his race, instincts, training, mentality and whole outlook of life are usually widely different from ours. We cannot blame him if he adheres to them and attempts to convert us to them, even by force. But we must see that he can never succeed.

The Jew is a more complex problem. His abilities are great, he contributes much to any country where he lives. This is particularly true of the Western Jew, those of the stocks we have known so long. Their separation from us is more religious than racial. When freed from persecution these Jews have shown a tendency to disintegrate and amalgamate. We may hope that shortly, in the free atmosphere of America, Jews of this class will cease to be a problem. Quite different are the Eastern Jews of recent immigration, the Jews known as the Askhenasim. It is interesting to note that anthropologists now tell us that these are not true Jews, but only Judaized Mongols—Chazars. These, unlike the true Hebrew, show a divergence from the American type so great that there seems little hope of their assimilation.

The most menacing and most difficult problem facing America today is this of the permanently unassimilable alien. The only solution so far offered is that of Dr. Eliot, president emeritus of Harvard. After admitting that the melting pot has failed—thus supporting the primary position of the Klan!—he adds that there is no hope of creating here a single, homogeneous race-stock of the kind necessary for national unity. He then suggests that, instead, there shall be a congeries of diverse peoples, living together in sweet harmony, and all working for the good of all and of the nation! This solution is on a par with the optimism which foisted the melting pot on us. Diverse races never have lived together in such harmony; race antipathies are too deep and strong. If such a state were possible, the nation would be too disunited for progress. One race always ruled, one always must, and there will be struggle and reprisals till the mastery is established—and bitterness afterwards. And, speaking for us Americans, we have come to realize that if all this could possibly be done, still within a few years we should be supplanted by the "mere force of breeding" of the low standard peoples. We intend to see that the American stock remains supreme.

This is a problem which must shortly engage the best American minds. We can neither expel, exterminate nor enslave these low-standard aliens, yet their continued presence on the present basis means our doom. Those who know the American character know that if the problem is not soon solved by wisdom, it will be solved by one of those cataclysmic outbursts which have so often disgraced—and saved!—the race. Our attempt to find a sane solution is one of the best justifications of the Klan's existence.

Toward the Catholic as an individual the Klan has no "attitude" whatever. His religion is none of our business. But toward the Catholic Church as a political organization, and toward the individual Catholic who serves it as such, we have a definite intolerance. We are intolerant of the refusal of the Roman Church to accept equality in a democracy, and resent its attempts to use clerical power in our politics. We resent, too, the subservience of members who follow clerical commands in politics. We are intolerant, also, of the efforts of the Roman Church to prevent the assimilation of immigrant members. We demand that in politics and in education the Roman Church abandon its clutching after special and un-American privileges, and that it become content to depend for its strength on the truth of its teachings and the spiritual power of its leaders. Further than this we ask nothing. We admit that this is intolerant; we deny that it is either bigoted or unjust.

The Klan today, because of the position it has come to fill, is by far the strongest movement recorded for the defense and fulfillment of Americanism. It has a membership of millions, the support of millions more. If there be any truth in the statement that the voice of the people is the voice of God, then we hold a Divine commission. Our finances are sound as they have been for years; we permit no great accumulation, but have reduced our fees when we found them producing more than enough to carry on our crusade.

Our ritual is still incomplete. We have been too busy getting our army into shape and our crusade started, to perfect the higher degrees, but this is being done. Our first, and so far only largely used degree, inculcates and symbolizes loyalty—to America, to Protestantism, to law and order and to the Klan. The second, just coming into use, emphasizes patriotism. The third will center around Protestantism, and the fourth and last around race pride, loyalty and responsibility. It may be added that members of other orders who have seen such ritualism as we already use, agree that it is unexcelled in solemnity, dignity and beauty.

One of the outstanding principles of the Klan is secrecy. We have been much criticized for it, and accused of cowardice, though how any sane person can allege cowardice against men who stood unarmed while rioters beat and shot them down, as Klansmen were beaten and shot at Carnegie and other places, we cannot understand. Our secrecy is, in fact, necessary for our protection so long as the bitter intolerance and fanatic persecution lasts. Until the Klan becomes strong in a community, individual members have often found themselves in danger of loss of work, business, property and even life. There is also the advantage in secrecy that it gives us greater driving force, since our enemies are handicapped in not knowing just what, where or how great is the strength we can exert.

Both these reasons for secrecy will grow less in time, but it can safely be predicted that the Klan will never officially abandon its secrecy. The mask, by the way, is not a part of our secrecy at all, but of our ritual, and can never be abandoned. The personal secrecy occasionally disappears, as the Klan gains strength, from the zeal of members who wish to work openly, whereby the Klan can be seen emerging as Masonry did a century ago.

One more charge against the Klan is worth noting: that we are trying to cure prejudice by using new and stronger prejudice, to end disunity by setting up new barriers, to speed Americanization by discriminations and issues which are un-American. This is a plausible charge, if the facts alleged were true, for it is certain that prejudice is no cure for prejudice, nor can we hope to promote Americanism by violating its principles.

But the Klan does not stimulate prejudice, nor has it raised race or religious issues, nor violated the spirit of Americanism in any way. We simply recognize facts, and meet the situation they reveal, as it must be met. Non-resistance to the alien invasion, and ostrich-like optimism have already brought us to the verge of ruin. The time has come for positive action. The Klan is open to the same charge of creating discord that lies against any people who, under outside attack, finally begin resistance when injuries have become intolerable—it is blamable to that extent, but no more. There can be no hope of curing our evils so long as it is possible for leaders of alien groups to profit by them, and by preventing assimilation. Our first duty is to see to it that no man may grow rich or powerful by breeding and exploiting disloyalty.

The future of the Klan we believe in, though it is still in the hands of

God and of our own abilities and consecration as individuals and as a race. Previous movements of the kind have been short-lived, killed by internal jealousies and personal ambitions, and partly, too, by partial accomplishment of their purposes. If the Klan falls away from its mission, or fails in it, perhaps even if it succeeds—certainly whenever the time comes that it is not doing needed work—it will become a mere derelict, without purpose or force. If it fulfills its mission, its future power and service are beyond calculation so long as America has any part of her destiny unfulfilled. Meantime we of the Klan will continue, as best we know and as best we can, the crusade for Americanism to which we have been providentially called.

1926

Bibliography

Abel, Theodore. *The Nazi Movement: Why Hitler Came to Power.* New York: Atherton, 1965.

Arendt, Hannah. *The Origins of Totalitarianism.* New York: Harcourt, Brace and World, Inc., 1966.

Bell, Daniel (ed.). *The Radical Right.* Garden City: Doubleday, 1963.

Bensen, Ezra Taft. *The Red Carpet.* Salt Lake City, Utah: Bookcraft, 1962.

Boggs, James. *Racism and the Class Struggle: Further Pages from a Black Worker's Notebook.* New York: Monthly Review Press, 1970.

Bracher, Karl D. *The German Dictatorship: The Origins, Structure and Effects of National Socialism.* New York: Praeger, 1971.

Bullock, Alan. *Hitler, A Study in Tyranny.* New York: Bantam Books, 1955.

Chalmers, David Mark. *Hooded Americanism: The First Century of the Ku Klux Klan, 1865–1965.* Garden City: Doubleday, 1965.

Chamberlain, Houston Stewart. *The Foundations of the Nineteenth Century.* Translated by John Lees. 2 vols. London: Bodley Head, Ltd., 1912.

de Gobineau, Comte Arthur. *The Inequality of Human Races.* Translated by Adrian Collins. New York: G. P. Putnam's Sons, 1915.

Del Boca, Angelo, and Giovana, Mario. *Fascism Today: A World Survey.* Translated by R. H. Boothroyd. New York: Pantheon Books, 1969.

Eisenberg, Dennis. *The Re-Emergence of Fascism.* New York: A. S. Barnes, 1968.

Epstein, Benjamin R., and Forster, Benjamin. *The Radical Right: Report on the John Birch Society and Its Allies.* New York: Random House, 1967.

Fermi, Laura. *Mussolini.* Chicago: University of Chicago Press, 1961.

Friedrich, Carl J., and Brezezinski, Zbigniew K. *Totalitarian Dictatorship and Autocracy.* 2d ed. New York: Frederick A. Praeger, 1965.

Gentile, G. *The Genesis and Structure of Society.* Translated by H. S. Harris. Urbana, Ill.: University of Illinois Press, 1960.

Greene, Nathanael (ed.). *Fascism: An Anthology.* New York: Thomas Y. Crowell Co., 1968.

Gregor, A. James. *The Ideology of Fascism: The Rationale of Totalitarianism.* New York: The Free Press, 1969.

Halperin, S. William (ed.). *Mussolini and Italian Fascism.* Princeton, N.J.: D. Van Nostrand Co., 1964.

Hitler, Adolf. *The Speeches of Adolf Hitler.* Edited by Norman H. Baynes. 2 vols. London: Oxford University Press, 1942.

Jackel, Eberhard. *Hitler's Weltanschauung: A Blueprint for Power.* Translated by Herbert Arnold. Middleworth, Conn.: Wesleyan University Press, 1972.

John Birch Society. *The Blue Book.* Belmont, Mass.: John Birch Society, 1961.

Lipset, Seymour Martin, and Raab, Earl. *The Politics of Unreason: Right Wing Extremism in America, 1790–1970.* New York: Harper & Row, 1973.

McCarthy, Joseph. *McCarthyism: The Fight for America.* New York: Devin-Adair, 1952.

McEvoy, James. *Radicals or Conservatives: The Contemporary American Right.* Chicago: Rand McNally, 1971.

Matusow, Allen J. (ed.). *Joseph R. McCarthy.* Englewood Cliffs, N.J.: Prentice-Hall, 1970.

Mosse, George L. *The Crisis of German Ideology: Intellectual Origins of the Third Reich.* New York: Grosset & Dunlap, 1964.

Mussolini, Benito. *The Corporate State.* Florence, Italy: Vallecchi, 1936.

Mussolini, Benito. *Fascism: Doctrine and Institutions.* New York: Howard Fertig, 1968.

Mussolini, Benito. *My Autobiography.* New York: Charles Scribner's Sons, 1928.

Myrdal, Gunnar. *An American Dilemma.* New York: Harper & Brothers, 1944.

Neumann, Franz. *Behemoth: The Structure and Practice of National Socialism.* 2d ed. New York: Octagon Books, 1963.

Nolte, Ernst. *Three Faces of Fascism: Action Francaise, Italian Fascism, National Socialism.* Translated by Leila Vennewitz. New York: Holt, Rinehart & Winston, 1965.

Payne, Stanley G. *Falange: A History of Spanish Fascism.* Stanford, Calif: Stanford University Press, 1961.

Readings on Fascism and National Socialism. Denver, Colo.: Alan Swallow, Publisher, no date.

Rhoodie, N. J., and Jenter, H. J. *Apartheid: A Socio-Historical Exploration of the Origins and Development of the Apartheid Idea.* Pretoria: HAUM, 1960.

Ruchames, Louis. *Racial Thought in America.* Amherst: University of Mass. Press, 1969.

Salvemini, Gaetano. *Under the Axe of Fascism.* New York: Viking Press, 1936.

Shirer, William L. *The Rise and Fall of the Third Reich.* New York: Simon and Schuster, 1960.

Snyder, Louis L. *The Idea of Racialism: Its Meaning and History.* Princeton, N.J.: D. Van Nostrand, 1962.

van den Berghe, Pierre L. *Race and Racism.* New York: John Wiley & Sons, Inc., 1967.

Viereck, Peter. *Metapolitics, the Roots of the Nazi Mind.* Rev. ed. New York: Capricorn Books, 1961.

Weber, Eugen. *Varieties of Fascism; Doctrines of Revolution in the Twentieth Century.* Princeton, N.J.: D. Van Nostrand Co., 1964.

Weiss, John. *The Fascist Tradition: Radical Right-Wing Extremism in Modern Europe.* New York: Harper & Row, 1967.

Woolf, S. J. (ed.). *The Nature of Fascism.* London: Weidenfeld and Nicolson, 1968.

X, Malcolm. *The Autobiography of Malcolm X.* New York: Grove Press, 1964.

II Communism

Communism is one of the most complex systems of ideas for thinking about man, society, and the state that has hitherto evolved from human experience. In mankind's struggle against the sometimes hostile forces of nature, the communists argue, men have sought to widen the boundaries of their existence by continuous revolutions in the given mode of production. To each stage in the dialectic development of the material forces of production correspond definite relations of production, including property relations. These relations of production define the economic structure of society out of which legal and political superstructures arise together with corresponding forms of social consciousness. Any change in the mode of production in society, the communists maintain, requires changes not only in the relations of production but also in the superstructure: the legal and political institutions and the corresponding forms of social consciousness.

The communists link the inevitable need for change in hitherto existing societies, in turn, to basic divisions in society reflecting simultaneously the antagonisms between the "old" and the "new" and the antagonisms between the "exploiter" and the "exploited." Often portrayed in terms of a principle of historical development known as the dialectic, this social antagonism constitutes the basis of the related notions of "class" and "class conflict." The class structure of a society reflects the dominant relations of production and hence is determined by the stage of development of the society's mode of production. Statically, class conflict occurs because classes stand in an exploiter–exploited relation to one another. Dynamically, class conflict occurs through the repeated revolutions in the social mode of production. The arrangement of society into classes marks the existence of social inequality and exploitation among the members of society.

Communists see the state as an instrument of force for the suppression of one class by another. In communist doctrine the state is, therefore, the mechanism through which one class secures and maintains its interests at the direct cost and detriment of the interests of another class. Since the communists link the need for a state to the division of society into classes, they foresee a gradual withering away of the state, although not of the administrative mechanisms of society. This will come about after an extended dictatorship of the proletariat, because with the ultimate victory of the proletariat, society will eventually become classless. The prelude to this victory is the bourgeoisie–proletariat class conflict.

The primary condition for the existence of the bourgeoisie in capitalist societies is, in Marxist theory, the accumulation of capital. Emphasizing that the value of an object is equal to the labor required for its production, the communists argue that this accumulation of capital rests in turn upon wage-labor. The amount paid for wage-labor often represents little more than enough to secure the barest existence of the worker. Competing with other workers for jobs, the worker tends to sell his labor for the survival costs of himself and his family. But the bourgeoisie is also in competition with itself; hence it constantly revolutionizes the instruments of production to maximize efficiency and decrease costs.

Such revolutions in the instruments of production by the bourgeoisie lead to similar changes in the relations of production. The constant advances of industry rapidly increase the number of people whose interests and conditions in life are equalized through automation. Man becomes little more than an appendage of the machine. Because the machinery is highly centralized, argue the Marxists, the proletarian class becomes concentrated in greater masses. Recognizing their growing strength and similarity of interests, the proletariat substitutes for the competition of workers an association of workers designed to secure wages above the minimum subsistence level. (It is with the notion of "consciousness" that Marx's concept of "class" begins to resemble the spiritual expression of a corporate identity discussed in the selections for Chapter I.)

Under capitalist relations of production, the state is an agency for managing the affairs of the bourgeoisie. As the livelihood of the workers becomes more precarious, as commercial crises worsen, and as the bourgeoisie proves more and more incapable of adjusting to changes in the mode of production, the workers organize into a political party in order to wrest control of the state from the hands of the bourgeoisie or in order to destroy the organs of the bourgeois state, thus making way for the dictatorship of the proletariat.

Underlying the communist vision of the withering away of the state and the development of a classless society is a conception of human progress and human perfectibility. Man is capable of a rational understanding of himself and his society such that inequality and exploitation among men need no longer exist. It is through the dictatorship of the proletariat, the communists apparently assume that mankind will prepare itself for this new era in human existence and societal living.

The experience serving as a model from which the communist political ideology was abstracted is primarily economic experience of the industrial era. Such experience Lenin once called "trade union politics." It should not be surprising, given the existential organs of the communist ideology, that communism tends to emphasize the supranational character of the proletarian movement rather than to focus exclusively on more national concerns. The early internationalism of the communist movement was tempered somewhat, however, as the communists were increasingly forced to contend with the existing institutions of the modern nation–state. This can be readily seen, for example, in Lenin's concern with the doctrine and practice of communist party politics. Notwithstanding, the communists continue to emphasize the common interests of the entire proletariat, independent of nationality, even while seeking to capture power in the context of the modern nation–state. Unlike the fascists, communists tend to deemphasize the religious powers of nationalism, refusing to accept the modern nation–state as an end in itself.

The readings that follow illustrate some developments in the communist ideology starting from its inception in the writings of Karl Marx. For although Marx was a brilliant theorist and propagandist, his writings were nevertheless incomplete guides for the concrete political activity of the burgeoning communist movement. As was noted in the introduction to this book, political ideologies are abstractions of concrete political and politically related activities. The model upon which Marx and his collaborator, Friedrich Engels, relied for their insights was an abstraction of primarily economic activity. In a sense the subsequent history of the communist movement represents additions and revisions, as well as applications, of this basic model. These subsequent changes and additions to the basic Marxist ideology reflect the growing communist experience with the politics and institutions of the modern nation–state, and more recently, the growing communist experience with the problems of the third world.

Lenin's primary addition to the Marxist ideology is his theory of the totalitarian party: its relation to the proletariat and the role of a socialist revolutionary party in a backward society where the bourgeoisie has yet to gain political control. According to Lenin, the Russian Social-Democratic Party should lead in the struggle for the abolition of the existing feudal social system, in addition to obtaining better terms for the sale of labor power. Trade union politics—the struggle for the satisfaction of trade union demands and the improvement of labor conditions in each trade—represents the class struggle only on the economic level. To develop political consciousness in the worker, Lenin contends, it is necessary to expose autocracy as well as explain how the workers' interests differ from those of the bourgeoisie. Working-class consciousness is political consciousness, Lenin argues, only when the workers are trained to respond to all cases of tyranny, oppression, violence, and abuse, regardless of which class is affected.

Such consciousness requires the worker to observe every other social class—its intellectual, ethical, and political life—and to apply the materialist analysis to the activity of these classes. Since this cannot be learned through factory experience, Lenin argues that the intellectual must supply this political knowledge. With a vanguard of intellectuals acting as a disciplined revolutionary elite, the party in a backward society can organize all aspects of the political struggle against the existing social system under the leadership of the socialist revolutionary party.

As a guide for political action in China, the Marxist ideology proved similarly incomplete. In China the socialist revolutionary party fights both the feudal landlord classes and the bourgeois imperialists from foreign countries who exploit China's natural resources, according to Mao Tse-tung. Because of the strength of these enemies, and because of their strategic location in the cities, Mao Tse-tung contends, the Chinese revolution must be an armed revolution based in the backward villages. Aiming at a disintegration of enemy forces, the primary form of this revolutionary struggle must be guerrilla warfare. Acknowledging that the Chinese proletariat cannot win victory by virtue of its own strength alone, Mao argues that all revolutionary classes must organize a united front against imperialism and feudalism. Although the revolution would not be a socialist revolution, Mao argues in the selection below, the joint dictatorship of several revolutionary classes can prevent a bourgeois dictatorship and hence be free to nationalize big capital and big enterprises, even while preserving the small private capitalist enterprises. This new form of democratic revolution, Mao suggests, is a necessary step to the socialist revolution.

Che Guevara proposes yet another revision in the Marxian revolutionary strategy to more readily conform to the reality of Latin American society and politics. Rather than strengthen existing parties or create new parties, as Lenin urges, Guevara argues that the principal stress must be upon the development of guerrilla warfare. Guerrilla warfare must be understood as a political–military struggle, which has as its final goal the taking of political power. The major contribution to revolutionary strategy of the Cuban experience was that one does not always have to wait for all the conditions of revolution to exist—the insurrection itself can create them. Furthermore, Guevara maintains, in Latin America the struggle must and will be continental in scope. Since the reactionary forces of the hemisphere are united, the popular forces must meet them in a united front until the Cordillera of the Andes becomes the Sierra Maestra of America.

Although most of the selections in this chapter concentrate on the struggle for power in one form or another, Victor Perlo leads us through a brief analysis of conditions in present day U.S.A.—through the eyes of a Marxist. He points out, for example, the continued relevance of Marxist economics to the conditions of the working class in America. Further, he suggests connections between capitalist exploitation and racism in America. Perlo also concentrates on the varieties of financial–industrial imperialism.

Imperialism is, as Lenin once observed, the monopoly stage of capitalism. Perlo argues that a financial–industrial monopoly exists in the United States leading to imperialist exploitation both domestically and in the foreign affairs of the United States. There is a need, he contends, for the application of Marxist principles in solving the multitude of problems existing in American society today.

5 Manifesto of the Communist Party

KARL MARX and FRIEDRICH ENGELS

A specter is haunting Europe—the specter of communism. All the powers of old Europe have entered into a holy alliance to exorcise this specter: Pope and Czar, Metternich and Guizot, French Radicals, and German police spies.

Where is the party in opposition that has not been decried as communistic by its opponents in power? Where the Opposition that has not hurled back the branding reproach of communism, against the more advanced opposition parties, as well as against its reactionary adversaries?

Two things result from this fact:

1. Communism is already acknowledged by all European powers to be itself a power.
2. It is high time that Communists should openly, in the face of the whole world, publish their views, their aims, their tendencies, and meet this nursery tale of the specter of communism with a manifesto of the party itself.

To this end, Communists of various nationalities have assembled in London, and sketched the following manifesto, to be published in the English, French, German, Italian, Flemish, and Danish languages.

I. Bourgeois and Proletarians

The history of all hitherto existing society is the history of class struggles.

Freeman and slave, patrician and plebeian, lord and serf, guildmaster and journeyman, in a word, oppressor and oppressed, stood in constant opposition to one another, carried on an uninterrupted, now hidden, now open fight, a fight that each time ended, either in a revolutionary reconstitution of society at large, or in the common ruin of the contending classes.

In the earlier epochs of history, we find almost everywhere a complicated arrangement of society into various orders, a manifold gradation of social rank. In ancient Rome we have patricians, knights, plebeians, slaves; in the Middle Ages, feudal lords, vassals, guildmasters, journeymen, apprentices, serfs; in almost all of these classes, again, subordinate gradations.

The modern bourgeois society that has sprouted from the ruins of feudal society, has not done away with class antagonisms. It has but established

SOURCE: from *The Communist Manifesto,* Karl Marx and Friedrich Engels, edited by Samuel H. Beer (Crofts Classics Series).

new classes, new conditions of oppression, new forms of struggle in place of the old ones.

Our epoch, the epoch of the bourgeoisie, possesses, however, this distinctive feature: It has simplified the class antagonisms. Society as a whole is more and more splitting up into two great hostile camps, into two great classes directly facing each other—bourgeoisie and proletariat.

From the serfs of the Middle Ages sprang the chartered burghers of the earliest towns. From these burgesses the first elements of the bourgeoisie were developed.

The discovery of America, the rounding of the Cape, opened up fresh ground for the rising bourgeoisie. The East-Indian and Chinese markets, the colonization of America, trade with the colonies, the increase in the means of exchange and in commodities generally, gave to commerce, to navigation, to industry, an impulse never before known, and thereby, to the revolutionary element in the tottering feudal society, a rapid development.

The feudal system of industry, in which industrial production was monopolized by closed guilds, now no longer sufficed for the growing wants of the new markets. The manufacturing system took its place. The guild-masters were pushed aside by the manufacturing middle class; division of labor between the different corporate guilds vanished in the face of division of labor in each single workshop.

Meantime the markets kept ever growing, the demand ever rising. Even manufacture no longer sufficed. Thereupon, steam and machinery revolutionized industrial production. The place of manufacture was taken by the giant, modern industry, the place of the industrial middle class, by industrial millionaires—the leaders of whole industrial armies, the modern bourgeois.

Modern industry has established the world market, for which the discovery of America paved the way. This market has given an immense development to commerce, to navigation, to communication by land. This development has, in its turn, reacted on the extension of industry; and in proportion as industry, commerce, navigation, railways extended, in the same proportion the bourgeoisie developed, increased its capital, and pushed into the background every class handed down from the Middle Ages.

We see, therefore, how the modern bourgeoisie is itself the product of a long course of development, of a series of revolutions in the modes of production and of exchange.

Each step in the development of the bourgeoisie was accompanied by a corresponding political advance of that class. An oppressed class under the sway of the feudal nobility, it became an armed and self-governing association in the medieval commune; here independent urban republic (as in Italy and Germany), there taxable "third estate" of the monarchy (as in France); afterwards, in the period of manufacture proper, serving either the semi-feudal or the absolute monarchy as a counterpoise against the nobility, and, in fact, cornerstone of the great monarchies in general—the bourgeoisie has at last, since the establishment of modern industry and of the world market, conquered for itself, in the modern representative state, exclusive political sway. The executive of the modern state is but a committee for managing the common affairs of the whole bourgeoisie.

The bourgeoisie has played a most revolutionary role in history.

The bourgeoisie, wherever it has got the upper hand, has put an end to all feudal, patriarchal, idyllic relations. It has pitilessly torn asunder the motley feudal ties that bound man to his "natural superiors," and has left no other bond between man and man than naked self-interest, than callous "cash payment." It has drowned the most heavenly ecstasies of religious fervor, of chivalrous enthusiasm, of philistine sentimentalism, in the icy water of egotistical calculation. It has resolved personal worth into exchange value, and in place of the numberless indefeasible chartered freedoms, has set up that single, unconscionable freedom—Free Trade. In one word, for exploitation, veiled by religious and political illusions, it has substituted naked, shameless, direct, brutal exploitation.

The bourgeoisie has stripped of its halo every occupation hitherto honored and looked up to with reverent awe. It has converted the physician, the lawyer, the priest, the poet, the man of science, into its paid wage-laborers.

The bourgeoisie has torn away from the family its sentimental veil, and has reduced the family relation to a mere money relation.

The bourgeoisie has disclosed how it came to pass that the brutal display of vigor in the Middle Ages, which reactionaries so much admire, found its fitting complement in the most slothful indolence. It has been the first to show what man's activity can bring about. It has accomplished wonders far surpassing Egyptian pyramids, Roman aqueducts, and Gothic cathedrals; it has conducted expeditions that put in the shade all former migrations of nations and crusades.

The bourgeoisie cannot exist without constantly revolutionizing the instruments of production, and thereby the relations of production, and with them the whole relations of society. Conservation of the old modes of production in unaltered form, was, on the contrary, the first condition of existence for all earlier industrial classes. Constant revolutionizing of production, uninterrupted disturbance of all social conditions, everlasting uncertainty and agitation distinguish the bourgeois epoch from all earlier ones. All fixed, fast-frozen relations, with their train of ancient and venerable prejudices and opinions, are swept away, all new-formed ones become antiquated before they can ossify. All that is solid melts into air, all that is holy is profaned, and man is at last compelled to face with sober senses his real conditions of life and his relations with his kind.

The need of a constantly expanding market for its products chases the bourgeoisie over the whole surface of the globe. It must nestle everywhere, settle everywhere, establish connections everywhere.

The bourgeoisie has through its exploitation of the world market given a cosmopolitan character to production and consumption in every country. To the great chagrin of reactionaries, it has drawn from under the feet of industry the national ground on which it stood. All old-established national industries have been destroyed or are daily being destroyed. They are dislodged by new industries, whose introduction becomes a life and death question for all civilized nations, by industries that no longer work up indigenous raw material, but raw material drawn from the remotest zones; industries whose products are consumed, not only at home, but in every quarter of the globe. In place of the old wants, satisfied by the production of the country, we find new wants, requiring for their satisfaction the products of distant lands and climes. In place of the old local and national seclusion and self-sufficiency, we have intercourse in every direction, universal interdependence of nations. And as in material, so also in intellectual production. The intellectual creations of individual nations become common property. National one-sidedness and narrow-mindedness become more and more impossible, and from the numerous national and local literatures there arises a world literature.

The bourgeoisie, by the rapid improvement of all instruments of production, by the immensely facilitated means of communication, draws all nations, even the most barbarian, into civilization. The cheap prices of its commodities are the heavy artillery with which it batters down all Chinese walls, with which it forces the barbarians' intensely obstinate hatred of foreigners to capitulate. It compels all nations, on pain of extinction, to adopt the bourgeois mode of production; it compels them to introduce what it calls civilization into their midst, i.e., to become bourgeois themselves. In a word, it creates a world after its own image.

The bourgeoisie has subjected the country to the rule of the towns. It has created enormous cities, has greatly increased the urban population as compared with the rural, and has thus rescued a considerable part of the population from the idiocy of rural life. Just as it has made the country dependent on the towns, so it has made barbarian and semibarbarian countries dependent on the civilized ones, nations of peasants on nations of bourgeois, the East on the West.

More and more the bourgeoisie keeps doing away with the scattered state of the population, of the means of production, and of property. It has agglomerated population, centralized means of production, and has concentrated property in a few hands. The necessary consequence of this was political centralization. Independent, or but loosely connected provinces, with separate interests, laws, governments and systems of taxation, became lumped together into one nation, with one government, one code of laws, one national class interest, one frontier and one customs tariff.

The bourgeoisie, during its rule of scarce one hundred years, has created more massive and more colossal productive forces than have all preceding generations together. Subjection of nature's forces to man, machinery, application of chemistry to industry and agriculture, steam-navigation, railways, electric telegraphs, clearing of whole continents for cultivation, canalization of rivers, whole populations conjured out of the ground—what earlier century had even a presentiment that such productive forces slumbered in the lap of social labor?

We see then that the means of production and of exchange, which served as the foundation for the growth of the bourgeoisie, were generated in feudal society. At a certain stage in the development of these means of production and of exchange, the conditions under which feudal society produced and exchanged, the feudal organization of agriculture and manufacturing industry, in a word, the feudal relations of property became no longer compatible with the already developed productive forces; they became so many fetters. They had to be burst asunder; they were burst asunder.

Into their place stepped free competition, accompanied by a social and political constitution adapted to it, and by the economic and political sway of the bourgeois class.

A similar movement is going on before our own eyes. Modern bourgeois society with its relations of production, of exchange and of property, a society that has conjured up such gigantic means of production and of exchange, is like the sorcerer who is no longer able to control the powers of the nether world whom he has called up by his spells. For many a decade past the history of industry and commerce is but the history of the revolt of modern productive forces against modern conditions of production, against the property relations that are the conditions for the existence of the bourgeoisie and of its rule. It is enough to mention the commercial crises that by their periodical return put the existence of the entire bourgeois society on trial, each time more threateningly. In these crises a great part not only of the existing products, but also of the previously created productive forces, are periodically destroyed. In these crises there breaks out an epidemic that, in all earlier epochs, would have seemed an absurdity—the epidemic of overproduction. Society suddenly finds itself put back into a state of momentary barbarism; it appears as if a famine, a universal war of devastation had cut off the supply of every means of subsistence; industry and commerce seem to be destroyed. And why? Because there is too much civilization, too much means of subsistence, too much industry, too much commerce. The productive forces at the disposal of society no longer tend to further the development of the conditions of bourgeois property; on the contrary, they have become too powerful for these conditions, by which they are fettered, and no sooner do they overcome these fetters than they bring disorder into the whole of bourgeois society, endanger the existence of bourgeois property. The conditions of bourgeois society are too narrow to comprise the wealth created by them. And how does the bourgeoisie get over these crises? On the one hand by enforced destruction of a mass of productive forces; on the other, by the conquest of new markets, and by the more thorough exploitation of the old ones. That is to say, by paving the way for more extensive and more destructive crises, and by diminishing the means whereby crises are prevented.

The weapons with which the bourgeoisie felled feudalism to the ground are now turned against the bourgeoisie itself.

But not only has the bourgeoisie forged the weapons that bring death to itself; it has also called into existence the men who are to wield those weapons—the modern working class—the proletarians.

In proportion as the bourgeoisie, i.e., capital, is developed, in the same proportion is the proletariat, the modern working class, developed—a class of laborers, who live only so long as they find work, and who find work only so long as their labor increases capital. These laborers, who must sell themselves piecemeal, are a commodity, like every other article of commerce, and are consequently exposed to all the vicissitudes of competition, to all the fluctuations of the market.

Owing to the extensive use of machinery and to division of labor, the work of the proletarians has lost all individual character, and, consequently, all charm for the workman. He becomes an appendage of the machine, and it is only the most simple, most monotonous, and most easily acquired knack, that is required of him. Hence, the cost of production of a workman is restricted, almost entirely, to the means of subsistence that he requires for his maintenance, and for the propagation of his race. But the price of a commodity, and therefore also of labor, is equal to its cost of production. In proportion, therefore, as the repulsiveness of the work increases, the wage decreases. Nay more, in proportion as the use of machinery and division of labor increases, in the same proportion the burden of toil also increases, whether by prolongation of the working hours, by increase of the work exacted in a given time, or by increased speed of the machinery, etc.

Modern industry has converted the little workshop of the patriarchal master into the great factory of the industrial capitalist. Masses of laborers, crowded into the factory, are organized like soldiers. As privates of the industrial army they are placed under the command of a perfect hierarchy of officers and sergeants. Not only are they slaves of the bourgeois class, and of the bourgeois state; they are daily and hourly enslaved by the machine, by the overlooker, and, above all, by the individual bourgeois manufacturer himself. The more openly this despotism proclaims gain to be its end and aim, the more petty, the more hateful and the more embittering it is.

The less the skill and exertion of strength implied in manual labor, in other words, the more modern industry develops, the more is the labor of men superseded by that of women. Differences of age and sex have no longer any distinctive social validity for the working class. All are instruments of labor, more or less expensive to use, according to their age and sex.

No sooner has the laborer received his wages in cash, for the moment escaping exploitation by the manufacturer, than he is set upon by the other portions of the bourgeoisie, the landlord, the shopkeeper, the pawnbroker, etc.

The lower strata of the middle class—the small tradespeople, shopkeepers, and retired tradesmen generally, the handicraftsmen and peasants —all these sink gradually into the proletariat, partly because their diminutive capital does not suffice for the scale on which modern industry is carried on, and is swamped in the competition with the large capitalists, partly because their specialized skill is rendered worthless by new methods of production. Thus the proletariat is recruited from all classes of the population.

The proletariat goes through various stages of development. With its birth begins its struggle with the bourgeoisie. At first the contest is carried on by individual laborers, then by the work people of a factory, then by the operatives of one trade, in one locality, against the individual bourgeois who directly exploits them. They direct their attacks not against the bourgeois conditions of production, but against the instruments of production themselves; they destroy imported wares that compete with their labor, they smash machinery to pieces, they set factories ablaze, they seek to restore by force the vanished status of the workman of the Middle Ages.

At this stage the laborers still form an incoherent mass scattered over the whole country, and broken up by their mutual competition. If anywhere they unite to form more compact bodies, this is not yet the consequence of their own active union, but of the union of the bourgeoisie, which class, in order to attain its own political ends, is compelled to set the whole proletariat in motion, and is moreover still able to do so for a time. At this stage, therefore, the proletarians do not fight their enemies, but the enemies of their enemies, the remnants of absolute monarchy, the landowners, the nonindustrial bourgeois, the petty bourgeoisie. Thus the whole historical movement is concentrated in the hands of the bourgeoisie; every victory so obtained is a victory for the bourgeoisie.

But with the development of industry the proletariat not only increases in number; it becomes concentrated in greater masses, its strength grows, and it feels that strength more. The various interests and conditions of life within the ranks of the proletariat are more and more equalized, in proportion as machinery obliterates all distinctions of labor and nearly everywhere reduces wages to the same low level. The growing competition among the bourgeois, and the resulting commercial crises, makes the wages of the workers ever more fluctuating. The unceasing improvement of machinery, ever more rapidly developing, makes their livelihood more and more precarious; the collisions between individual workmen and individual bourgeois take more and more the character of collisions between two classes. Thereupon the workers begin to form combinations (trade unions) against the bourgeoisie; they club together in order to keep up the rate of wages; they found permanent associations in order to make provision beforehand for these occasional revolts. Here and there the contest breaks out into riots.

Now and then the workers are victorious, but only for a time. The real fruit of their battles lies, not in the immediate results, but in the ever expanding union of the workers. This union is furthered by the improved means of communication which are created by modern industry, and which place the workers of different localities in contact with one another. It was just this contact that was needed to centralize the numerous local struggles, all of the same character, into one national struggle between classes. But every class struggle is a political struggle. And that union, to attain which the burghers of the Middle Ages, with their miserable highways, required centuries, the modern proletarians, thanks to railways, achieve in a few years.

This organization of the proletarians into a class, and consequently into a political party, is continually being upset again by the competition between the workers themselves. But it ever rises up again, stronger, firmer, mightier. It compels legislative recognition of particular interests of the workers, by taking advantage of the divisions among the bourgeoisie itself. Thus the ten-hour bill in England was carried.

Altogether, collisions between the classes of the old society further the course of development of the proletariat in many ways. The bourgeoisie finds itself involved in a constant battle. At first with the aristocracy; later on, with those portions of the bourgeoisie itself whose interests have become antagonistic to the progress of industry; at all times with the bourgeoisie of foreign countries. In all these battles it sees itself compelled to appeal to the proletariat, to ask for its help, and thus, to drag it into the political arena. The bourgeoisie itself, therefore, supplies the proletariat with its own elements of political and general education, in other words, it furnishes the proletariat with weapons for fighting the bourgeoisie.

Further, as we have already seen, entire sections of the ruling classes are, by the advance of industry, precipitated into the proletariat, or are at least threatened in their conditions of existence. These also supply the proletariat with fresh elements of enlightenment and progress.

Finally, in times when the class struggle nears the decisive hour, the process of dissolution going on within the ruling class, in fact within the whole range of old society, assumes such a violent, glaring character, that a small section of the ruling class cuts itself adrift, and joins the revolutionary class, the class that holds the future in its hands. Just as, therefore, at an earlier period, a section of the nobility went over to the bourgeoisie, so now a portion of the bourgeoisie goes over to the proletariat, and in particular, a portion of the bourgeois ideologists, who have raised themselves to the level of comprehending theoretically the historical movement as a whole.

Of all the classes that stand face to face with the bourgeoisie today, the proletariat alone is a really revolutionary class. The other classes decay and finally disappear in the face of modern industry; the proletariat is its special and essential product.

The lower middle class, the small manufacturer, the shopkeeper, the artisan, the peasant, all these fight against the bourgeoisie, to save from extinction their existence as fractions of the middle class. They are therefore not revolutionary, but conservative. Nay more, they are reactionary, for they try to roll back the wheel of history. If by chance they are revolutionary, they are so only in view of their impending transfer into the proletariat; they thus defend not their present, but their future interests; they desert their own standpoint to adopt that of the proletariat.

The "dangerous class," the social scum (*Lumpenproletariat*), that passively rotting mass thrown off by the lowest layers of old society, may, here and there, be swept into the movement by a proletarian revolution; its conditions of life, however, prepare it far more for the part of a bribed tool of reactionary intrigue.

The social conditions of the old society no longer exist for the proletariat. The proletarian is without property; his relation to his wife and children has no longer anything in common with bourgeois family relations; modern industrial labor, modern subjection to capital, the same in England as in France, in America as in Germany, has stripped him of every trace of national character. Law, morality, religion, are to him so many bourgeois prejudices, behind which lurk in ambush just as many bourgeois interests.

All the preceding classes that got the upper hand, sought to fortify their already acquired status by subjecting society at large to their conditions of appropriation. The proletarians cannot become masters of the productive forces of society, except by abolishing their own previous mode of appropriation, and thereby also every other previous mode of appropriation. They have nothing of their own to secure and to fortify; their mission is to destroy all previous securities for, and insurances of, individual property.

All previous historical movements were movements of minorities, or in the interest of minorities. The proletarian movement is the self-conscious, independent movement of the immense majority, in the interest of the immense majority. The proletariat, the lowest stratum of our present society, cannot stir, cannot raise itself up, without the whole superincumbent strata of official society being sprung into the air.

Though not in substance, yet in form, the struggle of the proletariat with the bourgeoisie is at first a national struggle. The proletariat of each country must, of course, first of all settle matters with its own bourgeoisie.

In depicting the most general phases of the development of the proletariat, we traced the more or less veiled civil war, raging within existing society, up to the point where that war breaks out into open revolution, and where the violent overthrow of the bourgeoisie lays the foundation for the sway of the proletariat.

Hitherto, every form of society has been based, as we have already seen, on the antagonism of oppressing and oppressed classes. But in order to oppress a class, certain conditions must be assured to it under which it can, at least, continue its slavish existence. The serf, in the period of serfdom, raised himself to membership in the commune, just as the petty bourgeois, under the yoke of feudal absolutism, managed to develop into a bourgeois. The modern laborer, on the contrary, instead of rising with the progress of industry, sinks deeper and deeper below the conditions of existence of his own class. He becomes a pauper, and pauperism develops more rapidly than population and wealth. And here it becomes evident, that the bourgeoisie is unfit any longer to be the ruling class in society, and to impose its conditions of existence upon society as an overriding law. It is unfit to rule because it is incompetent to assure an existence to its slave within his slavery, because it cannot help letting him sink into such a state, that it has to feed him, instead of being fed by him. Society can no longer live under this bourgeoisie, in other words, its existence is no longer compatible with society.

The essential condition for the existence and sway of the bourgeois class, is the formation and augmentation of capital; the condition for capital is wage-labor. Wage-labor rests exclusively on competition between the laborers. The advance of industry, whose involuntary promoter is the bourgeoisie, replaces the isolation of the laborers, due to competition, by their revolutionary combination, due to association. The development of modern industry, therefore, cuts from under its feet the very foundation on which the bourgeoisie produces and appropriates products. What the bourgeoisie therefore produces, above all, are its own gravediggers. Its fall and the victory of the proletariat are equally inevitable.

II. Proletarians and Communists

In what relation do the Communists stand to the proletarians as a whole?

The Communists do not form a separate party opposed to other working-class parties.

They have no interests separate and apart from those of the proletariat as a whole.

They do not set up any sectarian principles of their own, by which to shape and mold the proletarian movement.

The Communists are distinguished from the other working-class parties by this only:

1. In the national struggles of the proletarians of the different countries, they point out and bring to the front the common interests of the entire proletariat, independently of all nationality.
2. In the various stages of development which the struggle of the working class against the bourgeoisie has to pass through, they always and everywhere represent the interests of the movement as a whole.

The Communists, therefore, are on the one hand, practically, the most advanced and resolute section of the working-class parties of every country, that section which pushes forward all others; on the other hand, theoretically, they have over the great mass of the proletariat the advantage of clearly understanding the line of march, the conditions, and the ultimate general results of the proletarian movement.

The immediate aim of the Communists is the same as that of all the other proletarian parties: Formation of the proletariat into a class, overthrow of bourgeois supremacy, conquest of political power by the proletariat.

The theoretical conclusions of the Communists are in no way based on ideas or principles that have been invented, or discovered, by this or that would-be universal reformer.

They merely express, in general terms, actual relations springing from an existing class struggle, from a historical movement going on under our very eyes. The abolition of existing property relations is not at all a distinctive feature of communism.

All property relations in the past have continually been subject to historical change consequent upon the change in historical conditions.

The French Revolution, for example, abolished feudal property in favor of bourgeois property.

The distinguishing feature of communism is not the abolition of property generally, but the abolition of bourgeois property. But modern bourgeois private property is the final and most complete expression of the system of producing and appropriating products that is based on class antagonisms, on the exploitation of the many by the few.

In this sense, the theory of the Communists may be summed up in the single sentence: Abolition of private property.

We Communists have been reproached with the desire of abolishing the right of personally acquiring property as the fruit of a man's own labor, which property is alleged to be the groundwork of all personal freedom, activity and independence.

Hard-won, self-acquired, self-earned property! Do you mean the property of the petty artisan and of the small peasant, a form of property that preceded the bourgeois form? There is no need to abolish that; the development of industry has to a great extent already destroyed it, and is still destroying it daily.

Or do you mean modern bourgeois private property?

But does wage-labor create any property for the laborer? Not a bit. It creates capital, i.e., that kind of property which exploits wage-labor, and which cannot increase except upon condition of begetting a new supply of wage-labor for fresh exploitation. Property, in its present form, is based on the antagonism of capital and wage-labor. Let us examine both sides of this antagonism.

To be a capitalist, is to have not only a purely personal, but a social *status* in production. Capital is a collective product, and only by the united action of many members, nay, in the last resort, only by the united action of all members of society, can it be set in motion.

Capital is therefore not a personal, it is a social, power.

When, therefore, capital is converted into common property, into the property of all members of society, personal property is not thereby transformed into social property. It is only the social character of the property that is changed. It loses its class character.

Let us now take wage-labor.

The average price of wage-labor is the minimum wage, i.e., that quantum of the means of subsistence which is absolutely requisite to keep the laborer in bare existence as a laborer. What, therefore, the wage-laborer appropriates by means of his labor, merely suffices to prolong and reproduce a bare existence. We by no means intend to abolish this personal appropriation of the products of labor, an appropriation that is made for the maintenance and reproduction of human life, and that leaves no surplus wherewith to command the labor of others. All that we want to do away with is the miserable character of this appropriation, under which the laborer lives merely to increase capital, and is allowed to live only insofar as the interest of the ruling class requires it.

In bourgeois society, living labor is but a means to increase accumulated labor. In Communist society, accumulated labor is but a means to widen, to enrich, to promote the existence of the laborer.

In bourgeois society, therefore, the past dominates the present; in Communist society, the present dominates the past. In bourgeois society capital is independent and has individuality, while the living person is dependent and has no individuality.

And the abolition of this state of things is called by the bourgeois, abolition of individuality and freedom! And rightly so. The abolition of bourgeois individuality, bourgeois independence, and bourgeois freedom is undoubtedly aimed at.

By freedom is meant, under the present bourgeois conditions of production, free trade, free selling and buying.

But if selling and buying disappear, free selling and buying disappear also. This talk about free selling and buying, and all the other "brave words" of our bourgeoisie about freedom in general, have a meaning, if any, only in contrast with restricted selling and buying, with the fettered traders of the Middle Ages, but have no meaning when opposed to the Communist abolition of buying and selling, of the bourgeois conditions of production, and of the bourgeoisie itself.

You are horrified at our intending to do away with private property. But in your existing society, private property is already done away with for nine-tenths of the population; its existence for the few is solely due to its nonexistence in the hands of those nine-tenths. You reproach us, therefore, with intending to do away with a form of property, the necessary condition for whose existence is the nonexistence of any property for the immense majority of society.

In a word, you reproach us with intending to do away with your property. Precisely so; that is just what we intend.

From the moment when labor can no longer be converted into capital, money, or rent, into a social power capable of being monopolized, i.e., from the moment when individual property can no longer be transformed into bourgeois property, into capital, from that moment, you say, individuality vanishes.

You must, therefore, confess that by "individual" you mean no other person than the bourgeois, than the middle-class owner of property. This person must, indeed, be swept out of the way, and made impossible.

Communism deprives no man of the power to appropriate the products of society; all that it does is to deprive him of the power to subjugate the labor of others by means of such appropriation.

It has been objected, that upon the abolition of private property all work will cease, and universal laziness will overtake us.

According to this, bourgeois society ought long ago to have gone to the dogs through sheer idleness; for those of its members who work, acquire nothing, and those who acquire anything, do not work. The whole of this objection is but another expression of the tautology: There can no longer be any wage-labor when there is no longer any capital.

All objections urged against the Communist mode of producing and appropriating material products, have, in the same way, been urged against the Communist modes of producing and appropriating intellectual products. Just as, to the bourgeois, the disappearance of class property is the disappearance of production itself, so the disappearance of class culture is to him identical with the disappearance of all culture.

That culture, the loss of which he laments, is, for the enormous majority, a mere training to act as a machine.

But don't wrangle with us so long as you apply, to our intended abolition of bourgeois property, the standard of your bourgeois notions of freedom, culture, law, etc. Your very ideas are but the outgrowth of the conditions of your bourgeois production and bourgeois property, just as your jurisprudence is but the will of your class made into a law for all, a will whose essential character and direction are determined by the economic conditions of existence of your class.

The selfish misconception that induces you to transform into eternal laws of nature and of reason, the social forms springing from your present mode of production and form of property—historical relations that rise and disappear in the progress of production—this misconception you share with every ruling class that has preceded you. What you see clearly in the case of ancient property, what you admit in the case of feudal property, you are of course forbidden to admit in the case of your own bourgeois form of property.

Abolition of the family! Even the most radical flare up at this infamous proposal of the Communists.

On what foundation is the present family, the bourgeois family, based? On capital, on private gain. In its completely developed form this family exists only among the bourgeoisie. But this state of things finds its complement in the practical absence of the family among the proletarians, and in public prostitution.

The bourgeois family will vanish as a matter of course when its complement vanishes, and both will vanish with the vanishing of capital.

Do you charge us with wanting to stop the exploitation of children by their parents? To this crime we plead guilty.

But, you will say, we destroy the most hallowed of relations, when we replace home education by social.

And your education! Is not that also social, and determined by the social conditions under which you educate, by the intervention of society, direct or indirect, by means of schools, etc.? The Communists have not invented the intervention of society in education; they do but seek to alter the character of that intervention, and to rescue education from the influence of the ruling class.

The bourgeois claptrap about the family and education, about the hallowed co-relation of parent and child, becomes all the more disgusting, the more, by the action of modern industry, all family ties among the proletarians are torn asunder, and their children transformed into simple articles of commerce and instruments of labor.

But you Communists would introduce community of women, screams the whole bourgeoisie in chorus.

The bourgeois sees in his wife a mere instrument of production. He hears that the instruments of production are to be exploited in common, and, naturally, can come to no other conclusion than that the lot of being common to all will likewise fall to the women.

He has not even a suspicion that the real point aimed at is to do away with the status of women as mere instruments of production.

For the rest, nothing is more ridiculous than the virtuous indignation of our bourgeois at the community of women which, they pretend, is to be openly and officially established by the Communists. The Communists have no need to introduce community of women; it has existed almost from time immemorial.

Our bourgeois, not content with having the wives and daughters of their proletarians at their disposal, not to speak of common prostitutes, take the greatest pleasure in seducing each other's wives.

Bourgeois marriage is in reality a system of wives in common and thus, at the most, what the Communists might possibly be reproached with is that they desire to introduce, in substitution for a hypocritically concealed, an openly legalized community of women. For the rest, it is self-evident, that the abolition of the present system of production must bring with it the abolition of the community of women springing from that system, i.e., of prostitution both public and private.

The Communists are further reproached with desiring to abolish countries and nationality.

The workingmen have no country. We cannot take from them what they have not got. Since the proletariat must first of all acquire political supremacy, must rise to be the leading class of the nation, must constitute itself *the* nation, it is, so far, itself national, though not in the bourgeois sense of the word.

National differences and antagonisms between peoples are vanishing gradually from day to day, owing to the development of the bourgeoisie, to freedom of commerce, to the world market, to uniformity in the mode of production and in the conditions of life corresponding thereto.

The supremacy of the proletariat will cause them to vanish still faster. United action, of the leading civilized countries at least, is one of the first conditions for the emancipation of the proletariat.

In proportion as the exploitation of one individual by another is put an end to, the exploitation of one nation by another will also be put an end to. In proportion as the antagonism between classes within the nation vanishes, the hostility of one nation to another will come to an end.

The charges against communism made from a religious, a philosophical, and, generally, from an ideological standpoint, are not deserving of serious examination.

Does it require deep intuition to comprehend that man's ideas, views, and conceptions, in one word, man's consciousness, changes with every change in the conditions of his material existence, in his social relations and in his social life?

What else does the history of ideas prove, than that intellectual production changes its character in proportion as material production is changed? The ruling ideas of each age have ever been the ideas of its ruling class.

When people speak of ideas that revolutionize society, they do but express the fact that within the old society the elements of a new one have been created, and that the dissolution of the old ideas keeps even pace with the dissolution of the old conditions of existence.

When the ancient world was in its last throes, the ancient religions were overcome by Christianity. When Christian ideas succumbed in the eighteenth century to rationalist ideas, feudal society fought its death-battle with the then revolutionary bourgeoisie. The ideas of religious liberty and freedom of conscience, merely gave expression to the sway of free competition within the domain of knowledge.

"Undoubtedly," it will be said, "religion, moral, philosophical and juridical ideas have been modified in the course of historical development. But religion, morality, philosophy, political science, and law, constantly survived this change."

"There are, besides, eternal truths, such as Freedom, Justice, etc., that are common to all states of society. But communism abolishes eternal truths, it abolishes all religion, and all morality, instead of constituting them on a new basis; it therefore acts in contradiction to all past historical experience."

What does this accusation reduce itself too? The history of all past society has consisted in the development of class antagonisms, antagonisms that assumed different forms at different epochs.

But whatever form they may have taken, one fact is common to all past ages, viz., the exploitation of one part of society by the other. No wonder, then, that the social consciousness of past ages, despite all the multiplicity and variety it displays, moves within certain common forms, or general ideas, which cannot completely vanish except with the total disappearance of class antagonisms.

The Communist revolution is the most radical rupture with traditional property relations; no wonder that its development involves the most radical rupture with traditional ideas.

But let us have done with the bourgeois objections to communism.

We have seen above, that the first step in the revolution by the working class, is to raise the proletariat to the position of ruling class, to establish democracy.

The proletariat will use its political supremacy to wrest, by degrees, all capital from the bourgeoisie, to centralize all instruments of production in the hands of the state, i.e., of the proletariat organized as the ruling class; and to increase the total of productive forces as rapidly as possible.

Of course, in the beginning, this cannot be effected except by means of despotic inroads on the rights of property, and on the conditions of bourgeois production; by means of measures, therefore, which appear economically insufficient and untenable, but which, in the course of the movement, outstrip themselves, necessitate further inroads upon the old social order, and are unavoidable as a means of entirely revolutionizing the mode of production.

These measures will of course be different in different countries.

Nevertheless in the most advanced countries, the following will be pretty generally applicable.

1. Abolition of property in land and application of all rents of land to public purposes.
2. A heavy progressive or graduated income tax.
3. Abolition of all right of inheritance.
4. Confiscation of the property of all emigrants and rebels.
5. Centralization of credit in the hands of the state, by means of a national bank with state capital and an exclusive monopoly.

6. Centralization of the means of communication and transport in the hands of the state.
7. Extension of factories and instruments of production owned by the state; the bringing into cultivation of waste lands, and the improvement of the soil generally in accordance with a common plan.
8. Equal obligation of all to work. Establishment of industrial armies, especially for agriculture.
9. Combination of agriculture with manufacturing industries; gradual abolition of the distinction between town and country, by a more equable distribution of the population over the country.
10. Free education for all children in public schools. Abolition of child factory labor in its present form. Combination of education with industrial production, etc.

When, in the course of development, class distinctions have disappeared, and all production has been concentrated in the hands of a vast association of the whole nation, the public power will lose its political character. Political power, properly so called, is merely the organized power of one class for oppressing another. If the proletariat during its contest with the bourgeoisie is compelled, by the force of circumstances, to organize itself as a class; if, by means of a revolution, it makes itself the ruling class, and, as such sweeps away by force the old conditions of production, then it will, along with these conditions, have swept away the conditions for the existence of class antagonisms, and of classes generally, and will thereby have abolished its own supremacy as a class.

In place of the old bourgeois society, with its classes and class antagonisms, we shall have an association, in which the free development of each is the condition for the free development of all.

III. Socialist and Communist Literature

1. Reactionary Socialism

a. Feudal Socialism Owing to their historical position, it became the vocation of the aristocracies of France and England to write pamphlets against modern bourgeois society. In the French Revolution of July, 1830, and in the English reform agitation, these aristocracies again succumbed to the hateful upstart. Thenceforth, a serious political struggle was altogether out of the question. A literary battle alone remained possible. But even in the domain of literature the old cries of the restoration period[1] had become impossible.

In order to arouse sympathy, the aristocracy was obliged to lose sight, apparently, of its own interests, and to formulate its indictment against the

[1] Not the English Restoration, 1660 to 1689, but the French Restoration, 1814 to 1830.

bourgeoisie in the interest of the exploited working class alone. Thus the aristocracy took its revenge by singing lampoons against its new master, and whispering in his ears sinister prophecies of coming catastrophe.

In this way arose feudal socialism: half lamentation, half lampoon; half echo of the past, half menace of the future; at times, by its bitter, witty, and incisive criticism, striking the bourgeoisie to the very heart's core, but always ludicrous in its effect through total incapacity to comprehend the march of modern history.

The aristocracy, in order to rally the people to them, waved the proletarian alms-bag in front for a banner. But the people, as often as it joined them, saw on their hindquarters the old feudal coats of arms, and deserted with loud and irreverent laughter.

One section of the French Legitimists, and "Young England," exhibited this spectacle.

In pointing out that their mode of exploitation was different from that of the bourgeoisie, the feudalists forget that they exploited under circumstances and conditions that were quite different, and that are now antiquated. In showing that, under their rule, the modern proletariat never existed, they forget that the modern bourgeoisie is the necessary offspring of their own form of society.

For the rest, so little do they conceal the reactionary character of their criticism, that their chief accusation against the bourgeoisie amounts to this, that under the bourgeois regime a class is being developed, which is destined to cut up root and branch the old order of society.

What they upbraid the bourgeoisie with is not so much that it creates a proletariat, as that it creates a *revolutionary* proletariat.

In political practice, therefore, they join in all coercive measures against the working class; and in ordinary life, despite their high-falutin phrases, they stoop to pick up the golden apples dropped from the tree of industry, and to barter truth, love, and honor for traffic in wool, beetroot-sugar, and potato spirits.[2]

As the parson has ever gone hand in hand with the landlord, so has Clerical Socialism with Feudal Socialism.

Nothing is easier than to give Christian asceticism a socialist tinge. Has not Christianity declaimed against private property, against marriage, against the state? Has it not preached in the place of these, charity and poverty, celibacy, and mortification of the flesh, monastic life and Mother Church? Christian socialism is but the holy water with which the priest consecrates the heartburnings of the aristocrat.

[2] This applies chiefly to Germany where the landed aristocracy and squirearchy have large portions of their estates cultivated for their own account by stewards, and are, moreover, extensive beetroot-sugar manufacturers and distillers of potato spirits. The wealthier British aristocrats are, as yet, rather above that; but they, too, know how to make up for declining rents by lending their names to floaters of more or less shady joint-stock companies.

b. Petty Bourgeois Socialism The feudal aristocracy was not the only class that was ruined by the bourgeoisie, not the only class whose conditions of existence pined and perished in the atmosphere of modern bourgeois society. The medieval burgesses and the small peasant proprietors were the precursors of the modern bourgeoisie. In those countries which are but little developed, industrially and commercially, these two classes still vegetate side by side with the rising bourgeoisie.

In countries where modern civilization has become fully developed, a new class of petty bourgeois has been formed, fluctuating between proletariat and bourgeoisie, and ever renewing itself as a supplementary part of bourgeois society. The individual members of this class, however, are being constantly hurled down into the proletariat by the action of competition, and, as modern industry develops, they even see the moment approaching when they will completely disappear as an independent section of modern society, to be replaced, in manufactures, agriculture, and commerce, by overlookers, bailiffs and shopmen.

In countries, like France, where the peasants constitute far more than half of the population, it was natural that writers who sided with the proletariat against the bourgeoisie, should use, in their criticism of the bourgeois regime, the standard of the peasant and petty bourgeois, and from the standpoint of these intermediate classes should take up the cudgels for the working class. Thus arose petty bourgeois socialism. Sismondi was the head of this school, not only in France but also in England.

This school of socialism dissected with great acuteness the contradictions in the conditions of modern production. It laid bare the hypocritical apologies of economists. It proved, incontrovertibly, the disastrous effects of machinery and division of labor; the concentration of capital and land in a few hands; overproduction and crises; it pointed out the inevitable ruin of the petty bourgeois and peasant, the misery of the proletariat, the anarchy in production, the crying inequalities in the distribution of wealth, the industrial war of extermination between nations, the dissolution of old moral bonds, of the old family relations, of the old nationalities.

In its positive aims, however, this form of socialism aspires either to restoring the old means of production and of exchange, and with them the old property relations, and the old society, or to cramping the modern means of production and of exchange within the framework of the old property relations that have been, and were bound to be, exploded by those means. In either case, it is both reactionary and utopian.

Its last words are: Corporate guilds for manufacture; patriarchal relations in agriculture.

Ultimately, when stubborn historical facts had dispersed all intoxicating effects of self-deception, this form of socialism ended in a miserable fit of the blues.

c. German or "True" Socialism The Socialist and Communist literature of France, a literature that originated under the pressure of a bourgeoisie in power, and that was the expression of the struggle against this power, was introduced into Germany at a time when the bourgeoisie, in that country, had just begun its contest with feudal absolutism.

German philosophers, would-be philosophers, and men of letters eagerly seized on this literature, only forgetting that when these writings immigrated from France into Germany, French social conditions had not immigrated along with them. In contact with German social conditions, this French literature lost all its immediate practical significance, and assumed a purely literary aspect. Thus, to the German philosophers of the eighteenth century, the demands of the first French Revolution were nothing more than the demands of "Practical Reason" in general, and the utterance of the will of the revolutionary French bourgeoisie signified in their eyes the laws of pure will, of will as it was bound to be, of true human will generally.

The work of the German *literati* consisted solely in bringing the new French ideas into harmony with their ancient philosophical conscience, or rather, in annexing the French ideas without deserting their own philosophic point of view.

This annexation took place in the same way in which a foreign language is appropriated, namely by translation.

It is well known how the monks wrote silly lives of Catholic saints *over* the manuscripts on which the classical works of ancient heathendom had been written. The German *literati* reversed this process with the profane French literature. They wrote their philosophical nonsense beneath the French original. For instance, beneath the French criticism of the economic functions of money, they wrote "alienation of humanity," and beneath the French criticism of the bourgeois state, they wrote, "dethronement of the category of the general," and so forth.

The introduction of these philosophical phrases at the back of the French historical criticisms they dubbed "Philosophy of Action," "True Socialism," "German Science of Socialism," "Philosophical Foundation of Socialism," and so on.

The French Socialist and Communist literature was thus completely emasculated. And, since it ceased in the hands of the German to express the struggle of one class with the other, he felt conscious of having overcome "French one-sidedness" and of representing, not true requirements, but the requirements of truth; not the interests of the proletariat, but the interests of human nature, of man in general, who belongs to no class, has no reality, who exists only in the misty realm of philosophical fantasy.

This German socialism, which took its school-boy task so seriously and solemnly, and extolled its poor stock-in-trade in such mountebank fashion, meanwhile gradually lost its pedantic innocence.

The fight of the German and especially of the Prussian bourgeoisie against feudal aristocracy and absolute monarchy, in other words, the liberal movement, became more earnest.

By this, the long-wished-for opportunity was offered to "true" socialism of confronting the political movement with the Socialist demands, of hurling the traditional anathemas against liberalism, against representative government, against bourgeois competition, bourgeois freedom of the press, bourgeois legislation, bourgeois liberty and equality, and of preaching to the masses that they had nothing to gain, and everything to lose, by this bourgeois movement. German socialism forgot, in the nick of time, that the French criticism, whose silly echo it was, presupposed the existence of modern bourgeois society, with its corresponding economic conditions of existence, and the political constitution adapted thereto, the very things whose attainment was the object of the pending struggle in Germany.

To the absolute governments with their following of parsons, professors, country squires and officials, it served as a welcome scarecrow against the threatening bourgeoisie.

It was a sweet finish after the bitter pills of floggings and bullets, with which these same governments, just at that time, dosed the risings of the German working class.

While this "true" socialism thus served the governments as a weapon for fighting the German bourgeoisie, it, at the same time, directly represented a reactionary interest, the interest of the German Philistines. In Germany the petty bourgeois class, a relic of the sixteenth century, and since then constantly cropping up again under various forms, is the real social basis of the existing state of things.

To preserve this class, is to preserve the existing state of things in Germany. The industrial and political supremacy of the bourgeoisie threatens it with certain destruction—on the one hand, from the concentration of capital; on the other, from the rise of a revolutionary proletariat. "True" socialism appeared to kill these two birds with one stone. It spread like an epidemic.

The robe of speculative cobwebs, embroidered with flowers of rhetoric, steeped in the dew of sickly sentiment, this transcendental robe in which the German Socialists wrapped their sorry "eternal truths," all skin and bone, served to increase wonderfully the sale of their goods amongst such a public.

And on its part, German socialism recognized, more and more, its own calling as the bombastic representative of the petty bourgeois Philistine.

It proclaimed the German nation to be the model nation, and the German petty Philistine to be the typical man. To every villainous meanness of this model man it gave a hidden, higher, socialistic interpretation, the exact contrary of his real character. It went to the extreme length of directly opposing the "brutally destructive" tendency of communism, and of proclaiming its supreme and impartial contempt of all class struggles. With very few exceptions, all the so-called Socialist and Communist publications that now (1847) circulate in Germany belong to the domain of this foul and enervating literature.

2. Conservative or Bourgeois Socialism

A part of the bourgeoisie is desirous of redressing social grievances, in order to secure the continued existence of bourgeois society.

To this section belong economists, philanthropists, humanitarians, improvers of the condition of the working class, organizers of charity, members of societies for the prevention of cruelty to animals, temperance fanatics, hole-and-corner reformers of every imaginable kind. This form of socialism has, moreover, been worked out into complete systems.

We may cite Proudhon's *Philosophy of Poverty* as an example of this form.

The socialistic bourgeois want all the advantages of modern social conditions without the struggles and dangers necessarily resulting therefrom. They desire the existing state of society minus its revolutionary and disintegrating elements. They wish for a bourgeoisie without a proletariat. The bourgeoisie naturally conceives the world in which it is supreme to be the best; and bourgeois socialism develops this comfortable conception into various more or less complete systems. In requiring the proletariat to carry out such a system, and thereby to march straightway into the social New Jerusalem, it but requires in reality, that the proletariat should remain within the bounds of existing society, but should cast away all its hateful ideas concerning the bourgeoisie.

A second and more practical, but less systematic, form of this socialism sought to depreciate every revolutionary movement in the eyes of the working class, by showing that no mere political reform, but only a change in the material conditions of existence, in economic relations, could be of any advantage to them. By changes in the material conditions of existence, this form of socialism, however, by no means understands abolition of the bourgeois relations of production, an abolition that can be effected only by a revolution, but administrative reforms, based on the continued existence of these relations; reforms, therefore, that in no respect affect the relations between capital and labor, but, at the best, lessen the cost, and simplify the administrative work of bourgeois government.

Bourgeois socialism attains adequate expression, when, and only when, it becomes a mere figure of speech.

Free trade: For the benefit of the working class. Protective duties: For the benefit of the working class. Prison reform: For the benefit of the working class. These are the last words and the only seriously meant words of bourgeois socialism.

It is summed up in the phrase: the bourgeois are bourgeois—for the benefit of the working class.

3. Critical-Utopian Socialism and Communism

We do not here refer to that literature which, in every great modern revolution, has always given voice to the demands of the proletariat, such as the writings of Babeuf and others.

The first direct attempts of the proletariat to attain its own ends—made in times of universal excitement, when feudal society was being overthrown—necessarily failed, owing to the then undeveloped state of the proletariat, as well as to the absence of the economic conditions for its emancipation, conditions that had yet to be produced, and could be produced by the impending bourgeois epoch alone. The revolutionary literature that accompanied these first movements of the proletariat had necessarily a reactionary character. It inculcated universal asceticism and social leveling in its crudest form.

The socialist and communist systems properly so called, those of St. Simon, Fourier, Owen and others, spring into existence in the early undeveloped period, described above, of the struggle between proletariat and bourgeoisie (see Section 1. Bourgeois and Proletarians).

The founders of these systems see, indeed, the class antagonisms, as well as the action of the decomposing elements in the prevailing form of society. But the proletariat, as yet in its infancy, offers to them the spectacle of a class without any historical initiative or any independent political movement.

Since the development of class antagonism keeps even pace with the development of industry, the economic situation, as such Socialists find it, does not as yet offer to them the material conditions for the emancipation of the proletariat. They therefore search after a new social science, after new social laws, that are to create these conditions.

Historical action is to yield to their personal inventive action; historically created conditions of emancipation to fantastic ones; and the gradual, spontaneous class organization of the proletariat to an organization of society specially contrived by these inventors. Future history, resolves itself, in their eyes, into the propaganda and the practical carrying out of their social plans.

In the formation of their plans they are conscious of caring chiefly for the interests of the working class, as being the most suffering class. Only from the point of view of being the most suffering class does the proletariat exist for them.

The undeveloped state of the class struggle, as well as their own surroundings, causes Socialists of this kind to consider themselves far superior to all class antagonisms. They want to improve the condition of every member of society, even that of the most favored. Hence, they habitually appeal to society at large, without distinction of class; nay, by preference, to the ruling class. For how can people, when once they understand their system, fail to see in it the best possible plan of the best possible state of society?

Hence, they reject all political, and especially all revolutionary action; they wish to attain their ends by peaceful means, and endeavor, by small experiments, necessarily doomed to failure, and by the force of example, to pave the way for the new social gospel.

Such fantastic pictures of future society, painted at a time when the proletariat is still in a very undeveloped state and has but a fantastic conception of its own position, correspond with the first instinctive yearnings of that class for a general reconstruction of society.

But these socialist and communist writings contain also a critical element. They attack every principle of existing society. Hence they are full of the most valuable materials for the enlightenment of the working class. The practical measures proposed in them—such as the abolition of the distinction between town and country; abolition of the family, of private gain and of the wage-system; the proclamation of social harmony; the conversion of the functions of the state into a mere superintendence of production—all these proposals point solely to the disappearance of class antagonisms which were, at that time, only just cropping up, and which, in these publications, are recognized in their earliest, indistinct, and undefined forms only. These proposals, therefore, are of a purely utopian character.

The significance of critical-utopian socialism and communism bears an inverse relation to historical development. In proportion as the modern class struggle develops and takes definite shape, this fantastic standing apart from the contest, these fantastic attacks on it, lose all practical value and all theoretical justification. Therefore, although the originators of these systems were, in many respects, revolutionary, their disciples have, in every case, formed mere reactionary sects. They hold fast by the original views of their masters, in opposition to the progressive historical development of the proletariat. They, therefore, endeavor, and that consistently, to deaden the class struggle and to reconcile the class antagonisms. They still dream of experimental realization of their social utopias, of founding isolated *phalanstères*, of establishing "Home Colonies," or setting up a "Little Icaria"[3]—pocket editions of the New Jerusalem—and to realize all these castles in the air, they are compelled to appeal to the feelings and purses of the bourgeois. By degrees they sink into the category of the reactionary conservative Socialists depicted above, differing from these only by more systematic pedantry, and by their fanatical and superstitious belief in the miraculous effects of their social science.

They, therefore, violently oppose all political action on the part of the

[3] *Phalanstères* were socialist colonies on the plan of Charles Fourier; *Icaria* was the name given by Cabet to his utopia and, later on, to his American communist colony. "Home Colonies" were what Owen called his communist model societies.

working class; such action, according to them, can only result from blind unbelief in the new gospel.

The Owenites in England, and the Fourierists in France, respectively, oppose the Chartists and the *Réformistes.*

IV. Position of the Communists in Relation to the Various Existing Opposition Parties

Section II has made clear the relations of the Communists to the existing working-class parties, such as the Chartists in England and the Agrarian Reformers in America.

The Communists fight for the attainment of the immediate aims, for the enforcement of the momentary interests of the working class; but in the movement of the present, they also represent and take care of the future of that movement. In France the Communists ally themselves with the Social-Democrats,[4] against the conservative and radical bourgeoisie, reserving, however, the right to take up a critical position in regard to phrases and illusions traditionally handed down from the great Revolution.

In Switzerland they support the Radicals, without losing sight of the fact that this party consists of antagonistic elements, partly of Democratic Socialists, in the French sense, partly of radical bourgeois.

In Poland they support the party that insists on an agrarian revolution as the prime condition for national emancipation, that party which fomented the insurrection of Cracow in 1846.

In Germany they fight with the bourgeoisie whenever it acts in a revolutionary way, against the absolute monarchy, the feudal squirearchy, and the petty bourgeoisie.

But they never cease, for a single instant, to instill into the working class the clearest possible recognition of the hostile antagonism between bourgeoisie and proletariat, in order that the German workers may straightway use, as so many weapons against the bourgeoisie, the social and political conditions that the bourgeoisie must necessarily introduce along with its supremacy, and in order that, after the fall of the reactionary classes in Germany, the fight against the bourgeoisie itself may immediately begin.

The Communists turn their attention chiefly to Germany, because that country is on the eve of a bourgeois revolution that is bound to be carried out under more advanced conditions of European civilization and with a much more developed proletariat than what existed in England in the seventeenth and in France in the eighteenth century, and because the bourgeois revolution in Germany will be but the prelude to an immediately following proletarian revolution.

[4] The party then represented in Parliament by Ledru-Rollin [Alexander Auguste, 1807–1874], in literature by Louis Blanc [1811–1882], in the daily press by the *Réforme.* The name of social-democracy signified, with these its inventors, a section of the democratic or republican party more or less tinged with socialism.

In short, the Communists everywhere support every revolutionary movement against the existing social and political order of things.

In all these movements they bring to the front, as the leading question in each case, the property question, no matter what its degree of development at the time.

Finally, they labor everywhere for the union and agreement of the democratic parties of all countries.

The Communists disdain to conceal their views and aims. They openly declare that their ends can be attained only by the forcible overthrow of all existing social conditions. Let the ruling classes tremble at a Communist revolution. The proletarians have nothing to lose but their chains. They have a world to win.

Workingmen of all countries, unite!

1848

6 Trade-Union Politics and Social Democratic Politics

V. I. LENIN

A. Political Agitation and Its Restriction by the Economists

Everyone knows that the economic[1] struggle of the Russian workers underwent widespread development and consolidation simultaneously with the production of "literature" exposing economic (factory and occupational) conditions. The "leaflets" were devoted mainly to the exposure of the factory system, and very soon a veritable passion for exposures was roused among the workers. As soon as the workers realised that the Social-Democratic study circles desired to, and could, supply them with a new kind of leaflet that told the whole truth about their miserable existence, about their unbearably hard toil, and their lack of rights, they began to send in, actually flood us with, correspondence from the factories and workshops. This "exposure literature" created a tremendous sensation, not only in the particular

SOURCE: from V. I. Lenin, "What Is to Be Done?" *V. I. Lenin Collected Works,* Vol. 5. Moscow: Progress Publishers, 1964, pp. 397–401, 404–407, 412–414, 417–425, 429–440.

[1] To avoid misunderstanding, we must point out that here, and throughout this pamphlet, by economic struggle, we imply (in keeping with the accepted usage among us) the "practical economic struggle", which Engels described as "resistance to the capitalists", and which in free countries is known as the organized-labour, syndical, or trade-union struggle [Lenin].

factory exposed in the given leaflet, but in all the factories to which news of the revealed facts spread. And since the poverty and want among the workers in the various enterprises and in the various trades are much the same, the "truth about the life of the workers" stirred *everyone.* Even among the most backward workers, a veritable passion arose to "get into print"—a noble passion for this rudimentary form of war against the whole of the present social system which is based upon robbery and oppression. And in the overwhelming majority of cases these "leaflets" were in truth a declaration of war, because the exposures served greatly to agitate the workers; they evoked among them common demands for the removal of the most glaring outrages and roused in them a readiness to support the demands with strikes. Finally, the employers themselves were compelled to recognise the significance of these leaflets as a declaration of war, so much so that in a large number of cases they did not even wait for the outbreak of hostilities. As is always the case, the mere publication of these exposures made them effective, and they acquired the significance of a strong moral influence. On more than one occasion, the mere appearance of a leaflet proved sufficient to secure the satisfaction of all or part of the demands put forward. In a word, economic (factory) exposures were and remain an important lever in the economic struggle. And they will continue to retain this significance as long as there is capitalism, which makes it necessary for the workers to defend themselves. Even in the most advanced countries of Europe it can still be seen that the exposure of abuses in some backward trade, or in some forgotten branch of domestic industry, serves as a starting-point for the awakening of class-consciousness, for the beginning of a trade-union struggle, and for the spread of socialism.[2]

The overwhelming majority of Russian Social-Democrats have of late been almost entirely absorbed by this work of organising the exposure of factory conditions. Suffice it to recall *Rabochaya Mysl,** to see the extent to which they have been absorbed by it—so much so, indeed, that they have lost sight of the fact that this, *taken by itself,* is in essence still not Social-Democratic work, but merely trade-union work. As a matter of fact, the exposures merely dealt with the relations between the workers *in a given trade* and their employers, and all they achieved was that the sellers of labour-power learned to sell their "commodity" on better terms and to fight the purchasers over a purely commercial deal. These exposures could have served (if properly utilised by an organisation of revolutionaries) as a be-

[2] [Here] we deal only with the *political* struggle, in its broader or narrower meaning [Lenin].

* *Rabochaya Mysl* (*Worker's Thought*) is the economists' newspaper published irregularly between 1897 and 1902. The economists were influenced by Eduard Bernstein, a leading theoretician of the German Social Democratic Party, who in *Evolutionary Socialism* (1899) documented the failure of Marx's predictions and called for socialists to reassess their movements. The economists appealed for an internally democratic, socialist party that would work solely to secure better wages and working conditions for the proletariat and would put aside both revolutionary sloganeering and conspiratorial methods.—Ed.

ginning and a component part of Social-Democratic activity; but they could also have led (and, given a worshipful attitude towards spontaneity, were bound to lead) to a "purely trade-union" struggle and to a non-Social-Democratic working-class movement. Social-Democracy leads the struggle of the working-class movement. Social-Democracy leads the struggle of the working class, not only for better terms for the sale of labour-power, but for the abolition of the social system that compels the propertyless to sell themselves to the rich. Social-Democracy represents the working class, not in its relation to a given group of employers alone, but in its relation to all classes of modern society and to the state as an organised political force. Hence, it follows that not only must Social-Democrats not confine themselves exclusively to the economic struggle, but that they must not allow the organisation of economic exposures to become the predominant part of their activities. We must take up actively the political education of the working class and the development of its political consciousness.

The question arises, what should political education consist in? Can it be confined to the propaganda of working-class hostility to the autocracy? Of course not. It is not enough *to explain* to the workers that they are politically oppressed (any more than it is *to explain* to them that their interests are antagonistic to the interests of the employers). Agitation must be conducted with regard to every concrete example of this oppression (as we have begun to carry on agitation round concrete examples of economic oppression). Inasmuch as *this* oppression affects the most diverse classes of society, inasmuch as it manifests itself in the most varied spheres of life and activity —vocational, civic, personal, family, religious, scientific, etc., etc.—is it not evident that *we shall not be fulfilling our task* of developing the political consciousness of the workers if we do not *undertake* the organisation of the *political exposure* of the autocracy *in all its aspects?* In order to carry on agitation round concrete instances of oppression, these instances must be exposed (as it is necessary to expose factory abuses in order to carry on economic agitation). . . .

What concrete, real meaning attaches to Martynov's * words when he sets before Social-Democracy the task of "lending the economic struggle itself a political character"? The economic struggle is the collective struggle of the workers against their employers for better terms *in the sale of their labour-power,* for better living and working conditions. This struggle is necessarily a trade-union struggle, because working conditions differ greatly in different trades, and, consequently, the struggle *to improve* them can only be conducted on the basis of trade organisations (in the Western countries, through trade unions; in Russia, through temporary trade associations and through leaflets, etc.). Lending "the economic struggle itself a political char-

* A. S. Martynov, an Economist-theoretician.—Ed.

acter" means, therefore, striving to secure satisfaction of these trade demands, the improvement of working conditions in each separate trade by means of "legislative and administrative measures."... This is precisely what all workers' trade unions do and always have done. Read the works of the soundly scientific (and "soundly" opportunist) Mr. and Mrs. Webb * and you will see that the British trade unions long ago recognised, and have long been carrying out, the task of "lending the economic struggle itself a political character"; they have long been fighting for the right to strike, for the removal of all legal hindrances to the co-operative and trade-union movements, for laws to protect women and children, for the improvement of labour conditions by means of health and factory legislation, etc.

Thus, the pompous phrase about "lending the economic struggle *itself* a political character", which sounds so "terrifically" profound and revolutionary, serves as a screen to conceal what is in fact the traditional striving *to degrade* Social-Democratic politics to the level of trade-union politics. Under the guise of rectifying the one-sidedness of *Iskra,*† which, it is alleged, places "the revolutionising of dogma higher than the revolutionising of life", we are presented with the *struggle for economic reforms* as if it were something entirely new. In point of fact, the phrase "lending the economic struggle itself a political character" means nothing more than the struggle for economic reforms. Martynov himself might have come to this simple conclusion, had he pondered over the significance of his own words. "Our Party," he says, training his heaviest guns on *Iskra,* "could and should have presented concrete demands to the government for legislative and administrative measures against economic exploitation, unemployment, famine, etc." Concrete demands for measures—does not this mean demands for social reforms? Again we ask the impartial reader: Are we slandering the *Rabocheye Dyelo*-‡ ites (may I be forgiven for this awkward, currently used designation!) by calling them concealed Bernsteinians when, as their point of *disagreement* with *Iskra,* they advance their thesis on the necessity of struggling for economic reforms?

Revolutionary Social-Democracy has always included the struggle for reforms as part of its activities. But it utilises "economic" agitation for the purpose of presenting to the government, not only demands for all sorts of measures, but also (and primarily) the demand that it cease to be an autocratic government. Moreover, it considers it its duty to present this demand to the government on the basis, not of the economic struggle *alone,* but of all manifestations in general of public and political life. In a word, it subordinates

* British Socialists.—Ed.

† *Iskra (The Spark)* was a Russian Marxist paper founded in 1900 by Lenin and other Russian Social Democrats.—Ed.

‡ *Rabocheye Dyelo (Workers' Cause)* was a journal of the Union of Russian Social Democrats that was published in Switzerland. Its ideological and political stance placed it in the right wing of the Social-Democratic movement.—Ed.

the struggle for reforms, as the part of the whole, to the revolutionary struggle for freedom and for socialism. Martynov, however, resuscitates the theory of stages in a new form and strives to prescribe, as it were, an exclusively economic path of development for the political struggle. By advancing at this moment, when the revolutionary movement is on the upgrade, an alleged special "task" of struggling for reforms, he is dragging the party backwards and is playing into the hands of both "Economist" and liberal opportunism.

To proceed. Shamefacedly hiding the struggle for reforms behind the pompous thesis of "lending the economic struggle itself a political character", Martynov advanced, as if it were a special point, *exclusively economic* (indeed, exclusively factory) *reforms.* As to the reason for his doing that, we do not know it. Carelessness, perhaps? Yet if he had in mind something else besides "factory" reforms, then the whole of his thesis, which we have cited, loses all sense. Perhaps he did it because he considers it possible and probable that the government will make "concessions" only in the economic sphere? If so, then it is a strange delusion. Concessions are also possible and are made in the sphere of legislation concerning flogging, passports, land redemption payments, religious sects, the censorship, etc., etc. "Economic" concessions (or pseudo-concessions) are, of course, the cheapest and most advantageous from the government's point of view, because by these means it hopes to win the confidence of the working masses. For this very reason, we Social-Democrats *must not* under any circumstances or in any way whatever create grounds for the belief (or the misunderstanding) that we attach greater value to economic reforms, or that we regard them as being particularly important, etc. "Such demands," writes Martynov, speaking of the concrete demands for legislative and administrative measures referred to above, "would not be merely a hollow sound, because, promising certain palpable results, they might be actively supported by the working masses. . . ." We are not Economists, oh no! We only cringe as slavishly before the "palpableness" of concrete results as do the Bernsteins. We only wish to make it understood . . . that all which "does not promise palpable results" is merely a "hollow sound"! We are only trying to argue as if the working masses were incapable (and had not already proved their capabilities, notwithstanding those who ascribe their own philistinism to them) of actively supporting *every* protest against the autocracy, even if it *promises absolutely no palpable results whatever!*

Let us take, for example, the very "measures" for the relief of unemployment and the famine that Martynov himself advances. *Rabocheye Dyelo* is engaged, judging by what it has promised, in drawing up and elaborating a programme of "concrete [in the form of bills?] demands for legislative and administrative measures", "promising palpable results", while *Iskra,* which "constantly places the revolutionising of dogma higher than the revolutionising of life", has tried to explain the inseparable connection between "famine is coming", has exposed the police "fight against the famine-stricken," and the outrageous "provisional penal servitude regulations"; and *Zarya* * has published a special reprint, in the form of an agitational pamphlet, of a section of its "Review of Home Affairs", dealing with the famine. But good God! How "one-sided" were these incorrigibly narrow and orthodox doctrinaires, how deaf to the calls of "life itself"! Their articles contained—oh horror!—*not a single,* can you imagine it?—not a single "concrete demand" "promising palpable results"! Poor doctrinaires! They ought . . . to be taught that tactics are a process of growth, of that which grows, etc., and that the economic struggle *itself* should be given a political character!

"In addition to its immediate revolutionary significance, the economic struggle of the workers against the employers and the government [*"economic* struggle against the government"!] has also this significance: it constantly brings home to the workers the fact that they have no political rights." We quote this passage, not in order to repeat for the hundredth and thousandth time what has been said above, but in order to express particular thanks to Martynov for this excellent new formula: "the economic struggle of the workers against the employers and the government." What a pearl! With what inimitable skill and mastery in eliminating all partial disagreements and shades of differences among Economists this clear and concise proposition expresses the *quintessence* of Economism, from summoning the workers "to the political struggle, which they carry on in the general interest, for the improvement of the conditions of all the workers", continuing through the theory of stages, and ending in the resolution of the Conference on the "most widely applicable", etc. "Economic struggle against the government" is precisely trade-unionist politics, which is still very far from being Social-Democratic politics. . . .

B. Political Exposures and "Training in Revolutionary Activity"

. . . In reality, it is possible to "raise the activity of the working masses" *only* when this activity *is not restricted* to "political agitation on an economic basis". A basic condition for the necessary expansion of political agitation is the organisation of *comprehensive* political exposure. *In no way* except by means of such exposures *can* the masses be trained in political consciousness and revolutionary activity. Hence, activity of this kind is one of the most important functions of international Social-Democracy as a whole, for even political freedom does not in any way eliminate exposures; it merely shifts somewhat their sphere of direction. Thus, the German party is especially

* *Zarya* (*Dawn*) was a Marxist "scientific" and political magazine published in Stuttgart in 1901–1902 by the *Iskra* Editorial Board.—Ed.

strengthening its positions and spreading its influence, thanks particularly to the untiring energy with which it is conducting its campaign of political exposure. Working-class consciousness cannot be genuine political consciousness unless the workers are trained to respond to *all* cases of tyranny, oppression, violence, and abuse, no matter *what class* is affected—unless they are trained, moreover, to respond from a Social-Democratic point of view and no other. The consciousness of the working masses cannot be genuine class-consciousness, unless the workers learn, from concrete, and above all from topical, political facts and events to observe *every* other social class in *all* the manifestations of its intellectual, ethical, and political life; unless they learn to apply in practice the materialist analysis and the materialist estimate of *all* aspects of the life and activity of *all* classes, strata, and groups of the population. Those who concentrate the attention, observation, and consciousness of the working class exclusively, or even mainly, upon itself alone are not Social-Democrats; for the self-knowledge of the working class is indissolubly bound up, not solely with a fully clear theoretical understanding—it would be even truer to say, not so much with the theoretical, as with the practical, understanding—of the relationships between *all* the various classes of modern society, acquired through the experience of political life. For this reason the conception of the economic struggle as the most widely applicable means of drawing the masses into the political movement, which our Economists preach, is so extremely harmful and reactionary in its practical significance. In order to become a Social-Democrat, the worker must have a clear picture in his mind of the economic nature and the social and political features of the landlord and the priest, the high state official and the peasant, the student and the vagabond; he must know their strong and weak points; he must grasp the meaning of all the catchwords and sophisms by which each class and each stratum *camouflages* its selfish strivings and its real "inner workings"; he must understand what interests are reflected by certain institutions and certain laws and how they are reflected. But this "clear picture" cannot be obtained from any book. It can be obtained only from living examples and from exposures that follow close upon what is going on about us at a given moment; upon what is being discussed, in whispers perhaps, by each one in his own way; upon what finds expression in such and such events, in such and such statistics, in such and such court sentences, etc., etc. These comprehensive political exposures are an essential and *fundamental* condition for training the masses in revolutionary activity.

Why do the Russian workers still manifest little revolutionary activity in response to the brutal treatment of the people by the police, the persecution of religious sects, the flogging of peasants, the outrageous censorship, the torture of soldiers, the persecution of the most innocent cultural undertakings, etc.? Is it because the "economic struggle" does not "stimulate" them to this, because such activity does not "promise palpable results", because it produces little that is "positive"? To adopt such an opinion, we repeat, is merely to direct the charge where it does not belong, to blame the working masses for one's own philistinism. . . . We must blame ourselves, our lagging behind the mass movement, for still being unable to organise sufficiently wide, striking, and rapid exposures of all the shameful outrages. When we do that (and we must and can do it), the most backward worker will understand, *or will feel,* that the students and religious sects, the peasants and the authors are being abused and outraged by those same dark forces that are oppressing and crushing him at every step of his life. Feeling that, he himself will be filled with an irresistible desire to react, and he will know how to hoot the censors one day, on another day to demonstrate outside the house of a governor who has brutally suppressed a peasant uprising, on still another day to teach a lesson to the gendarmes in surplices who are doing the work of the Holy Inquisition, etc. As yet we have done very little, almost nothing, *to bring* before the working masses prompt exposures on all possible issues. Many of us as yet do not recognise this as our *bounden duty* but trail spontaneously in the wake of the "drab everyday struggle", in the narrow confines of factory life. . . .

As for calling the masses to action, that will come of itself as soon as energetic political agitation, live and striking exposures come into play. To catch some criminal red-handed and immediately to brand him publicly in all places is of itself far more effective than any number of "calls"; the effect very often is such as will make it impossible to tell exactly who it was that "called" upon the masses and who suggested this or that plan of demonstration, etc. Calls for action, not in the general, but in the concrete, sense of the term can be made only at the place of action; only those who themselves go into action, and do so immediately, can sound such calls. Our business as Social-Democratic publicists is to deepen, expand, and intensify political exposures and political agitation. . . .

C. What Is There in Common Between Economism and Terrorism?

[Elsewhere] we cited the opinion of an Economist and of a non-Social-Democratic terrorist, who showed themselves to be accidentally in agreement. Speaking generally, however, there is not an accidental, but a necessary, inherent connection between the two, of which we shall have need to speak later, and which must be mentioned here in connection with the question of education for revolutionary activity. The Economists and the present-day terrorists have one common root, namely, *subservience to spontaneity,* with which we dealt in the preceding chapter as a general phenomenon and which we shall now examine in relation to its effect upon political activity and the political struggle. At first sight, our assertion may appear paradoxical, so great is the difference between those who stress the "drab everyday struggle" and those who call for the most self-sacrificing struggle of individuals. But this is no paradox. The Economists and the terrorists merely bow to different poles of spontaneity; the Economists bow to the spontaneity of "the labour movement pure and simple", while the terrorists bow to the spontaneity of the passionate indignation of intellectuals, who lack the ability or opportunity to connect the revolutionary struggle and the working-class movement into an integral whole. It is difficult indeed for those who have lost their belief, or who have never believed, that this is possible, to find some outlet for their indignation and revolutionary energy other than terror. Thus, both forms of subservience to spontaneity we have mentioned are nothing but *the beginning of the implementation* of the notorious *Credo* * programme: Let the workers wage their "economic struggle against the employers and the government" . . . and let the intellectuals conduct the political struggle by their own efforts—with the aid of terror, of course! This is an absolutely logical and inevitable *conclusion* which must be insisted on—*even though those* who are beginning to carry out this programme *do not themselves realise* that it is inevitable. Political activity has its logic quite apart from the consciousness of those who, with the best intentions, call either for terror or for lending the economic struggle itself a political character. The road to hell is paved with good intentions, and, in this case, good intentions cannot save one from being spontaneously drawn "along the line of least resistance", along the line of the *purely bourgeois Credo* programme. Surely it is no accident either that many Russian liberals —avowed liberals and liberals that wear the mask of Marxism—wholeheartedly sympathise with terror and try to foster the terrorist moods that have surged up in the present time. . . .

. . . Are there not enough outrages committed in Russian life without special "excitants" having to be invented? On the other hand, is it not obvious that those who are not, and cannot be, roused to excitement even by Russian tyranny will stand by "twiddling their thumbs" and watch a handful of terrorists engaged in single combat with the government? The fact is that the working masses are roused to a high pitch of excitement by the social evils in Russian life, but we are unable to gather, if one may so put it, and concentrate all these drops and streamlets of popular resentment that are brought forth to a far larger extent than we imagine by the conditions of Russian life, and that must be combined into a *single* gigantic torrent. That this can be accomplished is irrefutably proved by the enormous growth of the working-class movement and the eagerness, noted above, with which the workers clamour for political literature. On the other hand, calls for terror and calls to lend the economic struggle itself a political character are merely two different forms of *evading* the most pressing duty now resting upon Russian revolutionaries, namely, the organisation of comprehensive political agitation. . . .

* Written by a group of "Economists."—Ed.

D. The Working Class as Vanguard Fighter for Democracy

We have seen that the conduct of the broadest political agitation and, consequently, of all-sided political exposures is an absolutely necessary and a *paramount* task of our activity, if this activity is to be truly Social-Democratic. However, we arrived at this conclusion *solely* on the grounds of the pressing needs of the working class for political knowledge and political training. But such a presentation of the question is too narrow, for it ignores the general democratic tasks of Social-Democracy, in particular of present-day Russian Social-Democracy. In order to explain the point more concretely we shall approach the subject from an aspect that is "nearest" to the Economist, namely, from the practical aspect. "Everyone agrees" that it is necessary to develop the political consciousness of the working class. The question is, *how* that is to be done and what is required to do it. The economic struggle merely "impels" the workers to realise the government's attitude towards the working class. Consequently, *however much we may try* to "lend the economic struggle itself a political character", we *shall never be able* to develop the political consciousness of the workers (to the level of Social-Democratic political consciousness) by keeping within the framework of the economic struggle, for *that framework is too narrow.* The Martynov formula has some value for us, not because it illustrates Martynov's aptitude for confusing things, but because it pointedly expresses the basic error that all the Economists commit, namely, their conviction that it is possible to develop the class political consciousness of the workers *from without,* that is, only from outside the economic struggle, from outside the exclusive (or, at least, the main) starting-point, by making it the exclusive (or, at least, the main) basis. Such a view is radically wrong. Piqued by our polemics against them, the Economists refuse to ponder deeply over the origins of these disagreements, with the result that we simply cannot understand one another. It is as if we spoke in different tongues.

Class political consciousness can be brought to the workers *only from without,* that is, only from outside the economic struggle, from outside the sphere of relations between workers and employers. The sphere from which alone it is possible to obtain this knowledge is the sphere of relationships of *all* classes and strata to the state and the government, the sphere of the interrelations between *all* classes. For that reason, the reply to the question as to what must be done to bring political knowledge to the workers cannot be merely the answer with which, in the majority of cases, the practical workers, especially those inclined towards Economism, mostly content themselves, namely: "To go among the workers." To bring political knowledge to the *workers* the Social-Democrats must *go among all classes of the population;* they must dispatch units of their army *in all directions.*

We deliberately select this blunt formula, we deliberately express ourselves in this sharply simplified manner, not because we desire to indulge in paradoxes, but in order to "impel" the Economists to a realisation of their tasks which they unpardonably ignore, to suggest to them strongly the difference between trade-unionist and Social-Democratic politics, which they refuse to understand. We therefore beg the reader not to get wrought up, but to hear us patiently to the end.

Let us take the type of Social-Democratic study circle that has become most widespread in the past few years and examine its work. It has "contacts with the workers" and rests content with this, issuing leaflets in which abuses in the factories, the government's partiality towards the capitalists, and the tyranny of the police are strongly condemned. At workers' meetings the discussions never, or rarely ever, go beyond the limits of these subjects. Extremely rare are the lectures and discussions held on the history of the revolutionary movement, on questions of the government's home and foreign policy, on questions of the economic evolution of Russia and Europe, on the position of the various classes in modern society, etc. As to systematically acquiring and extending contact with other classes of society, no one even dreams of that. In fact, the ideal leader, as the majority of the members of such circles picture him, is something far more in the nature of a trade-union secretary than a socialist political leader. For the secretary of any, say English, trade union always helps the workers to carry on the economic struggle, he helps them to expose factory abuses, explains the injustice of the laws and of measures that hamper the freedom to strike and to picket (i.e., to warn all and sundry that a strike is proceeding at a certain factory), explains the partiality of arbitration court judges who belong to the bourgeois classes, etc., etc. In a word, every trade-union secretary conducts and helps to conduct "the economic struggle against the employers and the government". It cannot be too strongly maintained that *this is still not* Social-Democracy, that the Social-Democrat's ideal should not be the trade-union secretary, but *the tribune of the people,* who is able to react to every manifestation of tyranny and oppression, no matter where it appears, no matter what stratum or class of the people it affects; who is able to generalise all these manifestations and produce a single picture of police violence and capitalist exploitation; who is able to take advantage of every event, however small, in order to set forth *before all* his socialist convictions and his democratic demands, in order to clarify for *all* and everyone the world-historic significance of the struggle for the emancipation of the proletariat. . . .

. . . We said that a Social-Democrat, if he really believes it necessary to develop comprehensively the political consciousness of the proletariat, must "go among all classes of the population". This gives rise to the questions: how is this to be done? have we enough forces to do this? is there a basis for such work among all the other classes? will this not mean a retreat, or lead to a retreat, from the class point of view? Let us deal with these questions.

We must "go among all classes of the population" as theoreticians, as propagandists, as agitators, and as organisers. No one doubts that the theoretical work of Social-Democrats should aim at studying all the specific features of the social and political condition of the various classes. But extremely little is done in this direction, as compared with the work that is done in studying the specific features of factory life. In the committees and study circles, one can meet people who are immersed in the study even of some special branch of the metal industry; but one can hardly ever find members of organisations (obliged, as often happens, for some reason or other to give up practical work) who are especially engaged in gathering material on some pressing question of social and political life in our country which could serve as a means for conducting Social-Democratic work among other strata of the population. In dwelling upon the fact that the majority of the present-day leaders of the working-class movement lack training, we cannot refrain from mentioning training in this respect also, for it too is bound up with the "Economist" conception of "close organic connection with the proletarian struggle". The principal thing, of course, is *propaganda* and *agitation* among all strata of the people. The work of the West-European Social-Democrat is in this respect facilitated by the public meetings and rallies which *all* are free to attend, and by the fact that in parliament he addresses the representatives of *all* classes. We have neither a parliament nor freedom of assembly; nevertheless, we are able to arrange meetings of workers who desire to listen to *a Social-Democrat.* We must also find ways and means of calling meetings of representatives of all social classes that desire to listen to *a democrat;* for he is no Social-Democrat who forgets in practice that "the Communists support every revolutionary movement", that we are obliged for that reason to expound and emphasise *general democratic tasks before the whole people,* without for a moment concealing our socialist convictions. He is no Social-Democrat who forgets in practice his obligation to be *ahead of all* in raising, accentuating, and solving *every* general democratic question. . . .

. . . Have we sufficient forces to direct our propaganda and agitation among *all* social classes? Most certainly. Our Economists, who are frequently inclined to deny this, lose sight of the gigantic progress our movement has made from (approximately) 1894 to 1901. Like real "tail-enders", they often go on living in the bygone stages of the movement's inception. In the earlier period, indeed, we had astonishingly few forces, and it was perfectly natural and legitimate then to devote ourselves exclusively to activities among the workers and to condemn severely any deviation from this course. The entire task then was to consolidate our position in the working class. At the present time, however, gigantic forces have been attracted to the movement. The best representatives of the younger generation of the educated classes are coming over to us. Everywhere in the provinces there are people, resident there by dint of circumstance, who have taken part in the movement in the past or who desire to do so now and who are gravitating towards Social-

Democracy (whereas in 1894 one could count the Social-Democrats on the fingers of one's hand). A basic political and organisational shortcoming of our movement is our *inability* to utilise all these forces and give them appropriate work (we shall deal with this more fully in the next chapter). The overwhelming majority of these forces entirely lack the opportunity of "going among the workers", so that there are no grounds for fearing that we shall divert forces from our main work. In order to be able to provide the workers with real, comprehensive, and live political knowledge, we must have "our own people", Social-Democrats, everywhere, among all social strata, and in all positions from which we can learn the inner springs of our state mechanism. Such people are required, not only for propaganda and agitation, but in a still larger measure for organisation.

Is there a basis for activity among all classes of the population? Whoever doubts this lags in his consciousness behind the spontaneous awakening of the masses. The working-class movement has aroused and is continuing to arouse discontent in some, hopes of support for the opposition in others, and in still others the realisation that the autocracy is unbearable and must inevitably fall. We would be "politicians" and Social-Democrats in name only (as all too often happens in reality), if we failed to realise that our task is to utilise every manifestation of discontent, and to gather and turn to the best account every protest, however small. This is quite apart from the fact that the millions of the labouring peasantry, handicraftsmen, petty artisans, etc., would always listen eagerly to the speech of any Social-Democrat who is at all qualified. Indeed, is there a single social class in which there are no individuals, groups, or circles that are discontented with the lack of rights and with tyranny and, therefore, accessible to the propaganda of Social-Democrats as the spokesmen of the most pressing general democratic needs? To those who desire to have a clear idea of what the political agitation of a Social-Democrat among *all* classes and strata of the population should be like, we would point to *political exposures* in the broad sense of the word as the principal (but, of course, not the sole) form of this agitation.

> "We must arouse in every section of the population that is at all politically conscious a passion for *political* exposure," I wrote in my article "Where to Begin" [*Iskra,* May (No. 4) 1901], with which I shall deal in greater detail later. "We must not be discouraged by the fact that the voice of political exposure is today so feeble, timid, and infrequent. This is not because of a wholesale submission to police despotism, but because those who are able and ready to make exposures have no tribune from which to speak, no eager and encouraging audience, they do not see anywhere among the people that force to which it would be worth while directing their complaint against the 'omnipotent' Russian Government. . . . We are now in a position to provide a tribune for the nation-wide exposure of the tsarist government, and it is our duty to do this. That tribune must be a Social-Democratic newspaper."

The ideal audience for political exposure is the working class, which is first and foremost in need of all-round and live political knowledge, and is most capable of converting this knowledge into active struggle, even when that struggle does not promise "palpable results". A tribune for *nation-wide* exposures can be only an All-Russian newspaper. "Without a political organ, a political movement deserving that name is inconceivable in the Europe of today"; in this respect Russia must undoubtedly be included in present-day Europe. The press long ago became a power in our country, otherwise the government would not spend tens of thousands of rubles to bribe it and to subsidise the Katkovs and Meshcherskys.* And it is no novelty in autocratic Russia for the underground press to break through the wall of censorship and *compel* the legal and conservative press to speak openly of it. This was the case in the seventies and even in the fifties. How much broader and deeper are now the sections of the people willing to read the illegal underground press, and to learn from it "how to live and how to die", to use the expression of a worker who sent a letter to *Iskra*. Political exposures are as much a declaration of war against the *government* as economic exposures are a declaration of war against the factory owners. The moral significance of this declaration of war will be all the greater, the wider and more powerful the campaign of exposure will be and the more numerous and determined the social *class* that has *declared war in order to begin the war*. Hence, political exposures in themselves serve as a powerful instrument for *disintegrating* the system we oppose, as a means for diverting from the enemy his casual or temporary allies, as a means for spreading hostility and distrust among the permanent partners of the autocracy.

In our time only a party that will *organise* really *nation-wide* exposures can become the vanguard of the revolutionary forces. The word "nation-wide" has a very profound meaning. The overwhelming majority of the non-working-class exposers (be it remembered that in order to become the vanguard, we must attract other classes) are sober politicians and level-headed men of affairs. They know perfectly well how dangerous it is to "complain" even against a minor official, let alone against the "omnipotent" Russian Government. And they will come *to us* with their complaints only when they see that these complaints can really have effect, and that we represent *a political force*. In order to become such a force in the eyes of outsiders, much persistent and stubborn work is required *to raise* our own consciousness, initiative, and energy. To accomplish this it is not enough to attach a "vanguard" label to rearguard theory and practice.

But if we have to undertake the organisation of a really nation-wide exposure of the government, in what way will then the class character of our movement be expressed?—the overzealous advocate of "close organic contact with the proletarian struggle" will ask us, as indeed he does. The reply is manifold: we Social-Democrats will organise these nation-wide

* M. F. Katkov and V. P. Meshchersky were extreme Tsarist propagandists whose publications heavily depended on funds from the government.—Ed.

exposures; all questions raised by the agitation will be explained in a consistently Social-Democratic spirit, without any concessions to deliberate or undeliberate distortions of Marxism; the all-round political agitation will be conducted by a party which unites into one inseparable whole the assault on the government in the name of the entire people, the revolutionary training of the proletariat, and the safeguarding of its political independence, the guidance of the economic struggle of the working class, and the utilisation of all its spontaneous conflicts with its exploiters which rouse and bring into our camp increasing numbers of the proletariat.

But a most characteristic feature of Economism is its failure to understand this connection, more, this identity of the most pressing need of the proletariat (a comprehensive political education through the medium of political agitation and political exposures) with the need of the general democratic movement. This lack of understanding is expressed, not only in "Martynovite" phrases, but in the references to a supposedly class point of view identical in meaning with these phrases. Thus, the authors of the "Economist" letter in *Iskra,* No. 12, state: "This basic drawback of *Iskra* [overestimation of ideology] is also the cause of its inconsistency on the question of the attitude of Social-Democracy to the various social classes and tendencies. By theoretical reasoning [not by "the growth of Party tasks, which grow together with the Party"], *Iskra* solved the problem of the immediate transition to the struggle against absolutism. In all probability it senses the difficulty of such a task for the workers under the present state of affairs [not only senses, but knows fully well that this task appears less difficult to the workers than to the "Economist" intellectuals with their nursemaid concern, for the workers are prepared to fight even for demands which, to use the language of the never-to-be-forgotten Martynov, do not "promise palpable results"] but lacking the patience to wait until the workers will have gathered sufficient forces for this struggle, *Iskra* begins to seek allies in the ranks of the liberals and intellectuals". . . .

Yes, we have indeed lost all "patience" "waiting" for the blessed time, long promised us by divers "conciliators", when the Economists will have stopped charging the workers with *their own* backwardness and justifying their own lack of energy with allegations that the workers lack strength. We ask our Economists: What do they mean by "the gathering of working-class strength for the struggle"? Is it not evident that this means the political training of the workers, so that *all* the aspects of our vile autocracy are revealed to them? And is it not clear that *precisely for this work* we need "allies in the ranks of the liberals and intellectuals", who are prepared to join us in the exposure of the political attack on the Zemstvos,* on the

* In 1864 Alexander I had introduced into cities and provinces organs of local self-rule (municipal councils and Zemstvo). They were not meant to compete with the imperial bureaucracy but to assist it by assuming a variety of responsibilities previously left unattended.—Ed.

teachers, on the statisticians, on the students, etc.? Is this surprisingly "intricate mechanism" really so difficult to understand? Has not P. B. Axelrod * constantly repeated since 1897 that "the task before the Russian Social-Democrats of acquiring adherents and direct and indirect allies among the non-proletarian classes will be solved principally and primarily by the character of the propagandist activities conducted among the proletariat itself"? But the Martynovs and the other Economists continue to imagine that "by economic struggle against the employers and the government" the workers must *first* gather strength (for trade-unionist politics) and *then* "go over"—we presume from trade-unionist "training for activity"—to Social-Democratic activity!

"... In this quest," continue the Economists, "*Iskra* not infrequently departs from the class point of view, obscures class antagonisms, and puts into the forefront the common nature of the discontent with the government, although the causes and the degree of the discontent vary considerably among the 'allies.' Such, for example, is *Iskra's* attitude towards the Zemstvo. . . ." *Iskra,* it is alleged, "promises the nobles that are dissatisfied with the government's sops the assistance of the working class, but it does not say a word about the class antagonism that exists between these social strata". If the reader will turn to the article "The Autocracy and the Zemstvo" (*Iskra,* Nos. 2 and 4), to which, *in all probability,* the authors of the letter refer, he will find that they deal with the attitude of the *government* towards the "mild agitation of the bureaucratic Zemstvo, which is based on the social-estates", and towards the "independent activity of even the propertied classes". The article states that the workers cannot look on indifferently while the government is waging a struggle against the Zemstvo, and the Zemstvos are called upon to stop making mild speeches and to speak firmly and resolutely when revolutionary Social-Democracy confronts the government in all its strength. What the authors of the letter do not agree with here is not clear. Do they think that the workers will "not understand" the phrases "propertied classes" and "bureaucratic Zemstvo based on the social-estates"? Do they think that *urging* the Zemstvo to abandon mild speeches and to speak firmly is "overestimating ideology"? Do they imagine the workers can "gather strength" for the struggle against the autocracy if they know nothing about the attitude of the autocracy towards the Zemstvo *as well?* All this too remains unknown. One thing alone is clear and that is that the authors of the letter have a very vague idea of what the political tasks of Social-Democracy are. This is revealed still more clearly by their remark: "Such, too, is *Iskra*'s attitude towards the student movement" (i.e., it also "obscures the class antagonisms"). Instead of calling on the workers to declare by means of public demonstrations that the real breeding-place of unbridled violence, disorder, and outrage is not the university youth but the Russian Government (*Iskra,*

* Axelrod was a member of the Editorial Board of *Iskra.*—Ed.

No. 2), we ought probably to have inserted arguments in the spirit of *Rabochaya Mysl!* Such ideas were expressed by Social-Democrats in the autumn of 1901, after the events of February and March, on the eve of a fresh upsurge of the student movement, which reveals that even in this sphere the "spontaneous protest against the autocracy is *outstripping* the conscious Social-Democratic leadership of the movement. The spontaneous striving of the workers to defend the students who are being assaulted by the police and the Cossacks surpasses the conscious activity of the Social-Democratic organisation!

"And yet in other articles," continue the authors of the letter, "*Iskra* sharply condemns all compromise and defends, for instance, the intolerant conduct of the Guesdists." We would advise those who are wont so conceitedly and frivolously to declare that the present disagreements among the Social-Democrats are unessential and do not justify a split, to ponder these words. Is it possible for people to work together in the same organisation, when some among them contend that we have done extremely little to explain the hostility of the autocracy to the various classes and to inform the workers of the opposition displayed by the various social strata to the autocracy, while others among them see in this clarification a "compromise"—evidently a compromise with the theory of "economic struggle against the employers and the government"?

We urged the necessity of carrying the class struggle into the rural districts in connection with the fortieth anniversary of the emancipation of the peasantry (issue No. 3), and spoke of the irreconcilability of the local government bodies and the autocracy in relation to Witte's secret Memorandum (No. 4). In connection with the new law we attacked the feudal landlords and the government which serves them (No. 8) and we welcomed the illegal Zemstvo congress. We urged the Zemstvo to pass over from abject petitions (No. 8) to struggle. We encouraged the students, who had begun to understand the need for the political struggle, and to undertake this struggle (No. 3), while, at the same time, we lashed out at the "outrageous incomprehension" revealed by the adherents of the "purely student" movement, who called upon the students to abstain from participating in the street demonstrations (No. 3, in connection with the manifesto issued by the Executive Committee of the Moscow students on February 25). We exposed the "senseless dreams" and the "lying hypocrisy" of the cunning liberals of *Rossiya* (No. 5), while pointing to the violent fury with which the government-gaoler persecuted "peaceful writers, aged professors, scientists, and well-known liberal Zemstvo members" (No. 5, "Police Raid on Literature"). We exposed the real significance of the programme of "state protection for the welfare of the workers" and welcomed the "valuable admission" that "it is better, by granting reforms from above, to forestall the demand for such reforms from below than to wait for those demands to be put forward" (No. 6). We encouraged the protesting statisticians (No. 7) and censured the strike-breaking statisticians (No. 9). He who sees in these tactics an obscuring of the class-consciousness of the proletariat and *a compromise with liberalism* reveals his utter failure to understand the true significance of the programme of the *Credo* and *carries out that programme de facto,* however much he may repudiate it. For by *such an approach* he drags Social-Democracy towards the "economic struggle against the employers and the government" and *yields to liberalism,* abandons the task of actively intervening in *every* "liberal" issue and of determining *his own,* Social-Democratic, attitude towards this question.

E. Once More "Slanderers", Once More "Mystifiers"

These polite expressions, as the reader will recall, belong to *Rabocheye Dyelo,* which in this way answers our charge that it "is indirectly preparing the ground for converting the working-class movement into an instrument of bourgeois democracy". In its simplicity of heart *Rabocheye Dyelo* decided that this accusation was nothing more than a polemical sally: these malicious doctrinaires are bent on saying all sorts of unpleasant things about us, and, what can be more unpleasant than being an instrument of bourgeois democracy? And so they print in bold type a "refutation": "Nothing but downright slander", "mystification", "mummery".... *Rabocheye Dyelo* (although bearing little resemblance to that deity) is wrathful because it is wrong, and proves by its hasty abuse that it is incapable of understanding its opponents' mode of reasoning. And yet, with only a little reflection it would have understood why *any* subservience to the spontaneity of the mass movement and *any* degrading of Social-Democratic politics to the level of trade-unionist politics mean preparing the ground for converting the working-class movement into an instrument of bourgeois democracy. The spontaneous working-class movement is by itself able to create (and inevitably does create) only trade-unionism, and working-class trade-unionist politics is precisely working-class bourgeois politics. The fact that the working class participates in the political struggle, and even in the political revolution, does not in itself make its politics Social-Democratic politics. Will *Rabocheye Dyelo* make bold to deny this? Will it, at long last, publicly, plainly, and without equivocation explain how it understands the urgent questions of international and of Russian Social-Democracy? Hardly. It will never do anything of the kind, because it holds fast to the trick, which might be described as the "not here" method—"It's not me, it's not my horse, I'm not the driver. We are not Economists; *Rabochaya Mysl* does not stand for Economism; there is no Economism at all in Russia." This is a remarkably adroit and "political" trick, which suffers from the slight defect, however, that the publications practising it are usually nicknamed, "At your service, sir".

Rabocheye Dyelo imagines that bourgeois democracy in Russia is, in general, merely a "phantom". Happy people! Ostrich-like, they bury their heads in the sand and imagine that everything around has disappeared. Liberal publicists who month after month proclaim to the world their triumph over the collapse and even the disappearance of Marxism; liberal newspapers (*S. Peterburgskiye Vedomosti, Russkiye Vedomosti,* and many others) which encourage the liberals who bring to the workers the Brentano * conception of the class struggle and the trade-unionist conception of politics; the galaxy of critics of Marxism, whose real tendencies were so very well disclosed by the *Credo* and whose literary products alone circulate in Russia without let or hindrance; the revival of revolutionary *non*-Social-Democratic tendencies, particularly after the February and March events—all these, apparently, are just phantoms! All these have nothing at all to do with bourgeois democracy!

Rabocheye Dyelo and the authors of the Economist letter published in *Iskra,* No. 12, should "ponder over the reason why the events of the spring brought about such a revival of revolutionary non-Social-Democratic tendencies instead of increasing the authority and the prestige of Social-Democracy".

The reason lies in the fact that we failed to cope with our tasks. The masses of the workers proved to be more active than we. We lacked adequately trained revolutionary leaders and organisers possessed of a thorough knowledge of the mood prevailing among all the opposition strata and able to head the movement, to turn a spontaneous demonstration into a political one, broaden its political character, etc. Under such circumstances, our backwardness will inevitably be utilised by the more mobile and more energetic non-Social-Democratic revolutionaries, and the workers, however energetically and self-sacrificingly they may fight the police and the troops, however revolutionary their actions may be, will prove to be merely a force supporting those revolutionaries, the rearguard of bourgeois democracy, and not the Social-Democratic vanguard. Let us take, for example, the German Social-Democrats, whose weak aspects alone our Economists desire to emulate. Why is there *not a single* political event in Germany that does not add to the authority and prestige of Social-Democracy? Because Social-Democracy is always found to be in advance of all others in furnishing the most revolutionary appraisal of every given event and in championing every protest against tyranny. It does not lull itself with arguments that the economic struggle brings the workers to realise that they have no political rights and that the concrete conditions unavoidably impel the working-class movement on to the path of revolution. It intervenes in every sphere and in every question of social and political life; in the matter of Wilhelm's refusal to endorse a bourgeois progressist as city mayor (our Economists have not

* L. Brentano was a German economist who championed "state socialism." He tried to prove the possibility of achieving social equality within the framework of capitalism through reforms and through the reconciliation of the interests of the capitalists and the workers.—Ed.

yet managed to educate the Germans to the understanding that such an act is, in fact, a compromise with liberalism!); in the matter of the law against "obscene" publications and pictures; in the matter of governmental influence on the election of professors, etc., etc. Everywhere the Social-Democrats are found in the forefront, rousing political discontent among all classes, rousing the sluggards, stimulating the laggards, and providing a wealth of material for the development of the political consciousness and the political activity of the proletariat. As a result, even the avowed enemies of socialism are filled with respect for this advanced political fighter, and not infrequently an important document from bourgeois, and even from bureaucratic and Court circles, makes its way by some miraculous means into the editorial office of *Vorwärts.**

This, then, is the resolution of the seeming "contradiction" that surpasses *Rabocheye Dyelo*'s powers of understanding to such an extent that it can only throw up its hands and cry, "Mummery!" Indeed, just think of it: We, *Rabocheye Dyelo,* regard the *mass* working-class movement as the *corner-stone* (and say so in bold type!); we warn all and sundry against belittling the significance of the element of spontaneity; we desire to lend the economic struggle itself—*itself*—a political character; we desire to maintain close and organic contact with the proletarian struggle. And yet we are told that we are preparing the ground for the conversion of the working-class movement into an instrument of bourgeois democracy! And who are they that presume to say this? People who "compromise" with liberalism by intervening in every "liberal" issue (what a gross misunderstanding of "organic contact with the proletarian struggle"!), by devoting so much attention to the students and even (oh horror!) to the Zemstvos! People who in general wish to devote a greater percentage (compared with the Economists) of their efforts to activity among non-proletarian classes of the population! What is this but "mummery"?

Poor *Rabocheye Dyelo!* Will it ever find the solution to this perplexing puzzle?

1902

* *Vorwärts (Forward)* was the central organ of German Social-Democracy.—Ed.

7 The Chinese Revolution

MAO TSE-TUNG

Section 1. The Revolutionary Movements in the Last Hundred Years

The process of the transformation of China into a semi-colony and colony by imperialism allying with Chinese feudalism is at the same time the process of the struggle of the Chinese people against imperialism and its lackeys. The Opium War, the Movement of the T'aip'ing Heavenly Kingdom, the Sino-French War, the Sino-Japanese War, the *Coup d'état* of 1898, the Yi Ho Tuan (Boxer) Movement, the Revolution of 1911, the May 4 Movement, the May 30 Movement, the Northern Expedition, the Agrarian Revolutionary War and the present Anti-Japanese War all testify to the stubborn resistance of the Chinese people who refuse to submit to imperialism and its lackeys.

Thanks to the unyielding and ever-renewed heroic struggles waged by the Chinese people during the last hundred years, imperialism has not been and will never be able to subjugate China.

At present, although Japanese imperialism is putting forth all its strength in an all-out offensive against China, and many landlords and big bourgeois, like the Wang Ching-weis in the open or under cover, have capitulated or are prepared to capitulate to the enemy, yet the heroic Chinese people will certainly fight on. They certainly will not cease fighting until Japanese imperialism is driven out of China and China achieves complete liberation.

The national revolutionary struggle of the Chinese people has a history of exactly one hundred years dating from the Opium War of 1840, and of thirty years dating from the Revolution of 1911. As this revolution has not yet run its full course and there has not yet been any signal achievement with regard to the revolutionary tasks, it is still necessary for all the Chinese people, and above all the Chinese Communist Party, to assume the responsibility for a resolute fight.

Then, what are the targets of this revolution? What are its tasks? What are its motive forces? What is its character? And what are its perspectives? These are the questions we shall answer in the following pages.

Section 2. The Targets of the Chinese Revolution

. . . we already know that present-day Chinese society is a colonial, semi-colonial and semi-feudal society. Only when we clearly understand the

SOURCE: from *The Chinese Revolution and the Chinese Communist Party* by Mao Tse-tung, pp. 24–56. Copyright Foreign Languages Press, Peking, 1954.

character of Chinese society can we clearly understand the targets of the Chinese revolution, its tasks, its motive forces, its character and its perspectives and transition. Therefore a clear understanding of the character of Chinese society, i.e., of the country's situation, is the basic premise for an understanding of all problems of the revolution.

Since the character of present-day Chinese society is colonial, semi-colonial and semi-feudal, then what after all are our chief targets or enemies at this stage of the Chinese revolution?

They are none other than imperialism and feudalism, namely, the bourgeoisie of the imperialist countries and the landlord class at home. For these and none other are the principal agents that carry out oppression in Chinese society at the present stage and obstruct its advance. These agents conspire to oppress the Chinese people and, since national oppression by imperialism is the heaviest oppression, imperialism has become the foremost and fiercest enemy of the Chinese people.

Since Japan's armed invasion of China, the principal enemies of the Chinese revolution have been Japanese imperialism and all the collaborators and reactionaries who are in collusion with it, who have either openly capitulated or are prepared to capitulate.

The Chinese bourgeoisie, also actually oppressed by imperialism, once led revolutionary struggles; it played a principal leading role, for instance, in the Revolution of 1911, and also has joined such revolutionary struggles as the Northern Expedition and the present Anti-Japanese War. In the long period from 1927 to 1937, however, the upper stratum of the bourgeoisie, as represented by the reactionary bloc of the Kuomintang, was in collusion with imperialism and formed a reactionary alliance with the landlord class, turning against the friends who had helped it—the Communist Party, the proletariat, the peasantry, and other sections of the petty bourgeoisie, betraying the Chinese revolution, and thereby causing its defeat. At that time, therefore, the revolutionary people and their political party, the Communist Party, could only regard these bourgeois elements as a target of the revolution. During the Anti-Japanese War a section of the big landlords and the big bourgeois, as represented by Wang Ching-wei, has already deserted to the enemy and turned collaborator. Consequently the anti-Japanese people can only regard these big bourgeois, who have betrayed our national interests, as a target in the revolution.

It is clear then that the enemies of the Chinese revolution are quite powerful. Among them is not only powerful imperialism, but are also powerful feudal forces and, at certain times, the reactionaries among the bourgeoisie who, in collusion with the other two, regard the people as their enemy. Thus the view is incorrect that belittles the strength of the enemies of the revolutionary Chinese people.

Confronted with such enemies, the Chinese revolution becomes protracted and ruthless in nature. Since the enemies are extremely powerful, the revolutionary forces, unless allowed a long period of time, cannot be massed and steeled into a power that will finally crush them. Since the enemy's suppression of the Chinese revolution is exceedingly ruthless, the revolutionary forces cannot hold their own positions and take over the enemy's unless they steel themselves and develop their tenacity. The view that the forces of the Chinese revolution can be built up in a twinkling and the Chinese revolutionary struggle can triumph overnight is therefore incorrect.

Confronted with such enemies, the Chinese revolution must, in so far as its principal means or the principal form is concerned, be an armed rather than a peaceful one. This is because our enemy makes it impossible for the Chinese people—a people deprived of all political freedoms and rights—to take any peaceful political action. Stalin said, "In China, armed revolution is fighting against armed counter-revolution. This is one of the peculiarities and one of the advantages of the Chinese revolution."[1] This is a perfectly correct formulation. The view which belittles armed struggle, revolutionary war, guerrilla war and army work is therefore incorrect.

Confronted with such enemies, the Chinese revolution has also to tackle the question of revolutionary base areas. Since powerful imperialism, and its allies, the reactionary forces in China, have occupied China's key cities for a long time, if the revolutionary forces do not wish to compromise with them but want to carry on the struggle staunchly, and if they intend to accumulate strength and steel themselves and avoid decisive battles with their powerful enemy before they have mustered enough strength, then they must build the backward villages into advanced, consolidated base areas, into great military, political, economic, and cultural revolutionary bastions, so that they can fight the fierce enemy who utilises the cities to attack the rural districts and, through a protracted struggle, gradually win an over-all victory for the revolution. In these circumstances, owing to the unevenness in China's economic development (not a unified capitalist economy), to the immensity of China's territory (which gives the revolutionary forces sufficient room to manoeuvre in), to the disunity inside China's counter-revolutionary camp which is fraught with contradictions, and to the fact that the struggle of the peasants, the main force in the Chinese revolution, is led by the party of the proletariat—the Communist Party, a situation arises in which, on the one hand, the Chinese revolution can triumph first in the rural districts and, on the other hand, a state of unevenness is created in the revolution and the task of winning complete victory in the revolution becomes a protracted and arduous one. It is thus clear that the protracted revolutionary struggle conducted in such revolutionary base areas is chiefly a

[1] J. V. Stalin, "On the Perspectives of the Revolution in China," as translated in *Political Affairs* (New York: December 1950), p. 29.

peasant guerrilla war led by the Chinese Communist Party. To neglect building up revolutionary base areas in the rural districts, to neglect performing arduous work among the peasants, and to neglect guerrilla war are therefore all incorrect views.

However, to emphasise armed struggle does not mean giving up other forms of struggle; on the contrary, armed struggle will not succeed unless coordinated with other forms of struggle. And to emphasise the work in rural base areas does not mean giving up our work in the cities and in the vast rural districts under the enemy's rule; on the contrary, without the work in the cities and in other rural districts, the rural base areas will be isolated and the revolution will suffer defeat. Moreover, the capture of the cities now serving as the enemy's main bases is the final objective of the revolution, an objective which cannot be achieved without adequate work in the cities.

This shows clearly that it is impossible for the revolution to triumph in both the cities and the countryside unless the enemy's principal instrument for fighting the people—his armed forces—is destroyed. Thus besides annihilating enemy troops in war, it is important to work for their disintegration.

This shows clearly that, in the Communist Party's propaganda and organisational work in the cities and the countryside long occupied by the enemy and dominated by the forces of reaction and darkness, we must adopt, instead of an impetuous and adventurist line, a line of hiding the crack forces, accumulating strength and biding our time. In leading the people's struggle against the enemy we must adopt the tactics of advancing slowly but surely, by making use of all forms of open and legal activities permitted by laws and decrees and social customs and basing ourselves on the principles of justifiability, expediency and restraint; vociferous cries and rash actions can never lead to success.

Section 3. The Tasks of the Chinese Revolution

Imperialism and the feudal landlord class being the chief enemies of the Chinese revolution at the present stage, what are the present tasks of the revolution?

Unquestionably, the major tasks are to strike at these two enemies, to carry out a national revolution to overthrow imperialist oppression from the outside and a democratic revolution to overthrow the oppression of the feudal landlords at home, and of the two tasks the primary one is the national revolution for the overthrow of imperialism.

The two major tasks of the Chinese revolution are interrelated. Unless the rule of imperialism is overthrown, the rule of the feudal landlord class cannot be ended, because imperialism is the principal support of the feudal landlord class. On the other hand, as the feudal landlord class forms the principal social basis for the rule of imperialism over China and the peasantry is the main force in the Chinese revolution, no powerful contingents of the Chinese revolution can be formed to overthrow the imperialist rule unless help is given to the peasantry in overthrowing the feudal landlord class. Therefore the two basic tasks, the national revolution and the democratic revolution, are at once distinguished from and related to each other.

As the main task of China's national revolution today is to oppose Japanese imperialism that has invaded her territory, and the task of her democratic revolution must be fulfilled in order to win the war, the two revolutionary tasks are already linked with each other. To regard the national revolution and the democratic revolution as two distinctly different stages is an incorrect view.

Section 4. The Motive Forces of the Chinese Revolution

According to the foregoing analysis and definition of the character of Chinese society and of the targets and tasks of the Chinese revolution at the present stage, what are the motive forces of the Chinese revolution?

Since Chinese society is a colonial, semi-colonial and semi-feudal society, since the targets against which the Chinese revolution is directed are principally foreign imperialist rule in China and domestic feudalism and since the task of the Chinese revolution is to overthrow the two oppressors, then among the classes and strata in Chinese society, which are the forces capable of fighting imperialism and feudalism? This is a question of the motive forces of the Chinese revolution at the present stage. The problem of the basic tactics of the Chinese revolution can be correctly solved only through a clear understanding of this question.

What classes are there in present-day Chinese society? There are the landlord class and the bourgeoisie; the landlord class and the upper strata of the bourgeoisie are the ruling classes in Chinese society. There are also the proletariat, the peasantry and all types of the petty bourgeoisie other than the peasantry which, over the greatest part of Chinese soil, still remain the subject classes.

The attitudes and positions of all these classes in relation to the Chinese revolution are entirely determined by their socio-economic status. Thus the character of China's socio-economy determines not only the targets and tasks of the revolution but also its motive forces.

We shall now proceed to an analysis of the classes in Chinese society.

1. The Landlord Class

The landlord class forms the principal social basis for imperialist rule over China, the class that uses the feudal system to exploit and oppress the peasantry and obstructs the political, economic and cultural development of Chinese society rather than plays any progressive role.

Therefore the landlords, as a class, are a target and not a motive force of the revolution.

In the Anti-Japanese War a section of the big landlords, following a section of the big bourgeoisie (the capitulators), has surrendered to the Japanese invaders and turned collaborator, while another section, following the other section of the big bourgeoisie (the die-hards), has been very vacillating though it remains yet in the anti-Japanese camp. But as many of the enlightened gentry who are middle and small landlords, i.e., landlords more or less of a capitalist complexion, display some enthusiasm for resistance to Japan, we still have to unite with them for the common fight.

2. The Bourgeoisie

Among the bourgeoisie there is a distinction between the big bourgeoisie of a comprador character and the national bourgeoisie.

The big bourgeoisie of a comprador character is a class that directly serves the capitalists of imperialist countries and is fed by them; countless ties connect it closely with the feudal forces in the countryside. Therefore in the history of the Chinese revolution the big bourgeoisie of a comprador character has never been a motive force, but has always been a target of the Chinese revolution.

However, the different sections of the Chinese big bourgeoisie of a comprador character owe allegiance to different imperialist powers; when the contradictions among these powers grow into sharp antagonisms, and one of these powers becomes the particular object of the revolution, the sections owing allegiance to other imperialist groups may join the current anti-imperialist front to a certain extent and for a certain period of time. But as soon as their masters start to oppose the Chinese revolution, they will follow suit.

In the Anti-Japanese War the pro-Japanese big bourgeois (the capitulators) have either surrendered or are getting ready to do so. The pro-European and pro-American big bourgeois (the die-hards), though remaining in the anti-Japanese camp, are very vacillating, for they are double dealers, anti-Japanese on the one hand and anti-Communist on the other. Our policy towards the big-bourgeois capitulators is to treat them as enemies and resolutely strike them down. As to the die-hards of the big bourgeoisie, we deal with them by a revolutionary twofold policy, that is, on the one hand uniting with them for they are still anti-Japanese and we should still utilise the contradiction between them and Japanese imperialism; and on the other hand waging struggles against them resolutely for they are pursuing a high-handed anti-Communist and anti-popular policy to undermine resistance and unity, and without such struggles resistance and unity will be jeopardised.

The national bourgeoisie is a class with a dual character.

On the one hand, this class is oppressed by imperialism and fettered by feudalism and is consequently in contradiction with both. In this respect it constitutes one of the revolutionary forces. In the history of Chinese revolution it has shown some enthusiasm for fighting imperialism and the government of bureaucrats and warlords.

But on the other hand, it lacks the courage to oppose imperialism and feudalism thoroughly because it is economically and politically flabby and its economic ties with imperialism and feudalism are not yet completely severed. This is most clearly revealed when the people's revolutionary strength grows.

This dual character of the national bourgeoisie determines that at certain periods and to a certain extent this class can take part in the revolution against imperialism and against the government of bureaucrats and warlords and become a revolutionary force. But in other periods there is the danger that it may follow the big comprador bourgeoisie as its accomplice in counter-revolution.

The national bourgeoisie in China consists mainly of the middle bourgeoisie which, though having followed the big landlord class and the big bourgeoisie in opposing the revolution in the period between 1927 and 1931 (before the Incident of September 18), has never really held political power, but has suffered from restrictions imposed by the reactionary policies of the big landlord class and the big bourgeoisie in power. During the War of Resistance to Japan, it distinguishes itself not only from the capitulators of the big landlord class and the big bourgeoisie but also from the big bourgeois die-hards and, up to now, remains a comparatively good ally of ours. Hence it is entirely necessary to adopt a cautious policy towards the national bourgeoisie.

3. Various Types of the Petty Bourgeoisie Other Than the Peasantry

The petty bourgeoisie other than the peasantry consists of the vast numbers of intellectuals, small merchants, handicraftsmen and professionals.

With a status somewhat like that of the middle peasants among the peasantry, all these types of the petty bourgeoisie suffer from the oppression of imperialism, feudalism and the big bourgeoisie, and are driven daily nearer bankruptcy and ruin.

Hence these sections of the petty bourgeoisie form one of the motive forces of the revolution and a reliable ally of the proletariat. They can achieve their liberation only under the leadership of the proletariat.

Now we shall analyse the various types of the petty bourgeoisie other than the peasantry.

First, the intellectuals and student youth. The intellectuals and student youth do not constitute a class or stratum. But judging from their family origin, their living conditions and their political viewpoints, most of the intellectuals and student youth in present-day China may be classed with the petty bourgeoisie. For decades in the past a large group of intellectuals and student youth has emerged in China. Apart from a section of the intellectuals who are closely connected with imperialism and the big bourgeoisie and serve them in opposing the people, the intellectuals and student youth are generally oppressed by imperialism, feudalism, and the big bourgeoisie, and are in danger of losing their jobs or the opportunity to go to school. Hence they are quite revolutionary. They are more or less equipped with bourgeois scientific knowledge, have a keen political sense, and often serve as the spearhead or as a bridge in the present stage of the Chinese revolution. The campaign to send students to study abroad before the Revolution of 1911, the May 4 Movement of 1919, the May 30 Movement of 1925, and the December 9 Movement of 1935 are striking proofs of this. In particular, the great masses of the more or less impoverished intellectuals can join and support the revolution together with the workers and peasants. It was also among the intellectuals and the student youth that Marxist–Leninist ideology was first widely disseminated and accepted in China. No success can be achieved in organising the revolutionary forces and carrying on revolutionary work without the participation of the revolutionary intellectuals. But before the intellectuals identify themselves with the cause of the people's revolutionary struggles or resolve to serve the interests of the masses and become one with them, they often tend towards subjectivism and individualism, illusory in views and irresolute in action. Hence though the great masses of China's revolutionary intellectuals can serve as a spearhead or a bridge, not all of them can remain staunch revolutionaries. A section of the intellectuals often leaves the revolutionary ranks at critical moments and becomes passive, while a few may even become enemies of the revolution. The intellectuals can overcome these defects only after they have gone through a long period of mass struggle.

Second, the small merchants. Generally they run small stores and hire only a few or no assistants. They are threatened with bankruptcy because of the exploitation by imperialism, the big bourgeoisie and the usurers.

Third, the handicraftsmen. They constitute a great mass of people. They have their own means of production, and hire no workers or only have one or two apprentices or helpers. Their position resembles that of the middle peasants.

Fourth, the professionals. They are men of various professions, such as the doctors. They do not or only slightly exploit other people. Their position resembles that of the handicraftsman.

The above-mentioned sections of the petty bourgeoisie form a great multitude and must be won over and attended to because they generally can join and support the revolution and are its good allies. The drawback is that some of them are easily influenced by the bourgeoisie; hence it is necessary to pay attention to carrying out revolutionary propaganda and organisational work among them.

4. The Peasantry

The peasantry constitutes approximately 80 per cent of the nation's total population and is the mainstay of China's present-day national economy.

A process of radical differentiation is taking place inside the peasantry.

First, the rich peasants. The rich peasants constitute about 5 per cent of the rural population (about 10 per cent together with the landlords), and are called the rural bourgeoisie. Most of the rich peasants in China let a part of their land, practise usury, ruthlessly exploit the farm labourers and are semi-feudal in character. But generally the rich peasants engage in labour themselves, and in this sense they are part of the peasantry. Their productive activities will remain useful for some time to come. And generally they might contribute some effort to the anti-imperialist struggles of the peasant masses and might stay neutral in the agrarian revolutionary struggles against the landlords. Therefore we should neither consider them as of the same class as the landlords nor adopt prematurely a policy of liquidating them.

Second, the middle peasants. The middle peasants constitute about 20 per cent of China's rural population. Economically self-supporting (possibly having a surplus when the crops are good and occasionally hiring a limited amount of labour or lending a little money at interest), they generally do not exploit others but suffer from exploitation by imperialism, the landlord class and the bourgeoisie. The middle peasants have no political rights. A section of the middle peasants does not have enough land, and only the section of well-to-do middle peasants has a little surplus land. The middle peasants not only can join the anti-imperialist revolution and the agrarian revolution, but also accept socialism. Therefore the whole middle peasantry can become a reliable ally of the proletariat and is among the important motive forces of the revolution. The attitude of the middle peasants towards the revolution—whether they are for or against it—is a factor determining its victory or defeat, and this is especially true when the middle peasants become the majority in the countryside after the agrarian revolution.

Third, the poor peasants. The poor peasants in China, together with the farm labourers, constitute about 70 per cent of the rural population. The poor peasants are the broad peasant masses with no land or insufficient land—the semi-proletariat in the countryside, the biggest motive force of the Chinese revolution, and by nature the most reliable ally of the proletariat and the main contingent of China's revolutionary forces. The poor peasants and the middle peasants can achieve their liberation only under the leadership of the proletariat, and only when the proletariat has concluded a firm alliance with the poor peasants and middle peasants can it lead the revolution to victory, a thing otherwise impossible. The term "peasantry" refers mainly to the poor and middle peasants.

5. *The Proletariat*

Among the Chinese proletariat, the modern industrial workers number about 2,500,000 to 3,000,000; the hired labourers in small-scale industries and handicrafts in the city and the shop assistants total about 12,000,000; and the rural proletariat (farm labourers) and other urban and rural proletarians also constitute a great number.

In addition to the basic good qualities of the proletariat in general—that it is associated with the most advanced form of economy, that it has a strong sense of organisation and discipline and that it owns no private means of production—the Chinese proletariat has many outstanding qualities.

What are the outstanding qualities of the Chinese proletariat?

First, the Chinese proletariat is subjected to threefold oppression (oppression by imperialism, by the bourgeoisie and by the feudal forces) with a severity and ruthlessness seldom found in other nations of the world, and consequently it is more resolute and more thoroughgoing in the revolutionary struggle than any other class. Since there is no such economic basis for social reformism in colonial and semi-colonial China as in Europe, the proletariat, with the exception of a few scabs, is most revolutionary as a whole.

Secondly, ever since its appearance on the revolutionary scene, the Chinese proletariat has been under the leadership of its own revolutionary political party—the Chinese Communist Party—and has become the most politically conscious class in Chinese society.

Thirdly, because the Chinese proletariat is largely made up of bankrupt peasants, it has natural ties with the vast peasantry, which facilitate their close alliance.

Therefore, in spite of certain unavoidable weaknesses—for example, its small size (as compared with the peasantry), its young age (as compared with the proletariat in capitalist countries), and its low cultural level (as compared with the bourgeoisie), the Chinese proletariat has nonetheless become the basic motive force of the Chinese revolution. The Chinese revolution certainly will not succeed without the leadership of the proletariat. To take an earlier example, the Revolution of 1911 was abortive because the proletariat did not consciously participate in it and because there was yet no Communist Party. More recently, the revolution of 1924–27 achieved great success for a time because of the conscious participation and leadership of the proletariat and the existence of the Communist Party, but later on it suffered defeat because the big bourgeoisie betrayed its alliance with the proletariat and abandoned the common revolutionary programme, and also because the Chinese proletariat and its political party still lacked ample revolutionary experience. Subsequently, because of the leadership of the proletariat and the Chinese Communist Party in the Anti-Japanese National United Front, the whole nation has been united and the great Anti-Japanese War has been launched and resolutely carried on.

The Chinese proletariat ought to understand that, although it is the class with the highest political consciousness and sense of organisation, it cannot win victory by virtue of its own strength alone. In order to win victory it must unite, under various conditions, with all possible revolutionary classes and strata and organise a revolutionary united front. Of all the classes in Chinese society, the peasantry is the firm ally of the working class, the urban petty bourgeoisie is a reliable ally and the national bourgeoisie is an ally in certain periods and to a certain extent; this is one of the fundamental laws proved by the history of modern Chinese revolution.

6. The Vagrants

China's colonial and semi-colonial status has created a multitude of unemployed people both in the countryside and in the cities. Denied of any legitimate way of making a living, many of them are forced to resort to illegitimate means, hence the robbers, gangsters, beggars, prostitutes and all those who live upon superstitious practices. This social stratum is vacillating in character: while one section is liable to be bought over by the reactionary forces, another section can join the revolution. Lacking the constructive quality and given more to destruction than to construction, these people, after joining the revolution, become the source of the ideology of the roving insurgents and of anarchism among the ranks of the revolution. Therefore we should know how to remould them and forestall their destructiveness.

The above is our analysis of the motive forces of the Chinese revolution.

Section 5. The Character of the Chinese Revolution

Now we have come to understand the character of Chinese society, i.e., the special conditions in China, which form the most fundamental premise for solving all China's revolutionary problems. We have also come to know the targets of the Chinese revolution, its tasks and its motive forces, which are the basic issues at the present stage of the Chinese revolution, arising from the special character of Chinese society and the special conditions in China. Having come to understand all these, we can now understand another basic issue of the Chinese revolution at the present stage, i.e., the character of the Chinese revolution.

What, after all, is the character of the Chinese revolution at the present stage? Is it a bourgeois-democratic or a proletarian-socialist revolution? Obviously, not the latter but the former.

It is now clear that Chinese society is still a colonial, semi-colonial, and semi-feudal society, that the principal enemies of the Chinese revolution are still imperialism and the feudal forces, that the task of the Chinese revolution consists in a national revolution and a democratic revolution for overthrowing these two principal enemies, and furthermore that the bourgeoisie sometimes also takes part in this revolution and, even if the big bourgeoisie betrays the revolution and becomes its enemy, the spearhead of the revolution will still be directed at imperialism and feudalism rather than at capitalism and capitalist private property in general. That being so, the character of the Chinese revolution at the present stage is not proletarian-socialist but bourgeois-democratic.

However, the bourgeois-democratic revolution in present-day China is no longer one of the general, old type, which is now obsolete, but one of the special, new type. This kind of revolution is developing in China as well as in all colonial and semi-colonial countries, and we call it the new-democratic revolution. This new-democratic revolution is part of the world proletarian-socialist revolution, which resolutely opposes imperialism, i.e., international capitalism. Politically, it means the joint dictatorship of several revolutionary classes over the imperialists, collaborators and reactionaries, and opposition to the transformation of Chinese society into a society under bourgeois dictatorship. Economically, it means nationalisation of all big capital and big enterprises of the imperialists, collaborators and reactionaries, distribution of the land of the landlords among the peasants, and at the same time general preservation of private capitalist enterprises without the elimination of rich-peasant economy. While clearing the way for capitalism, this democratic revolution of a new type creates the pre-condition for socialism. The present stage of the Chinese revolution is a transitional stage between putting an end to the colonial, semi-colonial, and semi-feudal society and establishing a socialist society—a process of new-democratic revolution. This process, begun only after the First World War and the Russian October Revolution, started in China with the May 4 Movement of 1919. A new-democratic revolution is a revolution of the broad masses of the people led by the proletariat and directed against imperialism and feudalism. China must go through this revolution before she can advance to a socialist society; otherwise she cannot advance to socialism.

This kind of new-democratic revolution differs greatly from the democratic revolutions in the history of European and American countries in that it results not in the dictatorship of the bourgeoisie but in the dictatorship of the united front of all revolutionary classes under the leadership of the proletariat. During the Anti-Japanese War, the anti-Japanese democratic political power built up in the anti-Japanese base areas under the leadership of the Chinese Communist Party is a political power of the Anti-Japanese National United Front, which is neither a one-class dictatorship of the bourgeoisie nor a one-class dictatorship of the proletariat, but a joint dictatorship of several revolutionary classes under the leadership of the proletariat. All those who stand for resistance to Japan and for democracy are qualified to share this political power, regardless of their party affiliations.

This kind of new-democratic revolution differs also from a socialist revolution in that it aims only at overthrowing the rule of the imperialists, collaborators and reactionaries in China, but not at injuring any capitalist sections which can still take part in the anti-imperialist, anti-feudal struggles.

This kind of new-democratic revolution is basically in line with the revolution of the Three People's Principles as advocated by Sun Yat-sen in 1924. In the Manifesto of the First National Congress of the Kuomintang issued in that year, Sun Yat-sen stated:

> The so-called democratic system in modern nations is usually monopolised by the bourgeoisie and has simply become an instrument for oppressing the common people. As to the Principle of Democracy of the Kuomintang, it stands for something to be shared by all the common people and not to be monopolised by a few.

Further:

> Enterprises, whether Chinese-owned or foreign-owned, which are monopolistic in character or which are on too large a scale for private management, such as banks, railways and air lines, shall be operated by the state, so that private capital cannot dominate the livelihood of the people: This is the main principle of the control of capital.

And again in his Testament, Sun Yat-sen pointed out the fundamental principle for domestic and foreign policies:

> . . . We must arouse the masses of the people and unite in a common fight with those nations of the world who treat us on the basis of equality. . . .

The Three People's Principles of the old democracy adapted to old circumstances at home and abroad were thus remoulded into the Three People's Principles of the New Democracy adapted to new circumstances at home and abroad. The Chinese Communist Party was referring to the Three People's Principles of the latter kind and not to anything else when it announced in its Manifesto of September 22, 1937, that "The Three People's Principles being what China needs today, our Party pledges itself to fight for their complete realisation." It is the Three People's Principles of this kind that underlie Sun Yat-sen's three cardinal policies—alliance with Russia, co-operation with the Communists and assistance to the peasants and workers. Under the new international and domestic conditions, any kind of Three People's Principles which departs from the three cardinal policies cannot be the revolutionary Three People's Principles. (That communism and the Three People's Principles agree only in the basic political programmes for the democratic revolution and differ in all other respects, is a question that will not be treated here.)

Thus whether in the alignment for struggle (the united front) or in the composition of the state, the position of the proletariat, peasantry and the other sections of the petty bourgeoisie should not be ignored in China's bourgeois-democratic revolution. Whoever tries to exclude China's proletariat, peasantry, and other sections of the petty bourgeoisie from the picture certainly cannot shape China's destiny or solve any of her problems. The democratic republic which the Chinese revolution is striving to create at the present stage must be one in which the workers, peasants, and other sections of the petty bourgeoisie occupy definite places and play definite roles. In other words, it is to be a democratic republic with a revolutionary alliance of the workers, the peasants, the urban petty bourgeoisie, and all other anti-imperialist and anti-feudal people. Only under the leadership of the proletariat can such a republic be completely realised.

Section 6. The Perspectives of the Chinese Revolution

Now that the basic problems as to the character of Chinese society and the targets, tasks, motive forces and character of the Chinese revolution at the present stage have been clarified, it is easy to understand the problem of the perspectives of the Chinese revolution, the problem of the relation between China's bourgeois-democratic and proletarian-socialist revolutions or between the present and future stages of the Chinese revolution.

Since China's bourgeois-democratic revolution at the present stage is not a bourgeois-democratic revolution of the general, old type, but a democratic revolution of a special, new type, a new-democratic revolution, and furthermore the Chinese revolution is now taking place in the new international setting of the 1930s and 1940s, characterised by the rise of socialism and the decline of capitalism, and in the period of the Second World War and of revolutions, there can be no doubt whatever that the ultimate perspective of the Chinese revolution is not capitalism but socialism and communism.

Since the Chinese revolution at the present stage aims at changing the existing colonial, semi-colonial, and semi-feudal status of society, and is a struggle to complete a new-democratic revolution, it is conceivable and not surprising that, after the victory of the revolution, capitalist economy will develop to a certain extent in Chinese society because the obstacles to the development of capitalism will have been swept away. It is an inevitable result of the victory of the democratic revolution in the economically backward China that capitalism will develop to a certain degree. But this will be only the result of the Chinese revolution in one aspect, not its whole outcome. The whole outcome of the Chinese revolution will be the development of the capitalist factors on the one hand, and of the socialist factors on the other. What are the socialist factors? They are the growing political weight of the proletariat and the Communist Party in the whole country; the leadership of the proletariat and the Communist Party that has been or may be recognised by the peasantry, the intelligentsia, and the urban petty bourgeoisie; and the state enterprises of the people's republic and the co-operatives of the labouring people. All these are the socialist factors. Together with the favourable international situation, they are bound to make it highly possible that the Chinese bourgeois–democratic revolution will finally steer away from a capitalist future and head towards the realisation of socialism.

Section 7. The Twofold Task of the Chinese Revolution and the Chinese Communist Party

Recapitulating the points in the foregoing sections of this chapter, we can see that the Chinese revolution taken as a whole involves a twofold task. That is to say, it embraces a revolution that is bourgeois–democratic in character (a new-democratic revolution) and a revolution that is proletarian–socialist in character—it embraces the twofold task of the revolution at both the present and the future stages. The leadership in this twofold revolutionary task rests on the shoulders of the party of the Chinese proletariat, the Chinese Communist Party, for without its leadership no revolution can succeed.

To complete China's bourgeois–democratic revolution (the new-democratic revolution) and to prepare to transform it into a socialist revolution when all the necessary conditions are present: that is the sum total of the great glorious revolutionary task for the Communist Party of China. All members of the Party should strive for its accomplishment and should never give up half way. Some immature Communists think that we have only the task of democratic revolution at the present stage, but not that of the socialist revolution at the future stage; or that the present revolution or the agrarian revolution is in fact the socialist revolution. It must be emphatically pointed out that both views are erroneous. Every Communist must know that the whole Chinese revolutionary movement led by the Chinese Communist Party is a complete revolutionary movement embracing the two revolutionary stages, democratic and socialist, which are two revolutionary processes differing in character, and that the socialist stage can be reached only after the democratic stage is completed. The democratic revolution is the necessary preparation for the socialist revolution, and the socialist revolution is the inevitable trend of the democratic revolution. And the ultimate aim of all Communists is to strive for the final building of socialist society and Communist society. We can give correct leadership to the Chinese revolution only on the basis of a clear understanding of both the differences between the democratic and socialist revolutions and their interconnections.

Except the Communist Party, none of the political parties, bourgeois or petty-bourgeois, is equal to the task of leading China's two great revolutions, democratic and socialist, to their complete realisation. And the Chinese Communist Party, from the very day of its birth, has placed this twofold task upon its own shoulders and has already strenuously fought for it for a full eighteen years.

A task like this is at once most glorious and most arduous. It cannot be accomplished without a bolshevised Chinese Communist Party of a nation-wide scope and a broad mass character, fully consolidated ideologically, politically and organisationally. It is therefore the duty of every Communist to take an active part in building up such a Communist Party.

1939

8 Guerrilla Warfare: A Method

ERNESTO "CHE" GUEVARA

Guerrilla warfare has been used innumerable times in history under different conditions and to achieve different ends. Lately it has been used in various people's wars of liberation where the vanguard of the people chose the path of armed irregular struggle against enemies of greater military strength. Asia, Africa, and America have been the scene of these actions when power was sought in the struggle against feudal, neocolonial or colonial exploitation. In Europe it was used as a supplement to the regular armies themselves or allies.

In America recourse has been made to guerrilla warfare on different occasions. As a precedent closer to home, the experience of Augusto Cesar Sandino, fighting against the Yankee expeditionary forces on the Segovia in Nicaragua can be noted; and recently the revolutionary war in Cuba. Since then, the problems of guerrilla war in America have arisen in theoretical discussions of the progressive parties of the continent, and the possibility of appropriateness of its utilization is the subject of heated controversies.

These notes will try to express our ideas about guerrilla warfare and what its correct use would be.

SOURCE: from Ernesto "Che" Guevara, "Guerrilla Warfare: A Method," in *Cuba Socialista,* September 1963. Translated by Betty M. Shaw.

Above all, it must be made clear that this form of struggle is a method—a means to an end. That end, essential and inescapable for all revolutionaries, is the winning of political power. Therefore, in analyzing specific situations in different countries in America, the concept of guerrilla warfare must be reduced to the simple category of a method of fighting to gain that end.

Almost immediately the question arises: Is the method of guerrilla warfare the only formula for the taking of power throughout America? Or will it be, in any case, the predominant form? Or simply, will it be one formula among many used in the struggle? And in the final analysis it may be asked: Will the Cuban example be applicable to other continental realities? For argument's sake those who wish to use guerrilla warfare are often criticized for forgetting the struggle of the masses, almost as if they were opposing methods. We reject this implication; guerrilla warfare is a war of the people, a mass struggle. To try to realize this type of warfare without the support of the population is a prelude to inevitable disaster. The guerrilla is the fighting vanguard of the people stationed in a specific place in some given territory, armed and prepared to carry out a series of belligerent acts leading to the only possible strategic end—the taking of power. It is supported by the rural peasant masses and workers of the zone and of the whole territory in which they operate. Without those preconditions guerrilla warfare cannot be permitted.

> In our American situation we consider three fundamental contributions the Cuban Revolution made to the mechanics of the revolutionary movement. They are: First, popular forces can win a war against the army. Second, one does not always have to wait for all the conditions of revolution to exist—the insurrection itself can create them. Third, in the underdeveloped part of America the territory for armed insurrection should be fundamentally the countryside (*Guerrilla Warfare*).

Such are the contributions to the development of the revolutionary struggle in America and they can be applied to any of the countries of our continent where guerrilla warfare may be developed.

The *Second Declaration of Havana* points out:

> In our countries are united the circumstances of underdeveloped industry and an agrarian regime with a feudal character. For that reason no matter how hard the conditions of the urban worker's life are, the rural population lives in even more horrible conditions of oppression and exploitation; but it is also, with some exceptions, the absolute majority sector, sometimes more than seventy percent of the Latin American populations.
>
> Discounting the landlords that many times live in the cities, the rest of that large free mass sustain themselves working as peons on the haciendas for miserable salaries, or labor on the land under conditions of exploitation which are indistinguishable from those of the Middle Ages. These circumstances are the

ones that make the rural poor of Latin America constitute a tremendous potential revolutionary force.

The armies, structured and equipped for conventional war, are the force which sustains the power of the exploiting classes, and when they have to confront the irregular warfare of the rural peasants on their own ground they are absolutely impotent, losing ten men for every revolutionary that falls. Demoralization spreads rapidly when they have to confront an invisible and invincible enemy that does not offer them an occasion to display their academic tactics and their martial fanfares of which they boast so much to repress the workers and students in the city.

The initial struggle of the small nucleus of combatants is constantly nurtured by new forces, the mass movement begins to break loose, the old order little by little cracks into a thousand pieces and that is the moment when the working class and the urban masses decide the battle.

What is it that from the very beginning of the fight makes that first nucleus invincible, regardless of the number, strength or resources of their enemies? The support of the people; and they can count on mass support to an ever increasing degree.

But the peasantry is a class that because of the lack of culture in which it has been maintained and the isolation in which it lives needs revolutionary direction and the political leadership of the working class and revolutionary intellectuals, without which it would not be able by itself to launch the fight and capture the victory.

Under the present historical conditions of Latin America, the national bourgeoisie cannot lead the antifeudal antiimperialist fight. Experience demonstrates that in our nations this class—even though its interests are contradictory to those of the Yankee imperialists—has been incapable of confronting them, paralyzed by the fear of social revolution and by the clamor of the exploited masses.

Supplementing the significance of these affirmations that constitute the crux of the revolutionary declaration of America, the *Second Declaration of Havana* in other paragraphs expresses the following:

The subjective conditions of each country, that is, awareness, organization and leadership, can accelerate or retard the revolution according to the state of their development, but sooner or later in each historic epoch, when the objective conditions mature, the consciousness is acquired, the organization is attained, the leadership comes forth and the revolution is produced.

Whether the struggle takes place peacefully or comes to the world after painful labor, does not depend on the revolutionaries; it depends on the reactionary forces of the old society; it depends on their resistance against allowing the new society to be born, a society engendered by the contradictions of the old society. The revolution is, in history, as the doctor that assists in the birth of a new life: The instruments of force are not used unless necessary, but are used without hesitation each time it is necessary in order to help the delivery. It is a birth that brings the enslaved and exploited masses hope of a better life.

In many Latin American countries revolution is today inevitable. This has not been voluntarily determined by anybody. It has been determined by the awful conditions in which the American man lives, the development of a revolutionary

> consciousness in the masses, the world crisis of imperialism and the universal movement of struggle of the world's subjugated peoples.

We will start from this basis to analyze the whole question of guerrilla warfare in America.

We have established that it is a method of struggle to obtain an end. Our first interest is to analyze the end and see if the conquest of power can be attained in a manner other than armed struggle here in America.

The peaceful struggle can be carried out by means of mass movements and can—in special situations of crisis—compel governments to yield so that eventually the popular forces take power and establish a dictatorship of the proletariat. This is theoretically correct. On analyzing the past in the American panorama we must arrive at the following conclusion: Generally speaking, on this continent there exists the objective conditions that impel the masses to violent action against the bourgeoisie and landlord governments; in many countries a power crisis exists and some subjective conditions also. Of course, in all the countries where all the given conditions exist it would be criminal not to act in order to seize power. In those others in which this has not occurred, it is right that distinct alternatives appear and that from the theoretical discussion a decision applicable to each country arise. The only thing that history does not permit is that the analysts and executors of the politics of the proletariat blunder. Nobody can seek to be part of the vanguard as he would seek an official diploma from the university. To be part of the vanguard is to be at the front of the working class in the fight for seizing power, to know how to guide it to success, including how to lead it through short cuts. That is the mission of our revolutionary party and the analysis ought to be profound and exhaustive in order that there be no mistakes.

Day by day one sees in America a state of unstable equilibrium between the oligarchic dictatorship and popular pressure. We call it oligarchy, trying to define the reactionary alliance between the bourgeoisie of each country and its class of landowners, with a greater or lesser preponderance of feudal structures. These dictatorships continue within certain frameworks of legality which they set up for themselves to facilitate their work during the whole unrestricted period of class domination; but we are passing through a period in which popular pressures are very strong; they are knocking at the doors of bourgeois legality which its own authors must violate in order to hold back the impetus of the masses. The shameless violations of all preestablished legislation—or of legislation established a posteriori in order to legitimize their deeds—heighten the tension of the popular forces. Therefore the oligarchic dictatorship tries to use the old legal ordinances in order to change the constitution and further suffocate the proletariat without a head-on collision. In spite of that, here is where the contradiction is produced: The people no longer support the old and even less the new coercive methods established by the dictatorship and try to break them. We must never forget the authoritarian and restrictive class character of the bourgeois state. Lenin referred to it thus:

> The state is the product and manifestation of the irreconcilable character of class contradictions. The state appears in the place and at the moment and to the degree that class contradictions cannot objectively be reconciled. And conversely, the existence of the state demonstrates that class contradictions are irreconcilable (*The State and Revolution*).

In other words, we ought not to allow the word democracy, used in an apologetic form to represent the dictatorship of the exploiting classes, to lose its deeper meaning and acquire the meaning of giving more or less optimal liberties to citizens. To struggle only for the restoration of certain bourgeois legality without raising, on the other hand, the problem of revolutionary power is to struggle to return to a certain dictatorial order established by the dominant social classes; it is, in any case, to struggle only for the establishment of a lighter ball at the end of the convict's chains.

Under these conditions of conflict the oligarchy breaks its own contracts, its own appearance of "democracy" and attacks the people, although it always tries to use the superstructure it has formed for oppression. At that moment, the question then arises: What is to be done? We answer: Violence is not the patrimony of the exploiters; the exploited can use it too, and moreover they ought to use it at this time. Marti said, "He who promotes war in a country where it can be avoided is a criminal and so is he who fails to promote an inevitable war."

Lenin, on the other hand said:

> Social democracy has never viewed, nor does it now view war from a sentimental perspective. It condemns absolutely war as a savage recourse for deciding differences among men, but it knows that wars are inevitable while society is divided into classes, while exploitation of man by man exists. And to do away with that exploitation we cannot disregard war which is always and everywhere begun by the very classes that exploit, dominate and oppress.

He said this in 1905. Later, in "The War Program of the Proletarian Revolution," in a profound analysis of the nature of class struggle, he affirmed:

> Whoever admits class struggle cannot help but admit civil wars which in any society of classes represents, the continuation, development and outbreak—natural and in certain circumstances inevitable—of the class struggle. All great revolutions confirm it. To deny civil wars or forget them would be to fall into extreme opportunism and deny the socialist revolution.

That is to say, we should not fear violence, the midwife of new societies; only that violence should be unleashed precisely at the moment when the leaders of the people have encountered the most favorable circumstances.

What will these be? Subjectively, they depend on two factors that complement each other and that in turn deepen in the course of the struggle: The consciousness of the necessity for change and the certainty of the possibility of this revolutionary change. These objective conditions—that are greatly favorable in almost all (Latin) America for the development of our struggle—coupled with a firm will to obtain it and a new balance of forces in the world, determine the method of action.

However far away the socialist countries may be, their favorable influence will make itself felt in the popular struggle, and their enlightening example will give them more force. Fidel Castro said last July 26 [1963]:

> Above all, it is the duty of the revolutionary in this instance to know how to recognize and how to take advantage of the changes in the correlation of forces that have taken place in the world, and to understand that these changes facilitate the people's struggle. It is the duty of revolutionaries of the Latin American revolution not to wait for the change in the balance of forces to produce a miracle of social revolutions in Latin America, but to take full advantage of everything the change in the balance of forces presents to the revolutionary movement—and to make the revolution!

There are those who say: "We admit revolutionary war is the proper method in certain specific cases for the seizing of political power. Where do we find the great leaders, the Fidel Castros who will bring us to triumph? The military and political leaders that direct the insurrections in America, united if it were possible in a single person, will learn the art of war in the practice of war itself. There is no office or profession that can be learned exclusively in textbooks. In this case struggle is the great teacher."

During the development of the armed struggle there are two moments of extreme danger for the future of the revolution. The first of these is in the stage of preparation, and the way with which it is dealt gives the measure of determination for struggle and clarity of purpose of the popular forces. When the bourgeois state advances against the positions of the people, obviously there must be produced a defensive process against the enemy who attacks at this moment of superiority. If the minimum objective and subjective conditions have already developed, the defense ought to be armed, but in such a way that the popular forces are not converted into mere recipients of the blows of the enemy; nor should the stage for armed defense simply be a last refuge for the pursued. The guerrilla, the defensive movement of the people at a given moment, has within itself and should constantly develop the ability to attack the enemy. This capacity is what, in time, is going to determine its nature as a catalyst of the popular forces. That is to say, guerrilla activity is not passively self-defensive; it is defense with attack and, from the moment in which it is recognized as such, it has as its final goal the conquest of political power.

This moment is important. In the social process the difference between violence and nonviolence cannot be measured by the number of shots exchanged; it depends on the concrete and fluctuating situations. And it is necessary to be able to see the instant in which the popular forces, conscious of their relative weakness, but at the same time, of their strategic strength, must force the enemy to take the necessary steps so that the situation does not worsen. The balance between the dictatorial oligarchy and popular pressure must be upset. The dictatorship tries constantly to operate without the apparent use of force. Forcing the dictatorship to appear undisguised, that is, in its true aspect as a violent dictatorship of the reactionary classes, will contribute to its unmasking, and that will intensify the fighting to such an extent that it will not be able to turn back.

The firm beginning of long-range armed action depends on how the people's forces fulfill their function, which is the task of forcing the dictatorship to define itself—to draw back or unleash the struggle.

Escape from the other dangerous moment depends on the power of growing development of the people's army. Marx always maintained that once the revolutionary process had begun, the proletariat had to strike and strike unceasingly. Revolution that does not constantly become more profound is a revolution that regresses. Tired combatants begin to lose faith and then some of the maneuvers to which the bourgeoisie have so accustomed us may appear. These can be elections with the transfer of power to another man with a more honeyed voice and a more angelic face than the current dictator, or a coup by the reactionaries, generally led by the army and directly or indirectly supported by the progressive forces. There are others as well, but it is not our intention to analyze such tactical stratagems.

Principally we call attention to the maneuver of the military coup mentioned above. What can militarists contribute to the true democracy? What loyalty can be asked of them if they are merely the instrument of domination of the reactionary classes and the imperialist monopolies and, as a caste whose worth depends upon the arms it possesses, aspire only to maintain their privileges?

When in difficult situations for the oppressors, the military conspire and overthrow a dictator, who in fact is finished, it can be taken for granted that they do it because they are unable to preserve their class prerogatives without extreme violence, a procedure which, in general, does not now suit the interests of the oligarchs.

This affirmation does not in any manner mean the rejection of the use of the military as individual fighters, separated from the social milieu in which they have acted and against which they have, in fact, rebelled. And they should be made use of within the framework of the revolutionary line they adopt as fighters and not as representatives of a caste.

In times past, in the preface to the third edition of *The Civil War in France,* Engels said:

> The workers, after each revolution, were armed. For that reason, the disarmament of the workers was the first order of the bourgeois that headed the state. Hence, after each revolution gained by the workers, a new struggle arose that culminated with their overthrow. (Quoted in Lenin, *The State and Revolution.*)

This play of continual struggles in which a formal change of some kind is brought about only to be strategically withdrawn has been repeated for decades in the capitalist world. But continuous deception of the proletariat in this respect has been going on periodically for more than a century.

There is also a danger that at certain times, moved by the desire to maintain the most favorable conditions for revolutionary action by using certain aspects of bourgeois legality, the leaders of the progressive parties confuse terms, a thing very common in the course of action, and forget the final strategic objective, the taking of power.

These two difficult moments of the revolution that we have briefly analyzed are obviated when the leading Marxist–Leninist parties are able to see clearly the implications of the moment and to mobilize the masses to the maximum, leading them onto the correct path of resolving fundamental contradictions.

In the development of this theme we have assumed that eventually the idea of armed struggle and also the formula of guerrilla warfare as a method of combat will be accepted. Why do we estimate that guerrilla warfare is the correct way under the present conditions in America? There are fundamental arguments that in our opinion determine the necessity for guerrilla action in America as the central axis of the struggle.

First, accepting as truth that the enemy will fight to maintain himself in power, it is necessary to consider the destruction of the oppressing army; in order to destroy it, it is necessary to oppose it with a popular army. That army is not born spontaneously; they have to arm themselves from the enemy's arsenal, and this causes a very long struggle in which the popular forces and their leaders will be always exposed to attack by superior forces without suitable conditions for defense and maneuverability.

On the other hand, the guerrilla nucleus settled in a terrain favorable for the struggle guarantees the security and permanence of the revolutionary command. Urban forces directed from the general staff of the people's army can carry out actions of incalculable importance. The eventual destruction of these groups would not kill the soul of the revolution or its leadership that, from its rural fortress, would continue catalyzing the revolutionary spirit of the masses and organizing new forces for other battles.

Furthermore, in this zone begins the construction of the future state apparatus charged with directing efficiently the class dictatorship during the entire period of transition. The longer the battle the greater and more complex will be the administrative problems. To solve them, cadres will be trained for the difficult task of consolidating power and economic development in a future stage.

Second, there is the general situation of the Latin American peasants and the progressively explosive nature of their struggle against feudal structures in the framework of a social situation of alliance between local and foreign exploiters.

Returning to the *Second Declaration of Havana:*

> The people of America freed themselves from Spanish colonialism at the beginning of the last century, but they did not free themselves from exploitation. The feudal landowners assumed the authority of the Spanish governors; the Indians continued in painful servitude; the Latin American man, in one form or another, continued enslaved; and the slightest hopes of the people crumbled under the power of the oligarchs and the yoke of foreign capital. This has been the situation in [Latin] America in one form or another. Today Latin America is under a much more ferocious imperialism, far more powerful and ruthless than Spanish colonial imperialism.
>
> And faced with the objective and historically inexorable reality of the Latin American revolution, what is the attitude of Yankee imperialism? To prepare to begin a colonial war with the people of Latin America; to create an apparatus of force, political pretexts and peudo-legal instruments signed with the representatives of the reactionary oligarchies in order to repress by blood and fire the struggle of the Latin American people.

This objective situation demonstrates the force that sleeps unproductive in our peasants and the necessity of utilizing it for the liberation of America.

Third is the continental character of the struggle.

Could this new stage in the emancipation of America be conceived of as the meeting of two local forces fighting for power on a given territory? Only with difficulty. The struggle will be to the death between all the popular forces and all the forces of repression. The paragraphs cited above also predict this.

The Yankees will intervene out of solidarity of interests and because the struggle in [Latin] America is a decisive one. In fact, they are now intervening in the preparation of the repressive forces and the organization of a continental fighting apparatus. But from now on they will do it with all the arms of destruction at their disposal; they will not permit revolutionary power to consolidate and if anyone should succeed in doing it, they will again attack, they will not recognize it, they will try to divide the revolutionary forces, they will introduce saboteurs of every type, they will create border problems, they will turn other reactionary states against them, they will try to smother the economy of the new state, in a word, to annihilate it.

Given this American panorama, it is difficult to achieve and consolidate victory in an isolated country. A union of the repressive forces ought to be answered by a union of the popular forces. In all the countries in which oppression reaches unbearable levels, the banner of rebellion must be raised and this banner of rebellion will have, by historical necessity, a continental character. The Cordillera of the Andes will be called the Sierra Maestra of America as Fidel has said and all the vast territories that make up this continent will become the scene of a struggle to the death against imperialist power.

We cannot say when it will achieve this continental character nor how long the struggle will last; but we can predict its coming and its triumph because it is the inevitable result of historic, economic, and political circumstances and its course cannot be turned aside. The task of the revolutionary force in each country is to begin it when the conditions are present, regardless of the situation in other countries. The way in which the struggle develops conditions the general strategy. The prediction of the continental character of the struggle is borne out by analysis of the forces of each contender, but this does not in the least exclude independent outbreaks. Just as the beginning of the struggle in one part of a country is intended to carry it throughout the country, the beginning of the revolutionary war contributes to the development of new conditions in neighboring countries.

The development of revolutions has normally been produced by inversely proportional ebbs and flows; the counterrevolutionary ebb corresponds to the revolutionary flow, and, conversely, in moments of revolutionary decline there is a counterrevolutionary rise. In these instances the situation of the popular forces becomes difficult and they must resort to the best means of defense in order to suffer the least damage. The enemy is extremely strong, continentally. For this reason the relative weakness of local bourgeoisie cannot be analyzed for the purpose of making decisions within restricted limits. Even less would we be able to think of the eventual alliance of these oligarchs with an armed people. The Cuban Revolution has sounded the alarm. The polarization of forces will be total; exploited on one side and exploiters on the other. The mass of small bourgeoisie will be inclined toward one side or the other according to their interests and the political skill with which they are handled; neutrality will be an exception. This is how the revolutionary war will be.

Let us think about how the guerrilla center would begin. A relatively small nucleus of persons choose favorable places for guerrilla war, either to begin a counterattack, or to weather a storm, and then begin to attack. But the following have to be clearly established: At the beginning the relative weakness of the guerrilla is such that he ought only to work on settling in the terrain in order to get to know the area, establishing connections with the population and reinforcing the place that will eventually be converted into his base of support.

There are three conditions for the survival of a guerrilla movement that begins its development under the premises expressed here: Constant mobility, constant vigilance, constant distrust. Without the adequate use of these three tactical military elements, the movement would have difficulty surviving. It must be remembered that the heroism of the guerrilla in these times consists in the scope of his planned objective and the enormous sacrifices that must be made in order to achieve it.

These sacrifices will not be in daily combat, the face to face struggle with the enemy; they will take more subtle and more difficult-to-resist forms for the guerrilla both physically and mentally.

They will perhaps be severely punished by the enemy army, divided into groups at times, taken prisoner and martyred. They will be persecuted like hunted animals in those areas in which they have chosen to operate; theirs will be the constant worry of having the enemy on their track, and the constant doubt that the frightened peasants will betray them to the repressive troops in order to save their own lives. They have no alternative but death or victory at times when death is an ever present thought and victory is the myth that only a revolutionary can dream.

That is the heroism of the guerrilla. For this reason it is said that walking is another form of fighting. The plan is, faced with the general superiority of the enemy, to find the tactical form of achieving relative superiority at a chosen point whether it be to concentrate more troops than the enemy or by use of terrain to assure an advantage upsetting the balance of forces. Under these conditions a tactical victory is assured. If relative superiority is not clear it is preferable not to attack. One ought not to engage in combat that does not produce a victory as long as the "how" and "when" can be chosen. In the framework of the grand political–military action of which it is a part, the guerrilla will grow and consolidate. Bases of support, a fundamental element for the prosperity of the guerrilla, will be formed. These bases of support are the points at which the enemy army can penetrate only with great losses. They are bastions of the revolution, refuge and starting point for guerrilla incursions, each time more daring and distant.

This moment arrives if the tactical and political difficulties have been overcome simultaneously. The guerrillas can never forget their function as vanguard of the people, a mandate that they personify, and consequently, they must create the political conditions necessary for the establishment of revolutionary power based on the total support of the masses. The great claims of the peasants must be satisfied to the extent and in the form that circumstances warrant, making all of the population a compact and decided unit.

If the military situation is difficult at first, the political situation will be no less delicate; and if only one military error can liquidate the guerrilla movement, a political error can stop its development for long periods.

The struggle is political–military; thus it must develop and consequently be understood.

The guerrilla, in his process of growth, reaches a point in which his capacity for action covers a specific region for which there is a surplus of men and too great a concentration in the zone. Then the beehive activity begins, when one of the leaders, an outstanding guerrilla, moves to another region and repeats the chain of development of guerrilla warfare, subject of course, to central command.

Now, it is necessary to point out that one cannot aspire to victory without the formation of a popular army. The guerrilla forces will be able to extend themselves to a certain size; the popular forces, in the cities and in other penetrable enemy zones, can cause damage to him, but the military potential of the reactionaries would remain intact. It must always be remembered that the final result must be the annihilation of the enemy. Therefore, all the new zones which are created, plus the penetrated zones behind enemy lines, plus the forces that operate in the principal cities must have a subordinate relation to the (central) command. It cannot be claimed that the tight chain of command that characterizes an army exists, but there must be a strategic chain of command. Within determined conditions of freedom of action, the guerrillas must comply with all strategic orders of central command set up in one of the strongest and most secure zones, preparing the conditions for the union of forces at a given moment.

Guerrilla war, or war of liberation, will, in general, have three stages: The first; the defensive stage where a small hunted force nibbles away at the enemy; it is not protected for a passive defense in a small circle but its defense consists in limited attacks that can be carried out. After this a point of equilibrium arrives in which the possibilities of action for the guerilla and the enemy are stabilized and, later, the final stage of overrunning the repressive army that will lead to the taking of the large cities and to the great decisive encounters and to the total annihilation of the adversary.

After the point of equilibrium is reached, where both forces respect each other, guerrilla war acquires new characteristics. The concept of maneuver begins to be introduced; large columns attack strong points. It is a war of movements with a transfer of forces and means of attack of relative strength. But, because of the capacity for resistance and counterattack which the enemy still possesses, the war of maneuver does not definitely replace the guerrillas; it is only another form of action, a superior magnitude of the guerrilla forces that finally crystalizes a popular army into an army corps. Even at this time, marching at the head of the action of the main forces, the guerrillas will go in their state of "purity," destroying communications, sabotaging the whole defensive apparatus of the enemy.

We had predicted that the war would be continental. This means it will also be prolonged; it will have many fronts, it will cost much blood, innumerable lives for a long time. But even more, the phenomenon of polarization of forces that will be occurring in America, the clear division between exploiters and exploited that will exist in future revolutionary wars, means that when power is taken over by the armed vanguard of the people, the country or countries that obtain it will have simultaneously liquidated the oppressor in liquidating the imperialists and the national exploiters. The first stage of the socialist revolution will have crystalized; people will be ready to stanch their wounds and begin the construction of socialism.

Will there be other, less bloody possibilities?

Some time ago the last partition of the world was made in which the United States took for itself the lion's share of our continent; today the imperialists of the Old World are expanding again and the power of the European Common Market is threatening the North Americans as well. All this would make one think it will be possible to watch as spectators the interimperialist fight in order to gain advances, perhaps in alliance with the strongest national bourgeoisie. Without mentioning that passive politics never brings good results in the class struggle and that alliances with the bourgeoisie, however revolutionary it may seem at a given time, have only a transitory character, there are reasons of time that induce the taking of another position. The sharpening of the fundamental conditions appears to be so rapid in America that it disturbs the "normal" development of the contradictions in the imperialist camp in the fight for markets.

The national bourgeoisie has been tied to North American imperialism, in most cases, and must suffer the same fate as the latter in each country. Even in the cases in which there are pacts or identity of contradictions between the national bourgeoisie and other imperialists with the North Americans, this happens in the framework of a fundamental struggle that necessarily, in the course of its development, will include *all the exploited and all the exploiters.* The polarization of antagonistic forces, of classes, is until now more rapid than the development of the contradictions of the forces between exploiters over the division of the spoils. There are two camps: The alternative is becoming clearer for each individual and for each special stratum of the population.

The Alliance for Progress is an attempt to check the unrestrainable.

But if the advance of the European Common Market or any other imperialist group on the American market were more rapid than the development of the fundamental contradiction, the only thing remaining would be the introduction of the popular forces as a wedge in the open breach, the latter leading the whole struggle and using the new intruders with full awareness of their final intentions.

One ought not to surrender any position, any arms, or any secret to the enemy class under pain of losing everything.

In fact, the birth of the American struggle has begun. Will the center of the storm be in Venezuela, Guatemala, Colombia, Peru, Ecuador—? Will these present skirmishes be only manifestations of unrest that do not bear fruit? The results of today's struggles are not important. It is not important for the final result that one or another movement be temporarily defeated. What counts is the decision to struggle that matures day by day; the awareness of the need for revolutionary change, and the certainty of its possibility.

This is a prediction. We make it with the conviction that history will prove us right. The analysis of the objective and subjective factors in America and in the imperialist world indicates to us the certainty of these statements based on the Second Havana Declaration.

1963

9 Relevance of Marxist Economics to U.S. Conditions

VICTOR PERLO

It is the custom of the vulgar critics of Marxism to say: "Marx predicted so-and-so. But the opposite happened. This proves that Marx was an oaf." Often these assertions are based on a crudely distorted version of what Marx actually said.

But Marx was not in the game of prediction. He was a student of society who sought to probe it to its very depths, to learn its basic laws of development, and to draw appropriate political conclusions therefrom. Occasionally, he made short-range estimates of the outcome of this or that situation, some of which proved wrong and some right. But his basic conclusions of a predictive character were not like those of the race-track handicapper; they were theorems derived by the most rigorous social science.

The given conditions in social life change infinitely more rapidly than those in nature. Therefore, even the best of theorems in social science must be tested continually against reality and are subject to being revised or supplanted. Still, if we take the more or less purely economic conclusions of Marx, and compare them with those of any other economist of the nineteenth century, we will see that Marx's conclusions stand up infinitely better to the realities of modern capitalism. Most to the point, however, is that Marx's fundamental *political* conclusions have been the most brilliantly vindicated in all history: a) that the fundamental conflict of capitalism was between the capitalists and the working class; and b) that the dynamics of this conflict must inevitably lead to the proletarian revolution, to working class power and the construction of socialist and communist society.

Marx and Engels believed in the unity of theory and practice. They were prime organizers of that Communist movement, based on scientific socialism,

SOURCE: from Victor Perlo, "Relevance of Marxist Economics to U.S. Conditions," *Political Affairs LVIII,* 2 (February 1969), pp. 41–50. Reprinted by permission.

which has achieved victory in one-third of the world, population-wise, and is a growing factor globally.

Marxists, if they are to be effective, must combine ardent partisanship in the class struggle with scientific rigor in the study of reality. Subjective evaluation, substitution of the wish for the fact, invariably leads to defeat.

To assess the applicability of Marxist economics to modern America, you cannot limit yourself to the teachings of Marx and Engels. You must also take into account the development of theory by later Marxists, of whom the most significant, undoubtedly, has been Lenin. There have been important post-World War II contributions by Marxist economists in Western countries and in the USSR as well.

Most of bourgeois economic theory is devoted to the attempt to rebut Marxism, and a particularly significant part of that is the attempt to rebut Marxism from the Left, so to speak, by claiming to be "more revolutionary" than Marxism.

It is my experience, in a lifetime of economic research motivated by partisanship to the American working class and Negro people, that Marxism provides an approach which permits the solution of most research problems, enables one to tear away the confusions perpetrated by apologist economists and establishment statisticians, enables one to really relate the dynamics of economic development with the struggles of the people, to develop programs and to help in particular campaigns, strikes, etc.

I want to discuss this more concretely with reference to five specific themes.

1. Theory of Surplus Value and the Exploitation of Labor

We begin with the separation of workers from the means of production, the ownership of plants and equipment by the ruling class of capitalists. The workers have nothing to sell but their labor power. It becomes a commodity bought by the capitalists.

The value of a commodity is equal to the average number of hours of labor socially necessary to produce or reproduce it. The labor theory of value was formulated by the so-called classical economists, Adam Smith and David Recardo and further developed by Marx. It remains valid today.

The value of the commodity labor power is determined in the same way. It is equal to the number of hours of labor socially necessary to reproduce the worker—to keep him going and working and raising his successors at a given standard of living. The value produced in the extra hours, or surplus value, is the basic source of capitalist profits, shared out in many parts among the capitalists and their top aides. This is the essence of exploitation.

Is this applicable to U.S. conditions? By all means; and as an increasing factor; and to *all* workers, other than bosses.

Take the latest statistics for U.S. manufacturing for the year of 1966. The value added by manufacture came to $251 billion. Total payrolls of clerical and manual workers combined came to $117 billion. So the owners got $134 billion out of the labor of their workers, or 115 per cent of what the workers got. This is a rate of surplus value of 115 per cent. It is subject to various adjustments, mostly upward, which would bring it to 140 per cent. The rate of surplus value, that is, of the exploitation of labor, has been increasing. Marx used as an example a figure of 100 per cent as of a century ago. Actually, it was probably realistic at that time. Recent U.S. statistics show a rapidly rising trend over the past fifteen years.

Paul Sweezy, in *Monopoly Capital,* chooses the term "economic surplus" rather than "surplus value" because, he says, "the latter is probably identified in the minds of most people with Marxian economic theory as equal to the sum of profits + interests + rents." He then implies it should include other items also. But that is a very flimsy reason. In the first place, who does he mean by "most people"? In most Marxist literature dealing with surplus value the emphasis is not on the breakdown of its distribution, but on the conditions and amount of its extraction.

It seems that the real reason for Sweezy's discarding of the term "surplus value" is related to his political interpretation—he considers the exploitation of labor within the United States as mainly a thing of the past. The bulk of white workers, in his view, have been "coopted" by capitalism, integrated as consumers and ideologically conditioned members of society. They only suffer psychically from capitalism's irrationality.

But that is obviously not the case. The wages of American workers fall far below the U.S. Labor Department estimates of what is needed for a "moderate" living standard; 65 per cent of workers—including white collar and blue collar, white as well as black—are able to consume much less than the so-called "affluent American standard of living." The concept of "stuffed-goose capitalism" does not correspond to reality.

The exploitation of labor does not depend on the worker realizing it, or his understanding of the class struggle, but on its objective reality. The reality of exploitation and of the class struggle is revealed by the strike wave and many other signs of mass labor dissatisfaction.

The conditions of labor under capitalism provide powerful evidence of the oppressive nature of the system, over and beyond the statistical fact of exploitation. Marx stressed that the misery of the workers was due to many causes connected with the accumulation of capital: "the lot of the laborer, be his payment high or low, must grow worse," he wrote. Of course, as Marx indicated, such laws can be modified through organization and struggle. Still, miserable conditions prevail in American industry today—speedup, lack of safety provisions, job insecurity, monotony, excessive hours, degradation of labor, arbitrary bosses, etc. Every intellectual should read the [July 24, 1967] account of *Wall Street Journal* correspondent Roger Rapoport's one-week stint at Ford's:

> Working on the line is gruelling and frustrating, and while it may be repetitive, it's not simple. I learned at first-hand why 250,000 auto workers are unhappy about working conditions. I'm in fairly good physical shape, but I ached all over after each day's work on the line. Nobody seemed to take any particular pride in his work.

He described the breakneck speed of the line, the frequent violation of safety rules, the gulped lunch—all in one of Ford's newest, best plants.

Marxism provides the strategic key to the efforts of radicals to orient on the working class, to help workers in the struggle to organize, to merge with the working class in strike battles against employers, to raise the consciousness of workers to an understanding of their own historic revolutionary role in ending exploitation through working-class power and socialism.

2. Capitalism and Racism

You all know Marx's famous statement: the worker in a white skin cannot be free while the worker in a black skin is branded.

Genuine Marxists have always been aware of this and have fought for the liberation of black men, for the unity of white and black labor, as an essential for the socialist revolution. In this country the record goes back to the abolitionists and the Communist General Joseph Weydemeyer, appointed by Lincoln, in the Civil War. And it continues in the entire history of the modern Communist Party, whose greatest glory, whose outstanding contribution in nearly fifty years, has been its pioneering in the struggle for black and white unity and in arousing widespread national support for the black liberation struggle.

Famous Communist-originated slogans chart the course of that history: Negro and White, Unite and Fight; Self-determination for the Black Belt; Free the Scottsboro Boys; James Ford for Vice President; Charlene Mitchell for President.

It is the particular contention of Marxists that only the capitalists are the real gainers from special exploitation of black workers. An example of this is the comparison of wages, North and South. The oppression of black workers, of course, is much worse in the South than in the North. In 1967, Negro families in the South earned $2,265 less, on the average, than Negro families in the North.

Did southern workers gain or lose from this, from supposedly being the beneficiaries of an open, undisguised system of complete priority? The facts show they lost. The extra oppression of black workers only subjected the white workers to stronger competition on the labor market, even though that competition remained generally potential. White families in the South, on the average, earned $1,212 less than white families in the North. Applied to 12,300,000 southern white families, this gives a loss of just under $15 billion a year. And this is over and above the losses suffered by all white workers,

North and South, from the economic discrimination against black workers.

The southern textile industry is a classic example. Southern white workers, as a "special privilege," were permitted to work in textile mills at wages and conditions radically undercutting those in the North. The northern textile industry was almost annihilated by this, and hundreds of thousands of white textile workers suffered cuts in real wages and then were thrown on the industrial scrap heap.

Strongholds of jim crow are often strongholds of successful employer resistance to trade unionism, to decency and dignity of labor, to providing minimum living conditions.

In the research field, I may say, I pioneered in the postwar period in establishing a quantitative measure of the superexploitation of black workers as a major source of superprofits of U.S. imperialism. This type of calculation has since become general. But the main point has yet to be fully worked out. And this is, the all-around proof of the harm to white workers from this superexploitation of the black workers, and the campaign to convince the masses of white workers that *in their own interest,* they must unite with black workers and join them in the fight for equality.

Thus the approach of Marxism is based on the following theses:

> The liberation of the black people is only possible together with and through the liberation of the working class as a whole.
>
> Such partial demands as black capitalism and black control of ghettos are limited, and do not provide the strategic solution.
>
> Even under capitalism gains can be won, however, primarily at the point of production, where black-white unity is the key.
>
> The main enemy and oppressor of the black people is the capitalist and not the misguided white workers. The former must be fought and exposed. The latter must be argued with and won over to unity.

3. Imperialism and Finance Capital

The great crisis of the 1930s led to the exposure in this country of the ugly reality of modern monopoly capital. Lenin's teaching became widespread, directly and indirectly. Congressional investigations, the Roosevelt electoral campaigns, the CIO organizing drive—all of these brought to light the rule of America by a handful of tycoons of merged banking and industrial monopolies, as explained by Lenin in his masterpiece, *Imperialism, the Highest Stage of Capitalism.*

After World War II there were a plethora of theories designed to undermine that understanding, to recreate faith in American capitalism. We had the managerial revolution, people's capitalism, the income revolution and, "from the Left," the cybercultural revolution. Sweezy and many other liberals and progressives tended to fall into the trap of these apologetic theories.

Sweezy, for example, talks of the vanishing of bank capital as an important factor.

However, Marxism provides the basis for studying the real facts and exposing all of this nonsense. Examples in my own work are: *The Empire of High Finance, People's Capitalism and Stock Ownership* and *The "Income Revolution."* Now with the spread of conglomerates, this is becoming obvious to everybody again as witness the work *Who Rules America* by G. William Domhoff, of Lampman on concentration of wealth, and now the latest material from the House Banking and Currency Committee.

Here are some key facts from this latest report: One hundred banks with $200 billion in trust assets control most of the giant corporations of the country. Most of these are controlled by 15 banks with $113 billion of trust assets. The First National Bank of Chicago has over 5 per cent of the stock of 401 companies. The Chemical Bank New York Trust Company has interlocking directorates with 278 companies. The Morgan Guaranty Trust Company has 5–20 per cent of the stock of all leading copper companies save Anaconda. In 55 years the assets of non-financial corporations increased 18 times, of financial corporations 40 times.

We have a picture of a few centers of financial-industrial power having absolute sway over the economy, over the government, and—yes—over the Pentagon.

These financial tycoons, despite all their demagogy, are the real organizers of racism—from the ghettos of U.S. cities to the mines of South Africa. They are the organizers of militarism and wars of aggression. They are the organizers of international runaway shops, of mine disasters and depressed areas, of inflation eating away the pension of old people and taxes cutting the living standards of workers, of multiversities thwarting the striving for truth and basic learning of student youth.

But do we expose them just to make a sensation? No. This analysis is a guide to action. We have the potential for an alliance of all anti-monopoly forces which in one way or another are exploited or oppressed or subordinated by these centers. An alliance is possible on such issues as peace, tax reform, aspects of black liberation, university reform, a new political party not dominated by Wall Street. That is how Marxists unite theory with practical politics. But in such an alliance, we strive always for the leading role of the working class, which by its position in society is most consistently pitched against the capitalist class, has the potential of leading in the struggle to a more revolutionary height, and preparing for further stages.

4. Export of Capital and External Imperialism

A key contribution of Lenin was the establishment of the decisive importance of the export of capital, as compared with the export of goods, in the era of imperialism. For many years, the illusion was spread in this country by apologists for capitalism, and by some Left circles, that the export of capital had lost its importance as a means of exploitation. The open apologists of imperialism spread the propaganda, in the universities and elsewhere, that investments were a form of foreign aid which were helping underdeveloped countries. Some progressives grossly underestimated its importance.

This mistake has now largely been recognized owing to the very boasting of the imperialists themselves on the enormous scale of foreign investments. Today, goods produced in mines and factories owned by U.S. corporations abroad, amount to over $100 billion yearly. As of nearly a decade ago, the 25 largest industrials made 29 per cent of their profits from foreign investments. Surely this percentage is higher now. The biggest banks, previously mentioned, have $14 billion, or up to one-third of all their deposits, in foreign branches. This sum has expanded with fabulous speed in just these last few years.

The object of foreign investment, the superexploitation of workers in other countries, remains paramount. A prime example is provided by Taiwan and South Korea, where the connection between military conquest by the U.S. and superprofits derived by U.S. corporations is most obvious. In these countries, such corporate giants as IBM, wearing a paternalistic veneer at home, ruthlessly exploit the girls of these occupied lands in the most modern electronic factories for wages of $15 per month.

Here is a gem from the *Journal of Commerce* (December 12, 1968):

> Some businessmen contend that the government should end the chronic deficit in its payments account, resulting from foreign aid and its vast military commitments around the world. Confronted with this argument at a recent business convention, the Director of the Office of Foreign Direct Investments of the U.S. Department of Commerce, Charles E. Fiero, asked: "What would happen to our investments in the Middle East, and the earnings and exports they bring, if the U.S. withdrew the Sixth Fleet from the Mediterranean?" No one answered him.

The struggle for national liberation on a global scale is today largely against the same corporations as black workers fight seeking escape from the ghettos, as industrial workers fight seeking decent wages, job security and relief from speedup. Hence the goal of international unity of anti-imperialist forces, the consistent attempts of Communists—going back to before World War I—to organize the struggle precisely against their own imperialists as the way to liberation and socialism. This applies fully to the United States today and again it is fair to say that the Communist-Marxists were pioneers in this respect. If we consider the postwar period, it was exactly because the Communists pioneered in exposing and organizing the struggle against the cold-war policies of aggression, the Marshall Plan, etc., that reaction turned on them so furiously, used endless pressure to try to destroy them organizationally, and threw their leadership into prison under the Smith Act.

Today, it is a great thing that the anti-imperialist movement within the United States has reached significant, broad proportions. History shows the value of Marxism, and Marxists, in developing that struggle. It is necessary in this period to broaden that struggle, to bring the main sections of the working class into it.

5. The USSR, the Working Class and the "Third World"

A major aspect of Marxism cannot be gotten in detail from the works of Marx and Lenin, because it represents developments after both of them. And that is the relationship of the modern highly developed, powerful socialist world to the working class of the capitalist countries and to the national liberation movement.

The pioneering achievements of the Soviet Union in realizing full employment, cradle-to-grave social security, socialized medicine, a shorter workweek, steadily rising real wages, have been an inspiration to the struggle of workers in capitalist countries and have helped them to win corresponding demands in these countries. This is especially evident in Western Europe.

The achievement of working-class power in the Soviet Union was the most powerful stimulant to the development of socialist and communist revolutionary movements in all the capitalist countries. The material and moral aid of the working class in power in the USSR to the workers of capitalist countries should not be minimized.

The achievement of true national equality within the USSR was a decisive stimulant of the anti-imperialist movement throughout Asia and Africa.

Today, the economically powerful Soviet Union provides tremendous material assistance to all countries striving for liberation from the yoke of imperialism. Yet, we have such absurdities in the United States as people, who consider themselves great friends of socialist Cuba, socialist North Vietnam and the National Liberation Front, simultaneously denouncing the Soviet Union as a "partner" of U.S. imperialism. The reality is, that with all of the heroism of the Cubans, the U.S. would have long since conquered that island without the enormous material and military aid of the USSR, without the readiness of the USSR to go to war with the U.S., if necessary, in the event of a U.S. invasion of Cuba.

Similar considerations prevail in relations to Vietnam. The liberation of Vietnam is mainly the effort of the Vietnamese themselves. But the enormous and growing assistance of the USSR is absolutely essential, as is the peace movement and resistance in the United States and other capitalist countries.

The study of the economic competition between the two world systems becomes one of the important areas of progressive research, one of the significant fields for the application of Marxism to American conditions, as the United States is the main factor in such competition on the side of capitalism.

The development of friendly relations between progressives in capitalist countries and the socialist lands is very important. The imperialists pay big rewards for just a little bit of anti-Sovietism. They know where their enemy is.

What is necessary is not to idealize or idolize the Soviet Union, but to appreciate its tremendous forward strides, its vital positive role in world affairs today and in the cause of liberation of all people.

Marxism and Progressive Economics Today

There are a multitude of unsolved problems, intimately related to the ongoing struggles in the United States. And there is a need for the application of Marxism to their solution.

Consider such complex problems as taxation, education, housing. Once you take a class approach in digging into these problems, you will find solutions opening up, answers as to who is responsible and why, how to organize, and around what programs to organize for change.

Today unions are at a great disadvantage in dealing with multi-national corporations and with employers able to shuffle around government contracts. Take the approach of Lenin and you will find the keys to the riddles, identify the allies for the anti-imperialist struggle, establish the real balance of forces within the so-called military-industrial complex and the power elite.

For radical economists there is an unlimited field of activity providing light and fighting material to the struggles of the American people—the struggle for full employment, for liberation of black people, for peace—and, further along the road, the struggle for the liberation from capitalist oppression and exploitation, for socialism.

Never have struggles been conducted on a more sophisticated level than today. Never have facts, research and informed propaganda been more necessary. Whether in the colleges teaching youth, whether in trade union research departments, or on the staffs of liberation organizations or peace organizations, whether on labor or progressive publications, there is an infinite field of creative work for progressive economists. Marxism will provide the approach and body of knowledge which will add enormously to the effectiveness, direction, optimistic outlook and success of that work.

1969

Bibliography

Adams, H. P. *Karl Marx in His Earlier Writings.* New York: Atheneum Press, 1972. (Originally published in 1940.)

Almond, Gabriel A. *The Appeals of Communism.* Princeton: Princeton University Press, 1954.

Avineri, Shlomo. *The Social and Political Thought of Karl Marx.* Cambridge: Cambridge University Press, 1968.

Baron, Paul A. *The Political Economy of Growth.* New York: Modern Reader Paperbacks, 1968.

Bell, Daniel. *Marxian Socialism in the United States.* Princeton, N.J.: Princeton University Press, 1967.

Berlin, Isaiah. *Karl Marx.* 3rd ed. New York: Oxford University Press, 1963.

Chai, Winberg (ed.). *Essential Works of Chinese Communism.* New York: Bantam Books, 1969.

Christman, Henry M. (ed.). *Communism in Action: A Documentary History.* New York: Bantam Books, 1969.

Cohen, Arthur A. *The Communism of Mao Tse-tung.* Chicago: University of Chicago Press, 1964.

Connor, James E. (ed.). *Lenin on Politics and Revolution: Selected Writings.* New York: Pegasus, 1968.

Crossman, Richard (ed.). *The God That Failed.* New York: Bantam Books, 1965.

Daniels, Robert V. (ed.). *Marxism and Communism: Essential Readings.* New York: Random House, 1967.

De George, Richard T. *The New Marxism: Soviet and European Marxism Since 1956.* New York: Pegasus, 1968.

Djilas, Milovan. *The New Class.* New York: Frederick A. Praeger, 1957.

Djilas, Milovan. *The Unperfect Society: Beyond the New Class.* New York: Harcourt, Brace & World, 1969.

Draper, Theodore. *Castroism: Theory and Practice.* New York: Frederick A. Praeger, 1965.

Easton, Lloyd D., and Guddat, Kurt H. (eds.). *Writings of the Young Marx on Philosophy and Society.* Garden City, N.Y.: Doubleday & Co., 1967.

Engels, Friedrich. *Selected Writings.* Edited by W. O. Henderson. Baltimore: Penguin Books, 1967.

Fall, Bernard (ed.). *Ho Chi Minh on Revolution.* New York: Frederick A. Praeger, 1967.

Freeman, Robert (ed.). *Marx on Economics.* New York: Harcourt, Brace & World, 1961.

Freeman, Robert. *Marxist Social Thought.* New York: Harcourt, Brace & World, 1968.

Fromm, Erich. *Marx's Concept of Man.* New York: Frederick Ungar Publishing Co., 1966.

Gregor, A. James. *A Survey of Marxism; Problems in Philosophy and the Theory of History.* New York: Random House, 1965.

Guevara, Ernesto "Che." *Socialism and Man.* New York: New American Library, 1967.

Halperin, Maurice. *The Rise and Decline of Fidel Castro.* Berkeley, Calif.: U. of California Press, 1973.

Hsiung, James Chieh. *Ideology and Practice: The Evolution of Chinese Communism.* New York: Praeger, 1970.

Hunt, R. N. Carew. *The Theory and Practice of Communism.* 5th ed. New York: Macmillan, 1960.

Jacobs, Dan N. *The New Communisms.* New York: Harper & Row, 1969.

Jacobs, Dan N. (ed.). *The New Communist Manifesto and Related Documents.* 3rd ed. New York: Harper Torchbacks, 1961.

Lefebvre, Henri. *The Sociology of Marx.* Translated by Norbert Guterman. New York: Random House, 1968.

Lenin, V. I. *Imperialism; The Highest Stage of Capitalism.* New York: International Publishers Co., 1939.

Lenin, V. I. *State and Revolution.* New York: International Publishers Co., 1943.

Lichtheim, George. *Marxism: An Historical and Critical Study.* 2d ed. New York: Frederick A. Praeger, 1965.

Lobkowicz, Nicholas (ed.). *Marx and the Western World.* Notre Dame, Ind.: University of Notre Dame Press, 1967.

Lowenthal, Richard. *World Communism: The Disintegration of a Secular Faith.* New York: Oxford University Press, 1966.

Mallin, Jay. *"Che" Guevara on Revolution.* Coral Gables, Fla.: University of Miami Press, 1972.

Mallin, Jay (ed.). *Strategy for Conquest: Communist Documents on Guerrilla Warfare.* Coral Gables, Fla.: University of Miami, 1972.

Mandel, Ernest. *An Introduction to Marxist Economic Theory.* New York: Merit Publishing Co., 1969.

Mao Tse-tung. *Selected Works of Mao Tse-tung.* 4 vols. Peking: Foreign Languages Press, 1961–1965.

Marcuse, Herbert. *Soviet Marxism; A Critical Analysis.* New York: Vintage Books, 1961.

Marx, Karl. *Capital.* Any edition.

Marx, Karl. *Selected Works.* New York: International Publishers, 1968.

Marx, Karl, and Engels, F. *The German Ideology.* New York: International Publishers. (Originally published in 1845–1846.)

Mayo, Henry B. *Introduction to Marxist Theory.* New York: Oxford University Press, 1960.

Meyer, Alfred G. *Communism.* 3rd ed. New York: Random House, 1967.

Meyer, Alfred G. *Leninism.* New York: Frederick A. Praeger, 1957.

Meyer, Alfred G. Marxism: *The Unity of Theory and Practice.* Ann Arbor: University of Michigan Press, 1963.

Parry, Albert. *The New Class Divided: Science and Technology Versus Communism.* New York: Macmillan, 1966.

Sanderson, John. *An Interpretation of the Political Ideas of Marx and Engels.* London: Longmans, Green and Co., 1969.

Schram, Stuart R. *The Political Thought of Mao Tse-tung.* Rev. ed. New York: Frederick A. Praeger, 1969.

Stalin, Josef. *The Foundations of Leninism.* Moscow: Foreign Languages Publishing House, 1924.

Starr, John Bryan. *Ideology and Culture.* New York: Harper & Row, 1973.

Tanham, George K. *Communist Revolutionary Warfare: from the Vietminh to the Viet Cong.* New York: Frederick A. Praeger, 1968.

Trotsky, Leon. *The Permanent Revolution.* Translated by Max Shachtman. New York: Pioneer Publishers, 1931.

Tucker, Robert C. *The Marxian Revolutionary Idea.* New York: W. W. Norton & Co., 1969.

Tucker, Robert C. (ed.). *The Marx–Engels Reader.* New York: W. W. Norton & Co., 1972.

Tucker, Robert C. *Philosophy and Myth in Karl Marx.* Cambridge: Cambridge University Press, 1961.

Ulam, Adam B. *The New Face of Soviet Totalitarianism.* Cambridge, Mass.: Harvard University Press, 1963.

Wetter, Gustav. *Soviet Ideology Today.* New York: Frederick A. Praeger, 1966.

Williams, William A. *The Great Evasion.* Chicago: Quadrangle Paperbacks, 1964.

Zeitlin, Irving M. *Marxism: A Re-Examination.* Princeton, N.J.: D. Van Nostrand, 1967.

III The Web of Democracy

We saw in the introduction that democracy is best understood as a set of political institutions to which an ideology has been "added." It should not be at all surprising, in consequence, that there are several rather distinct ideologies which correspond to democratic institutions in the modern nation–state. Although each of these ideologies represents a somewhat different way of thinking about man, society, and the state, still all the various democratic ideologies tend to share certain broad principles concerning man, society, and state. As Jefferson once stated: a difference in opinion need not signal a difference in principle. In many instances, however, democratic conservatism takes exception to some of these shared principles. This is due in part to the fact that the democratic conservatives have attempted to fuse together rather disparate views of man and society: those implicit in conservatism and traditionalism and those implicit in the structure of democratic institutions.

The core notion of all democratic ideologies is "consent" to the agency of government, whether that consent be tacitly or expressly granted. Often tracing the foundation of the state—and perhaps of society as well—to a social contract, either historical or analytical, democrats emphasize that the state and its agency of government are merely instruments of men, forged by men, for the pursuit of human goals and purposes. Government—as agency of the state—is the mechanism through which men attend to the arrangements of society. The democrats thus see the state as less real or more artificial than the individual; by so doing the democrats acknowledge a belief in the inherent worth and dignity of the individual. (With this last point the democratic conservatives tend to take issue: on the one hand, they might argue that some individuals have an inherent worth and dignity or competence, but not all; on the other hand, they might argue that some individuals are inherently more worthy or more competent to actually rule than others.)

Again with the exception of the democratic conservatives, the emphasis on consent implies that man possesses a capacity for self-direction, even if only through the process of electing officials. Further, the notion that men consent to a social contract, whether tacitly or expressly, implies the belief that man has a social character sufficient to guarantee the minimum of trust and good will necessary for social life. Finally, the notion of consent suggests that men do share some common interests, common goals, and common purposes, which can be addressed through the institutions of the modern democratic nation–state.

We noted before that democratic ideologies tend to portray the state as something artificial—a product of man's art created through his consent. This means, conversely, that the state is not something given by nature. The immediate implication of this conception of the state is that, unlike the fascists, the right of coercion does not inhere in an abstraction called "the state." Rather, the right of coercion is conferred upon the state by the individual members of the society contracting to form the state. The right to coercion is supposedly confined to the limits laid down in the articles of association—whether written or unwritten. Rather than emphasize force, power, and coercion, as we have seen to be characteristic of fascism, racism, and communism, the democratic ideologues emphasize the primacy of moral rules, not the least of which is the obligation of contract binding together the members of society. Finally, the democrats generally hold that, because of the consensual basis of the state and perhaps society as well, the primary function and goal of the state are to serve the various interests of its constituent members, both collective and individual.

It follows from the discussion above that the democrats seek to rest the ultimate control over the exercise of authority in the hands of the people, thereby to guarantee that the government, as agency of the state, attends to those arrangements of society serving the interests of the vast majority of its people. Such final control over the exercise of authority usually involves some effective determination of rulers by the public, together with a willingness, on the part of the incumbents, to retire from office should this be so decided.

Historically speaking, democracy has been associated with three creeds: liberty, equality, and fraternity. All three creeds are implicit in the doctrine of a social contract. The creed of liberty is generally associated with the democratic emphasis on the ultimate popular control over the exercise of authority. Coupled with a doctrine of natural rights and natural law, the creed of liberty extends the guarantee of freedom from coercion to the minorities as well as to the majority. The creed of equality is often associated with the democratic emphasis on numbers in the political calculus of power. And it is but a short step from a doctrine of a social contract to the creed of fraternity: the organization of a group of people for common goals and common interests. To this creed of fraternity the democratic conservatives add the importance of tradition as a source of fraternal bonds among men.

The modes of experience from which models of democratic ideologies have been abstracted are far too complex and wide-ranging to discuss adequately here. There are, however, some core elements common to all democratic ideologies which we can identify. From the practices of the ancient Greek democracy, the democratic ideologues derived the notion of citizenship (participation in political life) and the notion of equality before the law. There is a further parallel between the emphasis in early Greek tradition on the "fundamental rule of law" and the democratic presuppositions of articles of association constituting the basis of a social contract. From the Roman government the democratic ideologues borrowed the notion of popular sovereignty: that in some manner the final authority of the state rested in the hands of the people. From the Christian understanding of man as made in the image of God, the democratic ideologues constructed a model of the inherent worth and dignity of the individual. From the Protestant emphasis on the priesthood of all believers and the congregational method of decision-making, the democratic ideologues derived models of grassroots or participatory democracy. Finally, from the discoveries generated through scientific activity, particularly advances in physics in the seventeenth and eighteenth centuries, the democratic ideologues abstracted a model of society which ultimately reduced mankind to a collection of atomistic individuals to be molded into a society, whether by human design alone or human design sanctioned by divine intention.

The various selections in this chapter serve to illustrate the points raised above. Particular attention should be directed to the subtle shifts in emphasis between and among the creeds of liberty, equality, and fraternity as one moves from Locke to Sartori. Implicitly the readings to follow demonstrate how ill-adapted are the creeds of liberty, equality, and fraternity, one to another. That is to say, these creeds, and in a larger sense, the web of democratic principles discussed above, are not completely consistent with each other. It is this lack of internal consistency, which the chapters to follow indicate, that has allowed the growth of divergent democratic ideologies within the context of democratic institutions in the modern nation–state.

Since man is by nature free, equal, and independent, according to Locke, he cannot be subjected to the political power of others except by his own consent. With the end of all political societies and governments being the preservation of property, any number of men may consent to make one community or government in order to greater secure their property in civil society than in the state of nature. The will of the body politic, composed only of those who have consented to join, is, according to Locke, subsequently determined by majority rule. Such compacts, Locke argues, do not bind the children or posterity of the man who originally entered into the contract. Distinguishing between express and tacit consent, Locke suggests that only express consent makes a man a member of a society and a subject of the government to which he is obliged, by and large, to remain subject. That man who enjoys the benefits of any given government, but has not given his express consent, has tacitly consented to obey the laws of that government only so long as he chooses to enjoy its benefits.

Moving beyond Locke's emphasis on property, Jefferson sees government as a means to secure life, liberty, and the pursuit of happiness. In the event that these functions are not fulfilled, Jefferson argues the moral right to dissolve the political bonds forged through the social contract. (A century earlier Locke had similarly argued the right to dissolve a government when either the legislative or executive component acted contrary to the trust charged to them through the social contract.) Like Locke, Jefferson emphasizes that the will of the majority is to prevail, although that "will" must be tempered with reason, guaranteeing to minorities rights equal to those enjoyed by the majority.

Unlike Locke, who sees civil society merely as a better way to secure the enjoyment of property, Rousseau finds a point in the state of nature when the human race could simply no longer endure. By surrendering all rights to a civil association, according to Rousseau, mankind enlists the strength of the entire community for protection of person and property of each constituent member. Although the individual, in the association thus formed, has no claim against the community, the conditions of civil society will conform to the individual's real interests, Rousseau asserts, since the conditions of civil society are the same for all, and thus it would be to no one's interests to make onerous the conditions of any other. In rather stark contrast to Locke and Jefferson, Rousseau argues that the social contract creates a moral and collective body. Far from destroying natural equality, Rousseau urges, the contract substitutes moral and legal equality for the physical inequalities from which men suffer in the state of nature. Similarly, the unqualified right to lay hands on all that tempts man—his natural liberty—is replaced, in civil society, with a positive title to property. Finally, in civil society, Rousseau contends, man gains moral freedom: no longer subject to the appetites, man discovers that to obey the laws of society is to be free. Although man is no longer subject to the will of the stronger as in the state of nature, he may be compelled, in civil society, to obey the general will. But to be so compelled is, notes Rousseau, only forcing the individual to realize his moral freedom.

There is a rather strong similarity between the doctrine of Rousseau and the hopes expressed by the authors of the "Port Huron Statement." Like Rousseau, the Students for a Democratic Society (SDS) emphasize the need to cultivate the unrealized potential of mankind through the mechanisms of civil society. Much like Rousseau, the SDS envision politics as a means of bringing people out of isolation into community; only by so doing will man alleviate the loneliness, estrangement, and isolation characterizing the relations among men today. Subjectively, the SDS contends, apathy exists because ordinary people share a feeling of powerlessness in the face of human events. Objectively, according to the SDS, apathy exists because the ordinary people are separated from the seats of power. Calling for human relationships involving fraternity and honesty, the SDS seek a participatory democracy where the common man shares in the daily calculus of power, thereby encouraging his independence and self-development.

With Burke, the moral and corporate character attributed to civil society by Rousseau acquires such an overwhelming significance that Burke's notion of the social contract has receded into the background. For all intents and purposes, Burke informs us, once a people has formed a commonwealth, becoming a political personality, they have forever parted with any moral power to alter it. In fact, he points out, our fundamental obligations to mankind arise not from choice, as both Rousseau and the SDS contend, but from divine will. All voluntary agreements, including the sanctity of the original contract, necessarily depend upon these prior obligations. Burke emphasizes, in contrast to the other writers considered above, that there is no necessary reason why the general will need be determined by majority rule. For majority rule is, Burke points out, a matter of convention. Political leaders for Burke, unlike the legislators of Locke and Rousseau, are a natural aristocracy, inseparable from the interests of state and society. This does not mean that Burke rejects equality before the law—commutative justice. It does mean, as Burke argues, that the national harmony requires a balance between the common sort of men and their proper chieftains. (On this point the SDS stands in strong vocal opposition.) More than simply the father of modern conservatism, Burke offers one of the first complete statements of modern democratic elitism.

Sartori follows Burke's lead in emphasizing that the democratic theory of elites is the core of democratic theory. Prodemocratic elites are an essential guarantee to any democratic system. Democracy, he claims, has only functioned when an aristocracy has governed. Although the popular slogan rests sovereignty in the hands of the people, Sartori contends, the fact that we have recourse to elections demonstrates that the democratic system cannot be operated by the people. Sartori argues that the sovereign people do not (and should not) make political decisions; rather, political decisions are submitted to the people. Only in this last sense can it be said that the people govern (at the point of elections). Prescriptively, democracy may mean equal power for everybody; actually, democracy means that power resides in those persons who avail themselves of it. And the success, and even survival, of a democracy depends upon the quality of the leadership so defined.

10 Of the Beginning of Political Societies

JOHN LOCKE

Men being, as has been said, by Nature, all free, equal and independent, no one can be put out of this Estate, and subjected to the Political Power of another, without his own *Consent.* The only way whereby any one devests himself of his Natural Liberty, and *puts on the bonds of Civil Society* is by agreeing with other Men to joyn and unite into a Community, for their comfortable, safe, and peaceful living one amongst another, in a secure Enjoyment of their Properties, and a greater Security against any that are not of it. This any number of Men may do, because it injures not the Freedom of the rest; they are left as they were in the Liberty of the State of Nature. When any number of Men have so *consented to make one Community* or Government, they are thereby presently incorporated, and make *one Body Politick,* wherein the *Majority* have a Right to act and conclude the rest.

For when any number of Men have, by the consent of every individual, made a *Community,* they have thereby made that *Community* one Body, with a Power to Act as one Body, which is only by the will and determination of the *majority.* For that which acts any Community, being only the consent of the individuals of it, and it being necessary to that which is one body to move one way; it is necessary the Body should move that way whither the greater force carries it, which is the *consent of the majority:* or else it is impossible it should act or continue one Body, *one Community,* which the consent of every individual that united into it, agreed that it should; and so every one is bound by that consent to be concluded by the *majority.* And therefore we see that in Assemblies impowered to act by positive Laws where no number is set by that positive Law which impowers them, the *act of the Majority* passes for the act of the whole, and of course determines, as having by the Law of Nature and Reason, the power of the whole.

And thus every Man, by consenting with others to make one Body Politick under one Government, puts himself under an Obligation to every one of that Society, to submit to the determination of the *majority,* and to be concluded by it; or else this *original Compact,* whereby he with others incorporates into *one Society,* would signifie nothing, and be no Compact, if he be left free, and under no other ties, than he was in before in the State of Nature. For what appearance would there be of any Compact? What new Engage-

SOURCE: from *The Second Treatise of Government* by John Locke, edited by Peter Laslett, pp. 374–394.

ment if he were no farther tied by any Decrees of the Society, than he himself thought fit, and did actually consent to? This would be still as great a liberty, as he himself had before his Compact, or any one else in the State of Nature hath, who may submit himself and consent to any acts of it if he thinks fit.

For if *the consent of the majority* shall not in reason, be received, *as the act of the whole,* and conclude every individual; nothing but the consent of every individual can make any thing to be the act of the whole: But such a consent is next impossible ever to be had, if we consider the Infirmities of Health, and Avocations of Business, which in a number, though much less than that of a Common-wealth, will necessarily keep many away from the publick Assembly. To which if we add the variety of Opinions, and contrariety of Interests, which unavoidably happen in all Collections of Men, the coming into Society upon such terms, would be only like *Cato*'s coming into the Theatre, only to go out again. Such a Constitution as this would make the mighty *Leviathan* of a shorter duration, than the feeblest Creatures; and not let it outlast the day it was born in: which cannot be suppos'd till we can think, that Rational Creatures should desire and constitute Societies only to be dissolved. For where the *majority* cannot conclude the rest, there they cannot act as one Body, and consequently will be immediately dissolved again.

Whosoever therefore out of a state of Nature unite into a *Community,* must be understood to give up all the power, necessary to the ends for which they unite into Society, to the *majority* of the Community, unless they expressly agreed in any number greater than the majority. And this is done by barely agreeing to *unite into one Political Society,* which is *all the Compact that* is, or needs be, between the Individuals, that enter into, or make up a *Common-wealth.* And thus that, which begins and actually *constitutes any Political Society,* is nothing but the consent of any number of Freemen capable of a majority to unite and incorporate into such a Society. And this is that, and that only, which did, or could give *beginning* to any *lawful Government* in the World.

To this I find two Objections made.

First, *That there are no Instances to be found in Story of a Company of Men independent and equal one amongst another, that met together, and in this way began and set up a Government.*

Secondly, *'Tis impossible of right that Men should do so, because all Men being born under Government, they are to submit to that, and are not at liberty to begin a new one.*

To the first there is this to Answer. That it is not at all to be wonder'd, that *History* gives us but a very little account of Men, *that lived together in the State of Nature.* The inconveniencies of that condition, and the love, and want of Society no sooner brought any number of them together, but they presently united and incorporated, if they designed to continue together. And if we may not suppose *Men* ever to have been *in the State of Nature,* because we hear not much of them in such a State, we may as well suppose the Armies of *Salmanasser,* or *Xerxes* were never Children, because we hear little of them, till they were Men, and imbodied in Armies. Government is every where antecedent to Records, and Letters seldome come in amongst a People, till a long continuation of Civil Society has, by other more necessary Arts provided for their Safety, Ease, and Plenty. And then they begin to look after the History of their *Founders,* and search into their *original,* when they have out-lived the memory of it. For 'tis with *Common-wealths* as with particular Persons, they are commonly *ignorant of their own Births* and *Infancies:* And if they know any thing of their *Original,* they are beholding, for it, to the accidental Records, that others have kept of it. And those that we have, of the beginning of any Polities in the World, excepting that of the *Jews,* where God himself immediately interpos'd, and which favours not at all Paternal Dominion, are all either plain instances of such a beginning, as I have mentioned, or at least have manifest footsteps of it.

He must shew a strange inclination to deny evident matter of fact, when it agrees not with his Hypothesis, who will not allow that the *beginning* of *Rome* and *Venice* were by the uniting together of several Men free and independent one of another, amongst whom there was no natural Superiority or Subjection. And if *Josephus Acosta*'s word may be taken, he tells us, that in many parts of *America* there was no Government at all. *There are great and apparent Conjectures,* says he, *that these Men,* speaking of those of *Peru, for a long time had neither Kings nor Common-wealths, but lived in Troops, as they do this day in* Florida, *the* Cheriquanas, *those of* Bresil, *and many other Nations, which have no certain Kings, but as occasion is offered in Peace or War, they choose their Captains as they please.* 1. I. c. 25. If it be said, that every Man there was born subject to his Father, or the head of his Family. That the subjection due from a Child to a Father, took not away his freedom of uniting into what Political Society he thought fit, has been already proved. But be that as it will, these Men, 'tis evident, were actually *free;* and whatever superiority some Politicians now would place in any of them, they themselves claimed it not; but by consent were all *equal,* till by the same consent they set Rulers over themselves. So that their *Politick Societies* all *began* from a voluntary Union, and the mutual agreement of Men freely acting in the choice of their Governours, and forms of Government.

And I hope those who went away from *Sparta* with *Palantus,* mentioned by *Justin l. 3, c.* 4 will be allowed to have been *Freemen independent* one of another, and to have set up a Government over themselves, by their own consent. Thus I have given several Examples out of History, of *People free and in the State of Nature,* that being met together incorporated and *began a Common-wealth.* And if the want of such instances be an argument to prove that *Government* were not, nor could not be so *begun,* I suppose the contenders for Paternal Empire were better let it alone, than urge it against natural Liberty. For if they can give so many instances out of History, of

Governments begun upon Paternal Right, I think (though at best an Argument from what has been, to what should of right be, has no great force) one might, without any great danger, yield them the cause. But if I might advise them in the Case, they would do well not to search too much into the *Original of Governments,* as they have begun *de facto,* lest they should find at the foundation of most of them, something very little favourable to the design they promote, and such a power as they contend for.

But to conclude, Reason being plain on our side, that Men are naturally free, and the Examples of History shewing, that the *Governments* of the World, that were begun in Peace, had their beginning laid on that foundation, and were *made by the Consent of the People;* There can be little room for doubt, either where the Right is, or what has been the Opinion, or Practice of Mankind, about the *first erecting of Governments.*

I will not deny, that if we look back as far as History will direct us, towards the *Original of Common-wealths,* we shall generally find them under the Government and Administration of one Man. And I am also apt to believe, that where a Family was numerous enough to subsist by it self, and continued entire together, without mixing with others, as it often happens, where there is much Land and few People, the Government commonly began in the Father. For the Father having, by the Law of Nature, the same Power with every Man else to punish, as he thought fit, any Offences against that Law, might thereby punish his transgressing Children even when they were Men, and out of their Pupilage; and they were very likely to submit to his punishment, and all joyn with him against the Offender, in their turns, giving him thereby power to Execute his Sentence against any transgression, and so in effect make him the Law-maker, and Governour over all, that remained in Conjunction with his Family. He was fittest to be trusted; Paternal affection secured their Property, and Interest under his Care, and the Custom of obeying him, in their Childhood, made it easier to submit to him, rather than to any other. If therefore they must have one to rule them, as Government is hardly to be avoided amongst Men that live together; who so likely to be the Man, as he that was their common Father; unless Negligence, Cruelty, or any other defect of Mind, or Body made him unfit for it? But when either the Father died, and left his next Heir for want of Age, Wisdom, Courage, or any other Qualities, less fit for Rule: or where several Families met, and consented to continue together: There, 'tis not to be doubted, but they used their natural freedom, to set up him, whom they judged the ablest, and most likely, to Rule well over them. Conformable hereunto we find the People of *America,* who (living out of the reach of the Conquering Swords, and spreading domination of the two great Empires of *Peru* and *Mexico*) enjoy'd their own natural freedom, though, *caeteris paribus,* they commonly prefer the Heir of their deceased King; yet if they find him any way weak, or uncapable, they pass him by and set up the stoutest and bravest Man for their Ruler.

Thus, though looking back as far as Records give us any account of

Peopling the World, and the History of Nations, we commonly find the *Government* to be in one hand, yet it destroys not that, which I affirm, (*viz.*) That the *beginning of Politick Society* depends upon the consent of the Individuals, to joyn into and make one Society; who, when they are thus incorporated, might set up what form of Government they thought fit. But this having given occasion to Men to mistake, and think, that by Nature Government was Monarchical, and belong'd to the Father, it may not be amiss here to consider, why People in the beginning generally pitch'd upon this form, which though perhaps the Father's Preheminency might in the first institution of some Common-wealths, give a rise to, and place, in the beginning, the Power in one hand; Yet it is plain, that the reason, that continued the Form of *Government in a single Person,* was not any Regard, or Respect to Paternal Authority; since all petty Monarchies, that is, almost all *Monarchies,* near their Original, have been commonly, at least upon occasion, *Elective.*

First then, in the beginning of things, the Father's Government of the Childhood of those sprung from him, having accustomed them to the *Rule of one Man,* and taught them that where it was exercised with Care and Skill, with Affection and Love to those under it, it was sufficient to procure and preserve to Men all the Political Happiness they sought for, in Society. It was no wonder, that they should pitch upon, and naturally run into that Form of Government, which from their Infancy they had been all accustomed to; and which, by experience they had found both easie and safe. To which, if we add, that *Monarchy* being simple, and most obvious to Men, whom neither experience had instructed in Forms of Government, nor the Ambition or Insolence of Empire had taught to beware of the Encroachments of Prerogative, or the Inconveniencies of Absolute Power, which Monarchy, in Succession, was apt to lay claim to, and bring upon them, it was not at all strange, that they should not much trouble themselves to think of Methods of restraining any Exorbitances of those, to whom they had given the Authority over them, and of ballancing the Power of Government, by placing several parts of it in different hands. They had neither felt the Oppression of Tyrannical Dominion, nor did the Fashion of the Age, nor their Possessions, or way of living (which afforded little matter for Covetousness or Ambition) give them any reason to apprehend or provide against it: and therefore 'tis no wonder they put themselves into such a *Frame of Government,* as was not only as I said, most obvious and simple, but also best suited to their present State and Condition; which stood more in need of defence against foreign Invasions and Injuries, than of multiplicity of Laws. The equality of a simple poor way of liveing confineing their desires within the narrow bounds of each mans smal propertie made few controversies and so no need of many laws to decide them: And there wanted not of Justice where there were but few trespasses, and few Offenders. Since then those, who liked one another so well as to joyn into Society, cannot but be supposed to have some Acquaintance and Friendship together, and some Trust one in another; they coud not but have greater Apprehensions of others, than of one another: And therefore their first care and thought cannot but be supposed to be, how to secure themselves against foreign Force. 'Twas natural for them to put themselves under a *Frame of Government,* which might best serve to that end; and chuse the wisest and bravest Man to conduct them in their Wars, and lead them out against their Enemies, and in this chiefly be their *Ruler.*

Thus we see, that the *Kings* of the *Indians* in *America,* which is still a Pattern of the first Ages in *Asia* and *Europe,* whilst the Inhabitants were too few for the Country, and want of People and Money gave Men to Temptation to enlarge their Possessions of Land, or contest for wider extent of Ground, are little more than *Generals of their Armies;* and though they command absolutely in War, yet at home and in time of Peace they exercise very little Dominion, and have but a very moderate Sovereignty, the Resolutions of Peace and War, being ordinarily either in the People, or in a Council. Though the War it self, which admits not of Plurality of Governours, naturally devolves the Command into the *King's sole Authority.*

And thus in *Israel* it self, the *chief Business of their Judges, and first Kings* seems to have been *to be Captains in War,* and Leaders of their Armies; which, (besides what is signified by *going out and in before the People,* which was, to march forth to War, and home again in the Heads of their Forces) appears plainly in the Story of *Jephtha.* The *Ammonites* making War upon *Israel,* the *Gileadites,* in fear send to *Jephtha,* a Bastard of their Family, whom they had cast off, and article with him, if he will assist them against the *Ammonites,* to make him their Ruler; which they do in these words, *And the People made him head and captain over them,* Judg. 11. 11. which was, as it seems, all one as to be *Judge. And he judged Israel,* Judg. 12. 7. that is, was their *Captain-General, six Years.* So when *Jotham* upbraids the *Schechemites* with the Obligation they had to *Gideon,* who had been their *Judge* and Ruler, he tells them, *He fought for you, and adventured his life far, and delivered you out of the hands of Midian,* Judg. 9. 17. Nothing mentioned of him, but what he did as a *General,* and indeed that is all is found in his History, or in any of the rest of the Judges. And *Abimelech* particularly is called *King,* though at most he was but their *General.* And when, being weary of the ill Conduct of *Sammel's* Sons, the Children of *Israel* desired a King, *like all the nations to judge them, and to go out before them, and to fight their battles,* 1 Sam. 8. 20. God granting their Desire, says to *Samuel, I will send thee a Man, and thou shalt anoint him to be Captain over my People Israel, that he may save my People out of the hands of the Philistines,* c. 9. v. 16. As if the only *business of a King* had been to lead out their Armies, and fight in their Defence; and accordingly at his Inauguration, pouring a Vial of Oyl upon him, declares to *Saul,* that *the Lord had anointed him to be Captain over his inheritance,* c. 10. v. 1. And therefore those, who after *Saul*'s being solemnly chosen and saluted *King* by the *Tribes* at *Mispah,* were unwilling to have him their King, make no other Objection but this, *How shall this Man save us?* v. 27. as if they should have said, This Man is unfit to be our *King,* not having Skill and Conduct enough in War, to be able to defend us. And when God resolved to transfer the Government to *David,* it is in these Words, *But now thy kingdom shall not continue: The Lord hath sought him a Man after his own heart, and the Lord hath commanded him to be Captain over his People,* c. 13. v. 14. As if the whole *Kingly Authority* were nothing else but to be their *General:* And therefore the *Tribes* who had stuck to *Saul*'s Family, and opposed *David*'s Reign, when they came to *Hebron* with terms of Submission to him, they tell him, amongst other Arguments they had to submit to him as to their King, That he was in effect their *King* in *Saul*'s time, and therefore they had no reason but to receive him as their King now. *Also* (say they) *in time past, when Saul was King over us, thou wast he that leddest out and broughtest in Israel, and the Lord said unto thee, thou shalt feed my People Israel, and thou shalt be a Captain over Israel.*

Thus, whether *a Family* by degrees *grew up into a Common-wealth,* and the Fatherly Authority being continued on to the elder Son, every one in his turn growing up under it, tacitly submitted to it, and the easiness and equality of it not offending any one, every one acquiesced, till time seemed to have confirmed it, and settled a right of Succession by Prescription: or whether several Families, or the Descendants of several Families, whom Chance, Neighbourhood, or Business brought together, uniting into Society, the need of a General, whose Conduct might defend them against their Enemies in War, and the great confidence the Innocence and Sincerity of that poor but vertuous Age (such as are almost all those which begin Governments, that ever come to last in the World) gave Men one of another, made the first Beginners of Common-wealths generally put the Rule into one Man's hand, without any other express Limitation or Restraint, but what the Nature of the thing, and the End of Government required: which ever of these it was, that at first put the rule into the hands of a single person, certain it is that no body was ever intrusted with it but for the publick Good and Safety, and to those Ends in the Infancies of Commonwealths those who had it, commonly used it: And unless they had done so, young Societies could not have subsisted: without such nursing Fathers tender and carefull of the publick weale, all Governments would have sunk under the Weakness and Infirmities of their Infancy; and the Prince and the People had soon perished together.

But though the *Golden Age* (before vain Ambition, and *amor sceleratus habendi,* evil Concupiscence, had corrupted Mens minds into a Mistake of true Power and Honour) had more Virtue, and consequently better Governours, as well as less vicious Subjects; and there was then *no stretching Prerogative* on the one side to oppress the People; *nor* consequently on the other any *Dispute about Priviledge,* to lessen or restrain the Power of the Magistrate; and so no contest betwixt Rulers and People about Governours or Government: Yet, when Ambition and Luxury, in future Ages would retain and increase the Power, without doing the Business, for which it was given, and aided by Flattery, taught Princes to have distinct and separate Interests from their People, Men found it necessary to examine more carefully *the Original* and Rights of *Government;* and to find out ways to *restrain the Exorbitances,* and *prevent the Abuses* of that Power which they having intrusted in another's hands only for their own good, they found was made use of to hurt them.

Thus we may see how probable it is, that People that were naturally free, and by their own consent either submitted to the Government of their Father, or united together, out of different Families to make a Government, should generally put the *Rule into one Man's hands,* and chuse to be under the Conduct of a *single Person,* without so much as by express Conditions limiting or regulating his Power, which they thought safe enough in his Honesty and Prudence. Though they never dream'd of Monarchy being *Jure Divino,* which we never heard of among Mankind, till it was revealed to us by the Divinity of this last Age; nor ever allowed Paternal Power to have a right to Dominion, or to be the Foundation of all Government. And thus much may suffice to shew, that as far as we have any light from History, we have reason to conclude, that all peaceful beginnings of *Government* have been *laid in the Consent of the People.* I say *peaceful,* because I shall have occasion in another place to speak of Conquest, which some esteem a way of beginning of Governments.

The other Objection I find urged against the beginning of Polities, in the way I have mentioned, is this, viz.

That all Men being born under Government, some or other, it is impossible any of them should ever be free, and at liberty to unite together, and begin a new one, or ever be able to erect a lawful Government.

If this Argument be good; I ask, how came so many lawful Monarchies into the World? For if any body, upon this supposition, can shew me any one Man in any Age of the World *free* to begin a lawful Monarchy; I will be bound to shew him Ten other *free Men* at Liberty, at the same time to unite and begin a new Government under a Regal, or any other Form. It being demonstration, that if any one, *born under the Dominion* of another, may be so *free* as to have a right to command others in a new and distinct Empire; every one that is *born under the Dominion* of another may be so *free* too, and may become a Ruler, or Subject, of a distinct separate Government. And so by this their own Principle, either all Men, however *born,* are *free,* or else there is but one lawful Prince, one lawful Government in the World. And then they have nothing to do but barely to shew us, which that is. Which when they have done, I doubt not but all Mankind will easily agree to pay Obedience to him.

Though it be a sufficient Answer to their Objection to shew, that it involves them in the same difficulties that it doth those they use it against; yet I shall endeavour to discover the weakness of this Argument a little farther.

All Men, say they, *are born under Government, and therefore they cannot be at liberty to begin a new one. Every one is born a Subject to his Father, or his Prince, and is therefore under the perpetual tye of Subjection and Allegiance.* 'Tis plain Mankind never owned nor considered any such natural *subjection, that they were born in,* to one or to the other, that tied them, without their own Consents, to a Subjection to them and their Heirs.

For there are no Examples so frequent in History, both Sacred and Prophane, as those of Men withdrawing themselves, and their Obedience, from the Jurisdiction they were born under, and the Family or Community they were bred up in, and *setting up new Governments* in other places; from whence sprang all that number of petty Common-wealths in the beginning of Ages, and which always multiplyed, as long as there was room enough, till the stronger, or more fortunate swallowed the weaker; and those great ones again breaking to pieces, dissolved into lesser Dominions. All which are so many Testimonies against Paternal Sovereignty, and plainly prove, That it was not the natural right of the Father descending to his Heirs, that made Governments in the beginning, since it was impossible, upon that ground, there should have been so many little Kingdoms; all must have been but only one Universal Monarchy, if Men had not been *at liberty to separate* themselves from their Families, and the Government, be it what it will, that was set up in it, and go and make distinct Common-wealths and other Governments, as they thought fit.

This has been the practice of the World from its first beginning to this day: Nor is it now any more hindrance to the freedom of Mankind, that they are *born under constituted and ancient Polities,* that have established Laws and set Forms of Government, than if they were born in the Woods, amongst the unconfined Inhabitants that ran loose in them. For those who would perswade us, that *by being born under any Government, we are naturally Subjects to it,* and have no more any title or pretence to the freedom of the State of Nature, have no other reason (bating that of Paternal Power, which we have already answer'd) to produce for it, but only because our Fathers or Progenitors passed away their natural Liberty, and thereby bound up themselves and their Posterity to a perpetual subjection to the Government, which they themselves submitted to. 'Tis true, that whatever Engagements or Promises any one has made for himself, he is under the Obligation of them, but *cannot* by any *Compact* whatsoever, bind *his Children* or Posterity. For this Son, when a Man, being altogether as free as the Father, any *act of the Father can no more give away the liberty of the Son,* than it can of any body else: He may indeed annex such Conditions to the Land, he enjoyed as a Subject of any Commonwealth, as may oblige his Son to be of that Community, if he will enjoy those Possessions which were his Fathers;

because that Estate being his Fathers Property, he may dispose or settle it as he pleases.

And this has generally given the occasion to mistake in this matter; because Commonwealths not permitting any part of their Dominions to be dismembred, nor to be enjoyed by any but those of their Community, the Son cannot ordinarily enjoy the Possessions of his Father, but under the same terms his Father did; by becoming a Member of the Society: whereby he puts himself presently under the Government, he finds there established, as much as any other Subject of that Commonwealth. And thus *the Consent of Free-men, born under Government,* which only *makes them Members of it,* being given separately in their turns, as each comes to be of Age, and not in a multitude together; People take no notice of it, and thinking it not done at all, or not necessary, conclude they are naturally Subjects as they are Men.

But, 'tis plain, *Governments* themselves understand it otherwise; they *claim no Power over the Son, because of that they had over the Father;* nor look on Children as being their Subjects, by their Fathers being so. If a Subject of *England* have a Child by an *English* Woman in *France,* whose Subject is he? Not the King of *England*'s; for he must have leave to be admitted to the Priviledges of it. Nor the King of *France*'s; For how then has his Father a liberty to bring him away, and breed him as he pleases? And who ever was judged as a *Traytor* or *Deserter,* if he left, or warr'd against a Country, for being barely born in it of Parents that were Aliens there? 'Tis plain then, by the Practice of Governments themselves, as well as by the Law of right Reason, that *a Child is born a Subject of no Country or Government.* He is under his Fathers Tuition and Authority, till he come to Age of Discretion; and then he is a Free-man, at liberty what Government he will put himself under; what Body Politick he will unite himself to. For if an *English-Man*'s Son, born in *France,* be at liberty, and may do so, 'tis evident there is no Tye upon him by his Father being a Subject of this Kingdom; nor is he bound up, by any Compact of his Ancestors. And why then hath not his Son, by the same reason, the same liberty, though he be born any where else? Since the Power that a Father hath naturally over his Children, is the same, where-ever they be born; and the Tyes of Natural Obligations, are not bounded by the positive Limits of Kingdoms and Common-wealths.

Every Man being, as has been shewed, *naturally free,* and nothing being able to put him into subjection to any Earthly Power, but only his own Consent; it is to be considered, what shall be understood to be *a sufficient Declaration of* a Mans *Consent, to make him subject* to the Laws of any Government. There is a common distinction of an express and a tacit consent, which will concern our present Case. No body doubts but an *express Consent,* of any Man, entring into any Society, makes him a perfect Member of that Society, a Subject of that Government. The difficulty is, what ought to be look'd upon as a *tacit Consent,* and how far it binds, *i.e.* how far any one shall be looked on to have consented, and thereby submitted to any Government, where he has made no Expressions of it at all. And to this I say, that every Man, that hath any Possession, or Enjoyment, of any part of the Dominions of any Government, doth thereby give his *tacit Consent,* and is as far forth obliged to Obedience to the Laws of that Government, during such Enjoyment, as any one under it; whether this his Possession be of Land, to him and his Heirs for ever, or a Lodging only for a Week; or whether it be barely travelling freely on the Highway; and in Effect, it reaches as far as the very being of any one within the Territories of that Government.

To understand this the better, it is fit to consider, that every Man, when he, at first, incorporates himself into any Commonwealth, he, by his uniting himself thereunto, annexed also, and submits to the Community those Possessions, which he has, or shall acquire, that do not already belong to any other Government. For it would be a direct Contradiction, for any one, to enter into Society with others for the securing and regulating of Property: And yet to suppose his Land, whose Property is to be regulated by the Laws of the Society, should be exempt from the Jurisdiction of that Government, to which he himself the Proprietor of the Land, is a Subject. By the same Act therefore, whereby any one unites his Person, which was before free, to any Commonwealth; by the same he unites his Possessions, which were before free, to it also; and they become, both of them, Person and Possession, subject to the Government and Dominion of that Commonwealth, as long as it hath a being. *Whoever* therefore, from thenceforth, by Inheritance, Purchase, Permission, or otherways *enjoys any part of the Land,* so annext to, and under the Government *of that Commonwealth, must take it with the Condition* it is under; that is, *of submitting to the Government of the Commonwealth,* under whose Jurisdiction it is, as far forth, as any Subject of it.

But since the Government has a direct Jurisdiction only over the Land, and reaches the Possessor of it, (before he has actually incorporated himself in the Society) only as he dwells upon, and enjoys that: *The Obligation* any one is under, by Virtue of such Enjoyment, *to submit to the Government, begins and ends with the Enjoyment;* so that whenever the Owner, who has given nothing but such a *tacit Consent* to the Government, will, by Donation, Sale, or otherwise, quit the said Possession, he is at liberty to go and incorporate himself into any other Commonwealth, or to agree with others to begin a new one, *in vacuis locis,* in any part of the World, they can find free and unpossessed: Whereas he, that has once, by actual Agreement, and any *express* Declaration, given his *Consent* to be of any Commonweal, is perpetually and indispensably obliged to be and remain unalterably a Subject to it, and can never be again in the liberty of the state of Nature; unless by any Calamity, the Government, he was under, comes to be dissolved; or else by some publick Act cuts him off from being any longer a Member of it.

But submitting to the Laws of any Country, living quietly, and enjoying Priviledges and Protection under them, *makes not a Man a Member of that*

Society: This is only a local Protection and Homage due to, and from all those, who, not being in a state of War, come within the Territories belonging to any Government, to all parts whereof the force of its Law extends. But this no more *makes a Man a Member of that Society,* a perpetual Subject of that Commonwealth, than it would make a Man a Subject to another in whose Family he found it convenient to abide for some time; though, whilst he continued in it, he were obliged to comply with the Laws, and submit to the Government he found there. And thus we see, that *Foreigners,* by living all their Lives under another Government, and enjoying the Priviledges and Protection of it, though they are bound, even in Conscience, to submit to its Administration, as far forth as any Denison; yet do not thereby come to be *Subjects or Members of that Commonwealth.* Nothing can make any Man so, but his actually entering into it by positive Engagement, and express Promise and Compact. This is that, which I think, concerning the beginning of Political Societies, and that *Consent which makes any one a Member* of any Commonwealth.

1690

11 The Declaration of Independence

(As it reads in the parchment copy)

THOMAS JEFFERSON

The Unanimous Declaration of the Thirteen United States of America

When in the Course of human events, it becomes necessary for one people to dissolve the political bands, which have connected them with another, and to assume among the powers of the earth, the separate and equal station to which the Laws of Nature and of Nature's God entitle them, a decent respect to the opinions of mankind requires that they should declare the causes which impel them to the separation.—We hold these truths to be self-evident, that all men are created equal, that they are endowed by their Creator with certain unalienable Rights, that among these are Life, Liberty and the pursuit of Happiness.—That to secure these rights, Governments are instituted among Men, deriving their just powers from the consent of the governed,—That whenever any Form of Government becomes destructive of these ends, it is the Right of the People to alter or to abolish it, and to institute new Government, laying its foundation on such principles and organizing its powers in such form, as to them shall seem most likely to effect their Safety and Happiness. Prudence, indeed, will dictate that Governments long established should not be changed for light and transient causes; and accordingly all experience hath shewn, that mankind are more disposed to suffer, while evils are sufferable, than to right themselves by abolishing the forms to which they are accustomed. But when a long train of abuses and usurpations, pursuing invariably the same Object evinces a design to reduce them under absolute Despotism, it is their right, it is their duty, to throw off such Government, and to provide new Guards for their future security.—Such has been the patient sufferance of these Colonies; and such is now the necessity which constrains them to alter their former Systems of Government. The history of the present King of Great Britain is a history of repeated injuries and usurpations, all having in direct object the establishment of an absolute Tyranny over these States. To prove this, let Facts be submitted to a candid world.—He has refused his Assent to Laws, the most wholesome and necessary for the public good.—He has forbidden his Governors to pass Laws of immediate and pressing importance, unless suspended in their operation till his Assent should be obtained; and when so suspended, he has utterly neglected to attend to them.—He has refused to pass other Laws for the accommodation of large districts of people, unless those people would relinquish the right of Representation in the Legislature, a right inestimable to them and formidable to tyrants only.—He has called together legislative bodies at places unusual, uncomfortable, and distant from the depository of their public Records, for the sole purpose of fatiguing them into compliance with his measures.—He has dissolved Representative Houses repeatedly, for opposing with manly firmness his invasions on the rights of the people.—He has refused for a long time, after such dissolutions, to cause others to be elected; whereby the Legislative powers, incapable of Annihilation, have returned to the People at large for their exercise; the State remaining in the meantime exposed to all the dangers of invasion from without, and convulsions within.—He has endeavoured to prevent the population of these States; for that purpose obstructing the Laws for Naturalization of Foreigners; refusing to pass others to encourage their migrations hither, and raising the conditions of new Appropriations of Lands.—He has obstructed the Administration of Justice, by refusing his Assent to Laws for establishing Judiciary powers.—He has made Judges dependent on his Will alone, for the tenure of their offices, and the amount and payment of their salaries.—He has erected a multitude of New Offices, and sent hither swarms of Officers to harass our people, and eat out their substance.—He has kept among us, in times of peace, Standing Armies without the Consent of our legislatures.—He has affected to render the Military independent of and superior to the Civil power.—He has combined with others to subject us to a jurisdiction foreign to our constitution, and unacknowledged by our laws; giving his Assent to their Acts of pretended Legislation.—For quartering large bodies of armed troops among us:—For protecting them, by a mock Trial, from punishment for any Murders which they should commit on the Inhabitants of these States:—For cutting off our Trade with all parts of the world:—For imposing Taxes on us without our Consent:—For depriving us in many cases, of the benefits of Trial by Jury:—For transporting us beyond Seas to be tried for pretended offenses:—For abolishing the free System of English Laws in a neighboring Province, establishing therein an Arbitrary government, and enlarging its Boundaries so as to render it at once an example and fit instrument for introducing the same absolute rule into these Colonies:—For taking away our Charters, abolishing our most valuable Laws, and altering fundamentally the Forms of our Governments:—For suspending our own Legislatures, and declaring themselves invested with power to legislate for us in all cases whatsoever.—He has abdicated Government here, by declaring us out of his Protection and waging War against us.—He has plundered our seas, ravaged our Coasts, burnt our towns, and destroyed the lives of our people.—He is at this time transporting large Armies of foreign Mercenaries to compleat the works of death, desolation and tyranny, already begun with circumstances of Cruelty & perfidy, scarcely paralleled in the most barbarous ages, and totally unworthy the Head of a civilized nation.—He has constrained our fellow Citizens taken Captive on the high Seas to bear Arms against their Country, to become the executioners of their friends and Brethren, or to fall themselves by their hands.—He has excited domestic insurrections amongst us, and has endeavoured to bring on the inhabitants of our frontiers, the merciless Indian Savages, whose known rule of warfare, is an undistinguished destruction of all ages, sexes and conditions. In every stage of these Oppressions We have Petitioned for Redress in the most humble terms: Our repeated Petitions have been answered only by repeated injury. A Prince whose character is thus marked by every act which may define a Tyrant, is unfit to be the ruler of a free people. Nor have We been wanting in attentions to our Brittish brethren. We have warned them from time to time of attempts by their legislature to extend an unwarrantable jurisdiction over us. We have reminded them of the circumstances of our emigration and settlement here. We have appealed to their native justice and magnanimity, and we have conjured them by the ties of our common kindred to disavow these usurpations, which would inevitably interrupt our connections and correspondence. They too have been deaf to the voice of justice and of consanguinity. We must, therefore, acquiesce in the necessity, which denounces our Separation, and hold them, as we hold the rest of mankind, Enemies in War, in Peace Friends.—

We, therefore, the Representatives of the united States of America, in General Congress, Assembled, appealing to the Supreme Judge of the world for the rectitude of our intentions do, in the Name, and by the Authority of the good People of these Colonies, solemnly publish and declare, That these United Colonies are, and of Right ought to be Free and Independent States; that they are Absolved from all Allegiance to the British Crown, and that all political connection between them and the State of Great Britain, is and ought to be totally dissolved; and that as Free and Independent States, they have full Power to levy War, conclude Peace, contract Alliances, establish Commerce, and to do all other Acts and Things which Independent States may of right do.—And for the support of this Declaration, with a firm reliance on the protection of divine Providence, we mutually pledge to each other our Lives, our Fortunes and our sacred Honor.

1776

12 First Inaugural Address

THOMAS JEFFERSON

Friends and Fellow Citizens:

Called upon to undertake the duties of the first executive office of our country, I avail myself of the presence of that portion of my fellow citizens which is here assembled to express my grateful thanks for the favor with which they have been pleased to look toward me, to declare a sincere consciousness that the task is above my talents, and that I approach it with those anxious and awful presentiments which the greatness of the charge and the weakness of my powers so justly inspire. A rising nation, spread over a wide and fruitful land, traversing all the seas with the rich productions of their industry, engaged in commerce with nations who feel power and forget right, advancing rapidly to destinies beyond the reach of mortal eye—when I contemplate these transcendent objects and see the honor, the happiness, and the hopes of this beloved country committed to the issue and the auspices of this day, I shrink from the contemplation and humble myself before the magnitude of the undertaking. Utterly indeed should I despair did not the presence of many whom I here see remind me that in the other high authorities provided by our Constitution I shall find resources of wisdom, of virtue, and of zeal on which to rely under all difficulties. To you then, gentlemen, who are charged with the sovereign functions of legislation, and to those associated with you, I look with encouragement for that guidance and support which may enable us to steer with safety the vessel in which we are all embarked amidst the conflicting elements of a troubled world.

During the contest of opinion through which we have passed, the animation of discussions and of exertions has sometimes worn an aspect which might impose on strangers unused to think freely and to speak and to write what they think. But this being now decided by the voice of the nation, enounced according to the rules of the Constitution, all will of course arrange themselves under the will of the law and unite in common efforts for the common good. All, too, will bear in mind this sacred principle that, though the will of the majority is in all cases to prevail, that will, to be rightful, must be reasonable; that the minority possess their equal rights, which equal laws must protect and to violate which would be oppression. Let us then, fellow citizens, unite with one heart and one mind; let us restore to social intercourse that harmony and affection without which liberty, and even life itself, are but dreary things. And let us reflect that, having banished from our land that religious intolerance under which mankind so long bled and suffered, we have yet gained little if we countenance a political intolerance as despotic, as wicked, and capable of as bitter and bloody persecutions. During the throes and convulsions of the ancient world, during the agonizing spasms of infuriated man, seeking through blood and slaughter his long-lost liberty, it was not wonderful that the agitation of the billows should reach even this distant and peaceful shore, that this should be more felt and feared by some and less by others, and should divide opinions as to measures of safety.

But every difference of opinion is not a difference of principle. We have called by different names brethren of the same principle. We are all republicans; we are all federalists. If there be any among us who would wish to dissolve this Union or to change its republican form, let them stand undisturbed as monuments of the safety with which error of opinion may be tolerated, where reason is left free to combat it. I know, indeed, that some honest men fear that a republican government cannot be strong; that this government is not strong enough. But would the honest patriot, in the full tide of successful experiment, abandon a government which has so far kept us free and firm, on the theoretic and visionary fear that this government, the world's best hope, may by possibility want energy to preserve itself? I trust not. I believe this, on the contrary, the strongest government on earth. I believe it the only one where every man, at the call of the law, would fly to the standard of the law and would meet invasions of the public order as his own personal concern. Sometimes it is said that man cannot be trusted with the government of himself. Can he then be trusted with the government of others? Or have we found angels, in the form of kings, to govern him? Let history answer this question.

Let us then, with courage and confidence, pursue our own federal and republican principles, our attachment to Union and representative government. Kindly separated by nature and a wide ocean from the exterminating havoc of one quarter of the globe; too high-minded to endure the degradations of the others; possessing a chosen country, with room enough for our descendants to the thousandth and thousandth generation; entertaining a due sense of our equal right to the use of our own faculties, to the acquisitions of our own industry, to honor and confidence from our fellow citizens, resulting not from birth but from our actions and their sense of them; enlightened by a benign religion, professed indeed and practiced in various forms, yet all of them including honesty, truth, temperance, gratitude, and the love of man; acknowledging and adoring an overruling Providence which, by all its dispensations, proves that It delights in the happiness of man here and his greater happiness hereafter; with all these blessings, what more is necessary to make us a happy and a prosperous people? Still one thing more, fellow citizens—a wise and frugal government which shall restrain men from injuring one another, shall leave them otherwise free to regulate their own pursuits of industry and improvement, and shall not take from the mouth of labor the bread it has earned. This is the sum of good government, and this is necessary to close the circle of our felicities.

About to enter, fellow citizens, on the exercise of duties which comprehend everything dear and valuable to you, it is proper you should understand what I deem the essential principles of our government and, consequently, those which ought to shape its administration. I will compress them within the narrowest compass they will bear, stating the general principle but not all its limitations: Equal and exact justice to all men, of whatever state or persuasion, religious or political; peace, commerce, and honest friendship with all nations, entangling alliances with none; the support of the State governments in all their rights, as the most competent administrations for our domestic concerns and the surest bulwarks against anti-republican tendencies; the preservation of the general government in its whole constitutional vigor, as the sheet anchor of our peace at home and safety abroad; a jealous care of the right of election by the people, a mild and safe corrective of abuses which are lopped by the sword of revolution where peaceable remedies are unprovided; absolute acquiescence in the decisions of the majority, the vital principle of republics from which there is no appeal but to force, the vital principle and immediate parent of despotism; a well-disciplined militia, our best reliance in peace and for the first moments of war till regulars may relieve them; the supremacy of the civil over the military authority; economy in the public expense, that labor may be lightly burdened; the honest payment of our debts and sacred preservation of the public faith; encouragement of agriculture, and of commerce as its handmaid; the diffusion of information, and arraignment of all abuses at the bar of the public reason; freedom of religion; freedom of the press; freedom of person, under the protection of the habeas corpus; and trial by juries, impartially selected. These principles form the bright constellation which has gone before us and guided our steps through an age of revolution and reformation. The wisdom of our sages and blood of our heroes have been devoted to their attainment; they should be the creed of our political faith, the text of civic instruction, the touchstone by which to try the services of those we trust; and should we wander from them in moments of error or of alarm, let us hasten to retrace our steps and to regain the road which alone leads to peace, liberty, and safety.

I repair then, fellow citizens, to the post you have assigned me. With experience enough in subordinate offices to have seen the difficulties of this, the greatest of all, I have learned to expect that it will rarely fall to the lot of imperfect man to retire from this station with the reputation and the favor which bring him into it. Without pretensions to that high confidence you reposed in our first and great revolutionary character, whose pre-eminent services had entitled him to the first place in his country's love and destined for him the fairest page in the volume of faithful history, I ask so much confidence only as may give firmness and effect to the legal administration of your affairs. I shall often go wrong through defect of judgment. When right, I shall often be thought wrong by those whose positions will not command a view of the whole ground. I ask your indulgence for my own errors, which will never be intentional, and your support against the errors of others who may condemn what they would not if seen in all its parts. The approbation implied by your suffrage is a great consolation to me for the past, and my future solicitude will be to retain the good opinion of those who have bestowed it in advance, to conciliate that of others by doing them all the good in my power, and to be instrumental to the happiness and freedom of all.

Relying then on the patronage of your good will, I advance with obedience to the work, ready to retire from it whenever you become sensible how much better choice it is in your power to make. And may that Infinite Power which rules the destinies of the universe lead our councils to what is best and give them a favorable issue for your peace and prosperity.

1801

13 The Social Contract

JEAN-JACQUES ROUSSEAU

The Social Pact

I assume that men have reached a point at which the obstacles that endanger their preservation in the state of nature overcome by their resistance the forces which each individual can exert with a view to maintaining himself in that state. Then this primitive condition cannot longer subsist, and the human race would perish unless it changed its mode of existence.

SOURCE: from Jean-Jacques Rousseau, "Social Contract," in *Ideal Empires and Republics*, Wm. H. Wise & Co., Publishers, New York, 1901, pp. 13–20.

Now as men cannot create any new forces, but only combine and direct those that exist, they have no other means of self-preservation than to form by aggregation a sum of forces which may overcome the resistance, to put them in action by a single motive power, and to make them work in concert.

This sum of forces can be produced only by the combination of many; but the strength and freedom of each man being the chief instruments of his preservation, how can he pledge them without injuring himself, and without neglecting the cares which he owes to himself? This difficulty, applied to my subject, may be expressed in these terms:

"To find a form of association which may defend and protect with the whole force of the community the person and property of every associate, and by means of which, coalescing with all, may nevertheless obey only himself, and remain as free as before." Such is the fundamental problem of which the social contract furnishes the solution.

The clauses of this contract are so determined by the nature of the act that the slightest modification would render them vain and ineffectual; so that, although they have never perhaps been formally enunciated, they are everywhere the same, everywhere tacitly admitted and recognized, until, the social pact being violated, each man regains his original rights and recovers his natural liberty while losing the conventional liberty for which he renounced it.

These clauses, rightly understood, are reducible to one only, viz., the total alienation to the whole community of each associate with all his rights; for, in the first place, since each gives himself up entirely, the conditions are equal for all; and, the conditions being equal for all, no one has any interest in making them burdensome to others.

Further, the alienation being made without reserve, the union is as perfect as it can be, and an individual associate can no longer claim anything; for, if rights were left to individuals, since there would be no common superior who could judge between them and the public, each, being on some point his own judge, would soon claim to be so on all; the state of nature would still subsist, and the association would necessarily become tyrannical or useless.

In short, each giving himself to all, gives himself to nobody; and as there is not one associate over whom we do not acquire the same rights which we concede to him over ourselves, we gain the equivalent of all that we lose, and more power to preserve what we have.

If, then, we set aside what is not of the essence of the social contract, we shall find that it is reducible to the following terms: "Each of us puts in common his person and his whole power under the supreme direction of the general will; and in return we receive every member as an indivisible part of the whole."

Forthwith, instead of the individual personalities of all the contracting parties, this act of association produces a moral and collective body, which is composed of as many members as the assembly has voices, and which receives from this same act its unity, its common self (*moi*), its life, and its will. This public person, which is thus formed by the union of all the individual members, formerly took the name of CITY, and now takes that of REPUBLIC or BODY POLITIC, which is called by its members STATE when it is passive, SOVEREIGN when it is active, POWER when it is compared to similar bodies. With regard to the associates, they take collectively the name of PEOPLE, and are called individually CITIZENS, as participating in the sovereign power, and SUBJECTS, as subjected to the laws of the State. But these terms are often confused and are mistaken one for another; it is sufficient to know how to distinguish them when they are used with complete precision.

The Sovereign

We see from this formula that the act of association contains a reciprocal engagement between the public and individuals, and that every individual, contracting so to speak with himself, is engaged in a double relation, viz., as a member of the sovereign toward individuals, and as a member of the State toward the sovereign. But we cannot apply here the maxim of civil law that no one is bound by engagements made with himself; for there is a great difference between being bound to oneself and to a whole of which one forms part.

We must further observe that the public resolution which can bind all subjects to the sovereign in consequence of the two different relations under which each of them is regarded cannot, for a contrary reason, bind the sovereign to itself; and that accordingly it is contrary to the nature of the body politic for the sovereign to impose on itself a law which it cannot transgress. As it can only be considered under one and the same relation, it is in the position of an individual contracting with himself; whence we see that there is not, nor can be, any kind of fundamental law binding upon the body of the people, not even the social contract. This does not imply that such a body cannot perfectly well enter into engagements with others in what does not derogate from this contract; for, with regard to foreigners, it becomes a simple being, an individual.

But the body politic or sovereign, deriving its existence only from the sanctity of the contract, can never bind itself, even to others, in anything that derogates from the original act, such as alienation of some portion of itself, or submission to another sovereign. To violate the act by which it exists would be to annihilate itself; and what is nothing produces nothing.

So soon as the multitude is thus united in one body, it is impossible to injure one of the members without attacking the body, still less to injure the body without the members feeling the effects. Thus duty and interest alike oblige the two contracting parties to give mutual assistance; and the men themselves should seek to combine in this twofold relationship all the advantages which are attendant on it.

Now, the sovereign, being formed only of the individuals that compose it, neither has nor can have any interest contrary to theirs; consequently the sovereign power needs no guarantee toward its subjects, because it is impossible that the body should wish to injure all its members; and we shall see hereafter that it can injure no one as an individual. The sovereign, for the simple reason that it is so, is always everything that it ought to be.

But this is not the case as regards the relation of subjects to the sovereign, which, notwithstanding the common interest, would have no security for the performance of their engagements, unless it found means to ensure their fidelity.

Indeed, every individual may, as a man, have a particular will contrary to, or divergent from, the general will which he has as a citizen; his private interest may prompt him quite differently from the common interest; his absolute and naturally independent existence may make him regard what he owes to the common cause as a gratuitous contribution, the loss of which will be less harmful to others than the payment of it will be burdensome to him; and, regarding the moral person that constitutes the State as an imaginary being because it is not a man, he would be willing to enjoy the rights of a citizen without being willing to fulfil the duties of a subject. The progress of such injustice would bring about the ruin of the body politic.

In order, then, that the social pact may not be a vain formulary, it tacitly includes this engagement, which can alone give force to the others, that whoever refuses to obey the general will shall be constrained to do so by the whole body; which means nothing else than that he shall be forced to be free; for such is the condition which, uniting every citizen to his native land, guarantees him from all personal dependence, a condition that insures the control and working of the political machine, and alone renders legitimate civil engagements, which, without it, would be absurd and tyrannical, and subject to the most enormous abuses.

The Civil State

The passage from the state of nature to the civil state produces in man a very remarkable change, by substituting in his conduct justice for instinct, and by giving his actions the moral quality that they previously lacked. It is only when the voice of duty succeeds physical impulse, and law succeeds appetite, that man, who till then had regarded only himself, sees that he is obliged to act on other principles, and to consult his reason before listening to his inclinations. Although, in this state, he is deprived of many advantages that he derives from nature, he acquires equally great ones in return; his faculties are exercised and developed; his ideas are expanded; his feelings are ennobled; his whole soul is exalted to such a degree that, if the abuses of this new condition did not often degrade him below that from which he has emerged, he ought to bless without ceasing the happy moment that released him from it for ever, and transformed him from a stupid and ignorant animal into an intelligent being and a man.

Let us reduce this whole balance to terms easy to compare. What man loses by the social contract is his natural liberty and an unlimited right to anything which tempts him and which he is able to attain; what he gains is civil liberty and property in all that he possesses. In order that we may not be mistaken about these compensations, we must clearly distinguish natural liberty, which is limited only by the powers of the individual, from civil liberty, which is limited by the general will; and possession, which is nothing but the result of force or the right of first occupancy, from property, which can be based only on a positive title.

Besides the preceding, we might add to the acquisitions of the civil state moral freedom, which alone renders man truly master of himself; for the impulse of mere appetite is slavery, while obedience to a self-prescribed law is liberty. But I have already said too much on this head, and the philosophical meaning of the term LIBERTY does not belong to my present subject.

Real Property

Every member of the community at the moment of its formation gives himself up to it, just as he actually is, himself and all his powers, of which the property that he possesses forms part. By this act, possession does not change its nature when it changes hands, and become property in those of the sovereign; but, as the powers of the State (*cité*) are incomparably greater than those of an individual, public possession is also, in fact, more secure and more irrevocable, without being more legitimate, at least in respect of foreigners; for the State, with regard to its members, is owner of all their property by the social contract, which, in the State, serves as the basis of all rights; but with regard to other powers, it is owner only by the right of first occupancy which it derives from individuals.

The right of first occupancy, although more real than that of the strongest, becomes a true right only after the establishment of that of property. Every man has by nature a right to all that is necessary to him; but the positive act which makes him proprietor of certain property excludes him from all the residue. His portion having been allotted, he ought to confine himself to it, and he has no further right to the undivided property. That is why the right of first occupancy, so weak in the state of nature, is respected by every member of a State. In this right men regard not so much what belongs to others as what does not belong to themselves.

In order to legalize the right of first occupancy over any domain whatsoever, the following conditions are, in general, necessary: first, the land must not yet be inhabited by any one; secondly, a man must occupy only the area required for his subsistence; thirdly, he must take possession of it, not by an empty ceremony, but by labor and cultivation, the only mark of ownership which, in default of legal title, ought to be respected by others.

Indeed, if we accord the right of first occupancy to necessity and labor, do we not extend it as far as it can go? Is it impossible to assign limits to this right? Will the mere setting foot on common ground be sufficient to give an immediate claim to the ownership of it? Will the power of driving away other men from it for a moment suffice to deprive them for ever of the right of returning to it? How can a man or a people take possession of an immense territory and rob the whole human race of it except by a punishable usurpation, since other men are deprived of the place of residence and the sustenance which nature gives to them in common. When Nuñez Balboa on the seashore took possession of the Pacific Ocean and of the whole of South America in the name of the crown of Castile, was this sufficient to dispossess all the inhabitants, and exclude from it all the princes in the world? On this supposition such ceremonies might have been multiplied vainly enough; and the Catholic king in his cabinet might, by a single stroke, have taken possession of the whole world, only cutting off afterward from his empire what was previously occupied by other princes.

We perceive how the lands of individuals, united and contiguous, become public territory, and how the right of sovereignty, extending itself from the subjects to the land which they occupy, becomes at once real and personal; which places the possessors in greater dependence, and makes their own powers a guarantee for their fidelity—an advantage which ancient monarchs do not appear to have clearly perceived, for, calling themselves only kings of the Persians or Scythians or Macedonians, they seem to have regarded themselves as chiefs of men rather than as owners of countries. Monarchs of to-day call themselves more cleverly kings of France, Spain, England, etc.; in thus holding the land they are quite sure of holding its inhabitants.

The peculiarity of this alienation is that the community, in receiving the property of individuals, so far from robbing them of it, only assures them lawful possession, and changes usurpation into true right, enjoyment into ownership. Also, the possessors being considered as depositaries of the public property, and their rights being respected by all the members of the State, as well as maintained by all its power against foreigners, they have, as it were, by a transfer advantageous to the public and still more to themselves, acquired all that they have given up—a paradox which is easily explained by distinguishing between the rights which the sovereign and the proprietor have over the same property, as we shall see hereafter.

It may also happen that men begin to unite before they possess anything, and that afterward occupying territory sufficient for all, they enjoy it in common, or share it among themselves, either equally or in proportions fixed by the sovereign. In whatever way this acquisition is made, the right which every individual has over his own property is always subordinate to the right which the community has over all; otherwise there would be no stability in the social union, and no real force in the exercise of sovereignty.

I shall close . . . with a remark which ought to serve as a basis for the whole social system; it is that instead of destroying natural equality, the fundamental pact, on the contrary, substitutes a moral and lawful equality for the physical inequality which nature imposed upon men, so that, although unequal in strength or intellect, they all become equal by convention and legal right.

1762

14 Port Huron Statement

STUDENTS FOR A DEMOCRATIC SOCIETY

Introduction: Agenda for a Generation

We are people of this generation, bred in at least modest comfort, housed now in universities, looking uncomfortably to the world we inherit.

When we were kids the United States was the wealthiest and strongest country in the world; the only one with the atom bomb, the least scarred by modern war, an initiator of the United Nations that we thought would distribute Western influence throughout the world. Freedom and equality for each individual, government of, by, and for the people—these American values we found good, principles by which we could live as men. Many of us began maturing in complacency.

As we grew, however, our comfort was penetrated by events too troubling to dismiss. First, the permeating and victimizing fact of human degradation, symbolized by the Southern struggle against racial bigotry, compelled most of us from silence to activism. Second, the enclosing fact of the Cold War, symbolized by the presence of the Bomb, brought awareness that we ourselves, and our friends, and millions of abstract "others" we knew more directly because of our common peril, might die at any time. We might deliberately ignore, or avoid, or fail to feel all other human problems, but not these two, for these were too immediate and crushing in their impact, too challenging in the demand that we as individuals take the responsibility for encounter and resolution.

SOURCE: from the document produced by the Students for a Democratic Society at the 1962 SDS National Convention, Port Huron, Michigan.

While these and other problems either directly oppressed us or rankled our consciences and became our own subjective concerns, we began to see complicated and disturbing paradoxes in our surrounding America. The declaration "all men are created equal . . ." rang hollow before the facts of Negro life in the South and the big cities of the North. The proclaimed peaceful intentions of the United States contradicted its economic and military investments in the Cold War status quo.

We witnessed, and continue to witness, other paradoxes. With nuclear energy whole cities can easily be powered, yet the dominant nation-states seem more likely to unleash destruction greater than that incurred in all wars of human history. Although our own technology is destroying old and creating new forms of social organization, men still tolerate meaningless work and idleness. While two-thirds of mankind suffers undernourishment, our own upper classes revel amidst superfluous abundance. Although world population is expected to double in forty years, the nations still tolerate anarchy as a major principle of international conduct and uncontrolled exploitation governs the sapping of the earth's physical resources. Although mankind desperately needs revolutionary leadership, America rests in national stalemate, its goals ambiguous and tradition-bound instead of informed and clear, its democratic system apathetic and manipulated rather than "of, by, and for the people."

Not only did tarnish appear on our image of American virtue, not only did disillusion occur when the hypocrisy of American ideals was discovered, but we began to sense that what we had originally seen as the American Golden Age was actually the decline of an era. The worldwide outbreak of revolution against colonialism and imperialism, the entrenchment of totalitarian states, the menace of war, overpopulation, international disorder, supertechnology—these trends were testing the tenacity of our own commitment to democracy and freedom and our abilities to visualize their application to a world in upheaval.

Our work is guided by the sense that we may be the last generation in the experiment with living. But we are a minority—the vast majority of our people regard the temporary equilibriums of our society and world as eternally functional parts. In this is perhaps the outstanding paradox: we ourselves are imbued with urgency, yet the message of our society is that there is no viable alternative to the present. Beneath the reassuring tones of the politicians, beneath the common opinion that America will "muddle through," beneath the stagnation of those who have closed their minds to the future, is the pervading feeling that there simply are no alternatives, that our times have witnessed the exhaustion not only of Utopias, but of any new departures as well. Feeling the press of complexity upon the emptiness of life, people are fearful of the thought that at any moment things might be thrust out of control. They fear change itself, since change might smash whatever invisible framework seems to hold back chaos for them now. For most Americans, all crusades are suspect, threatening. The fact that each individual sees apathy in his fellows perpetuates the common reluctance to organize for change. The dominant institutions are complex enough to blunt the minds of their potential critics, and entrenched enough to swiftly dissipate or entirely repel the energies of protest and reform, thus limiting human expectancies. Then, too, we are a materially improved society, and by our own improvements we seem to have weakened the case for further change.

Some would have us believe that Americans feel contentment amidst prosperity—but might it not better be called a glaze above deeply felt anxieties about their role in the new world? And if these anxieties produce a developed indifference to human affairs, do they not as well produce a yearning to believe there *is* an alternative to the present, that something *can* be done to change circumstances in the school, the workplaces, the bureaucracies, the government? It is to this latter yearning, at once the spark and engine of change, that we direct our present appeal. The search for truly democratic alternatives to the present, and a commitment to social experimentation with them, is a worthy and fulfilling human enterprise, one which moves us and, we hope, others today. On such a basis do we offer this document of our convictions and analysis: as an effort in understanding and changing the conditions of humanity in the late twentieth century, an effort rooted in the ancient, still unfulfilled conception of man attaining determining influence over his circumstances of life.

Values

Making values explicit—an initial task in establishing alternatives—is an activity that has been devalued and corrupted. The conventional moral terms of the age, the politician moralities—"free world," "people's democracies"—reflect realities poorly, if at all, and seem to function more as ruling myths than as descriptive principles. But neither has our experience in the universities brought us moral enlightenment. Our professors and administrators sacrifice controversy to public relations; their curriculums change more slowly than the living events of the world; their skills and silence are purchased by investors in the arms race; passion is called unscholastic. The questions we might want raised—what is really important? can we live in a different and better way? if we wanted to change society, how would we do it?—are not thought to be questions of a "fruitful, empirical nature," and thus are brushed aside.

Unlike youth in other countries we are used to moral leadership being exercised and moral dimensions being clarified by our elders. But today, for us, not even the liberal and socialist preachments of the past seem adequate to the forms of the present. Consider the old slogans: Capitalism Cannot Reform Itself, United Front Against Fascism, General Strike, All Out on May Day. Or, more recently, No Cooperation with Commies and Fellow Travelers,

Ideologies are Exhausted, Bipartisanship, No Utopias. These are incomplete, and there are few new prophets. It has been said that our liberal and socialist predecessors were plagued by vision without program, while our own generation is plagued by program without vision. All around us there is astute grasp of method, technique—the committee, the *ad hoc* group, the lobbyist, the hard and soft sell, the make, the projected image—but, if pressed critically, such expertise is incompetent to explain its implicit ideals. It is highly fashionable to identify oneself by old categories, or by naming a respected political figure, or by explaining "how we would vote" on various issues.

Theoretic chaos has replaced the idealistic thinking of old—and, unable to reconstitute theoretic order, men have condemned idealism itself. Doubt has replaced hopefulness—and men act out a defeatism that is labeled realistic. The decline of utopia and hope is in fact one of the defining features of social life today. The reasons are various: the dreams of the older left were perverted by Stalinism and never recreated; the congressional stalemate makes men narrow their view of the possible; the specialization of human activity leaves little room for sweeping thought; the horrors of the twentieth century, symbolized in the gas ovens and concentration camps and atom bombs, have blasted hopefulness. To be idealistic is to be considered apocalyptic, deluded. To have no serious aspirations, on the contrary, is to be "tough-minded."

In suggesting social goals and values, therefore, we are aware of entering a sphere of some disrepute. Perhaps matured by the past, we have no sure formulas, no closed theories—but that does not mean values are beyond discussion and tentative determination. A first task of any social movement is to convince people that the search for orienting theories and the creation of human values is complex but worthwhile. We are aware that to avoid platitudes we must analyze the concrete conditions of social order. But to direct such an analysis we must use the guideposts of basic principles. Our own social values involve conceptions of human beings, human relationships, and social systems.

We regard *men* as infinitely precious and possessed of unfulfilled capacities for reason, freedom, and love. In affirming these principles we are aware of countering perhaps the dominant conceptions of man in the twentieth century: that he is a thing to be manipulated, and that he is inherently incapable of directing his own affairs. We oppose the depersonalization that reduces human beings to the status of things—if anything, the brutalities of the twentieth century teach that means and ends are intimately related, that vague appeals to "posterity" cannot justify the mutilations of the present. We oppose, too, the doctrine of human incompetence because it rests essentially on the modern fact that men have been "competently" manipulated into incompetence—we see little reason why men cannot meet with increasing skill the complexities and responsibilities of the situation, if society is organized not for minority, but for majority, participation in decision-making.

Men have unrealized potential for self-cultivation, self-direction, self-understanding, and creativity. It is this potential that we regard as crucial and to which we appeal, not to the human potentiality for violence, unreason, and submission to authority. The goal of man and society should be human independence: a concern not with image of popularity but with finding a meaning in life that is personally authentic; a quality of mind not compulsively driven by a sense of powerlessness, nor one which unthinkingly adopts status values, nor one which represses all threats to its habits, but one which has full, spontaneous access to present and past experiences, one which easily unites the fragmented parts of personal history, one which openly faces problems which are troubling and unresolved; one with an intuitive awareness of possibilities, an active sense of curiosity, an ability and willingness to learn.

This kind of independence does not mean egotistic individualism—the object is not to have one's way so much as it is to have a way that is one's own. Nor do we deify man—we merely have faith in his potential.

Human relationships should involve fraternity and honesty. Human interdependence is contemporary fact; human brotherhood must be willed, however, as a condition of future survival and as the most appropriate form of social relations. Personal links between man and man are needed, especially to go beyond the partial and fragmentary bonds of function that bind men only as worker to worker, employer to employee, teacher to student, American to Russian.

Loneliness, estrangement, isolation describe the vast distance between man and man today. These dominant tendencies cannot be overcome by better personnel management, nor by improved gadgets, but only when a love of man overcomes the idolatrous worship of things by man. As the individualism we affirm is not egoism, the selflessness we affirm is not self-elimination. On the contrary, we believe in generosity of a kind that imprints one's unique individual qualities in the relation to other men, and to all human activity. Further, to dislike isolation is not to favor the abolition of privacy; the latter differs from isolation in that it occurs or is abolished according to individual will.

We would replace power rooted in possession, privilege, or circumstance by power and uniqueness rooted in love, reflectiveness, reason, and creativity. As a *social system* we seek the establishment of a democracy of individual participation, governed by two central aims: that the individual share in those social decisions determining the quality and direction of his life; that society be organized to encourage independence in men and provide the media for their common participation.

In a participatory democracy, the political life would be based in several root principles:

> that decision-making of basic social consequence be carried on by public groupings;
>
> that politics be seen positively, as the art of collectively creating an acceptable pattern of social relations;
>
> that politics has the function of bringing people out of isolation and into community, thus being a necessary, though not sufficient, means of finding meaning in personal life;
>
> that the political order should serve to clarify problems in a way instrumental to their solution; it should provide outlets for the expression of personal grievance and aspiration; opposing views should be organized so as to illuminate choices and facilitate the attainment of goals; channels should be commonly available to relate men to knowledge and to power so that private problems—from bad recreation facilities to personal alienation—are formulated as general issues.
>
> The economic sphere would have as its basis the principles:
>
> that work should involve incentives worthier than money or survival. It should be educative, not stultifying; creative, not mechanical; self-directed, not manipulated, encouraging independence, a respect for others, a sense of dignity and a willingness to accept social responsibility, since it is this experience that has crucial influence on habits, perceptions and individual ethics;
>
> that the economic experience is so personally decisive that the individual must share in its full determination;
>
> that the economy itself is of such social importance that its major resources and means of production should be open to democratic participation and subject to democratic social regulation.

Like the political and economic ones, major social institutions—cultural, educational, rehabilitative, and others—should be generally organized with the well-being and dignity of man as the essential measure of success.

In social change or interchange, we find violence to be abhorrent because it requires generally the transformation of the target, be it a human being or a community of people, into a depersonalized object of hate. It is imperative that the means of violence be abolished and the institutions—local, national, international—that encourage nonviolence as a condition of conflict be developed.

These are our central values, in skeletal form. It remains vital to understand their denial or attainment in the context of the modern world.

The Students

In the last few years, thousands of American students demonstrated that they at least felt the urgency of the times. They moved actively and directly against racial injustices, the threat of war, violations of individual rights of conscience and, less frequently, against economic manipulation. They succeeded in restoring a small measure of controversy to the campuses after the stillness of the McCarthy period. They succeeded, too, in gaining some concessions from the people and institutions they opposed, especially in the fight against racial bigotry.

The significance of these scattered movements lies not in their success or failure in gaining objectives—at least not yet. Nor does the significance lie in the intellectual "competence" or "maturity" of the students involved—as some pedantic elders allege. The significance is in the fact the students are breaking the crust of apathy and overcoming the inner alienation that remain the defining characteristics of American college life.

If student movements for change are still rarities on the campus scene, what is commonplace there? The real campus, the familiar campus, is a place of private people, engaged in their notorious "inner emigration." It is a place of commitment to business-as-usual, getting ahead, playing it cool. It is a place of mass affirmation of the Twist, but mass reluctance toward the controversial public stance. Rules are accepted as "inevitable," bureaucracy as "just circumstances," irrelevance as "scholarship," selflessness as "martyrdom," politics as "just another way to make people, and an unprofitable one, too."

Almost no students value activity as citizens. Passive in public, they are hardly more idealistic in arranging their private lives: Gallup concludes they will settle for "low success, and won't risk high failure." There is not much willingness to take risks (not even in business), no setting of dangerous goals, no real conception of personal identity except one manufactured in the image of others, no real urge for personal fulfillment except to be almost as successful as the very successful people. Attention is being paid to social status (the quality of shirt collars, meeting people, getting wives or husbands, making solid contacts for later on); much, too, is paid to academic status (grades, honors, the med school rat race). But neglected generally is real intellectual status, the personal cultivation of the mind.

"Students don't even give a damn about the apathy," one has said. Apathy toward apathy begets a privately constructed universe, a place of systematic study schedules, two nights each week for beer, a girl or two, and early marriage; a framework infused with personality, warmth, and under control, no matter how unsatisfying otherwise.

Under these conditions university life loses all relevance to some. Four hundred thousand of our classmates leave college every year.

But apathy is not simply an attitude; it is a product of social institutions, and of the structure and organization of higher education itself. The extracurricular life is ordered according to *in loco parentis* theory, which ratifies the administration as the moral guardian of the young.

The accompanying "let's pretend" theory of student extracurricular affairs validates student government as a training center for those who want to spend their lives in political pretense, and discourages initiative from the more articulate, honest, and sensitive students. The bounds and style of controversy are delimited before controversy begins. The university "prepares" the student for "citizenship" through perpetual rehearsals and, usually, through emasculation of what creative spirit there is in the individual.

The academic life contains reinforcing counterparts to the way in which extracurricular life is organized. The academic world is founded on a teacher-student relation analogous to the parent-child relation which characterizes *in loco parentis.* Further, academia includes a radical separation of the student from the material of study. That which is studied, the social reality, is "objectified" to sterility, dividing the student from life—just as he is restrained in active involvement by the deans controlling student government. The specialization of function and knowledge, admittedly necessary to our complex technological and social structure, has produced an exaggerated compartmentalization of study and understanding. This has contributed to an overly parochial view, by faculty, of the role of its research and scholarship, to a discontinuous and truncated understanding, by students, of the surrounding social order; and to a loss of personal attachment, by nearly all, to the worth of study as a humanistic enterprise.

There is, finally, the cumbersome academic bureaucracy extending throughout the academic as well as the extracurricular structures, contributing to the sense of outer complexity and inner powerlessness that transforms the honest searching of many students to a ratification of convention and, worse, to a numbness to present and future catastrophes. The size and financing systems of the university enhance the permanent trusteeship of the administrative bureaucracy, their power leading to a shift within the university toward the value standards of business and the administrative mentality. Huge foundations and other private financial interests shape the under-financed colleges and universities, not only making them more commercial, but less disposed to diagnose society critically, less open to dissent. Many social and physical scientists, neglecting the liberating heritage of higher learning, develop "human relations" or "morale-producing" techniques for the corporate economy, while others exercise their intellectual skills to accelerate the arms race. . . .

There are no convincing apologies for the contemporary malaise. While the world tumbles toward the final war, while men in other nations are trying desperately to alter events, while the very future qua future is uncertain—America is without community, impulse, without the inner momentum necessary for an age when societies cannot successfully perpetuate themselves by their military weapons, when democracy must be viable because of the quality of life, not its quantity of rockets.

The apathy here is, first, *subjective*—the felt powerlessness of ordinary people, the resignation before the enormity of events. But subjective apathy is encouraged by the *objective* American situation—the actual structural separation of people from power, from relevant knowledge, from pinnacles of decision-making. Just as the university influences the student way of life, so do major social institutions create the circumstances in which the isolated citizen will try hopelessly to understand his world and himself.

The very isolation of the individual—from power and community and ability to aspire—means the rise of a democracy without publics. With the great mass of people structurally remote and psychologically hesitant with respect to democratic institutions, those institutions themselves attenuate and become, in the fashion of the vicious circle, progressively less accessible to those few who aspire to serious participation in social affairs. The vital democratic connection between community and leadership, between the mass and the several elites, has been so wrenched and perverted that disastrous policies go unchallenged time and again.

Politics Without Publics

The American political system is not the democratic model of which its glorifiers speak. In actuality it frustrates democracy by confusing the individual citizen, paralyzing policy discussion, and consolidating the irresponsible power of military and business interests.

A crucial feature of the political apparatus in America is that greater differences are harbored within each major party than the differences existing between them. Instead of two parties presenting distinctive and significant differences of approach, what dominates the system is a natural interlocking of Democrats from Southern states with the more conservative elements of the Republican Party. This arrangement of forces is blessed by the seniority system of Congress which guarantees Congressional committee domination by conservatives—ten of seventeen committees in the Senate and thirteen of twenty-one in the House of Representatives are chaired currently by Dixiecrats.

The party overlap, however, is not the only structural antagonist of democracy in politics. First, the localized nature of the party system does not encourage discussion of national and international issues: thus problems are not raised by and for people, and political representatives usually are unfettered from any responsibilities to the general public except those regarding parochial matters. Second, whole constituencies are divested of the full political power they might have: many Negroes in the South are prevented from voting, migrant workers are disenfranchised by various residence requirements, some urban and suburban dwellers are victimized by gerrymandering, and poor people are too often without the power to obtain political representation. Third, the focus of political attention is significantly distorted by the enormous lobby force, composed predominantly of business interests, spending hundreds of millions each year in an attempt to conform facts about productivity, agriculture, defense, and social services, to the wants of private economic groupings.

What emerges from the party contradiction and insulation of privately held power is the organized political stalemate: calcification dominates flexibility as the principle of parliamentary organization, frustration is the expectancy of legislators intending liberal reform, and Congress becomes less and less central to national decision-making, especially in the area of foreign policy. In this context, confusion and blurring are built into the formulation of issues, long-range priorities are not discussed in the rational manner needed for policy-making, the politics of personality and "image" become a more important mechanism than the construction of issues in a way that affords each voter a challenging and real option. The American voter is buffeted from all directions by pseudo-problems, by the structurally initiated sense that nothing political is subject to human mastery. Worried by his mundane problems which never get solved, but constrained by the common belief that politics is an agonizingly slow accommodation of views, he quits all pretense of bothering.

A most alarming fact is that few, if any, politicians are calling for changes in these conditions. Only a handful even are calling on the President to "live up to" platform pledges; no one is demanding structural changes, such as the shuttling of Southern Democrats out of the Democratic Party. Rather than protesting the state of politics, most politicians are reinforcing and aggravating that state. While in practice they rig public opinion to suit their own interests, in word and ritual they enshrine "the sovereign public" and call for more and more letters. Their speeches and campaign actions are banal, based on a degrading conception of what people want to hear. They respond not to dialogue, but to pressure: and knowing this, the ordinary citizen sees even greater inclination to shun the political sphere. The politician is usually a trumpeter to "citizenship" and "service to the nation," but since he is unwilling to seriously rearrange power relationships, his trumpetings only increase apathy by creating no outlets. Much of the time the call to "service" is justified not in idealistic terms, but in the crasser terms of "defending the free world from Communism"—thus making future idealistic impulses harder to justify in anything but Cold War terms.

In such a setting of status quo politics, where most if not all government activity is rationalized in Cold War anti-Communist terms, it is somewhat natural that discontented, super-patriotic groups would emerge through political channels and explain their ultra-conservatism as the best means of Victory over Communism. They have become a politically influential force within the Republican Party, at a national level through Senator Goldwater, and at a local level through their important social and economic roles. Their political views are defined generally as the opposite of the supposed views of Communists: complete individual freedom in the economic sphere, non-participation by the government in the machinery of production. But actually "anti-Communism" becomes an umbrella by which to protest liberalism, internationalism, welfareism, the active civil rights and labor movements. It is to the disgrace of the United States that such a movement should become a prominent kind of public participation in the modern world—but, ironically, it is somewhat to the interests of the United States that such a movement should be a public constituency pointed toward realignment of the political parties, demanding a conservative Republican Party in the South and an exclusion of the "leftist" elements of the national GOP. . . .

1962

15 An Appeal from the New to the Old Whigs

EDMUND BURKE

I do not wish to enter very much at large into the discussions which diverge and ramify in all ways from this productive subject. But there is one topic upon which I hope I shall be excused in going a little beyond my design. The factions now so busy amongst us, in order to divest men of all love for their country, and to remove from their minds all duty with regard to the state, endeavor to propagate an opinion, that the *people,* in forming their commonwealth, have by no means parted with their power over it. This is an impregnable citadel, to which these gentlemen retreat, whenever they are pushed by the battery of laws and usages and positive conventions. Indeed, it is such, and of so great force, that all they have done in defending their outworks is so much time and labor thrown away. Discuss any of their schemes, their answer is, It is the act of the *people,* and that is sufficient. Are we to deny to a *majority* of the people the right of altering even the whole frame of their society, if such should be their pleasure? They may change it, say they, from a monarchy to a republic to-day, and to-morrow back again from a republic to a monarchy; and so backward and forward as often as they like. They are masters of the commonwealth, because in

SOURCE: from *An Appeal from the New to the Old Whigs,* by Edmund Burke in *The Writings and Speeches of the Right Honourable Edmund Burke* (Vol. 4) Beaconsfield edition, 1791, pp. 161–177.

substance they are themselves the commonwealth. The French Revolution, say they, was the act of the majority of the people; and if the majority of any other people, the people of England, for instance, wish to make the same change, they have the same right.

Just the same, undoubtedly. That is, none at all. Neither the few nor the many have a right to act merely by their will, in any matter connected with duty, trust, engagement, or obligation. The Constitution of a country being once settled upon some compact, tacit or expressed, there is no power existing of force to alter it, without the breach of the covenant, or the consent of all the parties. Such is the nature of a contract. And the votes of a majority of the people, whatever their infamous flatterers may teach in order to corrupt their minds, cannot alter the moral any more than they can alter the physical essence of things. The people are not to be taught to think lightly of their engagements to their governors; else they teach governors to think lightly of their engagements towards them. In that kind of game, in the end, the people are sure to be losers. To flatter them into a contempt of faith, truth, and justice is to ruin them; for in these virtues consists their whole safety. To flatter any man, or any part of mankind, in any description, by asserting that in engagements he or they are free, whilst any other human creature is bound, is ultimately to vest the rule of morality in the pleasure of those who ought to be rigidly submitted to it,—to subject the sovereign reason of the world to the caprices of weak and giddy men.

But, as no one of us men can dispense with public or private faith, or with any other tie of moral obligation, so neither can any number of us. The number engaged in crimes, instead of turning them into laudable acts, only augments the quantity and intensity of the guilt. I am well aware that men love to hear of their power, but have an extreme disrelish to be told of their duty. This is of course; because every duty is a limitation of some power. Indeed, arbitrary power is so much to the depraved taste of the vulgar, of the vulgar of every description, that almost all the dissensions which lacerate the commonwealth are not concerning the manner in which it is to be exercised, but concerning the hands in which it is to be placed. Somewhere they are resolved to have it. Whether they desire it to be vested in the many or the few depends with most men upon the chance which they imagine they themselves may have of partaking in the exercise of that arbitrary sway, in the one mode or in the other.

It is not necessary to teach men to thirst after power. But it is very expedient that by moral instruction they should be taught, and by their civil constitutions they should be compelled, to put many restrictions upon the immoderate exercise of it, and the inordinate desire. The best method of obtaining these two great points forms the important, but at the same time the difficult problem to the true statesman. He thinks of the place in which political power is to be lodged with no other attention than as it may render the more or the less practicable its salutary restraint and its prudent direction. For this reason, no legislator, at any period of the world, has willingly placed the seat of active power in the hands of the multitude; because there it admits of no control, no regulation, no steady direction whatsoever. The people are the natural control on authority; but to exercise and to control together is contradictory and impossible.

As the exorbitant exercise of power cannot, under popular sway, be effectually restrained, the other great object of political arrangement, the means of abating an excessive desire of it, is in such a state still worse provided for. The democratic commonwealth is the foodful nurse of ambition. Under the other forms it meets with many restraints. Whenever, in states which have had a democratic basis, the legislators have endeavored to put restraints upon ambition, their methods were as violent as in the end they were ineffectual,—as violent, indeed, as any the most jealous despotism could invent. The ostracism could not very long save itself, and much less the state which it was meant to guard, from the attempts of ambition,—one of the natural, inbred, incurable distempers of a powerful democracy.

But to return from this short digression,—which, however, is not wholly foreign to the question of the effect of the will of the majority upon the form or the existence of their society. I cannot too often recommend it to the serious consideration of all men who think civil society to be within the province of moral jurisdiction, that, if we owe to it any duty, it is not subject to our will. Duties are not voluntary. Duty and will are even contradictory terms. Now, though civil society might be at first a voluntary act, (which in many cases it undoubtedly was,) its continuance is under a permanent standing covenant, coexisting with the society; and it attaches upon every individual of that society, without any formal act of his own. This is warranted by the general practice, arising out of the general sense of mankind. Men without their choice derive benefits from that association; without their choice they are subjected to duties in consequence of these benefits; and without their choice they enter into a virtual obligation as binding as any that is actual. Look through the whole of life and the whole system of duties. Much the strongest moral obligations are such as were never the results of our option. I allow, that, if no Supreme Ruler exists, wise to form, and potent to enforce, the moral law, there is no sanction to any contract, virtual or even actual, against the will of prevalent power. On that hypothesis, let any set of men be strong enough to set their duties at defiance, and they cease to be duties any longer. We have but this one appeal against irresistible power,—

> *Si genus humanum et mortalia temnitis arma,*
> *At sperate Deos memores fandi atque nefandi.*

Taking it for granted that I do not write to the disciples of the Parisian philosophy, I may assume that the awful Author of our being is the Author of our place in the order of existence,—and that, having disposed and marshalled us by a divine tactic, not according to our will, but according to His, He has in and by that disposition virtually subjected us to act the part which belongs to the place assigned us. We have obligations to mankind at large, which are not in consequence of any special voluntary pact. They arise from the relation of man to man, and the relation of man to God, which relations are not matters of choice. On the contrary, the force of all the pacts which we enter into with any particular person or number of persons amongst mankind depends upon those prior obligations. In some cases the subordinate relations are voluntary, in others they are necessary,—but the duties are all compulsive. When we marry, the choice is voluntary, but the duties are not matter of choice: they are dictated by the nature of the situation. Dark and inscrutable are the ways by which we come into the world. The instincts which give rise to this mysterious process of Nature are not of our making. But out of physical causes, unknown to us, perhaps unknowable, arise moral duties, which, as we are able perfectly to comprehend, we are bound indispensably to perform. Parents may not be consenting to their moral relation; but, consenting or not, they are bound to a long train of burdensome duties towards those with whom they have never made a convention of any sort. Children are not consenting to their relation; but their relation, without their actual consent, binds them to its duties,—or rather it implies their consent, because the presumed consent of every rational creature is in unison with the predisposed order of things. Men come in that manner into a community with the social state of their parents, endowed with all the benefits, loaded with all the duties of their situation. If the social ties and ligaments, spun out of those physical relations which are the elements of the commonwealth, in most cases begin, and always continue, independently of our will, so, without any stipulation on our own part, are we bound by that relation called our country, which comprehends (as it has been well said) "all the charities of all." Nor are we left without powerful instincts to make this duty as dear and grateful to us as it is awful and coercive. Our country is not a thing of mere physical locality. It consists, in a great measure, in the ancient order into which we are born. We may have the same geographical situation, but another country; as we may have the same country in another soil. The place that determines our duty to our country is a social, civil relation.

These are the opinions of the author whose cause I defend. I lay them down, not to enforce them upon others by disputation, but as an account of his proceedings. On them he acts; and from them he is convinced that neither he, nor any man, or number of men, have a right (except what necessity, which is out of and above all rule, rather imposes than bestows) to free themselves from that primary engagement into which every man born into a community as much contracts by his being born into it as he contracts an obligation to certain parents by his having been derived from their bodies.

The place of every man determines his duty. If you ask, *Quem te Deus esse jussit?* you will be answered when you resolve this other question, *Humana qua parte locatus es in re?*

I admit, indeed, that in morals, as in all things else, difficulties will sometimes occur. Duties will sometimes cross one another. Then questions will arise, which of them is to be placed in subordination? which of them may be entirely superseded? These doubts give rise to that part of moral science called *casuistry,* which though necessary to be well studied by those who would become expert in that learning, who aim at becoming what I think Cicero somewhere calls *artifices officiorum,* it requires a very solid and discriminating judgment, great modesty and caution, and much sobriety of mind in the handling; else there is a danger that it may totally subvert those offices which it is its object only to methodize and reconcile. Duties, at their extreme bounds, are drawn very fine, so as to become almost evanescent. In that state some shade of doubt will always rest on these questions, when they are pursued with great subtilty. But the very habit of stating these extreme cases is not very laudable or safe; because, in general, it is not right to turn our duties into doubts. They are imposed to govern our conduct, not to exercise our ingenuity; and therefore our opinions about them ought not to be in a state of fluctuation, but steady, sure, and resolved.

Amongst these nice, and therefore dangerous points of casuistry, may be reckoned the question so much agitated in the present hour,—Whether, after the people have discharged themselves of their original power by an habitual delegation, no occasion can possibly occur which may justify the resumption of it? This question, in this latitude, is very hard to affirm or deny: but I am satisfied that no occasion can justify such a resumption, which would not equally authorize a dispensation with any other moral duty, perhaps with all of them together. However, if in general it be not easy to determine concerning the lawfulness of such devious proceedings, which must be ever on the edge of crimes, it is far from difficult to foresee the perilous consequences of the resuscitation of such a power in the people. The practical consequences of any political tenet go a great way in deciding upon its value. Political problems do not primarily concern truth or falsehood. They relate to good or evil. What in the result is likely to produce evil is politically false; that which is productive of good, politically true.

Believing it, therefore, a question at least arduous in the theory, and in the practice very critical, it would become us to ascertain as well as we can what form it is that our incantations are about to call up from darkness and the sleep of ages. When the supreme authority of the people is in question, before we attempt to extend or to confine it, we ought to fix in our minds, with some degree of distinctness, an idea of what it is we mean, when we say, the PEOPLE.

In a state of *rude* Nature there is no such thing as a people. A number of men in themselves have no collective capacity. The idea of a people is the idea of a corporation. It is wholly artificial, and made, like all other legal fictions, by common agreement. What the particular nature of that agreement was is collected from the form into which the particular society has been cast. Any other is not *their* covenant. When men, therefore, break up the original compact or agreement which gives its corporate form and capacity to a state, they are no longer a people,—they have no longer a corporate existence,—they have no longer a legal coactive force to bind within, nor a claim to be recognized abroad. They are a number of vague, loose individuals, and nothing more. With them all is to begin again. Alas! they little know how many a weary step is to be taken before they can form themselves into a mass which has a true politic personality.

We hear much, from men who have not acquired their hardiness of assertion from the profundity of their thinking, about the omnipotence of a *majority,* in such a dissolution of an ancient society as hath taken place in France. But amongst men so disbanded there can be no such thing as majority or minority, or power in any one person to bind another. The power of acting by a majority, which the gentlemen theorists seem to assume so readily, after they have violated the contract out of which it has arisen, (if at all it existed,) must be grounded on two assumptions: first, that of an incorporation produced by unanimity; and secondly, an unanimous agreement that the act of a mere majority (say of one) shall pass with them and with others as the act of the whole.

We are so little affected by things which are habitual, that we consider this idea of the decision of a *majority* as if it were a law of our original nature. But such constructive whole, residing in a part only, is one of the most violent fictions of positive law that ever has been or can be made on the principles of artificial incorporation. Out of civil society Nature knows nothing of it; nor are men, even when arranged according to civil order, otherwise than by very long training, brought at all to submit to it. The mind is brought far more easily to acquiesce in the proceedings of one man, or a few, who act under a general procuration for the state, than in the vote of a victorious majority in councils in which every man has his share in the deliberation. For there the beaten party are exasperated and soured by the previous contention, and mortified by the conclusive defeat. This mode of decision, where wills may be so nearly equal, where, according to circumstances, the smaller number may be the stronger force, and where apparent reason may be all upon one side, and on the other little else than impetuous appetite,—all this must be the result of a very particular and special convention, confirmed afterwards by long habits of obedience, by a sort of discipline in society, and by a strong hand, vested with stationary, permanent power to enforce this sort of constructive general will. What organ it is that shall declare the corporate mind is so much a matter of positive arrangement, that several states, for the validity of several of their acts, have required a proportion of voices much greater than that of a mere majority. These proportions are so entirely governed by convention that in some cases the minority decides. The laws in many countries to *condemn* require more than a mere majority; less than an equal number to *acquit.* In our judicial trials we require unanimity either to condemn or to absolve. In some incorporations one man speaks for the whole; in others, a few. Until the other day, in the Constitution of Poland unanimity was required to give validity to any act of their great national council or diet. This approaches much more nearly to rude Nature than the institutions of any other country. Such, indeed, every commonwealth must be, without a positive law to recognize in a certain number the will of the entire body.

If men dissolve their ancient incorporation in order to regenerate their community, in that state of things each man has a right, if he pleases, to remain an individual. Any number of individuals, who can agree upon it, have an undoubted right to form themselves into a state apart and wholly independent. If any of these is forced into the fellowship of another, this is conquest and not compact. On every principle which supposes society to be in virtue of a free covenant, this compulsive incorporation must be null and void.

As a people can have no right to a corporate capacity without universal consent, so neither have they a right to hold exclusively any lands in the name and title of a corporation. On the scheme of the present rulers in our neighboring country, regenerated as they are, they have no more right to the territory called France than I have. I have a right to pitch my tent in any unoccupied place I can find for it; and I may apply to my own maintenance any part of their unoccupied soil. I may purchase the house or vineyard of any individual proprietor who refuses his consent (and most proprietors have, as far as they dared, refused it) to the new incorporation. I stand in his independent place. Who are these insolent men, calling themselves the French nation, that would monopolize this fair domain of Nature? Is it because they speak a certain jargon? Is it their mode of chattering, to me unintelligible, that forms their title to my land? Who are they who claim by prescription and descent from certain gangs of banditti called Franks, and Burgundians, and Visigoths, of whom I may have never heard, and ninety-nine out of an hundred of themselves certainly never have heard, whilst at the very time they tell me that prescription and long possession form no title to property? Who are they that presume to assert that the land which I purchased of the individual, a natural person, and not a fiction of state, belongs to them, who in the very capacity in which they make their claim can exist only as an imaginary being, and in virtue of the very prescription which they reject and disown? This mode of arguing might be pushed into all the detail, so as to leave no sort of doubt, that, on their principles, and on the sort of footing on which they have thought proper to place themselves, the crowd of men, on the other side of the Channel, who have the impudence to call themselves a people, can never be the lawful, exclusive possessors of the soil. By what they call reasoning without prejudice, they leave not one stone upon another in the fabric of human society. They subvert all the authority which they hold, as well as all that which they have destroyed.

As in the abstract it is perfectly clear, that, out of a state of civil society, majority and minority are relations which can have no existence, and that, in civil society, its own specific conventions in each corporation determine what it is that constitutes the people, so as to make their act the signification of the general will,—to come to particulars, it is equally clear that neither in France nor in England has the original or any subsequent compact of the state, expressed or implied, constituted *a majority of men, told by the head,* to be the acting people of their several communities. And I see as little of policy or utility as there is of right, in laying down a principle that a majority of men told by the head are to be considered as the people, and that as such their will is to be law. What policy can there be found in arrangements made in defiance of every political principle? To enable men to act with the weight and character of a people, and to answer the ends for which they are incorporated into that capacity, we must suppose them (by means immediate or consequential) to be in that state of habitual social discipline in which the wiser, the more expert, and the more opulent conduct, and by conducting enlighten and protect, the weaker, the less knowing, and the less provided with the goods of fortune. When the multitude are not under this discipline, they can scarcely be said to be in civil society. Give once a certain constitution of things which produces a variety of conditions and circumstances in a state, and there is in Nature and reason a principle which, for their own benefit, postpones, not the interest, but the judgment, of those who are *numero plures,* to those who are *virtute et honore majores.* Numbers in a state (supposing, which is not the case in France, that a state does exist) are always of consideration,—but they are not the whole consideration. It is in things more serious than a play, that it may be truly said, *Satis est equitem mihi plaudere.*

A true natural aristocracy is not a separate interest in the state, or separable from it. It is an essential integrant part of any large body rightly constituted. It is formed out of a class of legitimate presumptions, which, taken as generalities, must be admitted for actual truths. To be bred in a place of estimation; to see nothing low and sordid from one's infancy; to be taught to respect one's self; to be habituated to the censorial inspection of the public eye; to look early to public opinion; to stand upon such elevated ground as to be enabled to take a large view of the wide-spread and infinitely diversified combinations of men and affairs in a large society; to have leisure to read, to reflect, to converse; to be enabled to draw the court and attention of the wise and learned, wherever they are to be found; to be habituated in armies to command and to obey; to be taught to despise danger in the pursuit of honor and duty; to be formed to the greatest degree of vigilance, foresight, and circumspection, in a state of things in which no fault is committed with impunity and the slightest mistakes draw on the most ruinous consequences; to be led to a guarded and regulated conduct, from a sense that you are considered as an instructor of your fellow-citizens in their highest concerns, and that you act as a reconciler between God and man; to be employed as an administrator of law and justice, and to be thereby amongst the first benefactors to mankind; to be a professor of high science, or of liberal and ingenuous art; to be amongst rich traders, who from their success are presumed to have sharp and vigorous understandings, and to possess the virtues of diligence, order, constancy, and regularity, and to have cultivated an habitual regard to commutative justice: these are the circumstances of men that form what I should call a *natural* aristocracy, without which there is no nation.

The state of civil society which necessarily generates this aristocracy is a state of Nature,—and much more truly so than a savage and incoherent mode of life. For man is by nature reasonable; and he is never perfectly in his natural state, but when he is placed where reason may be best cultivated and most predominates. Art is man's nature. We are as much, at least, in a state of Nature in formed manhood as in immature and helpless infancy. Men, qualified in the manner I have just described, form in Nature, as she operates in the common modification of society, the leading, guiding, and governing part. It is the soul to the body, without which the man does not exist. To give, therefore, no more importance, in the social order, to such descriptions of men than that of so many units is a horrible usurpation.

When great multitudes act together, under that discipline of Nature, I recognize the PEOPLE. I acknowledge something that perhaps equals, and ought always to guide, the sovereignty of convention. In all things the voice of this grand chorus of national harmony ought to have a mighty and decisive influence. But when you disturb this harmony,—when you break up this beautiful order, this array of truth and Nature, as well as of habit and prejudice,—when you separate the common sort of men from their proper chieftains, so as to form them into an adverse army,—I no longer know that venerable object called the people in such a disbanded race of deserters and vagabonds. For a while they may be terrible, indeed,—but in such a manner as wild beasts are terrible. The mind owes to them no sort of submission. They are, as they have always been reputed, rebels. They may lawfully be fought with, and brought under, whenever an advantage offers. Those who attempt by outrage and violence to deprive men of any advantage which they hold under the laws, and to destroy the natural order of life, proclaim war against them.

1791

16 Governed Democracy and Governing Democracy

GIOVANNI SARTORI

Elections, Phantom Public, and Public Opinion

Politics is ultimately the relationship between the governing and the governed —a relationship which may take the outright form of a direct power *over* the governed or work out smoothly as a power to get things done. It has been argued that the dichotomy between the governed and the governing holds for all systems but democracy, as the peculiar feature of a democratic government is that it makes nobody entirely subject or entirely sovereign. Now it is quite true that democratic decision-making makes it impossible, if we follow its entire course, to locate a dividing line between the positions of the governed and the governing. Nevertheless, to say that it is difficult to indicate the exact boundary between obedience and command is not the same as saying there is no boundary. And even if there were none, our frame of reference would still be useful, for it would lead us to define democracy as the only system which succeeds in escaping the eternal dilemma of politics by making the governed and the governing one and the same.

This, however, is not the case. But we may well ask to what degree is this limiting hypothesis realized. We all agree that in order to have democracy we must have, to some degree, a government of the people; but we also know that if there is a government, it has to be a government over the people. The problem is how these two requirements can be reconciled. And the thorny point is obviously not raised by saying "government over the people" but by the phrase "the governing people."

The question, then, is: When do we find the *demos* in the act or the role of governing? The answer is easy—during elections. The assertion that in a democracy power is exercised by the sovereign people, is warranted because we are measuring the system in electoral terms. And not only are we perfectly justified in doing so but it would be very wrong to overlook the importance of elections. If it were not for elections, if it were not for the fact that we do not trust presumed consensus of opinion, there would be no bridge between governed and governing and hence no democracy. However, we still must consider that elections are a discontinuous and very elementary performance. Between elections the people's power remains quiescent, and

SOURCE: reprinted from *Democratic Theory* by Giovanni Sartori, pp. 72–79, 90–91, 108–110, 118–119, 124–128, by permission of Wayne State University Press.

there is also a wide margin of discretion between elementary electoral choices and the concrete governmental decisions that follow.

Elections are only the time when single expressions of will are counted. Elections register the voter's decisions; but how are these decisions arrived at? Elections compute opinions; but where do these opinions come from and how are they formed? What, in a word, is the genesis of the will and opinion that elections limit themselves to recording? Voting has a pre-voting background. While, then, we must not forget the importance of elections, we cannot isolate the electoral event from the whole circle of the opinion-making process. If the actual sovereign is not the citizen but the voter, in his turn the voter is none other than the citizen in the critical instant in which he is asked to act as sovereign. And when we shift our attention to this larger picture, we see that popular sovereignty is only a phase of the over-all political process.

The actual weight and importance of this obligatory path of the political process through the sieve of popular sovereignty remains to be determined case by case, and depends on a series of conditions, the most important of these being the circumstances in which so-called public opinion is formed. Electoral power per se is the mechanical guarantee of the system, but the substantive guarantee is given by the conditions under which the citizen gets the information and is exposed to the pressure of the opinion-makers. Elections are the means to an end—the end being a "government of opinion" of the kind so masterfully described by Dicey, that is, a government responsive to and responsible towards public opinion.[1]

We say that elections must be free. This is indeed true, but it may not be enough; for opinion too must be, in some basic sense, free. Free elections with unfree opinion—that is, with no public opinion—express nothing. The retort will be, I suppose, that in every society, be it democratic or not, there is always, inevitably, a public opinion. This answer, however, calls our attention to the need of distinguishing between (1) an opinion that is public merely in the sense that it is disseminated *among* the public, and (2) an opinion which the public to some degree has formed by itself. In the first sense, we have an opinion *made* public but in no way produced *by* the public: therefore public only in the geographical meaning that it is located *in* the public. In the second sense, we have instead an opinion *of* the public, meaning that the public is the subject. In the first sense, any society can be credited with a public opinion. In the second sense, no public opinion exists unless it is based on, or related to, personal and private opinions; and therefore a present-day totalitarian mass society has no public opinion, but only State-made opinions enforced *upon* the public.

Until a few decades ago there was no reason to draw this distinction.

[1] Cf. A. V. Dicey, *Lectures on the Relation Between Law and Public Opinion in England During the Nineteenth Century,* 3rd ed. (London, 1924), *passim.*

Until the advent of mass media and of totalitarian control of the public, to say "popular opinion" meant, and could only mean, "opinion *of* the people," that which the subjects, not the sovereign, had in mind. But nowadays we can find a popular opinion which is in no meaningful sense the people's opinion. Hence the distinction is crucial, and ambiguity as to the meaning of public opinion should be carefully avoided.[2] I shall therefore refer to public opinion only when it is a relatively free and autonomous opinion, that is, to the extent that it expresses a relatively independent will of the people and not when it becomes a mere reflection of the will of the State.

Of course, even a free and autonomous public opinion is, in many senses, neither free nor autonomous. What is actually meant by these requirements is free from State control of the opinion-making process and instrumentalities. As a rule of thumb, the conditions for a relatively self-sufficient public opinion are provided by a system of plural and alternative centers of influence and information—we might say by free competition among mass media and between opinion leaders. This does not imply that the audience usually plays one source of information against another, and that it makes up its mind after having compared and discussed the various arguments. This is seldom the case. Actually, the benefits of mass media decentralization and competition are largely mechanical and unintentional. They are so, mainly because a polycentric system of opinion-making helps to produce a plural, heterogeneous, and—above all—unpredictable and uncontrollable distribution of opinions. In short, a plurality of persuaders reflects itself in a plurality of publics, and a plurality of publics is the minimal but already sufficient condition for a successful operation of the system as a whole—I mean, of a system in which we can truthfully speak of the power of public opinion.

To acknowledge that whenever we meet with an efficient, unrestrained totalitarian monopoly of mass media there is no true public opinion,[3] does not settle the question of just how true public opinion is in the case of a loose, plural system of opinion formation. If the expression "public opinion" is supposed to evoke the image of the common man, we may still ask: to what extent does the public of the common people actually play a role of its own and exert a real influence in all this? Voting studies have, in effect, brought out a very poor picture of the ordinary voter, so poor that one is forced to wonder whether the public in question is anything more than a merely passive audience.[4] The average citizen is neither interested nor active

[2] For a general orientation, a helpful anthology of material relative to the problem of public opinion is *Reader in Public Opinion and Communication*, eds. B. Berelson and M. Janowitz (Glencoe, 1953).

[3] I shall make this point more definite in [a later] section.

[4] Until now, political and social scientists have generally been rather cautious in assessing the bearing of their findings on the theory of democracy. Cf., however, B. Berelson's "Democratic Theory and Public Opinion," *Public Opinion Quarterly* (Fall 1952), as well as *Voting* (Chicago, 1954), Chap. XIV. Cf. also the volume edited by E. Burdick and A. J. Brodbeck, *American Voting Behavior* (Glencoe, 1959), in which Burdick and a number of contributors attempt generalizations from the electoral data to political theory.

in the political discourse. His information is indeed thin and his perception of the issues is distorted and aprioristic. His choices correspond to patterns of identification connected with a prevailing allegiance or with overlapping affiliations to the family, the peer group, the class, the church, etc.[5] Psephology, the study of electoral behavior, has abundantly shown to what extent the citizen's vote depends on his social, economic, and religious environment, and also—as the French electoral sociology points out—on historically-based collective electoral predispositions.[6] We are thus forced to recognize that the expression "public opinion" stands for an *optimum.* In many respects and instances the public has no opinion, but only a very inarticulate public feeling, made up of moods and drifts of sentiment. In matters of internal policy no less than in foreign affairs, behind the so-called public will what we often find is, as Walter Lippmann says, a "phantom public."[7] But this conclusion needs some qualifications.

When we invest public opinion with the responsibility of making intelligent and rational decisions on definite questions, it is true that we are dealing with a phantom public. Schumpeter exaggerates little, I believe, when he writes that "the typical citizen drops down to a lower level of mental performance as soon as he enters the political field. He argues and analyzes in a way which he would readily recognize as infantile within the sphere of his real interests. He becomes a primitive again. His thinking becomes associative and affective. . . ."[8] He exaggerates little because a similar drop in mental performance can be observed whenever we cross the border from our field of specialization and interest. An astronomer who discusses philosophy, a chemist who speaks about music, or a poet who talks about mathematics will not utter less nonsense than the average citizen interviewed by a pollster. The difference is that the astronomer, the chemist, and the poet will generally avoid making fools of themselves by pleading ignorance, whereas the citizen is forced to concern himself with politics and in the

[5] In this connection the most relevant evidence is provided by ecological analysis and survey studies. For the United States, cf. Lazarsfeld *et al., The People's Choice,* 2nd ed. (New York, 1948); Berelson *et al., Voting;* Campbell *et al., The Voter Decides* (Evanston, 1954) and the subsequent Michigan Survey Research Center studies. All this literature has been extensively surveyed by R. E. Lane, *Political Life: Why People Get Involved in Politics* (Glencoe, 1959). A condensed, useful synthesis is Lipset, Lazarsfeld, Barton, and Linz, "The Psychology of Voting," in *Handbook of Social Psychology,* Vol. II, Chap. XXX. British scholars have paid more attention to trend reports. However, three small-scale survey studies are comparable with and relevant to the American findings: Benney *et al., How People Vote* (New York, 1956), for the Greenwich, 1950 survey; R. S. Milne and H. C. Mckenzie, *Straight Fight* (London, 1954); Milne and Mckenzie, *Marginal Seat 1955* (London, 1958). For the French findings, the representative volume is *Les Elections du 2 janvier 1956,* eds. Duverger, Goguel and Touchard (Paris, 1957). With respect to the French ecological analysis cf. note 6.

[6] French electoral sociology derives from the electoral geography of André Siegfried. Cf. the joint studies *Études de sociologie électorale* (Paris, 1947), and *Nouvelles études de sociologie électorale,* ed. F. Goguel (Paris, 1954).

[7] Lippmann's *The Phantom Public* (1920) and his *Public Opinion* (1922) are not only pioneer but still standard works.

[8] Cf. *Capitalism, Socialism and Democracy,* 2nd ed. (New York, 1947), p. 262, and all of Chap. XXI, where Schumpeter criticizes the "classical doctrine of democracy," meaning its "will of the people" conception.

midst of the general incompetence he no longer realizes that he is an ass. So the only difference is that in other zones of ignorance we are warned to mind our own business, while in the political realm we are encouraged to take the opposite attitude, and thus we end by not knowing that we know nothing.

But there is another side to the question. If, instead of asking public opinion to express ad hoc judgments that are articulate, informed, and rational, we think of public opinion as a pattern of attitudes and a cluster of basic demands, then our phantom takes on consistency and stability. In this connection Berelson has suggested an illuminating analogy. "For many voters," Berelson writes, "political preferences may be considered analogous to cultural tastes. . . . Both have their origin in ethnic, sectional, class, and family traditions. Both exhibit stability and resistance to change for individuals, but flexibility and adjustment over generations for the society as a whole. Both seem to be matters of sentiment and disposition rather than 'reasoned preferences.' While both are responsive to changed conditions and unusual stimuli, they are relatively invulnerable to direct argumentation. . . . Both are characterized more by faith than by conviction and by wishful expectation rather than careful prediction of consequences."[9] From this angle, then, public opinion reveals a formidable inertia and a gluey resistance; and therein lies its strength and its limitations, which are correlative.

Therefore, as long as the public is allowed to have an opinion, public opinion is a protagonist which should not be underestimated. It would be entirely mistaken to infer from the poor quality of the ordinary citizen that he amounts to an absentee. He may well be politically illiterate, but he is there. Tenacious in its tastes, identifications, and expectations, impervious to direct argument, public opinion enters the circle of political decision-making demanding a heavy toll. But it is just that—a toll. Policy-making does not spring from a "cultural taste" any more than music from the people who attend a concert, or literature from readers. Public opinion assures the success or failure of a policy. But it does not initiate it. The average voter does not act, he reacts. Political decisions are not arrived at by the sovereign people, they are submitted to them. The processes of forming opinion do not start *from* the people, they pass *through* them.

Thus, it is only by looking at elections and forgetting about electioneering and all the rest that democracy may be viewed as a one-way decision-making process going from bottom to top. Actually, we are confronted with a continuous circular process whose dynamics are activated from the top rather than from the bottom. Even in the most favorable circumstances it almost never happens that popular sovereignty is the real starting point. Before exerting an influence the people are influenced. Before they want something, they are often made to want it. "What we are confronted with in

[9] *Voting*, p. 311.

the analysis of political processes is largely not a genuine but a manufactured will. . . . The will of the people is the product and not the motive power of the political process." [10]

Moreover, elections should not be considered only *a parte ante,* but *a parte post* as well. In the latter focus, it is only in a very vague sense that elections can tell those who have been elected how to govern.[11] Primarily the results of voting establish who shall govern. And it is not the fault of the instrument, i.e., the imperfection of the electoral system employed, if elections can reveal only rarely and inadequately the will of the majority in regard to specific policy issues. I mean that the remedy for this cannot be found in creating more refined channels and more sensitive electoral techniques, because if the machine is imperfect it is not cruder than its mechanics, the voters.

Let us be honest. The average voter is called on to make decisions on questions about which he knows nothing. In other words, he is incompetent. And the decisions that each of us makes in fields in which we have no skill are, obviously, decisions that have been suggested by someone else, either a competent or a pseudo-competent person. And attention must be paid to the pseudo-competent person, because incompetence consists precisely in not being able to tell the difference between competence and incompetence. How then can we reasonably expect electoral instrumentalities to say more than the voter has to say? We are lucky enough if the voter is not tricked by an erroneous identification into choosing a representative that in no way impersonates his feelings and desires.[12] It would be almost a miracle if he managed to indicate a policy for every issue. Therefore, I see no grounds for complaint if voting does nothing more than indicate, within a general political orientation, the person or the party that we are "coinciding in opinion with." [13]

If this is the actual meaning and performance of elections, then the assertion that voting power is a "governing" power is metaphorical. There is power and power, and in this process the *demos* exercises a power of control and/or of pressure which amounts to a set of vetoes and basic claims in regard to those who govern. But while the people condition a government, they do not themselves govern. This means that when we talk about governing or governed democracy the verb "govern" is used in two

[10] Schumpeter, *op. cit.,* p. 263.

[11] Cf. Robert T. Dahl: "I have shown both that elections are a crucial device for controlling leaders and that they are quite ineffective as indicators of majority preference. These statements are really not in contradiction. A good deal of traditional democratic theory leads us to expect more from national elections than they can possibly provide. We expect elections to reveal the 'will' or the preferences of a majority on a set of issues. This is one thing elections rarely do. . . ." *A Preface to Democratic Theory,* p. 131.

[12] Let us not forget that *impersonare,* to impersonate, was one of the original basic meanings of *repraesentare.* Cf. H. F. Gosnell, *Democracy, the Threshold of Freedom* (New York, 1948), p. 132.

[13] This is how W. Bagehot expressed the idea of representation. Cf. "Parliamentary Reform" in N. St. John-Stevas, *Walter Bagehot* (London, 1959), p. 432.

very different senses, or with different intensity and accuracy. When we speak of the people as governing, we exaggerate, or we give the verb a vague, feeble meaning. When we speak of the people as governed we use the verb "govern" in its narrow and proper sense. And there is quite a difference. The difference is so great that we may end up with the conclusion that while the ideal would require a governing democracy, observation of the real world shows that what we actually have is a governed democracy.

So the unvarnished answer to the question, "To what degree and in what sense is the *demos* governing?" could be that a realistic examination of existing democracies shows us the exact reverse of the ideal: namely, that democracy has functioned only when an aristocracy has governed. The deontology postulates a government of the people, observation shows that the people are governed by minorities. Democracy is supposed to be a system of self-government but it turns out to be a polyarchy.

• • •

Democracy Defined: The Power of the Active "Demos"

Politics is, and always will be, the output of the politically active. Thus democracy is, and can only be, the political system in which the power resides in the active *demos.* Of course, looking at the figures, we shall discover that the active *demos* is only a *minor pars:* but this discovery should not be taken with dismay. Even if the *demos* turns out to be a numerical minority or rather a constellation of minorities, the principle remains intact as long as the rule is respected that opportunities are offered to all without exception. The foregoing definition can be implemented accordingly by saying that democracy is the power of active democratic minorities, the word "democratic" meaning that the recruitment of these minorities must be open, and that they must compete according to the rules of a multi-party system.

We arrive at similar conclusions if, instead of starting from *demo*-cracy, we start with the concept of *iso*-cracy. We can say either that democracy *ought to be* equal power for everybody, or that democracy *is* equal power for each and all. In the first case we establish a norm, with a corresponding right; and it is clear that the right has not been violated just because it is not exercised. In the second case, as the sentence has a descriptive formulation, it can only mean that an isocracy offers the whole *demos* the opportunity to participate actively and equally in policy-making.

I have said that democracy *can* only mean that the power resides in the active people. Let me add that this is right; I mean, this is also what it *should* mean. For if we do not accept this conclusion as valid, there are two possibilities. Either we ask that political apathy be met by coercion, or that those who are politically active be penalized in favor of the politically inert.

And these solutions are both absurd. In the first hypothesis it is evident that a democracy cannot impose more than the obligation to vote; otherwise we can no longer speak of free people. Moreover, initiative—i.e., the capacity to intervene actively in the political process—cannot be produced by coercion, for coercion obtains compliance but can hardly make a citizen qualitatively better than he is. In the second hypothesis, which calls for penalizing active minorities because of the apathy of the majority, the result would be general apathy and this would be indeed a queer way to obviate apathy.

Let me sum up. Prescriptively—and therefore potentially—democracy is "equal power for everybody." Actually, democracy is "the power of the active demos," which amounts to saying that power resides in those who avail themselves of it. We may complain that the gap between the prescriptive definition of democracy and its actual performance is very great. This is indeed so. But, again, whose fault is it?

For a long time we have blamed the norm; that is, our complaint has been that the norm "the people must be sovereign" was not fully realized. But we must not confuse the enactment of a prescription with its utilization by those to whom it is addressed. To enact the democratic or isocratic rule means that we have to remove the obstacles which prevent its utilization. It cannot mean more than this, for the actual utilization is a matter for those whom it concerns. It is high time, therefore, that we realized that when we complain about democracy, we are complaining about the *demos*. The defects of our systems are democratic defects, and it does not make sense to maintain that the power belongs to the people and then bewail the fact that they do not use it, or use it badly, or what you will. For this is precisely what observation of the rule that the people are the rulers implies. This point should therefore be stressed: the distance that separates the prescriptive from the descriptive definition of democracy depends on the *demos*, on the quality and intensity of its political output. For it is clear that if the right to the equal exercise of power were made use of by all of the nominal holders of power in the same way, the descriptive definition would merge, in the last analysis, with the prescriptive definition.

• • •

Democracy, Leadership and Elites

... (T)he issue as to which system provides the truest kind of representation has to be tested against this question: representation of what? Of the articulate knowledge and will of each voter? No doubt if there were any such thing, "true representation" would be important. But hardly so in the light of the actual voting performance.[14] On the other hand, it can hardly be main-

[14] As previously stated, elections are in no significant way indicators of majority preference. Dahl, among others, has made the point very well by stating that "all an election reveals is the first preference of some citizen among the candidates standing for office" (*A Preface to Democratic Theory*, p. 125, and pp. 125–132 *passim*).

tained that one electoral system is more democratic than another because it makes leaders more responsive to the voice of the people: there is no significant difference in this respect between single-member and proportional systems. Actually, if we wish to make the system still more democratic the only real progress in this direction would be—as Rousseau well knew—to lessen the scope and the bearing of elections by having the citizen replace the voter. At the limit, the most democratic method would be not to vote at all. If we vote, then, it is not to make a democracy more democratic, but to make democracy possible: that is, to make it function. In the very moment that we admit the need of having recourse to elections, we minimize democracy, for we realize that the system cannot be operated by the *demos* itself. Clearly, then, the purpose of elections is to select leadership, not to maximize democracy.[15] And if the *raison d'être* of elections is to select leadership, then the best electoral system will be the most selective system, the one which best provides for the qualitative choice of leaders.

The distressing implication of the aforesaid conclusion is that it highlights the fact that for about half a century we have failed to meet the question. For, clearly, to say that the best electoral system is the most democratic system is as good as saying that the best airplane is the one that never flies. How helpful! What is worse, despite the impressive record of failures of democratic leadership, there are still very few people who seem to realize that unless the *major pars* becomes concerned with the choice of the *melior pars,* democracies have little chance of surviving;[16] and even fewer seem to be concerned with finding the devices that could make electoral systems more selective.[17]

It may be that after mature reflection we shall be forced to come to the conclusion that the problem cannot be solved because there is no adequate corrective for the law of numbers. I say "may be" because until the question is raised and everybody becomes aware of its existence, we cannot be sure. However, even if we eventually discover that internalized norms of behavior cannot, in themselves, cope with the problem, we can try to deal with it through constitutional techniques. Once we realize that this is *the* critical issue, we can solve it on one level or another. It is a question of finding the strategic point. But unless we have the courage to raise the question openly it is quite certain that we shall never be able to solve it at all. Let me add in this connection that if the problem were to be approached on the constitu-

[15] The old-fashioned way of making this statement would be that we vote to appoint "executors." However, this is precisely one of those myths that election studies have dispelled: actually we need leaders, not mere executors.

[16] Among the few exceptions see Luigi Einaudi's essay, "Major et sanior pars" in *Il buongoverno* (Bari, 1954), esp. pp. 92–93.

[17] In this respect, instead of resuming contact with the problems, we have if anything been losing it more and more. For instance, John Stuart Mill, although a follower of Hare's system of proportional representation, was always mindful of the qualitative problem, so much so that he took particular care to insure the influence of "the best" by means of a plural voting based on educational criteria.

tional level, even then we should have to start from zero. Our constitutional theory is hardly more mature—as far as the problems of the future are concerned—than our electoral theory. We speak about "more democratic" constitutions just as *hors de propos* as we speak about more democratic electoral systems;[18] for we forget once again that if citizens do not obtain a good government they cannot be satisfied with the promise of some mythical future self-government.

Curiously enough, it is the same people who bombastically complain about how little the values of democracy are revered, who forget values altogether when the examination of a value problem confronts them with an unpopular issue. It is well to stress, therefore, that we have to be concerned not only with the values that the enemies of democracy deny, but even more with the values that are given so little weight by democrats themselves. In our specific case, a democracy that is unable to produce valuable leadership, or that surrenders to worthless leadership, is a democracy which the *demos* itself ends by feeling is not worth preserving. Let us not delude ourselves. The law of numbers, as such, is no better than the law of chance. The proof can be seen in the fact that the frequency with which mathematical chance has placed in office inept and irresponsible individuals, can be matched by the frequency with which the democracies of the twentieth century have revived the cult of the man sent by Providence.

Let us not be tempted to forget, therefore, that a democracy cannot pass the test, in the long run, unless it succeeds as a system of government. For if a democracy does not succeed in being a system of government, it does not succeed—and that is that.

• • •

. . . Pro-democratic elites are not an imperfection but an essential guarantee of the system. The more we study democracy, the more we realize how complicated and precarious it is. And the more we seek ways and means for assuring its survival, the more we become aware that a democratic society asserts itself and gains ground as government *for* the people insofar as responsible and reliable minorities devote themselves to that purpose.

The truth is that democracies depend—as the most thoughtful scholars have observed—on the quality of their leadership. Thucydides reminds us that the greatness of Athens reached its height with Pericles precisely because "by his rank, ability, and known integrity [he] was enabled to exercise an independent control over the multitude."[19] Bryce said: "Perhaps no form of government needs great leaders so much as democracy does."[20] Fifty years later, in 1937, after all the experience of the intervening period, De Madariaga wrote: "Despite appearances, liberal democracies are de-

[18] Cf. Sartori, *Democratic Theory*, Chap. XIII, 7.

[19] *History of the Peloponnesian War*, trans. Richard Crawley (New York, 1950), Bk. II, Chap. VII, pp. 142–143.

[20] *The American Commonwealth* (New York, 1888), III, p. 337.

pendent on leadership even more so perhaps than other, more authoritarian forms of government; for . . . their natural tendency to weaken the springs of political authority must be counterbalanced by a higher level of . . . authority on the part of their leaders."[21] In the same years Karl Mannheim had reached the same conclusion: "The lack of leadership in the late liberal mass society can be . . . diagnosed as the result of the change for the worse in selecting the elite. . . . It is this general lack of direction that gives the opportunity to groups with dictatorial ambitions."[22]

Democracy is the most daring experiment in man's faith that has ever been, or ever can be tried. It moves along the tightrope created by the greatest possible axiological and deontological tension. It is therefore very much exposed to the danger of extremes, and consequently of breaking the delicate balance between *is* and *ought,* between what can and what ought to be done. In short, democracy is terribly difficult. It is so difficult that only expert and accountable elites can save it from the excesses of perfectionism, from the vortex of demagogy, and from the degeneration of the *lex majoris partis.* And this is why adequate leadership is vital to democracy. It has been said that leadership is needed only to the extent that the role of the people remains secondary. But I had rather say that it is when the pressure from below is greatest that eminent leadership is more necessary than ever. For it is at this point that perfectionism on the one hand, and mass manipulation and mobilization on the other, throw the system off balance.

In the light of this, distrust and fear of elites is an anachronism that blinds us to the problems of the future. For we must really be behind the times if we think that democracy is still threatened by the existence of a ruling aristocracy, in the feudal sense of the term. What really threatens us is the opposite danger—that the reaction against rulership might lead us to the extreme of an absence of leadership. I am not saying that democracy should not oppose aristocracy; I am only pointing out that the time is past when democracy has to be on guard against it, and that it is unintelligent to fear a danger that has been largely overcome when the opposite danger—mediocracy—is looming ahead.[23]

• • •

Democracy Defined Vertically: An Elective Polyarchy

The subject matter of this [section] is the stumbling block of most discussions about democracy. This is because it is not easy to grasp how the

[21] S. de Madariaga, *Anarchie ou hiérarchie* (Paris, 1936), p. 56.

[22] *Man and Society in an Age of Reconstruction* (London, rev. 1940 English ed.), p. 87. One could keep on citing at length. Cf. finally Lester G. Seligman: "The question may thus be seriously raised as to whether the democracies have been defective by impeding the . . . rise of adequate leadership." *American Political Science Review,* Dec. 1950, pp. 904–915.

[23] Cf. A. D. Lindsay, *The Modern Democratic State* (London, 1943), p. 261.

system really works. The classic theory of democracy is unable to explain it, because it leans too heavily on the role of the individual voter and the majority, i.e., on the assumption that for the system to be democratic it must be the output of a majority will.[24] If this were the case or if this were all, we might well wonder how democracy could ever solve its problems and survive as a going political organization. The point is, however, that the classic approach loses sight of the part, vital for democratic purposes, that is played by the mechanisms of the system, which oblige its operators to compete vis-à-vis the consumer market. Therefore, in order to understand how the system actually works, we have to formulate the question this way: Why does an elective polyarchy produce democratic results?

In defining democracy as an elective polyarchy I follow, on the whole, the definition put forward by Dahl. There is, however, a difference, for in my opinion what characterizes democracy is not so much that it is an *egalitarian* polyarchy—as Dahl says—[25] as that it is an *electoral* polyarchy. By this I do not mean that the egalitarian tension is not a typical element in the system. But as far as the vertical aspect of a democracy is concerned, its importance is secondary, and the element of egalitarianism that goes into the construction of the power pyramid tends, if anything, to obstruct its vertical dimension (equality, as such, does not postulate the need for leaders). On the other hand, the amount of equality that actually goes into the vertical construction can be inferred from the conditions that make elections democratic.

Democracy, then, is an elective polyarchy, and we must say "elective" because some polyarchal systems are not based on popular suffrage. In that case the system will be competitive without being democratic. There will be a leader-leader relationship, but hardly a leader-led relationship other than as a unidirectional all-to-one relation. That is to say that in a non-elective polyarchy we will find a reciprocal control *among* leaders, but no reliable kind of control *of* leaders, or *upon* leaders. In order that the non-leaders may be able to restrain, influence, and control leaders, they must have the power to choose them—that is, regular elections must regularly occur.

It will be noted that the descriptive definition of democracy that we have arrived at is ostensibly distant from the prescriptive ideal and the etymological definition that we started with. Yet, a closer examination will show that the gap is not so wide. For when we call democracy a polyarchy, we are not simply saying that many leaders take the place of one. If that were all the difference, there would not be much to rejoice over. Likewise, when we specify that we are talking of an elective polyarchy, we are not saying that

[24] Cf., although in a somewhat different perspective, Walter Lippmann, *Public Opinion*, p. 312: "The democratic fallacy has been its preoccupation with the origin of government rather than with the processes and results. The democrat has always assumed that if political power could be derived in the right way, it would be beneficent. . . . But . . . the crucial interest is how power is exercised. . . . And that use cannot be controlled at the source."

[25] Cf. *A Preface to Democratic Theory*, p. 87, for his classification of political systems and equalitarian and non-equalitarian polyarchies.

we are simply allowed to choose among various possible leaders. If that were all, one might again conclude, in a disillusioned vein, that the leaders change but the domination remains. However, this is not the case. For we must not forget that the definition in question has to be understood dynamically. It means that democracy consists in the procedure (i) that continuously creates open, competitive minorities, (ii) whose behavior is guided by the "rule of anticipated reactions,"[26] that is, by the expectation of how the voters will react at the next elections. In full, our definition says that democracy is a procedure that produces a polyarchy in which competition on the electoral market results in the attribution of power to the people.

According to the main argument developed in this chapter, our definition can be reformulated as follows: democracy is a political system in which *the influence of the majority is assured by elective and competitive minorities to whom it is entrusted.* This definition not only stresses that "If we cannot expect citizens always to check leaders . . . then we are forced to rely heavily on checks exerted by other leaders,"[27] but also has the virtue of bringing out the vital role of leadership, as it implies that minorities are a *sine qua non* condition of the system.

The above definition, however, is only descriptive, in that it does not bring out the requisite conditions for the good functioning of the system. Electoral competition does not assure the quality of the results but only their democratic character. The rest—the worth of the output, so to speak—depends on the quality of leadership. So if we are considering specifically the qualitative aspect of the problem, our definition will have to be rephrased as follows: democracy should be *a polyarchy of elected elites.* We may also put it this way: democracy ought to be a *selective system of competing elected minorities.*

All of this may seem very complicated. But that is because democracy is indeed a complicated form. And our definitions cannot make it simpler than it is; they can only trick us into making it *seem* simple. It is easy to say that democracy is the "people's power." The question is to understand how this is possible, and in what way the people's will can make itself usefully felt. What is required is thus a reply to the question: On what does the proper functioning of an experiment in democratic government depend? This is the question that I have attempted to answer.

Do my conclusions add up to "another theory" of democracy? At first sight it may seem so. It has been said that there are two theories of democracy, the mandate theory, which is the orthodox one, and the competitive theory, developed by Pendleton Herring in *Politics of Democracy,* and especially by Schumpeter in *Capitalism, Socialism and Democracy.* I have un-

[26] This is Friedrich's felicitous wording. Cf. his 2nd (1941) ed. of *Constitutional Government and Democracy* (Boston), pp. 589–591. The chapter in question, XXV, has been omitted from the 1950 ed.

[27] R. A. Dahl in *Research Frontiers in Politics and Government* (Washington, 1955), p. 62.

doubtedly been working along these lines. Yet, I am unwilling to accept the so-called new theory as another theory. For I by no means reject the mandate theory; I have only said that it has a prescriptive validity. And if I have followed the competitive theory, I have done so stating that it is the descriptive theory. Therefore the definition that has been suggested in this chapter does not contradict the classical theory and does not attempt to replace it. It is rather an extension and completion of it. For the fault of the classical doctrine is that it stops midway and does not go to the end of the road.

In other words, the inadequacy of the orthodox theory of democracy does not imply that it should be replaced (for in doing that I would be stating a theory about something else), but that it should be developed to its complete extent. The classical conception is simply an unfinished picture, and my point is that the time has come to finish it. Up to now we have not had enough evidence at our disposal to know what landfall we might make. But now we do. It can be understood why at an early stage all the emphasis had to be placed on the *demos*. But now that we have reached maturity, the theory has to be balanced. And that is why I have laid emphasis on democracy as a system of government, and thus on the importance of admitting—in our over-all outlook—the principle of leadership openly, without the usual guilt complexes. Otherwise our theory will remain unbalanced, only prescriptive and not sufficiently (if at all) operational, continuing the unhappy results that our unrealistic attitude and our head-in-the-sand policies have long been causing.

It is pertinent to wonder in this connection why this completion is so laborious. This is chiefly because we fail to make the distinction between the scientific validity and the ideocratic (and subordinately ideologic) use of a statement,[28] or at any rate we fail to place the distinction between its scientific exactness and its ideocratic value at the proper juncture. Thus, the elite argument is classified *en bloc* as aristocratic. Methodologically speaking, this single-package way of disposing of the problem is definitely wrong, and I fear that little progress will be achieved by political theory unless we realize—speaking in general—that when an argument is based on a finding, this finding can only be true or false, and that it is only its subsequent ideocratic or ideological role that falls under the aristocratic-democratic categorization. It follows that the elite concept (i) cannot be classified either as aristocratic or democratic until the purpose is taken into account, and that (ii) it can be *both* aristocratic and democratic, depending on how it is put to use. To assert from the outset that the elite concept is aristocratic amounts to (i) passing an ideological judgment on a statement of fact, and to (ii) disguising a biased premise as the conclusion that it is not. For the correct conclusion is that the elite findings which are put to use for the purpose

[28] I make a sharp distinction between ideocratic and ideological function. Cf. *Democratic Theory*, Chap. XVIII, 2.

of showing that democracy is impossible make for an aristocratic theory of elites; whereas elite findings which serve the purpose of helping to constitute the best possible democracy are precisely a democratic theory of elites.

One might say that this is an aristocratic theory of democracy as against its demolatric version. However, what is the value of the demolatric theory of democracy? The voting studies and the opinion polls have confirmed beyond the point of doubt that we have to reckon with a leader-seeking and leader-needing public. On the other hand, our findings prove that the imagery of a self-governing *demos* is either a deceptive myth or a demagogic device, and that in both cases it can only foster the bankruptcy of the system. All the evidence points out, then, that our goal cannot be a headless society but a political community in which coercion yields to inducement, a *vis coactiva* is replaced by a *vis directiva.* I therefore venture to suggest that the democratic theory of elites is in the light of present-day factual knowledge the core of democratic theory itself. To know the facts and to refuse to acknowledge them by putting two and two together—as many people are still doing—is an unhealthy and, in the long run, suicidal policy.

1962

Bibliography

Barker, Ernest. *Principles of Social and Political Theory.* Oxford: Clarendon, 1951.

Becker, Carl L. *Modern Democracy.* New Haven: Yale University Press, 1941.

Benn, S. I., and Peters, R. S. *The Principles of Political Thought.* New York: Free Press, 1959.

Berg, Elias. *Democracy and the Majority Rule.* Stockholm: Akademiförlaget, 1965.

Barbu, Zevedei. *Democracy and Dictatorship; Their Psychology and Patterns of Life.* New York: Grove Press, 1956.

Cassinelli, C. W. *The Politics of Freedom: An Analysis of the Modern Democratic State.* Seattle: University of Washington Press, 1961.

Cohen, Carl. *Democracy.* New York: Free Press, 1973.

Cook, Terrance E. (ed.). *Participatory Democracy.* San Francisco: Candfield Press, 1971.

Dahl, Robert. *Polyarchy.* New Haven: Yale University Press, 1972.

Dahl, Robert. *A Preface to Democratic Theory.* Chicago: University of Chicago Press, 1956.

Dewey, John. "Democracy and Educational Administration," *School and Society,* April 3, 1937.

Dumbauld, Edward (ed.). *The Political Writings of Thomas Jefferson.* Indianapolis, Ind.: Bobbs-Merrill Co., Inc., 1955.

Frankel, Charles. *The Democratic Prospect.* New York: Harper & Row, 1964.

Friedrich, Carl. *The New Belief in the Common Man.* Boston: Little, Brown & Co., 1942.

Girvetz, Harry K. (ed.). *Democracy and Elitism.* New York: Charles Scribner's Sons, 1967.

Hallowell, John H. *The Moral Foundation of Democracy.* Chicago: University of Chicago Press, 1956.

Hudson, Joy William. *Why Democracy: A Study in the Philosophy of the State.* New York: Appleton Century Co., Inc., 1936.

Kariel, Henry S. (ed.). *Frontiers of Democratic Theory.* New York: Random House, 1970.

Kendall, Willmore. *John Locke and the Doctrine of Majority Rule.* Urbana: University of Illinois Press, 1941.

Lakoff, Sanford A. *Equality in Political Philosophy.* Cambridge, Mass.: Harvard University Press, 1964.

Lindsay, A. D. *The Modern Democratic State.* New York: Oxford University Press, 1967.

Lippincott, Benjamin. *Victorian Critics of Democracy.* Minneapolis: University of Minnesota Press, 1938.

Lipson, Leslie. *The Democratic Civilization.* New York: Oxford University Press, 1964.

MacPherson, C. B. *The Real World of Democracy.* Oxford: Clarendon Press, 1966.

Mayo, Henry B. *An Introduction to Democratic Theory.* New York: Oxford University Press, 1960.

Megill, Kenneth. *The New Democratic Theory.* New York: Free Press, 1970.

Mims, Edwin, Jr. *The Majority of the People.* New York: Modern Age Books, 1941.

Niebuhr, Reinhold. *Children of Light and Children of Darkness.* New York: Charles Scribner's Sons, 1944.

Pateman, Carole. *Participation and Democratic Theory.* Cambridge: Cambridge University Press, 1970.

Pickles, Dorothy. *Democracy.* New York: Basic Books, 1970.

Ranney, Austin, and Kendall, Willmore. *Democracy and the American Party System.* New York: Harcourt, Brace & World, 1956.

Rejai, M. (ed.). *Democracy: The Contemporary Theories.* New York: Atherton, 1967.

Ricci, David. *Community Power and Democratic Theory.* New York: Random House, 1971.

Riemer, Neal. *The Revival of Democratic Theory.* New York: Appleton-Century-Crofts, 1962.

Shell, Kurt L. (ed.). *The Democratic Political Process: A Cross National Reader.* Waltham, Mass.: Blaisdell, 1969.

Simon, Yves R. *Philosophy of Democratic Government.* Chicago: University of Chicago Press, 1951.

Smith, T. V., and Lindeman, Edward C. *The Democratic Way of Life.* New York: New American Library, 1951.

Swabey, Marie Collins. *Theory of the Democratic State.* Cambridge, Mass.: Harvard University Press, 1937.

Talmon, J. L. *The Rise of Totalitarian Democracy.* Boston: Beacon Press, 1952.

Thorson, Thomas L. *The Logic of Democracy.* New York: Holt, Rinehart and Winston, 1962.

Verba, Sidney, and Nie, Norman H. *Participation in America: Political Democracy and Social Equality. New York:* Harper and Row, 1972.

IV Liberal Democracy

None of the democratic ideologies portrays an individualistic conception of the nature of man more so than liberal democracy. Descendants of Locke and the Utilitarian tradition, the liberals assume that enlightened self-interest, unencumbered by the various positive conventions of human society, will lead the individual to conduct his life coincident with the public interest—sometimes by the individual's design, but more often as an automatic outcome of the rational pursuit of one's self-interest. As a movement of liberation, vindicating the personal, civil, and economic freedom of the individual, liberalism seeks a clearance of all obstructions to the progress of mankind. Never a matter of mechanical contrivance, progress is thought possible only through the spontaneous activity of the individual. To enhance progress, in turn, the liberals oppose arbitrary government and even the more informal mechanisms of social control.

Ostensibly, the liberal democratic emphasis on liberty—personal, civil, and economic—applies to all members of society. Notwithstanding, the liberal democratic ideology, with its emphasis on minimal governmental regulation, reflects most clearly the social vantage point of entrepreneurial activity in a predominantly market economy. It is the case, however, that liberal democrats generally argue that benefits realized by capital and private enterprise indirectly accrue to all members of society. Quite often, the mechanism connecting the individual's interest to the public interest is an assumed natural harmony of interests between and among the members of society.

In the above respect, therefore, the activity from which the liberal democratic ideology was first abstracted is primarily economic activity. (This is in addition to the core experiences common to the various democratic ideologies.) The liberal democratic model reflects, first in historical sequence, the activities and needs of the mercantilists. Later, with the continued growth and expansion of the Industrial Revolution, the liberal democratic model reflects the economic demands and activities of the capitalist entrepreneurs in the dual struggle for the rapid social change necessitated by an industrializing society and for a competitive position in the growing capitalist economy.

Arguing the liberal case for free trade, Adam Smith suggests that governmental regulations of trade introduce some degree of disorder into the natural harmony of the state. No regulation of commerce, he contends, can increase the quantity of industry in a society beyond the means of its capital. In fact, Smith maintains that industry is somewhat retarded by governmental regulation. Without the regulation of commerce, capital is directed to the production of commodities of apparently higher value than those articles which, under a system of regulation, are made at a cost higher than they can be bought elsewhere. The production of commodities of higher value increases revenue which, in turn, augments capital and can then be used to further the expansion of industry.

Extending the liberal position to personal freedom, John Stuart Mill argues that the only case in which mankind is warranted to interfere with personal liberty is that of self-protection. Freedom, for Mill, consists in pursuing our own good in our own way, so long as we neither deprive others of their liberty nor impede the efforts of others to obtain it. It is important to note, however, that liberty, according to Mill, is not a universal principle applicable to all men and all societies, although the principle is relevant to the vast majority of mankind. The principle is not universal because liberty is relevant to the arrangements of society only among men capable of being improved by free and equal discussion. It is Mill's contention, further, that well-developed human beings are possible only through the cultivation of individuality. Thus the public has no business interfering with an individual's personal tastes and self-regarding concerns.

Milton Friedman, University of Chicago economist and self-proclaimed classical liberal, argues that government control of the economic order (central planning) results in political slavery for the ordinary man. Friedman suggests that where the private market is the main organizing device of the economy, there too is individual freedom. Progress in the availability of material comforts, and the hope for further progress, Friedman contends, are inextricably bound with the capitalist order.

17 Free Trade

ADAM SMITH

By restraining, either by high duties, or by absolute prohibitions, the importation of such goods from foreign countries as can be produced at home, the monopoly of the home-market is more or less secured to the domestic industry employed in producing them. Thus the prohibition of importing either live cattle or salt provisions from foreign countries, secures to the graziers of Great Britain the monopoly of the home-market for butchers' meat. The high duties upon the importation of corn, which in times of moderate plenty amount to a prohibition, give a like advantage to the growers of that commodity. The prohibition of the importation of foreign woollens is equally favourable to the woollen manufactures. . . . The variety of goods, of which the importation into Great Britain is prohibited, either absolutely, or under certain circumstances, greatly exceeds what can easily be suspected by those who are not well acquainted with the laws of the customs.

That this monopoly of the home-market frequently gives great encouragement to that particular species of industry which enjoys it, and frequently turns towards that employment a greater share of both the labour and stock of the society than would otherwise have gone to it, cannot be doubted. But whether it tends either to increase the general industry of the society, or to give it the most advantageous direction, is not, perhaps, altogether so evident.

The general industry of the society never can exceed what the capital of the society can employ. As the number of workmen that can be kept in employment by any particular person, must bear a certain proportion to his capital; so the number of those that can be continually employed by all the members of a great society, must bear a certain proportion to the capital of that society, and never can exceed that proportion. No regulation of commerce can increase the quantity of industry in any society beyond what its capital can maintain. It can only divert a part of it into a direction into which it might not otherwise have gone; and it is by no means certain that this artificial direction is likely to be more advantageous to the society, than that into which it would have gone of its own accord.

Every individual is continually exerting himself to find out the most advantageous employment for whatever capital he can command. It is his own advantage, indeed, and not that of the society, which he has in view. But the

SOURCE: from Adam Smith, *An Inquiry into the Nature and Causes of the Wealth of Nations* (Edinburgh and London: William Creech Mundell, Doug and Stevenson, Arch Constable and Co. and Ostell, 1806), pp. 247–266.

study of his own advantage naturally, or rather necessarily, leads him to prefer that employment which is most advantageous to the society.

First, every individual endeavours to employ his capital as near home as he can, and consequently as much as he can in the support of domestic industry; provided always that he can thereby obtain the ordinary, or not a great deal less than the ordinary profits of stock.

Thus, upon equal, or nearly equal profits, every wholesale merchant naturally prefers the home-trade to the foreign trade of consumption, and the foreign trade of consumption to the carrying trade. In the home-trade his capital is never so long out of his sight as it frequently is in the foreign trade of consumption. He can know better the character and situation of the persons whom he trusts; and if he should happen to be deceived, he knows better the laws of the country from which he must seek redress. In the carrying trade, the capital of the merchant is, as it were, divided between two foreign countries, and no part of it is ever necessarily brought home, or placed under his own immediate view and command. The capital which an Amsterdam merchant employs in carrying corn from Konningsberg to Lisbon, and fruit and wine from Lisbon to Konningsberg, must generally be the one half of it at Konningsberg and the other half at Lisbon. No part of it need ever come to Amsterdam. The natural residence of such a merchant should either be at Konningsberg or Lisbon, and it can only be some very particular circumstances which can make him prefer the residence of Amsterdam. The uneasiness, however, which he feels at being separated so far from his capital, generally determines him to bring part, both of the Konningsberg goods which he destines for the market of Lisbon, and of the Lisbon goods which he destines for that of Konningsberg, to Amsterdam: and though this necessarily subjects him to a double charge of loading and unloading, as well as to the payment of some duties and customs, yet, for the sake of having some part of his capital always under his own view and command, he willingly submits to this extraordinary charge; and it is in this manner that every country which has any considerable share of the carrying trade, becomes always the emporium, or general market, for the goods of all the different countries whose trade it carries on. The merchant, in order to save a second loading and unloading, endeavours always to sell in the home-market, as much of the goods of all those different countries as he can; and thus, so far as he can, to convert his carrying trade into a foreign trade of consumption. A merchant, in the same manner, who is engaged in the foreign trade of consumption, when he collects goods for foreign markets, will always be glad, upon equal or nearly equal profits, to sell as great a part of them at home as he can. He saves himself the risk and trouble of exportation, when, so far as he can, he thus converts his foreign trade of consumption into a home-trade. Home is in this manner the centre, if I may say so, round which the capitals of the inhabitants of every country are continually circulating, and towards which they are always tending, though, by particular causes, they may sometimes be driven off and repelled from it towards more distant employments. But a capital employed in the home-trade, it has already been shewn, necessarily puts into motion a greater quantity of domestic industry, and gives revenue and employment to a greater number of the inhabitants of the country, than an equal capital employed in the foreign trade of consumption: and one employed in the foreign trade of consumption has the same advantage over an equal capital employed in the carrying trade. Upon equal, or only nearly equal profits, therefore, every individual naturally inclines to employ his capital in the manner in which it is likely to afford the greatest support to domestic industry, and to give revenue and employment to the greatest number of people of his own country.

Secondly, every individual who employs his capital in the support of domestic industry, necessarily endeavours so to direct that industry, that its produce may be of the greatest possible value.

The produce of industry is what it adds to the subject or materials upon which it is employed. In proportion as the value of this produce is great or small, so will likewise be the profits of the employer. But it is only for the sake of profit that any man employs a capital in the support of industry; and he will always, therefore, endeavour to employ it in the support of that industry of which the produce is likely to be of the greatest value, or to exchange for the greatest quantity either of money or of other goods.

But the annual revenue of every society is always precisely equal to the exchangeable value of the whole annual produce of its industry, or rather is precisely the same thing with that exchangeable value. As every individual, therefore, endeavours as much as he can, both to employ his capital in the support of domestic industry, and so to direct that industry that its produce may be of the greatest value; every individual necessarily labours to render the annual revenue of the society as great as he can. He generally, indeed, neither intends to promote the public interest, nor knows how much he is promoting it. By preferring the support of domestic to that of foreign industry, he intends only his own security; and by directing that industry in such a manner as its produce may be of the greatest value, he intends only his own gain; and he is in this, as in many other cases, led by an invisible hand to promote an end which was no part of his intention. Nor is it always the worse for the society that it was no part of it. By pursuing his own interest, he frequently promotes that of the society more effectually than when he really intends to promote it. I have never known much good done by those who affected to trade for the public good. It is an affectation, indeed, not very common among merchants, and very few words need be employed in dissuading them from it.

What is the species of domestic industry which his capital can employ, and of which the produce is likely to be of the greatest value, every individual, it is evident, can, in his local situation, judge much better than any statesman or lawgiver can do for him. The statesman, who should attempt to direct private people in what manner they ought to employ their capitals, would not only load himself with a most unnecessary attention, but assume an authority which could safely be trusted, not only to no single person, but to no council or senate whatever, and which would nowhere be so dangerous as in the hands of a man who had folly and presumption enough to fancy himself fit to exercise it.

To give the monopoly of the home-market to the produce of domestic industry, in any particular art or manufacture, is in some measure to direct private people in what manner they ought to employ their capitals, and must, in almost all cases, be either a useless or a hurtful regulation. If the produce of domestic can be brought there as cheap as that of foreign industry, the regulation is evidently useless. If it cannot, it must generally be hurtful. It is the maxim of every prudent master of a family, never to attempt to make at home what it will cost him more to make than to buy. The tailor does not attempt to make his own shoes, but buys them of the shoemaker. The shoemaker does not attempt to make his own cloths, but employs a tailor. The farmer attempts to make neither the one nor the other, but employs those different artificers. All of them find it for their interest, to employ their whole industry in a way in which they have some advantage over their neighbours, and to purchase with a part of its produce, or what is the same thing, with the price of a part of it, whatever else they have occasion for.

What is prudence in the conduct of every private family, can scarce be folly in that of a great kingdom. If a foreign country can supply us with a commodity cheaper than we ourselves can make it, better buy it of them with some part of the produce of our own industry, employed in a way in which we have some advantage. The general industry of the country, being always in proportion to the capital which employs it, will not thereby be diminished, no more than that of the above-mentioned artificers; but only left to find out the way in which it can be employed with the greatest advantage. It is certainly not employed to the greatest advantage, when it is thus directed towards an object which it can buy cheaper that it can make. The value of its annual produce is certainly more or less diminished, when it is thus turned away from producing commodities evidently of more value than the commodity which it is directed to produce. According to the supposition, that commodity could be purchased from foreign countries cheaper than it can be made at home: it could, therefore, have been purchased with a part only of the commodities, or, what is the same thing, with a part only of the price of the commodities, which the industry employed by an equal capital would have produced at home, had it been left to follow its natural course. The industry of the country, therefore, is thus turned away from a more to a less advantageous employment; and the exchangeable value of its annual produce, instead of being increased, according to the intention of the lawgiver, must necessarily be diminished by every such regulation.

By means of such regulations, indeed, a particular manufacture may sometimes be acquired sooner than it could have been otherwise, and, after a certain time, may be made at home as cheap or cheaper than in the foreign country. But though the industry of the society may be thus carried with advantage into a particular channel sooner than it could have been otherwise, it will by no means follow that the sum total, either of its industry, or of its revenue, can ever be augmented by any such regulation. The industry of the society can augment only in proportion as its capital augments, and its capital can augment only in proportion to what can be gradually saved out of its revenue. But the immediate effect of every such regulation is to diminish its revenue; and what diminishes its revenue is certainly not very likely to augment its capital faster than it would have augmented of its own accord, had both capital and industry been left to find out their natural employments.

Though for want of such regulations, the society should never acquire the proposed manufacture, it would not, upon that account, necessarily be the poorer in any one period of its duration. In every period of its duration its whole capital and industry might still have been employed, though upon different objects, in the manner that was most advantageous at the time. In every period its revenue might have been the greatest which its capital could afford, and both capital and revenue might have been augmented with the greatest possible rapidity.

The natural advantages which one country has over another in producing particular commodities, are sometimes so great, that it is acknowledged by all the world to be in vain to struggle with them. By means of glasses, hot-beds, and hot-walls, very good grapes can be raised in Scotland, and very good wine too can be made of them, at about thirty times the expence for which at least equally good can be brought from foreign countries. Would it be a reasonable law to prohibit the importation of all foreign wines, merely to encourage the making of claret and burgundy in Scotland? But if there would be a manifest absurdity in turning towards any employment, thirty times more of the capital and industry of the country, than would be necessary to purchase from foreign countries an equal quantity of the commodities wanted, there must be an absurdity, though not altogether so glaring, yet exactly of the same kind, in turning towards any such employment a thirtieth, or even a three hundredth part more of either. Whether the advantages which one country has over another, be natural or acquired, is in this respect of no consequence. As long as the one country has those advantages, and the other wants them, it will always be more advantageous for the latter, rather to buy the former than to make. It is an acquired advantage only, which one artificer has over his neighbour, who exercises another trade; and yet they both find it more advantageous to buy of one another, than to make what does not belong to their particular trades.

Merchants and manufacturers are the people who derive the greatest advantage from this monopoly of the home-market. The prohibition of the importation of foreign cattle, and of salt provisions, together with the high duties upon foreign corn, which in times of moderate plenty amount to a prohibition, are not near so advantageous to the graziers and farmers of Great Britain, as other regulations of the same kind are to its merchants and manufacturers. Manufactures, those of the finer kind especially, are more easily transported from one country to another than corn or cattle. It is in the fetching and carrying manufactures, accordingly, that foreign trade is chiefly employed. In manufactures, a very small advantage will enable foreigners to undersell our own workmen, even in the home-market. It will require a very great one to enable them to do so in the rude produce of the soil. If the free importation of foreign manufactures were permitted, several of the home-manufactures would probably suffer, and some of them, perhaps, go to ruin altogether, and a considerable part of the stock and industry at present employed in them would be forced to find out some other employment. But the freest importation of the rude produce of the soil could have no such effect upon the agriculture of the country.

If the importation of foreign cattle, for example, were made ever so free, so few could be imported, that the grazing trade of Great Britain could be little affected by it. . . .

Even the free importation of foreign corn could very little affect the interest of the farmers of Great Britain. Corn is a much more bulky commodity than butchers' meat. A pound of wheat at a penny, is as dear as a pound of butchers' meat at four pence. The small quantity of foreign corn imported even in times of the greatest scarcity, may satisfy our farmers, that they can have nothing to fear from the freest importation. The average quantity imported, one year with another, amounts only, according to the very well informed author of the Tracts upon the corn trade, to 23,728 quarters of all sorts of grain, and does not exceed the five hundredth and seventy-one part of the annual consumption. But as the bounty upon corn occasions a greater exportation in years of plenty, so it must of consequence occasion a greater importation in years of scarcity, than in the actual state of tillage would otherwise take place. By means of it, the plenty of one year does not compensate the scarcity of another; and as the average quantity exported is necessarily augmented by it, so must likewise, in the actual state of tillage, the average quantity imported. If there were no bounty, as less corn would be exported, so it is probable that, one year with another, less would be imported than at present. The corn merchants, the fetchers and carriers of corn between Great Britain and foreign countries, would have much less employment, and might suffer considerably; but the country gentlemen and farmers could suffer very little. It is in the corn merchants accordingly, rather than in the country gentlemen and farmers, that I have observed the greatest anxiety for the renewal and continuation of the bounty.

Country gentlemen and farmers are, to their great honour, of all people, the least subject to the wretched spirit of monopoly. The undertaker of a great manufactory is sometimes alarmed, if another work of the same kind is established within twenty miles of him. The Dutch undertaker of the woollen manufacture at Abbeville stipulated, that no work of the same kind should be established within thirty leagues of that city. Farmers and country gentlemen, on the contrary, are generally disposed rather to promote, than to obstruct, the cultivation and improvement of their neighbours' farms and estates. They have no secrets, such as those of the greater part of manufacturers, but are generally rather fond of communicating to their neighbours, and of extending, as far as possible, any new practice which they have found to be advantageous. *Pius Questus,* says old Cato, *stabilissimusque, minimeque invidiosus; minimeque male cogitantes sunt, qui in eo studio occupati sunt.* Country gentlemen and farmers, dispersed in different parts of the country, cannot so easily combine as merchants and manufacturers, who, being collected into towns, and accustomed to that exclusive corporation spirit which prevails in them, naturally endeavour to obtain, against all their countrymen, the same exclusive privilege which they generally possess against the inhabitants of their respective towns. They accordingly seem to have been the original inventors of those restraints upon the importation of foreign goods, which secure to them the monopoly of the home-market. It was probably in imitation of them, and to put themselves upon a level with those who, they found, were disposed to oppress them, that the country gentlemen and farmers of Great Britain so far forgot the generosity which is natural to their station, as to demand the exclusive privilege of supplying their countrymen with corn and butchers' meat. They did not, perhaps, take time to consider, how much less their interest could be affected by the freedom of trade, than that of the people whose example they followed.

To prohibit, by a perpetual law, the importation of foreign corn and cattle, is in reality to enact, that the population and industry of the country shall, at no time, exceed what the rude produce of its own soil can maintain.

There seem, however, to be two cases, in which it will generally be advantageous to lay some burden upon foreign, for the encouragement of domestic, industry.

The first is, when some particular sort of industry is necessary for the defence of the country. The defence of Great Britain, for example, depends very much upon the number of its sailors and shipping. The act of navigation, therefore, very properly endeavours to give the sailors and shipping of Great Britain the monopoly of the trade of their own country, in some cases, by absolute prohibitions, and in others, by heavy burdens upon the shipping of foreign countries. . . .

The second case, in which it will generally be advantageous to lay some burden upon foreign for the encouragement of domestic industry, is, when some tax is imposed at home upon the produce of the latter. In this case, it seems reasonable that an equal tax should be imposed upon the like produce of the former. This would not give the monopoly of the home-market to domestic industry, nor turn towards a particular employment a greater share of the stock and labour of the country, than what would naturally go to it. It would only hinder any part of what would naturally go to it from being turned away by the tax, into a less natural direction, and would leave the competition between foreign and domestic industry, after the tax, as nearly as possible upon the same footing as before it. In Great Britain, when any such tax is laid upon the produce of domestic industry, it is usual, at the same time, in order to stop the clamorous complaints of our merchants and manufacturers, that they will be undersold at home, to lay a much heavier duty upon the importation of all foreign goods of the same kind.

This second limitation of the freedom of trade, according to some people, should, upon some occasions, be extended much farther than to the precise foreign commodities which could come into competition with those which had been taxed at home. When the necessaries of life have been taxed in any country, it becomes proper, they pretend, to tax not only the like necessaries of life imported from other countries, but all sorts of foreign goods which can come into competition with any thing that is the produce of domestic industry. Subsistence, they say, becomes necessarily dearer in consequence of such taxes; and the price of labour must always rise with the price of the labourer's subsistence. Every commodity, therefore, which is the produce of domestic industry, though not immediately taxed itself, becomes dearer in consequence of such taxes, because the labour which produces it becomes so. Such taxes, therefore, are really equivalent, they say, to a tax upon every particular commodity produced at home. In order to put domestic upon the same footing with foreign industry, therefore, it becomes necessary, they think, to lay some duty upon every foreign commodity, equal to this enhancement of the price of the home commodities with which it can come into competition.

Whether taxes upon the necessaries of life, such as those in Great Britain upon soap, salt, leather, candles, &c. necessarily raise the price of labour, and consequently that of all other commodities, I shall consider hereafter, when I come to treat of taxes. Supposing, however, in the meantime, that they have this effect, and they have it undoubtedly, this general enhancement of the price of all commodities, in consequence of that labour, is a case which differs in the two following respects from that of a particular commodity, of which the price was enhanced by a particular tax immediately imposed upon it.

First, it might always be known with great exactness, how far the price of such a commodity could be enhanced by such a tax: but how far the general enhancement of the price of labour might affect that of every different commodity about which labour was employed, could never be known with any tolerable exactness. It would be impossible, therefore, to proportion, with any tolerable exactness, the tax upon every foreign, to this enhancement of the price of every home, commodity.

Secondly, taxes upon the necessaries of life have nearly the same effect upon the circumstances of the people as a poor soil and a bad climate. Provisions are thereby rendered dearer, in the same manner as if it required extraordinary labour and expence to raise them. As in the natural scarcity arising from soil and climate, it would be absurd to direct the people in what manner they ought to employ their capitals and industry, so is it likewise in the artificial scarcity arising from such taxes. To be left to accommodate, as well as they could, their industry to their situation, and to find out those employments, in which, notwithstanding their unfavourable circumstances, they might have some advantage either in the home or in the foreign market, is what, in both cases, would evidently be most for their advantage. To lay a new tax upon them, because they are already overburdened with taxes, and, because they already pay too dear for the necessaries of life, to make them likewise pay too dear for the greater part of other commodities, is certainly a most absurd way of making amends.

Such taxes, when they have grown up to a certain height, are a curse equal to the barrenness of the earth and the inclemency of the heavens; and yet it is in the richest and most industrious countries that they have been most generally imposed. No other countries could support so great a disorder. As the strongest bodies only can live and enjoy health, under an unwholesome regimen; so the nations only, that in every sort of industry have the greatest natural and acquired advantages, can subsist and prosper under such taxes. Holland is the country in Europe in which they abound most, and which, from peculiar circumstances, continues to prosper, not by means of them, as has been most absurdly supposed, but in spite of them.

As there are two cases, in which it will generally be advantageous to lay some burden upon foreign for the encouragement of domestic industry; so there are two others, in which it may sometimes be a matter of deliberation: in the one, how far it is proper to continue the free importation of certain foreign goods; and in the other, how far, or in what manner, it may be proper to restore that free importation, after it has been for some time interrupted.

The case in which it may sometimes be a matter of deliberation how far it is proper to continue the free importation of certain foreign goods, is, when some foreign nation restrains, by high duties or prohibitions, the importation of some of our manufactures into their country. Revenge in this case naturally dictates retaliation, and that we should impose the like duties and prohibitions upon the importation of some or all of their manufactures into ours. Nations accordingly seldom fail to retaliate in this manner. . . .

There may be good policy in retaliations of this kind, when there is a probability that they will procure the repeal of the high duties or prohibitions complained of. The recovery of a great foreign market will generally more than compensate the transitory inconveniency of paying dearer during a short time for some sorts of goods. To judge whether such retaliations are likely to produce such an effect, does not, perhaps, belong so much to the science of a legislator, whose deliberations ought to be governed by general principles which are always the same, as to the skill of that insidious and crafty animal, vulgarly called a statesman or politician, whose councils are directed by the momentary fluctuations of affairs. When there is no probability that any such repeal can be procured, it seems a bad method of compensating the injury done to certain classes of our people, to do another injury ourselves, not only to those classes, but almost all the other classes of them. When our neighbours prohibit some manufacture of ours, we generally prohibit, not only the same, for that alone would seldom affect them considerably, but some other manufacture of theirs. This may no doubt give encouragement to some particular class of workmen among ourselves, and, by excluding some of their rivals, may enable them to raise their price in the home-market. These workmen, however, who suffered by our neighbours' prohibition, will not be benefited by ours. On the contrary, they, and almost all the other classes of our citizens, will thereby be obliged to pay dearer than before for certain goods. Every such law, therefore, imposes a real tax upon the whole country, not in favour of that particular class of workmen who were injured by our neighbours' prohibition, but of some other class.

The case in which it may sometimes be a matter of deliberation, how far, or in what manner, it is proper to restore the free importation of foreign goods, after it has been for some time interrupted, is, when particular manufactures, by means of high duties or prohibitions upon all foreign goods, which can come into competition with them, have been so far extended as to employ a great multitude of hands. Humanity may, in this case, require that the freedom of trade should be restored only by slow gradations, and with a good deal of reserve and circumspection. Were those high duties and prohibitions taken away all at once, cheaper foreign goods of the same kind might be poured so fast into the home-market, as to deprive, all at once, many thousands of our people of their ordinary employment, and means of subsistence. The disorder which this would occasion might, no doubt, be very considerable. It would in all probability, however, be much less than is commonly imagined, for the two following reasons.

First, all those manufactures, of which any part is commonly exported to other European countries without a bounty, could be very little affected by the freest importation of foreign goods. Such manufactures must be sold as cheap abroad as any other foreign goods of the same quality and kind, and consequently must be sold cheaper at home. They would still, therefore, keep possession of the home-market; and though a capricious man of fashion might sometimes prefer foreign wares, merely because they were foreign, to cheaper and better goods of the same kind that were made at home, this folly could, from the nature of things, extend to so few, that it could make no sensible impression upon the general employment of the people. But a great part of all the different branches of our woollen manufacture, of our tanned leather, and of our hard-ware, are annually exported to other European countries without any bounty, and these are the manufactures which employ the greatest number of hands. The silk, perhaps, is the manufacture which would suffer the most by this freedom of trade, and after it the linen, though the latter much less than the former.

Secondly, though a great number of people should, by thus restoring the freedom of trade, be thrown all at once out of their ordinary employment and common method of subsistence, it would by no means follow that they would thereby be deprived either of employment or subsistence. By the reduction of the army and navy at the end of the late war, more than 100,000 soldiers and seamen, a number equal to what is employed in the greatest manufactures, were all at once thrown out of their ordinary employment; but, though they no doubt suffered some inconveniency, they were not thereby deprived of all employment and subsistence. The greater part of the seamen, it is probable, gradually betook themselves to the merchant-service as they could find occasion, and, in the meantime, both they and the soldiers were absorbed in the great mass of the people, and employed in a great variety of occupations. Not only no great convulsion, but no sensible disorder, arose from so great a change in the situation of more than 100,000 men, all accustomed to the use of arms, and many of them to rapine and plunder. The number of vagrants was scarce anywhere sensibly increased by it; even the wages of labour were not reduced by it in any occupation, so far as I have been able to learn, except in that of seamen in the merchant-service. But if we compare together the habits of a soldier and of any sort of manufacturer, we shall find that those of the latter do not tend so much to disqualify him from being employed in a new trade, as those of the former from being employed in any. The manufacturer has always been accustomed to look for his subsistence from his labour only: the soldier to expect it from his pay. Application and industry have been familiar to the one; idleness and dissipation to the other. But it is surely much easier to change the direction of industry from one sort of labour to another, than to turn idleness and dissipation to any. To the greater part of manufactures, besides, it has already been observed, there are other collateral manufactures of so similar a nature, that a workman can easily transfer his industry from one of them to another. The greater part of such workmen, too, are occasionally employed in country labour. The stock which employed them in a particular manufacture before, will still remain in the country, to employ an equal number of people in some other way. The capital of the country remaining the same, the demand for labour will likewise be the same, or very nearly the same, though it may be exerted in different places, and for different occupations. Soldiers and seamen, indeed, when discharged from the king's service, are at liberty to exercise any trade within any town or place of Great Britain or Ireland. Let the same natural liberty of exercising what species of industry they please, be restored to all his majesty's subjects, in the same manner as to soldiers and seamen; that is, break down the exclusive privileges of corporations, and repeal the statute of apprenticeship, both which are real encroachments upon natural liberty, and add to these the repeal of the law of settlements, so that a poor workman, when thrown out of employment, either in one trade or in one place, may seek for it in another trade or in another place, without the fear either of a prosecution or of a removal; and neither the public nor the individuals will suffer much more from the occasional disbanding some particular classes of manufacturers, than from that of soldiers. Our manufacturers have no doubt great merit with their country, but they cannot have more than those who defend it with their blood, nor deserve to be treated with more delicacy.

To expect, indeed, that the freedom of trade should ever be entirely restored in Great Britain, is as absurd as to expect that an Oceana or Utopia should ever be established in it. Not only the prejudices of the public, but what is much more unconquerable, the private interests of many individuals, irresistibly oppose it. Were the officers of the army to oppose, with the same zeal and unanimity, any reduction in the number of forces, with which master manufacturers set themselves against every law that is likely to increase the number of their rivals in the home-market; were the former to animate their soldiers, in the same manner as the latter inflame their workmen, to attack with violence and outrage the proposers of any such regulation; to attempt to reduce the army would be as dangerous as it has now become to attempt to diminish, in any respect, the monopoly which our manufacturers have obtained against us. This monopoly has so much increased the number of some particular tribes of them, that, like an overgrown standing army, they have become formidable to the government, and, upon many occasions, intimidate the legislature. The member of parliament who supports every proposal for strengthening this monopoly, is sure to acquire not only the reputation of understanding trade, but great popularity and influence with an order of men whose numbers and wealth render them of great importance. If he opposes them, on the contrary, and still more if he has authority enough to be able to thwart them, neither the most acknowledged probity, nor the highest rank, nor the greatest public services, can protect him from the most infamous abuse and detraction, from personal insults, nor sometimes from real danger, arising from the insolent outrage of furious and disappointed monopolists.

The undertaker of a great manufacture, who, by the home-markets being suddenly laid open to the competition of foreigners, should be obliged to abandon his trade, would no doubt suffer very considerably. That part of his capital which had usually been employed in purchasing materials, and in paying his workmen, might, without much difficulty, perhaps, find another employment. But that part of it which was fixed in workhouses, and in the instruments of trade, could scarce be disposed of without considerable loss. The equitable regard, therefore, to his interest, requires that changes of this kind should never be introduced suddenly, but slowly, gradually, and after a very long warning. The legislature, were it possible that its deliberations could be always directed, not by the clamorous importunity of partial interests, but by an extensive view of the general good, ought, upon this very account, perhaps, to be particularly careful, neither to establish any new monopolies of this kind, nor to extend further those which are already established. Every such regulation introduces some degree of real disorder into the constitution of the state, which it will be difficult afterwards to cure without occasioning another disorder. . . .

1776

18 On Liberty

JOHN STUART MILL

The subject of this Essay is not the so-called Liberty of the Will, so unfortunately opposed to the misnamed doctrine of Philosophical Necessity; but Civil, or Social Liberty: the nature and limits of the power which can be legitimately exercised by society over the individual. A question seldom stated, and hardly ever discussed, in general terms, but which profoundly influences the practical controversies of the age by its latent presence, and is likely soon to make itself recognized as the vital question of the future. It is so far from being new, that, in a certain sense, it has divided mankind, almost from the remotest ages; but in the stage of progress into which the more civilized portions of the species have now entered, it presents itself under new conditions, and requires a different and more fundamental treatment.

The struggle between Liberty and Authority is the most conspicuous feature in the portions of history with which we are earliest familiar, particularly in that of Greece, Rome, and England. But in old times this contest was between subjects, or some classes of subjects, and the Government. By liberty, was meant protection against the tyranny of the political rulers. The rulers were conceived (except in some of the popular governments of

SOURCE: from John Stuart Mill: *On Liberty*, edited by Alburey Castell (Crofts Classics Series). Copyright 1947. By permission of Appleton-Century-Crofts, Educational Division, Meredith Corporation.

Greece) as in a necessarily antagonistic position to the people whom they ruled. They consisted of a governing One, or a governing tribe or caste, who derived their authority from inheritance or conquest, who, at all events, did not hold it at the pleasure of the governed, and whose supremacy men did not venture, perhaps did not desire, to contest, whatever precautions might be taken against its oppressive exercise. Their power was regarded as necessary, but also as highly dangerous; as a weapon which they would attempt to use against their subjects, no less than against external enemies. To prevent the weaker members of the community from being preyed upon by innumerable vultures, it was needful that there should be an animal of prey stronger than the rest, commissioned to keep them down. But as the king of the vultures would be no less bent upon preying on the flock than any of the minor harpies, it was indispensable to be in a perpetual attitude of defense against his beak and claws. The aim, therefore, of patriots was to set limits to the power which the ruler should be suffered to exercise over the community; and this limitation was what they meant by liberty. It was attempted in two ways. First, by obtaining a recognition of certain immunities, called political liberties or rights, which it was to be regarded as a breach of duty in the ruler to infringe, and which, if he did infringe, specific resistance, or general rebellion, was held to be justifiable. A second, and generally a later expedient, was the establishment of constitutional checks, by which the consent of the community, or of a body of some sort, supposed to represent its interests, was made a necessary condition to some of the more important acts of the governing power. To the first of these modes of limitation, the ruling power, in most European countries, was compelled, more or less, to submit. It was not so with the second; and, to attain this, or when already in some degree possessed, to attain it more completely, became everywhere the principal object of the lovers of liberty. And so long as mankind were content to combat one enemy by another, and to be ruled by a master, on condition of being guaranteed more or less efficaciously against his tyranny, they did not carry their aspirations beyond this point.

A time, however, came, in the progress of human affairs, when men ceased to think it a necessity of nature that their governors should be an independent power, opposed in interest to themselves. It appeared to them much better that the various magistrates of the State should be their tenants or delegates, revocable at their pleasure. In that way alone, it seemed, could they have complete security that the powers of government would never be abused to their disadvantage. By degrees this new demand for elective and temporary rulers became the prominent object of the exertions of the popular party, wherever any such party existed; and superseded, to a considerable extent, the previous efforts to limit the power of rulers. As the struggle proceeded for making the ruling power emanate from the periodical choice of the ruled, some persons began to think that too much importance had been attached to the limitation of the power itself. *That* (it might seem) was a resource against rulers whose interests were habitually opposed to those of the people. What was now wanted was, that the rulers should be identified with the people; that their interest and will should be the interest and will of the nation. The nation did not need to be protected against its own will. There was no fear of its tyrannizing over itself. Let the rulers be effectually responsible to it, promptly removable by it, and it could afford to trust them with power of which it could itself dictate the use to be made. Their power was but the nation's own power, concentrated, and in a form convenient for exercise. This mode of thought, or rather perhaps of feeling, was common among the last generation of European liberalism, in the Continental section of which it still apparently predominates. Those who admit any limit to what a government may do, except in the case of such governments as they think ought not to exist, stand out as brilliant exceptions among the political thinkers of the Continent. A similar tone of sentiment might by this time have been prevalent in our own country, if the circumstances which for a time encouraged it, had continued unaltered.

But, in political and philosophical theories, as well as in persons, success discloses faults and infirmities which failure might have concealed from observation. The notion, that the people have no need to limit their power over themselves, might seem axiomatic, when popular government was a thing only dreamed about, or read of as having existed at some distant period of the past. Neither was that notion necessarily disturbed by such temporary aberrations as those of the French Revolution, the worst of which were the work of an usurping few, and which, in any case, belonged, not to the permanent working of popular institutions, but to a sudden and convulsive outbreak against monarchical and aristocratic despotism. In time, however, a democratic republic came to occupy a large portion of the earth's surface, and made itself felt as one of the most powerful members of the community of nations; and elective and responsible government became subject to the observations and criticisms which wait upon a great existing fact. It was now perceived that such phrases as "self-government," and "the power of the people over themselves," do not express the true state of the case. The "people" who exercise the power are not always the same people with those over whom it is exercised; and the "self-government" spoken of is not the government of each by himself, but of each by all the rest. The will of the people, moreover, practically means the will of the most numerous or the most active *part* of the people; the majority, or those who succeed in making themselves accepted as the majority; the people, consequently, *may* desire to oppress a part of their number; and precautions are as much needed against this as against any other abuse of power. The limitation, therefore, of the power of government over individuals loses none of its importance when the holders of power are regularly accountable to the community, that is, to the strongest party therein. This view of things, recommending itself equally to the intelligence of thinkers and to the inclination of those important classes in European society to whose real or supposed interests democracy is adverse, has had no difficulty in establishing itself; and in political speculations "the tyranny of the majority" is now generally included among the evils against which society requires to be on its guard.

Like other tyrannies, the tyranny of the majority was at first, and is still vulgarly, held in dread, chiefly as operating through the acts of the public authorities. But reflecting persons perceived that when society is itself the tyrant—society collectively, over the separate individuals who compose it—its means of tyrannizing are not restricted to the acts which it may do by the hands of its political functionaries. Society can and does execute its own mandates: and if it issues wrong mandates instead of right, or any mandates at all in things with which it ought not to meddle, it practices a social tyranny more formidable than many kinds of political oppression, since, though not usually upheld by such extreme penalties, it leaves fewer means of escape, penetrating much more deeply into the details of life, and enslaving the soul itself. Protection, therefore, against the tyranny of the magistrate is not enough: there needs protection also against the tyranny of the prevailing opinion and feeling; against the tendency of society to impose, by other means than civil penalties, its own ideas and practices as rules of conduct on those who dissent from them; to fetter the development, and, if possible, prevent the formation, of any individuality not in harmony with its ways, and compel all characters to fashion themselves upon the model of its own. There is a limit to the legitimate interference of collective opinion with individual independence: and to find that limit, and maintain it against encroachment, is as indispensable to a good condition of human affairs, as protection against political despotism.

But though this proposition is not likely to be contested in general terms, the practical question, where to place the limit—how to make the fitting adjustment between individual independence and social control—is a subject on which nearly everything remains to be done. All that makes existence valuable to any one, depends on the enforcement of restraints upon the actions of other people. Some rules of conduct, therefore, must be imposed, by law in the first place, and by opinion on many things which are not fit subjects for the operation of law. What these rules should be, is the principal question in human affairs; but if we except a few of the most obvious cases, it is one of those which least progress has been made in resolving. No two ages, and scarcely any two countries, have decided it alike; and the decision of one age or country is a wonder to another. Yet the people of any given age and country no more suspect any difficulty in it, than if it were a subject on which mankind had always been agreed. The rules which obtain among themselves appear to them self-evident and self-justifying. This all but universal illusion is one of the examples of the magical influence of custom, which is not only, as the proverb says, a second nature, but is continually mistaken for the first. The effect of custom, in preventing any misgiving respecting the rules of conduct which mankind impose on one another, is all the more complete because the subject is one on which it is not generally considered necessary that reasons should be given, either by one person to others, or by each to himself. People are accustomed to believe, and have been encouraged in the belief by some who aspire to the character of philosophers, that their feelings, on subjects of this nature, are better than reasons, and render reasons unnecessary. The practical principle which guides them to their opinions on the regulation of human conduct, is the feeling in each person's mind that everybody should be required to act as he, and those with whom he sympathizes, would like them to act. No one, indeed, acknowledges to himself that his standard of judgment is his own liking; but an opinion on a point of conduct, not supported by reasons, can only count as one person's preference; and if the reasons, when given are a mere appeal to a similar preference felt by other people, it is still only many people's liking instead of one. To an ordinary man, however, his own preference, thus supported, is not only a perfectly satisfactory reason, but the only one he generally has for any of his notions of morality, taste, or propriety, which are not expressly written in his religious creed; and his chief guide in the interpretation even of that. Men's opinions, accordingly, on what is laudable or blameable, are affected by all the multifarious causes which influence their wishes in regard to the conduct of others, and which are as numerous as those which determine their wishes on any other subject. Sometimes their reason—at other times their prejudices or superstitions: often their social affections, not seldom their antisocial ones, their envy or jealousy, their arrogance or contemptuousness: but most commonly, their desires or fears for themselves—their legitimate or illegitimate self-interest. Wherever there is an ascendant class, a large portion of the morality of the country emanates from its class interests, and its feelings of class superiority. The morality between Spartans and Helots, between planters and negroes, between princes and subjects, between nobles and roturiers, between men and women, has been for the most part the creation of these class interests and feelings: and the sentiments thus generated, react in turn upon the moral feelings of the members of the ascendant class, in their relations among themselves. Where, on the other hand, a class, formerly ascendant, has lost its ascendancy, or where its ascendancy is unpopular, the prevailing moral sentiments frequently bear the impress of an impatient dislike of superiority. Another grand determining principle of the rules of conduct, both in act and forbearance, which have been enforced by law or opinion, has been the servility of mankind towards the supposed preferences or aversions of their temporal masters, or of their gods. This servility, though essentially selfish, is not hypocrisy; it gives rise to perfectly genuine sentiments of abhorrence; it made men burn magicians and heretics. Among so many baser influences, the general and obvious interests of society have of course had a share, and a large one, in the direction of the moral sentiments: less, however, as a matter of reason, and on their own account, than as a consequence of the sympathies and antipathies which grew out of them: and sympathies and antipathies which had little or nothing to do with the interests of society, have made themselves felt in the establishment of moralities with quite as great force.

The likings and dislikings of society, or of some powerful portion of it, are thus the main thing which has practically determined the rules laid down for general observance, under the penalties of law or opinion. And in general, those who have been in advance of society in thought and feeling, have left this condition of things unassailed in principle, however they may have come into conflict with it in some of its details. They have occupied themselves rather in inquiring what things society ought to like or dislike, than in questioning whether its likings or dislikings should be a law to individuals. They preferred endeavoring to alter the feelings of mankind on the particular points on which they were themselves heretical, rather than make common cause in defense of freedom, with heretics generally. The only case in which the higher ground has been taken on principle and maintained with consistency, by any but an individual here and there, is that of religious belief: a case instructive in many ways, and not least so as forming a most striking instance of the fallibility of what is called the moral sense: for the *odium theologicum,* in a sincere bigot, is one of the most unequivocal cases of moral feeling. Those who first broke the yoke of what called itself the Universal Church, were in general as little willing to permit difference of religious opinion as that church itself. But when the heat of the conflict was over, without giving a complete victory to any party, and each church or sect was reduced to limit its hopes to retaining possession of the ground it already occupied; minorities, seeing that they had no chance of becoming majorities, were under the necessity of pleading to those whom they could not convert, for permission to differ. It is accordingly on this battle-field, almost solely, that the rights of the individual against society have been asserted on broad grounds of principle, and the claim of society to exercise authority over dissentients, openly controverted. The great writers to whom the world owes what religious liberty it possesses, have mostly asserted freedom of conscience as an indefeasible right, and denied absolutely that a human being is accountable to others for his religious belief. Yet so natural to mankind is intolerance in whatever they really care about, that religious freedom has hardly anywhere been practically realized, except where religious indifference, which dislikes to have its peace disturbed by theological quarrels, has added its weight to the scale. In the minds of almost all religious persons, even in the most tolerant countries, the duty of toleration is admitted with tacit reserves. One person will bear with dissent in matters of church government, but not of dogma; another can tolerate everybody, short of a Papist or a Unitarian; another, every one who believes in revealed religion; a few extend their charity a little further, but stop at the belief in a God and in a future state. Wherever the sentiment of the majority is still genuine and intense, it is found to have abated little of its claim to be obeyed.

In England, from the peculiar circumstances of our political history, though the yoke of opinion is perhaps heavier, that of law is lighter, than in most other countries of Europe; and there is considerable jealousy of direct interference, by the legislative or the executive power, with private conduct; not so much from any just regard for the independence of the individual, as from the still subsisting habit of looking on the government as representing an opposite interest to the public. The majority have not yet learnt to feel the power of the government their power, or its opinions their opinions. When they do so, individual liberty will probably be as much exposed to invasion from the government, as it already is from public opinion. But, as yet, there is a considerable amount of feeling ready to be called forth against any attempt of the law to control individuals in things in which they have not hitherto been accustomed to be controlled by it; and this with very little discrimination as to whether the matter is, or is not, within the legitimate sphere of legal control; insomuch that the feeling, highly salutary on the whole, is perhaps quite as often misplaced as well grounded in the particular instances of its application. There is, in fact, no recognized principle by which the propriety or impropriety of government interference is customarily tested. People decide according to their personal preferences. Some, whenever they see any good to be done, or evil to be remedied, would willingly instigate the government to undertake the business; while others prefer to bear almost any amount of social evil, rather than add one to the departments of human interests amenable to governmental control. And men range themselves on one or the other side in any particular case, according to this general direction of their sentiments; or according to the degree of interest which they feel in the particular thing which it is proposed that the government should do, or according to the belief they entertain that the government would, or would not, do it in the manner they prefer; but very rarely on account of any opinion to which they consistently adhere, as to what things are fit to be done by a government. And it seems to me that in consequence of this absence of rule or principle, one side is at present as often wrong as the other; the interference of government is, with about equal frequency, improperly invoked and improperly condemned.

The object of this Essay is to assert one very simple principle, as entitled to govern absolutely the dealings of society with the individual in the way of compulsion and control, whether the means used be physical force in the form of legal penalties, or the moral coercion of public opinion. That principle is, that the sole end for which mankind are warranted, individually or collectively, in interfering with the liberty of action of any of their number, is self-protection. That the only purpose for which power can be rightfully exercised over any member of a civilized community, against his will, is to prevent harm to others. His own good, either physical or moral, is not a sufficient warrant. He cannot rightfully be compelled to do or forbear because it will be better for him to do so, because it will make him happier, because, in the opinions of others, to do so would be wise, or even right. These are good reasons for remonstrating with him, or reasoning with him, or persuading him, or entreating him, but not for compelling him, or visiting him with any evil in case he do otherwise. To justify that, the conduct from which it is desired to deter him, must be calculated to produce evil to some one else. The only part of the conduct of any one, for which he is amenable to society, is that which concerns others. In the part which merely concerns himself, his independence is, of right, absolute. Over himself, over his own body and mind, the individual is sovereign.

It is, perhaps, hardly necessary to say that this doctrine is meant to apply only to human beings in the maturity of their faculties. We are not speaking of children, or of young persons below the age which the law may fix as that of manhood or womanhood. Those who are still in a state to require being taken care of by others, must be protected against their own actions as well as against external injury. For the same reason, we may leave out of consideration those backward states of society in which the race itself may be considered as in its nonage. The early difficulties in the way of spontaneous progress are so great, that there is seldom any choice of means for overcoming them; and a ruler full of the spirit of improvement is warranted in the use of any expedients that will attain an end, perhaps otherwise unattainable. Despotism is a legitimate mode of government in dealing with barbarians, provided the end be their improvement, and the means justified by actually effecting that end. Liberty, as a principle, has no application to any state of things anterior to the time when mankind have become capable of being improved by free and equal discussion. Until then, there is nothing for them but implicit obedience to an Akbar or a Charlemagne, if they are so fortunate as to find one. But as soon as mankind have attained the capacity of being guided to their own improvement by conviction or persuasion (a period long since reached in all nations with whom we need here concern ourselves), compulsion, either in the direct form or in that of pains and penalties for non-compliance, is no longer admissible as a means to their own good, and justifiable only for the security of others.

It is proper to state that I forgo any advantage which could be derived to my argument from the idea of abstract right, as a thing independent of utility. I regard utility as the ultimate appeal on all ethical questions; but it must be utility in the largest sense, grounded on the permanent interests of man as a progressive being. Those interests, I contend, authorize the subjection of individual spontaneity to external control, only in respect to those actions of each, which concern the interest of other people. If any one does an act hurtful to others, there is a prima facie case for punishing him, by law, or, where legal penalties are not safely applicable, by general disapprobation. There are also many positive acts for the benefit of others, which he may rightfully be compelled to perform; such as, to give evidence in a court of justice; to bear his fair share in the common defense, or in any other joint work necessary to the interest of the society of which he enjoys the protection; and to perform certain acts of individual beneficence, such as saving a fellow creature's life, or interposing to protect the defenseless against ill-usage, things which whenever it is obviously a man's duty to do, he may rightfully be made responsible to society for not doing. A person may cause evil to others not only by his actions but by his inaction, and in either case he is justly accountable to them for the injury. The latter case, it is true, requires a much more cautious exercise of compulsion than the former. To make any one answerable for doing evil to others, is the rule; to make him answerable for not preventing evil, is, comparatively speaking, the exception. Yet there are many cases clear enough and grave enough to justify that exception. In all things which regard the external relations of the individual, he is *de jure* amenable to those whose interests are concerned, and if need be, to society as their protector. There are often good reasons for not holding him to the responsibility; but these reasons must arise from the special expediencies of the case: either because it is a kind of case in which he is on the whole likely to act better, when left to his own discretion, than when controlled in any way in which society have it in their power to control him; or because the attempt to exercise control would produce other evils, greater than those which it would prevent. When such reasons as these preclude the enforcement of responsibility, the conscience of the agent himself should step into the vacant judgment-seat, and protect those interests of others which have no external protection; judging himself all the more rigidly, because the case does not admit of his being made accountable to the judgment of his fellow creatures.

But there is a sphere of action in which society, as distinguished from the individual, has, if any, only an indirect interest; comprehending all that portion of a person's life and conduct which affects only himself, or if it also affects others, only with their free, voluntary, and undeceived consent and participation. When I say only himself, I mean directly, and in the first instance: for whatever affects himself, may affect others through himself; and the objection which may be grounded on this contingency will receive consideration in the sequel. This, then, is the appropriate region of human liberty. It comprises, first, the inward domain of consciousness; demanding liberty of conscience, in the most comprehensive sense; liberty of thought and feeling; absolute freedom of opinion and sentiment on all subjects, practical or speculative, scientific, moral, or theological. The liberty of expressing and publishing opinions may seem to fall under a different principle, since it belongs to that part of the conduct of an individual which concerns other people; but, being almost of as much importance as the liberty of thought itself, and resting in great part on the same reasons, is practically inseparable from it. Secondly, the principle requires liberty of tastes and pursuits; of framing the plan of our life to suit our own character; of doing as we like, subject to such consequences as may follow: without impediment from our fellow creatures, so long as what we do does not harm them, even though they should think our conduct foolish, perverse, or wrong. Thirdly, from this liberty of each individual, follows the liberty, within the same limits, of combination among individuals; freedom to unite, for any purpose not involving harm to others: the persons combining being supposed to be of full age, and not forced or deceived.

No society in which these liberties are not, on the whole, respected, is free, whatever may be its form of government; and none is completely free in which they do not exist absolute and unqualified. The only freedom which deserves the name, is that of pursuing our own good in our own way, so long as we do not attempt to deprive others of theirs, or impede their efforts to obtain it. Each is the proper guardian of his own health, whether bodily, or mental and spiritual. Mankind are greater gainers by suffering each other to live as seems good to themselves, than by compelling each to live as seems good to the rest.

Though this doctrine is anything but new, and, to some persons, may have the air of a truism, there is no doctrine which stands more directly opposed to the general tendency of existing opinion and practice. Society has expended fully as much effort in the attempt (according to its lights) to compel people to conform to its notions of personal, as of social excellence. The ancient commonwealths thought themselves entitled to practice, and the ancient philosophers countenanced, the regulation of every part of private conduct by public authority, on the ground that the State had a deep interest in the whole bodily and mental discipline of every one of its citizens; a mode of thinking which may have been admissible in small republics surrounded by powerful enemies, in constant peril of being subverted by foreign attack or internal commotion, and to which even a short interval of relaxed energy and self-command might so easily be fatal, that they could not afford to wait for the salutary permanent effects of freedom. In the modern world, the greater size of political communities, and, above all, the separation between spiritual and temporal authority (which placed the direction of men's consciences in other hands than those which controlled their worldly affairs), prevented so great an interference by law in the details of private life; but the engines of moral repression have been wielded more strenuously against divergence from the reigning opinion in self-regarding, than even in social matters; religion, the most powerful of the elements which have entered into the formation of moral feeling, having almost always been governed either by the ambition of a hierarchy, seeking control over every department of human conduct, or by the spirit of Puritanism. And some of those modern reformers who have placed themselves in strongest opposition to the religions of the past, have been no way behind either churches or sects in their assertion of the right of spiritual domination: M. Comte, in particular, whose social system, as unfolded in his *Système Politique de Positive,* aims at establishing (though by moral more than by legal appliances) a despotism of society over the individual, surpassing anything contemplated in the political ideal of the most rigid disciplinarian among the ancient philosophers.

Apart from the peculiar tenets of individual thinkers, there is also in the world at large an increasing inclination to stretch unduly the powers of society over the individual, both by the force of opinion and even by that of legislation: and as the tendency of all the changes taking place in the world is to strengthen society, and diminish the power of the individual, this encroachment is not one of the evils which tend spontaneously to disappear, but, on the contrary, to grow more and more formidable. The disposition of mankind, whether as rulers or as fellow citizens, to impose their own opinions and inclinations as a rule of conduct on others, is so energetically supported by some of the best and by some of the worst feelings incident to human nature, that it is hardly ever kept under restraint by anything but want of power; and as the power is not declining, but growing, unless a strong barrier of moral conviction can be raised against the mischief, we must expect, in the present circumstances of the world, to see it increase.

It will be convenient for the argument, if, instead of at once entering upon the general thesis, we confine ourselves in the first instance to a single branch of it, on which the principle here stated is, if not fully, yet to a certain point, recognized by the current opinions. This one branch is the Liberty of Thought: from which it is impossible to separate the cognate liberty of speaking and of writing. Although these liberties, to some considerable amount, form part of the political morality of all countries which profess religious toleration and free institutions, the grounds, both philosophical and practical, on which they rest, are perhaps not so familiar to the general mind, nor so thoroughly appreciated by many even of the leaders of opinion, as might have been expected. Those grounds, when rightly understood, are of much wider application than to only one division of the subject, and a thorough consideration of this part of the question will be found the best introduction to the remainder. Those to whom nothing which I am about to say will be new, may therefore, I hope, excuse me, if on a subject which for now three centuries has been so often discussed, I venture on one discussion more.

• • •

What, then, is the rightful limit to the sovereignty of the individual over himself? Where does the authority of society begin? How much of human life should be assigned to individuality, and how much to society?

Each will receive its proper share, if each has that which more particularly concerns it. To individuality should belong the part of life in which it is chiefly the individual that is interested; to society, the part which chiefly interests society.

Though society is not founded on a contract, and though no good purpose is answered by inventing a contract in order to deduce social obligations from it, every one who receives the protection of society owes a return for the benefit, and the fact of living in society renders it indispensable that each should be bound to observe a certain line of conduct towards the rest. This conduct consists, first, in not injuring the interests of one another; or rather certain interests, which, either by express legal provision or by tacit understanding, ought to be considered as rights; and secondly, in each person's bearing his share (to be fixed on some equitable principle) of the labors and sacrifices incurred for defending the society or its members from injury and molestation. These conditions society is justified in enforcing at all costs to those who endeavor to withhold fulfilment. Nor is this all that society may do. The acts of an individual may be hurtful to others, or wanting in due consideration for their welfare, without going the length of violating any of their constituted rights. The offender may then be justly punished by opinion, though not by law. As soon as any part of a person's conduct affects prejudicially the interests of others, society has jurisdiction over it, and the question whether the general welfare will or will not be promoted by interfering with it, becomes open to discussion. But there is no room for entertaining any such question when a person's conduct affects the interests of no persons besides himself, or needs not affect them unless they like (all the persons concerned being of full age, and the ordinary amount of understanding). In all such cases there should be perfect freedom, legal and social, to do the action and stand the consequences.

It would be a great misunderstanding of this doctrine to suppose that it is one of selfish indifference, which pretends that human beings have no business with each other's conduct in life, and that they should not concern themselves about the well-doing or well-being of one another, unless their own interest is involved. Instead of any diminution, there is need of a great increase of disinterested exertion to promote the good of others. But disinterested benevolence can find other instruments to persuade people to their good, than whips and scourges, either of the literal or the metaphorical sort. I am the last person to undervalue the self-regarding virtues; they are only second in importance, if even second, to the social. It is equally the business of education to cultivate both. But even education works by conviction and persuasion as well as by compulsion, and it is by the former only that, when the period of education is past, the self-regarding virtues should be inculcated. Human beings owe to each other help to distinguish the better from the worse, and encouragement to choose the former and avoid the latter. They should be for ever stimulating each other to increased exercise of their higher faculties, and increased direction of their feelings and aims towards wise instead of foolish, elevating instead of degrading, objects and contemplations. But neither one person, nor any number of persons, is warranted in saying to another human creature of ripe years, that he shall not do with his life for his own benefit what he chooses to do with it. He is the person most interested in his own well-being; the interest which any other person, except in cases of strong personal attachment, can have in it, is trifling, compared with that which he himself has; the interest which society has in him individually (except as to his conduct to others) is fractional, and altogether indirect: while, with respect to his own feelings and circumstances, the most ordinary man or woman has means of knowledge immeasurably surpassing those that can be possessed by any one else. The interference of society to overrule his judgment and purposes in what only regards himself, must be grounded on general presumptions; which may be altogether wrong, and even if right, are as likely as not to be misapplied to individual cases, by persons no better acquainted with the circumstances of such cases than those are who look at them merely from without. In this department, therefore, of human affairs, Individuality has its proper field of action. In the conduct of human beings towards one another, it is necessary that general rules should for the most part be observed, in order that people may know what they have to expect; but in each person's own concerns, his individual spontaneity is entitled to free exercise. Considerations to aid his judgment, exhortations to strengthen his will, may be offered to him, even obtruded on him, by others; but he himself is the final judge. All errors which he is likely to commit against advice and warning, are far outweighed by the evil of allowing others to constrain him to what they deem his good.

I do not mean that the feelings with which a person is regarded by others, ought not to be in any way affected by his self-regarding qualities or deficiencies. This is neither possible nor desirable. If he is eminent in any of the qualities which conduce to his own good, he is, so far, a proper object of admiration. He is so much the nearer to the ideal perfection of human nature. If he is grossly deficient in those qualities, a sentiment the opposite of admiration will follow. There is a degree of folly, and a degree of what may be called (though the phrase is not unobjectionable) lowness or depravation of taste, which, though it cannot justify doing harm to the person who manifests it, renders him necessarily and properly a subject of distaste, or, in extreme cases, even of contempt: a person could not have the opposite qualities in due strength without entertaining these feelings. Though doing no wrong to any one, a person may so act as to compel us to judge him, and feel to him, as a fool, or as a being of an inferior order: and since this judgment and feeling are a fact which he would prefer to avoid, it is doing him a service to warn him of it beforehand, as of any other disagreeable consequence to which he exposes himself. It would be well, indeed, if this good office were much more freely rendered than the common notions of politeness at present permit, and if one person could honestly point out to another that he thinks him in fault, without being considered unmannerly or presuming. We have a right, also, in various ways, to act upon our unfavorable opinion of any one, not to the oppression of his individuality, but in the exercise of ours. We are not bound, for example, to seek his society; we have a right to avoid it (though not to parade the avoidance), for we have a right to choose the society most acceptable to us. We have a right, and it may be our duty, to caution others against him, if we think his example or conversation likely to have a pernicious effect on those with whom he associates. We may give others a preference over him in optional good offices, except those which tend to his improvement. In these various modes a person may suffer very severe penalties at the hands of others, for faults which directly concern only himself; but he suffers these penalties only in so far as they are the natural, and, as it were, the spontaneous consequences of the faults themselves, not because they are purposely inflicted on him for the sake of punishment. A person who shows rashness, obstinacy, self-conceit—who cannot live within moderate means—who cannot restrain himself from hurtful indulgences—who pursues animal pleasures at the expense of those of feeling and intellect—must expect to be lowered in the opinion of others, and to have a less share of their favorable sentiments; but of this he has no right to complain, unless he has merited their favor by special excellence in his social relations, and has thus established a title to their good offices, which is not affected by his demerits towards himself.

What I contend for is, that the inconveniences which are strictly inseparable from the unfavorable judgment of others, are the only ones to which a person should ever be subjected for that portion of his conduct and character which concerns his own good, but which does not affect the interests of others in their relations with him. Acts injurious to others require a totally different treatment. Encroachment on their rights; infliction on them of any loss or damage not justified by his own rights; falsehood or duplicity in dealing with them; unfair or ungenerous use of advantages over them; even selfish abstinence from defending them against injury—these are fit objects of moral reprobation, and, in grave cases, of moral retribution and punishment. And not only these acts, but the dispositions which lead to them, are properly immoral, and fit subjects of disapprobation which may rise to abhorrence. Cruelty of disposition; malice and ill nature; that most anti-social and odious of all passions, envy; dissimulation and insincerity; irascibility on insufficient cause, and resentment disproportioned to the provocation; the love of domineering over others; the desire to engross more than one's share of advantages (the πλεονεξια of the Greeks); the pride which derives gratification from the abasement of others; the egotism which thinks self and its concerns more important than everything else, and decides all doubtful questions in its own favor;—these are moral vices, and constitute a bad and odious moral character: unlike the self-regarding faults previously mentioned, which are not properly immoralities, and to whatever pitch they may be carried, do not constitute wickedness. They may be proofs of any amount of folly, or want of personal dignity and self-respect; but they are only a subject of moral reprobation when they involve a breach of duty to others, for whose sake the individual is bound to have care for himself. What are called duties to ourselves are not socially obligatory, unless circumstances render them at the same time duties to others. The term duty to oneself, when it means anything more than prudence, means self-respect or self-development; and for none of these is any one accountable to his fellow creatures, because for none of them is it for the good of mankind that he be held accountable to them.

The distinction between the loss of consideration which a person may rightly incur by defect of prudence or of personal dignity, and the reprobation which is due to him for an offense against the rights of others, is not a merely nominal distinction. It makes a vast difference both in our feelings and in our conduct towards him, whether he displeases us in things in which we think we have a right to control him, or in things in which we know that we have not. If he displeases us, we may express our distaste, and we may stand aloof from a person as well as from a thing that displeases us; but we shall not therefore feel called on to make his life uncomfortable. We shall reflect that he already bears, or will bear, the whole penalty of his error; if he spoils his life by mismanagement, we shall not, for that reason, desire to spoil it still further: instead of wishing to punish him, we shall rather endeavor to alleviate his punishment, by showing him how he may avoid or cure the evils his conduct tends to bring upon him. He may be to us an object of pity, perhaps of dislike, but not of anger or resentment; we shall not treat him like an enemy of society: the worst we shall think ourselves jusified in doing is leaving him to himself, if we do not interfere benevolently by showing interest or concern for him. It is far otherwise if he has infringed the rules necessary for the protection of his fellow creatures, individually or collectively. The evil consequences of his acts do not then fall on himself, but on others; and society, as the protector of all its members, must retaliate on him; must inflict pain on him for the express purpose of punishment, and must take care that it be sufficiently severe. In the one case, he is an offender at our bar, and we are called on not only to sit in judgment on him, but, in one shape or another, to execute our own sentence; in the other case, it is not our part to inflict any suffering on him, except what may incidentally follow from our using the same liberty in the regulation of our own affairs, which we allow to him in his.

The distinction here pointed out between the part of a person's life which concerns only himself, and that which concerns others, many persons will refuse to admit. How (it may be asked) can any part of the conduct of a member of society be a matter of indifference to the other members? No person is an entirely isolated being; it is impossible for a person to do anything seriously or permanently hurtful to himself, without mischief reaching at least to his near connections, and often far beyond them. If he injures his property, he does harm to those who directly or indirectly derived support from it, and usually diminishes, by a greater or less amount, the general resources of the community. If he deteriorates his bodily or mental faculties, he not only brings evil upon all who depended on him for any portion of their happiness, but disqualifies himself for rendering the services which he owes to his fellow creatures generally; perhaps becomes a burthen on their affection or benevolence; and if such conduct were very frequent, hardly any offense that is committed would detract more from the general sum of good. Finally, if by his vices or follies a person does no direct harm to others, he is nevertheless (it may be said) injurious by his example; and ought to be compelled to control himself, for the sake of those whom the sight or knowledge of his conduct might corrupt or mislead.

And even (it will be added) if the consequences of misconduct could be confined to the vicious or thoughtless individual, ought society to abandon to their own guidance those who are manifestly unfit for it? If protection against themselves is confessedly due to children and persons under age, is not society equally bound to afford it to persons of mature years who are equally incapable of self-government? If gambling, or drunkenness, or incontinence, or idleness, or uncleanliness, are as injurious to happiness, and as great a hindrance to improvement, as many or most of the acts prohibited by law, why (it may be asked) should not law, so far as is consistent with practicability and social convenience, endeavor to repress these also? And as a supplement to the unavoidable imperfections of law, ought not opinion at least to organize a powerful police against these vices, and visit rigidly with social penalties those who are known to practice them? There is no question here (it may be said) about restricting individuality, or impeding the trial of new and original experiments in living. The only things it is sought to prevent are things which have been tried and condemned from the beginning of the world until now; things which experience has shown not to be useful or suitable to any person's individuality. There must be some length of time and amount of experience, after which a moral or prudential truth may be regarded as established: and it is merely desired to prevent generation after generation from falling over the same precipice which has been fatal to their predecessors.

I fully admit that the mischief which a person does to himself may seriously affect, both through their sympathies and their interests, those nearly connected with him, and in a minor degree, society at large. When, by conduct of this sort, a person is led to violate a distinct and assignable obligation to any other person or persons, the case is taken out of the self-regarding class, and becomes amenable to moral disapprobation in the proper sense of the term. If, for example, a man, through intemperance or extravagance, becomes unable to pay his debts, or, having undertaken the moral responsibility of a family, becomes from the same cause incapable of supporting or educating them, he is deservedly reprobated, and might be justly punished; but it is for the breach of duty to his family or creditors, not for the extravagance. If the resources which ought to have been devoted to them, had been diverted from them for the most prudent investment, the moral culpability would have been the same. George Barnwell murdered his uncle to get money for his mistress, but if he had done it to set himself up in business, he would equally have been hanged. Again, in the frequent case of a man who causes grief to his family by addiction to bad habits, he deserves reproach for his unkindness or ingratitude; but so he may for cultivating habits not in themselves vicious, if they are painful to those with whom he passes his life, or who from personal ties are dependent on him for their comfort. Whoever fails in the consideration generally due to the interests and feelings of others, not being compelled by some more imperative duty, or justified by allowable self-preference, is a subject of moral disapprobation for that failure, but not for the cause of it, nor for the errors, merely personal to himself, which may have remotely led to it. In like manner, when a person disables himself, by conduct purely self-regarding, from the performance of some definite duty incumbent on him to the public, he is guilty of a social offense. No person ought to be punished simply for being drunk; but a soldier or a policeman should be punished for being drunk on duty. Whenever, in short, there is a definite damage, or a definite risk of damage, either to an individual or to the public, the case is taken out of the province of liberty, and placed in that of morality or law.

But with regard to the merely contingent, or, as it may be called, constructive injury which a person causes to society, by conduct which neither violates any specific duty to the public, nor occasions perceptible hurt to any assignable individual except himself; the inconvenience is one which society can afford to bear, for the sake of the greater good of human freedom. If grown persons are to be punished for not taking proper care of themselves, I would rather it were for their own sake, than under pretense of preventing them from impairing their capacity of rendering to society benefits which society does not pretend it has a right to exact. But I cannot consent to argue the point as if society had no means of bringing its weaker members up to its ordinary standard of rational conduct, except waiting till they do something irrational, and then punishing them, legally or morally, for it. Society has had absolute power over them during all the early portion of their existence: it has had the whole period of childhood and nonage in which to try whether it could make them capable of rational conduct in life. The existing generation is master both of the training and the entire circumstances of the generation to come; it cannot indeed make them perfectly wise and good, because it is itself so lamentably deficient in goodness and wisdom; and its best efforts are not always, in individual cases, its most successful ones; but it is perfectly well able to make the rising generation, as a whole, as good as, and a little better than, itself. If society lets any considerable number of its members grow up mere children, incapable of being acted on by rational consideration of distant motives, society has itself to blame for the consequences. Armed not only with all the powers of education, but with the ascendancy which the authority of a received opinion always exercises over the minds who are least fitted to judge for themselves; and aided by the *natural* penalties which cannot be prevented from falling on those who incur the distaste or the contempt of those who know them; let not society pretend that it needs, besides all this, the power to issue commands and enforce obedience in the personal concerns of individuals, in which, on all principles of justice and policy, the decision ought to rest with those who are to abide the consequences. Nor is there anything which tends more to discredit and frustrate the better means of influencing conduct, than a resort to the worse. If there be among those whom it is attempted to coerce into prudence or temperance, any of the material of which vigorous and independent characters are made, they will infallibly rebel against the yoke. No such person will ever feel that others have a right to control him in his concerns, such as they have to prevent him from injuring them in theirs; and it easily comes to be considered a mark of spirit and courage to fly in the face of such usurped authority, and do with ostentation the exact opposite of what it enjoins; as in the fashion of grossness which succeeded, in the time of Charles II, to the fanatical moral intolerance of the Puritans. With respect to what is said of the necessity of protecting society from the bad example set to others by the vicious or the self-indulgent; it is true that bad example may have a pernicious effect, especially the example of doing wrong to others with impunity to the wrong-doer. But we are now speaking of conduct which, while it does no wrong to others, is supposed to do great harm to the agent himself: and I do not see how those who believe this, can think otherwise than that the example, on the whole, must be more salutary than hurtful, since, if it displays the misconduct, it displays also the painful or degrading consequences which, if the conduct is justly censured, must be supposed to be in all or most cases attendant on it.

But the strongest of all the arguments against the interference of the public with purely personal conduct, is that when it does interfere, the odds are that it interferes wrongly, and in the wrong place. On questions of social morality, of duty to others, the opinion of the public, that is, of an overruling majority, though often wrong, is likely to be still oftener right; because on such questions they are only required to judge of their own interests; of the manner in which some mode of conduct, if allowed to be practiced, would affect themselves. But the opinion of a similar majority, imposed as a law on the minority, on questions of self-regarding conduct, is quite as likely to be wrong as right; for in these cases public opinion means, at the best, some people's opinion of what is good or bad for other people; while very often it does not even mean that; the public, with the most perfect indifference, passing over the pleasure or convenience of those whose conduct they censure, and considering only their own preference. There are many who consider as an injury to themselves any conduct which they have a distaste for, and resent it as an outrage to their feelings; as a religious bigot, when charged with disregarding the religious feelings of others, has been known to retort that they disregard his feelings, by persisting in their abominable worship or creed. But there is no parity between the feeling of a person for his own opinion, and the feeling of another who is offended at his holding it; no more than between the desire of a thief to take a purse, and the desire of the right owner to keep it. And a person's taste is as much his own peculiar concern as his opinion or his purse. It is easy for any one to imagine an ideal public, which leaves the freedom and choice of individuals in all uncertain matters undisturbed, and only requires them to abstain from modes of conduct which universal experience has condemned. But where has there been seen a public which set any such limit to its censorship? or when does the public trouble itself about universal experience? In its interferences with personal conduct it is seldom thinking of anything but the enormity of acting or feeling differently from itself; and this standard of judgment, thinly disguised, is held up to mankind as the dictate of religion and philosophy, by nine-tenths of all moralists and speculative writers. These teach that things are right because they are right; because we feel them to be so. They tell us to search in our own minds and hearts for laws of conduct binding on ourselves and on all others. What can the poor public do but apply these instructions, and make their own personal feelings of good and evil, if they are tolerably unanimous in them, obligatory on all the world?

The evil here pointed out is not one which exists only in theory; and it may perhaps be expected that I should specify the instances in which the public of this age and country improperly invests its own preferences with the character of moral laws. I am not writing an essay on the aberrations of existing moral feeling. That is too weighty a subject to be discussed parenthetically, and by way of illustration. Yet examples are necessary, to show that the principle I maintain is of serious and practical moment, and that I am not endeavoring to erect a barrier against imaginary evils. And it is not difficult to show, by abundant instances, that to extend the bounds of what may be called moral police, until it encroaches on the most unquestionably legitimate liberty of the individual, is one of the most universal of all human propensities.

As a first instance, consider the antipathies which men cherish on no better grounds than that persons whose religious opinions are different from theirs, do not practice their religious observances, especially their religious abstinences. . . .

. . . Wherever the Puritans have been sufficiently powerful, as in New England, and in Great Britain at the time of the Commonwealth, they have endeavored, with considerable success, to put down all public, and nearly all private, amusements: especially music, dancing, public games, or other assemblages for purposes of diversion, and the theater. There are still in this country large bodies of persons by whose notions of morality and religion these recreations are condemned; and those persons belonging chiefly to the middle class, who are the ascendant power in the present social and political condition of the kingdom, it is by no means impossible that persons of these sentiments may at some time or other command a majority in Parliament. How will the remaining portion of the community like to have the amusements that shall be permitted to them regulated by the religious and moral sentiments of the stricter Calvinists and Methodists? Would they not, with considerable peremtoriness, desire these intrusively pious members of society to mind their own business? This is precisely what should be said to every government and every public, who have the pretension that no person shall enjoy any pleasure which they think wrong. But if the principle of the pretension be admitted, no one can reasonably object to its being acted on in the sense of the majority, or other preponderating power in the country; and all persons must be ready to conform to the idea of a Christian commonwealth, as understood by the early settlers in New England, if a religious profession similar to theirs should ever succeed in regaining its lost ground, as religions supposed to be declining have so often been known to do.

To imagine another contingency, perhaps more likely to be realized than the one last mentioned. There is confessedly a strong tendency in the modern world towards a democratic constitution of society, accompanied or not by popular political institutions. It is affirmed that in the country where this tendency is most completely realized—where both society and the government are most democratic—the United States—the feeling of the majority, to whom any appearance of a more showy or costly style of living than they can hope to rival is disagreeable, operates as a tolerably effectual sumptuary law, and that in many parts of the Union it is really difficult for a person possessing a very large income, to find any mode of spending it, which will not incur popular disapprobation. Though such statements as these are doubtless much exaggerated as a representation of existing facts, the state of things they describe is not only a conceivable and possible, but a probable result of democratic feeling, combined with the notion that the public has a right to a veto on the manner in which individuals shall spend their incomes. We have only further to suppose a considerable diffusion of Socialist opinions, and it may become infamous in the eyes of the majority to possess more property than some very small amount, or any income not earned by manual labor. Opinions similar in principle to these, already prevail widely among the artisan class, and weigh oppressively on those who are amenable to the opinion chiefly of that class, namely, its own members. It is known that the bad workmen who form the majority of the operatives in many branches of industry, are decidedly of opinion that bad workmen ought to receive the same wages as good, and that no one ought to be allowed, through piecework or otherwise, to earn by superior skill or industry more than others can without it. And they employ a moral police, which occasionally becomes a physical one, to deter skillful workmen from receiving, and employers from giving, a larger remuneration for a more useful service. If the public have any jurisdiction over private concerns, I cannot see that these people are in fault, or that any individual's particular public can be blamed for asserting the same authority over his individual conduct, which the general public asserts over people in general.

But, without dwelling upon supposititious cases, there are, in our own day, gross usurpations upon the liberty of private life actually practiced, and still greater ones threatened with some expectation of success, and opinions propounded which assert an unlimited right in the public not only to prohibit by law everything which it thinks wrong, but in order to get at what it thinks wrong, to prohibit any number of things which it admits to be innocent.

Under the name of preventing intemperance, the people of one English colony, and of nearly half the United States, have been interdicted by law from making any use whatever of fermented drinks, except for medical purposes: for prohibition of their sale is in fact, as it is intended to be, prohibition of their use. And though the impracticability of executing the law has caused its repeal in several of the States which had adopted it, including the one from which it derives its name, an attempt has notwithstanding been commenced, and is prosecuted with considerable zeal by many of the professed philanthropists, to agitate for a similar law in this country. The association, or "Alliance" as it terms itself, which has been formed for this purpose, has acquired some notoriety through the publicity given to a correspondence between its Secretary and one of the very few English public men who hold that a politician's opinions ought to be founded on principles. Lord Stanley's share in this correspondence is calculated to strengthen the hopes already built on him, by those who know how rare such qualities as are manifested in some of his public appearances, unhappily are among those who figure in political life. The organ of the Alliance, who would "deeply deplore the recognition of any principle which could be wrested to justify bigotry and persecution," undertakes to point out the "broad and impassable barrier" which divides such principles from those of the association. "All matters relating to thought, opinion, conscience, appear to me," he says, "to be without the sphere of legislation; all pertaining to social act, habit, relation, subject only to a discretionary power vested in the State itself, and not in the individual, to be within it." No mention is made of a third class, different from either of these, viz. acts and habits which are not social, but individual; although it is to this class, surely, that the act of drinking fermented liquors belongs. Selling fermented liquors, however, is trading, and trading is a social act. But the infringement complained of is not on the liberty of the seller, but on that of the buyer and consumer; since the State might just as well forbid him to drink wine, as purposely make it impossible for him to obtain it. The Secretary, however, says, "I claim, as a citizen, a right to legislate whenever my social rights are invaded by the social act of another." And now for the definition of these "social rights." "If anything invades my social rights, certainly the traffic in strong drink does. It destroys my primary right of security, by constantly creating and stimulating social disorder. It invades my right of equality, by deriving a profit from the creation of a misery I am taxed to support. It impedes my right to free moral and intellectual development, by surrounding my path with dangers, and by weakening and demoralizing society, from which I have a right to claim mutual aid and intercourse." A theory of "social rights," the like of which probably never before found its way into distinct language: being nothing short of this—that it is the absolute social right of every individual, that every other individual shall act in every respect exactly as he ought; that whosoever fails thereof in the smallest particular, violates my social right, and entitles me to demand from the legislature the removal of the grievance. So monstrous a principle is far more dangerous than any single interference with liberty; there is no violation of liberty which it would not justify; it acknowledges no right to any freedom whatever, except perhaps to that of holding opinions in secret, without ever disclosing them: for, the moment an opinion which I consider noxious passes any one's lips, it invades all the "social rights" attributed to me by the Alliance. The doctrine ascribes to all mankind a vested interest in each other's moral, intellectual, and even physical perfection, to be defined by each claimant according to his own standard.

Another important example of illegitimate interference with the rightful liberty of the individual, not simply threatened, but long since carried into triumphant effect, is Sabbatarian legislation. Without doubt, abstinence on one day in the week, so far as the exigencies of life permit, from the usual daily occupation, though in no respect religiously binding on any except Jews, is a highly beneficial custom. And inasmuch as this custom cannot be observed without a general consent to that effect among the industrious classes, therefore, in so far as some persons by working may impose the same necessity on others, it may be allowable and right that the law should guarantee to each the observance by others of the custom, by suspending the greater operations of industry on a particular day. But this justification, grounded on the direct interest which others have in each individual's observance of the practice, does not apply to the self-chosen occupations in which a person may think fit to employ his leisure; nor does it hold good, in the smallest degree, for legal restrictions on amusements. It is true that the amusement of some is the day's work of others; but the pleasure, not to say the useful recreation, of many, is worth the labor of a few, provided the occupation is freely chosen, and can be freely resigned. The operatives are perfectly right in thinking that if all worked on Sunday, seven days' work would have to be given for six days' wages: but so long as the great mass of employments are suspended, the small number who for the enjoyment of others must still work, obtain a proportional increase of earnings; and they are not obliged to follow those occupations, if they prefer leisure to emolument. If a further remedy is sought, it might be found in the establishment by custom of a holiday on some other day of the week for those particular classes of persons. The only ground, therefore, on which restrictions on Sunday amusements can be defended, must be that they are religiously wrong; a motive of legislation which never can be too earnestly protested against. *"Deorum injuriae Diis curae."* It remains to be proved that society or any of its officers holds a commission from on high to avenge any supposed offense to Omnipotence, which is not also a wrong to our fellow creatures. The notion that it is one man's duty that another should be religious, was the foundation of all the religious persecutions ever perpetrated, and if admitted, would fully justify them. Though the feeling which breaks out in the repeated attempts to stop railway traveling on Sunday, in the resistance to the opening of Museums, and the like, has not the cruelty of the old persecutors, the state of mind indicated by it is fundamentally the same. It is a determination not to tolerate others in doing what is permitted by their religion, because it is not permitted by the persecutor's religion. It is a belief that God not only abominates the act of the misbeliever, but will not hold us guiltless if we leave him unmolested.

I cannot refrain from adding to these examples of the little account commonly made of human liberty, the language of downright persecution which breaks out from the press of this country, whenever it feels called on to notice the remarkable phenomenon of Mormonism. Much might be said on the unexpected and instructive fact, that an alleged new revelation, and a religion founded on it, the product of palpable imposture, not even supported by the *prestige* of extraordinary qualities in its founder, is believed by hundreds of thousands, and has been made the foundation of a society, in the age of newspapers, railways, and the electric telegraph. What here concerns us is, that this religion, like other and better religions, has its martyrs; that its prophet and founder was, for his teaching, put to death by a mob; that others of its adherents lost their lives by the same lawless violence; that they were forcibly expelled, in a body, from the country in which they first grew up; while, now that they have been chased into a solitary recess in the midst of a desert, many in this country openly declare that it would be right (only that it is not convenient) to send an expedition against them, and compel them by force to conform to the opinions of other people. The article of the Mormonite doctrine which is the chief provocative to the antipathy which thus breaks through the ordinary restraints of religious tolerance, is its sanction of polygamy; which, though permitted to Mohammedans, and Hindoos, and Chinese, seems to excite unquenchable animosity when practiced by persons who speak English, and profess to be a kind of Christians. No one has a deeper disapprobation than I have of this Mormon institution; both for other reasons, and because, far from being in any way countenanced by the principle of liberty, it is a direct infraction of that principle, being a mere riveting of the chains of one-half of the community, and an emancipation of the other from reciprocity of obligation towards them. Still, it must be remembered that this relation is as much voluntary on the part of the women concerned in it, and who may be deemed the sufferers by it, as is the case with any other form of the marriage institution; and however surprising this fact may appear, it has its explanation in the common ideas and customs of the world, which teaching women to think marriage the one thing needful, make it intelligible that many a woman should prefer being one of several wives, to not being a wife at all. Other countries are not asked to recognize such unions, or release any portion of their inhabitants from their own laws on the score of Mormonite opinions. But when the dissentients have conceded to the hostile sentiments of others, far more than could justly be demanded; when they have left the countries to which their doctrines were unacceptable, and established themselves in a remote corner of the earth, which they have been the first to render habitable to human beings; it is difficult to see on what principles but those of tyranny they can be prevented from living there under what laws they please, provided they commit no aggression on other nations, and allow perfect freedom of departure to those who are dissatisfied with their ways. A recent writer, in some respects of considerable merit, proposes (to use his own words) not a crusade, but a *civilizade,* against this polygamous community, to put an end to what seems to him a retrograde step in civilization. It also appears so to me, but I am not aware that any community has a right to force another to be civilized. So long as the sufferers by the bad law do not invoke assistance from other communities, I cannot admit that persons entirely unconnected with them ought to step in and require that a condition of things with which all who are directly interested appear to be satisfied, should be put an end to because it is a scandal to persons some thousands of miles distant, who have no part or concern in it. Let them send missionaries, if they please, to preach against it; and let them, by any fair means (of which silencing the teachers is not one), oppose the progress of similar doctrines among their own people. If civilization has got the better of barbarism when barbarism had the world to itself, it is too much to profess to be afraid lest barbarism, after having been fairly got under, should revive and conquer civilization. A civilization that can thus succumb to its vanquished enemy, must first have become so degenerate, that neither its appointed priests and teachers, nor anybody else, has the capacity, or will take the trouble, to stand up for it. If this be so, the sooner such a civilization receives notice to quit, the better. It can only go on from bad to worse, until destroyed and regenerated (like the Western Empire) by energetic barbarians.

1859

19 Myths That Keep People Hungry

MILTON FRIEDMAN

Some time ago my wife and I spent a year traveling through Eastern Europe, the Middle East, and the Far East. In country after country we were deeply impressed by the striking contrast between the facts, as they appeared to us, and the ideas about the facts held by intellectuals.

Wherever we found any large element of individual freedom, some beauty in the ordinary life of the ordinary man, some measure of real progress in the material comforts at his disposal, and a live hope of further progress in the future—there we also found that the private market was the main device being used to organize economic activity. Wherever the private market was largely suppressed and the state undertook to control in detail the economic activities of its citizens (wherever, that is, detailed central economic planning reigned)—there the ordinary man was in political fetters, had a low standard of living, and was largely bereft of any conception of controlling his own destiny. The state might prosper and accomplish mighty material works. Privileged classes might enjoy a full measure of material comforts. But the ordinary man was an instrument to be used for the state's purpose, receiving no more than necessary to keep him docile and reasonably productive.

By contrast, the intellectuals everywhere took it for granted that capitalism and the market were devices for exploiting the masses, while central economic planning was the wave of the future that would set their countries on the road to rapid economic progress. I shall not soon forget the tongue-lashing I received from a prominent, highly successful, and extremely literate Indian manufacturer when I made remarks that he correctly interpreted as criticism of India's detailed central planning. Or the numerous discussions with professors at government-supported universities in India, where I was told again and again that in a country as poor as India it was essential for the government to control imports, domestic production, and the allocation of investment in order to assure that *social* priorities and not the market demand for luxuries dominated. Many of these discussions took place in comfortable university guesthouses, or relatively luxurious seminar rooms or lounges, well shielded from the nearby hovels where the common people live. One even took place in the magnificent Ashoka Hotel in New Delhi, a showplace built by the government. Yet not once was any question raised about the appropriateness of the "social priorities" reflected in the allocation of governmental funds for these amenities.

I remember, also, the attitude of my audience at the University of Malaya in Kuala Lumpur. They listened politely, though with clear signs of rising hostility, as I expounded the merits of the market and the demerits of central planning for underdeveloped countries. The one remark that brought down the house was by the Malay chairman—the head of the economics department of the university. India's current difficulties, he instructed me, were not the result of central planning but rather of the suppression of India by colonialism (this nearly two decades after Indian independence).

"Don't Bother Me with Facts"

A few examples show how clear the facts are. East and West Germany provide almost a controlled scientific experiment. Here are people of the same blood, the same civilization, the same level of technical skill and knowledge, torn asunder by the accidents of warfare. On the one side of the frontier, communism, tyranny, and misery; on the other, capitalism, freedom, and affluence.

Even two communist countries, Russia and Yugoslavia, offer a similar contrast. Russia is far more closely controlled from the center; private property and a moderately free market have almost no scope. In agriculture only 3 per cent of the cultivated area is in private plots whose produce the owners are free to market privately—though this 3 per cent produces one-third of the total agricultural output of the Soviet Union. In industry there is no legal scope at all for private activity, though apparently there is substantial black-market activity. In Yugoslavia, on the other hand, the great bulk of agricultural land is privately owned, there are many private handicrafts, and a deliberate attempt has been made to decentralize industry. Yugoslavia is far from free and its ordinary people are from affluent by Western standards. Yet it strikes the traveler as a paradise in both respects compared with Russia.

As it happened, we went from Russia directly to Yugoslavia, and both our departure from Russia and our arrival in Yugoslavia emphasized the contrast. On our way to the airport in Moscow, we had an Intourist guide assigned to us, as we had at every arrival and departure in Russia. This one turned out to be a young man who was in his final year of studies in American and English literature at the university. After desultory discussion of authors, I asked him what he was going to do after he finished school. "I do not know," he replied; "they haven't decided yet where I can be most useful"—no annoyance at having his career decided for him, simply a matter-of-fact statement. Three key questions were asked us as we went through the formalities for embarkation: "Are you taking any papers or letters out for any Russian?" "Do you have relatives in Russia?" "Did you visit anyone except as arranged by Intourist?" Having truthfully answered no, we were permitted to embark on a plane headed for Accra via Belgrade and carrying mostly Ghanaians returning home after an extended stay in Russia for military training. (To judge by the unrestrained comments of our seatmates, whatever the stay might have added to the military effectiveness of the Ghanaians, it had certainly inspired strong hostility toward the Russians and a heightened admiration of the West.)

When we landed in Belgrade, questions by the authorities were strictly perfunctory. What surprised us even more, after our Russian experience, was the absence of any governmental official to meet and shepherd us. We were left on our own, much to our great delight. Without difficulty we were able to wangle, for a modest side payment, a ride into town on the one vehicle that was going there. The dinars for the payment were advanced to us at the hotel where we had privately made reservations. (In Russia, we had been required to pay in full in advance and did not know what hotel we were to stay in until informed by Intourist on arrival.)

In the Middle East, Israel and Egypt offer the same contrast as West and East Germany; in the Far East, Malaya, Singapore, Thailand, Formosa, Hong Kong, and Japan—all relying primarily on free markets—are thriving and their people full of hope, a far call from India, Cambodia, Indonesia, and Communist China—all relying heavily on central planning.

We were struck most forcibly by the contrast between facts and ideas in Malaysia. This country is a testimonial to the potentialities of competitive capitalism. Singapore, which was still part of Malaysia when we were there, was built on free trade. It has a vigorous industry and the standard of living of the ordinary Chinese or Malay citizen is many times higher than in neighboring Indonesia or nearby India. Malaya itself was mostly an unsettled jungle three-quarters of a century ago. Today it is an attractive country with widespread cultivated areas. The standard of life of its citizens, though somewhat lower than that of Singapore, is much higher than that of its other neighbors. Rubber and tin are its main export crops. Yet rubber is not even native to Malaya. The rubber tree was imported by private enterprises from South America; the tin mines were developed entirely by private concerns.

Malaysia, now independent, is in the process of deciding what economic policy to follow. Its own past offers one example. Its populous neighbors, Indonesia and India, offer another. Both have embraced widespread and detailed central planning, with results that are as depressing as they are clear. In Indonesia, the standard of living and the condition of the ordinary man has clearly deteriorated in the nearly two decades since independence—a major factor in the recent political turmoil. In India, the situation is only a little better.

Which example does Malaysia propose to follow? If the intellectuals have their way, as it appears they will, the new nation will follow India and Indonesia. The chairman of my meeting at the university, his colleagues, and the civil servants had no doubt that it was they who should control the direction of investment and development. A central bank had been established and a government development agency was already making long-range plans. A World Bank mission, headed by Jacques Rueff of France, a liberal in the nineteenth-century sense, had nonetheless bowed sufficiently to the temper of the times to recommend tariff protection, government development subsidies, and other measures of central planning. How clear it is that the world is ruled by ideas—not facts—and that ideas can for long periods live a life of their own, little affected by the facts.

Japan offers another striking example of the importance of ideas and the intellectual climate—less present-day Japan than its experience a century ago. We were much impressed by modern Japan: by the high level of income, its wide distribution, and its rapid growth; the aesthetic content of everyday life and common household goods; the dignity of the Japanese people, and their courteous hospitality to the visitor.

A century ago, just prior to the Meiji restoration in 1868, the situation of Japan was very different. Japan had experienced centuries of deliberate and enforced isolation from the rest of the world. Though by no means completely stagnant, Japan's social and economic structure had altered little in that time, and it had fallen far behind the advanced Western countries in scientific knowledge and productive techniques.

Why the Japanese Succeeded

There is a remarkable parallel between Japan just after the Meiji restoration and India after it achieved independence eight decades later in 1948. In both cases a major political change permitted drastic alteration in economic arrangements and the rigid class relations among men. In both cases the political change placed in power a group of able and patriotic men determined to convert prior economic stagnation into rapid economic progress—though for somewhat different objectives. In both cases these events occurred in countries with ancient cultures and a high artistic and literary civilization. And in both cases the countries were technologically far behind the leading economic powers of the time. Both had an opportunity to make major economic gains by using techniques developed at great cost in the West.

There were also, of course, differences—mostly favoring India. India's physical resources are distinctly superior to Japan's—except only for the sea around Japan, with its easy transportation and potential supply of food. Japan had been almost completely out of touch with the rest of the world; India had had extensive and widespread contact. The British, moreover, left India an excellent railroad system, many factories, much physical equipment, and—even more important—functioning political institutions, numerous skilled administrators, and many men trained in modern industrial techniques.

In my own contacts, the top Indian civil servants impressed me as man-for-man the ablest people in any civil service with which I have had experience—including the American. True, they are few and there is a tremendous gap between them and lower-level civil servants, but progress in any area has always depended on small numbers of people.

Finally, in the years since 1948, the rest of the world has made available to India—largely as gifts—an enormous volume of resources, roughly equal to a quarter of India's total capital formation. Japan had no comparable advantage. The closest parallel was the fortuitous failure of the European silk crops in the early years of the Meiji restoration, which enabled Japan to earn more foreign exchange by silk exports than she otherwise could have earned. Japan herself financed the training of Japanese abroad and the importation of foreigners with technical skills. During the whole of the first half-century after the Meiji restoration, Japan had not only no net grants from abroad but not even any net capital import; she provided the whole of her own capital from domestic sources.

There is a widespread tendency to attribute India's difficulties to its social institutions, the character of its people, and the climatic conditions under which they live. Religious taboos, the caste system, a fatalistic philosophy are said to imprison the society in a straitjacket of tradition; the people are thought to be unenterprising and slothful. I find it impossible to accept any of these explanations. The Indians who have migrated to Africa or to Southeast Asia have in country after country formed a major part of the entrepreneurial class, and have often been the dynamic element initiating and promoting progress. In the Punjab, an industrial revolution is taking place in towns like Ludhiana with thousands of small and medium-size workshops, reproducing, or so it seemed to me, the experience of Manchester and Birmingham at the end of the eighteenth century. There is no shortage of enterprise, drive, or technical skill; on the contrary, there is a self-confident, strident capitalism bursting at the seams.

For a nation to progress, it is not necessary for every individual to be an enterprising, risk-taking economic man. The history of every developed nation shows that a tiny percentage of the community sets the pace, undertakes the path-breaking ventures, and coordinates the economic activity of hosts of others. Most people everywhere are hewers of wood and drawers of water. But their hewing of wood and drawing of water is made far more productive by the activities of the minority of industrial and commercial innovators, and the much larger but still small number of imitators. I have no doubt whatever that India has an adequate supply of potential entrepreneurs, both innovators and imitators. The appearance of sloth and lack of enterprise is surely a reflection of the absence of rewards for different behavior, not a reason; the fatalistic philosophy is more likely an accommodation to stagnation, not a cause.

Many early foreign residents in Japan reported similar impressions.

Wrote one: "Wealthy we do not think it [Japan] will ever become: the advantages conferred by Nature, with the exception of the climate, and the love of indolence and pleasure of the people themselves forbid it. The Japanese are a happy race, and being content with little are not likely to achieve much." Wrote another: "In this part of the world principles, established and recognized in the West, appear to lose whatever virtue and vitality they originally possessed and to tend fatally towards weediness and corruption." They were wrong and so too, in my opinion, are those who are similarly pessimistic about India.

Although the circumstances of Japan in 1868 and India in 1948 were highly similar and the opportunities much the same, yet the outcome was vastly different. In Japan there was a thorough dismantling of the feudal structure, a vast extension of social and economic opportunity, rapid economic growth, and widespread improvement in the lot of the ordinary man—though, unfortunately, nothing approaching real democracy in the political sphere. In India there was much lip service to the elimination of caste barriers yet shockingly little actual progress; differences in income and wealth between the few and the many have widened not narrowed; economic output per capita has been nearly stationary; and there has probably been an actual deterioration in the standard of life of the poorest third of the population. With all this has come a growing network of deadening and restrictive controls.

Why the difference in results? I believe the contrast between the two countries reflects primarily the difference in the techniques of economic organization adopted, though no doubt other factors played some part. Japan followed essentially a free-market policy, taking the Britain of its time as its model. True, the state intervened in many and diverse ways, and played a key role in the process of development. It subsidized the technical training of many Japanese and the importation of foreign experts, established pilot plants in many industries, and gave numerous subsidies.

Yet at no time did it ever try to control the total amount or direction of investment or the structure of output. It sold off most of its pilot plants to private firms within a few years. The state maintained a large interest only in shipbuilding and iron and steel, industries that it deemed necessary to build military power. It retained even these industries only because they were not attractive to private enterprise and required heavy government subsidies. These subsidies were a drain on Japanese resources. They impeded rather than stimulated Japanese economic progress. Finally, by international treaty, Japan was prohibited during the first three decades after the Meiji restoration from imposing tariffs higher than 5 per cent. This restriction was an unmitigated boon to Japan, though naturally it was resented at the time, and tariffs were imposed after the treaty prohibitions expired.

India has followed a very different policy. Its leaders, schooled in the doctrines of Fabian socialism and central planning, have regarded capitalism as synonymous with imperialism, to be avoided at all costs. They have taken Russia as their model and embarked on a series of five-year plans with detailed programs of investment allocated between government and private firms and among industries. Certain areas of production are reserved to government. Tariffs, quotas, and subsidies to exports are widely used to shape foreign trade. When exchange difficulties arose, detailed and extensive exchange control was imposed. The Indian government controls wages and prices, prohibits private enterprises from building factories or making other investments without government permits, and levies taxes that are highly graduated on paper though largely evaded in practice.

Reliance on the market in Japan released hidden and unsuspected resources of energy and ingenuity, prevented vested interests from blocking change, and forced development to conform to the harsh test of efficiency. Reliance on governmental controls in India frustrates initiative, or diverts it into wasteful channels, protects vested interests from the forces of change, and substitutes bureaucratic approval for market efficiency as the criterion of survival.

An instructive specific example is the different experience with home-made and factory-made textiles in the two countries. Both Japan and India had extensive production of textiles in the home at the outset of their development. In Japan home production of silk was for long little affected, but home spinning of cotton, and later, hand-loom weaving of cotton cloth, unable to meet the competition of foreign spun yarn and factory-made cloth, were all but wiped out. A Japanese factory industry developed, at first manufacturing only the coarsest and lowest-grade fabrics, but then moving on to higher and higher grades and ultimately becoming a major export industry. In India, hand-loom weaving was subsidized and guaranteed a market, allegedly to ease the transition to factory production. Factory production is growing gradually, yet there is no sign of an end to the subsidy. Indeed, hand-loom production is now larger than it was when the subsidy was introduced. Had Japan followed a similar policy, it still would have an extensive home cotton-textile industry—and a drastically lower level of living.

The most dramatic illustration of the waste that has been created by substituting government for market control in India is in automobile production. For some time now, the importing of both secondhand and new cars has been prohibited, supposedly to save foreign exchange by reducing "luxury" imports. Naturally the price of secondhand cars has skyrocketed. When I was in Bombay in 1963, a 1950 Buick—much like one I had sold in New Hampshire a few months earlier for $22—was selling for $1,500. The government has licensed the production of new cars, mostly copies of foreign makes. Their manufacture is proceeding in uneconomical small runs and at extremely high cost. India, its government apparently believes, is too poor to use secondhand cars; it must have new ones. I estimated in 1963 that about one-tenth of total American aid was being absorbed in the extra cost to India of getting motor vehicle transportation by building new cars instead of importing used ones—a glaring example of the wastes of conspicuous production.

The tragedy of the industrial revolution in the Punjab lies in this same waste and misdirection. Businessman after businessman told me that one-quarter of his time was usually devoted to getting around governmental restrictions—price control, rationing, and so on. Even more important, the distortion of prices and costs through governmental intervention means that the businessman's energy and ability are being directed toward doing the wrong things in the wrong ways.

An Erroneous Notion in the West

Ironically, the men who took charge of Japan in 1867 were dedicated principally to strengthening the power and glory of their country. They attached no special value to individual freedom or political liberty; on the contrary, they believed in aristocracy and political control by an elite. Their political ideas were the basis for later tragic totalitarian excesses. The men who took charge of India in 1948 had very different ideas. They were ardently devoted to political freedom, personal liberty, and democracy. Their aim was not national power, but improvement in the economic conditions of the masses. Yet it was the Japanese leaders who adopted a liberal economic policy that led to the widening of opportunities for the masses and, during the early decades, a great gain in their personal liberty. It was the Indian leaders who adopted a collectivist economic policy that hamstrings their people with restrictions and continues to undermine the large measure of individual freedom and political liberty encouraged by the British.

The difference in policies reflects faithfully the different intellectual climates of the two eras. In the mid-nineteenth century, liberalism (in its original, not its current American sense) was the dominant view. It was simply taken for granted that a modern economy should be conducted by free trade and private enterprise. It probably never occurred to the Japanese leaders to follow any other course. In the mid-twentieth century, collectivism was the dominant view. It was simply taken for granted that a modern economy should be conducted by centralized control and five-year plans. It probably never occurred to the Indian leaders to follow any other course.

Ideas can for a time lead a life of their own, independent of reality. But sooner or later they must meet the test of evidence. It may be crucial for the fate of mankind that they do so soon.

We, who are fortunate enough to live in the West, take for granted the freedom and affluence we enjoy and regard them as the natural lot of mankind. They are not. They have been achieved only for brief intervals in the long history of mankind. At no time, and certainly not now, have they been achieved by more than a small fraction of the world's population. We have been generous in our material aid to the less fortunate; we have given them a fine set of aspirations and an example of a free and affluent society. But we have also transmitted a climate of opinion hostile to the market arrangements that appear to be a necessary condition for both freedom and affluence.

We have a sufficient margin of protection to survive such ideas for a long time. The less-developed nations do not. In their failure, they may destroy us as well. The continuing ascendancy of such ideas may doom mankind to a renewed era of universal tyranny and misery.

1967

Bibliography

Acton, Lord. *Essays on Freedom and Power.* Edited with introduction by Gertrude Himmelfarb. Cleveland: World Publishing Co., 1962.

Chase, Harold W., and Dolan, Paul. *The Case for Democratic Capitalism.* New York: Thomas Y. Crowell, 1964.

Cohen, Morris Raphael. *The Faith of a Liberal.* New York: H. Holt & Co., 1946.

Friedman, Milton. *Capitalism and Freedom.* Chicago: University of Chicago Press, 1962.

Friedrich, Carl (ed.). *Liberty.* Nomos IV. New York: Atherton Press, 1966.

Girvetz, Harry K. *The Evolution of Liberalism.* New York: Collier Books, 1963.

Hartz, Louis. *The Liberal Tradition in America.* New York: Harcourt, Brace & World, 1955.

Hayek, Friedrich. *The Constitution of Liberty.* Chicago: Henry Regnery, Galeway Edition, 1972.

Hayek, Friedrich. *The Road to Serfdom.* Chicago: University of Chicago Press, 1944.

Held, Virginia. *The Public Interest and Individual Interests.* New York: Basic Books, Inc., 1970.

Hobhouse, L. T. *Liberalism.* London: Oxford University Press, 1964.

Meiklejohn, Alexander. *Political Freedom.* New York: Harper & Brothers, 1960.

Mill, John Stuart. *Considerations on Representative Government.* Indianapolis, Ind.: Bobbs-Merrill Co., Inc., 1958 (first published in London 1861).

Minogue, Kenneth. *The Liberal Mind.* New York: Vintage Books, 1963.

Paine, Thomas. *Common Sense and Other Political Writings.* Indianapolis, Ind.: Bobbs-Merrill, 1953 (originally published 1776).

Pennock, J. Roland. *Liberal Democracy: Its Merits and Prospects.* New York: Rinehart and Co., Inc., 1950.

Schapiro, J. Salwyn. *Liberalism: Its Meaning and History.* Princeton, N.J.: D. Van Nostrand Co., 1958.

Shonfield, Andrew. *Modern Capitalism.* New York: Oxford University Press, 1965.

Spitz, David. *Essays on the Liberal Idea of Freedom.* Tucson: The University of Arizona Press, 1964.

Stephen, Sir James Fitzjames. *Liberty, Equality, Fraternity.* Edited with an introduction by R. J. White. London: Cambridge University Press, 1967.

Wheeler, Harvey. *The Rise and Fall of Liberal Democracy.* Santa Barbara: Center for Study of Democratic Institutions, 1966.

Volkomer, Walter E. *The Liberal Tradition in American Thought.* New York: Capricorn Books, 1969.

Zeitlan, Irving. *Capitalism and Imperialism.* Chicago: Markham, 1973.

V Pluralist Democracy

Rather than concentrate upon the individual, as does liberal democratic ideology, pluralist ideology focuses upon groups and associations as the primary unit of analysis in democratic society. An association is, broadly speaking, a group of people organized for the pursuit of common goals or purposes. It is through associations, the pluralists contend, that individuals can rely upon their own efforts in pursuit of the "good life." By no means hostile to personal liberty, the pluralists argue that no association, including the state, is vested with absolute sovereignty in society. In fact, the pluralists generally assume that, within broadly defined limits, multiple centers of power in society ensure, more or less naturally, at least a modicum of liberty and social harmony. The pluralists view the state, in consequence, as simply one among many human associations for the security and improvement of life.

It is important to note that the "group basis of politics" can be understood in two quite distinct ways, a fact which has led to a great deal of confusion in pluralist thought. There is a rather obvious difference between a group of people sharing a common life style and habit of living, on the one hand, and a number of people, otherwise unrelated, who share a common interest in a particular concern, on the other hand. It is to the former that the notion of "community" corresponds; with the latter can be associated little more than the articulation of a common interest, devoid of any clearly defined group solidarity. It is often assumed, and quite erroneously, that where a common interest exists there also "community" exists.

The pluralist democratic ideology reflects the social vantage point of those groups in society capable of organizing for the articulate expression of their interests. This includes vast sections of modern industrial society, but by no means all. The premium is, in fact, awarded to those groups in society possessing the requisite expertise and resources necessary for the definition and pursuit of the common interests. Emphasizing the importance of bargaining activity in intergroup relations—more akin to reasoned academic discourse than social conflict—the pluralists often assume that divergent group interests are susceptible to mutual adjustment in order that the supposed prevailing harmony in society might be further assured.

The pluralist democratic ideology is an abstraction, in the first instance, of political activities in a society of self-asserted individualists traditionally suspicious of far-reaching social authority who nevertheless find some form of social authority necessary to the individual's well-being. Further, in addition to reflecting those core experiences common to the various democratic ideologies, pluralism reflects an essentially economic activity: bargaining, under threat of potential deadlock, between business and labor. The latter is an experience common to modern industrial society since the growth of trade unions. Finally, reflecting both the existence and the continued activities of the modern nation–state, the pluralists attempt to define a more positive role for the modern state, particularly in comparison with the liberal democrats, in the process of attending to the arrangements of society.

Madison's concern is with the need for institutions to break and control the possible violence of faction. By faction he means a group of citizens, whether that group be a majority or minority in society, united by passion or interest, acting either to the detriment of the rights of other citizens or to the detriment of the community interests. Finding it impossible to control the cause of faction, Madison suggests two means by which the effects of faction can be controlled, depending upon whether the faction is a minority or a majority. If a minority, Madison argues, then the republican principle of majority rule through representation will effectively diminish the threat of faction. If a majority constitutes the faction, then it is necessary, according to Madison, not only to filter popular sentiment through the more select body of representatives but also to increase the size of the republic in order to increase the variety of interests in society and make it less likely that a majority of men will act in concert against a minority.

Alexis de Tocqueville further develops Madison's last check on the power of faction. The most natural privilege of man, Tocqueville points out, next to acting for himself, is the right to combine his exertions with his fellow men in order to act in common with them. For Tocqueville, the right of association is as inalienable as the right of personal liberty. Uniting the minds of several individuals toward the pursuit of a single end, associations are established to promote public order, commerce, industry, morality, and even religion, while serving as a check on the despotism of faction under a democratic system of government. In the United States, Tocqueville suggests, associations are formed first, to show numerical strength and, thus, diminish the moral power of the majority, and second, to stimulate competition and discover those arguments most persuasive among those people constituting the majority.

Dewey begins by affirming a basic distinction between democracy as an idea and democracy as a system of government. Emphasizing that governments are but mechanisms for realizing an idea, Dewey suggests that a government designed to serve the community cannot fulfill this purpose unless the community itself shares in selecting its governors and determining their policies. The democratic idea, Dewey explains, consists in each individual, according to capacity, sharing in the direction of the activities of the groups to which he belongs and reaping, according to need, those values sustained through the group effort. Demanding liberation of the potentialities of the members of a group, while emphasizing that those group interests must be in harmony with the interests and goods which are common to all members of society, democracy is the idea of community life itself.

American political scientist Robert Dahl argues that, in the pluralist conception of politics, there are some fundamental constraints imposed upon groups by the modern nation–state, although several matters of policy are effectively outside the legal authority of the nation–state, being the prerogative of private, semi-public, and local governmental associations. Groups adversely affected by national policy are further given an ample opportunity to present their case against the given policy. Benefits accruing from multiple centers of power, none of which is wholly sovereign, include, according to Dahl, the taming of power, a guarantee of some semblance of minority rights, and the cultivation of the art of peaceful conflict resolution.

John Maynard Keynes, perhaps the most brilliant economist of the past generation, assigns to the modern nation–state economic activities designed to establish conditions necessary for the functioning of the economy according to the model of classical economical analysis. It is the duty of the state, Keynes argues, to determine the aggregate amount of resources invested in the instruments of production and the basic rate of reward for ownership. The state, Keynes maintains, must guide the propensity to consume in order to ensure the growth of capital, except perhaps in conditions of full employment, through such mechanisms as taxation and government spending. Once the volume of output is assured by the state, then, following classical analysis, private self-interest can determine what is produced, in what proportions the factors of production will be combined in order to produce the items, and finally, how the value of the finished product is to be distributed.

As a center of power in the modern economy, the corporation is the principal planning agent, according to the Harvard economist John Kenneth Galbraith. Because of the extensive use of technology, involving both capital and time for preparation, the modern economy demands planning, suggests Galbraith. This planning, in turn, requires relative stability of costs and prices, together with a security of return on investment and the potential for further expansion. In meeting these needs, the corporation can fix minimum prices, manage consumer wants, and extract from revenues the capital needed for growth and expansion. But because the corporation, like the state, is not wholly sovereign in the modern economy, certain tasks fall to the state in order to ensure a healthy economy. In addition to Keynesian economic policies, the state must, particularly in times of crisis, set maximum wages and prices. Further, according to Galbraith, the state, through publicly subsidized advanced education, must supply the specialization of manpower that technology, organization, and planning of the modern industrial state require. Finally, it falls to the lot of the state to absorb the risks and costs associated with the advancement of scientific and technological knowledge.

20 The Federalist #10

JAMES MADISON

Among the numerous advantages promised by a well-constructed Union, none deserves to be more accurately developed than its tendency to break and control the violence of faction. The friend of popular governments never finds himself so much alarmed for their character and fate as when he contemplates their propensity to this dangerous vice. He will not fail, therefore, to set a due value on any plan which, without violating the principles to which he is attached, provides a proper cure for it. The instability, injustice, and confusion introduced into the public councils have, in truth, been the mortal diseases under which popular governments have everywhere perished, as they continue to be the favorite and fruitful topics from which the adversaries to liberty derive their most specious declamations. The valuable improvements made by the American constitutions on the popular models, both ancient and modern, cannot certainly be too much admired; but it would be an unwarrantable partiality to contend that they have as effectually obviated the danger on this side, as was wished and expected. Complaints are everywhere heard from our most considerate and virtuous citizens, equally the friends of public and private faith and of public and personal liberty, that our governments are too unstable, that the public good is disregarded in the conflicts of rival parties, and that measures are too often decided, not according to the rules of justice and the rights of the minor party, but by the superior force of an interested and overbearing majority. However anxiously we may wish that these complaints had no foundation, the evidence of known facts will not permit us to deny that they are in some degree true. It will be found, indeed, on a candid review of our situation, that some of the distresses under which we labor have been erroneously charged on the operation of our governments; but it will be found, at the same time, that other causes will not alone account for many of our heaviest misfortunes; and, particularly, for that prevailing and increasing distrust of public engagements and alarm for private rights which are echoed from one end of the continent to the other. These must be chiefly, if not wholly, effects of the unsteadiness and injustice with which a factious spirit has tainted our public administration.

By a faction I understand a number of citizens, whether amounting to a majority or minority of the whole, who are united and actuated by some common impulse of passion, or of interest, adverse to the rights of other citizens, or to the permanent and aggregate interests of the community.

There are two methods of curing the mischiefs of faction: the one, by removing its causes; the other, by controlling its effects.

There are again two methods of removing the causes of faction: the one, by destroying the liberty which is essential to its existence; the other, by giving to every citizen the same opinions, the same passions, and the same interests.

It could never be more truly said than of the first remedy that it was worse than the disease. Liberty is to faction what air is to fire, an aliment without which it instantly expires. But it could not be a less folly to abolish liberty, which is essential to political life, because it nourishes faction than it would be to wish the annihilation of air, which is essential to animal life, because it imparts to fire its destructive agency.

The second expedient is as impracticable as the first would be unwise. As long as the reason of man continues fallible, and he is at liberty to exercise it, different opinions will be formed. As long as the connection subsists between his reason and his self-love, his opinions and his passions will have a reciprocal influence on each other; and the former will be objects to which the latter will attach themselves. The diversity in the faculties of men, from which the rights of property originate, is not less an insuperable obstacle to a uniformity of interests. The protection of these faculties is the first object of government. From the protection of different and unequal faculties of acquiring property, the possession of different degrees and kinds of property immediately results; and from the influence of these on the sentiments and views of the respective proprietors ensues a division of the society into different interests and parties.

The latent causes of faction are thus sown in the nature of man; and we see them everywhere brought into different degrees of activity, according to the different circumstances of civil society. A zeal for different opinions concerning religion, concerning government, and many other points, as well of speculation as of practice; an attachment to different leaders ambitiously contending for pre-eminence and power; or to persons of other descriptions whose fortunes have been interesting to the human passions, have, in turn, divided mankind into parties, inflamed them with mutual animosity, and rendered them much more disposed to vex and oppress each other than to co-operate for their common good. So strong is this propensity of mankind to fall into mutual animosities that where no substantial occasion presents itself the most frivolous and fanciful distinctions have been sufficient to kindle their unfriendly passions and excite their most violent conflicts. But the most common and durable source of factions has been the verious and unequal distribution of property. Those who hold and those who are without property have ever formed distinct interests in society. Those who are creditors, and those who are debtors, fall under a like discrimination. A landed interest, a manufacturing interest, a mercantile interest, a moneyed interest, with many lesser interests, grow up of necessity in civilized nations, and divide them into different classes, actuated by different sentiments and views. The regulation of these various and interfering interests forms the principal task of modern legislation and involves the spirit of party and faction in the necessary and ordinary operations of government.

No man is allowed to be a judge in his own cause, because his interest would certainly bias his judgment, and, not improbably, corrupt his integrity. With equal, nay with greater reason, a body of men are unfit to be both judges and parties at the same time; yet what are many of the most important acts of legislation but so many judicial determinations, not indeed concerning the rights of single persons, but concerning the rights of large bodies of citizens? And what are the different classes of legislators but advocates and parties to the causes which they determine? Is a law proposed concerning private debts? It is a question to which the creditors are parties on one side and the debtors on the other. Justice ought to hold the balance between them. Yet the parties are, and must be, themselves the judges; and the most numerous party, or in other words, the most powerful faction must be expected to prevail. Shall domestic manufacturers be encouraged, and in what degree, by restrictions on foreign manufacturers? are questions which would be differently decided by the landed and the manufacturing classes, and probably by neither with a sole regard to justice and the public good. The apportionment of taxes on the various descriptions of property is an act which seems to require the most exact impartiality; yet there is, perhaps, no legislative act in which greater opportunity and temptation are given to a predominant party to trample on the rules of justice. Every shilling with which they overburden the inferior number is a shilling saved to their own pockets.

It is in vain to say that enlightened statesmen will be able to adjust these clashing interests and render them all subservient to the public good. Enlightened statesmen will not always be at the helm. Nor, in many cases, can such an adjustment be made at all without taking into view indirect and remote considerations, which will rarely prevail over the immediate interest which one party may find in disregarding the rights of another or the good of the whole.

The inference to which we are brought is that the *causes* of faction cannot be removed and that relief is only to be sought in the means of controlling its *effects.*

If a faction consists of less than a majority, relief is supplied by the republican principle, which enables the majority to defeat its sinister views by regular vote. It may clog the administration, it may convulse the society; but it will be unable to execute and mask its violence under the forms of the Constitution. When a majority is included in a faction, the form of popular government, on the other hand, enables it to sacrifice to its ruling passion or interest both the public good and the rights of other citizens. To secure the public good and private rights against the danger of such a faction, and at the same time to preserve the spirit and the form of popular government, is then the great object to which our inquiries are directed. Let me add that it is the great desideratum by which alone this form of government can be rescued from the opprobrium under which it has so long labored and be recommended to the esteem and adoption of mankind.

By what means is this object attainable? Evidently by one of two only. Either the existence of the same passion or interest in a majority at the same time must be prevented, or the majority, having such coexistent passion or interest, must be rendered, by their number and local situation, unable to concert and carry into effect schemes of oppression. If the impulse and the opportunity be suffered to coincide, we well know that neither moral nor religious motives can be relied on as an adequate control. They are not found to be such on the injustice and violence of individuals, and lose their efficacy in proportion to the number combined together, that is, in proportion as their efficacy becomes needful.

From this view of the subject it may be concluded that a pure democracy, by which I mean a society consisting of a small number of citizens, who assemble and administer the government in person, can admit of no cure for the mischiefs of faction. A common passion or interest will, in almost every case, be felt by a majority of the whole; a communication and concert results from the form of government itself; and there is nothing to check the inducements to sacrifice the weaker party or an obnoxious individual. Hence it is that such democracies have ever been spectacles of turbulence and contention; have ever been found incompatible with personal security or the rights of property; and have in general been as short in their lives as they have been violent in their deaths. Theoretic politicians, who have patronized this species of government, have erroneously supposed that by reducing mankind to a perfect equality in their political rights, they would at the same time be perfectly equalized and assimilated in their possessions, their opinions, and their passions.

A republic, by which I mean a government in which the scheme of representation takes place, opens a different prospect and promises the cure for which we are seeking. Let us examine the points in which it varies from pure democracy, and we shall comprehend both the nature of the cure and the efficacy which it must derive from the Union.

The two great points of difference between a democracy and a republic are: first, the delegation of the government, in the latter, to a small number of citizens elected by the rest; secondly, the greater number of citizens and greater sphere of country over which the latter may be extended.

The effect of the first difference is, on the one hand, to refine and enlarge the public views by passing them through the medium of a chosen body of citizens, whose wisdom may best discern the true interest of their country and whose patriotism and love of justice will be least likely to sacrifice it to temporary or partial considerations. Under such a regulation it may well happen that the public voice, pronounced by the representatives of the people, will be more consonant to the public good than if pronounced by the people themselves, convened for the purpose. On the other hand, the effect may be inverted. Men of factious tempers, of local prejudices, or of sinister designs, may, by intrigue, by corruption, or by other means, first obtain the suffrages, and then betray the interests of the people. The question resulting is, whether small or extensive republics are most favorable to the election of proper guardians of the public weal; and it is clearly decided in favor of the latter by two obvious considerations.

In the first place it is to be remarked that however small the republic may be the representatives must be raised to a certain number in order to guard against the cabals of a few; and that however large it may be they must be limited to a certain number in order to guard against the confusion of a multitude. Hence, the number of representatives in the two cases not being in proportion to that of the constituents, and being proportionally greatest in the small republic, it follows that if the proportion of fit characters be not less in the large than in the small republic, the former will present a greater option, and consequently a greater probability of a fit choice.

In the next place, as each representative will be chosen by a greater number of citizens in the large than in the small republic, it will be more difficult for unworthy candidates to practise with success the vicious arts by which elections are too often carried; and the suffrages of the people being more free, will be more likely to center on men who possess the most attractive merit and the most diffusive and established characters.

It must be confessed that in this, as in most other cases, there is a mean, on both sides of which inconveniencies will be found to lie. By enlarging too much the number of electors, you render the representative too little acquainted with all their local circumstances and lesser interests; as by reducing it too much, you render him unduly attached to these, and too little fit to comprehend and pursue great and national objects. The federal Constitution forms a happy combination in this respect; the great and aggregate interests being referred to the national, the local and particular to the State legislatures.

The other point of difference is the greater number of citizens and extent of territory which may be brought within the compass of republican than of democratic government; and it is this circumstance principally which renders factious combinations less to be dreaded in the former than in the latter. The smaller the society, the fewer probably will be the distinct parties and interests composing it; the fewer the distinct parties and interests, the more frequently will a majority be found of the same party; and the smaller the number of individuals composing a majority, and the smaller the compass within which they are placed, the more easily will they concert and execute their plans of oppression. Extend the sphere and you take in a greater variety of parties and interests; you make it less probable that a majority of the whole will have a common motive to invade the rights of other citizens; or if such a common motive exists, it will be more difficult for all who feel it to discover their own strength and to act in unison with each other. Besides other impediments, it may be remarked that, where there is a consciousness of unjust or dishonorable purposes, communication is always checked by distrust in proportion to the number whose concurrence is necessary.

Hence, it clearly appears that the same advantage which a republic has over a democracy in controlling the effects of faction is enjoyed by a large over a small republic—is enjoyed by the Union over the States composing it. Does this advantage consist in the substitution of representatives whose enlightened views and virtuous sentiments render them superior to local prejudices and to schemes of injustice? It will not be denied that the representation of the Union will be most likely to possess these requisite endowments. Does it consist in the greater security afforded by a greater variety of parties, against the event of any one party being able to outnumber and oppress the rest? In an equal degree does the increased variety of parties comprised within the Union increase this security? Does it, in fine, consist in the greater obstacles opposed to the concert and accomplishment of the secret wishes of an unjust and interested majority? Here again the extent of the Union gives it the most palpable advantage.

The influence of factious leaders may kindle a flame within their particular States but will be unable to spread a general conflagration through the other States. A religious sect may degenerate into a political faction in a part of the Confederacy; but the variety of sects dispersed over the entire face of it must secure the national councils against any danger from that source. A rage for paper money, for an abolition of debts, for an equal division of property, or for any other improper or wicked project, will be less apt to pervade the whole body of the Union than a particular member of it, in the same proportion as such a malady is more likely to taint a particular county or district than an entire State.

In the extent and proper structure of the Union, therefore, we behold a republican remedy for the diseases most incident to republican government. And according to the degree of pleasure and pride we feel in being republicans ought to be our zeal in cherishing the spirit and supporting the character of federalists.

1787

21 Political Associations in the United States

ALEXIS DE TOCQUEVILLE

In no country in the world has the principle of association been more successfully used, or more unsparingly applied to a multitude of different objects, than in America. Besides the permanent associations which are established by law under the names of townships, cities, and counties, a vast number of others are formed and maintained by the agency of private individuals.

The citizen of the United States is taught from his earliest infancy to rely upon his own exertions in order to resist the evils and the difficulties of life; he looks upon social authority with an eye of mistrust and anxiety, and he only claims its assistance when he is quite unable to shift without it. This habit may even be traced in the schools of the rising generation, where the children in their games are wont to submit to rules which they have themselves established, and to punish misdemeanours which they have themselves defined. The same spirit pervades every act of social life. If a stoppage occurs in a thoroughfare, and the circulation of the public is hindered, the neighbours immediately constitute a deliberative body; and this extemporaneous assembly gives rise to an executive power which remedies the inconvenience before anybody has thought of recurring to an authority superior to that of the persons immediately concerned. If the public pleasures are concerned, an association is formed to provide for the splendour and the regularity of the entertainment. Societies are formed to resist enemies which are exclusively of a moral nature, and to diminish the vice of intemperance: in the United States associations are established to promote public order, commerce, industry, morality, and religion; for there is no end which the human will, seconded by the collective exertions of individuals, despairs of attaining.

Hereafter I shall have occasion to show the effects of association upon the course of society, and I must confine myself for the present to the political world. When once the right of association is recognised, the citizens may employ it in several different ways.

An association consists simply in the public assent which a number of individuals give to certain doctrines, and in the engagement which they contract to promote the spread of those doctrines by their exertions. The

SOURCE: from Alexis de Tocqueville, *Democracy in America,* translated by Henry Reeve (New York: J. & H. G. Langley, 1841), Vol. *I,* Chapter XII, pp. 204–212.

right of association with these views is very analogous to the liberty of unlicensed writing; but societies thus formed possess more authority than the press. When an opinion is represented by a society, it necessarily assumes a more exact and explicit form. It numbers its partisans, and compromises their welfare in its cause: they, on the other hand, become acquainted with each other, and their zeal is increased by their number. An association unites the efforts of minds which have a tendency to diverge in one single channel, and urges them vigorously toward one single end which it points out.

The second degree in the right of association is the power of meeting. When an association is allowed to establish centres of action at certain important points in the country, its activity is increased and its influence extended. Men have the opportunity of seeing each other; means of execution are more readily combined, and opinions are maintained with a degree of warmth and energy which written language can not approach.

Lastly, in the exercise of the right of political association, there is a third degree: the partisans of an opinion may unite in electoral bodies, and choose delegates to represent them in a central assembly. This is, properly speaking, the application of the representative system to a party

Thus, in the first instance, a society is formed between individuals professing the same opinion, and the tie which keeps it together is of a purely intellectual nature; in the second case, small assemblies are formed which only represent a fraction of the party. Lastly, in the third case, they constitute a separate nation in the midst of the nation, a government within the Government. Their delegates, like the real delegates of the majority, represent the entire collective force of their party; and they enjoy a certain degree of that national dignity and great influence which belong to the chosen representatives of the people. It is true that they have not the right of making the laws, but they have the power of attacking those which are in being, and of drawing up beforehand those which they may afterward cause to be adopted.

If, in a people which is imperfectly accustomed to the exercise of freedom, or which is exposed to violent political passions, a deliberating minority, which confines itself to the contemplation of future laws, be placed in juxtaposition to the legislative majority, I can not but believe that public tranquility incurs very great risks in that nation. There is doubtless a very wide difference between proving that one law is in itself better than another and proving that the former ought to be substituted for the latter. But the imagination of the populace is very apt to overlook this difference, which is so apparent to the minds of thinking men. It sometimes happens that a nation is divided into two nearly equal parties, each of which affects to represent the majority. If, in immediate contiguity to the directing power, another power be established, which exercises almost as much moral authority as the former, it is not to be believed that it will long be content to speak without acting; or that it will always be restrained by the abstract consideration of the nature of associations which are meant to direct but not to enforce opinions, to suggest but not to make the laws.

The more we consider the independence of the press in its principal consequences, the more are we convinced that it is the chief and, so to speak, the constitutive element of freedom in the modern world. A nation which is determined to remain free is therefore right in demanding the unrestrained exercise of this independence. But the unrestrained liberty of political association can not be entirely assimilated to the liberty of the press. The one is at the same time less necessary and more dangerous than the other. A nation may confine it within certain limits without forfeiting any part of its self-control; and it may sometimes be obliged to do so in order to maintain its own authority.

In America the liberty of association for political purposes is unbounded. An example will show in the clearest light to what an extent this privilege is tolerated.

The question of the tariff, or of free trade, produced a great manifestation of party feeling in America; the tariff was not only a subject of debate as a matter of opinion, but it exercised a favourable or a prejudicial influence upon several very powerful interests of the States. The North attributed a great portion of its prosperity, and the South all its sufferings, to this system; insomuch that for a long time the tariff was the sole source of the political animosities which agitated the Union.

In 1831, when the dispute was raging with the utmost virulence, a private citizen of Massachusetts proposed to all the enemies of the tariff, by means of the public prints, to send delegates to Philadelphia in order to consult together upon the means which were most fitted to promote freedom of trade. This proposal circulated in a few days from Maine to New Orleans by the power of the printing-press: the opponents of the tariff adopted it with enthusiasm; meetings were formed on all sides, and delegates were named. The majority of these individuals were well known, and some of them had earned a considerable degree of celebrity. South Carolina alone, which afterward took up arms in the same cause, sent sixty-three delegates. On the 1st of October, 1831, this assembly, which according to the American custom had taken the name of a Convention, met at Philadelphia; it consisted of more than two hundred members. Its debates were public, and they at once assumed a legislative character; the extent of the powers of Congress, the theories of free trade, and the different clauses of the tariff, were discussed in turn. At the end of ten days' deliberation the Convention broke up, after having published an address to the American people, in which it declared:

I. That Congress had not the right of making a tariff, and that the existing tariff was unconstitutional;

II. That the prohibition of free trade was prejudicial to the interests of all nations, and to that of the American people in particular.

It must be acknowledged that the unrestrained liberty of political association has not hitherto produced, in the United States, those fatal consequences which might perhaps be expected from it elsewhere. The right of association was imported from England, and it has always existed in America; so that the exercise of this privilege is now amalgamated with the manners and customs of the people. At the present time the liberty of association is become a necessary guarantee against the tyranny of the majority. In the United States, as soon as a party is become preponderant, all public authority passes under its control; its private supporters occupy all the places, and have all the force of the administration at their disposal. As the most distinguished partisans of the other side of the question are unable to surmount the obstacles which exclude them from power, they require some means of establishing themselves upon their own basis, and of opposing the moral authority of the minority to the physical power which domineers over it. Thus a dangerous expedient is used to obviate a still more formidable danger.

The omnipotence of the majority appears to me to present such extreme perils to the American republics that the dangerous measure which is used to repress it seems to be more advantageous than prejudicial. And here I am about to advance a proposition which may remind the reader of what I said before in speaking of municipal freedom: There are no countries in which associations are more needed, to prevent the despotism of faction or the arbitrary power of a prince, than those which are democratically constituted. In aristocratic nations the body of the nobles and the more opulent part of the community are in themselves natural associations, which act as checks upon the abuses of power. In countries in which these associations do not exist, if private individuals are unable to create an artificial and a temporary substitute for them, I can imagine no permanent protection against the most galling tyranny; and a great people may be oppressed by a small faction, or by a single individual, with impunity.

The meeting of a great political Convention (for there are Conventions of all kinds), which may frequently become a necessary measure, is always a serious occurrence, even in America, and one which is never looked forward to, by the judicious friends of the country, without alarm. This was very perceptible in the Convention of 1831, at which the exertions of all the most distinguished members of the assembly tended to moderate its language, and to restrain the subjects which it treated within certain limits. It is probable, in fact, that the Convention of 1831 exercised a very great influence upon the minds of the malcontents, and prepared them for the open revolt against the commercial laws of the Union which took place in 1832.

It can not be denied that the unrestrained liberty of association for political purposes is the privilege which a people is longest in learning how to exercise. If it does not throw the nation into anarchy, it perpetually augments the chances of that calamity. On one point, however, this perilous liberty offers a security against dangers of another kind; in countries where associations are free, secret societies are unknown. In America there are numerous factions, but no conspiracies.

The most natural privilege of man, next to the right of acting for himself, is that of combining his exertions with those of his fellow-creatures, and of acting in common with them. I am therefore led to conclude that the right of association is almost as inalienable as the right of personal liberty. No legislator can attack it without impairing the very foundations of society. Nevertheless, if the liberty of association is a fruitful source of advantages and prosperity to some nations, it may be perverted or carried to excess by others, and the element of life may be changed into an element of destruction. A comparison of the different methods which associations pursue in those countries in which they are managed with discretion, as well as in those where liberty degenerates into license, may perhaps be thought useful both to governments and to parties.

The greater part of Europeans look upon an association as a weapon which is to be hastily fashioned, and immediately tried in the conflict. A society is formed for discussion; but the idea of impending action prevails in the minds of those who constitute it: it is, in fact, an army; and the time given to parley serves to reckon up the strength and to animate the courage of the host, after which they direct their march against the enemy. Resources which lie within the bounds of the law may suggest themselves to the persons who compose it as means, but never as the only means, of success.

Such, however, is not the manner in which the right of association is understood in the United States. In America the citizens who form the minority associate, in order, in the first place, to show their numerical strength, and so to diminish the moral authority of the majority; and, in the second place, to stimulate competition, and to discover those arguments which are most fitted to act upon the majority; for they always entertain hopes of drawing over their opponents to their own side, and of afterward disposing of the supreme power in their name. Political associations in the United States are therefore peaceable in their intentions, and strictly legal in the means which they employ; and they assert with perfect truth that they only aim at success by lawful expedients.

The difference which exists between the Americans and ourselves depends on several causes. In Europe there are numerous parties so diametrically opposed to the majority that they can never hope to acquire its support, and at the same time they think that they are sufficiently strong in themselves to struggle and to defend their cause. When a party of this kind forms an association, its object is, not to conquer, but to fight. In America the individuals who hold opinions very much opposed to those of the majority are no sort of impediment to its power, and all other parties hope to win it over to their own principles in the end. The exercise of the right of association becomes dangerous in proportion to the impossibility which excludes great parties from acquiring the majority. In a country like the United States, in which the differences of opinion are mere differences of hue, the right of association may remain unrestrained without evil consequences. The inexperience of many of the European nations in the enjoyment of liberty leads them only to look upon the liberty of association as a right of attacking the Government. The first notion which presents itself to a party, as well as to an individual, when it has acquired a consciousness of its own strength, is that of violence: the notion of persuasion arises at a later period and is only derived from experience. The English, who are divided into parties which differ most essentially from each other, rarely abuse the right of association, because they have long been accustomed to exercise it. In France the passion for war is so intense that there is no undertaking so mad, or so injurious to the welfare of the State, that a man does not consider himself honoured in defending it, at the risk of his life.

But perhaps the most powerful of the causes which tend to mitigate the excesses of political association in the United States is Universal Suffrage. In countries in which universal suffrage exists the majority is never doubtful, because neither party can pretend to represent that portion of the community which has not voted. The associations which are formed are aware, as well as the nation at large, that they do not represent the majority: this is, indeed, a condition inseparable from their existence; for if they did represent the preponderating power, they would change the law instead of soliciting its reform. The consequence of this is that the moral influence of the Government which they attack is very much increased, and their own power is very much enfeebled.

In Europe there are few associations which do not affect to represent the majority, or which do not believe that they represent it. This conviction or this pretension tends to augment their force amazingly, and contributes no less to legalize their measures. Violence may seem to be excusable in defence of the cause of oppressed right. Thus it is, in the vast labyrinth of human laws, that extreme liberty sometimes corrects the abuses of license, and that extreme democracy obviates the dangers of democratic government. In Europe associations consider themselves, in some degree, as the legislative and executive councils of the people, which is unable to speak for itself. In America, where they only represent a minority of the nation, they argue and they petition.

The means which the associations of Europe employ are in accordance with the end which they propose to obtain. As the principal aim of these bodies is to act, and not to debate, to fight rather than to persuade, they are naturally led to adopt a form of organization which differs from the ordinary customs of civil bodies, and which assumes the habits and the maxims of military life. They centralize the direction of their resources as much as possible, and they intrust the power of the whole party to a very small number of leaders.

The members of these associations respond to a watchword, like soldiers on duty; they profess the doctrine of passive obedience; say rather, that in uniting together they at once abjure the exercise of their own judgment and free will; and the tyrannical control which these societies exercise is often far more insupportable than the authority possessed over society by the Government which they attack. Their moral force is much diminished by these excesses, and they lose the powerful interest which is always excited by a struggle between oppressors and the oppressed. The man who in given cases consents to obey his fellows with servility, and who submits his activity and even his opinions to their control, can have no claim to rank as a free citizen.

The Americans have also established certain forms of government which are applied to their associations, but these are invariably borrowed from the forms of the civil administration. The independence of each individual is formally recognised; the tendency of the members of the association points, as it does in the body of the community, toward the same end, but they are not obliged to follow the same track. No one abjures the exercise of his reason and his free will; but every one exerts that reason and that will for the benefit of a common undertaking.

1835

22 Search for the Great Community

JOHN DEWEY

We have had occasion to refer in passing to the distinction between democracy as a social idea and political democracy as a system of government. The two are, of course, connected. The idea remains barren and empty save as it is incarnated in human relationships. Yet in discussion they must be distinguished. The idea of democracy is a wider and fuller idea than can be exemplified in the state even at its best. To be realized it must affect all modes of human association, the family, the school, industry, religion. And even as far as political arrangements are concerned, governmental institu-

SOURCE: John Dewey, "Search for the Great Community," reprinted from *The Public and Its Problems* © 1927, 1954, by permission of the Swallow Press, Chicago.

tions are but a mechanism for securing to an idea channels of effective operation. It will hardly do to say that criticisms of the political machinery leave the believer in the idea untouched. For, as far as they are justified—and no candid believer can deny that many of them are only too well grounded—they arouse him to bestir himself in order that the idea may find a more adequate machinery through which to work. What the faithful insist upon, however, is that the idea and its external organs and structures are not to be identified. We object to the common supposition of the foes of existing democratic government that the accusations against it touch the social and moral aspirations and ideas which underlie the political forms. The old saying that the cure for the ills of democracy is more democracy is not apt if it means that the evils may be remedied by introducing more machinery of the same kind as that which already exists, or by refining and perfecting that machinery. But the phrase may also indicate the need of returning to the idea itself, of clarifying and deepening our apprehension of it, and of employing our sense of its meaning to criticize and re-make its political manifestations.

Confining ourselves, for the moment, to political democracy, we must, in any case, renew our protest against the assumption that the idea has itself produced the governmental practices which obtain in democratic states: General suffrage, elected representatives, majority rule, and so on. The idea has influenced the concrete political movement, but it has not caused it. The transition from family and dynastic government supported by the loyalties of tradition to popular government was the outcome primarily of technological discoveries and inventions working a change in the customs by which men had been bound together. It was not due to the doctrines of doctrinaires. The forms to which we are accustomed in democratic governments represent the cumulative effect of a multitude of events, unpremeditated as far as political effects were concerned and having unpredictable consequences. There is no sanctity in universal suffrage, frequent elections, majority rule, congressional and cabinet government. These things are devices evolved in the direction in which the current was moving, each wave of which involved at the time of its impulsion a minimum of departure from antecedent custom and law. The devices served a purpose; but the purpose was rather that of meeting existing needs which had become too intense to be ignored, than that of forwarding the democratic idea. In spite of all defects, they served their own purpose well.

Looking back, with the aid which *ex post facto* experience can give, it would be hard for the wisest to devise schemes which, under the circumstances, would have met the needs better. In this retrospective glance, it is possible, however, to see how the doctrinal formulations which accompanied them were inadequate, one-sided and positively erroneous. In fact they were hardly more than political war-cries adopted to help in carrying on some immediate agitation or in justifying some particular practical polity struggling for recognition, even though they were asserted to be absolute truths of human nature or of morals. The doctrines served a particular local pragmatic need. But often their very adaptation to immediate circumstances unfitted them, pragmatically, to meet more enduring and more extensive needs. They lived to cumber the political ground, obstructing progress, all the more so because they were uttered and held not as hypotheses with which to direct social experimentation but as final truths, dogmas. No wonder they call urgently for revision and displacement.

Nevertheless the current has set steadily in one direction: toward democratic forms. That government exists to serve its community, and that this purpose cannot be achieved unless the community itself shares in selecting its governors and determining their policies, are a deposit of fact left, as far as we can see, permanently in the wake of doctrines and forms, however transitory the latter. They are not the whole of the democratic idea, but they express it in its political phase. Belief in this political aspect is not a mystic faith as if in some overruling providence that cares for children, drunkards and others unable to help themselves. It marks a well-attested conclusion from historic facts. We have every reason to think that whatever changes may take place in existing democratic machinery, they will be of a sort to make the interest of the public a more supreme guide and criterion of governmental activity, and to enable the public to form and manifest its purposes still more authoritatively. In this sense the cure for the ailments of democracy is more democracy. The prime difficulty, as we have seen, is that of discovering the means by which a scattered, mobile and manifold public may so recognize itself as to define and express its interests. This discovery is necessarily precedent to any fundamental change in the machinery. We are not concerned therefore to set forth counsels as to advisable improvements in the political forms of democracy. Many have been suggested. It is no derogation of their relative worth to say that consideration of these changes is not at present an affair of primary importance. The problem lies deeper; it is in the first instance an intellectual problem: the search for conditions under which the Great Society may become the Great Community. When these conditions are brought into being they will make their own forms. Until they have come about, it is somewhat futile to consider what political machinery will suit them.

In a search for the conditions under which the inchoate public now extant may function democratically, we may proceed from a statement of the nature of the democratic idea in its generic social sense.[1] From the standpoint of the individual, it consists in having a responsible share according to capacity in forming and directing the activities of the groups to which one belongs and in participating according to need in the values which the groups

[1] The most adequate discussion of this ideal with which I am acquainted is T. V. Smith's "The Democratic Way of Life."

sustain. From the standpoint of the groups, it demands liberation of the potentialities of members of a group in harmony with the interests and goods which are common. Since every individual is a member of many groups, this specification cannot be fulfilled except when different groups interact flexibly and fully in connection with other groups. A member of a robber band may express his powers in a way consonant with belonging to that group and be directed by the interest common to its members. But he does so only at the cost of repression of those of his potentialities which can be realized only through membership in other groups. The robber band cannot interact flexibly with other groups; it can act only through isolating itself. It must prevent the operation of all interests save those which circumscribe it in its separateness. But a good citizen finds his conduct as a member of a political group enriching and enriched by his participation in family life, industry, scientific and artistic associations. There is a free give-and-take: fullness of integrated personality is therefore possible of achievement, since the pulls and responses of different groups reënforce one another and their values accord.

Regarded as an idea, democracy is not an alternative to other principles of associated life. It is the idea of community life itself. It is an ideal in the only intelligible sense of an ideal: namely, the tendency and movement of some thing which exists carried to its final limit, viewed as completed, perfected. Since things do not attain such fulfillment but are in actuality distracted and interfered with, democracy in this sense is not a fact and never will be. But neither in this sense is there or has there ever been anything which is a community in its full measure, a community unalloyed by alien elements. The idea or ideal of a community presents, however, actual phases of associated life as they are freed from restrictive and disturbing elements, and are contemplated as having attained their limit of development. Wherever there is conjoint activity whose consequences are appreciated as good by all singular persons who take part in it, and where the realization of the good is such as to effect an energetic desire and effort to sustain it in being just because it is a good shared by all, there is in so far a community. The clear consciousness of a communal life, in all its implications, constitutes the idea of democracy.

1927

23 A Pluralist Solution

ROBERT A. DAHL

The practical solutions that democratic countries have evolved are a good deal less clear than a straightforward application of the principle of majority rule. These solutions seem less 'logical,' less coherent, more untidy, and a good deal more attainable. Patterns of democratic government do not reflect a logically conceived philosophical plan so much as a series of responses to problems of diversity and conflict, by leaders who have sought to build and maintain a nation, to gain the loyalty and obedience of citizens, to win general and continuing approval of political institutions, and at the same time to conform to aspirations for democracy. However, some common elements can be discovered.

For one thing, in practise, countries with democratic regimes use force, just as other regimes do, to repel threats to the integrity of the national territory. Consequently secession is, as a practical matter, usually either impossible or extremely costly. (Colonies thought to lie outside the territory of the 'nation' may, of course, be granted independence.) To a considerable extent, then, large minorities are virtually 'compelled' to remain within the territorial limits of the nation. To make compulsory citizenship tolerable, great efforts are made to create and sustain a common sense of nationhood, so that minorities of all kinds will identify themselves with the nation. Hence secession or mass emigration are not usually thought of as practical alternatives.

Second, many matters of policy—religious beliefs and practises, for example—are effectively outside the legal authority of any government. Often they are placed beyond the legal authority of government through understandings and agreements widely shared and respected. In many cases these understandings and agreements are expressed in written constitutions that cannot be quickly or easily amended. Such a constitution is regarded as peculiarly binding; and ordinary laws that run counter to the constitution will be invalid, or, at the very least, subject to special scrutiny.

Third, a great many questions of policy are placed in the hands of private, semi-public, and local governmental organizations such as churches, families, business firms, trade unions, towns, cities, provinces, and the like. These questions of policy, like those left to individuals, are also effectively beyond the reach of national majorities, the national legislature, or indeed

SOURCE: from Robert A. Dahl, *Pluralist Democracy in the United States: Conflict and Consent*, any national policy-makers acting in their legal and official capacities. In fact, whenever uniform policies are likely to be costly, difficult, or troublesome, in pluralistic democracies the tendency is to find ways by which these policies can be made by smaller groups of like-minded people who enjoy a high degree of legal independence.

Fourth, whenever a group of people believe that they are adversely affected by national policies or are about to be, they generally have extensive opportunities for presenting their case and for negotiations that may produce a more acceptable alternative. In some cases, they may have enough power to delay, to obstruct, and even to veto the attempt to impose policies on them.

Now in addition to all these characteristics, the United States has limited the sovereignty of the majority in still other ways. In fact, the United States has gone so far in this direction that it is sometimes called a pluralistic system, a term I propose to use here.

The fundamental axiom in the theory and practise of American pluralism is, I believe, this: Instead of a single center of sovereign power there must be multiple centers of power, none of which is or can be wholly sovereign. Although the only legitimate sovereign is the people, in the perspective of American pluralism even the people ought never to be an absolute sovereign; consequently no part of the people, such as a majority, ought to be absolutely sovereign.

Why this axiom? The theory and practise of American pluralism tend to assume, as I see it, that the existence of multiple centers of power, none of which is wholly sovereign, will help (may indeed be necessary) to tame power, to secure the consent of all, and to settle conflicts peacefully:

> Because one center of power is set against another, power itself will be tamed, civilized, controlled, and limited to decent human purposes, while coercion, the most evil form of power, will be reduced to a minimum.
>
> Because even minorities are provided with opportunities to veto solutions they strongly object to, the consent of all will be won in the long run.
>
> Because constant negotiations among different centers of power are necessary in order to make decisions, citizens and leaders will perfect the precious art of dealing peacefully with their conflicts, and not merely to the benefit of one partisan but to the mutual benefit of all the parties to a conflict.

These are, I think, the basic postulates and even the unconscious ways of thought that are central to the American attempt to cope with the inescapable problems of power, conflict, and consent....

1967

24 Government and the Economy

JOHN MAYNARD KEYNES

I

The outstanding faults of the economic society in which we live are its failure to provide for full employment and its arbitrary and inequitable distribution of wealth and incomes. The bearing of [my] theory on the first of these is obvious. But there are also two important respects in which it is relevant to the second.

Since the end of the nineteenth century significant progress towards the removal of very great disparities of wealth and income has been achieved through the instrument of direct taxation—income tax and surtax and death duties—especially in Great Britain. Many people would wish to see this process carried much further, but they are deterred by two considerations; partly by the fear of making skilful evasions too much worth while and also of diminishing unduly the motive towards risk-taking, but mainly, I think, by the belief that the growth of capital depends upon the strength of the motive towards individual saving and that for a large proportion of this growth we are dependent on the savings of the rich out of their superfluity. Our argument does not affect the first of these considerations. But it may considerably modify our attitude towards the second. For we have seen that, up to the point where full employment prevails, the growth of capital depends not at all on a low propensity to consume but is, on the contrary, held back by it; and only in conditions of full employment is a low propensity to consume conducive to the growth of capital. Moreover, experience suggests that in existing conditions saving by institutions and through sinking funds is more than adequate, and that measures for the redistribution of incomes in a way likely to raise the propensity to consume may prove positively favourable to the growth of capital.

The existing confusion of the public mind on the matter is well illustrated by the very common belief that the death duties are responsible for a reduction in the capital wealth of the country. Assuming that the State applies the proceeds of these duties to its ordinary outgoings so that taxes on incomes and consumption are correspondingly reduced or avoided, it is, of course, true that a fiscal policy of heavy death duties has the effect of increasing the community's propensity to consume. But inasmuch as an increase in the habitual propensity to consume will in general (i.e. except

SOURCE: from John Maynard Keynes, *The General Theory of Employment, Interest, and Money*, pp. 372–384. Reprinted by permission of Harcourt Brace Jovanovich, Inc.

in conditions of full employment) serve to increase at the same time the inducement to invest, the inference commonly drawn is the exact opposite of the truth.

Thus our argument leads towards the conclusion that in contemporary conditions the growth of wealth, so far from being dependent on the abstinence of the rich, as is commonly supposed, is more likely to be impeded by it. One of the chief social justifications of great inequality of wealth is, therefore, removed. I am not saying that there are no other reasons, unaffected by our theory, capable of justifying some measure of inequality in some circumstances. But it does dispose of the most important of the reasons why hitherto we have thought it prudent to move carefully. This particularly affects our attitude towards death duties; for there are certain justifications for inequality of incomes which do not apply equally to inequality of inheritances.

For my own part, I believe that there is social and psychological justification for significant inequalities of incomes and wealth, but not for such large disparities as exist to-day. There are valuable human activities which require the motive of money-making and the environment of private wealth-ownership for their full fruition. Moreover, dangerous human proclivities can be canalised into comparatively harmless channels by the existence of opportunities for money-making and private wealth, which, if they cannot be satisfied in this way, may find their outlet in cruelty, the reckless pursuit of personal power and authority, and other forms of self-aggrandisement. It is better that a man should tyrannise over his bank balance than over his fellow-citizens; and whilst the former is sometimes denounced as being but a means to the latter, sometimes at least it is an alternative. But it is not necessary for the stimulation of these activities and the satisfaction of these proclivities that the game should be played for such high stakes as at present. Much lower stakes will serve the purpose equally well, as soon as the players are accustomed to them. The task of transmuting human nature must not be confused with the task of managing it. Though in the ideal commonwealth men may have been taught or inspired or bred to take no interest in the stakes, it may still be wise and prudent statesmanship to allow the game to be played, subject to rules and limitations, so long as the average man, or even a significant section of the community, is in fact strongly addicted to the money-making passion.

II

There is, however, a second, much more fundamental inference from our argument which has a bearing on the future of inequalities of wealth; namely, our theory of the rate of interest. The justification for a moderately high rate of interest has been found hitherto in the necessity of providing a sufficient inducement to save. But we have shown that the extent of effective saving is necessarily determined by the scale of investment and that the scale of investment is promoted by a *low* rate of interest, provided that we do not attempt to stimulate it in this way beyond the point which corresponds to full employment. Thus it is to our best advantage to reduce the rate of interest to that point relatively to the schedule of the marginal efficiency of capital at which there is full employment.

There can be no doubt that this criterion will lead to a much lower rate of interest than has ruled hitherto; and, so far as one can guess at the schedules of the marginal efficiency of capital corresponding to increasing amounts of capital, the rate of interest is likely to fall steadily, if it should be practicable to maintain conditions of more or less continuous full employment—unless, indeed, there is an excessive change in the aggregate propensity to consume (including the State).

I feel sure that the demand for capital is strictly limited in the sense that it would not be difficult to increase the stock of capital up to a point where its marginal efficiency had fallen to a very low figure. This would not mean that the use of capital instruments would cost almost nothing, but only that the return from them would have to cover little more than their exhaustion by wastage and obsolescence together with some margin to cover risk and the exercise of skill and judgment. In short, the aggregate return from durable goods in the course of their life would, as in the case of short-lived goods, just cover their labour-costs of production *plus* an allowance for risk and the costs of skill and supervision.

Now, though this state of affairs would be quite compatible with some measure of individualism, yet it would mean the euthanasia of the rentier, and, consequently, the euthanasia of the cumulative oppressive power of the capitalist to exploit the scarcity-value of capital. Interest to-day rewards no genuine sacrifice, any more than does the rent of land. The owner of capital can obtain interest because capital is scarce, just as the owner of land can obtain rent because land is scarce. But whilst there may be intrinsic reasons for the scarcity of land, there are no intrinsic reasons for the scarcity of capital. An intrinsic reason for such scarcity, in the sense of a genuine sacrifice which could only be called forth by the offer of a reward in the shape of interest, would not exist, in the long run, except in the event of the individual propensity to consume proving to be of such a character that net saving in conditions of full employment comes to an end before capital has become sufficiently abundant. But even so, it will still be possible for communal saving through the agency of the State to be maintained at a level which will allow the growth of capital up to the point where it ceases to be scarce.

I see, therefore, the rentier aspect of capitalism as a transitional phase which will disappear when it has done its work. And with the disappearance of its rentier aspect much else in it besides will suffer a sea-change. It will be, moreover, a great advantage of the order of events which I am advocating, that the euthanasia of the rentier, of the functionless investor, will be nothing sudden, merely a gradual but prolonged continuance of what we have seen recently in Great Britain, and will need no revolution.

Thus we might aim in practice (there being nothing in this which is unattainable) at an increase in the volume of capital until it ceases to be scarce, so that the functionless investor will no longer receive a bonus; and at a scheme of direct taxation which allows the intelligence and determination and executive skill of the financier, the entrepreneur *et hoc genus omne* (who are certainly so fond of their craft that their labour could be obtained much cheaper than at present), to be harnessed to the service of the community on reasonable terms of reward.

At the same time we must recognise that only experience can show how far the common will, embodied in the policy of the State, ought to be directed to increasing and supplementing the inducement to invest; and how far it is safe to stimulate the average propensity to consume, without forgoing our aim of depriving capital of its scarcity-value within one or two generations. It may turn out that the propensity to consume will be so easily strengthened by the effects of a falling rate of interest, that full employment can be reached with a rate of accumulation little greater than at present. In this event a scheme for the higher taxation of large incomes and inheritances might be open to the objection that it would lead to full employment with a rate of accumulation which was reduced considerably below the current level. I must not be supposed to deny the possibility, or even the probability, of this outcome. For in such matters it is rash to predict how the average man will react to a changed environment. If, however, it should prove easy to secure an approximation to full employment with a rate of accumulation not much greater than at present, an outstanding problem will at least have been solved. And it would remain for separate decision on what scale and by what means it is right and reasonable to call on the living generation to restrict their consumption, so as to establish, in course of time, a state of full investment for their successors.

III

In some other respects the foregoing theory is moderately conservative in its implications. For whilst it indicates the vital importance of establishing certain central controls in matters which are now left in the main to individual initiative, there are wide fields of activity which are unaffected. The State will have to exercise a guiding influence on the propensity to consume partly through its scheme of taxation, partly by fixing the rate of interest, and partly, perhaps, in other ways. Furthermore, it seems unlikely that the influence of banking policy on the rate of interest will be sufficient by itself to determine an optimum rate of investment. I conceive, therefore, that a somewhat comprehensive socialisation of investment will prove the only means of securing an approximation to full employment; though this need not exclude all manner of compromises and of devices by which public authority will co-operate with private initiative. But beyond this no obvious case is made out for a system of State Socialism which would embrace most of the economic life of the community. It is not the ownership of the instruments of production which it is important for the State to assume. If the State is able to determine the aggregate amount of resources devoted to augmenting the instruments and the basic rate of reward to those who own them, it will have accomplished all that is necessary. Moreover, the necessary measures of socialisation can be introduced gradually and without a break in the general traditions of society.

Our criticism of the accepted classical theory of economics has consisted not so much in finding logical flaws in its analysis as in pointing out that its tacit assumptions are seldom or never satisfied, with the result that it cannot solve the economic problems of the actual world. But if our central controls succeed in establishing an aggregate volume of output corresponding to full employment as nearly as is practicable, the classical theory comes into its own again from this point onwards. If we suppose the volume of output to be given, i.e. to be determined by forces outside the classical scheme of thought, then there is no objection to be raised against the classical analysis of the manner in which private self-interest will determine what in particular is produced, in what proportions the factors of production will be combined to produce it, and how the value of the final product will be distributed between them. Again, if we have dealt otherwise with the problem of thrift, there is no objection to be raised against the modern classical theory as to the degree of consilience between private and public advantage in conditions of perfect and imperfect competition respectively. Thus, apart from the necessity of central controls to bring about an adjustment to invest, there is no more reason to socialise economic life than there was before.

To put the point concretely, I see no reason to suppose that the existing system seriously misemploys the factors of production which are in use. There are, of course, errors of foresight; but these would not be avoided by centralising decisions. When 9,000,000 men are employed out of 10,000,000 willing and able to work, there is no evidence that the labour of these 9,000,000 men is misdirected. The complaint against the present system is not that these 9,000,000 men ought to be employed on different tasks, but that tasks should be available for the remaining 1,000,000 men. It is in determining the volume, not the direction, of actual employment that the existing system has broken down.

Thus I agree with Gesell that the result of filling in the gaps in the classical theory is not to dispose of the "Manchester System", but to indicate the nature of the environment which the free play of economic forces requires if it is to realise the full potentialities of production. The central controls necessary to ensure full employment will, of course, involve a large extension of the traditional functions of government. Furthermore, the modern classical theory has itself called attention to various conditions in which the free play of economic forces may need to be curbed or guided. But there will still remain a wide field for the exercise of private initiative and responsibility. Within this field the traditional advantages of individualism will still hold good.

Let us stop for a moment to remind ourselves what these advantages are. They are partly advantages of efficiency—the advantages of decentralisation and of the play of self-interest. The advantage to efficiency of the decentralisation of decisions and of individual responsibility is even greater, perhaps, than the nineteenth century supposed; and the reaction against the appeal to self-interest may have gone too far. But, above all, individualism, if it can be purged of its defects and its abuses, is the best safeguard of personal liberty in the sense that, compared with any other system, it greatly widens the field for the exercise of personal choice. It is also the best safeguard of the variety of life, which emerges precisely from this extended field of personal choice, and the loss of which is the greatest of all the losses of the homogeneous or totalitarian state. For this variety preserves the traditions which embody the most secure and successful choices of former generations; it colours the present with the diversification of its fancy; and, being the handmaid of experiment as well as of tradition and of fancy, it is the most powerful instrument to better the future.

Whilst, therefore, the enlargement of the functions of government, involved in the task of adjusting to one another the propensity to consume and the inducement to invest, would seem to a nineteenth-century publicist or to a contemporary American financier to be a terrific encroachment on individualism, I defend it, on the contrary, both as the only practicable means of avoiding the destruction of existing economic forms in their entirety and as the condition of the successful functioning of individual initiative.

For if effective demand is deficient, not only is the public scandal of wasted resources intolerable, but the individual enterpriser who seeks to bring these resources into action is operating with the odds loaded against him. The game of hazard which he plays is furnished with many zeros, so that the players *as a whole* will lose if they have the energy and hope to deal all the cards. Hitherto the increment of the world's wealth has fallen short of the aggregate of positive individual savings; and the difference has been made up by the losses of those whose courage and initiative have not been supplemented by exceptional skill or unusual good fortune. But if effective demand is adequate, average skill and average good fortune will be enough.

The authoritarian state systems of to-day seem to solve the problem of unemployment at the expense of efficiency and of freedom. It is certain that the world will not much longer tolerate the unemployment which, apart from brief intervals of excitement, is associated—and, in my opinion, inevitably associated—with present-day capitalistic individualism. But it may be possible by a right analysis of the problem to cure the disease whilst preserving efficiency and freedom.

IV

I have mentioned in passing that the new system might be more favourable to peace than the old has been. It is worth while to repeat and emphasise that aspect.

War has several causes. Dictators and others such, to whom war offers, in expectation at least, a pleasurable excitement, find it easy to work on the natural bellicosity of their peoples. But, over and above this, facilitating their task of fanning the popular flame, are the economic causes of war, namely, the pressure of population and the competitive struggle for markets. It is the second factor, which probably played a predominant part in the nineteenth century, and might again, that is germane to this discussion.

I have pointed out [previously] that, under the system of domestic *laissez-faire* and an international gold standard such as was orthodox in the latter half of the nineteenth century, there was no means open to a government whereby to mitigate economic distress at home except through the competitive struggle for markets. For all measures helpful to a state of chronic or intermittent under-employment were ruled out, except measures to improve the balance of trade on income account.

Thus, whilst economists were accustomed to applaud the prevailing international system as furnishing the fruits of the international division of labour and harmonising at the same time the interests of different nations, there lay concealed a less benign influence; and those statesmen were moved by common sense and a correct apprehension of the true course of events, who believed that if a rich, old country were to neglect the struggle for markets its prosperity would droop and fail. But if nations can learn to provide themselves with full employment by their domestic policy (and, we must add, if they can also attain equilibrium in the trend of their population), there need be no important economic forces calculated to set the interest of one country against that of its neighbours. There would still be room for the international division of labour and for international lending in appropriate conditions. But there would no longer be a pressing motive why one country need force its wares on another or repulse the offerings of its neighbour, not because this was necessary to enable it to pay for what it wished to purchase, but with the express object of upsetting the equilibrium of payments so as to develop a balance of trade in its own favour. International trade would cease to be what it is, namely, a desperate expedient to maintain employment at home by forcing sales on foreign markets and restricting purchases, which, if successful, will merely shift the problem of unemployment to the neighbour which is worsted in the struggle, but a willing and unimpeded exchange of goods and services in conditions of mutual advantage.

V

Is the fulfilment of these ideas a visionary hope? Have they insufficient roots in the motives which govern the evolution of political society? Are the interests which they will thwart stronger and more obvious than those which they will serve?

I do not attempt an answer in this place. It would need a volume of a different character from this one to indicate even in outline the practical measures in which they might be gradually clothed. But if the ideas are correct—an hypothesis on which the author himself must necessarily base what he writes—it would be a mistake, I predict, to dispute their potency over a period of time. At the present moment people are unusually expectant of a more fundamental diagnosis; more particularly ready to receive it; eager to try it out, if it should be even plausible. But apart from this contemporary mood, the ideas of economists and political philosophers, both when they are right and when they are wrong, are more powerful than is commonly understood. Indeed the world is ruled by little else. Practical men, who believe themselves to be quite exempt from any intellectual influences, are usually the slaves of some defunct economist. Madmen in authority, who hear voices in the air, are distilling their frenzy from some academic scribbler of a few years back. I am sure that the power of vested interests is vastly exaggerated compared with the gradual encroachment of ideas. Not, indeed, immediately, but after a certain interval; for in the field of economic and political philosophy there are not many who are influenced by new theories after they are twenty-five or thirty years of age, so that the ideas which civil servants and politicians and even agitators apply to current events are not likely to be the newest. But, soon or late, it is ideas, not vested interests, which are dangerous for good or evil.

1935

25 Market Planning and the Role of Government

JOHN KENNETH GALBRAITH

In fact since Adam and as a matter of settled doctrine since Adam Smith, the businessman has been assumed to be subordinate to the market. In last month's article I showed that modern highly technical processes and products and associated requirements of capital and time lead inevitably to planning—to the management of markets by those who supply them. It is technology, not ideology, that brings this result. The market serves admirably to supply simple things. But excellent as it may be on muskets, it is very bad on missiles. And not even the supply of components for the modern automobile can be trusted to the market; neither is it safe to assume that the market will absorb the necessary production at a remunerative price. There must be planning here as well.

The principal planning instrument in the modern economy is the large corporation. Within broad limits, it determines what the consumer shall have and at what price he shall have it. And it foresees the need for and arranges the necessary supply of capital, machinery, and materials.

The modern corporation is the direct descendant of the entrepreneur. This has kept us from seeing it in its new role. Had the corporation been an outgrowth of the state, which we readily associate with planning, we would not be in doubt. The modern corporation has, in fact, moved into a much closer association with the state than most of us imagine. And its planning activities are extensively and systematically supplemented by those of the state.

Let us consider first the regulation of prices in the modern economy and the means by which public behavior is accommodated to plan. Here, I should warn, we encounter some of the more deeply entrenched folk myths of our time, including a certain vested interest in error on the part of both economists and businessmen. If one takes faith in the market away from the economist, he is perilously barren of belief. So, he defends the market to defend his stock of knowledge. And the large corporate enterprise needs the concept of the market as a cover for the authority it exercises. It has great influence over our material existence and also our beliefs. But accepted doctrine holds that in all of its behavior it is subordinate to the

SOURCE: from John Kenneth Galbraith, "Market Planning and the Role of Government," *Atlantic Monthly,* May 1967, pp. 69–72, 77–79, which is taken from John Kenneth Galbraith, *The New Industrial State.* Reprinted by permission of Houghton Mifflin Company.

market. It is merely an automaton responding to instructions therefrom. Any complaint as to the use or misuse of power can be met by the answer that there is none.

Control of prices is an intrinsic feature of all planning. And it is made urgent by the special vagaries of the market for highly technical products. In the formally planned economies—that of the Soviet Union, for example—price control is a forthright function of the state, although there has been some tendency in recent times to allow some of the power over prices to devolve on the socialist firm. In the Western-type economies, comprehensive systems of price control have come about by evolution and adaptation. Nobody willed them. They were simply required by circumstance.

The power to set minimum industrial prices exists whenever a small number of firms share a market. The innocent at the universities have long been taught that small numbers of firms in the market—oligopoly, as it is known—accord to sellers the same power in imperfect form that has anciently been associated with monopoly. The principal difference is the imperfect nature of this monopoly power. It does not permit the exploitation of the consumer in quite such efficient fashion as was possible under the patents of monopoly accorded by the first Elizabeth to her favorites or by John D. Rockefeller to himself.

But in fact, the modern market shared by a few large firms is combined, in one of the more disconcerting contradictions of economic theory, with efficient production, expansive output, and prices that are generally thought rather favorable to the public. The consequences of oligopoly (few sellers) are greatly condemned in principle as being like those of monopoly but greatly approved in practice. Professor Paul Samuelson, the most distinguished of contemporary economists, warns in his famous textbook on economics that "to reduce the imperfections of competition" (by which he means markets consisting of a small number of large firms or oligopoly) "a nation must struggle perpetually and must ever maintain vigilance." Since American markets are now dominated by a very small number of very large firms, the struggle, obviously, has been a losing one and is now lost. But the result is that the economy functions very well. Samuelson himself concludes that man-hour efficiency in the United States "can hardly help but grow at the rate of three per cent or more, even if we do not rouse ourselves." A similar conflict between the inefficiency of oligopoly and the efficiency of an economy composed thereof is present in every well-regarded economic textbook. Samuelson agrees that technology and associated capital use are what improve efficiency. But these are precisely what require that there be planning and price control.

And here we have the answer. Prices in the modern economy are controlled not for the purposes of monopolistic exploitation. They are controlled for purposes of planning. This comes about as an effortless consequence of the development of that economy. Modern industrial planning both requires and rewards great size. This means, in turn, that a comparatively small number of large firms will divide the production of most (though not all) products. Each, as a matter of ordinary prudence, will act with full consideration of its own needs and of the common need. Each must have control of its own prices. Each will recognize this to be a requirement of others. Each will foreswear any action, and notably any sanguinary or competitive price-cutting, which would be prejudicial to the common interest in price control. This control is not difficult either to achieve or to maintain. Additionally, one firm's prices are another firm's costs. So, stability in prices means stability in costs.

The fact of control is far more important than the precise level at which prices are established. In 1964 in the United States, the big automobile companies had profits on their sales ranging from 5 percent to over 10 percent. There was security against collapse of prices and earnings for firms at either level. Planning was possible at either level of return. All firms could function satisfactorily. But none could have functioned had the price of a standard model fluctuated, depending on whim and reaction to the current novelties, from, say, $1800 to $3600, with steel, glass, chrome, plastics, paint, tires, stereo music, and labor moving over a similar range.

However, the level of prices is not unimportant. And from time to time, in response to major changes in cost—often when the renegotiation of a wage contract provides a common signal to all firms in the industry—prices must be changed. The prices so established will reflect generally the goals of those who guide the enterprise, not of the owners but of those who make the decisions. Security of earnings will be a prime objective. This is necessary for autonomy—for freedom from interference by shareholders and creditors. The next most important goal will be the growth of the firm. This is almost certainly more important than maximum profits. The professional managers and technicians who direct and guide the modern firm do not themselves get the profits. These accrue mainly to the shareholders. But the managers and technicians do get the benefits of expansion. This brings the prestige which is associated with a larger firm and which is associated with growth as such. And as a very practical matter, it opens up new executive jobs, new opportunities for promotion, and better excuses for higher pay.

Prices, accordingly, will be set with a view to attracting customers and expanding sales. When price control is put in the context of planning, the contradiction between expectation of monopolistic exploitation and expectation of efficiency, which pervades all textbook discussion, disappears. Planning calls for stability of prices and costs, security of return, and expansion. With none of these is the consumer at odds. Reality has, by its nature, advantages of internal consistency.

I must mention here one practical consequence of this argument, namely, its bearing on legal action against monopoly. There is a remarkable discrimination in the way such measures, notably the antitrust laws, are now applied. A great corporation wielding vast power over its markets is substantially immune. It does not appear to misuse its power; accordingly, it is left alone. And in any case, to declare all large corporations illegal is, in effect, to declare the modern economy illegal. That is rather impractical—and would damage any President's consensus. But if two small firms making the same product seek to unite, this corporate union will be meticulously scrutinized. And very possibly, it will be forbidden. This may be so even though the merged firm is minuscule in size or market power as compared with the giant that is already a giant.

The explanation is that the modern antimonopoly and antitrust laws are substantially a charade. Their function is not to prevent exploitation of the public. If great size and great market power led to such exploitation, our case would long since have been hopeless. Their function is to persuade people, liberal economists in particular, that the market still exists, for here is the state vigilantly standing guard. It does so by exempting the large firms and swatting those that seek to become larger.

The French, Germans, and Japanese either do not have or do not enforce such laws. That is because they are not impelled similarly to worship at the altar of the market. They quietly accept the logic of planning and its requirements in size for effective market control. There is no indication that they suffer in consequence.

When prices for a particular product are set by a few large firms, there is little danger of price-cutting. This part of the control is secure. There does remain a danger of uncontrolled price increases.

In particular, when a few large firms bargain with a strong union, conflict can be avoided by acceding to union demands. And there is not much incentive to resist. There is a common understanding among the firms that all will raise their prices to compensate for such a settlement. If demand is strong enough to keep the economy near full employment, it will be strong enough to make such price increases feasible. These price increases, in turn, set in motion demands for further wage increases. Thus, the familiar upward spiral of wages and prices proceeds. And this too is prejudicial to planning. The individual firm, moreover, cannot prevent such price increases; they are beyond its control as a planning unit.

So here, more and more we follow the practice of the formally planned economies. We rely on the state to set maximum wages and prices. In the United States as in Britain this is done with great caution, circumspection, and diffidence, somewhat in the manner of a Victorian spinster viewing an erotic statue. Such action is held to be unnatural and temporary. Economists accord it little or no standing in economic policy. They say it interferes with the market. Unions also dislike it: they say it interferes with free collective bargaining. Businessmen disapprove: they say it interferes with their natural freedom of decision on prices. But what everyone opposes in principle, all advanced countries end up doing in practice. The answer once more is clear. In a market economy, such ceilings would be unnecessary. But they are an indispensable counterpart of economic planning and of the minimum price control that already exists.

This price- and wage-setting by the state could be dispensed with by having such a shortage of demand that it would be impossible for firms to raise prices and unions to raise wages. That is to say, we could do without such controls by rehabilitating the market for labor and industrial products. It would not then be possible to raise wages in response to prices or prices in response to wages. But that would mean unemployment or greater uncertainty of employment, and it would mean greater market uncertainty for producers—for businessmen. Despite everyone's affection for the market, almost no one wants these results. So we have strong demand, small unemployment, reliable purchases, and the maximum price and wage controls that these require. And we try to avert our eyes from this result. It would be simpler were we to recognize that we have planning and that this control is an indispensable aspect.

This leads to another subject, the management of what people buy at the controlled prices.

The key to the management of demand is effective influence over the purchases of final consumers. The latter include both private individuals and the state. If all such purchases are under effective control, there will then be a reliable demand throughout the system for raw materials, parts, machinery, and other items going into the ultimate product. If the demand for its automobiles is secure, an automobile company can accord its suppliers the certainty of long-term contracts for *their* planning. And, even in the absence of such contracts, there will still be a reliable and predictable flow of orders. How, then, are the individual consumers managed?

As so often happens, change in modern industrial society has made possible what change requires. The need to control consumer behavior arises from the exigencies of planning. Planning, in turn, is made necessary by extensive use of advanced technology and the time and capital this requires. This is an efficient way of producing goods; the result is a very large volume of production. As a further consequence in the economically advanced countries, goods that serve elementary physical sensation—that prevent hunger, protect against cold, provide shelter, suppress pain—include only a small and diminishing part of what people consume. Only a few goods serve needs that are made known to the individual by the palpable discomfort or pain that is experienced in their absence. Most are enjoyed because of some psychic or aesthetic response to their possession or use. They give the individual a sense of personal achievement; they accord him a feeling of equality with his neighbors; they make him feel superior; or they divert his mind from thought or the absence of thought; or they promote or satisfy sexual aspiration; or they promise social acceptability; or they enhance his subjective feelings of health, well-being, and adequate peristalsis; or they are thought to contribute to personal beauty.

Thus it comes about that as the industrial system develops to where it has need for planning and the management of the consumer that this requires, we find it serving wants which are psychological in origin. And these are admirably subject to appeal to the psyche. Hence they can be managed. A man whose stomach is totally empty cannot be persuaded that his need is for entertainment. Physical discomfort will tell him he needs food more. But though a hungry man cannot be persuaded to choose between bread and a circus, a well-fed man can. And he can be persuaded to choose between different circuses and different foods.

By giving a man a ration card or distributing to him the specific commodities he is to consume, the individual can be required to consume in accordance with plan. But this is an onerous form of control, and it is ill adapted to differences in personality. In advanced industrial societies, it is considered acceptable only in times of great stress or for the very poor. (Even in the formally planned economies—the Soviet Union and the Eastern European states—the ration card is a manifestation of failure.) It is easier, and if less precise, still sufficient, to manage people by persuasion rather than by fiat.

Though advertising will be thought of as the central feature of this persuasion, and is certainly important, it is but a part of a much larger apparatus for the management of demand. Nor does this consist alone in devising a sales strategy for a particular product. It often means devising a product, or features of a product, around which a sales strategy can be built. Product design, model change, packaging, and even performance reflect the need to provide what are called strong selling points. They are as much a part of the process of demand management as the advertising campaign.

The first step in this process, generally speaking, is to ensure a loyal or automatic corps of customers. This is known as building customer loyalty and brand recognition. If successful, it means that the firm has a stable body of customers who are secure against any large-scale defection. Being thus reliable and predictable, they allow planning.

A purely defensive strategy will not, however, suffice. In line with the goals of its directing organization, the firm will want to expand sales. And such effort is necessary to hold a given position. The same will be true of others. Out of these efforts, from firms that have the resources to play the game (another advantage of size), comes a crude equilibrating process which accords to each participant a reasonably reliable share of the market.

Specifically, when a firm is enjoying a steady patronage by its existing customers and recruiting new ones at what seems a satisfactory rate, the existing strategy for consumer management—advertising, selling methods, product design—will be considered satisfactory. The firm will not quarrel with success. However, if sales are stationary or slipping, this will call for a change in selling methods—in advertising, product design, or even in the product itself. Testing and experiment are possible. And sooner or later, a formula providing a suitable response is obtained. This will lead, in turn, to countering action by the firms that are then failing to make gains. And out of this process a rough but reliable equilibrium between the participants is achieved.

It does not always work. There are Edsels. But it is the everyday assumption of those who engage in management of demand that if sales of a product are slipping, a new selling formula can be found that will correct the situation. By and large, the assumption is justified. Means, in other words, can almost always be found to keep the exercise of consumer discretion within safe or planned limits.

Management of the consumer on the scale that I have just outlined requires that there be some comprehensive, repetitive, and compelling communication between the managers of demand and those who are managed. It must be possible to win the attention of those who are being managed for considerable periods of time without great effort on their part.

Technology, once again, solved the problem it created. Coincidentally with rising mass incomes came first radio and then television. In their capacity to hold effortless interest, their accessibility over the entire cultural spectrum, and their independence of any educational qualification, these were superbly suited to mass persuasion. Television was especially serviceable. Not since the invention of speech has any medium of communication appeared which is so readily accommodated to the whole spectrum of mental capacity.

There is an insistent tendency among social scientists, including economists, to think that any institution which features singing commercials, shows the human intestinal tract in full or impaired operation, equates the effortless elimination of human whiskers with the greatest happiness of man, and implies that exceptional but wholesome opportunities for seduction are associated with a particular make of automobile is inherently trivial. This is a great mistake. The modern industrial system is profoundly dependent on this art. What is called progress makes it increasingly so.

And the management of demand so provided is in all respects an admirably subtle arrangement in social design. It works not on the individual but on the mass. An individual of will and determination can, in principle, contract out from under its influence. This being the case, no individual compulsion in the purchase of any product can ever be established. To all who object there is a natural answer: You are at liberty to leave! Yet there is no danger that enough people will ever assert this choice—will ever leave—to impair the management of mass behavior.

In the nonsocialist economy, the modern large corporation is, to repeat, the basic planning unit. For some planning tasks, we see that it is exceedingly competent. It can fix minimum prices. It can sufficiently manage consumer wants. And it can extract from revenues the savings it needs for its own growth and expansion. But some things it cannot do. Though the modern corporation can set and maintain minimum prices, it cannot, we have seen, set maximum prices and wages; it cannot prevent wages from forcing up prices and prices from forcing up wages in the familiar spiral. And while it can manage the demand for individual products, it cannot control total demand—it cannot ensure that total purchasing power in the economy will be equal, or approximately equal, to the supply of goods that can be produced by the current working force.

There are two other planning tasks that the large corporation cannot perform. It cannot supply the specialized manpower that modern technology and complex organization and planning require. It can train, but on the whole, it cannot educate. And it cannot absorb the risks and costs that are associated with very advanced forms of scientific and technical development—with the development of atomic power, or supersonic air transports, or antimissile defenses, or weapons systems to pierce these defenses, or the like requirements of modern civilized living.

This leads to a conclusion of great importance. The shortcomings of the large corporation as a planning instrument define the role of the modern state in economic policy. Wherever the private corporation cannot plan, the state comes in and performs the required function. Wherever the modern corporation can do the job, as in setting minimum prices or managing consumer demand, the state must remain out, usually as a matter of principle. But the corporation cannot fix maximum prices, so we have the state establishing wage and price guideposts or otherwise limiting wage and price increases. The private firm cannot control aggregate demand, so the state comes in to manipulate taxes, public spending, and bank lending—to implement what we call modern Keynesian policy. The private firm cannot supply specialized manpower, so we have a great expansion in publicly supported education. Private firms cannot afford to underwrite supersonic aircraft. So governments—British, French, or American—come in to do so and with no taint of socialism.

Our attitudes on the proper role of the state are firmly fixed by what the private corporation can or cannot do. The latter can set minimum prices for cigarettes, persuade people to buy a new and implausible detergent, or develop a more drastic laxative. This being so, such planning activity is naturally held to be sacred to private enterprise.

The planning functions of the state are somewhat less sacred. Some still have an improvised or *ad hoc* aspect. Thus, restraints on wages and prices are perpetual emergency actions; though fully accepted, Keynesian regulation of aggregate demand is thought to be occasioned by the particular imperatives of full employment and growth; the expansion of education is regarded as the result of a new enlightenment following World War II; the underwriting of especially expensive technology is a pragmatic response to the urgent social need for faster travel, emigration to the moon, bigger explosions, and competition with the Soviet Union.

So to regard matters is to fail to see the nature of modern planning. It is to yield unduly to the desire to avert our eyes from the reality of economic life. The planning functions of the state are not *ad hoc* or separate developments. They are a closely articulated set of functions which supplement and fill the gaps in the planning of the modern large firm. Together these provide a comprehensive planning apparatus. It decides what people should have and then arranges that they will get it and that they will want it. Not the least of its achievements is in leaving them with the impression that the controlling decisions are all theirs.

The Keynesian regulation of aggregate demand also requires only a word. The need for it follows directly from modern industrial planning. As we have seen, corporations decide authoritatively what they will reserve from earnings for reinvestment and expansion. But in the non-Soviet economies, there is no mechanism that ensures that the amounts so withheld for investment will be matched in the economy as a whole by what is invested. So there must be direct action by the state to equate the two. This it does primarily by manipulating private investment (principally in housing) and public spending and taxation. The need to equate the planned savings and the planned investment of the large corporation is not, of course, the only reason for such action. Savings and investment elsewhere in the economy must also be matched. But savings and investment by the large planning corporations are by far the most important in the total.

The successful regulation of demand requires that the quantitative role of the state in the modern economy be relatively large. That is because demand is regulated primarily by increasing or decreasing the expenditures of the state or decreasing or increasing the taxes it collects. Only when the state is large and its revenues are substantial will these changes be large enough to serve. One effective way of ensuring the requisite scale of state activity is to have it underwrite modern technology, which is admirably expensive. Such is the case with modern weaponry, space exploration, even highway and airport design. Though technology helps destroy the market, it does make possible the planning that replaces the market.

The next function of the state is to provide the specialized and trained manpower which the industrial system cannot supply to itself. This has led in our time to a very great expansion in education, especially in higher education, as has been true in all of the advanced countries. In 1900, there were 24,000 teachers in colleges and universities in the United States; in 1920, there were 49,000; by 1970, three years hence, there will be 480,000. This is rarely pictured as an aspect of modern economic development; it is the vanity of educators that they consider themselves the moving force in a new enlightenment. But it may be significant that when industry, at a little earlier stage, required mostly unlettered proletarians, that is what the educational system supplied. As it has come to need engineers, sales executives, copywriters, computer programmers, personnel managers, information retrieval specialists, product planners, and executive panjandrums, these are what the educational system has come to provide.

Once the community or nation that wanted more industry gave first thought to its capital supply and how to reassure the bankers on its reliability. Now it gives first thought to its educational system.

We cannot be altogether happy about education that is so motivated. There is danger that it will be excessively vocational and that we shall have a race of men who are strong on telemetry and space communications but who cannot read anything but a blueprint or write anything but a computer program. There is currently some uneasiness about liberal education in the modern industrial society. But so far this has manifested itself only in speeches by university presidents. In this segment of society, unfortunately a solemn speech is regularly considered a substitute for action.

Much the most interesting of the planning functions of the state is the underwriting of expensive technology. Few changes in economic life have ever proceeded with such explosive rapidity. Few have so undermined conventional concepts of public and private enterprise. In 1962, the U.S. government spent an estimated $10.6 billion on research and development. This was more than its total dollar outlay for all purposes, military or civilian, before World War II. But this function also includes the underwriting of markets—the provision of a guaranteed demand for billions of dollars worth of highly technical products, from aircraft to missiles to electronic gear to space vehicles. Nearly all of this expenditure, some 80 to 85 percent, goes to the large corporation, which is to say that it is to the planned sector of the American economy. It also brings the modern large corporation into the most intimate association with the state. In the case of such public agencies as NASA, the Atomic Energy Commission, or the Air Force, and the corporations serving them, it is no longer easy to say where the public sector ends and the private sector begins. Individuals and organizations are intimately associated. The private sector becomes, in effect, an extended arm of the public bureaucracy. However, the banner of private enterprise can be quite aggressively flaunted by the firm that does 75 percent of its business with the government and yearns to do more.

In the past, Keynesians have argued that there is nothing very special about government business. Replying to standard Marxian charges that capitalism depends excessively on armaments, they have pointed out that spending for housing, theaters, automobiles, highways to allow more automobiles to exist, and for radios to supply more automobiles to amuse more people while they are sitting in the resulting traffic jams, and for other of the attributes of gracious living will serve to sustain demand just as well as spending on arms. This, we now see, is not the whole story. The expenditures I have just mentioned would not serve to underwrite technology. And this underwriting is beyond the reach of private planning. Replacement of military spending, with its emphasis on underwriting advanced technology, must be by other equally technical outlays if it is to serve the same purpose. Otherwise, technical development will have to be curtailed to that level where corporate planning units can underwrite on their own. And this curtailment under present circumstances would be very, very drastic.

This analysis makes a considerable case for the space race. It is not that exploring the moon, Mars, or even Saturn is of high social urgency. Rather, the space race allows for an extensive underwriting of advanced technology. And it does this in a field of activity where spending is large and where, in contrast with weapons and weapons systems, competition with the Soviets is comparatively safe and benign. At the same time, as in the case of competitive athletics, everyone can easily be persuaded that it is absolutely vital to win.

We now see the modern corporation, in the technological aspects of its activities, moving into a very close association with the state. The state is the principal customer for such technology and the underwriter of major risk. In the planning of tasks and missions, the mapping of development work, and the execution of contracts, there is nowadays a daily and intimate association between the bureaucracy and the large so-called private firm. But one thing, it will be said, keeps them apart. The state is in pursuit of broad national goals, whatever these may be. And the private firm seeks to make money—in the more solemn language of economics, to maximize profits. This difference in goals, it will be said, sufficiently differentiates the state from private enterprise.

But here again reality supplies that indispensable thread of consistency. For power, as I showed in the first of these articles, and in detail in the book on which I am drawing, has passed from the owners of the corporation to the managers and scientists and technicians. The latter now exercise largely autonomous power, and not surprisingly, they exercise it in *their* own interest. And this interest differs from that of the owners. As noted, security of return is more important than the level of total earnings. When earnings fail, the autonomy of the decision-makers is threatened. And growth is more important to managers and technicians than maximum earnings.

But a further and important conclusion follows, for economic security and growth are also prime goals of the modern state. Nothing has been more emphasized in modern economic policy than the prevention of depression or recession. Politicians promise it automatically and without perceptible thought. And no test of social achievement is so completely and totally accepted as the rate of economic growth. It is the common measure of accomplishment of all the economic systems. Transcending political faith, religion, occupation, or all except eccentric philosophical persuasion, it is something on which Americans, Russians, Englishmen, Frenchmen, Germans, Italians, and Yugoslavs, and even Irishmen, all agree.

We have seen that as an aspect of its planning, the modern industrial enterprise accommodates the behavior and beliefs of the individual consumer to its needs. It is reasonable to assume that it has also accommodated our social objectives and associated beliefs to what it needs. In any case, there has been an interaction between state and firm which has brought a unity of goals.

A somber thought will occur to many here. We have seen that the state is necessary for underwriting the technology of modern industrial enterprise. Much of this it does within the framework of military expenditure. In the consumer goods economy, the wants and beliefs of the consumer, including his conviction that happiness is associated all but exclusively with the consumption of goods, are accommodated, in greater or less measure, to producer need. Is this true also of the state? Does it respond in its military procurement to what the supplying firms need to sell—and the technology that they wish to have underwritten? Are images of foreign policy in the planned industrial communities—in the United States, the Soviet Union, Western Europe—shaped by industrial need? Do we have an image of conflict because that serves technological and therewith planning need?

We cannot exclude that possibility; on the contrary, it is most plausible. It is a conclusion that was reached, perhaps a bit more intuitively, by President Eisenhower while he was President of the United States. In his famous valedictory, he warned of the influence on public policy resulting from the "conjunction of an immense military establishment and a large arms industry." This will not be an agreeable thought for those for whom the mind is an instrument for evading reality. Others will see the possibility of a two-way flow of influence. Presumably it will be true of any planned economy, East or West. The image of the foreign policy affects the demand of the state on industry. But the needs of economic planning expressed in the intimate association between industry and the state will affect the state's view of military requirements and of foreign policy. It is a matter where we had best be guided by reality. . . .

1967

Bibliography

Anton, Thomas. "Power, Pluralism and Local Politics," *Administrative Science Quarterly* 7 (March 1962): 425–457.

Bachrach, Peter, and Baratz, Morton. *Power and Poverty. New York:* Oxford University Press, 1970, especially Part One.

Baskin, Darryl. *American Pluralist Democracy: A Critique.* New York: Van Nostrand Reinhold Co., 1971.

Beam, George D. *Usual Politics.* New York: Holt, Rinehart and Winston, 1970.

Bentley, Arthur F. *The Process of Government.* Evanston, Ill.: Principia Press, 1935 (originally published in 1908).

Bowen, Ralph. *German Theories of the Corporate State.* New York: McGraw-Hill, 1947.

Calhoun, John C. *A Disquisition on Government and Selections from the Discourses.* Indianapolis, Ind.: Bobbs-Merrill, 1953.

Carmichael, Stokely, and Hamilton, Charles V. *Black Power: The Politics of Liberation in America.* New York: Vintage Books, 1967.

Connolly, William E. (ed.). *The Bias of Pluralism.* New York: Atherton, 1969.

Dahl, Robert. *Pluralist Democracy in the United States.* Chicago: Rand McNally, 1967.

Dahl, Robert. *Who Governs?* New Haven: Yale University Press, 1961.

Dahl, Robert, and Lindblom, Charles E. *Politics, Economics and Welfare.* New York: Harper, 1953.

Elbow, Matthew H. *French Corporative Theory, 1789–1948.* New York: Columbia University Press, 1953.

Galbraith, John K. *American Capitalism: The Concept of Countervailing Power.* Boston: Houghton Mifflin, 1956.

Ginzberg, Eli, *et al. The Pluralistic Economy.* New York: W. W. Norton, 1964.

Greenstone, J. David. *Labor in American Politics.* New York: Vintage, Random House, 1969.

Golembiewski, Robert. "The Group Theory of Politics: Notes and Analyses and Development," *American Political Science Review LIV* (March 1960): 38–51.

Herring, E. Pendleton. *The Politics of Democracy.* New York: Rinehart, 1940.

Kariel, Henry S. "Pluralism," *International Encyclopedia of the Social Sciences,* Vol. *12.* New York: Macmillan and Free Press, pp. 164–169.

Kariel, Henry S. *The Promise of Politics.* Englewood Cliffs, N.J.: Prentice-Hall, Inc., 1966.

Kornhauser, William. *The Politics of Mass Society.* New York: Free Press, 1959.

Latham, Earl. *The Group Basis of Politics.* Ithaca, N.Y.: Cornell University Press, 1952.

Lowi, Theodore. *The End of Liberalism.* New York: W. W. Norton, 1969.

Lowi, Theodore. "The Public Philosophy: Interest Group Liberalism," *American Political Science Review, LXI* (March 1967): 13.

Magid, Henry M. *English Political Pluralism.* Columbia University Studies in Philosophy, No. 2. New York: Columbia University Press, 1941.

McConnell, Grant. *Private Power and American Democracy.* New York: Alfred A. Knopf, 1966.

McFarland, Andrew S. *Power and Leadership in Pluralist Systems.* Stanford, Calif.: Stanford University Press, 1969.

Pennock, J. Roland, and Chapman, John W. (eds.). *Voluntary Associations.* Nomos XI. New York: Atherton Press, 1969.

Polsby, Nelson. *Community Power and Political Theory.* New Haven: Yale University Press, 1963.

Rothman, Stanley. "Systematic Political Theory: Observations on the Group Approach," *American Political Science Review, LIV* (March 1960): 15–33.

Rose, Arnold M. *The Power Structure.* New York: Oxford University Press, 1967.

Truman, David. *The Governmental Process.* New York: Alfred A. Knopf, 1953.

Webb, Leicester C. (ed.). *Legal Personality and Political Pluralism.* Australian National University Social Science Monograph No. 12. New York: Cambridge University Press, 1958.

VI Democratic Socialism

Democratic socialists argue against the atomistic individualism and faith in a spontaneous social harmony so characteristic of the liberal tradition dominant in the United States and much of Europe during the eighteenth, nineteenth, and the earlier part of the twentieth centuries. Well aware that individual interests may conflict with the supposed interests of society as a whole, the democratic socialists argue that liberty is primarily a function of social solidarity. The ends of society as a whole being in a sense paramount to those of any given individual, the democratic socialists urge that the existence and well-being of each individual depend upon the continuance and sound health of the body politic. Like Rousseau, the democratic socialists tend to link the liberty and equality of the individual to an organic conception of society (but certainly not of the state).

Fusing the complex arrangement of modern society with the simplicity of community, the democratic socialists tend to argue that liberty and social harmony are intricately bound with a congruity of character, belief, language, and mode of life. What this means, at a minimum, is that liberty and social harmony are intricately bound with fraternal cooperation. In a sense this defines the goal of the social democratic doctrine. Like the pluralists, the democratic socialists see the state as an association for the pursuit of common goals and purposes. Unlike the pluralists, however, the socialists see the state as the most comprehensive association, making rules and providing security and welfare for the society as a whole. The state, particularly the legislative institutions of the government, is or at least ought to be, according to the democratic socialists, the locus of sovereign power. As an instrument of the people, the state exists to secure and maintain the public interest.

The primary social vantage point reflected by the democratic socialist ideology is that of the proletariat in the modern industrial nation–state. Like the liberal democrats, the democratic socialists purport to attend to the arrangements of society as a whole, although the former often claim this as a spontaneous consequence of maximizing personal, civil, and economic liberty, while the latter propose to achieve this through conscious social planning. Democratic socialist politics, in attending to the arrangements of society, involve the deliberate social control, by democratically constituted authorities, of the means of production and often the means of distribution as well. Consumption is still regarded primarily as a matter of individual choice.

Democratic socialism, as its name implies, reflects, in addition to the activities reflected by all democratic ideologies, economic activity in the modern nation–state. Proposing public (state) ownership of otherwise private or corporate enterprise, the democratic socialists reflect both the economic activities of the modern proletariat in attempting to control the use of private power and the problems of proletariat life in modern industrial society. Finally, as an abstract model and guide for political action, democratic socialism reflects the growth in importance and activity of the institutions of the modern nation–state, particularly with respect to the potentially democratic deployment of those institutions.

G. D. H. Cole cites three elements which are essential to "socialism": the provision of an equal chance for all, the guarantee of a decent standard of living for all, and democracy. To achieve this end, Cole argues, society must be organized on the basis of equal human rights. These equal rights extend not merely to the personal development of the individual, but also to the arena of politics, where the individual ought to have a chance at playing a role in public affairs. Further, the socialist vision seeks to arrange the affairs of state in such a manner that participation is maximized. Identifying democracy with the creed of freedom as well as equality, Cole argues that a socialist democracy must not only tolerate diversity but must encourage it as well. Economically, democratic socialism attempts to replace the irresponsibility of monopoly with the communal ownership of the means of production, although this is not an end in itself.

C. A. R. Crosland further delineates the ethical and emotional ideals common to the various conceptions of "socialism." According to Crosland, three broad categories obtain: first, a commitment to the "underdog"; second, censure of the material consequences of capitalism; third, an idealistic desire for a just, cooperative, classless society. Crosland admits that the third category is perhaps not an essential goal of socialism, even though it is morally desirable that man be motivated by consideration of common social purposes.

Benjamin Lippincott, distinguished political theorist and one of the earliest American students of the economic theory of socialism, addresses himself to two charges against socialism: that it is economically impracticable and that it is politically undesirable. In the first instance Lippincott argues that the socialist economy can ascertain the relative importance of the factors of production through trial and error, much as capitalism does, and, hence, can achieve a rational allocation of resources. Paralleling the function of prices in a capitalist system, the Central Planning Board can make adjustments for relative scarcity or plenty based on information of surplus or deficit in inventories. In the second instance, regarding the charge that socialism is politically undesirable, Lippincott argues that socialism removes autocratic control from industry. More consistent with both liberty and equality than capitalism, the socialist economy would allow a more generous provision of public goods and services.

Echoing Lippincott's analysis, Harrington points out that capitalism assigns resources where there will be the greatest commercial return, ignoring the very important consideration of social consequences. Somewhat more optimistic concerning the possibility of fraternal cooperation than Crosland, Harrington sees a movement from the capitalist psychology toward a vision of associated producers. Unlike Cole, Harrington sees a continuing role for and continuing importance of the working class in modern industrial society. The problems of economic redistribution are by no means solved, he observes. Throughout his article, Harrington emphasizes that the welfare state of modern day America cannot solve the problems of modern day America; not only does capitalism subvert social justice, not only will private power not tolerate democratic planning, but also the capitalist system itself tends to make affluence self-destructive.

26 Basic Socialism

G. D. H. COLE

I call myself a 'Socialist', and have so called myself ever since I was a boy. I became a Socialist, in those far-off days, because the world which I saw around me seemed, as soon as I began to look at it, to be full of injustice and very badly organized for the promotion of human happiness. I was one of the lucky ones, brought up in a well-to-do household, educated at a good school, and given every chance of thinking for myself by a father who believed in freedom, though he was a Conservative and could never be persuaded that Socialism did not mean 'dividing everything up equally'. I soon realised how exceptional my chances were, and began to wonder why I should be thus favoured. The only answer I could find was that there was no valid reason; and as soon as I had arrived at that answer I began wanting to reorganise society on a basis which would give everybody a decent chance.

That desire soon led me to Socialism, and has remained from that time the basis of my Socialist faith. For I could not, and cannot, see how everyone can be given a decent chance except in a society which is organised on the assumption of equal human rights. I do not mean by this that I suppose all men to be equal; for the phrase has no meaning. Equal in what? Certainly not in cleverness, or bodily attainments, or moral qualities, or capacity for service—or in any combination of these qualities, if one could add up things so different. The doctrine of social equality stands for something quite other than this meaningless assertion that men are equal. It means that all men, and of course all women, ought to be given an equal chance of developing whatever good there is in them, of being reasonably happy in their lives, and of being pleasant to live with—for one man's well-being and happiness are bound up with others', and what makes the individual good and happy helps to make other men good and happy as well.

Of course, the equal chance is not by itself enough. Some men will miss their chances, and make a mess of their lives. They will be punished for this by their own sense of failure; and there is no need for society to set about punishing them into the bargain, merely because they have failed. In addition to the equal chance for all we need compassion for those who fail to take advantage of it, whether by their own fault or not.

That means to me, and has meant ever since I began to think about

SOURCE: from G. D. H. Cole, *Fabian Socialism,* pp. 30–38.

politics, that society ought to afford to all its members, irrespective of their virtues or vices, their strength or weakness, a tolerable basic standard of living, high enough to keep them in health and reasonable comfort and to enable them to bring up their children after a fashion that will allow them, in their turn, as far as possible, an equal chance of making the best of their lives. No social measures can give a really equal chance to a child that has the misfortune to be reared in a bad or unhappy home; but society can do its best not to punish the children for the parents' shortcomings. I am not under the illusion that the best forms of social organisation can make everybody healthy and happy; but to recognise the limits of what can be done is no reason for not doing all we can.

These two ideas, of the equal chance for all and of the basic standard of living assured to all, led me to Socialism. I think it was only a little later that I added to them a third—always implicit in my attitude, but not fully realised at first. This third idea was that of democracy, which was inseparably linked in my mind with that of freedom—so that I think of them instinctively as one idea, and not two. By democracy I mean not only that everybody who is not out of his mind ought to have an equal chance of playing his part in public affairs, but also that these affairs ought to be so arranged as to make it easy for as many people as possible to play an active part in them, and further that society ought to encourage the fullest possible open discussion of public affairs, and allow men the greatest practicable liberty to organise for public and private purposes.

Gradually this notion of democratic freedom broadened out in my mind. It came to mean to me that society ought to be so arranged as to encourage difference, and not merely to tolerate it. It takes many sorts of men and women to make a satisfactory human society; and within certain very wide limits the more men differ the better, not only in tastes and habits but also in opinions. For democratic progress comes of the clash of contending outlooks and opinions. In a growing free society, minorities of to-day become majorities of to-morrow, and it is disastrous to impose uniformity of either thought or conduct. This idea, like all true ideas, has its limits; for there must be a certain underlying community of manners and ways of thinking to hold a society together. But in a healthy society this basic community will establish itself almost without being sought: there is much more danger of overstressing it, so as to crush out individuality, than of insisting on it too little.

Socialism, then, came to stand in my mind for the predominance of these three—or, if you prefer, these four—ideas, the equal chance for all, the basic standard of living assured to all, and democratic freedom. You will observe that there is in all this no single word of what many people suppose to be the fundamental Socialist tenet—that the means of production, distribution and exchange ought to be owned in common by the whole people. There is no word of it, so far, because for me, and I think for nearly all Socialists, common ownership is not an end in itself, but a means of bringing these ends I have spoken of into existence. There is no *absolute* validity about the proposition that the entire community ought to own the means of production. Indeed, I can quite imagine societies for which it would not hold good, and I find it difficult to imagine any society in which *all* the means of production ought to be owned in this way. I can, however, imagine no society which *ought* not to do its best to give to all its members an equal chance, an assured basic standard of living, and as much democratic freedom as possible. These things are *ends,* which all decent men *ought* at all times to desire and attempt to further. The communal ownership of the means of production is a *method* of bringing them about, appropriate in the main to the type of society in which you and I are living, but not in any sense morally imperative in all societies, irrespective of time and place.

Of course, even the ends of which I have spoken can be achieved in any society only in part. They are ends to aim at, and to achieve as far as lies within our power. Taking men as they are, we cannot hope to give everyone an equal chance, or to establish a perfect free democracy. We can hope to assure to all members of our own society, in our own time, a tolerable basic standard of life; but we cannot hope either to make that standard as high as we should wish it to be, or to extend a like standard to all the peoples of the world for a long time to come. We can hope for no more than the speedy banishment from among us of primary poverty in all its forms, and therewith a much nearer approximation to equality of opportunity for all our people, and a great growth among them of the democratic spirit. These, however, are ideals quite high enough to work for; and it will be enough for us if we can say on our death-beds that we have worked for them honestly, and have done our best to give a helping hand to other peoples who have been working for them.

This is a quiet way of stating a conviction which is felt with passion, if it is felt at all. If my reason tells me that this is what I ought to do, my emotions also tell me that this is what I want. I cannot be happy in a world full of unnecessary injustice and misery, unless I am doing what I can to help in putting things to rights. Or, at least, I cannot be happy unless I am doing *something* towards this, even if I do much less than I could. I have a conscience about my fellow-men; and this conscience wars with my private selfishness and laziness, which bid me attend to my own affairs, or let matters slide. I am no saint, to do all I should; but I should be acutely unhappy unless I could say to myself honestly that I am not living to myself alone, or to the narrow circle of those whom I love, but am also trying, though not with all my strength, to lessen the sum of human unhappiness and to promote the cause of democratic freedom.

This, surely, is the common experience. Our opportunities differ; and some of us find better chances of being useful to our fellow-men in a narrow, and others in a wider circle. But, in one way or another, we feel a responsibility for the well-being of our fellows, and are not happy unless we are being of some use. Some people feel this more strongly than others; and some find their sphere of service in personal, and others mainly in public acts. But it is all an expression of the same spirit, resting on a sense of justice and a sympathy with others which are part of the way we are made.

Of course, these sentiments do not make all men Socialists. Socialism implies, among those who profess it by conviction and not by the accident of environment, a keener sense than the ordinary that the ends of social justice and human fraternity need to be promoted by collective action. It implies regarding the State as, potentially, not so much a policeman to keep us in order as a means of promoting the good life. It implies a belief that, even though men cannot be made good or happy by legislation, good laws can greatly improve their chances of being good and happy. It implies a belief that human societies ought to be organised for the benefit of all their members, and not of any limited class or group. It implies therewith the belief that collective action for the common good ought to extend to all things which are both essential to men's happiness and capable of being organised collectively without destroying their essential quality. In particular, it implies a conviction that the economic life of society ought not to be left to the play of private forces, but ought to be organised under some form of public control.

As against this view, it used to be argued that a beneficent Providence had so arranged economic affairs as to cause each man, in pursuing his own private interest, to pursue unwittingly and without conscious purpose the good of all. It used to be said that competition to make profits provided the surest guarantee that the consumers would be well and cheaply served, and that accordingly the State ought in all events to refrain from meddling in economic concerns. This notion was never in any place or time followed out to the full in practice; and hardly anyone continues to believe in it now. For it is obvious that, whatever may have been the situation a century ago, to-day the absence of State intervention does not lead to this supposedly beneficent competition. On the contrary, in nearly all the key industries and services, what happens in the absence of State intervention is not free competition, but some form of monopoly. Not all industries are monopolistic in structure; but there is hardly one left that is not monopolistic at some stage. Even where competition survives between the makers of finished goods, the producers of the materials out of which these goods are made may form a powerful monopoly. Finance—the provision of credit to the producers—is almost everywhere a highly monopolistic affair; and even where monopoly is incomplete huge concerns in many cases so dominate the market that it is a mockery to speak of free competition. Wages, too, are regulated more and more by large-scale collective bargains between Trade Unions and associations of employers, and the selling prices of goods are often fixed by the manufacturer, so that one retailer may not undercut another, even if he wishes to do so. The absence of State intervention no longer means competition as the dominant characteristic of the economic world: it means regulation by irresponsible monopolies instead of regulation in the common interest.

This would not suffice to condemn the system, if these monopolies did in fact serve the public well. But the natural tendency is for most monopolists, and most combines aiming at monopoly, to live in perpetual fear of glutting the market. The aim of those who control them is to make as much profit as possible; and this *must* be their aim, as matters stand, for unless they make it so they will speedily go to the wall. The highest profit is in most cases to be won, or seems likeliest to be won, not by producing as much as possible, but, on the contrary, by limiting production to what can be sold at a fairly high price. There are exceptions to this rule, in the case of goods the demand for which can be expanded considerably even by a small reduction in price; for in such a situation it may suit the monopolist to increase his output. It suited Henry Ford to produce a very large number of motor-cars, in order to secure the full economy of mass-production. But such instances are exceptional. Much oftener, what happens is that the business concerns turn out many fewer goods than they could, with the consequence that many workers are left unemployed and have to look to the State for support.

This is so much a commonplace that a great many people have become accustomed to it, and regard it as quite natural that millions of people should be out of work when they themselves, and millions of others, are going short of the things they could make. Yet such a state of affairs is, when you come to think of it, plainly immoral and absurd. If the means of making things exist, and the things are needed to give people a decent standard of life, it is manifestly wrong not to make them; and any economic system which leads to such results stands condemned at the bar of morality and commonsense. It is no doubt, *possible* that men are so incompetent at managing these affairs as to be incapable of doing any better. But they ought to try; and the method most widely advocated of curing the evil is that of Socialism.

At this point, it used always to be answered that Socialism was no doubt a very beautiful and lofty ideal, but could not be made to work in practice. 'Human nature', we were told, made it impossible. That argument is now out of court. For Socialism *has* worked, over a period of more than two decades, in one of the largest countries in the world. The system which was set up in 1917 in the Soviet Union has many faults; but it has banished unemployment and set out to produce goods up to the very limit of its productive power. It used to be said that a Socialist State would inevitably break down because the citizens would insist on consuming all they could produce instead of setting aside adequate provision for the accumulation of new productive power. That argument also is out of court; for the Soviet Union has put into capital accumulation probably a larger proportion of its national income than has ever been put by any capitalist State—and that despite the necessity it has been under of spending vast sums on armaments in self-defence.

It can no longer be argued that Socialism is unworkable. But it can, of course, still be held to be undesirable. There, the favourite contention is that Socialism is destructive of the freedom of the common man. That is harder to answer; for the situation in Russia in respect of freedom is much less obvious. I have listened to many inconclusive arguments about the relative extent of freedom in Russia and in Great Britain. One side will stress the suppression of doctrines supposed to make against the security of the Soviet State, the insistence on Marxian orthodoxy as the basis of all thinking, the prosecution of 'comrades' who are held to have deviated from the true faith. The other side will argue that the Soviet workmen, conscious of owning the factories they work in and the State itself, emancipated from subservience to persons of a higher social class, much more able to live private lives after their chosen fashion than most people in a class-ridden society, enjoy a much larger real freedom than the workers in capitalist countries. In effect, each side puts the accent on certain particular aspects of freedom, and ignores other aspects. They are both right, and they are both wrong. However, the fact that the argument remains inconclusive does show that social control of the State and the means of production is not by itself enough to ensure freedom in all its desirable forms. The Soviet Union is not a free democracy, as we understand the term; but then—neither is Great Britain, as they understand it.

This suggests that there is real danger, if we concentrate on securing the equal chance for all and the basic standard of living for all, to the exclusion of the type of democratic freedom which I have discussed earlier in this chapter, of our getting into conflict with a tradition of free speech and free organisation which hardly existed in Russia, but is very powerful here. Each country, in amending its social institutions, has to build upon its own past. Soviet Communism in Russia is what it is, in many respects, because Czardom was what it was; and British Socialism, when and if it comes to power, will have on it the stamp of the British tradition. That is why it is foolish for Communists to call upon us to do just as the Russians did. Our circumstances are so different that our revolution, when it comes, will necessarily take a different form and lead to a different set of institutions. The kinds of freedom we value and enjoy now we must carry over into the new society we mean to build; and we must add to them other kinds of freedom which are now denied to most of our people.

1943

27 The Aspirations of Socialism

C. A. R. CROSLAND

I The Confusion Between Ends and Means

If we are to reformulate socialist doctrine, the first task is clearly to decide what precise meaning is to be attached to the word 'socialism'.

This is not an easy question to answer. The word does not describe any present or past society, which can be empirically observed, and so furnish unimpeachable evidence for what is or is not 'socialism'. Thus statements about socialism can never be definitely verified; and we cannot treat it as being an *exact* descriptive word at all. There is therefore no point in searching the encyclopaedias for a definitive meaning; it has none, and never could.

This can easily be seen by considering the numerous and . . . often inconsistent meanings attached to the word by people who have called themselves 'socialists'. Marx, defining it as the 'nationalisation of the means of production, distribution, and exchange', meant something quite different from Proudhon, who defined it as consisting of 'every aspiration towards the amelioration of our society'. Sir William Harcourt, declaring in 1892 that 'we are all socialists now', evidently had a different version from his contemporary Bradlaugh, to whom socialism meant that 'the State should own all wealth, direct all labour, and compel the equal distribution of all produce'. And any history of socialist thought will provide dozens of different definitions, some in terms of ownership, some of co-operation, some of planning, some of income-distribution; and it soon becomes simply a matter of subjective personal preference which is chosen as the 'correct' one. Many definitions, moreover, are so vague as to be virtually meaningless; one can read almost anything, for example, into Sidney Webb's definition: 'the economic side of the democratic ideal'.

The confusion has become worse inasmuch as the word is also charged with a high degree of emotional content, and so has acquired a range of purely persuasive meanings. It is either used to denote or win approval, as in Hitler's National 'Socialism' and 'Socialism' in Eastern Europe, or when Left-wing weeklies attack a policy which they dislike as not being 'Socialist'; or pejoratively, as when Right-wing Americans speak of 'creeping Socialism'.

But the worst source of confusion is the tendency to use the word to describe, not a certain kind of society, or certain values which might be attributes of a society, but particular policies which are, or are thought to

SOURCE: reprinted with permission of The Macmillan Company from *The Future of Socialism* by C. A. R. Crosland.

be, means to attaining this kind of society, or realising these attributes. To rescue the word from these confusions, and the debasement referred to above, one must begin by asking what, if anything, is common to the beliefs of all, or almost all, of those who have called themselves socialists. The only constant element, common to all the bewildering variety of different doctrines, consists of certain moral values and aspirations; and people have called themselves socialists because they shared these aspirations, which form the one connecting link between otherwise hopelessly divergent schools of thought.

Thus the word first came on the modern scene with the early nineteenth-century Owenites, whom Marx contemptuously termed 'Utopian' socialists. They based their 'socialism' explicitly on an ethical view of society, a belief in a certain way of life and certain moral values. The means by which they thought this 'good society' could be attained are irrelevant to-day; and in fact they were quickly challenged by other socialist schools of thought, since when a continuous debate has proceeded, with no agreement, about what constituted the most suitable means. This debate would have no particular interest to-day, but for the fact that all the protagonists tried to appropriate the word 'socialism' to describe the particular means which they themselves favoured.

Thus Marx appropriated it for the collective ownership of the means of production on the false assumption . . . that the pattern of ownership determined the character of the whole society, and that collective ownership was a sufficient condition of fulfilling the basic aspirations. And generally the word came to be applied to policies for the economic or institutional transformation of society, instead of to the ultimate social purposes which that transformation was intended to achieve; so one often hears socialism equated not only with the nationalisation of industry, but with government planning, or redistribution, or state collectivism. This of course is quite unhelpful, for although people may agree on ends, they may legitimately disagree about means. Moreover, the means most suitable in one generation may be wholly irrelevant in the next, and in any case (still more significant) a given means may lead to more than one possible end, as indeed has happened with each of the policies just mentioned.[1]

Thus if, for example, socialism is defined as the nationalisation of the means of production, distribution and exchange, we produce conclusions

[1] The use of the terms 'ends' and 'means' might seem to imply a Utopian or 'blueprint' view of society—a belief that society might, or could, settle down to a stable, unchanging state, analogous to the classical 'stationary' state of economics. And of course most early socialists did hold this view. But as used in the text, the word 'end' is to be understood simply as describing principles or values, such as equality, or justice, or democracy, or co-operativeness, which might or might not be embodied in, or determine the character of, a particular society: and the word 'means' as describing the essentially institutional changes required to realise, or at least promote, these values in practice.

which are impossible to reconcile with what the early socialists had in mind when they used the word: such as, that Soviet Russia is a completely socialist country (much more so, for instance, than Sweden)—even though it denies almost all the values which Western socialists have normally read into the word. Similarly, if socialism is defined as economic collectivism or State control of economic life, then Nazi Germany would correctly have been called a socialist country. But in neither case would the end-result be described as socialism by most socialists; the means of nationalisation and planning have proved adaptable to more than one purpose, which shows how unwise it is to identify the means with the end.

Not only is it unwise, but it is also semantically and historically incorrect. The various schools of thought which have called themselves, and been called by others, 'socialist'—Owenites and Marxists, Fabians and Christian Socialists, Syndicalists and Guild Socialists—have differed profoundly over the right means; and no one means has a better title to the label 'socialist' than any other. The one single element common to all the schools of thought has been the basic aspirations, the underlying moral values. It follows that these embody the only logically and historically permissible meaning of the word socialism; and to this meaning we must now revert.

II The Basic Socialist Aspirations

These ethical and emotional ideals have been partly negative—a protest against the visible results of capitalism—and partly positive, and related to definite views about the nature of the good society; though of course negative and positive strands are often inter-twined.

Perhaps one can list them roughly as follows. First, a protest against the material poverty and physical squalor which capitalism produced. Secondly, a wider concern for 'social welfare'—for the interests of those in need, or oppressed, or unfortunate, from whatever cause. Thirdly, a belief in equality and the 'classless society', and especially a desire to give the worker his 'just' rights and a responsible status at work. Fourthly, a rejection of competitive antagonism, and an ideal of fraternity and co-operation. Fifthly, a protest against the inefficiencies of capitalism as an economic system, and notably its tendency to mass unemployment. The first three formed the basis of socialism as 'a broad, human movement on behalf of the bottom dog'.[2] The first and last were censures on the material results of capitalism; while the other three stemmed from an idealistic desire for a just, co-operative and classless society.

(I have listed only the social and economic aspirations. But of course

[2] Cole, George D. *A Short History of the British Working-Class Movement,* Vol. *III* (London: G. Allen & Unwin Ltd., 1925–1927), p. 22.

underlying them, and taken for granted, was a passionate belief in liberty and democracy. It would never have occurred to most early socialists that socialism had any meaning except within a political framework of freedom for the individual. But since this political assumption is shared by British Conservatives as well as socialists, no further reference is made to it.)

As thus formulated, even these basic aspirations are not all equally relevant to present-day society. Some are expressed in language adapted to conditions that no longer exist, and in particular are too negative in character. This is natural, for they were, in large part, a reaction against the actual results of pre-war capitalism; and with two million unemployed, widespread poverty and malnutrition, and appalling slums set against a background of flamboyant wealth amongst the richer classes, it was natural that the negative desire to abolish evils should outweigh more positive and detailed aspirations.

But to the extent that evils are remedied and injustices removed, negative statements become less and less appropriate. And they are seen to be inappropriate by the electorate, a growing section of which has no recollection of unemployment, or poverty, or dole-queues, and finds Labour propaganda which plays on the themes and memories of the 1930s quite incomprehensible. To a population which has lost its fears, and now has every hope of a rapidly rising standard of living, a negative protest against past wrongs is merely a bore.

Thus even when we go back to the basic aspirations, we still find the same, welcome difficulty that the pace of change has overtaken the doctrine, and a re-formulation is needed. Of course if a Tory Government were to re-create all the old evils, matters would be simple. New thinking could be set aside 'for the duration', and negative statements would again suffice. But it is not likely that the Tories will act so recklessly, or that mere periodic counter-attacks to regain lost positions will remove the need for a map of the new terrain.

How should we re-formulate these aspirations to-day in such a way as to preserve their basic emotional and ethical content, yet discarding what is clearly not germane to present-day conditions? Of the original five, the first and last are rapidly losing their relevance in a British context. Such primary poverty as remains will disappear within a decade, given our present rate of economic growth; and the contemporary mixed economy is characterised by high levels both of employment and productivity and by a reasonable degree of stability. In other words, the aspirations relating to the economic consequences of capitalism are fast losing their relevance as capitalism itself becomes transformed.

But the remaining three more positive ideals, described above as stemming either from a concern with the 'bottom dog', or from a vision of a just, co-operative and classless society, have clearly not been fully realised. No doubt we should phrase them differently to-day, but their basic content is still perfectly relevant. We have plenty of less fortunate citizens still requiring aid; and we certainly have not got an equal or classless society, nor one characterised by 'co-operative' social relations.

III The Co-operative Aspiration

I propose to discuss the co-operative aspiration first, in order to get it out of the way—not because I think its content less important, but simply because I find it impossible to reach a definite conclusion about its relevance in contemporary conditions.

Most people would agree that Britain to-day is a markedly less competitive society than it was a century ago. This is especially true of industry; and it was industrial competition which drew down the strongest strictures of the early anti-competitive socialists. Such competition is now both more limited in extent, and less fierce in character; and business attitudes generally have taken on [a] more restrained and amenable character. . . .

But the change goes wider than this, and reflects a deep-seated change in the accepted ideology—from an uncompromising faith in individualism and self-help to a belief in group action and 'participation', and collective responsibility for social welfare. The consequence is a pronounced tightening of the conventional rules of competitive behaviour. A century ago competition was virtually unrestricted. It justified colonial aggression, child-labour, sweated workshops, violence against labour leaders, a callous ruthlessness towards competitors, and even interference with personal liberty. All these to-day would be excluded from the bounds of what was conventionally, and often legally, permissible. The moral consensus of opinion has altered; and the aggressive instinct has been civilised and circumscribed.

There is now probably no country in the world where competition is less aggressive, or individual exertion more suspect. The worker who exceeds his norm or works too hard, the employer who embarks on a price-offensive, are thought guilty at the least of not playing the game, and probably of flouting the principle of fair shares and showing disloyalty to comrades. To a large extent, security has replaced competition as the guiding rule of economic conduct. At any rate, it could scarcely be denied that the intensity of competition was significantly less.

The *extensive* frontier of competition may, it is true, have widened. But this, ironically, is partly the result of action and pressure by the Left, since it follows from the progressive equalisation of opportunities for advancement. This inevitably increases competition; and indeed the absence of competition for the highest posts is incompatible with democracy, and consistent only with a hierarchical caste or feudal society offering no possibility of social mobility. Thus the antithesis of competition is not always co-operation—it may be social ossification, and the denial of individual rights. This clearly raises an awkward potential conflict of values.

The extent of competition, or at least of the individual pursuit of differential rewards, may have widened in another respect. A century ago it was mainly the entrepreneur whose income fluctuated with individual effort or hard work. But since then . . . there has been a growing tendency for incomes to take the form of differential rewards for differential effort. The purpose of such differentials may be partially frustrated by the counter-force of group solidarity; but their existence must do something to foster individualistic attitudes and the motive of personal gain. But here again there may be a conflict of values, since differentials may be good for economic growth and the standard of living. Once again, the antithesis of competition might be not co-operation, but economic stagnation.

Thus matters look a good deal less clear-cut than when the co-operative ideal was first formulated over a century ago. On the one hand, the excesses of competitive individualism have been significantly moderated; on the other hand, competition is seen to have certain compensating advantages, not previously much discussed. However, let us consider the implications of endeavouring to realise the ideal more fully. There appear to be two spheres in which it might be relevant: personal motives and relations at work.

First, people should work not for private material gain, but for the social good—either because they will then find a greater self-fulfilment and so be more contented, or because they will work better and harder, or simply because it is held to be ethically good that self-regarding instincts should be suppressed, and other-regarding instincts encouraged.

This is partly a factual statement, that people *do* work harder and feel happier if certain incentives are present: and partly a normative statement, that people *should* work for certain motives and not for others. Unfortunately the first is difficult to prove or disprove, and the second hard to express in concrete, practical policies.

It is clear that under the right circumstances the consciousness of working for a common purpose can be an extremely strong incentive, capable of eliciting exceptionally hard and contented work. In British aircraft factories after Dunkirk, in voluntary societies or charitable bodies, in village development schemes in India, or co-operative farms in Israel, people do appear to find a fulfilment and satisfaction in working for a common goal, and in consequence work better, and feel fewer grievances.[3]

But it is equally clear that people can work both well and contentedly for personal material gain under a system where rewards vary with individual effort. This is the case, for example, in a progressive and efficient private firm operating an elaborate system of bonus payments and incentives.

Evidently both motives can, under the right conditions, work extremely

[3] *v.* W. Arthur Lewis, *The Theory of Economic Growth* (Allen and Unwin, 1955), Part III, Chapter 1, for an excellent discussion of this point.

well. So far as the second is concerned, the essential condition in the normal case is probably an efficient management, pursuing an enlightened labour policy. But the difficulty is to create the conditions under which the 'social' motive can operate effectively for more than a short emergency period. It is certainly not enough to tell people that they are working for the public good, nor even that they should in fact be working for the public good. They must see it, and feel it, themselves; and it is not easy to create the institutional framework within which they will.

This may be seen from the experience of nationalisation. The miners and railwaymen are in fact working for the public good as well as for themselves, and for an extremely urgent public good; and there are no shareholders or private profits to 'expropriate' any of the fruits of their labour. Yet this appears to make only a limited psychological difference; and neither industry has a contented atmosphere. This might be a matter of scale and distance. The villager working on a community scheme, and building a new road for his village, can see the result with his own eyes, can see his own personal contribution as being significant, and can see that his own community is in fact deriving the benefit. The miner cannot see the total result of his efforts, which is reflected merely in periodic output figures announced from Hobart House: he may think that his own contribution to the total result is insignificant; and he may be vague as to how the benefits are distributed. Thus he feels, it might be argued, no sense of personal indispensability; the scale is too large, and the distances too remote.

Yet there might, for all we know, be a quite different explanation—that the average miner and railwayman are not sufficiently interested in the public good or the total result. It could plausibly be maintained that in these two industries, much more, for example, than in mass-production factories, the worker is exceptionally well aware of his personal role and contribution—the crew of a train for obvious reasons, and the miner (at least at the face) because of the institution of the checkweighman. Yet this awareness, and such 'social' incentive as may follow from it, may be outweighed by other incentives or emotions—local group solidarity, resentment over wages or conditions, dislike of the local management, disappointment (in the case of the railways) with the form of nationalisation and the performance of the Transport Commission; and so on.

All it seems possible to say in practice is (a) that people can work hard and contentedly for personal (or family) gain,[4] (b) that people can work

[4] Indeed, material incentives for the worker are exceptionally strong to-day, since both the psychological expectation and the physical possibility of rising to an entirely new plateau of consumption, characterised by the ownership of expensive consumers' durable goods and reached with the help of hire-purchase, now exist on a wide scale. So strong are these incentives that Trade Union leaders, who would like to reduce overtime, often cannot persuade their members to forego it.

badly and discontentedly even when they are working for the common good, (c) that no doubt they work best of all when both motives are present, but (d) if it is desired, on moral grounds, to effect a general conversion from self-regarding to other-regarding motives, this will be hard to achieve, since it might require either a change in the basic 'social character' or the creation of a largely novel institutional framework. This conclusion was of course reached at an early stage by the Soviet rulers, who quickly gave up the struggle and simply introduced the old 'capitalist' incentives, under the new label of 'Stakhanovitism', in an extreme and indeed brutal version.

One cannot say that either of these means to a general conversion is strictly impossible, only that they are rather unlikely. A change in social character, altering the underlying balance between self-regarding and other-regarding instincts, cannot, I suppose, be ruled out as a matter of theory. Social anthropology and group psychology have shown that motivation and behaviour are not immutable, or biologically given, but to some (unknown) extent 'culturally' determined. But of course we know too little about the determinants to say anything very useful when it comes to practical policy.

Nor is it much easier to alter the institutional framework in such a way as to give more outlet to *existing* social motives. Clearly public ownership is not enough. We might even require a complete devolution and fragmentation of economic activity down to a local scale. Of course this simply will not happen, and could not work, in an advanced industrial economy. It is not merely that the result would be a catastrophic fall in living standards, but that one cannot turn back history in this way, or reverse the underlying social and technological trends. Some devolution within the present framework is no doubt possible; and enlightened managements, by increasing attention to group activity and to fostering a social spirit, will gradually do something to encourage the desired incentives. But I cannot see what *national* policy a Labour Government could have for inducing a general and deep-seated, as opposed to local and marginal, change in personal motives.

The second sphere in which the co-operative ideal is relevant (though it is closely linked with the first) is that of relations at work. The early socialists wanted people to work, not as separate individuals, but communally and co-operatively, organised in groups (co-operative guilds or communes) inspired with an altruistic collective purpose. To-day, since self-governing guilds are now impracticable, we should no doubt interpret this in terms of joint consultation or joint participation, that is, of groups within a large industrial unit (whether public or private) identified with, and working co-operatively for, the purposes of that unit.

But we now see that the difficulty is often not, as the early socialists thought it would be, to resolve a clash between individual and collective instincts, or to persuade people to form groups and adopt group standards. The human instinct towards gregariousness is so strong that groups form automatically, in industry as elsewhere, and quickly establish their own informal leaders and standards of behaviour.

The difficulty is that these natural, self-created groups may be far from expressing the co-operative ideal. It is not merely that groups may develop (as anyone with experience of small political or religious or refugee groups will know) extremely disagreeable characteristics—intolerance of dissent, excessive conformity, arbitrary cruelty in the exercise of their ultimate power to ostracise (in modern language, send to Coventry): but even if they do not, their purpose and function may be in no way communal or altruistic so far as objectives and institutions *outside* the group are concerned. On the contrary, their function and behaviour may be wholly selfish, and the element of identification or co-operation with the firm or industry entirely lacking. Thus they may, as industrial research has demonstrated, serve to restrict output, not to expand it: to worsen relations with management, not to improve them: to foster resentment and discontent, instead of harmony and a sense of common purpose.

The problem is to harness the group instinct in such a way as to create the desired social and co-operative atmosphere—to cause the natural groups to identify themselves with the larger unit in which they work. Unfortunately we scarcely know in detail how this is to be done. It does not follow automatically either from nationalisation, as the mines and the railways show, or from setting up joint consultation, which may simply impose a formal and rootless group on top of, and at cross-purposes with, the real groups below.

Indeed if we examine industry, we find a bewildering variety of experience which makes it exceedingly hard to draw conclusions. We can find firms with a loyal and contented labour force, yet with no formal 'participation' of any kind: others with elaborate schemes of joint consultation, yet with a sullen, unhappy labour force: and yet others where good relations do seem to depend on the existence of joint bodies. All we can say is that institutional change by itself is not enough: and that whether joint participation does or does not create a co-operative atmosphere depends on social forces on the exact nature of which industrial psychologists are not agreed —at any rate not to the extent that any clear national policy emerges.

This does not mean, of course, that there is no case for altering relations within industry, or for giving the worker more power. There is such a case. But it rests not on propositions about fraternity or social contentment, which our present knowledge does not justify, but on statements about social justice, the rights of workers, and equality. It is therefore subsumed, and so discussed in later chapters, under the aspiration towards social equality.

To sum up, the co-operative aspiration has at least been partially fulfilled, in that society is much less aggressively individualistic and competitive than a century ago; and indeed the trend toward 'sociability' is now so strong that we are more likely to be deprived of solitude than company.

On the other hand we do not yet live in a co-operative Utopia. Most people still work mainly for personal gain, and not for the social good; and the ideal of communal, co-operative participation has scarcely begun to be realised in industry.

Now there are one or two specific directions in which a clear choice exists between more or less competition—most notably in education.... There are one or two further directions in which a less clear choice exists between more or less communal activity, e.g. housing development and town planning. Furthermore, the *sense* of co-operation in industry may spread as management grows more progressive and enlightened; and a gradual increase in equality will itself . . . still further diminish the intensity of competition. But beyond this, at our present state of knowledge, we cannot go. We cannot assert definitely what would be the effect either on personal contentment, or attitudes to work, or the quality of our society, of a wholesale effort to suppress the motive of personal gain, or to elevate collective at the expense of individual relationships: nor can we even begin to see a feasible institutional framework within which these changes could be brought about: nor can we be sure that even if they were practicable, they might not lead to serious losses in other directions, such as privacy, individuality, personal independence, equality of opportunity, or the standard of living.

While, therefore, I realise that as a matter of verbal precision the co-operative ideal is certainly embraced by the word 'socialism', and while I accept that it would clearly be in some sense 'better' if there were a more general awareness of a common social purpose, I do not feel able, in what is intended to be a reasonably definite and practical statement of socialist aims, to include this as part of the goal. I shall no doubt be corrected by those with clearer views.

IV The Welfare and Equality Aspirations

The two remaining aspirations—the concern with social welfare, and the desire for an equal and classless society—still have a perfectly clear relevance. The first implies an acceptance of collective responsibility and an extremely high priority for the relief of social distress or misfortune, in contrast to the much lower priority which it would receive in a 'free' economy guided mainly by an individualistic philosophy. This is the contemporary version of the traditional welfare and social-service philosophy of the Labour movement, and of the instinct to side automatically with the less fortunate and those in need.

There is plenty of residual social distress in Britain. It is now caused less by primary poverty, though this can still be found, than by secondary poverty, natural misfortune, physical or mental illness, the decline in the size of the family, sudden fluctuations in income, and deficiencies in social capital. These last, for all the high level of average personal spending, are still appalling—ugly towns, mean streets, slum houses, overcrowded schools, inadequate hospitals, under-staffed mental institutions, too few homes for the aged, indeed a general, and often squalid, lack of social amenities.

The relief of this distress and the elimination of this squalor is the main object of social expenditure; and a socialist is identified as one who wishes to give this an exceptional priority over other claims on resources. This is not a matter of the overall vertical equality of incomes; the arguments are humanitarian and compassionate, not egalitarian. It is a matter of priorities in the distribution of the national output, and a belief that the first priority should always be given to the poor, the unfortunate, the 'have-nots', and generally to those in need; from which follows a certain view about collective social responsibility, and thence about the role of the state and the level of taxation. This represents the first major difference between a socialist and a conservative.

The second distinctive socialist ideal is social equality and the 'classless society'. The socialist seeks a distribution of rewards, status, and privileges egalitarian enough to minimise social resentment, to secure justice between individuals, and to equalise opportunities; and he seeks to weaken the existing deep-seated class stratification, with its concomitant feelings of envy and inferiority, and its barriers to uninhibited mingling between the classes. This belief in social equality, which has been the strongest ethical inspiration of virtually every socialist doctrine, still remains the most characteristic feature of socialist thought to-day.

1956

28 On the Economic Theory of Socialism

BENJAMIN E. LIPPINCOTT

I

Whatever may be the explanation for the widespread belief that socialism is impracticable, we are concerned here with whether or not socialism is workable from the economic angle. The problem of a socialist economy is twofold. First, will the authorities of a socialist economy dictate what products consumers shall buy or will consumers dictate to the authorities, as is the case more or less under capitalism? In more technical language, will there be free consumers' choice? Secondly, can resources be put to work so that the most will be made of them, that is, can resources be economized? In more technical language, is a rational allocation of resources possible in a socialist economy?

The first problem is, of course, easily solved; a socialist economy by definition presupposes free consumers' choice. A socialist economy in the classical sense is one that socializes production alone, as contrasted with communism, which socializes both production and consumption. The contributors to this volume, Taylor and Lange, deal with a socialist economy in the classical sense. Both assume freedom of choice in consumption and freedom of choice in occupation. Therefore, it naturally follows for these writers that the preferences of consumers, as expressed by their demand prices (the prices they are prepared to pay for a product), are the guiding criteria of production, and ultimately of the allocation of resources. Thus the citizens of a socialist state will virtually dictate what commodities the authorities shall produce, and in substantially the same way as the citizens of a capitalist state dictate what private industry shall produce.

The solution of the second problem is much more difficult; in fact, the problem of a rational allocation of resources is the central problem of socialist economics. In order to solve this problem a knowledge of the relative (or comparative) importance of the primary factors of production, such as land, minerals, water power, and various kinds of labor services, is crucial. At bottom the problem of a rational allocation of resources is one of valuation, of ascertaining the relative economic significance of the primary factors of production. We must be able to valuate these factors, even though

SOURCE: from Lange, Oskar, and Taylor, Fred. *On the Economic Theory of Socialism,* edited by B. E. Lippincott. University of Minnesota Press, Minneapolis.

it cannot be done very accurately, if we are to make calculations in regard to them. Economic calculation is necessary if the most appropriate use is to be made of scarce resources.

...In his notable essay, "The Ministry of Production in the Collectivist State," written in 1908, Barone * proved that in principle the accounting prices of a socialist economy would be as economically significant as the market prices of a competitive economy. By a mathematical demonstration using simultaneous equations, Barone, following suggestions of Pareto, was the first to demonstrate that it was possible for a socialist economy to make a rational allocation of resources. His analysis showed, moreover, the great formal similarity of a socialist regime to a competitive one; indeed, he maintained that production in a socialist regime would be ordered in substantially the same way as it was in a competitive one. Barone's paper was pathfinding. And apparently it served to turn the flank of the attack of orthodox economics.

Professors Hayek and Robbins of the London School of Economics, who next to Mises are the leading opponents of socialism among economists, have apparently been influenced by Barone. They have taken up a second line of attack, the line that is usually taken after a principle has been admitted. They admit that a rational allocation of resources is theoretically possible in a socialist state, but deny that it can be worked out in practice. They insist that in order to determine prices the Central Planning Board of a socialist state would have to have "complete lists of the different quantities of all commodities which would be bought at any possible combination of prices of the different commodities that might be available." They also argue that the Central Planning Board would have to solve thousands, even millions, of calculations—simultaneous equations—before economic decisions could be taken, and with any means known at present these calculations could not be solved in a lifetime.

"The Guidance of Production in a Socialist State," ... provides in substance the answer to the contention of Hayek and Robbins. Written by the late Professor Fred M. Taylor in 1928, before Hayek and Robbins had made their attack, this is the first writing to mark an advance on Barone's contribution. Though Barone indicated that it was possible to solve the calculations necessary to a rational allocation of resources in a socialist economy by a method of trial and error, he did not show how such a method could be carried out.

It was left to Taylor to point this out. The crucial problem is to determine the relative importance (what Taylor calls the "effective importance") of the primary factors of production. According to Taylor, the relative importance of each primary factor is derived from and determined by the importances of the innumerable commodities which emerge from the whole complex of

* An Italian economist.—Ed.

productive processes. The question is, how in a concrete way is the relative importance of each factor determined? Taylor's answer is that a provisional valuation, in terms of money, would be assigned to each factor. The managers of the socialist industries would then carry on their operations as if the provisional valuations were absolutely correct.

Then, if the authorities had assigned a valuation to any particular factor which was too high or too low, that fact would be disclosed in unmistakable ways. If too high an evaluation had been assigned, causing the authorities to be unduly economical in the use of that factor, a physical surplus would show at the end of the productive period. If too low an evaluation had been assigned, leading the authorities to be too lavish in the use of that factor, a deficit would show. Surplus or deficit—one or the other would result from every wrong valuation of a factor. By successive trials the correct valuation for each factor, showing its relative importance, could be found. In other words, by a method of trial and error the correct accounting price for each factor could be ascertained.

Lange, writing after Hayek and Robbins had made their attack, answers them directly, using Taylor's analysis as the basis of his argument. He shows their position to be unreal by pointing out that the method of trial and error for determining accounting prices in a socialist economy would be substantially the same as that by which prices are actually determined on a competitive market. The Central Planning Board, he says, would not need to have, as Hayek seems to think, complete lists of the different quantities of all commodities which would be bought at any possible combination of prices of the different quantities which might be available. "Neither would the Central Planning Board have to solve hundreds of thousands of equations. The only 'equations' which would have to be 'solved' would be those of the consumers and the managers of production. These are exactly the same 'equations' which are solved in the present economic system and the persons who do the 'solving' are the same also.... And only a few of them have been graduated in higher mathematics. Professor Hayek and Professor Robbins 'solve' at least hundreds of equations daily, for instance, in buying a newspaper or in deciding to take a meal in a restaurant, and presumably they do not use determinates or Jacobians for the purpose."

Thus Lange argues that neither mathematics nor a knowledge of the demand and supply functions is needed in finding out the "right" accounting prices. The "right" accounting prices are "simply found by watching the quantities demanded and the quantities supplied and by raising the price of a commodity or service whenever there is an excess of demand over supply and lowering it whenever the reverse is the case, until, by trial and error, the price is found at which demand and supply are in balance." It may be remarked that it is important to arrive at, or approximate, this "right" (equilibrium) price in order that there is neither a misdirection of resources and waste on the producer's (the supply) side, nor a maldistribution of wants on the consumer's (the demand) side.

• • •

II

. . . there is nothing inherent in a socialist economy that requires an autocratic system of government, nor that would impair democracy. On the contrary, a socialist economy is far more in harmony with democracy than is a capitalist.

The genius of democracy, Matthew Arnold observed, is equality; by this he meant that the thrust of democracy is toward the removal of privilege, of artificial inequalities that cannot be justified in terms of the common welfare. The privilege that exists today in democratic states is based largely on wealth, and rests at bottom on capitalist arrangements, on the private ownership of the means of production. A socialist economy would eliminate the privilege that arises from wealth, since it stands for an equal distribution of income. Democracy's aim is to govern in the interests of the whole community; therefore democracy stands, in principle, for the satisfaction of necessities before luxuries. A socialist economy stands for this same principle, for equality in the distribution of income means that needs will be satisfied in proportion to their urgency.

If equality is a fundamental characteristic of democracy, so also is liberty. In this regard also a socialist economy is more in harmony with democracy than a capitalist, for, with a more equal distribution of income, free consumer's choice would be still freer. Where many under a capitalist economy must choose between a coat and a pair of shoes, under a socialist many could choose between a radio and a telephone.

It will doubtless be argued that public ownership of a great segment of industry is the high road to dictatorship. The corollary of this argument is that private ownership is a bulwark against tyranny. The immediate comment on these arguments must be that the form of property ownership of itself, whether public or private, neither promotes nor hinders freedom. What is crucial is the character of the authority which administers it, or the way in which the property is controlled.

Under feudal arrangements, private ownership went hand in hand with a local tyranny that was only mitigated by the rise of monarchy and the establishment of a central power. The lesson of this change is that a central authority, even though autocratic, proved to be less arbitrary locally than private autocracy. At the present time the very place where tyranny exists in democratic states is in privately owned industry; here power is exercised autocratically and often ruthlessly. To be sure, private ownership of the means of production prevents government from tyrannizing over industry;

at the same time, it enables industry to dominate government and to tyrannize over workers. In view of this condition of things, government ownership of basic industry carried out by a democratic government offers a means of taking autocracy out of industry.

The reason men resort to public ownership is for the purpose of obtaining more responsible action. Toll roads, for example, were abolished because private management broke down. Government ownership and management of roads, it may be observed, has led to greater freedom, and government ownership and management of the postal service and electrical power has hardly led to tyranny. It is perfectly true that the administration of an industry, like the administration of a social service such as the department of health, must be organized to a considerable extent on the autocratic principle. But the socialization of industry under a democracy would mean that the autocratic principle would be tempered by the introduction of democratic methods of assuring responsible action and by the establishment of decent working conditions. It goes without saying that the democratic methods introduced must be compatible with efficiency.

Democratizing administrative authority in industry would involve bringing in constitutional ways of life for whole industries and effective consultation between workers and management. To consult men who live under and feel the results of rules and administrative action, to attach importance to their experience in this regard, and to represent it appropriately in the bodies that frame the rules which affect them must raise the moral tone and the morale of the whole working community. A socialized industry would work in an atmosphere of publicity; records would be open to the public. Few things would make for responsibility more surely than this. Where industry is publicly owned, measurement, however rough, is possible; this would make for efficiency as well as for responsibility.

In a socialized state industry would become a profession; that is, for positions requiring special training a show of qualification would be demanded of applicants, and openings would be filled on the competitive principle. A man's personnel record and not, as is so frequently the case today, the influence of his friends or the personality of his property would determine his position and responsibility. And this would be the case not only for entrance into positions but also for advancement. Thus in the socialized industries, as in the professions, the setting of standards would be a means of discovering excellence, and the existence of standards would act as a check on personal power. And in all positions a personnel policy that made room for flexibility would be substituted for a personal policy.

It will probably be argued that a Central Planning Board involves a dangerous concentration of power. There can be no doubt that the Central Planning Board would exercise great power, but would it be any greater than that exercised collectively by private boards of directors? Because the decisions of private boards are made here and there, this does not mean that the consumer does not feel their collective impact, even though it may take a depression to make him aware of it. The problem is not the form of the power, but whether it is exercised responsibly. There is reason to believe that it could be exercised more responsibly under a Central Planning Board than under private industry, for the first would operate with greater knowledge. Government has unrivaled access to the facts and unrivaled resources for their collection.

Nor would the Central Planning Board be the sovereign authority of the state. If it were not made up of members of the executive, which might be the best solution, it would be appointed by the executive and directly responsible to it. However it might be composed and appointed, it would be responsible to the legislature for general policy. Associated with the Central Planning Board would be a technical staff which would report on resources, supplies, deficits, and prices and carry on research and suggest economic policies. It would be removed, within reasonable limits, from political influence, that is, its chiefs would be semi-permanent, appointed by the executive for a ten- or fifteen-year period always with the possibility of renewal of the appointment. Nor would the Central Planning Board and its technical staff do all the planning. This function would to a great extent be decentralized. There would be regional and local planning boards and technical staffs. The Central Planning Board would co-ordinate data and plans of the subordinate boards; it would suggest to the executive plans for the economy as a whole.

Lange's discussion of income distribution is especially instructive for socialist writers who approach the problem of reward from the social and ethical angle. He fully appreciates, of course, the socialist stand for equality of income; that equality is essential if the demands of different consumers for commodities at the same price are to represent an equal urgency of need. At the same time he shows that a practical solution must involve an element of inequality; that a differential in remuneration is necessary if labor services are to be apportioned in the most advantageous way economically. Lange presents, as we saw above, an ingenious solution for this apparent conflict in principle. His solution enables the socialist's insistence on equality to be satisfied, and the demand of the economist that there be an equilibrium between the marginal productivity of labor and the relative marginal disutility of work.*

It would seem that Lange is right in holding that bureaucracy is the real danger in a socialist economy. The chief danger is, as with any large-scale organization, whether public or private, a resistance to novelty, an aversion to innovation. That a socialist industry would work in a climate

* The principle involved here is that labor be so apportioned among the different occupations that the value of the marginal product of labor equal the marginal disutility involved in the pursuit of these occupations. Hence leisure, safety, and the agreeableness of work are included in the scales of utility for the individual.—Ed.

of publicity, consultation, criticism, and measurement would make it more amenable than private monopoly to experiment, though special effort would still have to be made to maintain flexibility and openness to new ideas. As Frank Knight has said, the problem of a socialist economy is not an economic problem but a political and sociological one.

Socialists often say that a socialist economy would eliminate the enormous waste that characterizes capitalism. It seems reasonable to hold that a socialist economy could avoid a considerable amount of the waste that occurs under capitalism, yet it could hardly avoid waste. Nor should it strive to do so, for there is such a thing as necessary waste; that which is the product of experiment. As Barone pointed out, a socialist economy must experiment and therefore must incur waste, else it will be impossible to determine whether the best use is being made of available resources. And unless this is done the standard of living cannot be raised.

Lange's discussion of the problem of transition from a capitalist to a socialist economy would seem to be irrefutable, and should compel socialists and communists to rethink their stock notions. His suggestion for a labor plan, which seems to reflect the experience of Sweden, might make possible the achievement of that rare thing in history—a fundamental change in political control, or in class relations, without a conflict.

1938

29 Why We Need Socialism in America

MICHAEL HARRINGTON

America needs socialism. Our technology has produced unprecedented wealth, rotted great cities, threatened the very air and water, and embittered races, generations, and social classes.

Our vision of society, even when most liberal, is too conservative to resolve these contradictions, for they are aspects of a system that has a deep, even principled commitment to the wrong priorities. And while significant reforms—often socialist in inspiration—have modified some of the extreme forms of capitalist injustice, the post-Keynesian welfare state

SOURCE: from "Why We Need Socialism in America" by Michael Harrington, *Dissent,* May–June 1970, pp. 240–242, 253–258, 262–268, 273–274, 280–287.

still allows huge corporations to make decisions of fundamental social importance without consulting either those who are affected or those who work for them.

But isn't it an act of leftist nostalgia to indict American society in this way?* Today, one is told, the United States is the richest country in the history of mankind, and its remaining problems can be taken care of by pragmatic technicians acting within the framework of the welfare state.

It is precisely this conventional assumption about our present and future that I propose to challenge. I will show that our affluence is so misshapen that it does not even meet the needs of the majority of the people. The most humane of technocrats cannot cope with the basic causes of these anti-social policies, if only because they are located in an entrenched and possessive system of power. Only a democratic mass movement could challenge this vested interest in our current crises. And it is just possible that the "success" of American capitalism will accomplish what its sweat-shops failed to do: make socialism politically relevant.

I say these things with a full knowledge of the ways in which the socialist idea has been confused, betrayed, and eviscerated during the past 150 years. Indeed, one of the aims of this essay is to try to face up to these difficulties with candor and to make the idea of socialism more precise. If that attempt is successful, what will emerge at the end of this study will not be the promise of a magical cure-all to bring complete and eternal happiness to all men but a more modest yet still audacious program for making America a good society.

I Is Reform of the Welfare State Enough?

There are three basic reasons why the reform of the welfare state will not solve our most urgent problems:

1. The class structure of capitalist society vitiates, or subverts, almost every such effort toward social justice.
2. Private, corporate power cannot tolerate the comprehensive and democratic planning we desperately need.
3. And even if these first two obstacles to providing every citizen with a decent house, income, and job were overcome, the system still has an inherent tendency to make affluence self-destructive.

In thus documenting the limits of the welfare state it may seem that I am contemptuous of past reforms or of those liberals who do not share my

* This essay is confined to developing the case for socialism in the United States. That does not for a moment mean that the rest of the world doesn't matter, or that America's problems can be solved in isolation from the fate of the globe. These international dimensions of socialism are of the utmost importance and are treated at length in *Socialism: Past, Present and Future,* which also contains much of the material presented here.

conviction that there must be fundamental, structural change. Nothing could be further from the truth. The welfare state was an enormous advance over the cruelty and indifference to human suffering that characterized early capitalism. It was achieved through struggle and great sacrifice—sometimes of life itself—on the part of "ordinary" people who, even though they had usually been denied an adequate education, tutored the wealthy in some of the fundamentals of social decency. And to the extent that there is a mass "left wing" in the United States, it is composed largely of precisely those groups—trade unionists, minorities, middle-class idealists—which fought these great battles and are determined to preserve the gains they brought.

Far from being simply a matter of keeping the record straight, this point has profound political implications for the future. It is important that socialists demonstrate the inherent inability of the welfare state, based as it is upon a capitalist economy and social structure, to deal with problems that demand anticapitalist allocations of resources. But that does not mean, as some young leftists in recent times have thought, that the welfare state is to be dismissed as a "fraud" that prevents the people from coming to truly radical conclusions. For if millions of Americans are to become socialists they will do so because, in the struggle to make that welfare state respond to their immediate needs they will have discovered that they must go beyond it. If socialists were arrogantly to dismiss these battles as irrelevant, they would play no role when masses of their fellow citizens turned left.

Socialists, then, must be in the forefront of every fight to defend and extend the welfare state, even as they criticize its inability to solve fundamental problems and even as they propose alternatives to it. In this context, the following analysis of the severe limits capitalism imposes upon the welfare state is designed not to prove that liberals are foolish and deluded, but that their liberal values can only be completely realized on the basis of a socialist program.

The welfare state, for all its value, tends to provide benefits in inverse relationship to human need. And not—the point is crucial—because there is a conspiracy of the affluent, but as a "natural" consequence of the division of society into unequal social classes.

Through vigorous and radical reforms it is possible to offset—though not to remove—this inherent tendency within capitalist society to distribute public benefits according to the inequalities of private wealth. Any movement that attempts to carry out such reforms will be going against the grain of the system itself. This has not kept socialists from participating in every one of these struggles, nor will it in the future. But if the gains are to be permanent, if they are not to be reversed when a period of social innovation is followed by a swing back to capitalist normality, then there must be basic, structural changes. Instead of episodic victories within an antisocial environment, there must be a concerted effort to create a new human environment.

• • •

II The Face of Socialism

Classical Marxism offered a powerful argument of the objective need for a new society; it recognized the role of the working class as the conscious agency that was to lead humanity in the desired social transition; but about the content of the desired future, the substance of what socialism would be, it had little to say. That was unfortunate.

There were, to be sure, good reasons why Marx adopted this attitude. The Germany of the 1840s had more than its share of lofty and irrelevant blueprints for utopia; Marx saw no need to add still another. His profoundly democratic realism led him to argue that the good society would be fashioned, not by the dictates of some intellectual's plan, but according to the needs and creativity of the people themselves. In the bitter struggles that have occurred since Marx first formulated his position, the working-class movement, upon which he rested his main hopes, has indeed made significant modifications in the structure of such capitalist institutions as the factory and the state. But if there was good reason for Marx to refrain from speaking precisely about the face of socialism, there is no such reason today. We have seen too many tyrannical distortions of the socialist ideal; we have come to realize that socialism is not the "inevitable" successor to capitalism and that, indeed, there can be successors at least as inhumane and reactionary as the worst capitalist society. Hence anyone who says he believes in socialism must make plain what he means by it.

In Marx's view history was not predetermined; there was no "inevitable" upward curve of progress. The class struggle within capitalist society, he said, could lead to socialism—or to barbarism. The latter Marx saw as a stalemate, "the common ruin of the contending classes," which would keep the contradictions of society from being resolved on a new and higher plane.[1] In his comments on the "Asiatic mode of production" he even described a system in which state control of a decisive means of production (water in an economy based on irrigation) could provide the basis for a kind of bureaucratic class rule.[2] Yet Marx did not anticipate that a sort of anti-socialist "socialism" could be the successor to capitalism in one third of the world, or that capitalism itself could become planned and rationalized for an entire historical period.

[1] Karl Marx, *The Communist Manifesto*, quoted here from Karl Marx and Friedrich Engels, *Werke* (Berlin: Dietz Verlag, 1960–) 4:462. Cited hereafter as *MEW*.

[2] Karl Marx, *Pre-Capitalist Economic Formations*, Eric Hobsbawm, ed. (New York: International Publishers, 1966). See also Karl Wittfogel, *Oriental Despotism* (New Haven: Yale University Press, 1957).

Collectivism—but What Kind?

But Marx did clearly assert a basic value judgment that makes it possible to distinguish socialism from other forms of collectivism. Nationalization of industry, planning, cooperative production—all these, he insisted, were only means to an end. The crucial question about such techniques and institutions are: who employs them and according to what priorities? If the state owns the means of production, we must then ask, who owns the state? And there is only one way for the people to "own" the state which owns the means of production: through the exercise of their democratic right to determine its policies and personnel.

For capitalism it is "natural" to assign resources where there will be the greatest commercial return, and without regard for social consequence. For socialism, by contrast, it is "natural" to allocate them on the basis of human need as democratically determined. As a group of independent French leftists have put it, "By socialism . . . one means a global conception of man and the world which seeks to substitute the principle of conscious solidarity for the traditional resort to domination and private interest in the organization and functioning of society."[3] If this solidarity does not suffuse the new institutions, then it is possible to nationalize all the means of production, to plan the economy meticulously and yet to end up, not with democratic socialism, but with a new and oppressive form of class society.

The Port Authority in New York City is a useful example of such an antisocial collectivism. Originally it was given considerable autonomy in order to take it out of "politics." Even though it was designed to be high-minded and serve the public, and even though there are no private owners, it acts at least as irresponsibly as any private corporation. As Theodore Kheel has described the Port Authority:

> It has preferred to grow huge—and hugely profitable—by catering to motorists. Without even the flimsy justification of acting in the interests of stockholders—it has none—the Port Authority pursues money, not service, with the arrogance, indifference and contempt for the public welfare characteristic of nineteenth-century robber barons.[4]

And then, in a perceptive statement of the kind of economic calculation that should rule in a publicly-owned enterprise, Kheel writes:

> Austin J. Tobin, executive director [of the Port Authority] for 27 years, once said, "Above all else, the people expect their officials to give them prudent and conservative management of public funds." That is disingenuous. Public servants are expected to manage public funds as conservatively as their essential purpose

[3] "Claude Bruclain" [pseudonym for a group of members of the Club Jean Moulin], *Le Socialisme et L'Europe* (Paris: Le Seuil, 1965), p. 56.

[4] Theodore Kheel, "How the Port Authority is Strangling New York," *New York,* November 17, 1969.

permits. A seemingly unprofitable venture, such as helping mass transportation, might be more genuinely productive than any seemingly self-supporting service the Port Authority has yet turned its hand to—and ultimately would cost us far less.

The Port Authority in New York, like many of the nationalized industries in Europe, shows that public ownership in and of itself, especially within the framework of an economy still basically capitalist, is no guarantee that a corporation will follow social priorities. It behaves exactly like the capitalist enterprises that surround it. This would not be the case under socialism—even though such a society would still have to take costs and alternate uses of resources into account. Karl Kautsky, who prided himself on his Marxian orthodoxy, argued that accounting, and even interest, would exist in socialist undertakings, and he opposed the notion that the omnipotent state would simply command the economy to produce this or that good.[5] There is now a voluminous literature on this subject. Socialist planning would seek to get as precise a measure of costs as possible; yet an investment would not be made simply because it could bring a high return and in spite of its social cost, as is the case under capitalism; nor would totalitarian bureaucrats ruthlessly sacrifice the present needs of the masses in order to build up heavy industry and a war machine, as under Communism.

In the following attempt to make a rough outline of socialist institutions, the point will be to describe how the contradictions of capitalist society can be resolved so that the needs of the people, as they themselves democratically determine them, are met. But in imagining this future it is obviously not enough to invent "ideal" solutions. We begin with the specific problems that have just been identified, and within a context established by capitalism where resources are limited and choices have to be made. Then, after having described the social classes and strata which need such innovations and can become politically conscious of this fact, we come to an ultimate vision of socialism. This ultimate vision assumes that the basic material desires of the people have been satisfied and productivity has grown to such an extent that man can free himself from the psychology and economics of scarcity. That more distant future will be the subject of the last section of this essay.

In making this distinction between the immediate transition to socialism and the final goal, I am using a necessary if somewhat dangerous idea. Marx had insisted that the new society would be conceived within the womb of the old and therefore would be born with the heritage of the past as well as with the hopes of the future. He contended that only when men had learned to live cooperatively through a long experience and abundance was an economic fact, the old bourgeois limits could be transcended and society inscribe on its banner, "From each according to his talents, to each accord-

[5] Karl Kautsky, *The Labour Revolution*, trans. H. J. Stenning (London: Allen & Unwin, 1925).

ing to his needs."[6] But precisely this theory of the two stages of socialism was used by Joseph Stalin to justify murder and totalitarianism.[7] Whenever the injustices and oppressions of Soviet society were attacked, Stalin could reply that this was, after all, only the first and "imperfect" phase of the transition to the millennium. Yet long after Stalin died, and more than half a century after the Bolshevik Revolution, the "temporary" institutions of anti-freedom are still basic to Russian society.

If it is indeed impossible to take a single, giant stride into utopia, one surely cannot arrive at a society of brotherhood by way of gradual terror and coercion. So, if the changes in capitalist structure that are proposed in the following pages are only transitional, they must also move in the direction of the ultimate vision of socialism. They cannot, as under Communism, be the very antithesis of it.

For Socialization of Investment

First of all—and this is urgent, practical politics within the present confines of capitalism as well as a step toward socialism—investment must be socialized.

There are, as has just been seen, huge and decisive areas of economic life in which private capital will not invest because there is no prospect of sufficient profitability (or, what amounts to the same thing, where antisocial allocations are more profitable than social ones). This is true of the fundamental determinants of the urban environment, such as housing and transportation. Therefore, the society must shift resources from the privately profitable sector of the economy to the socially necessary. This decision can be made only by government and must be taken only as a result of a democratic process. It can be accomplished only on a national scale and within the framework of planning.

I do not mean to say that the housing design or the exact mix of public and private transport will be settled by a ukase from Washington. A qualitative increase in the rate of social spending can be channeled through the most diverse kinds of organizations: through departments of national, regional, and local government, public corporations, cooperatives, private nonprofit institutions, neighborhood associations, and so on. A progressive income tax, nationally administered, is the only source of funds for such a gigantic appropriation, and the various regional and local choices—where to build a new city, for instance—have to be integrated into a national plan.

John Strachey, the late British socialist theorist, thought that such a

[6] Karl Marx, *Kritik des Gothaer Programms,* in *MEW,* 19:20 ff.

[7] See, e.g., the attack on equality in "New Conditions, New Tasks in Economic Construction; June 23, 1931," Joseph Stalin, *Works* (Moscow: Foreign Language Publishing House, 1955), 13:59.

process of transforming "the social form taken by accumulation into a consciously set-aside fund" was the "essence of the transition to socialism." [8] That is, as will be seen, an overly optimistic assessment of this development, since more than investment must be socialized. Yet it does emphasize the fact that federal planning and Congressional appropriation could be one way of directing production for use rather than profit.

In areas such as housing and transportation, this program obviously requires much more than simply the spending of money. For even conservatives have come to realize that government programs have to be coordinated: the Nixon administration talks of a national urban policy and uses five-year projections in its 1970 Budget. The National Commission on Urban Problems (chaired by the liberal economist Paul Douglas) recommended that

> the President and his Economic Advisers, the Federal Reserve Board, the Treasury Department, and other major agencies of government be required to state what effect any major change in economic policy [e.g. interest-rate changes, tax reductions or increases, balance of payments proposals] would have on the successful building of the number of housing units set by the President in his annual housing construction goal message.[9]

All these suggestions, the liberal as well as the conservative, assume the continuation of the present structure of the housing "industry"—if so modern a word can be used to describe so backward a sector. Yet the government will fail in its commitments unless it creates a new industry. New cities cannot be built by a myriad of private developers, each making his own decisions about a small parcel of real estate. The present procedure of clearing areas that are already urban and then turning them over to profit-seekers has indeed had the disastrous effect of subtracting from the housing supply, increasing the rent on existing, inadequate dwellings, and in general making life more miserable for the poor and minorities. There must consequently be a social land bank, a new technology, an industry created to modern scale, and to national and regional plans. And that will take more ingenuity than just writing a federal check.

It All Must Be Done Democratically

This one case could be duplicated in every other area of social need, and it points up the second socialist proposal for changing our institutional structure: that decisive investments must be democratically planned as well as financially socialized.

There should be an Office of the Future in the White House. Each year

[8] John Strachey, *Contemporary Capitalism* (New York: Random House, 1965), p. 243.
[9] National Commission on Urban Problems, *Building the American City: Report,* p. 182.

the President should make a Report on the Future—with projections ranging 5, 10, or even 20 years ahead—which would be submitted to a Joint Congressional Committee where it would be debated, amended and then presented to the entire Congress for decision. This process should establish the broad priorities of the society and annually monitor the result of past efforts. It would be, for instance, the proper forum where the broad concept of regional planning would be established; but it would not engage in the actual planning of individual projects.

At this point, let me say, a candid admission is in order. The changes outlined in the previous paragraph could be welcomed by social engineers determined to impose their values on the people. They might even be used by sophisticated corporate leaders to make the status quo more rational and stable. And they might create an entrenched bureaucracy with a self-interest of its own. The critics of socialism who cite such dangers ignore, or conceal, the fact that these are the consequence of the complexity of *all forms* of modern, technological society and that socialism is the only movement which seeks to offer a structural and democratic challenge to that trend. Even more important, it must be understood that there is no institutional reform which, in and of itself, can "guarantee" genuine popular participation. Only a vibrant movement of the people can do that. That is why socialists do not foresee an ultimate stage of human existence in which all conflicts are resolved. In the very best of societies both the democratic majority and the critical minority must be on the alert.

There is, however, one important area where planning is made more simple because of tendencies within the economy itself. The dominant trend of this century is to move economic activity away from primary pursuits, such as agriculture, and even away from industry, into areas like service and education. This is one of the reasons why college expenditures have increased faster than has GNP since 1950, and that school teaching has been one of the fastest-growing professions.[10]

A great many of the areas thereby expanded have been traditionally public or private nonprofit: schools, hospitals, social services, and the like. A 1970 analysis in *Fortune* has even suggested that it is impossible for the nation to achieve its health goals unless there is an even greater increase in the employment of paraprofessionals.[11] When there was a renewal of social consciousness in the sixties, the corporations began to move into these new markets and designed various human care programs according to the logic of profit. Yet education, health, and personal problems are obviously antagonistic to commercialism, for these are spheres in which one should not stint in order to cut costs and increase the return. The only humane criterion

[10] Christopher Jencks and David Riesman, *The Academic Revolution* (Garden City, N.Y.: Doubleday, 1968), p. 111.
[11] Dan Cordtz, "Change Begins in the Doctor's Office," *Fortune,* January 1970.

is that of need, and these growth "industries" are therefore natural candidates for social investment.

• • •

III Images of the Future

The question of exactly how ownership is to be socialized is another area of difficulty in the socialist tradition. Vague metaphors—the state will "seize" or "take over" the means of production—provide no guide for political action in a complex, technological economy.

The nineteenth-century socialists were deeply confused about the status of ownership in the society they sought. There was one tradition, with origins in Saint-Simon, that emphasized state action, planning, and socialized investment; there was another, represented by Fourier and Proudhon, that envisioned communes and free associations carrying on production; and Marx, to complicate matters, borrowed from both lines of thought. As time went on, it became clear that the very complexity of a modern economy required that social property function within a context controlled by the state.

Yet this does not mean that the government should simply "take over" the giant enterprises. As Otto Bauer put it after World War I,

> If the government controlled as many undertakings as possible, it would be too powerful as against the people and the popular assembly; such an increase in government power would be dangerous to democracy. At the same time, the government would be a bad administrator of socialized industry; nobody manages undertakings worse than the state. For this reason we have never advocated the nationalization of industry but always its socialization.[12]

How prescient Bauer's insight was can be seen from our recent American experience, as well as from our current understanding of the sources of creativity within the corporation. There is a quite successful model in this country of what a public corporation can accomplish: the Tennessee Valley Authority. Like a private corporation, the TVA is able to accumulate capital for future investment out of present income; yet it is under the broad supervision of the federal government in Washington. (It is also under constant attack by private power industry, which cannot tolerate this demonstration of how a government-chartered enterprise can be more efficient, and produce cheaper power, than the private sector.) Moreover, in 1969 the TVA proposed an innovation in an important area of social need by coming forth with plans for an integrated new town and by pointing out that its compre-

[12] Quoted in Karl Kautsky, *The Labour Revolution* (New York: L. Macveagh, Dial Press, 1925), p. 267.

hensive structure would make it much easier for the TVA to plan and finance such a project than could a private developer.[13]

This initiative touches upon one of the most important aspects of corporate organization. As Robin Marris has noted, "the most fundamental difference between business firms and government departments lies in the former's capacity for autonomous growth." [14] Indeed, one can argue, as Marris has, that the essence of the most sophisticated stage of corporate capitalism is not the famous separation of ownership from control but the fact that an organization is financially independent, i.e. that it can use retained profits to fund growth and is therefore not subject to the constraints of the money market.[15]

When considering giant industries, one should think in terms of the TVA model of a public corporation—with considerable autonomy and the right to innovate—rather than of the Post Office, a public enterprise under the direct and political control of the government. But there are obvious risks to this approach. It is precisely the autonomy of the New York Port Authority, its independence from democratic control, that has allowed it to use its resources for creative antisocial purposes. This point is central to John Kenneth Galbraith's critique of socialism in *The New Industrial State.* In the last century, according to Galbraith, firms were run by entrepreneurs, and as a result the state, or the collective of workers, could take over from them without too much trouble. Now, however, there is the corporation with its intricate "technostructure" of scientists and administrators. If the socialist state tries to exercise too close a control over such an organization, it almost guarantees waste and incompetence; but if the socialized industry is granted the right to independent action, it will probably follow its own purposes rather than those of the national plan. "The technical complexity and planning and associated scale of operation," Galbraith concludes, "that took power from the capitalist entrepreneur and lodged it with the technostructure, removed it also from the reach of socialist control." [16]

To Whom Is the Corporation Accountable?

Galbraith correctly notes that this was one of the problems that caused the socialists in Europe to retreat from the commitment to public property after World War II. But then ironically—for he writes as an American liberal who is critical of socialist dogma—he takes up an ambiguous position somewhere to the Left of many of the revisionist social democrats.

[13] TVA, *Annual Report, 1968* (Washington, D.C.: GPO). See also TVA, "Draft Study, Tellicoe Town" (mimeo).
[14] Robin Marris, *The Economic Theory of "Managerial" Capitalism* (Glencoe: Free Press, 1964), p. 101.
[15] *Ibid.*, p. 33.
[16] John Kenneth Galbraith, *The New Industrial State* (Boston: Houghton Mifflin Co., 1967), pp. 103–104.

> It is possible that there is, in fact, more to the case for the autonomous public corporation that the modern socialist now sees. The problem of the technostructure . . . is whether it can be accommodated to social goals or whether society will have to be accommodated instead to its needs. *The nature of the legal ownership has an undoubted bearing on the amenability of the technostructure to social goals.*[17] [Emphasis added.]

The ambiguity in Galbraith's position is that he never really follows up this insight except in fairly vague references to the gradual withering away of the "functionless stockholder." I propose to be more specific. Granting that Galbraith has identified a serious problem—the Scylla represented by the Post Office, the Charybdis represented by the Port Authority—it is impossible for society to carry out liberal reform, to plan and allocate social costs properly, unless it asserts a decisive interest over the huge corporations. This means that there will indeed be an ever-present danger of inefficiency, dullness, poor service, and all the rest. But that is a risk infinitely preferable to the one incurred by leaving the corporate structure in its present, irresponsible form. There are, in short, no "perfect" solutions to these enormous problems, and any intelligent person can foresee difficulties in any proposal. Nevertheless, the public corporation with both the right to internal financing and the responsibility to democratically-elected representatives of the people is, with all problems acknowledged, a right step in the best direction.

Nor is it necessary to accept all of these dangers fatalistically; some can be dealt with and eliminated. And here early socialist theory was more advanced than later socialist practice. For when Jaurès, Bauer, Kautsky, and other social democratic leaders in the early part of the century rejected the anarchist and syndicalist proposals to vest title and control of each enterprise in its own workers, they also suggested a very important reform. . . . The administration of public property, they argued, should take a corporate form in which the board of directors of an industry would be divided between representatives of the workers directly involved, of the consumers at large, and of the state authority.

When, for instance, the Attlee government nationalized industry after World War II in Britain, it did not follow the principle of Clause Four of the Labour party's constitution and did not provide "the best obtainable system of popular administration and control of each industry and service." [18] And when the Wilson government renationalized steel in the sixties, it not only paid 450 million pounds in compensation to the owners but left many of the previous managers in control of the public enterprise.[19] The London *Economist* could thus summarize an interesting article about the attitude of the exprivate steel executives in January 1970: "The British Steel Corporation

[17] *Ibid.*, p. 104.
[18] Quoted in Harold Wilson, *Purpose and Politics* (Boston: Houghton Mifflin Co., 1964), p. 264.
[19] Paul Foot, *The Role of Harold Wilson* (Baltimore: Penguin Books, 1968), p. 189.

would like Labour to start nationalizing the industry before the elections—and the Tories not to denationalize it afterward."[20] In other words, social property was allowed to be as much like private property as possible.

Without succumbing to decentralist panaceas, one can easily see that a much more imaginative structure, with major elements of workers' and consumers' control, would have led to profound changes in the society. In their 1969 electoral campaign, the German Social Democrats understood at least part of this point and made the extension of "co-determination"—which provides for workers' representation on the boards of certain large and private corporations—a central political demand. However, when Willy Brandt required the support of the Free Democrats in order to form a government, he agreed, as a price of coalition, not to push this reform.

So far, this discussion has dealt primarily with huge units of modern production, but there are also many instances where cooperative, regional, and even neighborhood forms of social ownership are desirable. In the United States, to take but one example, the electrification of the rural areas was largely achieved through a New Deal measure that provided cheap federal credit to local cooperatives.

So the idea of functional socialization is not simply a political necessity; it is also an opportunity for innovation. In the old, apocalyptic proposals for the sudden and complete nationalization of basic industry, there was little room for promoting diversity and a variety of institutional forms. But if we proceed to socialize the specific functions of property over a period of time, there is much more of a chance for originality and imagination. There is also, of course, the possibility that such gradualism will be an excuse for not challenging the basic power of capital itself. That is why this process can only culminate in a fundamental transformation of power structures if there is a conscious socialist movement which aggressively educates and persuades the electorate to see these reforms as steps toward a new society.

Social Change and Human Psychology

Yet, all these previous images of the possible future of social property have a certain unimaginative quality. For they assume that the change of ownership will take place with the capitalist psychology intact, so that the urge to maximize profit and/or power and the pervasive egotism of economic man will still be the rule of life. It is necessary to take this bleak premise into account, if only because socialism is not going to emerge full-blown as the result of a sudden apocalyptic leap. But it is perhaps even more important to understand the degree to which change affects not simply the structure of the economy but the human spirit as well.

[20] *Economist*, January 31, 1970.

Discussion of this practical potential of man's idealism has been confused because it has so often turned on the experience of Communism, and on what happens to human psychology in a regime of totalitarian scarcity and class privileges. Alienation—and greed and invidious striving—can only be overcome, as Marx observed, when the means of production are so developed that they provide the material basis for general abundance. When an impoverished economy is socialized, he said, *"want is made general, and with want the need to struggle for necessities must begin again and all of the old crap will be reproduced. . . ."* [21] (Emphasis added.) And "the old crap" is precisely that pervasive venality that is to be found in any form of class society, capitalist or Communist.

Marx's prediction has been corroborated under Communism. The totalitarian accumulation of capital that Stalin ruthlessly carried out under conditions of economic backwardness has made inequality a basic principle of Soviet life. The privileges conferred upon the new Soviet elite have been institutionalized, and they persist to this day, long after the economic rationalization for them has disappeared. The Russians pioneered in the establishment of this new class system, and other East Europeans copied their model; and the Chinese, or at least the Maoist faction, criticized the fat Communists bitterly from the point of view of a nation that was only at the beginning of this process. But the basic source of all this Communist inequality—the persistence of the "old crap"—was that scarcity whose psychological effects Marx analyzed.

Must an analysis then conclude, as Robert Heilbroner has suggested, with an acknowledgment that the socialist aspiration toward equality necessarily and always conflicts with the socialist determination to produce enough for all? I think not. For as soon as one examines the question of motivation within the context of affluent societies there emerges the possibility of a productive egalitarianism—and trends in this direction can be seen despite the outrageous inequality still prevailing in these nations. The evidence is provided by the children of the rich and the mothers of the poor in contemporary America; the optimistic generalizations come from men as counterposed as Keynes and Trotsky.

Heilbroner speculates on how advanced capitalism may be changing economic psychology. It is possible, he writes, that in such a society "affluence will weaken the condition of economic dependency on which the market system is tacitly based, opening up the prospect that normal differentials of income payment will no longer suffice to attract men to less desirable jobs, and thereby requiring that capitalism resort more and more to planning and coercion." [22] Yet if Heilbroner's observations of this trend are accurate, his conclusions are overly pessimistic.

[21] Karl Marx, *Die Deutsche Ideologie, MEW,* 3:34–35.
[22] Robert Heilbroner, "Socialism and the Future," *Commentary,* December 1969.

For it has been noted in New York that when welfare benefits to the mothers of dependent children became competitive with or superior to the pay for unskilled jobs in the labor market, these people did not seek work. They were hardly enjoying affluence, yet they certainly exemplified a breakdown of the old market compulsions. There is, as Nathan Glazer commented on the phenomenon, "a massive change in values which makes various kinds of work which used to support families undesirable to a large number of potential workers today." [23] Now one possible conclusion is to force these women to work. That was the response of the Nixon administration in 1969, when it made the benefits of its proposed minimum family income program conditional on the recipient working or training for a job. It was, in effect, a vicious public policy forcing mothers into the labor market (by 1969 there were practically no able-bodied men on public assistance).

Advance in Human Aspirations

But there is another way of handling this situation, one that socialists propose here and now, even within the context of welfare capitalism.

The unwillingness of human beings to work at degrading, routine jobs should be welcomed, both as an advance in the level of men's aspirations and as an opportunity for channeling their talents into socially useful areas. Many dead-end jobs can be mechanized out of existence; as long ago as 1966, the President's Automation Commission demonstrated that there were then 5.3 million public-service jobs in education, health services, beautification, and the like, that could provide decent employment for people displaced by such mechanization—and for millions of the underemployed and unemployed—which would vastly improve the quality of the entire society.[24]

Among the most cruelly used people in the affluent society there seems to be arising a new sense of dignity (conservatives mistake it for laziness), which refutes the old motivations now that brutal compulsions are no longer in force. And this change in psychology could be utilized to help America solve its problems—or it could serve as an excuse—which Heilbroner fears as a possibility and Nixon embraces as a policy—to substitute the coercion of law for the weakened discipline of the market and thereby to drive people to do humiliating work.

Another change in psychology is taking place, not in the slums, but in the suburbs of the upper middle class and the rich. A *Fortune* survey taken in October 1968 reports that 8 million youths between 18 and 24 are or have been in college. Forty percent of these young people said that they were no longer primarily interested in preparing for commercial careers in the profit

[23] Nathan Glazer, "Beyond Income Maintenance," *Public Interest,* Summer 1969, p. 120.
[24] National Commission on Technology, Automation and Economic Progress, *Technology and the American Economy: Report 1966* (Washington, D.C.: GPO), p. 36.

sector.[25] This trend will be dealt with in more detail shortly, for it has enormous political consequences; it is cited here to show that socially conscious motivations are becoming more and more important.

The *Fortune* data describes liberal arts students for the most part. There is a similar trend in industry, among technicians and engineers. Capitalism went through two successive industrial revolutions—coal, steam, and textiles were the basis of the first, steel and electricity of the second; both of these resulted in a hierarchical structure with a detailed division of labor. But the third revolution—in electronics, data processing, and petrochemicals—is not so prone to bureaucracy and subordination. Cooperation and informal, transitory team relationships become the norm, replacing fixed and formal lines of authority; groups coalesce around problems and reforms when new issues arise.[26] In May 1968, in France, adult militancy in the general strike was concentrated in precisely these advanced areas of the economy, and the key demands concerned the organization of work rather than simple wage increases.

One of the most important American theorists of the corporation, A. A. Berle, has some fascinating speculations on this development. He argues that profit-oriented decision is not particularly innovative, and that the more secure and wealthy a company becomes the fewer are its incentives to change.[27] The greatest feats of invention, Berle continues, have been accomplished by defense corporations under conditions of war and with survival and patriotism as central motives. The Manhattan Project, which created the atom bomb, is an obvious example.

Berle considers it at least possible that such attitudes can be given a social rather than a military thrust: "A day may come when national glory and prestige, perhaps even national safety, are best established by a country's being the most beautiful, the best socially organized, or culturally the most advanced in the world." [28] If such a profound psychological mutation does not lie in the immediate future, the attitudes of the educated and affluent young suggest that it is not impossibly distant either. Were this to happen, some of the dreams of the anarchists and Guild socialists would become a realistic byproduct of technical and social change. One could then think of human and communal relationships within the socialized enterprise, and the classic socialist vision—that production will be carried out by the "associated producers"—would become newly relevant.

The socialization of private wealth remains therefore a central goal. It can be achieved through the progressive socialization of the functions of ownership and it is an essential measure to offset, and eventually abolish,

[25] The Editors of Fortune, *Youth in Turmoil* (New York: Time-Life Books, 1969), p. 43.
[26] Warren G. Bennis, "Post-Bureaucratic Leadership," *Trans-action*, July–August 1969.
[27] A. A. Berle, *Power* (New York: Harcourt, Brace & World, 1969), p. 211.
[28] *Ibid.*, p. 213.

the political power of private ownership. But on the far side of such a process—and verging toward that second phase of socialist transition Marx envisioned—it is not at all utopian to expect that the relative disappearance of scarcity will give rise to new social forms of motivation.

As Keynes, who was certainly not a radical dreamer, put it:

> the author of these essays, for all his croakings, still hopes and believes that the day is not far off when the Economic Problem will take the back seat where it belongs and that the arena of the heart and head will be occupied, or reoccupied, by our real problems—the problems of life and human relations, of creation and behavior and religion.

The economic basis of this possibility, Keynes thought, was "an increase in the volume of capital until it ceases to be scarce so that the functionless investor will no longer receive a bonus." Relating this to a change in motivation, Keynes foresaw a time when society would adopt

> a scheme of taxation which allows the intelligence and determination and executive skill of the financiers and the entrepreneurs, *et hoc genus omne* [and all that sort] (who are certainly so fond of their craft that their labor could be obtained much cheaper than at present) to be harnessed to the community on reasonable terms of reward.[29]

Trotsky made much the same point, though in typically soaring Marxist language. Competition, he said, will not disappear under socialism. It will

> to use the language of psychoanalysis . . . be sublimated, that is, will assume a higher and more fertile form. . . . People will divide into "parties" over the question of a new gigantic canal, or the distribution of oases in the Sahara . . . and over the regulation of the weather and climate, over a new theater, over chemical hypotheses, over two competing tendencies in art and over a best system of sports. Such parties will not be poisoned by the greed of class or caste.[30]

• • •

IV Is the Working Class Obsolete?

The working class is by no means "disappearing." And even as various academics were explaining how the proletariat had ceased to be a historical actor, there were tens of millions of workers who continued to face many of the old problems of working-class life. For, as the Bureau of Labor Statistics computed the figures, in late 1966 it took about $9,200 to support an urban family of four in the United States at a "moderate standard of living" (the definition allowed, for example, the purchase of a new suit and a two-

[29] John Maynard Keynes, *Essays in Persuasion* (New York: Norton, 1963), pp. vii, 3 ff.
[30] Leon Trotsky, *Literature and Revolution* (New York: Russell & Russell, 1957), p. 231.

year-old used car every four years).[31] With our rampant inflation, it is clear that this figure would have to be revised to somewhat more than $11,000 for 1970.

To achieve that 1966 level required a weekly pay check of $177; the average for industrial workers was actually $114. Indeed, a majority of the American people lacked the resources of this "moderate" budget. In addition to the poor there were tens of millions of working Americans who, if not hungry, had to struggle and scrape to make ends meet. And many of these citizens were concentrated in factory jobs that were physically grueling. So the "old" issues of wages and working conditions were still very much a factor in the experience of the majority of the people. And in Europe, where per capita wealth is inferior to that in the United States, this is still more true.

Political Clout of the Workers

Expressions of working-class discontent did not take the turbulent, near revolutionary forms that it did in France and Italy in 1968 and 1969, but it was still a powerful political force. In the elections of 1968 the supposedly decrepit trade unions were clearly the single most important element in the coalition which, despite the most difficult odds, almost elected Humphrey President in 1968. The labor organizations registered 4.6 million voters, printed more than 100 million leaflets and pamphlets; and supplied 72,225 canvassers and 94, 457 volunteers on election day.[32]

For—and this point is extremely important—the political potential of social classes cannot be determined by a simple head count. There are nations in which the overwhelming majority is peasant and yet the society is run in the cities. Peasants are dispersed, parochial and pre-modern. They can flare into a Jacquerie or even provide the troops for a Mao or a Ho Chi Minh. But the decisive technology of the contemporary economy is industrial, and the center of power is therefore urban. Workers, in the cities, are concentrated in very large numbers, subjected to a common discipline in the work process, and forced—in the defense of their most immediate interests—to build collective institutions. They therefore have a cohesion, a social weight, in excess of their numbers.

I stress this aspect of working-class life which is so often ignored by the affluent, college-educated, and issue-oriented people who must form coalitions with the unionists. The new constituency that is emerging as a result of mass higher education is important; but it does not have a solidarity imposed upon it by the very conditions of life and work, as the workers do. Therefore even if the percentage of blue-collar workers is declining and that

[31] Oswald, "The City Worker's Budget," *Federationist*, February 1969.
[32] Theodore H. White, *The Making of a President, 1968* (New York: Atheneum, 1969), p. 365.

of "professional, technical, and kindred workers" is on the increase, it is the working people with their own stable institutions who must be the decisive component in a socialist majority.

Paradoxically, affluence may yet provoke the workers to political struggle as much as poverty did. As far back as 1849, Marx had recognized the possibility that capitalist success would make labor rebel.

> The rapid growth of productive capital [Marx wrote] brings about an equally rapid growth of wealth, luxury, social wants, social employments. Thus, although the enjoyments of the worker have risen, the social satisfactions which they give him fall in comparison with the increased enjoyments of the capitalists which are inaccessible to the worker, and in comparison with the state of development of society in general. Our desires and pleasures spring from society; we measure them, therefore, by society. . . .[33]

If one updates Marx's insight into the radicalizing effect of good times, another aspect of recent working-class militancy can be brought into focus. For affluence does not simply narcotize and make men passive, as Herbert Marcuse seems to think. It also makes people angry when they compare what they have with the bountiful pretensions of the society. They contrast their standard of living, not with that of their parents or grandparents, but with the enchanted creatures of television. Affluence seems to subvert itself.

Moreover—and here we move toward the line separating the traditional blue-collar working class from the new professionals—there are changes in class structure in the affluent economy which occasion new kinds of discontent. Planned, rationalized capitalism demands higher and higher skills from its labor force, and this opens up the possibility of a very educated opposition among the technicians employed in the most advanced industries. So it was, for example, that in the French general strike of May 1968 the greatest militancy was not found among the coal miners, the classic source of proletarian intransigeance, but among men and women working in electronics, the chemical and auto industries, among teachers and the employees of the state-run radio and television network.[34] And these demands of sophisticated workers in advanced industries did not concern wages as much as the democratization of working conditions.

• • •

V The Vision of Socialism

Though the changes I have been talking about go far beyond any proposals by major political movements in neocapitalist society, they are still only transitional measures. They would profoundly improve and humanize the

[33] *MEW,* 6:412.
[34] Alain Touraine, *Le Mouvement de Mai ou le Communisme Utopique* (Paris: Seuil, 1968), pp. 162–168.

old order but would not yet constitute a new and revolutionary order. So it is now necessary to look beyond scarcity to the ultimate vision of socialism itself.

In envisaging the transcendent potential of social change I am not, I hope, indulging in holiday rhetoric to console those who spend their lives in mundane struggles—nor am I implying that history will one day enter paradise. But in the particulars of this or that conflict, each increment of progress can be better structured if it is related to the vision of a qualitative change in the human condition. If, as I will argue in a moment, the abolition of money and work are basic socialist values, that has some bearing on tomorrow's urgent trade union negotiations and on the next welfare measure in the legislature. It was, for example, a prophetic notion of more dignity for human beings which led the British socialists in 1945 to reject a means test for the new social services they were providing....

It is... important to insist upon the limitations of socialism as a prelude to describing how it seeks to break through some of our present limits. It proposes a solution, not to all human ills, but to those based upon the economic, social, and political conditions of life. In contrast to what Marx thought, it may well be that once man stops dying from famines and depressions and starts to die only from death, there will be a resurgence of the religious spirit, not an end to it. "Under Communism," Sidney Hook once wrote, "man ceases to suffer as an animal and suffers as a human. He therefore moves from the plane of the pitiful to the plane of the tragic." [35]

To grant that socialism is not a final redemption should not, however, paralyze the imagination, for even within these limits there are enormous possibilities...

In what follows there will be a "dialectical" tension. On the one hand, I want to avoid that absolutist view of socialism which is so transcendental that it drives its true believers to totalitarianism and an antisocialist society; on the other hand, I want to suggest the truly radical potential for human change that exists today. And with these caveats, I would stress two elements as crucial in my definition of the socialist future. Society should move toward, even if it never reaches, the abolition of work and money.

Can Work Be Abolished? Should It?

... Essentially Marx is saying that, in the fullness of socialism, all men will work like artists, out of an inner need and satisfaction, and not because they are forced to earn their daily bread. In arguing that even in the planned, socially controlled society, work is still unfree as long as it is compulsory, Marx was anticipating that passionate antisocialist, Friedrich Nietzsche, who

[35] Sidney Hook, *Towards the Understanding of Karl Marx* (New York: John Day & Co., 1933), p. 14.

wrote, "Phew! To speak as if an increase in the impersonality inside a mechanized plant will make a new society and turn the scandal of slavery into a virtue!" [36]

• • •

What Marx understood, however, and Nietzsche did not was that the application of science and technology makes it possible—even necessary—to change the very nature of work. Marx had glimpsed the coming of automation as early as the late 1850's. . . . He wrote, "The actual wealth of society and the possibility of a continued expansion of its process of reproduction do not depend upon the duration of surplus labor, but upon its productivity and the more or less fertile conditions of production under which it is performed." [37]

In other words, the evolution of technology would progressively reduce the need for human labor, and this economic trend would make possible the socialist realm of freedom. In his notes for *Das Kapital,* Marx was even more specific about the tendency he summarized in Volume Three of that work. He not only argued that the increasing productivity of machine production would make it possible for society progressively to reduce labor time; he held that it would become a necessity.[38] The output of an automated economy, Marx said, would increase so fast that, if title to consumption were still determined by labor time, society could not possibly use up its own production. Therefore, as a matter of survival, such an economy would have to shorten the working day and increase the consumption of the masses. In order to release these surging forces of production, a new mode of production becomes a practical necessity.

Is it poetic license to say that Marx was talking about automation? Now it is obvious that he did not have advance knowledge of the computers and cybernated equipment that were not invented until long after his death. But it is extraordinary that his analysis of the capitalist dynamic did lead him to anticipate in broad outline what automation would mean. Marx had rightly seen (and Joseph Schumpeter thought it his great accomplishment) that one of the basic laws of motion in capitalist society was for competition to beget monopoly and a consequent tendency to increase investment in machines (in the Marxist vocabulary, for constant capital to grow in relationship to variable capital, thus changing the "organic composition" of capital itself). "In this transformation," Marx said, "it is neither the immediate labor which man himself performs, nor the time during which he works, but the appropriation of his common productivity . . . in a word, the development

[36] Friedrich Nietzsche, *Morgenröte,* in *Nietzsche's Werke* (Salzburg: Bergland), 2:475.
[37] *MEW,* 25:828.
[38] Karl Marx, *Grundrisse der Kritik der Politischen Oeconomie* (Berlin: Dietz Verlag, 1953), p. 592.

of the socialized individual, which is the basic source of richness and production." [39]

This reference to the "socialized individual" has a very specific economic meaning. The increasing investment per worker who tends more and more sophisticated machines enables the individual to produce out of all proportion to his own physical powers. Through science and its application to industry, one man can do as much as a hundred, or a thousand men used to do. Moreover—and if this is not an anticipation of automation, what is it?—"men relate more and more to the productive process as watchers and regulators." [40]

• • •

Can All Men Be Creative?

Socialism would be free of precisely those constraints which make it structurally impossible for capitalism to make a truly social use of its productivity. In the immediate future, a democratically socialized society could use this enormous economic power to meet the needs of America and to aid in the industrialization of the world. There is so much work that needs to be done within this country and internationally that the next several generations, at least, must put the "socialized individual" to work meeting basic needs Yet in the more distant future it is not only possible, but perhaps necessary, for society to enter that Kingdom of Freedom which Marx described. Once the basic needs of all of mankind are provided for, and productivity still grows, men may be forced to live without compulsory work. The sentence decreed in the Garden of Eden will have been served.

I would not suggest that a psychic transition of this character will be easy. . . .

We may well be on the eve of psychic mutations. Our unprecedented, man-made environments produce new kinds of people. The question is not whether this will happen but how it will take place: under commercial priorities (Marcuse's pessimistic vision); under totalitarian control (Orwell's fear); or consciously chosen and shaped by a free political and social movement.

Men Freed of the Curse of Money

The end of compulsory labor is one socialist ultimate; the abolition of money is another.

As many economists have recognized, money is the basis of a system of "rationing by the purse." In a society of maldistributed incomes it is obviously unjust that an elite should enjoy luxuries while a mass are denied

[39] *Ibid.*, p. 593.
[40] *Ibid.*, p. 592.

necessities. Long before the socialist movement will even be in sight of its final aims, it can ameliorate this outrage by the redistribution of income, for then the rations will at least be more justly shared. But this reform might even be assimilated to an Adam Smithian model of the economy. As Paul Samuelson remarks, Smith would now agree that dollar wealth has to be distributed "in an 'ethically optimal' manner—and kept so by non-distorting, nonmarket intervention" in order to get the most efficient production and "to give people what they really deem is best for them."[41]

Socialists should propose to go well beyond such a change and eventually to challenge the principle of money itself. In a discussion of property which produces unearned income John Strachey argued that, given such a phenomenon, "a moral poison is bound to permeate the society."[42] And as long as access to goods and pleasures is rationed according to the possession of money, there is a pervasive venality, an invitation to miserliness and hostility to one's neighbor. Particularly in the area of necessities no one should be required to choose between needs or to sacrifice them in order to get luxuries—and that is what money makes inevitable.

Socialism should therefore work toward making more and more goods and services free: medicine, housing, transportation, a healthy diet, etc. The standard response of many economists to such a proposition is that cliché of Economics One: nothing is really free. All commodities cost something to produce and if the individual does not pay for them directly, then some one does indirectly. But this is to miss the enormous social gain that would occur if society were to make all the fundamentals of life free. There would, surely, be a collective payment for these goods but the change in moral atmosphere created by such a new mode of distribution would be profound.

The other standard criticism of free goods is the charge that they invite waste. People, one is told, will lavishly misuse their new rights, and a socialist society will therefore be the least efficient in human history. That prediction is partly based on the parochial assumption that man will act in a radically new environment exactly as he did in the old, that the greed and acquisitiveness of several hundred years of capitalism are of the human essence. It is not even necessary to become particularly visionary in responding to this, for the theory and practice of recent years has provided a basis for the socialist hope.

In his famous essay on the economics of socialism, Oskar Lange argued that those goods and services for which demand is relatively inelastic can be made free without running the risk of wastefulness. Salt is a classic example. The amount of it consumed in good times or in bad is relatively invariant. If it were made free it is doubtful that individuals would suddenly and vastly increase their use of it. Similarly with transportation within a city. If that

[41] Paul Samuelson, *Economics*, 7th ed. (New York: McGraw-Hill, 1967), pp. 610–611.
[42] Strachey, *Contemporary Capitalism*, p. 140.

were made free, there would unquestionably be a large increase in the use of transit facilities, since people would be much more likely to visit one another, to go on outings, etc. Yet who can say that such an increase in sociability and recreation is "wasteful"? And who would want to ride a subway simply because it is free?

There is some experience to go on. In California there is a private medical plan run by the Kaiser company. It has succeeded in sharply reducing the cost of care while improving the service. According to the thesis about the inherent greediness of men, the people who subscribe should use their rights more than the citizen who pays a higher cost. In fact, the Kaiser patients go to the doctor less than do the patients of expensive fee-for-service systems. As an article in *Fortune* put it, "Kaiser's experience refutes the widely held belief that if medical services are 'free,' or virtually free, the public will stampede to them." [43]

Socialism, then, is not simply a program for socializing investments and ownership and redistributing wealth, important as all those goals are. It retains the notion of a truly new order of things and it asserts this through the vision of seeking, in the distant but conceivable future, to abolish compulsory work and the rationing system of money as far as is humanly possible. Perhaps I can sum up this vision by retelling a famous socialist parable.

In desert societies—including the American Southwest—water is so precious that it is money. People fight and die and connive over it; governments covet it; marriages are made and broken because of it. If one had talked to a person who had only known that desert and told him that in the city there are public water fountains and that children are even sometimes allowed to turn on the fire hydrants in the summer and to frolic in the water, he would be sure that you were crazy. For he knows, with an existential certitude, that it is human nature to fight over water.

Mankind has lived now for several millennia in the desert. Our minds and emotions are conditioned by that bitter experience; we do not dare to think that things could be otherwise. Yet there are signs that we are, without really having planned it that way, marching out of the desert. There are some who loathe to leave behind the consolation of familiar brutalities; there are others who, in one way or another, would like to impose the law of the desert upon the Promised Land. It may even be possible that mankind cannot bear too much happiness.

It is also possible that we will seize this opportunity and make of the earth a homeland rather than an exile. That is the socialist project. It does not promise or even seek to abolish the human condition. That is impossible. It does propose to end that invidious competition and venality which, be-

[43] Edmund K. Faltermayer, "Better Care at Less Cost Without Miracles," *Fortune,* January 1970, p. 83. See also "NHI [National Health Insurance]: What It Is, What It Isn't," *Federationist,* January 1970.

cause scarcity allowed no other alternatives, we have come to think are inseparable from our humanity.

Under socialism there will be no end to history—but there may be a new history.

1970

Bibliography

Beckwith, B. P. *The Economic Theory of a Socialist Economy.* Palo Alto, Calif.: Stanford University Press, 1949.

Bernstein, Edward. *Evolutionary Socialism.* Translated by E. C. Harvey. New York: B. W. Huebsch, 1909.

Cole, G. D. H. *Communism and Social Democracy, 1914–1931.* London: St. Martin's Press, 1958.

Cole, G. D. H. *Guild Socialism Re-Stated.* London: Leonard Parsons, 1920.

Cole, G. D. H. *A History of Socialist Thought.* 5 Vols. New York: St. Martin's Press, 1953–1960.

Cole, Margarte. *The Story of Fabian Socialism.* New York: John Wiley, 1964.

Crosland, C. A. R. *The Future of Socialism.* New York: Macmillan, 1957.

Crossman, R. H. S. *The Politics of Socialism.* New York: Atheneum, 1965.

Crossman, R. H. S. (ed.). *New Fabian Essays.* London: Turnstile Press, 1952.

Durbin, E. F. M. *The Politics of Democratic Socialism: An Essay on Social Policy.* London: Routledge and Kegan Paul, Ltd., 1940.

Fried, Albert (ed.). *Socialism in America.* Garden City, N.Y.: Doubleday and Co., 1970.

Fried, Albert, and Sanders, Ronald (eds.). *Socialist Thought: A Documentary History.* Garden City, N.Y.: Doubleday and Co., 1964.

Friedland, William, and Rosberg, Carl G., Jr. (eds.). *African Socialism.* Stanford, Calif.: Stanford University Press, 1964.

Gay, Peter. *The Dilemma of Democratic Socialism.* New York: Columbia University Press, 1953.

Glass, S. T. *The Responsible Society: The Ideas of Guild Socialism.* Great Britain: Longmans, 1966.

Harrington, Michael. *Socialism.* New York: Saturday Review Press, 1972, especially Chapters 12 and 14.

Heilbroner, Robert. "The Future of Socialism." *Commentary 48* (December 1969): 35 ff.

Henderson, Fred. *The Case for Socialism.* Chicago: The Socialist Party, 1935.

Howe, Irving (ed.). *Essential Works of Socialism.* New York: Holt, Rinehart and Winston, 1970.

Howe, Irving. *The Socialist Case.* London: Faber and Faber Ltd., 1946.

Jay, Douglas. *Socialism in the New Society.* New York: St. Martin's Press, 1963.

Kautsky, Karl. *Communism and Socialism.* New York: Atheneum League for Democratic Socialism, 1932.

Kautsky, Karl. *The Dictatorship of the Proletariat.* Translated by H. J. Stenning. Manchester: The National Labour Press Ltd., 1924.

Landauer, Carl. *European Socialism: A History of Ideas and Movements from the Industrial Revolution to Hitler's Seizure of Power.* 2 Vols. Berkeley: University of Berkeley Press, 1959.

Laski, Harold. *Socialism and Freedom.* London: Fabian Society, 1925.

Laski, Harold. *Socialism and Internationalism.* London: Fabian Society, 1947.

Lichtheim, George. *The Origins of Socialism.* New York: Frederick A. Praeger, 1969.

Lippincott, Benjamin (ed.). *On the Economic Theory of Socialism.* Minneapolis: University of Minnesota Press, 1938.
Mill, John Stuart. *Principles of Political Economy.* Toronto: University of Toronto Press, 1965, especially Book Five.
Nehru, Jawaharlal. *Toward a Socialistic State.* New Delhi: All India Congress Committee, 1956.
Nyerere, Julius K. *Essays on Socialism.* Dar es Salaam: Oxford University Press, 1968.
Owen, Robert. *A New View of Society.* Glencoe, Ill.: Free Press, 1948.
Radia, Giles. *Democratic Socialism.* New York: Frederick A. Praeger, 1966.
Robinson, Joan. *Freedom and Necessity.* London: G. Allen and Unwin, 1970.
Schumpeter, Joseph A. *Capitalism, Socialism and Democracy.* New York: Harper & Row, 1950.
Shaw, G. Bernard, *et al. Fabian Essays on Socialism.* Boston: Ball Publishing Co., 1908.
Shaw, G. Bernard. *The Intelligent Woman's Guide to Socialism and Capitalism.* New York: Bretano's Publishers, 1928.
Thomas, Norman. *Socialism Re-Examined.* New York: W. W. Norton & Co., 1963.
Ulam, Adam. *The Philosophical Foundations of English Socialism.* Cambridge, Mass.: Harvard University Press, 1951.
Von Mises, Ludwig. *Socialism.* New Haven: Yale University Press, 1951.
Ward, Benjamin. *The Socialist Economy.* New York: Random House, 1967.
Wheeler, Harvey. *Democracy in a Revolutionary Era.* Santa Barbara, Calif.: Center for the Study of Democratic Institutions, 1970.
Wilson, Harold. *The Relevance of British Socialism.* London: Weidenfeld and Nicolson, 1964.
Wood, Ellen. *Mind and Politics: An Approach to the Meaning of Liberal and Socialist Individualism.* Berkeley, Calif.: University of California Press, 1973.

VII Democratic Conservatism

Although democrats more by convention than conviction, the democratic conservatives tend to view the common man with what might be best described as "qualified suspicion." The democratic conservatives argue that the common man, who is not by nature and social position of high reason and culture, needs guidance and leadership. The fundamental emphasis of the democratic conservatives is the organic nature of society: the matrix of traditions binding men, one to another. Like Burke, the democratic conservatives concentrate on the moral unity and traditional continuity of society. And much like the democratic socialists envision society, the democratic conservatives tend to fuse the complex arrangements of society with the simpler notion of community. The state, broadly defined as the *nation* in its collective and corporate character, holds public authority as a trust from society, delegated to the agency of government as an instrument for the pursuit of certain collective goals within the limits of social tradition and moral cohesion. Should there be a want of reasoned agreement and harmonious order in the agency of government, the democratic conservatives contend, then there is almost certainly a similar want in the nation as a whole.

Democratic conservatism reflects the social vantage point of a self-ordained elite supposedly superior in talent, intellect, or culture. Portraying a basic class structure of society, with an inequitable distribution of human virtues, the democratic conservative ideology characterizes the arrangements of society as a congruent or quasi-congruent whole rather than irrevocably antagonistic, as in Marxian analysis. Rather than proposing to serve the interests of all individuals directly or the interests of one group if not several groups, the democratic conservatives emphasize the fundamental importance of securing the interests of the national character, generally assuming that by so doing, whatever may be the implicit mechanism of transference, benefits will accrue to the interests of the constituent individuals.

The democratic conservative ideology reflects the experiences common to all democratic ideologies more as a consequence of existing democratic institutions and practice than as a consequence of those tensions giving rise to democratic institutions in the first place. Alternately stated, the democratic conservative ideology is, at least in part, more an abstract model of existing political institutions than it is a reflection of the basic principles which those institutions embody. In this sense democratic conservatism represents a "second-hand" theory of democracy. Further, democratic conservatism is more a model of the slow growth and change characterizing the community than a model of change characterizing a society defined by the modern nation–state. Finally, as implied in the conservative emphasis on community rather than societal activities, democratic conservatism tends to reflect only those activities of the modern nation–state marked by an apparent unity of purpose and subsequent lack of apparent conflict; such conditions exist, for example, when a nation is in a state of defensive warfare (although this is not always the case).

Social freedom or equality, Matthew Arnold suggests, is the conquest of democracy. To live in a society of equals, Arnold argues, allows man's spirit to expand, guaranteeing a more facile and active use of the individual's facilities. Making up for the weakness of each man taken by himself, democracy substitutes the concert of a great number of men for the weakness of each man taken individually. Yet the democrats, rather than possessing high ideals, are better suited for following ideals. The basic problem arises, therefore, in how to go about supplying ideals for a democratic society. The aristocracy, Arnold contends, is losing its influence on people. And the liberty and industry of the middle class, Arnold continues, are hardly sufficient to guarantee high reason and culture. Suggesting that English individualism will prove an adequate check on state power, Arnold urges that state action, through public education, must provide the ideals necessary for cultivation of the national character. Pointing out that the genius of the English nation is greater than the genius of any individual, Arnold maintains that the nation should expect the state to offer a worthy initiative and set a standard of rational and equitable action.

For economist Joseph Schumpeter, democracy means only that the people have the opportunity of accepting or refusing those persons who compete for their votes. Schumpeter sees legislation and administration in the modern democratic state as a by-product of the struggle for political office. In consequence, he contends, policies are bent to the exigencies of political warfare, the policy-making process is inefficient, and the policy makers tend to favor short-run interests over the longer range interests of the nation as an organic unity. The democratic method can be successful, however, according to Schumpeter, if the leaders are of sufficient quality. Additionally, the effective range of political decisions must be restricted and tradition must temper the democratic process with self-control. Finally, the democratic process, to be successful, requires a well-trained bureaucracy of good standing and tradition, which can provide efficient and competent service to the democratic policy makers.

Babbitt, a Harvard professor and literary critic, in extending the conservative analysis specifically to the American society during the 1920s, and writing somewhat before Schumpeter, charges Americans with a lack of moral cohesion. Lacking any standards but a reprehensible quantitative view of life, the American democracy embodies inferior types of leadership. The George Washington liberals, Babbitt reflects, see man with a higher self that acts restrictively on the ordinary self; and like the individual self, the state too needs a higher self, embodied in institutions such as the Constitution, which sets bounds to the will of the populace at any given moment. But with the progressive crumbling of traditional standards and the growing lawlessness in American society, Babbitt avers, America's foremost problem is the need to secure leaders with an allegiance to standards.

30 Democracy, the State, and Education

MATTHEW ARNOLD

In giving an account of education in certain countries of the Continent, I have often spoken of the State and its action in such a way as to offend, I fear, some of my readers, and to surprise others. With many Englishmen, perhaps with the majority, it is a maxim that the State, the executive power, ought to be entrusted with no more means of action than those which it is impossible to withhold from it; that the State neither would nor could make a safe use of any more extended liberty; would not, because it has in itself a natural instinct of despotism, which, if not jealously checked, would become outrageous; could not, because it is, in truth, not at all more enlightened, or fit to assume a lead, than the mass of this enlightened community.

No sensible man will lightly go counter to an opinion firmly held by a great body of his countrymen. He will take for granted, that for any opinion which has struck deep root among a people so powerful, so successful, and so well worthy of respect as the people of this country, there certainly either are, or have been, good and sound reasons. He will venture to impugn such an opinion with real hesitation, and only when he thinks he perceives that the reasons which once supported it exist no longer, or at any rate seem about to disappear very soon. For undoubtedly there arrive periods, when, the circumstances and conditions of government having changed, the guiding maxims of government ought to change also. *J'ai dit souvent,* says Mirabeau,[1] admonishing the Court of France in 1790, *qu'on devait changer de manière de gouverner, lorsque le gouvernement n'est plus le même.* And these decisive changes in the political situation of a people happen gradually as well as violently. "In the silent lapse of events," says Burke,[2] writing in England twenty years before the French Revolution, "as material alterations have been insensibly brought about in the policy and character of governments and nations, as those which have been marked by the tumult of public revolutions."

I propose to submit to those who have been accustomed to regard all State-action with jealousy, some reasons for thinking that the circumstances which once made that jealousy prudent and natural have undergone an

SOURCE: from Matthew Arnold, *Mixed Essays,* Vol. *4* (London: Macmillan & Co., 1883), pp. 1–35.

[1] *Correspondance entre le Comte de Mirabeau et le Comte de la Marck,* vol. ii (Paris: M. de Bacourt, 1851), p. 143.

[2] Burke's *Works* (1852 edition), vol. iii, p. 115.

essential change. I desire to lead them to consider with me, whether, in the present altered conjuncture, that State-action, which was once dangerous, may not become, not only without danger in itself, but the means of helping us against dangers from another quarter. To combine and present the considerations upon which these two propositions are based, is a task of some difficulty and delicacy. My aim is to invite impartial reflection upon the subject, not to make a hostile attack against old opinions, still less to set on foot and fully equip a new theory. In offering, therefore, the thoughts which have suggested themselves to me, I shall studiously avoid all particular applications of them likely to give offence, and shall use no more illustration and development than may be indispensable to enable the reader to seize and appreciate them.

The dissolution of the old political parties which have governed this country since the Revolution of 1688 has long been remarked. It was repeatedly declared to be happening long before it actually took place, while the vital energy of these parties still subsisted in full vigour, and was threatened only by some temporary obstruction. It has been eagerly deprecated long after it had actually begun to take place, when it was in full progress, and inevitable. These parties, differing in so much else, were yet alike in this, that they were both, in a certain broad sense, *aristocratical* parties. They were combinations of persons considerable, either by great family and estate, or by Court favour, or lastly, by eminent abilities and popularity; this last body, however, attaining participation in public affairs only through a conjunction with one or other of the former. These connections, though they contained men of very various degrees of birth and property, were still wholly leavened with the feelings and habits of the upper class of the nation. They had the bond of a common culture; and, however their political opinions and acts might differ, what they said and did had the stamp and style imparted by this culture, and by a common and elevated social condition.

Aristocratical bodies have no taste for a very imposing executive, or for a very active and penetrating domestic administration. They have a sense of equality among themselves, and of constituting in themselves what is greatest and most dignified in the realm, which makes their pride revolt against the overshadowing greatness and dignity of a commanding executive. They have a temper of independence, and a habit of uncontrolled action, which makes them impatient of encountering, in the management of the interior concerns of the country, the machinery and regulations of a superior and peremptory power. The different parties amongst them, as they successively get possession of the government, respect this jealous disposition in their opponents, because they share it themselves. It is a disposition proper to them as great personages, not as ministers; and as they are great personages for their whole life, while they may probably be ministers but for a very short time, the instinct of their social condition avails more with them than the instinct of their official function. To administer as little as possible, to make its weight felt in foreign affairs rather than in domestic, to see in ministerial station rather the means of power and dignity than a means of searching and useful administrative activity, is the natural tendency of an aristocratic executive. It is a tendency which is creditable to the good sense of aristocracies, honourable to their moderation, and at the same time fortunate for their country, of whose internal development they are not fitted to have the full direction.

One strong and beneficial influence, however, the administration of a vigorous and high-minded aristocracy is calculated to exert upon a robust and sound people. I have had occasion, in speaking of Homer, to say very often, and with much emphasis, that he is *in the grand style.* It is the chief virtue of a healthy and uncorrupted aristocracy, that it is, in general, in this grand style. That elevation of character, that noble way of thinking and behaving, which is an eminent gift of nature to some individuals, is also often generated in whole classes of men (at least when these come of a strong and good race) by the possession of power, by the importance and responsibility of high station, by habitual dealing with great things, by being placed above the necessity of constantly struggling for little things. And it is the source of great virtues. It may go along with a not very quick or open intelligence; but it cannot well go along with a conduct vulgar and ignoble. A governing class imbued with it may not be capable of intelligently leading the masses of a people to the highest pitch of welfare for them; but it sets them an invaluable example of qualities without which no really high welfare can exist. This has been done for their nation by the best aristocracies. The Roman aristocracy did it; the English aristocracy has done it. They each fostered in the mass of the peoples they governed,—peoples of sturdy moral constitution and apt to learn such lessons,—a greatness of spirit, the natural growth of the condition of magnates and rulers, but not the natural growth of the condition of the common people. They made, the one of the Roman, the other of the English people, in spite of all the shortcomings of each, great peoples, peoples *in the grand style.* And this they did, while wielding the people according to their own notions, and in the direction which seemed good to them; not as servants and instruments of the people, but as its commanders and heads; solicitous for the good of their country, indeed, but taking for granted that of that good they themselves were the supreme judges, and were to fix the conditions.

The time has arrived, however, when it is becoming impossible for the aristocracy of England to conduct and wield the English nation any longer. It still, indeed, administers public affairs; and it is a great error to suppose, as many persons in England suppose, that it administers but does not govern. He who administers, governs, because he infixes his own mark and stamps his own character on all public affairs as they pass through his hands; and, therefore, so long as the English aristocracy administers the commonwealth, it still governs it. But signs not to be mistaken show that its headship and leadership of the nation, by virtue of the substantial acquiescence of the body of the nation in its predominance and right to lead, is nearly over. That acquiescence was the tenure by which it held its power; and it is fast giving way. The superiority of the upper class over all others is no longer so great; the willingness of the others to recognize that superiority is no longer so ready.

This change has been brought about by natural and inevitable causes, and neither the great nor the multitude are to be blamed for it. The growing demands and audaciousness of the latter, the encroaching spirit of democracy, are, indeed, matters of loud complaint with some persons. But these persons are complaining of human nature itself, when they thus complain of a manifestation of its native and ineradicable impulse. Life itself consists, say the philosophers, in the effort *to affirm one's own essence;* meaning by this, to develop one's own existence fully and freely, to have ample light and air, to be neither cramped nor overshadowed. Democracy is trying *to affirm its own essence;* to live, to enjoy, to possess the world, as aristocracy has tried, and successfully tried, before it. Ever since Europe emerged from barbarism, ever since the condition of the common people began a little to improve, ever since their minds began to stir, this effort of democracy has been gaining strength; and the more their condition improves, the more strength this effort gains. So potent is the charm of life and expansion upon the living; the moment men are aware of them, they begin to desire them, and the more they have of them, the more they crave.

This movement of democracy, like other operations of nature, merits properly neither blame nor praise. Its partisans are apt to give it credit which it does not deserve, while its enemies are apt to upbraid it unjustly. Its friends celebrate it as the author of all freedom. But political freedom may very well be established by aristocratic founders; and, certainly, the political freedom of England owes more to the grasping English barons than to democracy. Social freedom,—equality,—that is rather the field of the conquests of democracy. And here what I must call the injustice of its enemies comes in. For its seeking after equality, democracy is often, in this country above all, vehemently and scornfully blamed; its temper contrasted with that worthier temper which can magnanimously endure social distinctions; its operations all referred, as of course, to the stirrings of a base and malignant envy. No doubt there is a gross and vulgar spirit of envy, prompting the hearts of many of those who cry for equality. No doubt there are ignoble natures which prefer equality to liberty. But what we have to ask is, when the life of democracy is admitted as something natural and inevitable, whether this or that product of democracy is a necessary growth from its parent stock, or merely an excrescence upon it. If it be the latter, certainly it may be due to the meanest and most culpable passions. But if it be the former, then this product, however base and blameworthy the passions which it may sometimes be made to serve, can in itself be no more reprehensible than the vital impulse of democracy is in itself reprehensible; and this impulse is, as has been shown, identical with the ceaseless vital effort of human nature itself.

Now, can it be denied, that a certain approach to equality, at any rate a certain reduction of signal inequalities, is a natural, instinctive demand of that impulse which drives society as a whole,—no longer individuals and limited classes only, but the mass of a community,—to develop itself with the utmost possible fulness and freedom? Can it be denied, that to live in a society of equals tends in general to make a man's spirits expand, and his faculties work easily and actively; while, to live in a society of superiors, although it may occasionally be a very good discipline, yet in general tends to tame the spirits and to make the play of the faculties less secure and active? Can it be denied, that to be heavily overshadowed, to be profoundly insignificant, has, on the whole, a depressing and benumbing effect on the character? I know that some individuals react against the strongest impediments, and owe success and greatness to the efforts which they are thus forced to make. But the question is not about individuals. The question is about the common bulk of mankind, persons without extraordinary gifts or exceptional energy, and who will ever require, in order to make the best of themselves, encouragement and directly favouring circumstances. Can any one deny, that for these the spectacle, when they would rise, of a condition of splendour, grandeur, and culture, which they cannot possibly reach, has the effect of making them flag in spirit, and of disposing them to sink despondingly back into their own condition? Can any one deny, that the knowledge how poor and insignificant the best condition of improvement and culture attainable by them must be esteemed by a class incomparably richer-endowed, tends to cheapen this modest possible amelioration in the account of those classes also for whom it would be relatively a real progress, and to disenchant their imaginations with it? It seems to me impossible to deny this. And therefore a philosophic observer, with no love for democracy, but rather with a terror of it, has been constrained to remark, that "the common people is more uncivilised in aristocratic countries than in any others;" because there "the lowly and the poor feel themselves, as it were, overwhelmed with the weight of their own inferiority." He has been constrained to remark, that "there is such a thing as a manly and legitimate passion for equality, prompting men to desire to be, *all* of them, in the enjoyment of power and consideration." And, in France, that very equality, which is by us so impetuously decried, while it has by no means improved (it is said) the upper classes of French society, has undoubtedly given to the lower classes, to the body of the common people, a self-respect, an enlargement of spirit, a consciousness of counting for something in their country's action, which has raised them in the scale of humanity. The common people, in France, seems to me the soundest part of the French nation. They seem to me more free from the two opposite degradations of multitudes, brutality and servility, to have a more developed human life, more of what distinguishes elsewhere the cultured classes from the vulgar, than the common people in any other country with which I am acquainted.

I do not say that grandeur and prosperity may not be attained by a nation divided into the most widely distinct classes, and presenting the most signal inequalities of rank and fortune. I do not say that great national virtues may not be developed in it. I do not even say that a popular order, accepting this demarcation of classes as an eternal providential arrangement, not questioning the natural right of a superior order to lead it, content within its own sphere, admiring the grandeur and high-mindedness of its ruling class, and catching on its own spirit some reflex of what it thus admires, may not be a happier body, as to the eye of the imagination it is certainly a more beautiful body, than a popular order, pushing, excited, and presumptuous; a popular order, jealous of recognising fixed superiorities, petulantly claiming to be as good as its betters, and tastelessly attiring itself with the fashions and designations which have become unalterably associated with a wealthy and refined class, and which, tricking out those who have neither wealth nor refinement, are ridiculous. But a popular order of that old-fashioned stamp exists now only for the imagination. It is not the force with which modern society has to reckon. Such a body may be a sturdy, honest, and sound-hearted lower class; but it is not a democratic people. It is not that power, which at the present day in all nations is to be found existing; in some, has obtained the mastery; in others, is yet in a state of expectation and preparation.

The power of France in Europe is at this day mainly owing to the completeness with which she has organised democratic institutions. The action of the French State is excessive; but it is too little understood in England that the French people has adopted this action for its own purposes, has in great measure attained those purposes by it, and owes to its having done so the chief part of its influence in Europe. The growing power in Europe is democracy; and France has organised democracy with a certain indisputable grandeur and success. The ideas of 1789 were working everywhere in the eighteenth century; but it was because in France the State adopted them that the French Revolution became an historic epoch for the world, and France the lode-star of Continental democracy. Her airs of superiority and her overweening pretensions come from her sense of the power which she derives from this cause. Every one knows how Frenchmen proclaim France to be at the head of civilisation, the French army to be the soldier of God, Paris to be the brain of Europe, and so on. All this is, no doubt, in a vein of sufficient fatuity and bad taste; but it means, at bottom, that France believes she has so organised herself as to facilitate for all members of her society full and free expansion; that she believes herself to have remodelled her institutions with an eye to reason rather than custom, and to right rather than fact; it means, that she believes the other peoples of Europe to be preparing themselves, more or less rapidly, for a like achievement, and that she is conscious of her power and influence upon them as an initiatress and example. In this belief there is a part of truth and a part of delusion. I think it is more profitable for a Frenchman to consider the part of delusion contained in it; for an Englishman, the part of truth.

It is because aristocracies almost inevitably fail to appreciate justly, or even to take into their mind, the instinct pushing the masses towards expansion and fuller life, that they lose their hold over them. It is the old story of the incapacity of aristocracies for ideas; the secret of their want of success in modern epochs. The people treats them with flagrant injustice, when it denies all obligation to them. They can, and often do, impart a high spirit, a fine ideal of grandeur, to the people; thus they lay the foundations of a great nation. But they leave the people still the multitude, the crowd; they have small belief in the power of the ideas which are its life. Themselves a power reposing on all which is most solid, material, and visible, they are slow to attach any great importance to influences impalpable, spiritual, and viewless. Although, therefore, a disinterested looker-on might often be disposed, seeing what has actually been achieved by aristocracies, to wish to retain or replace them in their preponderance, rather than commit a nation to the hazards of a new and untried future; yet the masses instinctively feel that they can never consent to this without renouncing the inmost impulse of their being; and that they should make such a renunciation cannot seriously be expected of them. Except on conditions which make its expansion, in the sense understood by itself, fully possible, democracy will never frankly ally itself with aristocracy; and on these conditions perhaps no aristocracy will ever frankly ally itself with it. Even the English aristocracy, so politic, so capable of compromises, has shown no signs of being able so to transform itself as to render such an alliance possible. The reception given by the Peers to the bill for establishing life-peerages was, in this respect, of ill omen. The separation between aristocracy and democracy will probably, therefore, go on still widening.

And it must in fairness be added, that as in one most important part of general human culture,—openness to ideas and ardour for them,—aristocracy is less advanced than democracy, to replace or keep the latter under the tutelage of the former would in some respects be actually unfavourable to the progress of the world. At epochs when new ideas are powerfully fermenting in a society, and profoundly changing its spirit, aristocracies, as they are in general not long suffered to guide it without question, so are they by nature not well fitted to guide it intelligently.

In England, democracy has been slow in developing itself, having met with much to withstand it, not only in the worth of the aristocracy, but also in the fine qualities of the common people. The aristocracy has been more in sympathy with the common people than perhaps any other aristocracy.

It has rarely given them great umbrage; it has neither been frivolous, so as to provoke their contempt, nor impertinent, so as to provoke their irritation. Above all, it has in general meant to act with justice, according to its own notions of justice. Therefore the feeling of admiring deference to such a class was more deep-rooted in the people of this country, more cordial, and more persistent, than in any people of the Continent. But, besides this, the vigour and high spirit of the English common people bred in them a self-reliance which disposed each man to act individually and independently; and so long as this disposition prevails through a nation divided into classes, the predominance of an aristocracy, of the class containing the greatest and strongest individuals of the nation, is secure. Democracy is a force in which the concert of a great number of men makes up for the weakness of each man taken by himself; democracy accepts a certain relative rise in their condition, obtainable by this concert for a great number, as something desirable in itself, because though this is undoubtedly far below grandeur, it is yet a good deal above insignificance. A very strong, self-reliant people neither easily learns to act in concert, nor easily brings itself to regard any middling good, any good short of the best, as an object ardently to be coveted and striven for. It keeps its eye on the grand prizes, and these are to be won only by distancing competitors, by getting before one's comrades, by succeeding all by one's self; and so long as a people works thus individually, it does not work democratically. The English people has all the qualities which dispose a people to work individually; may it never lose them! A people without the salt of these qualities, relying wholly on mutual co-operation, and proposing to itself second-rate ideals, would arrive at the pettiness and stationariness of China. But the English people is no longer so entirely ruled by them as not to show visible beginnings of democratic action; it becomes more and more sensible to the irresistible seduction of democratic ideas, promising to each individual of the multitude increased self-respect, and expansion with the increased importance and authority of the multitude to which he belongs, with the diminished preponderance of the aristocratic class above him.

While the habit and disposition of deference are thus dying out among the lower classes of the English nation, it seems to me indisputable that the advantages which command deference, that eminent superiority in high feeling, dignity, and culture, tend to diminish among the highest class. I shall not be suspected of any inclination to underrate the aristocracy of this country. I regard it as the worthiest, as it certainly has been the most successful aristocracy, of which history makes record. If it has not been able to develop excellences which do not belong to the nature of an aristocracy, yet it has been able to avoid defects to which the nature of an aristocracy is peculiarly prone. But I cannot read the history of the flowering time of the English aristocracy, the eighteenth century, and then look at this aristocracy in our own century, without feeling that there has been a change. I am not now thinking of private and domestic virtues, of morality, of decorum. Perhaps with respect to these there has in this class, as in society at large, been a change for the better. I am thinking of those public and conspicuous virtues by which the multitude is captivated and led,—lofty spirit, commanding character, exquisite culture. It is true that the advance of all classes in culture and refinement may make the culture of one class, which, isolated, appeared remarkable, appear so no longer; but exquisite culture and great dignity are always something rare and striking, and it is the distinction of the English aristocracy, in the eighteenth century, that not only was their culture something rare by comparison with the rawness of the masses, it was something rare and admirable in itself. It is rather that this rare culture of the highest class has actually somewhat declined, than that it has come to look less by juxtaposition with the augmented culture of other classes.

Probably democracy has something to answer for in this falling off of her rival. To feel itself raised on high, venerated, followed, no doubt stimulates a fine nature to keep itself worthy to be followed, venerated, raised on high; hence that lofty maxim, *noblesse oblige.* To feel its culture something precious and singular, makes such a nature zealous to retain and extend it. The elation and energy thus fostered by the sense of its advantages, certainly enhances the worth, strengthens the behaviour, and quickens all the active powers of the class enjoying it. *Possunt quia posse videntur.* The removal of the stimulus a little relaxes their energy. It is not so much that they sink to be somewhat less than themselves, as that they cease to be somewhat more than themselves. But, however this may be, whencesoever the change may proceed, I cannot doubt that in the aristocratic virtue, in the intrinsic commanding force of the English upper class, there is a diminution. Relics of a great generation are still, perhaps, to be seen amongst them, surviving exemplars of noble manners and consummate culture; but they disappear one after the other, and no one of their kind takes their place. At the very moment when democracy becomes less and less disposed to follow and to admire, aristocracy becomes less and less qualified to command and to captivate.

On the one hand, then, the masses of the people in this country are preparing to take a much more active part than formerly in controlling its destinies; on the other hand, the aristocracy (using this word in the widest sense, to include not only the nobility and landed gentry, but also those reinforcements from the classes bordering upon itself, which this class constantly attracts and assimilates), while it is threatened with losing its hold on the rudder of government, its power to give to public affairs its own bias and direction, is losing also that influence on the spirit and character of the people which it long exercised.

I know that this will be warmly denied by some persons. Those who have grown up amidst a certain state of things, those whose habits, and interests, and affections, are closely concerned with its continuance, are slow to believe that it is not a part of the order of nature, or that it can ever come to an end. But I think that what I have here laid down will not appear doubtful either to the most competent and friendly foreign observers of this country, or to those Englishmen who, clear of all influences of class or party, have applied themselves steadily to see the tendencies of their nation as they really are. Assuming it to be true, a great number of considerations are suggested by it; but it is my purpose here to insist upon one only.

That one consideration is: On what action may we rely to replace, for some time at any rate, that action of the aristocracy upon the people of this country, which we have seen exercise an influence in many respects elevating and beneficial, but which is rapidly, and from inevitable causes, ceasing? In other words, and to use a short and significant modern expression which every one understands, what influence may help us to prevent the English people from becoming, with the growth of democracy, *Americanised?* I confess I am disposed to answer: On the action of the State.

I know what a chorus of objectors will be ready. One will say: Rather repair and restore the influence of aristocracy. Another will say: It is not a bad thing, but a good thing, that the English people should be Americanised. But the most formidable and the most widely entertained objection, by far, will be that which founds itself upon the present actual state of things in another country; which says: Look at France! there you have a signal example of the alliance of democracy with a powerful State-action, and see how it works.

This last and principal objection I will notice at once. I have had occasion to touch upon the first already, and upon the second I shall touch presently. It seems to me, then, that one may save one's self from much idle terror at names and shadows if one will be at the pains to remember what different conditions the different character of two nations must necessarily impose on the operation of any principle. That which operates noxiously in one, may operate wholesomely in the other; because the unsound part of the one's character may be yet further inflamed and enlarged by it, the unsound part of the other's may find in it a corrective and an abatement. This is the great use which two unlike characters may find in observing each other. Neither is likely to have the other's faults, so each may safely adopt as much as suits him of the other's qualities. If I were a Frenchman I should never be weary of admiring the independent, individual, local habits of action in England, of directing attention to the evils occasioned in France by the excessive action of the State; for I should be very sure that, say what I might, the part of the State would never be too small in France, nor that of the individual too large. Being an Englishman, I see nothing but good in freely recognising the coherence, rationality, and efficaciousness which characterise the strong State-action of France, of acknowledging the want of method, reason, and result which attend the feeble State-action of England; because I am very sure that, strengthen in England the action of the State as one may, it will always find itself sufficiently controlled. But when either the *Constitutionnel* sneers at the do-little talkativeness of parliamentary government, or when the *Morning Star* inveighs against the despotism of a centralised administration, it seems to me that they lose their labour, because they are hardening themselves against dangers to which they are neither of them liable. Both the one and the other, in plain truth,

> Compound for sins they are inclined to,
> By damning those they have no mind to.

They should rather exchange doctrines one with the other, and each might thus, perhaps, be profited.

So that the exaggeration of the action of the State, in France, furnishes no reason for absolutely refusing to enlarge the action of the State in England; because the genius and temper of the people of this country are such as to render impossible that exaggeration which the genius and temper of the French rendered easy. There is no danger at all that the native independence and individualism of the English character will ever belie itself, and become either weakly prone to lean on others, or blindly confiding in them.

English democracy runs no risk of being overmastered by the State; it is almost certain that it will throw off the tutelage of aristocracy. Its real danger is, that it will have far too much its own way, and be left far too much to itself. "What harm will there be in that?" say some; "are we not a self-governing people?" I answer: "We have never yet been a *self-governing democracy,* or anything like it." The difficulty for democracy is, how to find and keep high ideals. The individuals who compose it are, the bulk of them, persons who need to follow an ideal, not to set one; and one ideal of greatness, high feeling, and fine culture, which an aristocracy once supplied to them, they lose by the very fact of ceasing to be a lower order and becoming a democracy. Nations are not truly great solely because the individuals composing them are numerous, free, and active; but they are great when these numbers, this freedom, and this activity are employed in the service of an ideal higher than that of an ordinary man, taken by himself. Our society is probably destined to become much more democratic; who or what will give a high tone to the nation then? That is the grave question.

The greatest men of America, her Washingtons, Hamiltons, Madisons, well understanding that aristocratical institutions are not in all times and places possible; well perceiving that in their Republic there was no place for these; comprehending, therefore, that from these that security for national dignity and greatness, an ideal commanding popular reverence, was not to be obtained, but knowing that this ideal was indispensable, would have been rejoiced to found a substitute for it in the dignity and authority of the State.

They deplored the weakness and insignificance of the executive power as a calamity. When the inevitable course of events has made our self-government something really like that of America, when it has removed or weakened that security for national dignity, which we possessed in *aristocracy,* will the substitute of the *State* be equally wanting to us? If it is, then the dangers of America will really be ours; the dangers which come from the multitude being in power, with no adequate ideal to elevate or guide the multitude.

It would really be wasting time to contend at length, that to give more prominence to the idea of the State is now possible in this country, without endangering liberty. In other countries the habits and dispositions of the people may be such that the State, if once it acts, may be easily suffered to usurp exorbitantly; here they certainly are not. Here the people will always sufficiently keep in mind that any public authority is a trust delegated by themselves, for certain purposes, and with certain limits; and if that authority pretends to an absolute, independent character, they will soon enough (and very rightly) remind it of its error. Here there can be no question of a paternal government, of an irresponsible executive power, professing to act for the people's good, but without the people's consent, and, if necessary, against the people's wishes; here no one dreams of removing a single constitutional control, of abolishing a single safeguard for securing a correspondence between the acts of government and the will of the nation. The question is, whether, retaining all its power of control over a government which should abuse its trust, the nation may not now find advantage in voluntarily allowing to it purposes somewhat ampler, and limits somewhat wider within which to execute them, than formerly; whether the nation may not thus acquire in the State an ideal of high reason and right feeling, representing its best self, commanding general respect, and forming a rallying-point for the intelligence and for the worthiest instincts of the community, which will herein find a true bond of union.

I am convinced that if the worst mischiefs of democracy ever happen in England, it will be, not because a new condition of things has come upon us unforeseen, but because, though we all foresaw it, our efforts to deal with it were in the wrong direction. At the present time, almost every one believes in the growth of democracy, almost every one talks of it, almost every one laments it; but the last thing people can be brought to do is to make timely preparation for it. Many of those who, if they would, could do most to forward this work of preparation, are made slack and hesitating by the belief that, after all, in England, things may probably never go very far; that it will be possible to keep much more of the past than speculators say. Others, with a more robust faith, think that all democracy wants is vigorous putting-down; and that, with a good will and strong hand, it is perfectly possible to retain or restore the whole system of the Middle Ages. Others, free from the prejudices of class and position which warp the judgment of these, and who would, I believe, be the first and greatest gainers by strengthening the hands of the State, are averse from doing so by reason of suspicions and fears, once perfectly well-grounded, but, in this age and in the present circumstances, well-grounded no longer.

I speak of the middle classes. I have already shown how it is the natural disposition of an aristocratical class to view with jealousy the development of a considerable State-power. But this disposition has in England found extraordinary favour and support in regions not aristocratical,—from the middle classes; and, above all, from the kernel of these classes, the Protestant Dissenters. And for a very good reason. In times when passions ran high, even an aristocratical executive was easily stimulated into using, for the gratification of its friends and the abasement of its enemies, those administrative engines which, the moment it chose to stretch its hand forth, stood ready for its grasp. Matters of domestic concern, matters of religious profession and religious exercise, offered a peculiar field for an intervention gainful and agreeable to friends, injurious and irritating to enemies. Such an intervention was attempted and practised. Government lent its machinery and authority to the aristocratical and ecclesiastical party, which it regarded as its best support. The party which suffered comprised the flower and strength of that middle class of society, always very flourishing and robust in this country. That powerful class, from this specimen of the administrative activity of government, conceived a strong antipathy against all intervention of the State in certain spheres. An active, stringent administration in those spheres, meant at that time a High Church and Prelatic administration in them, an administration galling to the Puritan party and to the middle class; and this aggrieved class had naturally no proneness to draw nice philosophical distinctions between State-action in these spheres, as a thing for abstract consideration, and State-action in them as they practically felt it and supposed themselves likely long to feel it, guided by their adversaries. In the minds of the English middle class, therefore, State-action in social and domestic concerns became inextricably associated with the idea of a Conventicle Act, a Five-Mile Act, an Act of Uniformity. Their abhorrence of such a State-action as this they extended to State-action in general; and, having never known a beneficent and just State-power, they enlarged their hatred of a cruel and partial State-power, the only one they had ever known, into a maxim that no State-power was to be trusted, that the least action, in certain provinces, was rigorously to be denied to the State, whenever this denial was possible.

Thus that jealousy of an important, sedulous, energetic executive, natural to grandees unwilling to suffer their personal authority to be circumscribed, their individual grandeur to be eclipsed, by the authority and grandeur of the State, became reinforced in this country by a like sentiment among the middle classes, who had no such authority or grandeur to lose, but who, by a hasty reasoning, had theoretically condemned for ever an agency which they had practically found at times oppressive. *Leave us to ourselves!*

magnates and middle classes alike cried to the State. Not only from those who were full and abounded went up this prayer, but also from those whose condition admitted of great amelioration. Not only did the whole repudiate the physician, but also those who were sick.

For it is evident, that the action of a diligent, an impartial, and a national government, while it can do little to better the condition, already fortunate enough, of the highest and richest class of its people, can really do much, by institution and regulation, to better that of the middle and lower classes. The State can bestow certain broad collective benefits, which are indeed not much if compared with the advantages already possessed by individual grandeur, but which are rich and valuable if compared with the make-shifts of mediocrity and poverty. A good thing meant for the many cannot well be so exquisite as the good things of the few; but it can easily, if it comes from a donor of great resources and wide power, be incomparably better than what the many could, unaided, provide for themselves.

In all the remarks which I have been making, I have hitherto abstained from any attempt to suggest a positive application of them. I have limited myself to simply pointing out in how changed a world of ideas we are living; I have not sought to go further, and to discuss in what particular manner the world of facts is to adapt itself to this changed world of ideas. This has been my rule so far; but from this rule I shall here venture to depart, in order to dwell for a moment on a matter of practical institution, designed to meet new social exigencies: on the intervention of the State in public education.

The public secondary schools of France, decreed by the Revolution and established under the Consulate, are said by many good judges to be inferior to the old colleges. By means of the old colleges and of private tutors, the French aristocracy could procure for its children (so it is said, and very likely with truth) a better training than that which is now given in the lyceums. Yes; but the boon conferred by the State, when it founded the lyceums, was not for the aristocracy; it was for the vast middle class of Frenchmen. This class, certainly, had not already the means of a better training for its children, before the State interfered. This class, certainly, would not have succeeded in procuring by its own efforts a better training for its children, if the State had not interfered. Through the intervention of the State this class enjoys better schools for its children, not than the great and rich enjoy (that is not the question), but than the same class enjoys in any country where the State has not interfered to found them. The lyceums may not be so good as Eton or Harrow; but they are a great deal better than a *Classical and Commercial Academy.*

The aristocratic classes in England may, perhaps, be well content to rest satisfied with their Eton and Harrow. The State is not likely to do better for them. Nay, the superior confidence, spirit, and style, engendered by a training in the great public schools, constitute for these classes a real privilege, a real engine of command, which they might, if they were selfish, be sorry to lose by the establishment of schools great enough to beget a like spirit in the classes below them. But the middle classes in England have every reason not to rest content with their private schools; the State can do a great deal better for them. By giving to schools for these classes a public character, it can bring the instruction in them under a criticism which the stock of knowledge and judgment in our middle classes is not of itself at present able to supply. By giving to them a national character, it can confer on them a greatness and a noble spirit, which the tone of these classes is not of itself at present adequate to impart. Such schools would soon prove notable competitors with the existing public schools; they would do these a great service by stimulating them, and making them look into their own weak points more closely. Economical, because with charges uniform and under severe revision, they would do a great service to that large body of persons who, at present, seeing that on the whole the best secondary instruction to be found is that of the existing public schools, obtain it for their children from a sense of duty, although they can ill afford it, and although its cost is certainly exorbitant. Thus the middle classes might, by the aid of the State, better their instruction, while still keeping its cost moderate. This in itself would be a gain; but this gain would be slight in comparison with that of acquiring the sense of belonging to great and honourable seats of learning, and of breathing in their youth the air of the best culture of their nation. This sense would be an educational influence for them of the highest value. It would really augment their self-respect and moral force; it would truly fuse them with the class above, and tend to bring about for them the equality which they are entitled to desire.

So it is not State-action in itself which the middle and lower classes of a nation ought to deprecate; it is State-action exercised by a hostile class, and for their oppression. From a State-action reasonably, equitably, and nationally exercised, they may derive great benefit; greater, by the very nature and necessity of things, than can be derived from this source by the class above them. For the middle or lower classes to obstruct such a State-action, to repel its benefits, is to play the game of their enemies, and to prolong for themselves a condition of real inferiority.

This, I know, is rather dangerous ground to tread upon. The great middle classes of this country are conscious of no weakness, no inferiority; they do not want any one to provide anything for them. Such as they are, they believe that the freedom and prosperity of England are their work, and that the future belongs to them. No one esteems them more than I do; but those who esteem them most, and who most believe in their capabilities, can render them no better service than by pointing out in what they underrate their deficiencies, and how their deficiencies, if unremedied, may impair their future. They want culture and dignity; they want ideas. Aristocracy has culture and dignity; democracy has readiness for new ideas, and ardour for what ideas it possesses. Of these, our middle class has the last only: ardour for the ideas it already possesses. It believes ardently in liberty, it believes ardently in industry; and, by its zealous belief in these two ideas, it has accomplished great things. What it has accomplished by its belief in industry is patent to all the world. The liberties of England are less its exclusive work than it supposes; for these, aristocracy has achieved nearly as much. Still, of one inestimable part of liberty, liberty of thought, the middle class has been (without precisely intending it) the principal champion. The intellectual action of the Church of England upon the nation has been insignificant; its social action has been great. The social action of Protestant Dissent, that genuine product of the English middle class, has not been civilising; its positive intellectual action has been insignificant; its negative intellectual action,—in so far as by strenuously maintaining for itself, against persecution, liberty of conscience and the right of free opinion, it at the same time maintained and established this right as a universal principle,—has been invaluable. But the actual results of this negative intellectual service rendered by Protestant Dissent,—by the middle class,—to the whole community, great as they undoubtedly are, must not be taken for something which they are not. It is a very great thing to be able to think as you like; but, after all, an important question remains: *what* you think. It is a fine thing to secure a free stage and no favour; but, after all, the part which you play on that stage will have to be criticised. Now, all the liberty and industry in the world will not ensure these two things: a high reason and a fine culture. They may favour them, but they will not of themselves produce them; they may exist without them. But it is by the appearance of these two things, in some shape or other, in the life of a nation, that it becomes something more than an independent, an energetic, a successful nation,—that it becomes a *great* nation.

In modern epochs the part of a high reason, of ideas, acquires constantly increasing importance in the conduct of the world's affairs. A fine culture is the complement of a high reason, and it is in the conjunction of both with character, with energy, that the ideal for men and nations is to be placed. It is common to hear remarks on the frequent divorce between culture and character, and to infer from this that culture is a mere varnish, and that character only deserves any serious attention. No error can be more fatal. Culture without character is, no doubt, something frivolous, vain, and weak; but character without culture is, on the other hand, something raw, blind, and dangerous. The most interesting, the most truly glorious peoples, are those in which the alliance of the two has been effected most successfully, and its result spread most widely. This is why the spectacle of ancient Athens has such profound interest for a rational man; that it is the spectacle of the culture of a *people.* It is not an aristocracy, leavening with its own high spirit the multitude which it wields, but leaving it the unformed multitude still; it is not a democracy, acute and energetic, but tasteless, narrow-minded, and ignoble; it is the middle and lower classes in the highest development of their humanity that these classes have yet reached. It was the *many* who relished those arts who were not satisfied with less than those monuments. In the conversations recorded by Plato, or even by the matter-of-fact Xenophon, which for the free yet refined discussion of ideas have set the tone for the whole cultivated world, shopkeepers and tradesmen of Athens mingle as speakers. For any one but a pedant, this is why a handful of Athenians of two thousand years ago are more interesting than the millions of most nations our contemporaries. Surely, if they knew this, those friends of progress, who have confidently pronounced the remains of the ancient world to be so much lumber, and a classical education an aristocratic impertinence, might be inclined to reconsider their sentence.

The course taken in the next fifty years by the middle classes of this nation will probably give a decisive turn to its history. If they will not seek the alliance of the State for their own elevation, if they go on exaggerating their spirit of individualism, if they persist in their jealousy of all governmental action, if they cannot learn that the antipathies and the shibboleths of a past age are now an anachronism for them—that will not prevent them, probably, from getting the rule of their country for a season, but they will certainly *Americanise* it. They will rule it by their energy, but they will deteriorate it by their low ideals and want of culture. In the decline of the aristocratical element, which in some sort supplied an ideal to ennoble the spirit of the nation and to keep it together, there will be no other element present to perform this service. It is of itself a serious calamity for a nation that its tone of feeling and grandeur of spirit should be lowered or dulled. But the calamity appears far more serious still when we consider that the middle classes, remaining as they are now, with their narrow, harsh, unintelligent, and unattractive spirit and culture, will almost certainly fail to mould or assimilate the masses below them, whose sympathies are at the present moment actually wider and more liberal than theirs. They arrive, these masses, eager to enter into possession of the world, to gain a more vivid sense of their own life and activity. In this their irrepressible development, their natural educators and initiators are those immediately above them, the middle classes. If these classes cannot win their sympathy or give them their direction, society is in danger of falling into anarchy.

Therefore, with all the force I can, I wish to urge upon the middle classes of this country, both that they might be very greatly profited by the action of the State, and also that they are continuing their opposition to such action out of an unfounded fear. But at the same time I say that the middle classes have the right, in admitting the action of government, to make the condition that this government shall be one of their own adoption, one that they can trust. To ensure this is now in their own power. If they do not as yet ensure this, they ought to do so, they have the means of doing so. Two centuries ago they had not; now they have. Having this security, let them now show themselves jealous to keep the action of the State equitable and rational, rather than to exclude the action of the State altogether. If the State acts amiss, let them check it, but let them no longer take it for granted that the State cannot possibly act usefully.

The State—but what is *the State?* cry many. Speculations on the idea of a State abound, but these do not satisfy them; of that which is to have practical effect and power they require a plain account. The full force of the term, *the State,* as the full force of any other important term, no one will master without going a little deeply, without resolutely entering the world of ideas; but it is possible to give in very plain language an account of it sufficient for all practical purposes. The State is properly just what Burke called it—*the nation in its collective and corporate character.* The State is the representative acting-power of the nation; the action of the State is the representative action of the nation. Nominally emanating from the Crown, as the ideal unity in which the nation concentrates itself, this action, by the constitution of our country, really emanates from the ministers of the Crown. It is common to hear the depreciators of State-action run through a string of ministers' names, and then say: "Here is really your *State;* would you accept the action of these men as your own representative action? In what respect is their judgment on national affairs likely to be any better than that of the rest of the world?" In the first place I answer: Even supposing them to be originally no better or wiser than the rest of the world, they have two great advantages from their position: access to almost boundless means of information, and the enlargement of mind which the habit of dealing with great affairs tends to produce. Their position itself, therefore, if they are men of only average honesty and capacity, tends to give them a fitness for acting on behalf of the nation superior to that of other men of equal honesty and capacity who are not in the same position. This fitness may be yet further increased by treating them as persons on whom, indeed, a very grave responsibility has fallen, and from whom very much will be expected;—nothing less than the representing, each of them in his own department, under the control of Parliament, and aided by the suggestions of public opinion, the collective energy and intelligence of his nation. By treating them as men on whom all this devolves to do, to their honour if they do it well, to their shame if they do it ill, one probably augments their faculty of well-doing; as it is excellently said: "To treat men as if they were better than they are, is the surest way to *make* them better than they are." But to treat them as if they had been shuffled into their places by a lucky accident, were most likely soon to be shuffled out of them again, and meanwhile ought to magnify themselves and their office as little as possible; to treat them as if they and their functions could without much inconvenience be quite dispensed with, and they ought perpetually to be admiring their own inconceivable good fortune in being permitted to discharge them;—this is the way to paralyse all high effort in the executive government, to extinguish all lofty sense of responsibility; to make its members either merely solicitous for the gross advantages, the emolument, and self-importance, which they derive from their offices, or else timid, apologetic, and self-mistrustful in filling them; in either case, formal and inefficient.

But in the second place I answer: If the executive government is really in the hands of men no wiser than the bulk of mankind, of men whose action an intelligent man would be unwilling to accept as representative of his own action, whose fault is that? It is the fault of the nation itself, which, not being in the hands of a despot or an oligarchy, being free to control the choice of those who are to sum up and concentrate its action, controls it in such a manner that it allows to be chosen agents so little in its confidence, or so mediocre, or so incompetent, that it thinks the best thing to be done with them is to reduce their action as near as possible to a nullity. Hesitating, blundering, unintelligent, inefficacious, the action of the State may be; but, such as it is, it is the collective action of the nation itself, and the nation is responsible for it. It is our own action which we suffer to be thus unsatisfactory. Nothing can free us from this responsibility. The conduct of our affairs is in our own power. To carry on into its executive proceedings the indecision, conflict, and discordance of its parliamentary debates, may be a natural defect of a free nation, but it is certainly a defect; it is a dangerous error to call it, as some do, a perfection. The want of concert, reason, and organisation in the State, is the want of concert, reason, and organisation in the collective nation.

Inasmuch, therefore, as collective action is more efficacious than isolated individual efforts, a nation having great and complicated matters to deal with must greatly gain by employing the action of the State. Only, the State-power which it employs should be a power which really represents its best self, and whose action its intelligence and justice can heartily avow and adopt; not a power which reflects its inferior self, and of whose action, as of its own second-rate action, it has perpetually to be ashamed. To offer a worthy initiative, and to set a standard of rational and equitable action,—this is what the nation should expect of the State; and the more the State fulfils this expectation, the more will it be accepted in practice for what in idea it must always be. People will not then ask the State, what title it has to commend or reward genius and merit, since commendation and reward imply an attitude of superiority, for it will then be felt that the State truly acts for the English nation; and the genius of the English nation is greater than the genius of any individual, greater even than Shakespeare's genius, for it includes the genius of Newton also.

I will not deny that to give a more prominent part to the State would be a considerable change in this country; that maxims once very sound, and habits once very salutary, may be appealed to against it. The sole question is, whether those maxims and habits are sound and salutary at this moment. A yet graver and more difficult change,—to reduce the all-effacing prominence of the State, to give a more prominent part to the individual,—is imperiously presenting itself to other countries. Both are the suggestions of one irresistible force, which is gradually making its way everywhere, removing old conditions and imposing new, altering long-fixed habits, undermining venerable institutions, even modifying national character: *the modern spirit.*

Undoubtedly we are drawing on towards great changes; and for every nation the thing most needful is to discern clearly its own condition, in order to know in what particular way it may best meet them. Openness and flexibility of mind are at such a time the first of virtues. *Be ye perfect,* said the Founder of Christianity; *I count not myself to have apprehended,* said its greatest Apostle. Perfection will never be reached; but to recognise a period of transformation when it comes, and to adapt themselves honestly and rationally to its laws, is perhaps the nearest approach to perfection of which men and nations are capable. No habits or attachments should prevent their trying to do this; nor indeed, in the long run, can they. Human thought, which made all institutions, inevitably saps them, resting only in that which is absolute and eternal.

1861

31 Democratic Elitism: A Limited Role for the "People"

JOSEPH A. SCHUMPETER

The theory of competitive leadership has proved a satisfactory interpretation of the facts of the democratic process. So we shall naturally use it in our attempt to unravel the relation between democracy and a socialist order of things. As has been stated before, socialists claim not only compatibility; they claim that democracy implies socialism and that there cannot be true democracy except in socialism. On the other hand, the reader cannot but be familiar with at least some of the numerous pamphlets that have been published in this country during the last few years in order to prove that a planned economy, let alone full-fledged socialism, is completely incompatible with democracy. Both standpoints are of course easy to understand from the psychological background of the contest and from the natural wish of both parties to it to secure the support of a people the great majority of whom fervently believes in democracy. But suppose we ask: where lies the truth?

SOURCE: Previously entitled "The Inference" (pp. 287–302) in *Capitalism, Socialism and Democracy,* 3rd ed., by Joseph A. Schumpeter.

Our analysis in this . . . readily yields an answer. Between socialism as we defined it and democracy as we defined it there is no necessary relation: the one can exist without the other. At the same time there is no incompatibility: in appropriate states of the social environment the socialist engine can be run on democratic principles.

But observe that these simple statements depend upon our view about what socialism and democracy are. Therefore they mean not only less than, but also something different from, what either party to the contest has in mind. For this reason and also because behind the question of mere compatibility there inevitably arises the further question whether the democratic method will work more or less effectively in a socialist as compared with a capitalist regime, we have still a lot of explaining to do. In particular we must try to formulate the conditions under which the democratic method can be expected to give satisfaction. This will be done in the second section of this chapter. Now we shall look at some of the implications of our analysis of the democratic process.

First of all, according to the view we have taken, democracy does not mean and cannot mean that the people actually rule in any obvious sense of the terms "people" and "rule." Democracy means only that the people have the opportunity of accepting or refusing the men who are to rule them. But since they might decide this also in entirely undemocratic ways, we have had to narrow our definition by adding a further criterion identifying the democratic method, viz., free competition among would-be leaders for the vote of the electorate. Now one aspect of this may be expressed by saying that democracy is the rule of the politician. It is of the utmost importance to realize clearly what this implies.

Many exponents of democratic doctrine have striven hard to divest political activity of any professional connotation. They have held strongly, sometimes passionately, that politics ought not to be a profession and that democracy degenerates whenever it becomes one. But this is just ideology. It is true that, say, businessmen or lawyers may be elected to serve in parliament and even taken office occasionally and still remain primarily businessmen and lawyers. It is also true that many who become primarily politicians continue to rely on other activities for their livelihood. But normally, personal success in politics, more than occasional rise to cabinet office in particular, will imply concentration of the professional kind and relegate a man's other activities to the rank of sidelines or necessary chores. If we wish to face facts squarely, we must recognize that, in modern democracies of any type other than the Swiss, politics will unavoidably be a career. This in turn spells recognition of a distinct professional interest in the individual politician and of a distinct group interest in the political profession as such. It is essential to insert this factor into our theory. Many a riddle is solved as soon as we take account of it. Among other things we immediately cease to wonder why it is that politicians so often fail to serve the interest of their class or of the groups with which they are personally connected. Politically speaking, the man is still in the nursery who has not absorbed, so as never to forget, the saying attributed to one of the most successful politicians that ever lived: "What businessmen do not understand is that exactly as they are dealing in oil so I am dealing in votes."

Let us note that there is no reason to believe that this will be either better or worse in a socialist organization of society. The doctor or engineer who means to fill the cup of his ambitions by means of success as a doctor or engineer will still be a distinct type of man and have a distinct pattern of interests; the doctor or engineer who means to work or reform the institutions of his country will still be another type and have another pattern of interests.

Second, students of political organization have always felt doubts concerning the administrative efficiency of democracy in large and complex societies. In particular it has been urged that, as compared with other arrangements, the efficiency of democratic government is inevitably impaired because of the tremendous loss of energy which the incessant battle in parliament and outside of it imposes upon the leading men. It is further impaired, for the same reason, by the necessity of bending policies to the exigencies of political warfare. Neither proposition is open to doubt. Both are but corollaries to our previous statement that the democratic method produces legislation and administration as by-products of the struggle for political office.

Visualize, for instance, the situation of a Prime Minister. Where governments are as unstable as they have been in France from 1871 to the breakdown in 1940, his attention must be almost monopolized by a task that is like trying to build a pyramid from billiard balls. Only men of quite unusual force under such conditions can have had any energy to spare for current administrative work on bills and so on; and only such exceptional men can have acquired any authority with their civil service subordinates who like everybody else knew that their chief would be out before long. Of course this is not anything like as bad in the English case. Unstable governmental combinations are exceptions, and normally a government can count on a life of about five or six years. Ministers can settle down in their offices and are not so easy to unhorse in Parliament. But this does not mean that they are exempt from fighting. There always is a current contest and if governments are not constantly on trial for their lives it is only because they are as a rule able to smother current attacks this side of the danger point. The Prime Minister has to watch his opponents all the time, to lead his own flock incessantly, to be ready to step into breaches that might open at any moment, to keep his hand on the measures under debate, to control his cabinet—all of which amounts to saying that, when Parliament is in session, he is lucky if he has a couple of hours in the morning left for thinking things over and for real work. Individual miscarriages and defeats of a government as a whole are not infrequently due to physical exhaustion of the leading man or men. How could he, so it might well be asked, undertake to lead and supervise an administrative organism that is to embrace all the problems of economic life?

But this wastage of governmental energy is not all. The incessant competitive struggle to get into office or to stay in it imparts to every consideration of policies and measures the bias so admirably expressed by the phrase about "dealing in votes." The fact that in a democracy government must attend primarily to the political values of a policy or a bill or an administrative act—that is to say, the very fact that enforces the democratic principle of the government's dependence upon the voting of parliament and of the electorate—is likely to distort all the pro's and con's. In particular, it forces upon the men at or near the helm a short-run view and makes it extremely difficult for them to serve such long-run interests of the nation as may require consistent work for far-off ends; foreign policy, for instance, is in danger of degenerating into domestic politics. And it makes it no less difficult to dose measures rationally. The dosing that a government decides on with an eye to its political chances is not necessarily the one that will produce the results most satisfactory to the nation.

Thus the prime minister in a democracy might be likened to a horseman who is so fully engrossed in trying to keep in the saddle that he cannot plan his ride, or to a general so fully occupied with making sure that his army will accept his orders that he must leave strategy to take care of itself. And this remains true (and must, in the case of some countries such as France and Italy, be frankly recognized as one of the sources from which anti-democratic feeling has spread) in spite of the facts that may be invoked in extenuation.

There is, to begin with, the fact that the instances in which those consequences show to an extent that may be felt to be unbearable can often be explained on the ground that the social pattern is not up to the task of working democratic institutions. As the examples of France and Italy show, this may happen in countries that are much more civilized than some which do succeed in that task. But nevertheless the weight of the criticism is thereby reduced to the statement that the satisfactory working of the democratic method is contingent upon fulfillment of certain conditions—a subject that will be taken up presently.

Then there is the question of the alternative. These weaknesses are obviously not absent in non-democratic patterns. Paving one's way to a leading position, say, at a court, may absorb quite as much energy and distort one's views about issues quite as much as does the democratic struggle though that waste or distortion does not stand out so publicly. This amounts to saying that attempts at comparative appraisal of engines of government will have to take account of many other factors besides the institutional principles involved.

Moreover, some of us will reply to the critic that a lower level of governmental efficiency may be exactly what we want. We certainly do not want to be the objects of dictatorial efficiency, mere material for deep games. Such a thing as the Gosplan may at present be impossible in the United States. But does not this prove precisely that, just like the Russian Gosplan, its hypothetical analogue in this country would violate the spirit as well as the organic structure of the commonwealth.

Finally, something can be done to reduce the pressure on the leading men by appropriate institutional devices. The American arrangement for instance shows up to advantage on this point. The American "prime minister" must no doubt keep his eye on his political chessboard. But he need not feel responsible for every individual measure. And, not sitting in Congress, he is at least exempt from the physical strain this would involve. He has all the opportunity he wants to nurse his strength.

Third, our [earlier] analysis . . . brings into bold relief the problem of the quality of the men the democratic method selects for positions of leadership. The well-known argument about this hardly needs recalling: the democratic method creates professional politicians whom it then turns into amateur administrators and "statesmen." Themselves lacking all the acquirements necessary for dealing with the tasks that confront them, they appoint Lord Macaulay's "judges without law and diplomatists without French," ruining the civil service and discouraging all the best elements in it. Worse still, there is another point, distinct from any question of specialized competence and experience: the qualities of intellect and character that make a good candidate are not necessarily those that make a good administrator, and selection by means of success at the polls may work against the people who would be successes at the head of affairs. And even if the products of this selection prove successes in office, these successes may well be failures for the nation. The politician who is a good tactician can successfully survive any number of administrative miscarriages.

Recognition of the elements of truth in all this should again be tempered by the recognition of the extenuating facts. In particular, the case for democracy stands to gain from a consideration of the alternatives: no system of selection whatever the social sphere—with the possible exception of competitive capitalism—tests exclusively the ability to perform and selects in the way a stable selects its Derby crack. Though to varying degrees, all systems put premiums on other qualities as well, qualities that are often inimical to performance. But we may perhaps go further than this. It is not quite true that in the average case political success proves nothing for a man or that the politician is nothing but an amateur. There is one very important thing that he knows professionally, viz., the handling of men. And, as a broad rule at least, the ability to win a position of political leadership will be associated with a certain amount of personal force and also of other aptitudes that will come in usefully in a prime minister's workshop. There are after all many rocks in the stream that carries politicians to national office which are not entirely ineffective in barring the progress of the moron or the windbag.

That in such matters general argument one way or another does not lead to a definite result is only what we should expect. It is much more curious and significant that factual evidence is not, at first sight at least, any more conclusive. Nothing is easier than to compile an impressive list of failures of the democratic method, especially if we include not only cases in which there was actual breakdown or national discomfiture but also those in which, though the nation led a healthy and prosperous life, the performance in the political sector was clearly substandard relative to the performance in others. But it is just as easy to marshal hardly less impressive evidence in favor of the politician. To cite one outstanding illustration: It is true that in antiquity war was not so technical an affair as it has become of late. Yet one would think that the ability to make a success at it had even then very little to do with the ability to get oneself elected to political office. All the Roman generals of the republican era however were politicians and all of them got their commands directly through the elective offices they held or had previously held. Some of the worst disasters were due to this. But on the whole, these politician-soldiers did remarkably well.

Why is that so? There can be only one answer to this question.

Conditions for the Success of the Democratic Method

If a physicist observes that the same mechanism works differently at different times and in different places, he concludes that its functioning depends upon conditions extraneous to it. We cannot but arrive at the same conclusion. And it is as easy to see what these conditions are as it was to see what the conditions were under which the classical doctrine of democracy might be expected to fit reality to an acceptable degree.

This conclusion definitely commits us to that strictly relativist view that has been indicated all along. Exactly as there is no case for or against socialism at all times and in all places, so there is no absolutely general case for or against the democratic method. And exactly as with socialism, this makes it difficult to argue by means of a *ceteris paribus* clause, for "other things" *cannot* be equal as between situations in which democracy is a workable, or the only workable, arrangement and situations in which it is not. Democracy thrives in social patterns that display certain characteristics and it might well be doubted whether there is any sense in asking how it would fare in others that lack those characteristics—or how the people in those other patterns would fare with it. The conditions which I hold must be fulfilled for the democratic method to be a success [1]—in societies in which

[1] By "success" I mean no more than that the democratic process reproduce itself steadily without creating situations that enforce resort to non-democratic methods and that it cope with current problems in a way which all interests that count politically find acceptable in the long run. I do not mean that every observer, from his own individual standpoint, need approve of the results.

it is possible for it to work at all—I shall group under four headings; and I shall confine myself to the great industrial nations of the modern type.

The first condition is that the human material of politics—the people who man the party machines, are elected to serve in parliament, rise to cabinet office—should be of sufficiently high quality. This means more than that individuals of adequate ability and moral character must exist in sufficient numbers. As has been pointed out before, the democratic method selects not simply from the population but only from those elements of the population that are available for the political vocation or, more precisely, that offer themselves for election. All methods of selection do this of course. All of them therefore may, according to the degree to which a given vocation attracts talent and character, produce in it a level of performance that is above or below the national average. But the competitive struggle for responsible office is, on the one hand, wasteful of personnel and energy. On the other hand, the democratic process may easily create conditions in the political sector that, once established, will repel most of the men who can make a success at anything else. For both these reasons, adequacy of material is particularly important for the success of democratic government. It is not true that in a democracy people always have the kind and quality of government they want or merit.

There may be many ways in which politicians of sufficiently good quality can be secured. Thus far however, experience seems to suggest that the only effective guarantee is in the existence of a social stratum, itself a product of a severely selective process, that takes to politics as a matter of course. If such a stratum be neither too exclusive nor too easily accessible for the outsider and if it be strong enough to assimilate most of the elements it currently absorbs, it not only will present for the political career products of stocks that have successfully passed many tests in other fields—served, as it were, an apprenticeship in private affairs—but it will also increase their fitness by endowing them with traditions that embody experience, with a professional code and with a common fund of views.

It is hardly mere coincidence that England, which is the only country to fulfill our condition completely, is also the only country to have a political society in this sense. Still more instructive is the case of Germany in the period of the Weimar Republic (1918–1933). . . . There was nothing about the German politicians of that period that would ordinarily be considered a glaring defect. The average member of parliament and the average prime and cabinet minister were honest, reasonable and conscientious. This applies to all parties. However, with due respect for the sprinkling of talent that showed here and there, though rarely in a position of or near high command, it must be added that most of them were distinctly below par, in some cases pitifully so. Obviously this cannot have been due to any lack of ability and energy in the nation as a whole. But ability and energy spurned the political career. And there was no class or group whose members looked upon politics as their predestined career. That political system missed fire for many reasons. But the fact that eventually it met smashing defeat at the hands of an anti-democratic leader is nevertheless indicative of the lack of inspiring democratic leadership.

The second condition for the success of democracy is that the effective range of political decision should not be extended too far. How far it can be extended depends not only on the general limitations of the democratic method which follow from the analysis presented in the preceding section but also on the particular circumstances of each individual case. To put this more concretely: the range does not only depend, for instance, on the kind and quantity of matters that can be successfully handled by a government subject to the strain of an incessant struggle for its political life; it also depends, at any given time and place, on the quality of the men who form that government and on the type of political machine and the pattern of public opinion they have to work with. From the standpoint of our theory of democracy it is not necessary to require, as it would be from the standpoint of the classical theory, that only such matters should be dealt with by the political apparatus which the people at large can fully understand and have a serious opinion about. But a less exacting requirement of the same nature still imposes itself. It calls for additional comment.

Of course there cannot be any legal limits to what a parliament, led by the prime minister, might subject to its decision, if need be, by means of a constitutional amendment. But, so Edmund Burke argued in discussing the behavior of the English government and Parliament with respect to the American colonies, in order to function properly that all-powerful parliament must impose limits upon itself. Similarly we may argue that, even within the range of matters that have to be submitted to parliamentary vote, it is often necessary for government and parliament to pass measures on which their decision is purely formal or, at most, of a purely supervisory nature. Otherwise the democratic method may turn out legislative freaks. Take for instance the case of so bulky and so technical a measure as a criminal code. The democratic method will apply to the question whether or not a country is to have such a codification at all. It will also apply to certain "issues" that the government may choose to select for political decision which is more than formal—for instance, whether certain practices of labor or employers' associations should or should not be considered criminal. But for the rest, government and parliament will have to accept the specialists' advice whatever they may think themselves. For crime is a complex phenomenon. The term in fact covers many phenomena that have very little in common. Popular slogans about it are almost invariably wrong. And a rational treatment of it requires that legislation in this matter should be protected from both the fits of vindictiveness and the fits of sentimentality in which the laymen in the government and in the parliament are alternatingly prone to indulge. This is what I meant to convey by stressing the limitations upon the *effective* range of political decision—the range within which politicians decide in truth as well as in form.

Again, the condition in question can indeed be fulfilled by a corresponding limitation of the activities of the state. But it would be a serious misunderstanding if the reader thought that such a limitation is necessarily implied. Democracy does not require that every function of the state be subject to its political method. For instance, in most democratic countries a large measure of independence from political agencies is granted to the judges. Another instance is the position held by the Bank of England until 1914. Some of its functions were in fact of a public nature. Nevertheless these functions were vested with what legally was just a business corporation that was sufficiently independent of the political sector to have a policy of its own. Certain federal agencies in this country are other cases in point. The Interstate Commerce Commission embodies an attempt to extend the sphere of public authority without extending the sphere of political decision. Or, to present still another example, certain of our states finance state universities "without any strings," that is to say, without interfering with what in some cases amounts to practically complete autonomy.

Thus, almost any type of human affairs may conceivably be made to enter the sphere of the state without becoming part of the material of the competitive struggle for political leadership beyond what is implied in passing the measure that grants the power and sets up the agency to wield it and the contact that is implied in the government's role of general supervisor. It is of course true that this supervision may degenerate into vitiating influence. The politician's power to appoint the personnel of non-political public agencies, if remorselessly used, will often suffice in itself to corrupt them. But that does not affect the principle in question.

As a third condition, democratic government in modern industrial society must be able to command, for all purposes the sphere of public activity is to include—no matter whether this be much or little—the services of a well-trained bureaucracy of good standing and tradition, endowed with a strong sense of duty and a no less strong *esprit de corps.* Such a bureaucracy is the main answer to the argument about government by amateurs. Potentially it is the only answer to the question so often heard in this country: democratic politics has proved itself unable to produce decent city government; how can we expect the nation to fare if everything, eventually including the whole of the productive process, is to be handed over to it? And finally, it is also the principal answer to the question about how our second condition can be fulfilled whenever the sphere of public control is wide.

It is not enough that the bureaucracy should be efficient in current administration and competent to give advice. It must also be strong enough to guide and, if need be, to instruct the politicians who head the ministries. In order to be able to do this it must be in a position to evolve principles of its own and sufficiently independent to assert them. It must be a power in its own right. This amounts to saying that in fact though not in form appointment, tenure and promotion must depend largely—within civil service rules that politicians hesitate to violate—on its own corporate opinion in spite of all the clamor that is sure to arise whenever politicians or the public find themselves crossed by it as they frequently must.

Again, as in the case of the personnel of politics, the question of the available human material is all-important. Training though essential is quite secondary to this. And again, both requisite material and the traditional code necessary for the functioning of an official class of this kind can be most easily secured if there is a social stratum of adequate quality and corresponding prestige that can be drawn upon for recruits—not too rich, not too poor, not too exclusive, not too accessible. The bureaucracies of Europe, in spite of the fact that they have drawn enough hostile criticism to blur their records, exemplify very well what I am trying to convey. They are the product of a long development that started with the *ministeriales* of medieval magnates (originally serfs selected for administrative and military purposes who thereby acquired the status of petty nobles) and went on through the centuries until the powerful engine emerged which we behold today. It cannot be created in a hurry. It cannot be "hired" with money. But it grows everywhere, whatever the political method a nation may adopt. Its expansion is the one certain thing about our future.

The fourth set of conditions may be summed up in the phrase Democratic Self-control. Everybody will of course agree that the democratic method cannot work smoothly unless all the groups that count in a nation are willing to accept any legislative measure as long as it is on the statute book and all executive orders issued by legally competent authorities. But democratic self-control implies much more than this.

Above all, electorates and parliaments must be on an intellectual and moral level high enough to be proof against the offerings of the crook and the crank, or else men who are neither will be driven into the ways of both. Moreover, miscarriages that will discredit democracy and undermine allegiance to it may also occur if measures are passed without regard to the claims of others or to the national situation. The individual proposals for legislative reform or executive action must, as it were, be content to stand in an orderly breadline; they must not attempt to rush the shop. Recalling what has been said in the preceding chapter about the *modus operandi* of the democratic method, the reader will realize that this involves a lot of voluntary subordination.

In particular, politicians in parliament must resist the temptation to upset or embarrass the government each time they could do so. No successful policy is possible if they do this. This means that the supporters of the government must accept its lead and allow it to frame and act upon a program and that the opposition should accept the lead of the "shadow cabinet" at its head and allow it to keep political warfare within certain rules. Fulfillment of this requirement, habitual violation of which spells the beginning of the end of a democracy, will be seen to call for just the right amount—not too much, not too little—of traditionalism. To protect this traditionalism is in fact one of the purposes for which rules of parliamentary procedure and etiquette exist.

The voters outside of parliament must respect the division of labor between themselves and the politicians they elect. They must not withdraw confidence too easily between elections and they must understand that, once they have elected an individual, political action is his business and not theirs. This means that they must refrain from instructing him about what he is to do—a principle that has indeed been universally recognized by constitutions and political theory ever since Edmund Burke's time. But its implications are not generally understood. On the one hand, few people realize that this principle clashes with the classical doctrine of democracy and really spells its abandonment. For if the people are to rule in the sense of deciding individual issues, what could be more natural for them to do than to issue instructions to their representatives as the voters for the French States-General did in and before 1789? On the other hand, it is still less recognized that if the principle be accepted, not only instructions as formal as those French *cahiers* but also less formal attempts at restricting the freedom of action of members of parliament—the practice of bombarding them with letters and telegrams for instance—ought to come under the same ban.

We cannot enter into the various delicate problems which this raises concerning the true nature of democracy as defined by us. All that matters here is that successful democratic practice in great and complicated societies has invariably been hostile to political back-seat driving—to the point of resorting to secret diplomacy and lying about intentions and commitments—and that it takes a lot of self-control on the part of the citizen to refrain from it.

Finally, effective competition for leadership requires a large measure of tolerance for difference of opinion. It has been pointed out before that this tolerance never is and never can be absolute. But it must be possible for every would-be leader who is not lawfully excluded to present his case without producing disorder. And this may imply that people stand by patiently while somebody is attacking their most vital interests or offending their most cherished ideals—or as an alternative, that the would-be leader who holds such views restrains himself correspondingly. Neither is possible without genuine respect for the opinions of one's fellow citizens amounting to a willingness to subordinate one's own opinions.

Every system can stand deviating practice to a certain extent. But even the necessary minimum of democratic self-control evidently requires a national character and national habits of a certain type which have not everywhere had the opportunity to evolve and which the democratic method itself cannot be relied on to produce. And nowhere will that self-control stand tests beyond a varying degree of severity. In fact the reader need only review our conditions in order to satisfy himself that democratic government will work to full advantage only if all the interests that matter are practically unanimous not only in their allegiance to the country but also in their allegiance to the structural principles of the existing society. Whenever these principles are called in question and issues arise that rend a nation into two hostile camps, democracy works at a disadvantage. And it may cease to work at all as soon as interests and ideals are involved on which people refuse to compromise.

This may be generalized to read that the democratic method will be at a disadvantage in troubled times. In fact, democracies of all types recognize with practical unanimity that there are situations in which it is reasonable to abandon competitive and to adopt monopolistic leadership. In ancient Rome a non-elective office conferring such a monopoly of leadership in emergencies was provided for by the constitution. The incumbent was called *magister populi* or *dictator.* Similar provisions are known to practically all constitutions, our own included: the President of the United States acquires in certain conditions a power that makes him to all intents and purposes a dictator in the Roman sense, however great the differences are both in legal construction and in practical details. If the monopoly is effectively limited either to a definite time (as it originally was in Rome) or to the duration of a definite short-run emergency, the democratic principle of competitive leadership is merely suspended. If the monopoly, either in law or in fact, is not limited as to time—and if not limited as to time it will of course tend to become unlimited as to everything else—the democratic principle is abrogated and we have the case of dictatorship in the present-day sense.

Democracy in the Socialist Order

1. In setting forth our conclusions we had better begin with the relation between democracy and the capitalist order of things.

The ideology of democracy as reflected by the classical doctrine rests on a rationalist scheme of human action and of the values of life. By virtue of a previous argument . . . this fact would in itself suffice to suggest that it is of bourgeois origin. History clearly confirms this suggestion: historically, the modern democracy rose along with capitalism, and in causal connection with it. But the same holds true for democratic practice: democracy in the sense of our theory of competitive leadership presided over the process of political and institutional change by which the bourgeoisie reshaped, and from its own point of view rationalized, the social and political structure that preceded its ascendancy: the democratic method was the political tool of that reconstruction. We have seen that the democratic method works, particularly well, also in certain extra- and pre-capitalist societies. But modern democracy is a product of the capitalist process.

Whether or not democracy is one of those products of capitalism which are to die out with it is of course another question. And still another is how well or ill capitalist society qualifies for the task of working the democratic method it evolved.

As regards the latter question, it is clear that capitalist society qualifies well in one respect. The bourgeoisie has a solution that is peculiar to it for the problem of how the sphere of political decision can be reduced to those proportions which are manageable by means of the method of competitive leadership. The bourgeois scheme of things limits the sphere of politics by limiting the sphere of public authority; its solution is in the ideal of the parsimonious state that exists primarily in order to guarantee bourgeois legality and to provide a firm frame for autonomous individual endeavor in all fields. If, moreover, account be taken of the pacific—at any rate, anti-militarist—and free-trade tendencies we have found to be inherent in bourgeois society, it will be seen that the importance of the role of political decision in the bourgeois state can, in principle at least, be scaled down to almost any extent that the disabilities of the political sector may require.

Now this kind of state has no doubt ceased to appeal to us. Bourgeois democracy is certainly a very special historical case and any claims that may be made on behalf of it are obviously contingent upon acceptance of standards which are no longer ours. But it is absurd to deny that this solution which we dislike is a solution and that bourgeois democracy is democracy. On the contrary, as its colors fade it is all the more important to recognize how colorful it was in the time of its vitality; how wide *and equal* the opportunities it offered to the families (if not to the individuals); how large the personal freedom it granted to those who passed its tests (or to their children). It is also important to recognize how well it stood, for some decades at least, the strain of uncongenial conditions and how well it functioned, when faced by demands that were outside of and hostile to the bourgeois interests.

Also in another respect capitalist society in its meridian qualified well for the task of making democracy a success. It is easier for a class whose interests are best served by being left alone to practice democratic self-restraint than it is for classes that naturally try to live on the state. The bourgeois who is primarily absorbed in his private concerns is in general—as long as these concerns are not seriously threatened—much more likely to display tolerance of political differences and respect for opinions he does not share than any other type of human being. Moreover so long as bourgeois standards are dominant in a society this attitude will tend to spread to other classes as well. The English landed interest accepted the defeat of 1845 with relatively good grace; English labor fought for the removal of disabilities but until the beginning of the present century was slow to claim privileges. It is true that in other countries such self-restraint was much less in evidence. These deviations from the principle were not always serious or always associated with capitalist interests only. But in some cases political life all but resolved itself into a struggle of pressure groups and in many cases practices that failed to conform to the spirit of the democratic method have become important enough to distort its *modus operandi.* That there "cannot" be true democracy in the capitalist order is nevertheless an obvious over-statement.[2]

In both respects however capitalism is rapidly losing the advantages it used to possess. Bourgeois democracy which is wedded to that ideal of the state has for some time been working with increasing friction. In part this was due to the fact that, as we have seen before, the democratic method never works at its best when nations are much divided on fundamental questions of social structure. And this difficulty in turn proved particularly serious, because bourgeois society signally failed to fulfill another condition for making the democratic method function. The bourgeoisie produced individuals who made a success at political leadership upon entering a political class of non-bourgeois origin, but it did not produce a successful political stratum of its own although, so one should think, the third generations of the industrial families had all the opportunity to form one. Why this was so has been fully explained. . . . All these facts together seem to suggest a pessimistic prognosis for this type of democracy. They also suggest an explanation of the apparent ease with which in some cases it surrendered to dictatorship.

2. The ideology of classical socialism is the offspring of bourgeois ideology. In particular, it fully shares the latter's rationalist and utilitarian background and many of the ideas and ideals that entered the classical doctrine of democracy. So far as this goes, socialists in fact experienced no difficulty whatever in appropriating this part of the bourgeois inheritance and in making out a case for the proposition that those elements of the classical doctrine which socialism is unable to absorb—the emphasis on protection of private property for instance—are really at variance with its fundamental principles. Creeds of this kind could survive even in entirely non-democratic forms of socialism and we may trust the scribes and pharisees to bridge by suitable phrases any gap there may be between creed and practice. But it is the practice that interests us—the fate of democratic practice as interpreted by the doctrine of competitive leadership. And so, since we have seen that non-democratic socialism is perfectly possible, the real question is again how well or ill socialism qualifies for the task of making the democratic method function should it attempt to do so.

The essential point to grasp is this. No responsible person can view

[2] What should be said is that there are some deviations from the principle of democracy which link up with the presence of organized capitalist interests. But thus corrected, the statement is true both from the standpoint of the classical and from the standpoint of our own theory of democracy. From the first standpoint, the result reads that the means at the disposal of private interests are often used in order to thwart the will of the people. From the second standpoint, the result reads that those private means are often used in order to interfere with the working of the mechanism of competitive leadership.

with equanimity the consequences of extending the democratic method, that is to say the sphere of "politics," to all economic affairs. Believing that democratic socialism means precisely this, such a person will naturally conclude that democratic socialism must fail. But this does not necessarily follow. As has been pointed out before, extension of the range of public management does not imply corresponding extension of the range of political management. Conceivably, the former may be extended so as to absorb a nation's economic affairs while the latter still remains within the boundaries set by the limitations of the democratic method.

It does follow however that in socialist society these limitations will raise a much more serious problem. For socialist society lacks the automatic restrictions imposed upon the political sphere by the bourgeois scheme of things. Moreover, in socialist society it will no longer be possible to find comfort in the thought that the inefficiencies of political procedure are after all a guarantee of freedom. Lack of efficient management will spell lack of bread. However, the agencies that are to operate the economic engine—the Central Board . . . as well as the subordinate bodies entrusted with the management of individual industries or concerns—may be so organized and manned as to be sufficiently exempt in the fulfillment of their current duties from interference by politicians or, for that matter, by fussing citizens' committees or by their workmen. That is to say, they may be sufficiently removed from the atmosphere of political strife as to display no inefficiencies other than those associated with the term Bureaucracy. And even these *can* be much reduced by an appropriate concentration of responsibility on individuals and by a system of well-chosen incentives and penalties, of which the methods of appointment and promotion are the most important part.

Serious socialists, when off the stump and in a responsible mood, have always been aware of this problem and also of the fact that "democracy" is no answer to it. An interesting illustration is afforded by the deliberations of the German Committee on Socialization (*Sozialisierungs Kommission*). In 1919, when the German Social Democratic party had definitely set its face against bolshevism, the more radical among its members still believed that some measure of socialization was imminent as a matter of practical necessity and a committee was accordingly appointed in order to define aims and to recommend methods. It did not consist exclusively of socialists but socialist influence was dominating. Karl Kautsky was chairman. Definite recommendations were made only about coal and even these, arrived at under the gathering clouds of anti-socialist sentiment, are not very interesting. All the more interesting are the views that emerged in discussion at the time when more ambitious hopes still prevailed. The idea that managers of plants should be elected by the workmen of the same plants was frankly and unanimously condemned. The workmen's councils that had grown up during the months of universal breakdown were objects of dislike and suspicion. The committee, trying to get way as far as possible from the popular ideas about Industrial Democracy[3] did its best to shape them into an innocuous mold and cared little for developing their functions. All the more did it care for strengthening the authority and safeguarding the independence of the managerial personnel. Much thought was bestowed on how to prevent managers from losing capitalist vitality and sinking into bureaucratic ruts. In fact—if it be possible to speak of results of discussions that were soon to lose practical importance—these socialist managers would not have differed very much from their capitalist predecessors, and in many cases the same individuals would have been reappointed. . . .

But we are now in a position to link up this conclusion with an answer to the problem of democracy in socialism. In a sense, of course, the present-day forms and organs of democratic procedure are as much the outgrowth of the structure and the issues of the bourgeois world as is the fundamental principle of democracy itself. But this is no reason why they should have to disappear along with capitalism. General elections, parties, parliaments, cabinets and prime ministers may still prove to be the most convenient instruments for dealing with the agenda that the socialist order may reserve for political decision. The list of these agenda will be relieved of all those items that at present arise from the clash of private interests and from the necessity of regulating them. Instead there will be new ones. There will be such questions to decide as what the volume of investment should be or how existing rules for the distribution of the social product should be amended and so on. General debates about efficiency, investigation committees of the type of the English Royal Commissions would continue to fulfill their present functions.

Thus the politicians in the cabinet, and in particular the politician at the head of the Ministry of Production, would no doubt assert the influence of the political element, both by their legislative measures concerning the general principles of running the economic engine and by their power to appoint which could not be entirely absent or entirely formal. But they need not do so to an extent incompatible with efficiency. And the Minister of Production need not interfere more with the internal working of individual industries than English Ministers of Health or of War interfere with the internal working of their respective departments.

3. It goes without saying that operating socialist democracy in the way

[3] Industrial or Economic Democracy is a phrase that figures in so many quasi-utopias that it has retained very little precise meaning. Mainly, I think, it means two things: first, the trade-union rule over industrial relations; second, democratization of the monarchic factory by workmen's representation on boards or other devices calculated to secure them influence on the introduction of technological improvements, business policy in general and, of course, discipline in the plant in particular, including methods of "hiring and firing." Profit-sharing is a nostrum of a subgroup of schemes. It is safe to say that much of this economic democracy will vanish into thin air in a socialist regime. Nor is this so offensive as it may sound. For many of the interests this kind of democracy is intended to safeguard will then cease to exist.

indicated would be a perfectly hopeless task except in the case of a society that fulfills all the requirements of "maturity" . . . including, in particular, the ability to establish the socialist order in a democratic way and the existence of a bureaucracy of adequate standing and experience. But a society that does fulfill these requirements—I shall not deal with any other—would first of all command an advantage of possibly decisive importance.

I have emphasized that democracy cannot be expected to function satisfactorily unless the vast majority of the people in all classes are resolved to abide by the rules of the democratic game and that this in turn implies that they are substantially agreed on the fundamentals of their institutional structure. At present the latter condition fails to be fulfilled. So many people have renounced, and so many more are going to renounce, allegiance to the standards of capitalist society that on this ground alone democracy is bound to work with increasing friction. At the stage visualized however, socialism may remove the rift. It may reestablish agreement as to the tectonic principles of the social fabric. If it does, then the remaining antagonisms will be exactly of the kind with which the democratic method is well able to cope.

It has also been pointed out . . . that those remaining antagonisms will be further decreased in number and importance by the elimination of clashing capitalist interests. The relations between agriculture and industry, small-scale and large-scale industry, steel-producing and steel-consuming industries, protectionist and export industries will—or may—cease to be political questions to be settled by the relative weights of pressure groups and become technical questions to which technicians would be able to give unemotional and unequivocal answers. Though it may be utopian to expect that there would be no distinct economic interests or conflicts between them, and still more utopian to expect that there would be no noneconomic issues to disagree about, a good case may be made out for expecting that the sum total of controversial matter would be decreased even as compared with what it was in intact capitalism. There would, for instance, be no silver men. Political life would be purified.

On the face of it, socialism has no obvious solution to offer for the problem solved in other forms of society by the presence of a political class of stable traditions. I have said before that there will be a political profession. There may evolve a political set, about the quality of which it is idle to speculate.

Thus far socialism scores. It might still be argued that this score can be easily balanced by the importance and likelihood of possible deviations. To some extent we have provided for this by insisting on economic maturity which among other things implies that no great sacrifices need be required of one generation for the benefit of a later one. But even if there is no necessity for sweating the people by means of a Gosplan, the task of keeping the democratic course may prove to be extremely delicate. Circumstances in which the individuals at the helm would normally succeed in solving it are perhaps no easier to imagine than circumstances in which, faced by a spectacle of paralysis spreading from the political sector all over the nation's economy, they might be driven into a course of action which must always have some temptation for men beholding the tremendous power over the people inherent in the socialist organization. After all, effective management of the socialist economy means dictatorship not *of* but *over* the proletariat in the factory. The men who are there so strictly disciplined would, it is true, be sovereign at the elections. But just as they may use this sovereignty in order to relax the discipline of the factory, so governments—precisely the governments which have the future of the nation at heart—may avail themselves of this discipline in order to restrict this sovereignty. As a matter of practical necessity, socialist democracy may eventually turn out to be more of a sham than capitalist democracy ever was.

In any case, that democracy will not mean increased personal freedom. And, once more, it will mean no closer approximation to the ideals enshrined in the classical doctrine.

1942

32 American Democracy, Standards and Leadership

IRVING BABBITT

Judged by any quantitative test, the American achievement is impressive. We have ninety per cent of the motors of the world and control seventy-five per cent of its oil; we produce sixty per cent of the world's steel, seventy per cent of its copper, and eighty per cent of its telephones and typewriters. This and similar statistical proof of our material preëminence, which would have made a Greek apprehensive of Nemesis, seems to inspire in many Americans an almost lyrical complacency. They are not only quantitative in their estimates of our present accomplishment, but even more so if possible in what they anticipate for the future. Now that we have fifteen million automobiles they feel, with Mr. Henry Ford, that we can have no higher ambition than to expand this number to thirty million. Our present output of fifty

SOURCE: from Irving Babbitt, *Democracy and Leadership*, pp. 239–264.

million tons of steel a year is, according to Mr. Schwab, a mere trifle compared with our probable output of twenty years hence. In short, an age that is already immersed in things to an unexampled degree is merely to prepare the way for an age still more material in its preoccupations and still more subservient to machinery. This, we are told, is progress. To a person with a proportionate view of life it might seem rather to be full-blown commercial insolence.

The reasons for the quantitative view of life that prevails in America are far from being purely political. This view has resulted in a large measure from the coming together of scientific discovery with the opening up of a new continent. It has been possible with the aid of science to accomplish in a hundred years what even the optimistic Thomas Jefferson thought might take a thousand. The explanation, it has been said, of much that is obscure to us in the Chinese may be summed up in the words "lack of elbow-room." We in this country, on the other hand, have received a peculiar psychic twist from the fact that we have had endless elbow-room. A chief danger both to ourselves and others is that we shall continue to have a frontier psychology long after we have ceased to have a frontier. For a frontier psychology is expansive, and expansiveness, I have tried to show, is, at least in its political manifestations, always imperialistic.

If quantitatively the American achievement is impressive, qualitatively it is somewhat less satisfying. What must one think of a country, asks one of our foreign critics, whose most popular orator is W. J. Bryan, whose favorite actor is Charlie Chaplin, whose most widely read novelist is Harold Bell Wright, whose best-known evangelist is Billy Sunday, and whose representative journalist is William Randolph Hearst? What one must evidently think of such a country, even after allowing liberally for overstatement, is that it lacks standards. Furthermore, America suffers not only from a lack of standards, but also not infrequently from a confusion or an inversion of standards. As an example of the inversion of standards we may take the bricklayer who, being able to lay two thousand bricks a day, is reduced by union rules to laying five hundred. There is confusion of standards, again, when we are so impressed by Mr. Henry Ford's abilities as organizer and master mechanic that we listen seriously to his views on money; or when, simply because Mr. Edison has shown inventive genius along certain lines, we receive him as an authority on education. One is reminded of the story of the French butcher who, having need of legal aid, finally, after looking over a number of lawyers, selected the fattest one.

The problem of standards, though not identical with the problem of democracy, touches it at many points and is not therefore the problem of any one country. Europeans, indeed, like to look upon the crudity and chaotic impressionism of people who are no longer guided by standards as something specifically American. "America," says the *Saturday Review*, "is the country of unbalanced minds, of provincial policies and of hysterical

Utopias." The deference for standards has, however, been diminished by a certain type of democracy in many other countries besides America. The resulting vulgarity and triviality are more or less visible in all of these countries;—for example, if we are to believe Lord Bryce, in New Zealand. If we in America are perhaps preëminent in lack of distinction, it is because of the very completeness of our emancipation from the past. Goethe's warning as to the retarding effect of the commonplace is well known (*Was uns alle bändigt, das Gemeine*). His explanation of what makes for the commonplace is less familiar: "Enjoyment," he says, "makes common." (*Geniessen macht gemein.*) Since every man desires happiness, it is evidently no small matter whether he conceives of happiness in terms of work or of enjoyment. If he work in the full ethical sense that I have attempted to define, he is pulling back and disciplining his temperamental self with reference to some standard. In short, his temperamental self is, in an almost literal sense, undergoing conversion. The whole of life may, indeed, be summed up in the words diversion and conversion. Along which of these two main paths are most of us seeking the happiness to the pursuit of which we are dedicated by our Declaration of Independence? The author of this phrase, Thomas Jefferson, remarks of himself: "I am an Epicurean." It cannot be gainsaid that an increasing number of our young people are, in this respect at least, good Jeffersonians. The phrase that reflects most clearly their philosophy of life is perhaps "good time." One might suppose that many of them see this phrase written in great blazing letters on the very face of the firmament. As "Punch" remarked, the United States is not a country, but a picnic. When the element of conversion with reference to a standard is eliminated from life, what remains is the irresponsible quest of thrills. The utilitarian and industrial side of the modern movement comes into play at this point. Commercialism is laying its great greasy paw upon everything (including the irresponsible quest of thrills); so that, whatever democracy may be theoretically, one is sometimes tempted to define it practically as standardized and commercialized melodrama. This definition will be found to fit many aspects of our national life besides the moving-picture industry. The tendency to steep and saturate ourselves in the impression of the moment without reference to any permanent pattern of human experience is even more marked, perhaps, in our newspapers and magazines. It was said of the inhabitants of a certain ancient Greek city that, though they were not fools, they did just the things that fools would do. It is hard to take a glance at one of our news-stands without reflecting that, though we may not be fools, we are reading just the things that fools would read. Our daily press in particular is given over to the most childish sensationalism. "The Americans are an excellent people," Matthew Arnold wrote from Boston in 1883, "but their press seems to me an awful symptom." This symptom was not so awful then as now; for that was before the day of the scarehead and the comic supplement. The American reading his Sunday paper in a state of lazy collapse is perhaps the most perfect symbol of the triumph of quantity over quality that the world has yet seen. Whole forests are being ground into pulp daily to minister to our triviality.

One is inclined, indeed, to ask, in certain moods, whether the net result of the movement that has been sweeping the Occident for several generations may not be a huge mass of standardized mediocrity; and whether in this country in particular we are not in danger of producing in the name of democracy one of the most trifling brands of the human species that the world has yet seen. To be sure, it may be urged that, though we may suffer loss of distinction as a result of the democratic drift, by way of compensation a great many average people will, in the Jeffersonian sense at least, be made "happy." If we are to judge by history, however, what supervenes upon the decline of standards and the disappearance of leaders who embody them is not some equalitarian paradise, but inferior types of leadership. We have already been reminded by certain developments in this country of Byron's definition of democracy as an "aristocracy of blackguards." At the very moment when we were most vociferous about making the world safe for democracy the citizens of New York City refused to reëlect an honest man as their mayor and put in his place a tool of Tammany, an action followed in due course by a "crime wave"; whereupon they returned the tool of Tammany by an increased majority. The industrial revolution has tended to produce everywhere great urban masses that seem to be increasingly careless of ethical standards. In the case of our American cities, the problem of securing some degree of moral cohesion is further complicated by the presence of numerous aliens of widely divergent racial stocks and cultural backgrounds. In addition our population is not only about half urban, but we cannot be said, like most other countries, to have any peasantry or yeomanry. Those Americans who actually dwell in the country are more and more urban in their psychology. The whole situation is so unusual as to suggest doubts even from a purely biological point of view. "As I watch the American nation speeding gaily, with invincible optimism down the road to destruction," says Professor William McDougall, an observer of the biological type, "I seem to be contemplating the greatest tragedy in the history of mankind."

We are assured, indeed, that the highly heterogeneous elements that enter into our population will, like various instruments in an orchestra, merely result in a richer harmony; they will, one may reply, provided that, like an orchestra, they be properly led. Otherwise the outcome may be an unexampled cacophony. This question of leadership is not primarily biological, but moral. Leaders may vary in quality from the man who is so loyal to sound standards that he inspires right conduct in others by the sheer rightness of his example, to the man who stands for nothing higher than the law of cunning and the law of force, and so is, in the sense I have sought to define, imperialistic. If democracy means simply the attempt to eliminate the qualitative and selective principle in favor of some general will, based in turn on a theory of natural rights, it may prove to be only a form of the vertigo of the abyss. As I have tried to show in dealing with the influence of Rousseau on the French Revolution, it will result practically, not in equality, but in a sort of inverted aristocracy. One's choice may be, not between a democracy that is properly led and a democracy that hopes to find the equivalent of standards and leadership in the appeal to a numerical majority, that indulges in other words in a sort of quantitative impressionism, but between a democracy that is properly led and a decadent imperialism. One should, therefore, in the interests of democracy itself seek to substitute the doctrine of the right man for the doctrine of the rights of man.

The opposition between traditional standards and an equalitarian democracy based on the supposed rights of man has played an important part in our own political history, and has meant practically the opposition between two types of leadership. The "quality" in the older sense of the word suffered its first decisive defeat in 1829 when Washington was invaded by the hungry hordes of Andrew Jackson. The imperialism latent in this type of democracy appears in the Jacksonian maxim: "To the victors belong the spoils." In his theory of democracy Jackson had, of course, much in common with Thomas Jefferson. If we go back, indeed, to the beginnings of our institutions, we find that America stood from the start for two different views of government that have their origin in different views of liberty and ultimately of human nature. The view that is set forth in the Declaration of Independence assumes that man has certain abstract rights; it has therefore important points of contact with the French revolutionary "idealism." The view that inspired our Constitution, on the other hand, has much in common with that of Burke. If the first of these political philosophies is properly associated with Jefferson, the second has its most distinguished representative in Washington. The Jeffersonian liberal has faith in the goodness of the natural man, and so tends to overlook the need of a veto power either in the individual or in the State. The liberals of whom I have taken Washington to be the type or less expansive in their attitude towards the natural man. Just as man has a higher self that acts restrictively on his ordinary self, so, they hold, the State should have a higher or permanent self, appropriately embodied in institutions, that should set bounds to its ordinary self as expressed by the popular will at any particular moment. The contrast that I am establishing is, of course, that between a constitutional and a direct democracy. There is an opposition of first principles between those who maintain that the popular will should prevail, but only after it has been purified of what is merely impulsive and ephemeral, and those who maintain that this will should prevail immediately and unrestrictedly. The American experiment in democracy has, therefore, from the outset been ambiguous, and will remain so until the irrepressible conflict between a Washingtonian and a Jeffersonian liberty has been fought to a conclusion.

The liberal of the type of Washington has always been very much concerned with what one may term the unionist aspect of liberty. This central preoccupation is summed up in the phrase of Webster: Union and liberty, one and inseparable. The liberty of the Jeffersonian, on the other hand, makes against ethical union like every liberty that rests on the assertion of abstract rights. Jefferson himself proclaimed not only human rights, but also state rights. Later the doctrine of state rights was developed with logical rigor by Calhoun, whereas the doctrine of human rights was carried through no less uncompromisingly by the abolitionists. The result was two opposing camps of extremists and fire-eaters; so that the whole question of union, instead of being settled on ethical lines, had to be submitted to the arbitrament of force.

The man who has grasped the full import of the conflict between the liberty of the unionist and that of the Jeffersonian has been put in possession of the key that unlocks American history. The conflict between the two conceptions is not, indeed, always clear-cut in particular individuals. There is much in Jefferson himself that contradicts what I have been saying about Jefferson. A chief business of criticism, however, is to distinguish, in spite of peripheral overlappings, between things that are at the centre different. For example, to link together in a common admiration Jefferson and John Marshall, our most eminent unionist after Washington himself, is proof of lack of critical discrimination rather than of piety towards the fathers. Jefferson and Marshall knew perfectly that they stood for incompatible things, and it is important that we should know it also. "Marshall," says John Quincy Adams in his Diary, "has cemented the Union which the crafty and quixotic democracy of Jefferson had a perpetual tendency to dissolve."

By his preoccupation with the question of the union, Lincoln became the true successor of Washington and Marshall. In making of Lincoln the great emancipator instead of the great unionist, in spite of his own most specific declarations on this point, we are simply creating a Lincoln myth, as we have already created a Washington myth. We are sometimes told that the good democrat needs merely to be like Lincoln. But to be like Lincoln one must know what Lincoln was like. This is not only a task for the critic, but, in view of the Lincoln myth, a more difficult task than is commonly supposed. It is especially easy to sentimentalize Lincoln because he had a strongly marked vein of sentimentalism. Nevertheless, in spite of the peripheral overlappings between the democracy of Lincoln and that of Jefferson or even between that of Lincoln and Walt Whitman, one should insist on the central difference. One has only to read, for example, the Second Inaugural along with the "Song of Myself" if one wishes to become aware of the gap that separates religious humility from romantic egotism. We should be careful again, in spite of peripheral overlappings, not to confound the democracy of Lincoln with that of Roosevelt. What we feel at the very centre in Roosevelt is the dynamic rush of an imperialistic personality. What we feel at the very centre in Lincoln, on the other hand, is an element of judicial control; and in close relation to this control a profound conception of the rôle of the courts in maintaining free institutions. The man who has studied the real Lincoln does not find it easy to imagine him advocating the recall of judicial decisions.

The Jeffersonian liberal is, as a rule, much more ostentatiously fraternal than the liberal in the other tradition. Yet he is usually inferior in human warmth and geniality to the unionist. Washington and Marshall and Lincoln at their best combined practical sagacity with a central benignity and unselfishness. Jefferson, on the other hand, though perhaps our most accomplished politician, did not show himself especially sagacious in dealing with specific emergencies. Furthermore, it is hard to read his "Anas" and reflect on the circumstances of its composition without concluding that what was central in his personality was not benignity and unselfishness but vindictiveness.

Statesmen who deserve the praise I have bestowed on our unionist leaders are, as every student of history knows, extremely rare. The type of constitutional liberty that we owe to these men before all others is one of the greatest blessings that has ever been vouchsafed to any people. And yet we are in danger of losing it. The Eighteenth Amendment is striking proof of our loss of grasp, not only on the principles that underlie our own Constitution, but that must underlie any constitution, as such, in opposition to mere legislative enactment.

Our present drift away from constitutional freedom can be understood only with reference to the progressive crumbling of traditional standards and the rise of a naturalistic philosophy that, in its treatment of specifically human problems, has been either sentimental or utilitarian. The significant changes in our own national temper in particular are finally due to the fact that Protestant Christianity, especially in the Puritanic form, has been giving way to humanitarianism. The point is worth making because the persons who have favored prohibition and other similar "reforms" have been attacked as Puritans. Genuine Puritanism was, however, a religion of the inner life. Our unionist leaders, Washington, Marshall, and Lincoln, though not narrowly orthodox, were still religious in the traditional sense. The struggle between good and evil, as they saw it, was still primarily not in society, but in the individual. Their conscious dependence on a higher or divine will could not fail to be reflected in their notion of liberty. Jefferson, on the contrary, associated his liberty, not with God, but with "nature." He admired, as is well known, the liberty of the American Indian. He was for diminishing to the utmost the rôle of government, but not for increasing the inner control that must, according to Burke, be in strict ratio to the relaxation of outer control. When evil actually appears, the Jeffersonian cannot appeal to the principle of inner control; he is not willing again to admit that the sole alternative to this type of control is force; and so he is led into what seems at first sight a paradoxical denial of his own principles: he has recourse to legislation. It should be clear at all events that our present attempt to substitute social control for self-control is Jeffersonian rather than Puritanical. So far as we are true children of the Puritans, we may accept the contrast established by Professor Stuart P. Sherman between our own point of view and that of the German: "The ideal of the German is external control and 'inner freedom'; the Government looks after his conduct and he looks after his liberty. The ideal of the American is external freedom and inner control; the individual looks after his conduct and the Government looks after his liberty. Thus *Verboten* in Germany is pronounced by the Government and enforced by the police. In America *Verboten* is pronounced by public opinion and enforced by the individual conscience. In this light it should appear that Puritanism, our national principle of concentration, is the indispensable check on democracy, our national principle of expansion. I use the word Puritanism in the sense given to it by German and German-American critics: *the inner check upon the expansion of natural impulse.*"

Professor Sherman's contrast has been true in the past and still has some truth—at least enough for the purposes of war-time propaganda. But what about our main drift at present? It is plainly away from the point of view that Professor Sherman ascribes to the Puritan and towards the point of view that he ascribes to the German. "The inner check upon the expansion of natural impulse" is precisely the missing element in the Jeffersonian philosophy. The Jeffersonian has therefore been led to deal with the problem of evil, not vitally and in terms of the inner life, but mechanically. Like the Jesuit he has fallen from law into legalism. It has been estimated that for one *Verboten* sign in Germany we already have a dozen in this country; only, having set up our *Verboten* sign, we get even by not observing it. Thus prohibition is pronounced by the Government, largely repudiated by the individual conscience, and enforced (very imperfectly) by the police. The multitude of laws we are passing is one of many proofs that we are growing increasingly lawless.

There are, to be sure, peripheral overlappings between the point of view of the Puritan and that of the humanitarian legalist. The Puritan inclined from the start to be meddlesome, as any one who has studied the activities of Calvin at Geneva will testify. But even here one may ask whether the decisive arguments by which we have been induced to submit to the meddling of the prohibitionist were not utilitarian rather than puritanical. "Booze," says Mr. Henry Ford, "had to go out when modern industry and the motor car came in." The truth may be that we are prepared to make any sacrifice to the Moloch of efficiency, including, apparently, that of our federal Constitution.

The persons who have been carrying on of late a campaign against the Puritans like to look on themselves as "intellectuals." But if the primary function of the intellect is to make accurate distinctions, it is plain that they do not deserve the title. For in dealing with this whole subject they have fallen into a twofold confusion. So far as they identify with Puritanism the defence of the principle of control in human nature, they are simply attacking under that name the wisdom of the ages and all its authentic representatives in both East and West. To bestow, on the other hand, the name of Puritans on the humanitarian legalists who are now sapping our spiritual virility is to pay them an extravagant and undeserved compliment. Let us take as a sample of the attacks on the Puritans that of Mr. Theodore Dreiser, culminating in the grotesque assertion regarding the United States: "No country has such a peculiar, such a seemingly fierce determination to make the Ten Commandments work." We are murdering one another at the rate of about ten thousand a year (with very few capital convictions) and are in general showing ourselves more criminally inclined than any other nation that is reputed to be civilized. The explanation is that we are trying to make, not the Ten Commandments, but humanitarianism work—and it is not working. If our courts are so ineffective in punishing crime, a chief reason is that they do not have the support of public opinion, and this is because the public is so largely composed of people who have set up sympathy for the underdog as a substitute for all the other virtues, or else of people who hold that the criminal is the product of his environment and so is not morally responsible. Here as elsewhere there is a coöperation between those who mechanize life and those who sentimentalize it.

The belief in moral responsibility must be based on a belief in the possibility of an inner working of some kind with reference to standards. The utilitarian, as I have sought to show, has put his main emphasis on outer working. The consequence of this emphasis, coinciding as it has with the multiplication of machines, has been the substitution of standardization for standards. The type of efficiency that our master commercialists pursue requires that a multitude of men should be deprived of their specifically human attributes, and become mere cogs in some vast machine. At the present rate even the grocer in a remote country town will soon not be left as much initiative as is needed to fix the price of a pound of butter.

Standardization is, however, a less serious menace to standards than what are currently known as "ideals." The person who breaks down standards in the name of ideals does not seem to be impelled by base commercial motives, but to be animated, on the contrary, by the purest commiseration for the lowly and the oppressed. We must have the courage to submit this humanitarian zeal to a close scrutiny. We may perhaps best start with the familiar dictum that America is only another name for opportunity. Opportunity to do what? To engage in a scramble for money and material success, until the multimillionaire emerges as the characteristic product of a country dedicated to the proposition that all men are created equal? According to Napoleon, the French Revolution was also only another name for opportunity (*la carrière ouverte aux talents*). Some of our commercial supermen have evidently been making use of their opportunity in a very Napoleonic fashion. In any case, opportunity has meaning only with reference to some true standard. The sentimentalist, instead of setting up some such standard by way of protest against the wrong type of superiority, inclines rather to bestow an unselective sympathy on those who have been left behind in the race for economic advantage. Even when less materialistic in his outlook, he is prone to dodge the question of justice. He does not ask whether a man is an underdog because he has already had his opportunity and failed to use it, whether, in short, the man that he takes to be a victim of the social order is not rather a victim of his own misconduct or at least of his own indolence and inattention. He thus exposes himself to the penalties visited on those who set out to be kinder than the moral law.

At bottom the point of view of the "uplifter" is so popular because it nourishes spiritual complacency; it enables a man to look on himself as "up" and on some one else as "down." But there is psychological if not theological truth in the assertion of Jonathan Edwards that complacent people are a "particular smoke" in God's nostrils. A man needs to look, not down, but up to standards set so much above his ordinary self as to make him feel that he is himself spiritually the underdog. The man who thus looks up is becoming worthy to be looked up to in turn, and, to this extent, qualifying for leadership. Leadership of this type, one may add, may prove to be, in the long run, the only effectual counterpoise to that of the imperialistic superman.

No amount of devotion to society and its supposed interests can take the place of this inner obeisance of the spirit to standards. The humanitarian would seem to be caught here in a vicious circle. If he turns from the inner life to serve his fellow men, he becomes a busybody. If he sets out again to become exemplary primarily with a view to the benefit of others, he becomes a prig. Nothing will avail short of humility. Humility, as Burke saw, is the ultimate root of the justice that should prevail in the secular order, as well as of the virtues that are specifically religious. The modern problem, I have been insisting, is to secure leaders with an allegiance to standards, now that the traditional order with which Burke associated his standards and leadership has been so seriously shaken. Those who have broken with the traditional beliefs have thus far shown themselves singularly ineffective in dealing with this problem of leadership, even when they have admitted the need of leaders at all. The persons who have piqued themselves especially on being positive have looked for leadership to the exponents of physical science. Auguste Comte, for example, not only regarded men of science as the true modern priesthood, but actually disparaged moral effort on the part of the individual. I scarcely need to repeat here what I have said elsewhere—that the net result of a merely scientific "progress" is to produce efficient megalomaniacs. Physical science, excellent in its proper place, is, when exalted out of this place, the ugliest and most maleficent idol before which man has as yet consented to prostrate himself. If the essence of genuine science is to face loyally all the facts as they present themselves without dogmatic prepossessions, one is justified in asking whether the man who forgets that physical science is, in Tennyson's phrase, the second, not the first, is genuinely scientific; whether the very sharpest discrimination does not need to be established between science and utilitarianism. Aristotle, for example, was a true man of science; he was not a utilitarian. Francis Bacon, on the other hand, is the prophet of the whole utilitarian movement, but one may doubt his eminence as a man of science. Quite apart from the fact that he failed to make important scientific discoveries, one may question the validity of the Baconian method. His failure to do justice to deduction as part of a sound scientific method has often been noted. A more serious defect is his failure to recognize the rôle of the imagination, or, what amounts to the same thing, the rôle of exceptional genius in the making of scientific discoveries.

One cannot grant that an aristocracy of scientific intellectuals or indeed any aristocracy of intellect is what we need. This would mean practically to encourage the *libido sciendi* and so to put pride in the place of humility. Still less acceptable would be an aristocracy of artists; as the word art has come to be understood in recent times, this would mean an aristocracy of aesthetes who would attempt to base their selection on the *libido sentiendi.* The Nietzschean attempt, again, to found the aristocratic and selective principle on the sheer expansion of the will to power (*libido dominandi*) would lead in practice to horrible violence and finally to the death of civilization. The attempts that were made during the past century to establish a scale of values with reference to the three main lusts of the human heart often took on a mystical coloring. Man likes to think that he has God as an ally of his expansive conceit, whatever this conceit may chance to be. When, indeed, one has passed in review the various mysticisms of the modern movement, as they are set forth, for example, in the volumes of M. Seillière, one is reminded of the saying of Bossuet: "True mysticism is so rare and unessential and false mysticism is so common and dangerous that one cannot oppose it too firmly."

If one discovers frequently a pseudo-mystical element in the claims to leadership of the aesthetes, the supermen and the scientific intellectuals, this element is even more visible in those who would, in the name of democracy, dispense with leadership altogether. Thus Walt Whitman, as we have seen, would put no check on his "spontaneous me"; he would have every one else indulge his "idiocrasy" to the same degree, be a "genius," in short, in the full romantic sense of the term. A liberty thus anarchical is to lead to equality and fraternity. If one tells the democrat of this type that his programme is contrary to common sense and the facts of experience, he is wont to take refuge in mystical "vision." One needs in effect to be very mystical to suppose that men can come together by flying off each on his temperamental tangent. Whitman does not admit the need of the leader who looks up humbly to some standard and so becomes worthy to be looked up to in turn. The only leadership he contemplates apparently is that of the ideal democratic bard who flatters the people's pride and chants the divine average. He represents in an extreme form the substitution for vital control of expansive emotion under the name of love. Pride and self-assertion, when tempered by love, will not, he holds, endanger the principle of union. The Union, though "always swarming with blatherers, is yet," he says, "always sure and impregnable." The records of the past are not reassuring as to the maintenance of ethical union in a community that is swarming with "blatherers." At all events, the offset to the blatherers will be found, not in any divine average, but in the true leader—the "still strong man in a blatant land." We come here to another opposition that is one of first principles and is not therefore subject to mediation or compromise—the opposition, namely, between the doctrine of the saving remnant and that of the divine average. If one deals with human nature realistically one may find here and there a person who is worthy of respect and occasionally one who is worthy of reverence. Any one, on the other hand, who puts his faith in the divinity of the average is destined, if we are to trust the records of history, to pass through disillusion to a final despair. We are reaching the stage of disillusion in this country at the present moment. According to the author of "Main Street," the average is not divine but trivial; according to the author of the "Spoon River Anthology," it is positively hideous. It can scarcely be gainsaid that contemporary America offers an opening for satire. A great many people are gradually drifting into materialism and often cherishing the conceit at the same time that they are radiant idealists. But satire, to be worth while, must be constructive. The opposite of the trivial is the distinguished; and one can determine what is distinguished only with reference to standards. To see Main Street on a background of standards would be decidedly helpful; but standards are precisely what our so-called realists lack. They are themselves a part of the disease that they are attempting to define.

The democratic idealist is prone to make light of the whole question of standards and leadership because of his unbounded faith in the plain people. How far is this appeal to the plain people justified and how far is it merely demagogic? There is undoubted truth in the saying that there is somebody who knows more than anybody, and that is everybody. Only one must allow everybody sufficient time to sift the evidence and add that, even so, everybody does not know very much. Burke told the electors of Bristol that he was not flattering their opinions of the moment, but uttering the views that both they and he must have five years thence. Even in this triumph of the sober judgment of the people over its passing impression, the rôle of the true leader should not be underestimated. Thus in the year 1795 the plain people of America were eager to give the fraternal accolade to the French Jacobins. The great and wise Washington opposed an alliance that would almost certainly have been disastrous, and as a result he had heaped upon him by journals like the "Aurora," the forerunner of our modern "journals of opinion," epithets that, as he himself complained, would not have been deserved by a common pickpocket. In a comparatively short time Washington and his group were seen to be right, and those who seemed to be the spokesmen of the plain people were seen to be wrong. It is not clear that one can have much faith even in the sober second thought of a community that has no enlightened minority. A Haytian statesman, for example, might not gain much in appealing from Haytian opinion of today to Haytian opinion of five years hence. The democratic idealist does not, however, mean as a rule by an appeal to the plain people an appeal to its sober second thought. He means rather the immediate putting into effect of the will of a numerical majority. Like the man in the comic song the people is supposed to "want what it wants when it wants it." Our American drift for a number of years has unquestionably been towards a democracy of this radical type, as is evident from the increasing vogue of the initiative, referendum, and recall (whether of judges or judicial decisions) as well as from popular primaries and the direct election of Senators. The feeling that the people should act directly on all measures has led to the appearance in certain States of ballots thirty feet long! Yet the notion that wisdom resides in a popular majority at any particular moment should be the most completely exploded of all fallacies. If the plain people at Jerusalem had registered their will with the aid of the most improved type of ballot box, there is no evidence that they would have preferred Christ to Barabbas. In view of the size of the jury that condemned Socrates, one may affirm confidently that he was the victim of a "great and solemn referendum." On the other hand, the plain people can be shown to have taken a special delight in Nero. But the plain people, it will be replied, has been educated and enlightened. The intelligence tests applied in connection with the selective draft indicate that the average mental age of our male voters is about fourteen. The intelligence testers are, to be sure, under some suspicion as to the quality of their own intelligence. A more convincing proof of the low mentality of our population is found, perhaps, in the fact that the Hearst publications have twenty-five million readers. . . .

1924

Bibliography

Arnold, Thurman. *Folklore of Capitalism.* New Haven: Yale University Press, 1937.

Arnold, Thurman. *Symbols of Government:* New Haven: Yale University Press, 1936.

Bachrach, Peter. *The Theory of Democratic Elitism.* Boston: Little, Brown, 1966.

Bachrach, Peter (ed.). *Political Elites in a Democracy.* New York: Atherton Press, 1971.

Berelson, B., Lazarsfeld, P., and McPhee, W. *Voting.* Chicago: University of Chicago Press, 1954, especially Chapter 14.

Bottomore, T. B. *Elites and Society.* Baltimore, Md.: Penguin Books, 1966.
Burke, Edmund. *Burke's Politics.* Edited by R. J. S. Hoffman, Paul Levack. New York: Alfred A. Knopf, 1949.
Burke, Edmund. *Reflections on the Revolution in France, 1790.* (Any edition.)
Dye, Thomas L., and Zeigler, L. Harmon. *The Irony of Democracy.* Belmont, Calif.: Duxbury Press, 1971.
Guttmann, Allen. *The Conservative Tradition in America.* New York: Oxford University Press, 1967.
Hogg, Quintin. *The Case for Conservatism.* London: Penguin Books, 1947.
Keller, Suzanne. *Beyond the Ruling Class.* New York: Random House, 1963.
Lippmann, Walter. *The Public Philosophy.* Boston: Little, Brown, 1966.
McCoy, C. A., and Playford, J. (eds.). *Apolitical Politics: A Critique of Behavioralism.* New York: Thomas Y. Crowell Co., 1967.
Mencken, H. L. *Notes on Democracy.* New York: Alfred A. Knopf, 1926.
Mosca, Gaetano. *The Ruling Class.* New York: McGraw-Hill, 1939.
Ortega Y Gasset, José. *The Revolt of the Masses.* New York: Norton, 1932.
Parry, Geraint. *Political Elites.* New York: Frederick A. Praeger, 1969.
Rossiter, Clinton. *Conservatism in America.* New York: Vintage, 1962.
Rossiter, Clinton, and Lare, James (eds.). *The Essential Lippmann.* New York: Vintage Books, 1963.
Sartori, Giovanni. *Democratic Theory.* New York: Frederick A. Praeger, 1965.
Schattschneider, E. E. *The Semi-Sovereign People: A Realist's View of Democracy in America.* New York: Holt, Rinehart & Winston, 1960.
Stephen, Sir James Fitzjames. *Liberty, Equality, Fraternity.* Edited by and with introduction by R. J. White. London: Cambridge University Press, 1967.
Viereck, Peter. *Conservatism.* Princeton, N.J.: D. Van Nostrand Co., 1956.
Walker, Jack L. "A Critique of the Elitist Theory of Democracy," *American Political Science Review, LX* (June 1966): 285–295.
Wahlke, John C. *Public Policy and Representative Government: The Role of the Represented.* A Report from the Laboratory of Political Research Department of Political Science, University of Iowa, Iowa City, Iowa, September 1967.

1 2 3 4 5 6 7 8 9 10